A Meeting of Minds

ABOUT THE AUTHORS

 Patsy Callaghan is Chair of the English Department at Central Washington University in Ellensburg, Washington, where she has been a professor and administrator for twenty years. She teaches rhetoric, composition, and world literature and has coordinated both the writing and English Education programs. This is her second book with Ann Dobyns, following *Literary Conversation: Thinking, Talking, and Writing About Literature,* published in 1996. She has held leadership roles in national professional associations and has served on many state and regional committees on writing assessment and teacher education.

 Ann Dobyns is Chair of the English Department at the University of Denver, where she is an Associate Professor of Rhetoric and Medieval Literature and teaches the graduate seminar on teaching argument as well as classes in writing theory, history of rhetoric, Kenneth Burke, Chaucer, the Pearl Poet, and medieval romance. She is the author of *The Voices of Romance: Studies in Dialogue and Character* (Delaware, 1989) and co-author, with Patsy Callaghan, of *Literary Conversation: Thinking, Talking, and Writing About Literature* (Allyn & Bacon, 1996).

A Meeting of Minds

A BRIEF RHETORIC FOR WRITERS AND READERS

Patsy Callaghan
Central Washington University

Ann Dobyns
University of Denver

PEARSON
Longman

New York San Francisco Boston
London Toronto Sydney Tokyo Singapore Madrid
Mexico City Munich Paris Cape Town Hong Kong Montreal

Senior Vice President and Publisher: Joseph Opiela
Vice President and Publisher: Eben W. Ludlow
Development Manager: Janet Lanphier
Senior Development Editor: Judith Fifer
Executive Marketing Manager: Ann Stypuloski
Senior Supplements Editor: Donna Campion
Media Supplements Editor: Nancy Garcia
Production Manager: Joseph Vella
Project Coordination, Text Design, and Electronic Page Makeup:
    Electronic Publishing Services Inc., NYC
Design Manager/Cover Designer: Wendy Ann Fredericks
Cover Art: © Rowan Moore/Getty Images, Inc.
Photo Research: Photosearch, Inc.
Manufacturing Buyer: Roy L. Pickering, Jr.
Printer and Binder: R.R. Donnelley & Sons, Crawfordsville
Cover Printer: The Lehigh Press

For permission to use copyrighted material, grateful acknowledgment is made to the copyright holders on pp. 537–540, which are hereby made part of this copyright page.

Library of Congress Cataloging-in-Publication Data

Callaghan, Patsy.
    A meeting of the minds: a brief rhetoric for writers and readers/Patsy Callaghan, Ann Dobyns.—1st ed.
        p. cm.
Includes bibliographical references and index.
ISBN 0-321-09216-3
1. English language—Rhetoric. 2. College readers. 3. Report writing. I Dobyns, Ann, 1946 - II. Title.

PE1408.C276 2004
808'.042—dc21

                                                                        2003054823

Please visit our Website at http://www.ablongman.com/callaghan

ISBN 0-321-09216-3

    2 3 4 5 6 7 8 9 10—DOC—06 05 04

BRIEF CONTENTS

DETAILED CONTENTS

PART 2   Reading and Writing as Dialogues   85

CHAPTER 4   Summarizing and Responding   87

PART 4 | A Meeting of Minds: Dialogues on Issues 407

PREFACE

Every day, we struggle to make sense of what is unfamiliar or complex or disturbing or intriguing. Winning that struggle requires that we fit new information and ideas into the intricate web of our experience. When we win, we understand something in a new way. In most cases, the struggle to make sense involves other people. In our communities, we work together to find solutions to complex problems. In our college classes, we work together to achieve an understanding of the subject matter. "Do you know what I mean?" we ask each other. "Do you see this the way I do?"

So, for our students, for other writing instructors, and for ourselves, we have written a book about the art of rhetoric. Rhetoric is the art of using words to make sense, and of using words artfully so that they make sense to others. Such a "meeting of the minds," as Chaim Perelman calls it, allows writers and readers to explore their differences in reasoned discourse, and their understanding of this meeting of minds informs all parts of the book.

Students may think that learning involves mastering information, and to a certain extent that is true, but facts and data have no use until we act on them with our intelligence and imagination to make them meaningful to someone else. When we read, we are attempting to understand the words of other writers. When we write, we are attempting to help others see our meaning the way we do. Conscious, guided practice in reading and writing with a clear sense of this dynamic relationship strengthens our ability to come to understanding. Such explorations require us to identify our initial responses, and then challenge them through discussion, reasoning, and research.

Here's how this book can help readers and writers meet other minds through informed conversation.

PART I: RHETORIC AS A MEETING OF MINDS

Part 1 comprises three short chapters that introduce the strategies and responsibilities of the art of rhetoric. In Chapter 1, students learn how to analyze rhetorical situations—the way reader, writer, subject, and purpose influence the writer's work—and they learn how good writers choose effective rhetorical strategies, words, structures, reasons, and appeals that fit the situation. They "listen in" as members of a community try to make sense of the shooting of a young bear in a suburban backyard. Reading the community's responses, students locate key rhetorical concepts—situation, strategy, context, dialogue—within their consideration of a community controversy. In Chapter 2, students investigate situations and strategies as they explore in writing the kinds of inquiry developed more fully in later chapters. They write inquiry essays that encourage exploration for learning. In Chapter 3, students consider the ways writers shape their writing to follow different sets of conventions, different sets of rules, depending on the rhetorical context. They examine the conventions of language use and patterns found in personal, public, and academic messages so that they will be prepared to participate in conversations in all of these contexts.

PART II: READING AND WRITING AS DIALOGUES

The chapters in Part 2 present reading and writing as ways of knowing and understanding through dialogues with others on shared issues. Students often seem to assume that we expect them to enter conversations on issues with their minds already made up, or they believe they have no authority to say anything. We reassure them that the qualifications they need to join conversations about issues are that they know how to listen responsibly and speak with respect.

In Chapter 4, we discuss reading and writing to understand and respond. We separate *reading to understand* from *reading to respond*, even though we know that those processes happen simultaneously, because many of our students have difficulty reading texts that they disagree with and critiquing texts that they agree with. Students write summaries to help them listen thoroughly and respectfully to the words of others. They write responses to see how new ideas compare to their own experience and prior knowledge.

In Chapter 5, we continue to develop critical and rhetorical awareness as students examine strategies professional writers use to find, plan, and structure arguments that encourage mutual understanding. They consider how stasis questions allow readers to identify the kinds of questions a writer is addressing, whether the issue is one of fact, definition, circumstance, policy, or value. They also explore writers' appeals to reason, values, and emotions and how these appeals determine language choice. As they examine these choices in others' writing, students learn to write rhetorical analyses.

Chapter 6 presents a unique approach to academic research. Instead of seeing research as a genre, a paper with sources, we present essential information about finding and evaluating sources. Early in the book, students are provided with the tools they need to explore any issue they need to know more about. They are invited to prepare not research papers, but research proposals, including working bibliographies and plans for further investigation. Projects proposed in response to this chapter can develop as students learn more about inquiry and reasoning in subsequent chapters.

Chapters 7, 8, 9, and 10 show students ways to apply their responsible and responsive reading to the inquiry process. Chapter 7 suggests ways that students might synthesize alternate perspectives—helping them to suspend the inclination to jump prematurely to a conclusion. In synthesis essays, students connect different points of view on questions at issue, reflecting the complexity of academic conversations. They learn how to discover, cite, and document the voices in those conversations as they become familiar with the methods and conventions of research. Chapter 8 focuses on the rhetoric of the academic argument, its purpose, audience expectations, and forms and structures of reasoning. The emphasis is not on winning but on arriving at the position that is most acceptable among alternatives. This chapter on argument translates technical vocabulary into practical strategies for reasoning to avoid the "algebraic" look of logic-based texts. Chapters 9 and 10 invite students to apply the skills they have been learning and practicing throughout the book—skills of analysis, response, and argument—to questions of interpretation and evaluation.

PART III: DESIGNING AND REFINING YOUR WRITING

The three chapters of Part 3 focus on how writers can refine and present their messages to address the specific needs of a rhetorical context. In Chapter 11, students learn to see the elements and strategies of visual messages as analogous to the rhetoric of verbal messages. Then, in the section on document design, students come to understand that presentational features such as space, typography, alignment, and graphics are also persuasive and must be chosen strategically. Finally, the chapter links the visual and verbal by analyzing the Web page as a rhetorical document containing both verbal and visual strategies.

Chapters 12 and 13 present the editing and revision processes within a rhetorical context as well. Often, students complain that we evaluate their work on skills we do not teach. Instructors often complain that every student comes equipped with some revision and editing skills, but no two students have the same ones. When and where should we include sentence and paragraph skills in the first-year composition course? Our answer: Anytime the students need them, within the context of their own work. Chapters 12 and 13 do not replace the reference function of a handbook, but they do provide students with strategies for revising and editing, including coverage of the twenty most frequent errors college writers make. The key concepts related to structure, grammar, and syntax, as well as coherence, cohesion, clarity, and conciseness are illustrated, and students are invited to practice achieving these qualities through exercises designed to encourage purposeful decision making. An Appendix on Documentation is included to help students integrate source material responsibly and accurately.

PART IV: A MEETING OF MINDS: DIALOGUES ON ISSUES

We have included readings as models for analysis throughout the text: examples of student writing, letters to editors, and published writings. But because we want to present a realistic model of inquiry, we have expanded the discussion of three of the topics addressed in the text itself into casebooks. Each casebook includes readings that are meant to function as texts in dialogue with each other. They are varied in source, genre, and purpose. They are concerned with elements of a common subject, but they do not address the same question. We think they are evocative, raise multiple opportunities for inquiry, and help avoid "pro-con" oversimplifications of complex issues. Casebook 1: The Vote has as its focus the rights, responsibilities, and difficulties of participating in a democracy. Casebook 2: English Only addresses the culturally thorny bilingualism question. Casebook 3: He Said/She Said begins with Deborah Tannen's controversial research on the differences in male and female communication styles and then includes several essays that respond to and critique her argument.

OUR PURPOSE

As students read this book, we hope that it offers

- Acknowledgement of their uniqueness—by giving them opportunities to introduce their prior knowledge and experience into the classroom conversation.
- Reassurance—by making clear that some qualities of good writing apply across disciplinary and professional boundaries.
- Orientation—by making familiar the expectations and strategies used in academic writing tasks.
- Challenge—by encouraging them to identify their own preconceived notions and the assumptions of other readers and writers, and by valuing reasoned critique and assessment.
- Respect—by assuming that they can find and make their own meaning through the art of rhetoric.

SUPPLEMENTS FOR *A MEETING OF MINDS*

Instructor's Manual

The Instructor's Manual was prepared by Betsy Gwyn in collaboration with the authors. Betsy Gwyn has taught introductory composition, as well as argument and research courses, at Oklahoma State University, Denver University, Arapahoe Community College, and the University of North Carolina, Charlotte. The Instructor's Manual includes a practical overview for using the text in different course structures and with a variety of approaches; complete chapter notes including sample responses and guidance for chapter exercises; notes on student online writing with website references; an essay on the rhetorical and critical assumptions that inform the text; and sections on pedagogy and resources for composition.

Companion Website

The Companion Website (www.ablongman.com/callaghan) includes additional student resources and exercises for each chapter, including Writing to Learn activities, links to online resources, a list of readings and bibliographies for paper topics, and additional sample student papers to supplement the extensive selection of student papers provided in the text. The Companion Website is authored by Hillory Oakes, Director of the Writing Center at St. Lawrence University.

ACKNOWLEDGMENTS

The title of our book acknowledges the extent to which our work emerges from ongoing conversations: between the two of us for the last twenty-five years; with the theorists who have influenced our thinking and practice; and with professors, mentors, colleagues, and friends. First, as a collaborative work, this book grows out of a long dialogue that began in the spring of 1978 when we shared an office in graduate school and discovered our similar academic backgrounds. Patsy had studied rhetoric with William Irmscher in the masters program at the University of Washington; Ann had studied communication theory in undergraduate school at Lewis and Clark College. Both of us had taught at the secondary level. Later, we were both fortunate to study rhetoric with John Gage, whose influence can be found in every chapter of this book, both his own scholarship and that of the major figures we studied in his classes and tutorials: Plato, Aristotle, Cicero, and Quintilian; Kenneth Burke, I.A. Richards, Chaim Perelman, and Wayne C. Booth. In addition to these theorists, we owe a debt to scholars such as Mikhail Bakhtin, Ann Berthoff, Martin Camargo, Thomas Conley, James Crosswhite, Jeanne Fahnestock, Lawrence Green, Louise Rosenblatt, Marie Secor, and Jeffrey Walker, whose work has enriched our understanding of rhetoric. The conversations we have had with colleagues and friends have given us opportunities to test ideas in dialogue with good interlocutors. We should like to thank, in particular, Janet Bland, who read most of the book in manuscript and offered many suggestions for revision, and, in addition, Linda Bensel-Meyers, Eric Gould, David Klooster, Christina Kreps, Terry Martin, Sally O'Friel, Eileen Turoff, and Margaret Whitt. And we are grateful to Betsy Gwyn and Hillory Oakes for class testing the book, reading and commenting on the manuscript, and composing the Instructors' Manual and Companion Website, and to Dell Vandever for all her support. We should also like to thank the editorial staff at Longman: Eben Ludlow for his continuing support and oversight of the project; Judith Fifer for her suggestions that helped us focus the format and presentation of our ideas and for her attentiveness to details throughout the process; and Lake Lloyd for her speed and care with production. And we owe thanks to the excellent readers for their careful, respectful reading and excellent advice for revision.

Thanks are due to all of the reviewers who commented on this manuscript prior to publication: Janet M. Atwill, University of Tennessee; Tracy Clark, Purdue University; Deborah Coxwell Teague, Florida State University; Gay Lynn Crossley, Marian College; Debra S. Knutson, Dakota State University; Carrie Leverenz, Texas Christian University; Jeff Ludwig, Illinois State University; Rolf Norgaard, University of Colorado at Boulder; Tim Peeples, Elon University; Lance Rivers, Lake Superior State University; Cynthia L. Walker, Faulkner University; and Stephen Wilhoit, University of Dayton.

And finally, our greatest supporters have been our families: Kevin and Chuck and our children, Ian and Ellen and Jeff and Sarah, for listening, questioning, encouraging, offering suggestions, and being patient.

PATSY CALLAGHAN
ANN DOBYNS

A Meeting of Minds

PART 1

Rhetoric as a Meeting of Minds

CHAPTER 1

A Meeting of Minds as a Rhetorical Act

Conversation is a meeting of minds with different memories and habits. When minds meet, they don't just exchange facts: they transform them, reshape them, draw different implications from them, engage in new trains of thought. Conversation doesn't just reshuffle the cards: it creates new cards.

Theodore Zeldin,
Conversation: How Talk Can Change Our Lives

WHAT IS RHETORIC?

In this chapter we will be talking about rhetoric. *Rhetoric* is a word you have probably heard often. News reporters sometimes refer to a politician's rhetoric or say that the words a public figure used were "all rhetoric." You probably have some sense of what these comments imply, but you may not be able to say precisely what the word means. Does it describe the way the politician is speaking, the way the public figure manipulates his or her listeners, or does it mean that the words are, to borrow a phrase from Shakespeare, "all sound and fury signifying nothing"? Or does rhetoric represent effective argument? Before talking about where these attitudes come from and what we mean by the term, let's consider a hypothetical situation where a person's understanding of rhetoric will influence her interaction with a friend.

Katie was a first year student at a large state college. Her roommate, Jen, had been her best friend since elementary school. Unlike Katie and their other friends, Jen always had to struggle to get decent grades, but because she worked hard and earned the necessary grade point average, she was admitted to college. Halfway through their first term, Jen told Katie that she was considering dropping out of school because she had decided that she wasn't smart enough to graduate. She said she felt stupid when she was in class, was terrified that the instructor might call on her, and knew that she could never pass her final exams. Besides, she had just received a failing grade on her first major assignment in a core class. She

3

thought that the grade proved her assessment of herself as not smart enough to earn a college degree.

Because Katie had known Jen for so long, she knew that her friend often felt insecure, but she also knew that in the past Jen had worked hard enough to do well. She wanted to find a way to convince her to stay in school. She thought she had three options:

- Give Jen a list of the values of a college education.
- Tell Jen how much she would miss her if she left.
- Answer Jen's own assertions about why she was leaving by explaining why staying in college might help her develop the confidence she seemed to lack.

Which choice do you think would have the best chance of changing Jen's mind? If you are like us, you would choose the third. An understanding of what rhetoric is and what elements it includes can help us see why. So, how are we defining rhetoric? According to one of the earliest teachers of rhetoric, the Greek philosopher Aristotle, rhetoric is the art of finding all the available means of persuasion. Our definition is similar but with a significant difference. We are defining rhetoric as the art of testing ideas with people who share our questions.

 ## KEY CONCEPT

A Definition of Rhetoric

Rhetoric is the art of testing ideas with people who share our questions. It involves not merely the language we use but all the decisions we make about how to communicate effectively with others.

THE RHETORICAL SITUATION

As our definition implies, rhetoric occurs in a situation that includes a speaker or writer, a reader or listener, and a subject under discussion. In addition to these three central elements, we may add two more: the speaker's purpose and the context in which the communication occurs. Understanding these elements of the rhetorical situation can help Katie make decisions about how to communicate. Giving her friend a list of the values of a college education might let Jen know quite a bit about the problem she was trying to solve but might not make her feel much better. Telling Jen that she would miss her says a great deal about the relationship between Katie and Jen but not much about the problem. Answering Jen's own assertions about her decision, though, addresses Jen's problems, demonstrates that Katie has listened to her friend and takes her words seriously, and shows her concern for Jen's feelings. In

KEY CONCEPT

The Elements of a Rhetorical Situation

A **rhetorical situation** includes all of the elements a writer or speaker needs to consider for communicating about a particular issue, and the way those elements determine all the decisions the writer or speaker makes. The elements in any rhetorical situation include:

SUBJECT: What is the writing about?

WRITER: Who is writing?

READER: Who is the intended audience?

SUBJECT: What is the message?

PURPOSE: Why is the writer communicating with the reader?

CONTEXT: What is the occasion for the writing? What social, historical, institutional, or cultural forces might influence the ways the writer communicates with the reader? What conventions of form and style are appropriate and expected for this subject and audience?

other words, the third option balances the three central elements of the rhetorical situation—the subject, the speaker, and the person addressed. Whenever you communicate with another person, you will need to consider all three of these elements.

The Rhetorical Triangle

The diagram in Figure 1.1 illustrates the major components of any rhetorical situation. The *subject* angle of the triangle represents the ideas you intend to present. The *writer* angle represents your particular way of seeing the issue and the particular way you choose to express it. The *reader* angle represents what your audience will need from you in order to hear, understand, and respond to your ideas. Your *purpose* is the way you meet your reader in the center, where you share common ground, where you attempt to see the issue in the same way. Your purpose guides your writing, so that your written text is the result of all of your rhetorical choices. Understanding your rhetorical situation is the key to making choices that will help your reader understand and evaluate your answer to the question you share.

The circle around the entire diagram represents another essential component of the situation that we will return to later in the book: *context*. The context is the occasion for the communication, and it includes all of the influences on how readers and writers make and interpret meanings. When writers communicate, they and their readers are influenced by their cultural and social backgrounds and ideas about what is appropriate and inappropriate.

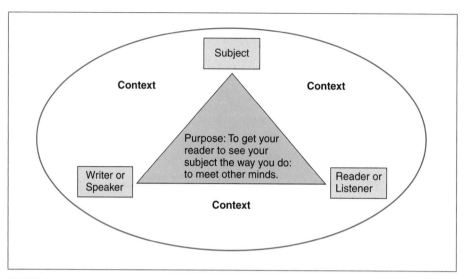

FIGURE 1.1   THE RHETORICAL TRIANGLE.

The major components of a rhetorical situation.

Writers need to know how these cultural and social situations will determine the effectiveness of their rhetorical decisions. They need to determine such things as what kinds of form they should use for the situation—a business letter, a memorandum, an academic argument? What kind of language—informal or formal? What kinds of examples—concrete or abstract? How many examples?

Our intuitive sense of rhetorical situations allows us to interact in everyday conversations with others. Even though you may think of yourself as having a certain personality or style, you make adjustments all the time to fit your social situation. You adjust your language choices to increase the likelihood that your messages will be heard and appreciated. You probably know some good jokes, but you may not tell the same joke the same way to your friends at a party as you do to your great aunt Doris at a family reunion. Making these kinds of distinctions shows that you have an intuitive understanding of the idea of the rhetorical situation because you are able to adjust language choices to meet the expectations and needs of particular audiences and subjects.

Most high school writing assignments help you develop your repertoire of language choices but rarely focus on developing your ability to *choose* from among your strategies those that will be most likely to address the needs of your rhetorical situation. There are reasons for that: most people are not ready until they are in college to figure out the complicated needs of other readers. In addition, the ideas and situations students confront often become more complicated in college. Your college writing classes should teach you ways to respond to a range of rhetorical situations using a variety of strategies, because as edu-

STRATEGY

How to Analyze a Rhetorical Situation

To analyze a writing situation, you will need to consider each element of the diagram in Figure 1.1: subject, writer, reader, purpose, and context. The following questions will help you do so:

1. **SUBJECT:** Why is this subject important to talk about? Do you have enough information about it? If you need more, where would you find it? If you are answering a question, how many answers can you think of, and how is your answer the best of those available? What are your key ideas? What evidence do you have to support them? What doubts do you have, and how can you inquire about them?

2. **WRITER:** Why are you writing? What is your stance in relation to your subject and reader: are you a friend, a mentor, a critic, a learner, a confidant, an expert?

3. **READER:** Who is your intended audience? How does your subject relate to their needs, interests, or expectations? Why might they need to know? What you would like to tell them? Are they receptive or resistant? If they are disinterested or resistant, how can you encourage interest and engagement?

4. **PURPOSE:** What would you like your reader to know, think, feel, or do about your subject? Is your intention to explain, explore, challenge, entertain, comfort, or persuade? Do you want to change your own understanding or behavior? Do you want to change the understanding or behavior of others?

5. **CONTEXT:** What social, historical, institutional, or cultural forces might influence your stance, your way of engaging an audience, or your way of presenting the subject? How does your understanding of the components of the rhetorical situation affect the form and content of your writing? In other words, what conventions of form and style are appropriate and expected for this subject and audience?

cated adults, you must address complicated issues while considering the needs of different audiences.

One of the most important advantages of a college education is that, through in-class and out-of-class experiences, you can broaden your understanding of contexts of all kinds. Interacting with people who are different from you helps you understand the ways others make decisions. Thus you not only develop your ability to work with others, but your own reasoning processes become more sophisticated as your repertoire of rhetorical strategies grows.

Understanding the elements of rhetoric will help you make good decisions as you write in real rhetorical situations. For example, what if you wanted to write a letter to the Director of the Writing Program at your college asking that you be excused from the first-year English requirement. You are doing so because you think that it doesn't make sense to require you to take a composition class when you took English all through high school and got decent grades. If you were to begin planning your letter by using the strategy questions listed in the "How to Analyze a Rhetorical Situation" strategy box, you might make the following notes:

> *Subject*: Why is the college composition course necessary? Need current course rationale, any justification for course in college catalog. Conversations with other students or teachers might help. Compare with high school course materials.
>
> *Writer*: I question the purposes of the course as stated in the syllabus because they look a lot like the ones for my high school class. I need to be informed about the materials of the class. Need to revise the letter for grammar and style and check conventions of a formal letter.
>
> *Reader:* Director of Writing, who evidently sees the necessity of the class and so might be resistant to the discussion. Knowledgeable about style, grammar, and writing conventions.
>
> *Context:* Current course rationale, Writing Director who will judge the quality of the writing against college-level standards, student as consumer, past experiences with writing classes, precedents for waiving the requirement.

This analysis would help you determine how to write the letter: what tone to use, what kinds of language might be appropriate, how formal to be, what information and supporting evidence to include, and so forth. We will be exploring all these decisions in the chapters that follow.

 APPLICATION

Analyzing Your Rhetorical Situation

Use the five elements of the Rhetorical Triangle—subject, writer, reader, purpose, and context—to determine what information the writer might need to explore the question below. Using the strategy questions in the "How to Analyze a Rhetorical Situation" box, list the questions that the writer should answer before writing the paper.

> "Why would we kill whales? It just doesn't make sense. Anything we get from whales we can get from other sources cheaper and more efficiently. So why go ahead and kill beautiful, intelligent animals?"

FIGURE 1.2

THE CONVERSATION,
PASTEL BY LOIS BAJOR

RHETORIC AND DIALOGUE

How do we test ideas with people who share our questions? If we are really interested in finding the best possible answers, we recognize the need to explore answers together, and that means we must exchange our ideas. We must engage in dialogue.

Seeing rhetoric as dialogue is quite different from the ways you might usually define the term. As we said earlier, people typically use the word *rhetoric* in one of two ways—either as the form of language or as logic. When people call someone's words "mere rhetoric," they mean that the message may sound impressive but lacks substance. Certainly, a speaker can convince a listener by using impressive language. You might remember times when you heard a speech or lecture that inspired or moved you by the words the speaker used. Politicians count on this kind of response when they use phrases that will be impressive and memorable. The other major way people talk about rhetoric is as the use of logic. When people talk about rhetoric this way, they imply that the way to change others' minds is by convincing them that only one answer makes sense. Sometimes debaters and attorneys in television shows imply this when they insist that their answers are the only logical conclusions to the facts presented.

Exploring ideas through dialogue means more than simply trying to change people's minds; it means trying to find good solutions to problems. A person using this kind of rhetoric is not trying to trick another person into accepting an answer to the question but rather to convince the other person to consider the strength of a position. This is the kind of conversation in which both participants seek to understand a mutual problem by identifying their question, analyzing their rhetorical situation, and considering the possible choices of language and the reasons they might use in proposing possible answers.

When people engage in this kind of dialogue about mutual questions, they must consider issues of identification, shared concerns, and responsibility. They must determine what questions they share, what assumptions they bring to the discussion, why their assumptions might differ, what information they need to solve their mutual question, how they interpret the information they will share, and how they might find points of agreement. The effectiveness of their dialogue depends on a level of integrity and responsibility beyond the concerns of simply changing another's mind; it requires the speaker or writer to be willing to change his or her mind as well.

Dialogue as a Meeting of Minds

An understanding of rhetoric, then, provides a way to address conflicts, to respect those whose positions you challenge, and to think in deeper and richer ways through dialogue. We call this a meeting of minds because when we test the strength of competing positions, we do so by putting our minds together. This dialogue occurs either in direct face-to-face interaction with others or by imagining the ways others concerned about the issue would respond.

Meeting other minds requires the speaker or writer to be in a two-way interaction with the listener. In dialogue, both participants are listening to and evaluating the other's positions. Rather than simply trying to change the other's mind, they are willing to change their own minds. People who define rhetoric as impressive and persuasive language or as convincing argument suggest that rhetorical choices are ones a writer makes to move readers to the writer's position, and thus only the listener's mind might change. For example, a candidate

 ## KEY CONCEPT

The Elements of Dialogue
Good dialogue includes the following characteristics:

A shared question.

Respectful listening.

Presentation of good ideas and reasons.

Consideration of the differences and similarities of competing answers.

Language choices that increase the likelihood that others will care enough to listen.

for congress in a midwestern farm state might argue that a law outlawing the sale of genetically engineered produce would unnecessarily deny farmers more efficient ways to increase their profits. As this congressional candidate makes the argument, she might talk about why she, unlike her opponent, is suspicious of "intrusive big government." In her choice of argument and language, the candidate would be asking her constituents to take on a particular attitude, to vote for her even if they might originally have considered voting for her opponent.

The irony of this kind of arguing is that it restricts both the speaker and the listener. When the congressional candidate defines the discussion in terms of a single concern of her listeners, she closes down her own exploration of the complexity of the issue. As a result, she not only makes her constituents see the election in simple terms, but she also limits her own perspective on the question.

This way of making rhetorical choices contradicts what we consider an essential part of dialogue. When you are in real dialogue with another person and genuinely care about the issue you are discussing and, perhaps most importantly, respect the other person in the dialogue, we doubt that you are making choices to manipulate or trick your listener into accepting your position. Instead, while you try to convince the person to understand and consider the position you are taking, you also attempt to understand and consider the other person's beliefs and assumptions. Making rhetorical choices in dialogue means that both the writer and person addressed participate in a mutual exploration of the issue and sometimes change their minds.

Identifying Through Dialogue

When we are in real dialogue with a person whose ideas we respect and take seriously, we say things like "I hear what you're saying" or "I'm not sure what you mean by that" or "I guess I can understand why you would see it that way." We suggest our own positions with statements like "But I've always thought" or "But if you look at it this way" or "But what if you considered." We use these phrases because we are trying to find where we agree and disagree and also because we are attempting to see the issue from someone else's perspective. As writers listen to different positions, attitudes, and reasons, they shape their own positions as a real response to others who share their questions.

When we realize that the person we are addressing does not see things in the same way we do, we need to step back and find the knowledge, ideas, beliefs, assumptions, and conventions we share. Finding what we have in common allows us to identify with another person. But to find what we hold in common often requires us to identify our differences. Sometimes our differences may have to do with nothing more than not speaking the same language. However, even when we speak the same language, we misunderstand each other because of our different national and regional differences. For example, in the United States we know that a large vehicle that has its own engine, travels on the highway, and carries goods is called a truck, but if we were in London it would be called a lorry. We know that football players score touchdowns and earn 6 points for doing so, unless we are in London, where football is a different sport and players score goals worth one point. Similar language differences exist even within the United States. In the northeast, people say they stand *on* line; most of the people in the rest of the country stand *in* line. While such differences seem small, recognizing them and understanding the underlying meaning can allow us to communicate more effectively.

More important than these differences in language are our political and cultural differences. Some Americans believe that education should be paid for by tax money, and others think a lottery is a more effective source of funding; some believe children should speak only when spoken to, and others want them to voice their opinions openly. In America we believe that each person has the right to vote in democratically held elections, that all citizens have the right to the pursuit of happiness, that women and men deserve equal pay for equal work. Not all cultures agree.

Knowing that belief systems are common only to those people who already share assumptions is important to you for two reasons. First, it means that if you are to communicate effectively with anyone whose background, experiences, or values are different from your own, you must be able to identify your own assumptions about what is reasonable or appropriate or right so that you can discuss them with others whose assumptions are different. Second, if you care about persuading your listeners or readers that your perspective is warranted, then you must be able to identify the assumptions you share. If you and another person disagree about how education should be funded, you can at least agree that it needs funding. Finding this point of agreement may allow you to consider the strengths and weaknesses of various competing proposals for providing the most effective means of funding.

Academic Dialogue

So far we have talked only about how rhetoric applies to dialogue in personal conversations, letters, or professional speeches or essays. You might wonder what possible connection this has to your college education. We think that the kind of rhetoric we have been describing is the heart of your studies because all disciplines rely on what is called shared critical inquiry, which is another term for this way of talking about rhetoric. Whatever your course of study, you will be asked at times to study a problem, take a position, and give good reasons for your opinion. When you do this, you will be writing like your instructors do when they publish their research. The articles and books they write may not look like they are engaging in dialogue, but they always write with the expectation that other scholars who are interested in the same questions will write responses to their inquiry. This is the way dialogue works in academic fields.

As you study the material in your classes, you will engage in inquiry in many different ways. You will need to summarize the positions and reasons of the instructor and the readings of the class, and to assess the strength of the arguments presented in a lecture or in the books and essays you read. When you have developed an understanding of the issues involved, you will conduct your own research about a question at issue in your class, then justify the conclusions you draw at the end of your study. Each of these situations will demand that you rely on your rhetorical skills.

As you do so, you will need to think about the rhetorical situation you are in. You may be able to see the danger of attempting to persuade your instructor of the strength of your position through impressive language, particularly if your argument lacks substance or if the language detracts from the strength of your argument. It may seem less obvious why you need to think about more than logic as you write your essay, but you should remember that real questions have more than one good answer. Your answer will be only one of many, and so you will need to consider what kinds of examples and information your instructor will consider convincing, to what extent you and your instructor agree, what questions, assumptions, and concerns you share, and whether your essay presents your position in a compelling way.

Conscious, guided practice in careful and attentive reading and writing strengthens your ability to explore questions. As you read, you see how writers are shaping their ideas into words to share with readers. As you write, you shape notions into words to share with others. In addition to sharing your ideas with others, you are also testing them against your own understanding, to clarify them for yourself, and to shape them the best way you can to reflect what it is you know and want to say. This interaction allows you to explore your initial ideas about the problem and to shape positions discovered through the initial inquiry.

 ## STRATEGY

How to Open Up a Dialogue

To meet other minds in shared understanding, you will need to do the following:

1. You must be able to identify the questions that people attempt to answer when they discuss ideas.
2. You must be able to listen carefully to what others are saying, keeping your mind open to good ideas and reasons.
3. You must give good reasons for the answers you propose.
4. You must consider how your answers differ from or parallel the answers others propose.
5. You must identify the assumptions and beliefs you hold in common with those you wish to address.
6. You must make language choices that will increase the likelihood that someone else will care enough to hear what you have to say.

APPLICATION

Opening Up a Dialogue
In small groups or with your whole class, brainstorm a list of questions on issues that interest the group. Choose one, then write a paragraph summarizing what you believe about the issue and how your position differs from what other people in the class believe.

RHETORICAL COMMUNITIES

What Is a Rhetorical Community?

One way to talk about the kind of dialogue we have been exploring is as conversations that take place within communities. They are conversations because they involve discussing various answers to a shared question. Being joined by their common interests and concerns, people who discuss common questions form what we call rhetorical communities.

Rhetorical communities may be groups of real people sitting down face to face as they try to solve immediate problems they share or people who do not know each other but enter Internet chatrooms to discuss their common concerns. What makes such communities rhetorical is their interest in the same question. Examples of communities engaging in this kind of dialogue might include a group of neighbors who meet to discuss whether their community organization should ask the city to reconsider building a half-way house in their district, a non-profit organization that explores ways to raise money for a new facility, a teachers' union that considers whether to demand a higher wage for beginning instructors, a student government subcommittee that is writing a policy statement on plagiarism, or even a group of poets in an artists' colony who exchange experimental poetry. These groups become rhetorical communities when they begin to explore a question the members have in common.

 KEY CONCEPT

Characteristics of a Rhetorical Community
Rhetorical communities have the following characteristics:

Its members share common questions.

Its members engage in dialogue to find answers to their common questions.

Its members have knowledge and experience that they bring to the discussion.

Kinds of Rhetorical Communities

Local Communities

Most geographical areas have many kinds of rhetorical communities that address the problems they share. Such organizations may be political units or simply neighbors who live on the same block, business owners in the district, homeowner associations in condominium units, religious groups, or parent-teacher organizations. Whatever joins them, the members share questions and problems. The issues they deal with may be as narrow and specific as how to organize an annual block party or what to do about noise complaints or as broad and general as how to address a region's problem of homelessness or how to improve the local schools. They become communities out of a need to engage in dialogue about their shared concerns.

Sharing concerns, however, does not mean that all members of the community are necessarily of one mind. Often such groups have members who are very different in gender, age, ethnic identity, religion, or socio-economic background. This means that the effectiveness of their dialogue depends on finding ways to identify common ground. They may do so by explaining their differences, then working together to identify what they might agree on as mutual goals. As they do so, they will be balancing their recognition and understanding of the differences in background, beliefs, and perhaps language with their expectation that they are a group of reasonable people willing to listen to each other.

The Academic Community

Like neighborhood and local organizations, college communities have shared issues. Because the members of a college community share a place of work and specific goals, their problems are not unlike those found in neighborhood groups. They often discuss questions related to parking on and around campus, living arrangements, relationships between faculty and students, community involvement, general education requirements, noise, and so forth. While the particular issues are specific to the individual school, these are questions that colleges all over the country address.

Because members of college communities also belong to the larger academic community, they share questions that have to do with how our society funds higher education, how that funding ought to be distributed, what admissions standards ought to be, whether there are shared views of general education requirements, or whether writing courses should be required. As members of the academic community address each other about the issues they explore, they use language characteristics that all members recognize as appropriate to academic discourse. When they engage in dialogue, they speak somewhat more formally than they might in conversations with friends. Rather than appealing primarily to the emotions of their audiences, they appeal to the reasoning of other members of the community. They also choose a genre appropriate for their message. Academic genres include the memorandum, public address, departmental or committee report, and academic essay, to mention a few. Whatever genre they choose, they do so according to the expectations of their audiences.

You may not think that you are a part of these discussions, but as members of your college community, you should have a voice in the dialogue about the issues of your school and higher education. Your experience and perspective should be represented. Throughout this book, we will be showing you ways to recognize and use academic discourse.

Specific Academic Communities: Disciplines and Classes

In addition to participating in the general academic conversation, you will be joining conversations in various academic communities. Every time you take a class, you are entering a particular rhetorical community. Whether the questions you are addressing have to do with mathematics, sciences, art, literature, or politics, the classroom is where students of that subject, or discipline, join to explore the questions they share. The questions will differ and depend on the material you will study, but each class will address very specific questions that your instructor should make clear on the course syllabus.

In addition to the rhetorical community of the entire class, smaller rhetorical communities may take shape within the classroom. Some instructors will assign issues to small discussion groups or teams, but students may also build their own communities such as writing groups to help each other revise their essays, or study groups to discuss research with other students who are studying related issues. In each of these situations, the group would benefit from practice in using the rhetorical triangle as the participants explore and try to find answers to their questions.

Just as the larger academic community shares language conventions, each discipline within the larger academic community has language characteristics particular to that discipline. A lab report requires you to use a form and language that is quite different from the kind of essay you might write in a political science class. When you first begin to study a subject, you begin by learning a new language and a new set of discourse conventions. Although this book will not teach you the language of every discipline, we hope that our discussions of discourse analysis will help you in learning those languages.

Forming a Rhetorical Community

What makes any group a rhetorical community is the questions they have in common and the activity of communicating about the questions. We will be discussing rhetorical communities in the classroom further in the following chapters, but for now, we will look at an example of the way a local issue caused a community to begin a discussion.

Every day, newspapers report on observed events and issues, and people respond to those reports in diverse ways through letters to the editor. Newspaper editorial pages are full of comments from people trying to understand the news. When we read these pages, we can witness communities attempting to meet other minds in response to questions they share. When these writers all address the same issue, they form a rhetorical community. Readers' responses often differ because they are influenced by the backgrounds and the experiences they bring to their reading. In the newspaper article that follows, a reporter begins a conversation when he reports on a seemingly minor event in a suburban community: a high school student shoots a bear out of a backyard tree. Just to the east of the location of the shooting is a mid-sized city. Just to the west of the location, beyond thousands of acres of orchard land, the Cascade Mountain wilderness area begins. The large Yakama Indian Reservation lies to the south. To the north, the Yakima River flows between ridges covered with sagebrush. In this location, the shooting triggers a community debate about values and priorities.

Taste for Pears Was Bruin's Undoin'

West Valley teen bags bear that wandered onto his grandfather's land near 84th and Summitview.

1.   An unwanted guest in West Valley went from orchard marauder to bedroom rug Thursday afternoon.

2.   Dubbed the "Pear Bear," a 3-year-old male black bear was shot in a backyard near the intersection of 84th and Summitview avenues after eluding authorities for more than a day.

3.   "He was dead after the first shot," said Dustin Trammel, a West Valley High School sophomore who bagged the treed bear.

4.   Wildlife biologist Lee Stream tried to shoot the bear Wednesday with a tranquilizer dart as it roamed through Congdon Orchards near 64th Avenue and Nob Hill Boulevard. Authorities were unable to track the bear.

5.   "Pear Bear was in the orchard doing what bears do at this time of year, eating as much food—in this case, apples and pears—as possible in order to survive a long winter hibernation," said Stream, with the state Department of Fish and Wildlife.

6.   "It has been a tough year for bears," said Scott McCorquedale, wildlife biologist with the Yakama Nation. He captured and tagged Pear Bear on the reservation a year ago as part of a research project.

7.   Record mountain snows lingering well into summer have hampered the growth of normal bear food, mainly berries. Many bears have wandered to lower elevations in search of food, he said.

8.   Pear Bear, who weighed 100 pounds at 2 years old, previously was not a problem, McCorquedale said.

9.   But the bear wandered closer to civilization than any bear in recent years. After eluding Stream and Yakima County sheriff's deputies Wednesday, the bear did not return to the wild as some had hoped. Instead, he blundered farther into suburbia.

FIGURE 1.3

WEST VALLEY TEEN BAGS
PEAR-EATING BEAR

10   "I drove up and saw the bear back by my cattle," said Don Trammel, a retired West Valley resident and hunter. "When I got out of my truck it climbed a tree."

11   Trammel immediately called the sheriff's office and the state Wildlife Department. The treed bear posed a safety risk for authorities.

12   "He didn't appear to be aggressive," Stream said Thursday. "But under the right circumstances, he could have been."

13   If the bear was shot with a tranquilizer-laden dart, it would likely run for five minutes until the drugs kicked in, authorities said.

14   "Bears run quickly," said sheriff's Lt. Dave Thompson, noting that Apple Valley Elementary School was only four blocks away.

15   "We were ready to lock down the school," said Sharon Allen, Apple Valley's principal.

16   "It is open season for bears, and hunting seemed to be the best option," Thompson said.

17   Don Trammel's grandson had a state permit to hunt bears. Thompson and Trammel went to the school and pulled 15-year-old Dustin from his fourth period class.

18   "He thought I was joking," the elder Trammel said.

19   The youth armed himself with a .30-caliber rifle and went to the back yard, where the bear remained in the tree.

20   A single 60-foot shot ended Pear Bear's life.

21   "It's going to be a rug," the obviously proud teenager said, while standing over the dead bear, which was unceremoniously loaded into the bed of his pickup.

22   "It's going in my bedroom."

After reading the article, you might wonder what the writer assumed about his readers, how he thought his story might affect the way they saw the incident, and whether he thought his story would start a discussion. Nearly forty letters were published in the *Yakima Herald-Republic* responding to this story. The following are representative of the very different responses elicited by the newspaper article.

___ __ __

Letters to the Editor of the *Yakima Herald-Republic*

To the editor:

1   Finally: a reasoned response to a fairly common occurrence.

2   To those who are critical of the measure taken to resolve this situation, remember, wild animals are nearly all hard-pressed to exist and all will take advantage of an easy meal. The resolution of this dilemma should be the simplest action that can be safely taken.

3   The recent killing of the bear west of Yakima was not cruel or uncalled for since the animal would revisit another easy meal whenever it could be found. And where can an animal be relocated where there are not "people"? Thank you Don Trammel for your solution.

Perry Boogard, *Yakima*

To the editor:

1   Are you joking? Dusty Trammel shoots a hungry, lost, scared bear out of a tree. He's quite the accomplished hunter. I'm sure he enjoyed the thrill of waking up and smelling the morning air, the challenge of finding an animal in his territory and stalking him, then enjoying the "fruits of his labor" by utilizing the animal to feed and sustain his family.

2   I'm sure he used the meat for food and the skin and pelt for this upcoming winter's harsh conditions. After all, is this not why people hunt? What a great policy the West Valley School District must have in allowing young boys to enjoy the thrill of the kill. Well done. What an educational experience.

3   A true "hunter" actually hunts. For the wildlife authorities to state that they were scared the bear could run after being shot with a tranquilizer dart, my better judgment tells me that the bear would have hung onto that tree in pure fear until it fell out.

4   Local officials deflect public attitude by coaxing a holder of a bear tag to be their scapegoat. They knew that shooting the bear would have led to a publicity nightmare for the county.

5   A boo and a hiss to all agencies and individuals who showed very poor judgment and character in their actions in this situation.

Tim Madden, *Yakima*

To the editor:

1   I would like to defend young Mr. Trammell before all the animal lovers and ban-the-guns people crucify him. I would also like to commend the boy's grandfather.

2   Dustin Trammell had the correct permits, issued by the state of Washington, to shoot the bear. Don Trammell went to the person he knew who had said permits were needed.

3   Regardless of the circumstances, the bear, a potential danger to the children of Apple Valley School, was tagged and bagged legally.

James Rogers, *Wapato*

To the editor:

1   There is nothing proud about gunning down a defenseless animal, and to think so is just as ridiculous as the grandfather who pulled a boy out of school to do a job that the so-called authorities couldn't handle.

2   If we as a society support decisions like that, we are truly in a state of peril. When we bore further and further into the mountains and natural forests with our condos, strip malls, and gas stations, where do we expect the animals to go?

3   This is nature, as it has evolved because of the human race. We exploit and exhaust everything we are given. We cannot expect to take over nature and not take care of it. What amuses me is the incompetence of the authorities involved. What kind of a biologist is eluded by a 200 pound bear? Also, if the bear was so hard to shoot with a tranquilizer gun, how was it so easy for a 15-year-old boy to shoot it?

4   Why couldn't it be trapped, taken to a refuge (there are plenty out there) and rehabilitated? Because Yakimans are so bored they would die without melodrama.

5   In closing I would just like to say, stop the insanity!

Jolene Calahan, *Yakima*

To the editor:

1   The great dominant culture's mentality and behavior strikes again with disrespect for life.

2   Bear is the medicine of healers within some of our cultures. Upon hearing of this magnificent creature's journey I thought to myself how sad it is that many people are blind to this medicine sign. When some part of the natural world captures our attention, it is to be noticed, honored, heeded.

3   Miserably, once again a group of individuals took part in killing a beautiful creature of medicine. From the rationalization that "Well, it could have become aggressive" (although no such behavior was observed) to the disrespectful manner in which the event was written about, the bear has been dishonored.

4   Some of us will burn candles and smudge sweetgrass in honor of our murdered brother. His violation? Searching for the fruit of life. For that he has become a bragged-about trophy rug.

5   My prayer is that each time someone walks upon bear's back they will hear great bear's whisper, "Mitakuye Oyasin" (we are related).

Sara Earthdove, *Selah*

To the editor:

1   Population growth is the single largest problem in the world. The Earth has doubled its own population since 1960. There's not much wilderness for wild animals to go to. There's not much wilderness for humans to go to. The carrying capacity of the wild land is at maximum for several species.

2   Would you, if you lived in the area where the bear had come to, have willingly given up your cat or dog to the bear? Would you have given up your child?

3   The shot was right and righteous. It's a hard world. The wind and water eat the rock. In the scope of things, there's little difference between a mustard seed and a bear, or between a bear and a human. This time the hunter got the bear. Sometimes it's the other way around.

Dan Donaldson, Prosser

To the editor:

1   There is a lesson to be learned here, and it is not about bear hunting. The Herald-Republic had a choice as to how they presented this article, and they chose to make it inflammatory. Choosing to call the bear "Pear Bear" had to be a deliberate attempt to subliminally relate to the warm and fuzzy "Care Bears."

2   Again we are hit with the old truth that "The pen is mightier than the sword." All you folks who are riled up by the Herald-Republic's treatment of this subject ought to sit back and consider how you have been manipulated. I think they call it "spin."

Judy Verbrugge, Wapato

These letters show that although members of a rhetorical community share an interest in an issue, their attitudes about the subject often differ radically. These writers have very different assumptions about what is good and evil, lawful and unlawful, acceptable and unacceptable. We're often told that newspaper reporting is generally assumed to be an objective account of events, but in this case something in the writer's account of the story invited these responses.

What was the rhetorical situation of the reporter who wrote the original article? His job was to report the facts, but as the writer of a human-interest story, the reporter also knew to take into account the needs and possible reactions of his readers. In his account of his subject, the reporter recognized that some of his readers would support the shooting because it took care of a problem. He knew that others might regret the shooting, maybe because the problem it solved was the fault of humans, not bears. In any case, his language choices recognized and predicted the split opinions of his audience. The bear was "just doing what bears do," especially in a "tough year." It didn't threaten civilization as much as it "blundered" into the neighborhood. The bear was "unceremoniously" loaded into the back of a truck, implying that some ceremony was in order. And we have to note that it's disturbing that a "guest," even an unwanted one, could wind up as a "bedroom rug."

We might say that the writer's purpose is simply to inform us about a community interest event. But the reporter's language also tweaks us, a little, into identifying with the bear so that we ask the question "Was the shooting necessary?"

The letter writers join the conversation as they consider the question the reporter raised. They offer varied reasons for their position, based on different assumptions: Yes, because the bear was a safety risk. No, because the bear was just trying to survive a harsh winter. The barrage of letters on this issue might have been written no matter what the original article said, but it's possible that the reporter's description of the event helped inspire the controversy.

If effective dialogue depends on shared understanding, then obviously, the group of letter writers who responded to the shooting of "Pear Bear" are not ready to solve their problem. They do not yet share a common understanding of what happened to the bear in the pear tree. But this "conversation" that occurred in the paper is exactly the way we communicate every day. The letter writers have different perspectives, and each one brings something unique to the conversation about the meaning of the bear and the bear's relationship to the community. If you know how to listen carefully to those different perspectives, and if you are able to analyze how your perspective is like and unlike those of others, you will be more likely to achieve better, stronger understandings of issues—for yourself, and when you want to, to share with others through a meeting of minds.

Is it really possible to put together opinions as different as those in the letters and come up with a meeting of minds? Yes—if readers and writers really listen to each other respectfully. Yes—because a meeting of minds does not have to end in complete agreement; the goal is that all parties understand each other better. Listening to all points of view with an open mind and trying to understand the reasoning of people whose ideas differ will increase the quality and breadth of knowledge of everyone in the conversation.

One way to begin the dialogue with other people is to ask questions that test the strength of the positions they present. The questions in the strategy box "How to Examine a Writer's Position" will help you begin such testing, a skill we will be developing further throughout this book.

STRATEGY

How to Examine a Writer's Position

When you seek to understand a piece of writing that expresses a position on an issue that interests you, try asking the following questions:

1. Does the writer know his or her subject, not only the facts but also the issues raised?

2. How does the writer pay respect to the ideas of others?

3. How does the writer attempt to convince us that he or she is equipped to answer the question? Why should we listen to him or her?

4. To what extent does the writing persuade you to agree with the writer? Why do you agree with the writer, or why not?

In the following article, a freelance writer for the newspaper enters the conversation. His understanding of the issue depends in many ways not only on the original news story but also on the discussion that took place in the community as a response to the original story.

JIM PEARSON

The Death of Pear Bear: Shooting Proved to Be Only Answer

1   By now you've heard about "Pear Bear." That's the one that 15-year-old Dustin Trammell shot last Thursday out on 84th Avenue in West Valley. Some people were outraged over the incident, and Don Trammell, Dustin's grandfather, has been getting phone calls, both pro and con.

2   Don came home last Thursday and saw a bear scooting up a tree on his property. He called the state Department of Fish and Wildlife office, and biologist Jeff Bernatowicz came out to have a look.

3   At that point, they had three possible courses of action:

1. Walk away and leave the bear alone.

2. Tranquilize the bear and move him away from humanity.

3. Kill him.

4   The first option was not a good one. The bear had moved in among people and was eating pretty well. He was in an area with lots of people, pets and livestock. The bear probably wasn't going away of his own accord because he had found food and evidently was not all that afraid of people.

5   The No. 2 option, tranquilizing and moving the bear to another area, also had its problems. In order to put the right amount of muscle relaxer/anesthetic into the syringe, the biologist has to guess the weight of the animal and how much fat is on the body. If the dart hits a vein, the drugs act quickly and the bear could fall from the tree, injuring itself. On the other hand, darted correctly in a muscle, the drug can take as long as 10 minutes to work. In the Spokane area, a number of bears have been darted, only to come out of the trees and take off running.

6   Either way, if he fell out of the tree and injured himself or if he came down the tree after being darted, they might be faced with having to shoot the critter. That's a problem in a crowded area, where the shot would be nearly horizontal.

7   Even if everything had worked out perfectly, it would have taken two men all day to haul the bear up to the mountains to be released. That costs money. After he's released, if he's in another bear's territory, he's going to get chased out. Even if he doesn't get chased out, he may come right back to the area where the pears are plentiful. Bears have a powerful homing instinct. You've no doubt read stories of bears that were trapped and moved repeatedly, only to return time and time again.

8   Option 3 looked better and better. Bear season was open, there are plenty of them, the bear was outside the city limits where discharge of a firearm was legal, no one else's property would have to be entered (hunting on private property is by permission only), the shot would be fired nearly straight up so as not to endanger anyone, and Don's grandson had a bear tag. In fact, he had already spent several days hunting for a bear.

9   The rest is history. Dustin is going to get a bear rug, the meat will be donated to Sportsmen Against Hunger, a program begun by Safari Club International that provides game meat to the needy, and the people in that area no longer have to worry about a bear.

10   But nuisance bears in the area west of town aren't a new thing. Pear Bear wasn't the first. In 1995, Tieton resident Bill Haney killed a huge black bear at the end of Tieton Drive, where the orchards end and the sagebrush begins. I reported that story in the Washington-Oregon Game and Fish Magazine. The bear was supposed to have weighed more than 600 pounds, but I wasn't able to confirm that. I did, however, show Dee Ruggles the picture of the bear. Dee, along with his partner, Bill Copeland, both Tieton residents, used to run bears with hounds on predator control.

11   Bill took one look at the photo and said, "I don't have any trouble believing that bear weighed 600 pounds." He pointed to a bear rug hanging on his wall. "That rug measures exactly six feet from nose to tail. It came off the biggest bear I ever saw and he weighed 450 pounds. The bear in this photo (the one Haney killed) is a lot bigger. It's turned diagonally across a 6-foot pick-up bed and the head is hanging over the tailgate. He's quite a bit longer than 6 feet."

12   I called Steve Pozzanghera, carnivore biologist for the Department of Fish and Wildlife to check out the story. He told me black bears could get that big, but they were usually "agricultural" bears. They can make terrific weight gains feeding on apples and other fruits, Pozzanghera said.

13   Bingo! Haney said the bear had about 40 pounds of Golden Delicious apples in his belly. Evidently, he had been making a nuisance of himself for some time because he had an old shotgun wound that was healed over and a newer rifle wound that was partially healed.

14   Let's face it, urban bears are a nuisance. Frankly, I think Dustin and his grandfather are owed a "thanks." They solved a problem in the only logical way available.

APPLICATION

Examining a Writer's Position

Using the questions in the strategy box "How to Examine a Writer's Position," examine Jim Pearson's opinion piece about the Pear Bear incident. Write a short paragraph summarizing your answers.

READING AND WRITING: A MEETING OF MINDS

In this chapter, we have introduced assumptions and concepts that relate to all of the practices included in this book. First, when you engage with others in conversations that seek good answers to shared questions, you will need to find what assumptions and ideas you share. This is important because if you are to help your readers understand you, then you must try to understand them. Second, understanding your rhetorical situation helps you share your ideas with others. Each new writing situation permits you to extend your knowledge by allowing you to learn new strategies or combine those you already know in a new way. Third, people respond to problems in different ways because their experiences and backgrounds differ. If you listen respectfully to others whose ideas are different from your own, you will not only understand your own positions more completely, but you will also increase the probability that others will understand you. Sometimes, with good reasons, you may even change your mind! This art, the art of rhetoric, is one of the most important and valuable arts you can employ both in and out of college.

A meeting of minds does not necessarily mean that you agree with others or that they agree with you; it only means that you understand each other and respect the fact that there are alternate perspectives on any issue that help define the issue as a whole. This kind of mutual respect is not just a matter of civility or tolerance, though it certainly relies on those qualities. Your knowledge will be increased and enriched through your ability to be open to new ideas and perspectives and to relate them to your old knowledge.

In this book, we will share with you the results of writers' attempts to understand experiences, situations, ideas, and issues through dialogue. We will introduce strategies for engaging in such dialogue that have been used successfully by writers—students and professionals—for ages. As you practice the strategies, you will discover how to choose the ones best suited for your reading and writing purposes.

Sometimes, you may be satisfied to have an opinion and not examine, explore, or question it, but for that, you don't need this book. This book begins with the assumption that questioning and exploring answers to questions will result in better, stronger understandings that can be shared with others and tested in that interaction.

Reading and writing are wonderful and powerful tools for helping you make sense of your experiences. As a capable reader, you enrich your experience and knowledge through meeting other minds. As a capable writer, you can find language to express complexities in comprehensible, coherent ways, and to express your conclusions in respectful, informed ways.

WRITING INVITATIONS

1. Select an issue that you find puzzling or questionable, perhaps one of the issues you identified in the application box "Opening Up a Dialogue." Then,

write several paragraphs that describe how you would go about exploring this subject or issue.

2. Part 4 of this text includes three casebooks of writings on various topics. Guided by your instructor or exploring on your own, select an article that challenges your thinking. Read it carefully, and then using questions from the strategy box "How to Examine a Writer's Position," explore possible reactions to the article in writing by imagining at least three different perspectives and writing letters to the author from those perspectives. Try as hard as you can to make each imaginary writer's perspective reasonable and believable.

3. Bring your local newspaper to class and, in groups, select an article that raises an issue for the group. Using the questions from the strategy box "How to Analyze a Rhetorical Situation," describe the rhetorical situation in which you think the author is writing. Individually, write letters responding to the article. You may go on to share your letters with your group.

DEVELOPING A WRITING PROJECT

Identify a question you might like to explore for an extended essay. Using the questions from the strategy box "How to Analyze a Rhetorical Situation," describe the elements of the rhetorical situation that would guide your exploration of the issue. Write a letter to your instructor in which you explain the issue and describe the rhetorical situation.

CHAPTER 2

Rhetoric and Inquiry

To meet at all, one must open one's eyes to another; and there is no true conversation no matter how many words are spoken, unless the eye, unveiled and listening, opens itself to the other.

Jessamyn West

Writing when properly managed…is but a different name for conversation.

Laurence Sterne

Never regard study as a duty but as an enviable opportunity to learn to know the liberating influence of beauty in the realm of the spirit for your own personal joy and to the profit of the community to which your later works belong.

Albert Einstein

WHAT IS INQUIRY?

In Chapter 1 we suggested that all learning, in or out of college, involves some exploration through dialogue. In dealing with our everyday problems, we might listen to others, consult authorities, read manuals written by others, or look at solutions others have discovered. Then we make decisions or take actions based on the best reasons we can come up with through these interactions. We also learn through a kind of dialogue when we read and write. When we read, we are listening in on a conversation about issues, a discussion that started before we began reading. When we write on a topic we have read or talked about, we are also entering a dialogue, because we address issues that others before us have addressed.

Conversations that we learn from occur all the time in our lives, and conducted in civil, informed ways, they can be wonderful—entertaining, engaging, informative. They occur among friends; they occur in response to public events, whether artistic, political, scientific, socio-cultural, or historical; they not only occur but are the point of that recently proliferating format, the talk show; and they occur more than ever before in the ever-present chat spaces on the Internet. All of these interactions are shared explorations, but not all lead to the kind of learning we hope you will acquire from your college discussions. But with experience and practice, you can make conversations like these into places to explore and test ideas—by practicing a kind of discussion we called shared inquiry.

Rather than talking merely about conversations then, we are using the more precise term *inquiry* in this chapter because we wish to look more specifically at the relationship between learning and inquiry. To inquire is to ask questions, but it is also to explore possible answers, reasons, and evidence that might support competing answers. An inquiry is an investigation in which inquirers ask questions and consider the strengths of possible competing answers. When we engage in shared inquiry, we are explicitly sharing the process of asking questions and exploring answers, and we are benefiting from the interaction. Through shared inquiry, we can learn about ourselves and others, as well as about the subject of the conversation.

The following transcribes a part of a college class inquiring together about a film they had watched in class. The film was Frances Ford Coppola's Vietnam war film *Apocalypse Now*, the story about an army captain named Willard who is sent on a mission up river into enemy territory to kill a former American army colonel who has set up a renegade camp of native warriors (see Figure 2.1). In addition to seeing the film, the students had also read a review of it by John Simon.

Apocalypse Now Discussion

INSTRUCTOR: How many of you had seen this film before or the new version issued in 2002? It came out originally in 1979, and many people call it a classic. Web sites are devoted to it, and Francis Ford Coppola is often called a genius. And yet, John Simon was extremely critical of it, as I'm sure you saw.

BRAD: Yeah, he said things like it was a "deeply depressing film." I agree that it was depressing.

INSTRUCTOR: Why?

JAMAAL: Well, Willard seemed like a good guy at first, but by the end he seemed amoral.

BETH: Yeah, I agree, and Simon says that we feel so numb by the time we get to Kurtz's compound that the violence loses its impact.

INSTRUCTOR: Do you agree with him?

ANTHONY: I don't know, I was thinking, "Oh, no, here we go again."

JAMAAL: Yeah, it kind of made it worse because it just became more and more horrible.

TRACY: I kind of thought, "Oh, more of the same."

BETH: Yeah, but I wasn't sure what to think when I was watching Willard changing in the last section, while he was being tortured.

FIGURE 2.1

APOCALYPSE NOW POSTER

JAMAAL: Remember when Kurtz said that Willard wasn't a real warrior? He seemed like one to me and he definitely was when he killed Kurtz.

BRAD: But he was because Kurtz made him one.

JAMAAL: What do you mean?

BRAD: Well, Kurtz tortured him and made him stronger somehow.

BETH: That's right. It was all kind of mythic, while Kurtz was talking about warriors and being strong enough to hurt people you love.

INSTRUCTOR: What do you mean by "mythic," Beth?

BETH: Kurtz seems like one of those gods, you know, like a Greek god who tests humans. I think Coppola wanted the film to have a kind of mythic quality. It goes along with everything somehow not being real.

INSTRUCTOR: That's interesting, Beth. Let's keep that in mind as we look at the section of the film that occurs in Kurtz's camp. Why don't we look at the scene after Willard hacks Kurtz to death then comes out all bloody and stands before the crowd and drops his machete and the people react by dropping their weapons too. What was that about?

JAMAAL: That seems pretty symbolic, but was he showing that Willard had become a killer or did it mean that the killing was over?

BETH: No, that would be too easy. I think he was being ironic.

BRAD: Yeah, but Kurtz was an instigator of war.

INSTRUCTOR: Maybe looking at the ending would help. How do you react to the ending? What is Coppola saying about war? Do we identify with anyone whose perspective might help us answer the question?

BRAD: I didn't.

BETH: But you don't identify with characters in myth. That's how myth is different from the novels we read. People in myths don't seem like real people. They're more like the people in fairy tales. Maybe that's what Coppola is doing—making us think about what the violence means.

CHRISTINE: Do you mean what war means?

BETH: I guess. Willard was changed. I don't know if he was amoral, but he was different. And I guess, if it's mythic, that says something about what war means. War changed him in a really deep way.

JAMAAL: I guess you could say that there were two enemies—the Viet Cong and the war itself. Maybe John Simon didn't like it because he was expecting a different kind of film.

CHRISTINE: I think I like the movie more now.

BETH: Me too. I want to see it again.

These students disagree at times, but they just as often agree or change their minds. They begin by considering the critic's objections to the film and reasons for his negative review. As they do so, they test his response against their own. The discussion is pretty freewheeling and associative as each student responds to the central issue and to the last comment made by a classmate. Their comments are exploratory and begin a conversation that allows them to decide what intrigued them most about the film. The discussion does not end with a definitive answer but rather with a kind of new understanding, and having had this initial inquiry, the students will probably discuss the issue again after thinking more about their questions and other answers.

 KEY CONCEPT

Elements of a Shared Inquiry Discussion

Discussions that are shared inquiries have the following elements:

- **Participants** interested in an issue.
- A **shared question** or questions.
- An **open-ended exploration** of the question or questions.
- At least **two possible answers** under consideration.
- **Reasons** for each plausible answer.
- **Information** that would contribute to finding an answer.
- **Interaction** that tests the strength of competing answers.

We call this kind of conversation "shared inquiry" because it involves a collaborative investigation of a question or questions at issue for the participants in a discussion. As this example shows, discussions using a shared inquiry model are open-ended and exploratory. They provide a place for a group of people interested in the similar questions to consider possible answers, reasons for accepting them as plausible, and details that would support the reasons.

Inquiry Questions

Most of the time, conversations about issues proceed without prompting or conscious direction. However, when you want to engage in a conversation in an informed way, it helps to be conscious of the kinds of questions that usually press good conversations deeper. The students who were discussing *Apocalypse Now* had many questions about the film: Was Willard amoral? How are we to react to the extreme violence? What was Coppola's attitude toward the Vietnam War? What does Coppola think war does to people? Because the film provided no definitive statements, the students could discuss possible answers and reasons for thinking some answers might be better than others.

As the dialogue about the film shows, discussions grow out of questions we share, questions that might be answered in a number of ways. We call such questions "at issue" because they are open to debate and exploration. In other words, there is no one absolute answer that everyone accepts, and therefore when we are investigating such questions, we do so in an open way. We may have hypothetical answers or initial positions, but as we talk, we try out different answers and, if we find good reasons, change our minds.

You may have heard about the five reporter's questions, *who, what, when, where,* and *why.* These questions are very helpful for reporting factual information in an efficient way, or for getting oriented in unfamiliar situations. But they don't invite much exploration or critique or evaluation. For productive and rich investigations of issues, the six generic questions in the "How to Use Exploratory Questions" strategy box may help you observe and articulate the significance and meaning that you find in your experiences, your conversations, your reading, and your written expressions. These questions are both

 KEY CONCEPT

Questions at Issue

Questions at issue are questions that have at least **two possible, supportable answers.** Although there many different types of questions you might explore, what they all have in common is that the person who raises the question and the person addressed share an **interest** in answering the question.

analytic and generative; that is, they can both help you figure out the component parts of and relationships among ideas, and they can help you reflect on, expand, and complicate those ideas for yourself. The questions help you explore the reasons certain ideas and experiences seem meaningful and significant to you, and, potentially, to others whose separate inquiries might converge with your own.

These questions can help you investigate almost any issue, behavior, or occurrence, from a drop in stock prices to the actions of a character in a movie. As you explore an issue using these questions, you will find that they are not separate and discrete but rather interdependent. In other words, although you may make one kind of question the central focus of your inquiry, you will find yourself exploring all of them to some extent as you do so. For example, you might be discussing whether a first-year English class should watch and discuss the film *Apocalypse Now*, which is a question of policy. As you discuss the question, you will need to talk about what happens in the film, a question of fact. As you consider the film's violence, you might wonder what kind of film it is, a question of definition. You could discuss what Coppola's treatment of the Vietnam War means, a question of interpretation. You might consider how the film might affect the students, a question of causality. If you talk about what the film's portrayal of war means, a question of definition, you might find yourself discussing whether it is a film that other first-year students might find worth seeing, a question of evaluation.

What makes these questions productive is that they open up the exploration at the same time that they help you find the approach that is most interesting to you, the question that is at issue for you. If you were to write about *Apocalypse Now* at the end of a discussion of the questions presented in the strategy box, you would probably choose one as your central focus, but you would also include some consideration of the others. Doing so would lead to a richer, more complicated and interesting paper.

 ## STRATEGY

How to Use Exploratory Questions

One good way to begin a discussion is by looking at an issue from different perspectives. You can do so by looking at it through six exploratory questions:

1. A question of fact: What happened?
2. A question of definition: What is it?
3. A question of interpretation: What does it mean?
4. A question of causation: Why did it happen? What might it cause?
5. A question of evaluation: Is it good?
6. A question of policy: What should be done about it?

Sample Student Writing

The following article appeared in the Kansas State University student newspaper, the *Collegian*. As you read, think about what questions are being shared and explored.

Takaki Speaks on Multicultural Requirement

Brooke Graber Fort

"You can take your multicultural class and shove it up your ass!"

These words proved to be the catalyst for the multicultural requirement at the University of California at Berkeley, Ron Takaki, professor of ethnic studies at Berkeley, said.

Takaki was the keynote speaker of Racial/Ethnic Harmony Week and the second Lou Douglas Lecture speaker this fall.

He said Berkeley passed the multicultural requirement in 1989.

"I have to confess the faculty didn't want to pass the requirement," Takaki said.

In the fall of 1987, students of color totaled 52 percent of the undergraduate population. Our faculty was over 90-percent white.

"These students were saying to the faculty 'Read our faces. We do not see ourselves in the books we read or hear our voices in the lectures we attend,'" Takaki said.

Takaki said these students came up with the idea of a multicultural-class requirement so they could learn about themselves and other cultures.

"The faculty, initially, was very defensive," he said. "The students began to have rallies. They sat in buildings," Takaki said.

There was a faculty club in the middle of campus, which faculty regarded as their reserve, he said.

Takaki said between 15 and 35 students had a sit-in in the narrow hallway leading from the faculty club to the sandwich lounge during lunchtime.

"Imagine the faculty showing up with all these bodies blocking the sandwich lounge. Some faculty members got angry. One angry faculty member was a conservative political science professor," Takaki said.

The political science professor shouted the fighting words, "You can take your multicultural class and shove it up your ass," he said.

"This led to an explosion," he said.

Takaki said professors began to reconsider the multicultural proposal as the debate went on.

"In the debate, many of us realized that this allowed us to more accurately understand the people that make up the American society," he said.

"All students at Berkeley must take two humanities courses and two social sciences courses, and one of these must meet the multicultural requirement," he said.

"Multicultural courses that meet the requirement are now offered by 26 departments, and about 80 courses meet the multicultural qualification," Takaki said.

"On a day-to-day basis, we should be learning about the people that make up the United States," he said.

Takaki said it would be common for K-State students to say the University doesn't need a multicultural program because Kansas is a predominantly white state.

However, he said, whites will become a minority in the 21st century.

Takaki said the University of Minnesota is a predominantly white university that approved a multicultural requirement before Berkeley.

"I remember having lunch with the dean of arts and sciences at the University of Minnesota. I asked him, 'Why Minnesota, when your state and student body is 98-percent white?' " Takaki said.

He said the dean gave two reasons.

First, faculty at Minnesota consider the university to be a national university and realized they needed to offer a national curriculum; and secondly, students move to other states following graduation.

"K-State should have a multicultural program because this is the reality of America," Takaki said.

"Where do K-State graduates go when they graduate from K-State? Many of you go to Chicago and Los Angeles. It might be a good idea for you to know about other cultures," he said.

Takaki said both *Time* and *Newsweek* magazines have documented the "culture wars" during the past few years.

He said the culture wars have emerged as a debate between the two ways of looking at history: "eurocentric exclusionism" and "ethnic particularism."

Both eurocentric exclusionism and ethnic particularism ignore certain cultures, Takaki said.

"There is a third way to look at history. This is the way that emphasizes a pluralistic society," he said.

"Here, if you want to have a pluralistic multicultural program, you have to emphasize the ways people have lived in America and how different paths have crossed," Takaki said.

He illustrated the ways different cultures interacted when two groups, the Irish and the Chinese, migrated to America.

He said about 4 million Irish immigrants came to America between 1800 and 1900 and about 400,000 Chinese immigrants came to America between 1850 and 1900.

Of these immigrants, 52 percent of the Irish were women, while only 15 percent of the Chinese were women, Takaki said.

He said the female Irish immigrants worked in factories in America, while the Chinese immigrants worked primarily on the transcontinental railroad.

Takaki said the American government did not want the Chinese to have children in America; they simply wanted the Chinese as a work force.

Many of the female Irish immigrants worked in textile factories processing cotton, which was tilled by African American slaves on land that belonged to American Indians, Takaki said.

Michael Ott, senior in pre-medicine and business administration, said he thinks all students should be required to take a multicultural class.

"If we don't receive a diverse education, we only hurt ourselves in the end," Ott said.

Jonathan Winkler, junior in math and physics, said he agreed K-State needs a multicultural program, but said it also needs a more global perspective.

"I think there's a great need for courses in our curriculum that will cover Asian Americans and African Americans as well as the European culture," Winkler said.

■ APPLICATION

Inquiring with Exploratory Questions

Review the "How to Use Exploratory Questions" strategy box. Many readers think that newspapers primarily report facts, but the article by Brooke Graber Fort in the Kansas State University *Collegian* illustrates that almost everything we read may raise questions at issue for us. After you have read the article, identify which exploratory questions the writer raises.

SHARED INQUIRY IN THE CLASSROOM

Because questions at issue have at least two possible, supportable answers, trying to answer them will involve learning. Although you may think you know the most probable answer, investigating the other possible answers will strengthen your understanding. Your investigation may lead you to verify your original thinking while strengthening your understanding and reasoning; it may lead you to modify and clarify your original thinking; or it may even cause you to change your mind. This kind of exploration is a process uniquely suited to the college classroom.

Many of your classes during your college years will involve shared inquiry. This is a very different educational model than the lecture model you may be used to. The Brazilian educator Paulo Freire called the lecture approach "the banking method." By this, he meant that the lecturer deposits information into the mind of the student, after which the student is tested on how well he or she retains that information.

Shared inquiry, in contrast, establishes a situation in which students engage in dialogue about the questions that are raised by the materials of the class—questions at issue. Together the members of the class identify the questions they share and explore answers to those questions. There are many such occasions for shared inquiry discussions: when the entire class meets to discuss materials or when small groups form. In either case, the model to follow is one of collaborative learning.

Working in Groups

Frequently in this book we will invite you to work in small groups to observe, discuss, and generalize about shared questions. You may be asked to take a few minutes in class to analyze a problem or you may work in study, reading, or writing groups outside of class. We suggest this kind of work because we believe such collaborative learning leads to better thinking and writing.

The British educator Kenneth Bruffee, who has written extensively about group work, makes a strong argument for the benefits of collaborative study. He tells the story of a British physician's innovative training program for medical students. The old model of medical training involved having the experienced physician lead a group of interns through their study. The doctor would lecture to the students about a case, then ask them questions that would allow them to apply that information to their diagnosis of the patient. The students would answer and the instructor would give positive reinforcement to those who provided the correct answers. The innovative physician, M. L. J. Abercrombie, decided to try a different educational model. Using a shared inquiry approach, Abercrombie asked the medical students to read the patient's medical record, then discuss the case as a group and come to a consensus on their diagnosis. What Abercrombie discovered was that not only did students make better diagnoses when they worked collaboratively, but they also learned the process of diagnosis better.

From this experiment and many like it in more traditional school settings, Bruffee concludes that an educational approach that empowers students to take responsibility for their own process of learning is more effective than one that relies predominantly on the authority and knowledge of the instructor. He suggests that classroom group work should replicate the model set by Abercrombie.

Small group discussions are good places to make this kind of learning happen. Like a discussion in which the entire class takes part, small group discussions work best when the participants are knowledgeable about the questions at issue. Being prepared and knowledgeable is perhaps even more important in the small group because small group discussions operate without the class instructor and require you to facilitate your own discussion.

In addition to bringing appropriate information to the conversation, participants need to make a commitment to active and responsible involvement. Shifting from passive reception of information to active engagement in learning requires energy and commitment from all members of the group. To make a discussion work well, all participants need to recognize their responsibilities. See the key concept box on "Responsibilities of Group Discussion Participants."

The Outcomes of Shared Inquiry

It may seem that the aim of shared inquiry is consensus—that the discussion is not successful unless, as if the group were a jury deciding the outcome of a trial, all members agree on the same conclusion. Sometimes consensus is achieved—different perspectives are considered, and one seems in all ways more acceptable than others. But even if consensus is not reached, all participants in a group discussion learn more about the subject at hand.

If some authoritative members of the group seem to support one answer and you have questions about it, it is important for their learning and for yours that your questions get asked and answered. If you don't change their minds,

KEY CONCEPT

Responsibilities of Group Discussion Participants

1. To be an informed participant, that is, to have read the material or to have thought carefully about the issues to be discussed.
2. To be ready to pose questions about the material.
3. To be willing to share your responses to the material and answers to questions you and others pose and to give reasons for your responses.
4. To listen carefully and respectfully to others' responses and to engage them in discussion about their positions.
5. To consider the reasons for and support of others' positions and to be willing to change your mind.

you have at least made them consider more carefully and thoroughly their reasons for supporting their positions. If they don't change your mind, at least they have made you consider more specifically the limits of their position, the strengths of your own, and the arguments that your position must address in order to make it acceptable to others.

Having an answer to a question isn't enough. To take an informed position, we need to know the alternative answers, and we need to be able to articulate the reasoning that supports our answer over the others. That is why knowing how to work as a group on a question you share is an essential part of learning and understanding, not just in college but in the workplace, where problems get solved every day as the mental energy of several thoughtful people is combined to address company or institutional needs.

Cybertalk as Shared Inquiry

In past times, opportunities for conversing about issues were considered entertainment. In the 19th and 20th centuries, salons, which are gatherings in private homes for the purpose of discussing notable ideas or works, were a popular and widespread social activity. In lieu of more sophisticated and immediate forms of communication about politics, town hall meetings used to perform the function of organizing debate and dialogue on the questions of the day to help everyone develop an informed judgment.

Radio and television have made salons and town hall meetings seem less compelling, and the fast pace of modern life has made them seem antiquated. However, radio and television are typically one-directional media. We listen to what we are told, and if we are lucky and there are others in the room, we might discuss the ideas with them.

STRATEGY

How to Engage in Shared Inquiry

To use shared inquiry in the most productive way, you will need to do the following:

1. You must be able to identify the kind of question your group is investigating.
2. You must be able to propose more than one plausible answer to the question.
3. You must give good reasons for each answer you consider.
4. You must weigh the strengths of the competing answers by testing them against the information you bring to the discussion.
5. You must consider the extent to which your answers reflect your prior knowledge and belief system.

Recently, though, our opportunities for discussing questions at issue with others have increased exponentially with our access to the Internet. Web sites devoted to identifying and discussing questions at issue are everywhere, and the participants are as diverse in knowledge and opinion as any group that could gather. Unlike letters to the editor in the newspaper, which encourage us to shape our ideas and present them as "finished," Web discussions are more *dialogic*: they invite give-and-take, changes of mind, clarifications of ideas. They are more like conversation because the language used is less formal, less crafted, more exploratory. Our society is once again practicing and valuing the idea of participation because more people have opportunities to make sense together, to meet others in the rhetorical space of the imaginary chatroom where we can engage in discussion.

The following Internet discussion occurred in a chatroom devoted to issues associated with the American health care system. The writers were responding to a comment one participant made that many nurses are leaving the profession, causing a crisis in the health care system.

WebLab.org Discussion on the Health Care System

Majestic mentioned nurses leaving the profession and that brings up the issue of What's Happening to our Health Care System? The 500# gorilla in the middle of the room that everybody in Washington, D.C. avoids. Hospitals are closing, nurses going to private duty, doctors starting new "premium care" practices only for the well-heeled (you pay big bucks, get personalized service, even house calls). More and more services are being excluded by insurers from coverage every year. Even seniors either fill their RX's or fill their stomach, but not both. Three times a week, full buses go to Canada from Seattle with seniors; filling RX's at cheaper prices. Any answers?

Posted by bas, 2/9/02

The answer is related to health care providers understanding that within the foreseeable future health care will go public and they will no longer be able to price gouge. They are all trying to get theirs now! The real American way. In home caregivers are some of the poorest paid in the country. If there is government sponsored program it needs to include benefits as well as providing the "entry level" i.e. low paying jobs.

Posted by unique, 2/9/02

And, with Bush's new budget giving more money to the wealthy in the form of tax cuts and rebates to corporations, not to mention an even more inflated budget for the military, there will be even less for health care. I work in the trenches - I'm a nurse. Back in the early 90s the medicaid cutbacks led to the wholesale firing of nurses - the hospital administrations used the euphemism "changing the skill mix"; all that meant was that minimum wage workers were taken from the kitchens and the housekeeping departments, given a couple of weeks training, and told to supplement the now depleted nursing staff. I worked in truly dangerous conditions - dangerous both for the nursing staff and the patients. We had 3 and even 4 times the number of patients we could care for safely, we worked 12.5 hour shifts without a single break, juggling way too many high risk patients. It was easy to get burned out under those conditions, and many good nurses left the profession as a result. In fact, the most experienced nurses were often harassed until they resigned - the hospitals saw that as a money saving endeavor, since the most experienced nurses were also the highest paid. Because nurses were being fired instead of hired, nursing schools all over the country closed. A few years later, hospital administrators began to realize what a mistake it had been to cut down on the numbers of nurses - but, with fewer nursing schools, there is now a severe, and dangerous nationwide shortage of nurses.

Posted by operabuff, 2/10/02

Great insight, OB! Two points; Bush's budget is a real piece of work..one point of contention shows his pervasive cuts of already obligated funding: federal retirees w/long service are under Civil Service. (I'm one) Bush wants to take away obligated funding of retirement and health benefits - change them to a discretionary expenditure of applicable agency and retirees wouldn't know from one year to the next if they had an annuity coming because yearly agency budgets are subject to the political whims of Congress. And last..because so many health care cuts are again coming, both House and Senate are tagging stuff like new clinics/other health care amendments as riders onto other bills (for the first time in history). Where they previously tagged on pork, they now have over 60 amendments pending for health care issues due to Bush's cuts.

Posted by bas, 2/10/02

■ **APPLICATION**

Engaging in Shared Inquiry

Having read the comments by the participants in the Internet chat on health care, meet in groups to do the following:

1. List the questions at issue that the participants raised and explored.
2. With other group members, choose a question from the list that you are all interested in discussing.
3. Together, compose at least two possible answers to the question, with reasons for each answer.
4. Discuss the answers, practicing the strategies in the "How to Engage in Shared Inquiry" strategy box.

Internet discussions blend our talking, reading, and writing skills in new ways: our participation can be immediate, reflective, or distant; our minds may be more open to change in the relatively anonymous environment of cyberspace. Even passive observation of Internet discussions can help us take inventory of possible points of view and challenge our preconceived notions and beliefs, leading to open, informed inquiry.

Unlike letters written to the editor of a newspaper, comments made in an Internet discussion more often respond directly to another writer. When the first writer ended the comment with "Any answers?" the next writer began by suggesting an answer and the third writer added another answer, which led the first writer to respond with "Great insight, OB!"

READING AND WRITING AS INQUIRY

Reading and Shared Inquiry

We've shown you a few examples that illustrate the way that conversation is inherently compelling and generative of ideas. The literary critic Gerald Graff considers conversation essential to the educational process. In his book *Beyond the Culture Wars*, he tells a story of his own experience in school. He says that he was a smart but indifferent student, especially in his literature and history classes. Somehow these classes didn't seem relevant to him. After years of feeling inadequate in these classes, he finally met a professor who asked the class to talk about questions that were at issue in a literary work, questions that various literary critics answered in different ways. As he discussed the various interpretations in class and read the critics, Graff felt an excitement and engagement with the work. He concludes that shared inquiry leads to better reading because it makes us care about what we read. We read knowing that we will be sharing our questions and tentative answers with others who are doing the same. When we explore ideas together and see competing answers to our questions, not only are we engaged and find the inquiry more interesting and compelling, but we also learn more about the subject and how to go about the process of learning.

Reading for Questions

Reading is an active, not a passive, process. We engage in the act of making sense by reacting to what we read. Just as you participate in a conversation with others by identifying shared questions, you can imagine yourself in dialogue with a writer by thinking about what questions you share with the writer. For example, a columnist might address the question, "What should the House of Representatives decide about how heavily Americans should be taxed?" A novelist might address the question, "What was it like to be a woman from the aristocracy during the French Revolution?" You react to what a writer says by thinking about how the writer's answers to the questions are similar to or different from your own answers. The writer's ideas may validate, contradict, explain, or complicate your own ideas. If you choose to write about the ideas in the reading, you can answer those shared questions for yourself, or evaluate the answers the writer gives.

Sometimes writers ask their questions directly and use them to organize their ideas. Most often, they do not, and readers have to discover them by thinking about what the writer was trying to answer for himself or herself. Students have compared "reading for the question" to the television game show *Jeopardy*. You see the answer, but what is the question?

How do you find questions in your reading? One way is to keep a record of questions that come up during discussion and comments and opinions that

 STRATEGY

How to Read for Questions

As you read essays, you may begin your attempt to understand what questions the writer is addressing by asking your own questions in the margin. Imagine that you are speaking directly to the writer. You might ask the following questions:

1. What does the title mean?
2. What does this word mean?
3. What does this information suggest?
4. What does this statement mean?
5. Why is the writer saying this?
6. What question does the essay address?

puzzle you. Some people keep large margins in their class notebooks and write interesting questions in that margin. Another way is to keep a record of questions you have while you read by underlining or marking any sentence, example, or section you find puzzling. After you complete your reading, return to the places you have marked or copied in your notebook. The questions you ask when you first begin studying a subject may be fairly simple, but you will find that they become more complex as you learn more about the material.

The following passage duplicates the opening paragraphs from an essay on voting and one student's questions. (For the full text of the essay, see Casebook 1, in Part 4 of this book.)

Evaluating Election Turnout

Richard Rose

In the contemporary world, virtually every country holds elections of one kind or another. The right of citizens to vote is now a defining attribute of democracy, and the franchise is a right of every adult citizen and no longer a privilege restricted to a narrowly defined group. Yet the fact that everyone has a right to vote is not sufficient to make a country democratic.

Global surveys invariably conclude that the majority of regimes in the world today are not democratic; the median regime has been aptly described as "partly free" (Freedom House, 1996). In countries of this nature, the failure to achieve democracy is not the result of denying most citizens the right to vote. It stems from the fact that such elections as are held are not freely competitive, and that regimes do not fully respect the rule of law, which includes the need to limit their own coercion. As long as it has the power to control competition and the counting of votes, a regime has nothing to fear from holding elections which are unfree and unfair.

Marginal questions:

The title seems to indicate that this will be an evaluative essay. Is he evaluating all elections?

How are these countries different?

What does it mean to be able to vote?

What does a vote mean?

What kind of election is necessary to show that a country is a democracy?

How can a regime allow voting if it isn't democratic?

How can a regime be "partly free"?

Then what is democracy?

What countries is he talking about?

How do regimes limit competition?

How does counting votes limit competition?

Why is he using all these negative terms—"nothing," "unfree," "unfair"?

APPLICATION

Reading for Questions

Read the following paragraphs from Jack G. Shaheen's essay, "The Media's Image of Arabs." As you read, write the questions you would ask the author if he were sitting in front of you. Use the questions in the "How to Read for Questions" strategy box as a guideline. Then decide what question the paragraphs seem to be answering.

The Media's Image of Arabs
Jack G. Shaheen

I can remember the Saturday afternoon when my son, Michael, who was seven, and my daughter, Michele, six, suddenly called out: "Daddy, Daddy, they've got some bad Arabs on TV." They were watching that great American morality play, TV wrestling. Akbar the Great, who liked to hear the cracking of bones, and Abdullah the Butcher, a dirty fighter who liked to inflict pain, were pinning their foes with "camel locks." From that day on, I knew I had to try to neutralize the media caricatures.

It hasn't been easy. With my children, I have watched animated heroes like Heckle and Jeckle pull the rug from under "Ali Boo-Boo, the Desert Rat," and Laverne and Shirley stop "Sheik Ha-Mean-Ie" from conquering "the U.S. and the world." I have read comic books like the "Fantastic Four" and G.I. Combat whose characters have sketched Arabs as "lowlifes" and "human hyenas." Negative stereotypes were everywhere. A dictionary informed my youngsters that an Arab is a "vagabond, drifter, hobo, and vagrant." Whatever happened, my wife wondered, to Aladdin's good genie?

WRITING AND SHARED INQUIRY

As we participate in shared inquiry, we are speakers and listeners discussing a subject at issue in a particular rhetorical situation. This means that our writing does not occur in a vacuum. We always write with one or more readers in mind, imagining their reactions. We are trying to make sense in a way that would make sense to someone else, but too often novice writers begin writing before they have really explored the potential of the assignment. They haven't taken the time to decide what questions really interest them, what possible answers they might have to those questions, what assumptions lie behind those answers, what details support them, and which answers are better than others. While it may be tempting to write papers this way because all of us have too much to do and too little time, doing so means missing an opportunity to learn more about the subject matter of the class, ourselves, and a thinking process that will make us better thinkers and learners.

One way to avoid this kind of writing is to begin with an inquiry paper. An inquiry paper is an investigation of some material you are studying. It is not a formal essay. Instead, it is exploratory and open-ended. It is thinking on paper.

KEY CONCEPT

Characteristics of an Inquiry Paper

- Begins with a **question at issue.**
- Suggests several possible **answers** to the question.
- Gives **reasons** why each answer might be the best answer.
- Includes **details** that support each reason.
- Identifies the **assumptions** each answer implies.
- Evaluates the **strengths** of each answer.
- Does not need to take a position.

When we write inquiries, we usually begin by identifying a question about the material and why it puzzles us. As we do so, we consider possible answers to the question and reasons we might find them valid. We may or may not decide which answer we find most compelling. We may simply end by writing about what more we need to know before we are able to answer the question.

Sample Student Writing: Inquiry Paper

The following inquiry paper was written by a student who was studying the rise of the Renaissance. Read the paper carefully and, referring to the "Characteristics of an Inquiry Paper" key concept box, evaluate how well it works as an exploration of a question at issue.

What Gave Rise to the Renaissance?

Leo Simonovich

As Europe entered the fifteenth century, it saw a fundamental change in its societal behavior: the Renaissance. This phenomenon originated in the Italian cities like Florence and Venice and continued to spread into the rest of Europe. A fundamental cultural and religious turning point in the western world, this period was dominated by influential musicians, famous painters and powerful politicians. From writers like Machiavelli writing the *Prince* to Michelangelo's *David*, great works of art were produced under the patronage of the Medici family, for example. And yet, the origins of this phenomenon are unclear, as different social factors contributed to the beginning of the Renaissance. To some, the Black Death, a dangerous disease that spread into Europe from the Middle East, was a factor, while to others the Crusades, the Holy War on the Muslim infidels, was the cause of the Renaissance. Did the Black Death or the Crusades play a bigger role in the birth of the Renaissance?

The Crusades played a role in the birth of the Renaissance. Indeed, when the Crusades began, they contributed to the establishment of the Renaissance. After all, the Crusades mobilized a largely immobile, feudal society in action. Sons of nobility—especially the young that could not inherit land or wealth—went into action on the call of the Church. These young men left their manors behind in search of glory, only to find themselves crushed in the battles against the Muslims. However, during the processes, these young men saw the wealth, the culture—the advancements of the Muslim world. As the Crusaders came back from the battle fields, they brought with them some of the samples of culture or at least told stories of the advanced civilization. Consequently, the stories spread and trade began to increase because the Christian merchants saw an opportunity for profit in the Middle East. New goods, new culture and a new way of life began to arrive in the Christian world. This, of course, helped revive interest in education, and the feudal bonds began to disappear (serfdom, however, remained, to be abolished many centuries later). The port cities, moreover, benefited the most from the trade, since the people there became the middle men between two civilizations. And so, the Crusades, an important mobilizing factor, helped shake the Christian world of the Dark Ages; the Feudal society began to change for the better.

Although the Crusades were important in bringing about the Renaissance, they were not the main reason for its birth. Since the Crusades began in the 11th century, they could not have been fully responsible for the Renaissance. That is, even though trade was increased in the Christian world during the Crusades, and the merchant class began to grow because of it, the Church still had a strong grip on the feudal society. The Church as an institution, moreover, did not change to adapt to the new, secular ideal. The Church still had control over education, culture and political life. For example, while new rulers consolidated their kingdoms and tried to loosen the grip of the Church, the Church fought back by excommunicating rebellious kings and princes. This phenomenon can be seen in Fiero's description of the court of Philip IV "the fair." Phillip, a powerful monarch in Normandy, fought back against the Church supremacy by trying to move the center of the Christian world to France. The Church, however, fought back and won the battle, as the center of Papal authority remained in Italy. Thus, the Church was still the dominant power in the Christian world, and the time was not ripe for the secular, humanistic Renaissance.

The most important turning point from the Medieval to the Renaissance was the recurrence of the bubonic plagues. As the Black Death spread from Mongolia, through the Middle East, into Europe, it changed the European society forever (Fiero 3). This period, in fact, altered both the European political and religious structure, as it helped revive secularism and education. That is, even though the bubonic plague was devastating, as it "destroyed one third to one half of its population," it also mobilized the European people to move away from the feudal world (Fiero 3). After all, the disease forced both the lower and the upper classes to move into the country side, for the cities were inundated with death and disease. Powerless to help, the Church was seen as weak, and religious bonds between the Vatican and the common people began to break (Fiero 9). Additionally, the lower classes—most wiped out by the deadly plague—began to demand more rights, since there were very few people to work and farm. From organizing into guilds to moving away from the Feudal manors, the lower classes began to climb up in society's ranks (of course, those changes were very minute).

Perhaps the most important change was made by the upper-middle classes and aristocracy, when they took secular education away from the Church. As the upper classes embraced the study of humanism—that is, the writers of ancient Greece and Rome—they looked to the past for cultural education. The Church, therefore, was left to perform one role: religious duties. As such, the Church had lost its grip on the people of Europe, and the door for secularism was open.

In conclusion, even though the Crusades were important in the birth of the Renaissance, it's the bubonic plague that helped open the door for the Renaissance.

STRATEGY

How to Write an Inquiry Paper

1. Identify your question: The "How to Use Exploratory Questions" strategy box will help you think through your interest in the issue and focus your inquiry.
2. Plan: List at least two possible answers to your question and reasons for believing them, and identify information that supports each answer.
3. Organize: Decide the order in which you will explore the answers.
4. Draft: The inquiry paper should include the following sections:
   An introduction that lets the reader know what your question is and why it is important
   A paragraph for each answer to the question that explores reasons for accepting the answer and information supporting the reason.
   A conclusion that reflects your new understanding now that you have explored the possible answers. The conclusion may be that all answers have merit but warrant further study or that one seems stronger than the others.
5. Revise: Rewrite so that your essay is understandable and clear.

 APPLICATION

Writing an Inquiry Paper

Later in the term you may choose to write inquiry papers about issues that arise in the readings, but for now, you may have many questions about being a college student, questions that are worth exploring. You might wonder "What makes college writing different from high school writing?" "What should I major in?" "What is the best place to live on campus?" Meet in your discussion groups to share questions you have and possible answers, then choose one issue and write an inquiry paper exploring it.

WRITING PROCESSES AND INQUIRY

Some of you may have had writing instruction that focused solely on the mastery of particular skills. Surely some of you who are in a composition course must think that you are here because you lack or have forgotten or have misunderstood the rules that govern the behavior of good writers. But if you see writing as a way to learn through exploring, inquiring, and testing answers, you will realize that a writing class is not about skills but rather about how to use writing to make your thinking sharper and more precise. As Roger Sale, a professor and writer who has taught literature and writing for many years, puts it, "a subject like writing…is not a subject at all but an action."

What we offer in this chapter should not be taken as prescriptions for good writing, then, but as descriptions of what successful writers do, or what successful writing looks like. Remember that the success of writing depends on the reader. We will offer suggestions to help avoid strategies or choices that *don't* work, uses of language that confuse or complicate or simply obstruct understanding. But it is important to understand from the outset that both writing and reading are activities that involve interaction with language, activities that involve thinking and discovering and shaping, activities that involve trial and error, reason and risk. English professor Ann Berthoff describes writing this way:

> You don't suddenly become another person when you sit down to write, though that may be what it feels like sometimes. Composing means putting things together—and that is something you do all the time. When you take in a scene or an event or a piece of news, you are interpreting, putting things together to make sense. When you see what is happening or understand what has happened or imagine what might happen, you are composing: figuring out relationships, working out implications, drawing conclusions. What is currently called "getting your head together" used to be known as "composing yourself."

You have learned many skills related to writing—as Berthoff refers to them, the "rules governing the use of the semicolon or the names of sentence structures"—and this knowledge can be usefully applied in the same way that tools of any craft can be applied. Just as we pick up a hammer when we need to pound a nail to construct something, when we write we use the tools of language toward the end of achieving a meaningful purpose.

Good writing is rarely the result of a spontaneous response to inspiration. Even experienced, successful writers go through the work of planning and drafting and revising, replanning, redrafting, and revising again. Writing involves several, often overlapping and repeating processes, including discovering what we mean to say, finding ways to say it, and shaping the language for readers whose needs we must address if they are to understand what we say.

As we write, we are constantly making choices regarding our general ideas and our specific support, our form and sequence, sentence structures, word choices, voice, and conventions. Because communication is an active, interactive process, it is not always easy to make meaning out of the signals somebody else sends us or to send signals that will be understood. Most of the time this happens fairly smoothly, but often enough, we misunderstand each other. Sometimes this is because we are so different: our experiences, backgrounds, ages, religions, or economic situations may create differences in the way we understand messages. However, we all know that even people in the same gene pool around the same dinner table can misunderstand each other disastrously! Because we want to understand and be understood, we should consider carefully how our language choices affect others and how theirs are intended to affect us.

When you read, you expect writers to fulfill their obligation to you as a reader. When you write, you must fulfill your responsibilities to your readers. To do this, it is important to use planning, drafting, and revising strategies to match your message with your language choices in ways that help your audience hear what you have to say.

Planning

Planning strategies include defining your subject, but also refining and clarifying it as you attempt to explore it. You might think about and describe your rhetorical situation and consider which rhetorical strategies would be most likely to help your audience see your subject the way you do, including strategies for what you will need to *do*, and for what you want to *say*. There are two kinds of planning processes, open-ended and systematic. Open-ended processes require an open mind and involve exploring possibilities without judging or editing. Systematic strategies involve going through a process of inquiry in a particular sequence to examine a subject or an idea analytically. The kind of strategy that will be most useful depends on the writing situation and your own preferences, but it is helpful to know a range of strategies to try. In the following chapters, we will introduce some useful planning strategies. The lists in the "How to Plan an Essay" strategy box may be familiar to you.

Some people suggest that you not write until you have finished planning, but planning involves writing—not always orderly writing, but writing nonetheless. As you draft and revise, new ideas—or new ways of seeing old ideas—may occur to you, and when that happens, you need to take the time to revisit your planning and change your mind. The results will be much more satisfying. The kinds of thinking involved in good planning—reflecting, questioning, listening, responding, and gathering material—are practiced with each new writing situation, and we have included strategies for practice in each chapter of this book.

 STRATEGY

How to Plan an Essay

Open-ended strategies include:
- Brainstorming ideas
- Sketching out connections with lines, shapes, and diagrams
- Talking to other people to get reactions to your observations

Systematic strategies include:
- Asking questions
- Arguing against your idea to test it
- Gathering information from your memory, your contacts, or your research and reading

Drafting

Drafting strategies include finding tentative shapes for your ideas and tentative connections among them as you produce text by filling blank pages with sentences and paragraphs. Your planning process generally leads you seamlessly (and repeatedly!) into attempts at drafting written material. Chunks of "sense" may emerge separately as you draft, showing you where you have connected your understanding or where you may still have gaps that need to be filled.

What kinds of structures are you choosing and combining as you draft? Not just sequences of paragraphs, but also forms and voices; kinds and orders of sentences, clauses, and phrases; particular and purposeful words, punctuation marks, and conventions; images, comparisons, and reasons. All of these choices are yours to make as you attempt to create sense. The more choices you have, the more likely it is that you will find a way to express your ideas clearly and effectively. (See the strategy box "How to Draft an Essay.")

Revising

Revising strategies are helpful ways to examine and improve your written message by adjusting the match of content to form until your message and expression of

---

 STRATEGY

How to Draft an Essay

Drafting is the process of articulating the relationships among your ideas in sentences and paragraphs. Some writers blend planning, drafting, and revising; others prefer to work in discrete stages. Some writers need to have a purpose clearly in mind to begin composing sentences and paragraphs; others discover their purpose in the physical and mental moves of composing. Even for those who plan consciously before they draft, ideas will change as they are translated into specific word choices that are connected to others. However you draft, the following general strategies can be helpful.

1. Draft casually. Drafting is "writer-centered," meaning that you are trying, at this stage, to make your ideas clear to yourself. When you begin to translate your ideas into text, just try to keep the ideas flowing. Don't be too critical about expression or mechanics. You can move, add, delete, and modify as you revise.

2. Choose your ideas consciously. You don't have to use everything you know related to your subject. Your purpose may evolve and grow clearer as you draft, so as that happens, become more conscientious about including ideas that advance the purpose.

3. Don't count words as you draft. Use your purpose to help you decide whether you have or have not completed articulating your ideas. The way to ensure that your paper does what it needs to do is to write until you have said everything that needs to be said about the question you have asked.

it are one and the same. In the same way that planning motivates drafting, so drafting motivates revising. When you draft, you are trying to "get it right" for yourself. When you revise, you are trying to "get it right" for a reader, and this process, literally "re-seeing" your writing as a reader might, requires some objective distance. Even though your writing process has allowed you to find connections among your ideas, it does not follow that your readers will see the connections unless you make them clear and explicit in your language choices. That is why revising usually involves several different kinds of changes.

In writing that is purposeful, all parts relate to all other parts. So when you revise, you need to think about how each part affects the effectiveness of the whole. When you draft, you are very concerned with composing the parts. But when you revise, you have to get a distant perspective on the whole in order to see it the way a reader would.

Within paragraphs, you can help readers understand your messages too; you can point directions with transition words and reader cues. Among paragraphs, you can let the reader know through topic sentences how each paragraph adds to or functions as a part of the whole. Usually, in introductory paragraphs, you try to provide a map or a preview of what is to come, and in what order, to encourage confident exploration. In concluding paragraphs, you review or comment on the journey in a way that will help the reader understand the significance of the trip.

It can be difficult to get the kind of objective distance necessary to map out your own messages for readers, because you understand your own words. Our best advice is to make sure your composing process allows for some time between drafting and revising so that you can come back to your writing with a fresh eye. Take a day or two if possible, but if you can't, then take a walk, eat a meal, or work on some other task for a couple of hours before returning to your writing. To increase your repertoire of "tried and true" strategies for revision, check out Chapter 12: Revising Effectively.

 ## STRATEGY

How to Revise an Essay

1. Add new material to develop or connect paragraphs or paragraph sequences.
2. Delete material that does not add specifically to the progression of ideas.
3. Reorder ideas within and among paragraphs.
4. Connect ideas within and among paragraphs.
5. Substitute or transform ways of expressing ideas for clarity, vividness, emphasis, or interest.

Editing

Editing means making adjustments in sentences, words, and punctuation for clarity, conciseness, and correctness. Many people claim to dislike editing. One student writer commented that editing was like "nitpicking," which, given the source of the expression, equates editing with picking bugs out of fur, a good deed, maybe, but not necessarily an appealing one. What appeals to most of us when we write is discovering new ideas, but editing our sentences, words, and punctuation is a meaningful, sense-making activity too.

In college and professional communities, the acceptable ways of editing are quite consistent. Being able to use the conventions of standard academic English is one of the conditions of membership in college and professional communities, and employing these conventions is no more difficult than employing the "smiley face" icons in an e-mail message. We just have to know (or know how to find out) what the guidelines are.

If you want to review some guidelines for polishing your writing, see the strategy box "How to Edit an Essay," as well as Chapter 13: Editing Effectively.

 STRATEGY

How to Edit an Essay

When you edit, you are reading for meaning, but you are also focused on the word, the phrase, or the symbol, instead of the larger conceptual connections among ideas. Some general strategies can help you switch from readng for revision to reading for editing.

1. Get some distance from the work by taking a break once your draft seems to say exactly what you want it to say. Return to your reading with a fresh eye.

2. Personalize your editing by reviewing your old papers and making a list of the kinds of errors you typically make.

3. Using an English handbook, resources on the Internet, or assistance through your college Writing Center, make sure you understand why specific error types result in communication problems.

4. Identify specific strategies for finding and fixing patterns of error and avoiding ineffective choices.

5. Create your own list of guidelines using sample sentences you have composed.

6. Read slowly. If you read at normal speed, your mind will fill in missing letters and correct problems because you already understand what you want to say. One way to slow down is to read out loud.

7. Slide a bookmark down the page as you read each line to help you focus on specific elements.

WRITING WITH PURPOSE

To write with purpose, you should be able to answer the following question: What do I want my reader to do, or know, or think, or feel about this subject? Writers who don't take the time to reflect on their purpose and to make conscious choices often struggle terribly with writing, because they have no clear basis on which to make language choices. When you write to explore ideas in the planning stages, you are writing to find a purpose. Once your purpose is clear, it becomes much easier to write. Again, referring to the rhetorical triangle, you write with purpose when all of your language choices are made with your subject and your audience in mind. When you've arrived at a sense of purpose, your decisions get easier because you have a basis on which to make them.

STRATEGY

How to Determine Your Purpose for Writing

To determine the purpose of your writing, ask yourself the following questions:

1. What question am I answering?
2. To whom am I talking, and why should they listen to me? Will they be sympathetic or critical? Will they respect my ideas, or will I need to gain their support by developing my credibility or relying on the authority of others?
3. How do I want my readers to respond? To act? To react? To stay the course? To change? To relax? To energize?
4. What choices of form, sequence, and expression will increase the likelihood that I will achieve my purpose?

APPLICATION

Determining Your Purpose for Writing

In a small group, identify several recent situations that have called for writing: personal letters, formal letters, memos, personal statements, requests, apologies, school assignments. Analyze the purpose for each by using the questions in the strategy box "How to Determine Your Purpose for Writing."

FIGURE 2.2   RAISING QUESTIONS IN THE PUBLIC ARENA

INQUIRY AND CONTROVERSY

We live in a time of protest and conflicts about ideas and policies (Figure 2.2). This makes it more important than ever that we learn to participate in shared inquiry. You have just joined a community of college students, a community that explores issues of all kinds from the very narrowest of specialized research to larger questions of how to live in the community in which the school finds itself. As a member of the community, you will choose how involved you will be in the life of the college and your classrooms. Because these issues often are quite controversial, knowing ways to explore them becomes paramount. We believe that experience and practice in shared inquiry will give you the knowledge and self-confidence to participate in and contribute to these discussions. As members of a classroom, college community, neighborhood, country, and the world, we all need to inquire together to learn about the questions we share and try to find good answers so that we might live together with all our differences.

> WRITING INVITATIONS

1. Using one of the articles in the casebooks in Part 4, a piece of writing selected by your instructor, or a reading you have discovered and selected, read the piece for the question or questions at issue. Name the article and write the

author's questions. Tell how the writer answers the questions. Then describe how the writer's answers validate, contradict, challenge, explain, or modify your own ideas.

2. Using the same article as above, or another of your choosing, analyze the writer's purpose. Then describe how the writer's techniques support or fail to support that purpose. End with a statement regarding the degree to which the writer has achieved his or her purpose.

3. Write a personal exploration and description of your own writing process. What planning, drafting, revising, and editing strategies have worked for you in the past? What is easy for you? Where do you get stuck? What kinds of strategies do you need help with? Share your answers with classmates. Offer each other strategies that may be helpful.

4. Identify a question that struck you as you listened to a recent news report, read an article in the newspaper, or attended a class. Write an inquiry paper in which you explore various possible answers to the question and reasons that might support the answers. End your paper by explaining what more you would need to know to be prepared to take a position on the question.

5. Francis Ford Coppola explained that he wished "to create a film experience that would give its audience a sense of the horror, the madness, the sensuousness, and the moral dilemma of the Vietnam War." The film *Apocalypse Now* is available in many video stores and libraries. Watch the film, and using the guidelines in the strategy box "How to Write an Inquiry Paper," write an inquiry exploring whether you find the violence of the film effective.

DEVELOPING A WRITING PROJECT

Identify a question at issue related to a personal area of interest, hobby, or academic field, one that you might like to explore for a term paper. Review the information in the "How to Use Exploratory Questions" strategy box, then make a list of questions that you might investigate in your inquiry. After making your list, write a paragraph explaining which question interests you the most and why.

CHAPTER 3

Rhetorical Thinking: Matching Situation and Strategy

As readers, we are made over every time we take up a piece of writing: we recognize that there are assumptions and expectations implied there and that as sympathetic listeners…we must share these assumptions.

Walker Gibson

What is reading but silent conversation?

Walter Savage Landor

EFFECTIVE COMMUNICATION

Effective communication requires more than just knowing what you want to say. You may be extremely knowledgeable and have strong and reasonable arguments but not be able to convince others that your ideas are worth considering unless you know how to present your positions in a way that is compelling to your listener. To appeal to a listener, you will need to craft your message in an artful way. Saying this may make it seem that we are back to the old definition of rhetoric as a way to trick a listener, but you may craft your language to convince a reader without trickery, and if you are genuinely concerned about dialogue, you will use language to appeal to your reader, not manipulate. Knowing how to do so requires that you understand the occasion for your writing and make effective rhetorical choices.

Consider, for example, the best high school class you remember. The teacher probably persuaded you to find the material interesting without tricking you into being interested. How did he or she do this? Was it just the subject matter that made you interested, or did the way the instructor presented the material affect your response? We suspect that the teacher had something to do with the effectiveness of the class. A dynamic teacher can make what may seem dull material come to life through the way he or she presents it.

KEY CONCEPT

Rhetorical Strategy

A **rhetorical strategy** is any decision a writer makes that makes the message more effective, clear, or compelling to a reader. **Strategies** may be as small as the words the writer chooses or as large as the overall shape of the writing. **A strategic decision** should make the writing more interesting, memorable, and persuasive.

So what can rhetoric teach you about how to make *your* message more compelling to your reader? The effective instructor you remember may provide a good model. What made that special teacher so remarkable? Was it humor? Knowledge of the subject matter? Clarity of presentation? Organization of the material? Effective examples? Interesting language? Patience? Special help for someone who was struggling? It was probably a combination of all of these—the most entertaining teacher will not be effective without joining a thorough knowledge of the material with an understanding of how to present it to students. More important, though, than the kinds of choices the teacher made was the appropriateness of those choices for the particular group of students. To know how to teach a group of individuals, a teacher needs to balance the material of the course with the learning styles of the students. This means thinking strategically.

To communicate effectively with a particular reader, a writer needs to think strategically. Because you will need to balance the information of the message with the interests of the individuals who will be reading the message, you will need to analyze the context in which you are writing and choose strategies that are appropriate for the occasion and purpose.

READING FOR RHETORICAL STRATEGY

In Chapter 1 we included a diagram to illustrate the major components of any rhetorical situation. To review the rhetorical triangle concept, see Figure 3.1. Here, we will consider how to craft messages while thinking about the components of the triangle.

Seeing Purpose, Context, and Strategy

As you look at the diagram in Figure 3.1, you will notice that all the lines and points that make up the triangle are contained within the larger circle we have labeled *context*. The context, we told you, is "the occasion for the communication, and it includes all of the influences on how readers and writers make and interpret meanings." You will also notice that at the center of the trian-

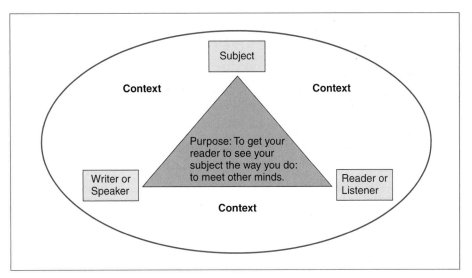

FIGURE 3.1   THE RHETORICAL TRIANGLE

gle is *purpose*, which we have defined generally as: "To get your reader to see your subject the way you do: to meet other minds." If you wish to convince a reader to see the subject the way you do, you will need to consider all the influences that might affect that reader's reaction, so purpose and context depend on each other. Together, they determine the ways writers interact with readers in the choice of material and manner of presentation. One contains all the elements the writer needs to consider and the other provides the focus for those elements.

We can see how understanding context and purpose determine strategy by returning to the example of the effective instructor. Her purpose was to teach you the material of the particular course within the context of the school, the year, a classroom of a certain type, a geographical area, the education level of the class, and so forth. To teach effectively, she analyzed all of the elements of the rhetorical situation, and then determined what choices of material and manner of presentation would help her achieve her purpose.

As you begin planning a paper, you will use a similar process. Your reason for writing will be influenced by the particular context in which you find yourself: the class you are taking in which the professor asks you to write a research paper, a discussion group concerned with a community issue that asked you to write a committee report, or an editorial in the newspaper that made you want to write a letter to the editor. In each of these cases, your purpose will depend on the subject matter, the people who will be reading what you write, and the issue you are addressing.

What purposes might you have for writing? The list in the "Purposes for Writing" key concept box includes many possibilities, among them: to raise questions, to present discoveries, to prove, to persuade.

KEY CONCEPT

Purposes for Writing

Most of the writing you do will be for one or several of the following reasons:

- To **raise questions**
- To **inform or report**
- To **criticize**
- To **entertain**
- To share **an experience or feeling**
- To **challenge**
- To **explore**
- To **present discoveries**

- To **understand**
- To **introduce**
- To **imagine**
- To **support**
- To **sell**
- To **teach**
- To **relate ideas**
- To **prove**
- To **persuade**

The purposes for writing overlap, and they can be combined in any piece of writing. Some people say that "to persuade" actually includes all of the others, because whenever writers write, they are attempting to persuade a reader to see the world the way they do. As you consider your purpose, you should be able to answer the following question: What do I want my readers to do, or know, or think, or feel about this subject? In addition to this question, we want you to consider the following: What do I need to do so that my particular readers will see the ideas in the way I would like them to? This is a question that asks you to consider how you communicate rather than simply what you communicate, but both the "how" and the "what" are dependent on your purpose and the context.

You have probably noticed many times the ways that advertisers choose details for the advertisements they place in magazines or the commercials they run on television. You may be amused or annoyed or intrigued by these ads and what they say, or about the way they are constructed, but you are certainly aware that the company hires the advertiser to compel you to buy their products. Like commercial companies, non-profit organizations also use advertising agencies, but often with a different attitude toward appealing to the viewer. Instead of wishing to manipulate you as a potential buyer, these organizations want to establish a relationship based on the kind of rhetoric we have been discussing. Thus they choose visual images that represent shared concerns and interests. In the following ad copy, a Web site established to provide such visual images to non-profit organizations describes the appeal of their photos, one of which is reproduced in Figure 3.2.

The Blackfoot River, known to many through the book and movie *A River Runs Through It*, begins along the Continental Divide high in the Scapegoat Wilderness. Its cold, clear waters are home to native west-slope

FIGURE 3.2   MARK ALAN WILSON, *BLACKFOOT RIVER #1*

cutthroat and bull trout—its watershed home to elk, grizzly bear, goshawk, ponderosa pine, aspen, calypso and coralroot orchids, and countless other species. Not far below its headwaters lies the site of a proposed open-pit gold mine. The mine's permit application calls for an open pit a mile across, and for hundreds of acres of forest and sage grasslands to be buried beneath cyanide leach pads as tall as the Washington Monument. All this within a few hundred yards of the Blackfoot.

HOW THE WRITING OF OTHERS REFLECTS CONTEXT AND PURPOSE

When you read, as when you look at advertisements, being aware of the writer's purpose and context helps you understand both the content and the sequence of the ideas. As is true in advertisements, sometimes in written texts the writer announces the purpose directly, and sometimes you must infer it, but in all cases, writers will have gone to the trouble of shaping their words with the hope that you will understand them and respond to them. In this way, words are actions. They are intended to have an effect on you, the reader. Aware of the writer's purpose and the context in which the words are written, you can decide whether you will do, know, think, or feel about this subject as the writer wishes.

To see the purpose of a piece of writing, ask yourself, "Why is the writer writing this and what does the writer say that makes me think so?" To answer the question, you might fill in the blanks in this sentence:

The writer wants me to (do, know, think, or feel) _____, because _____.

For example, read the following sentences that appear in Jack Shaheen's essay "The Media's Image of Arabs" and consider his purpose, including the reason for his purpose. Knowing the context in which the work was written will help you answer the question. He wrote the essay in the early 1990s when the American newspapers were beginning to write about the threat of terrorism and news stories were full of anti-Arab "rhetoric."

> To me, the Arab demon of today is much like the Jewish demon of yesterday. We deplore the false portrait of Jews as a swarthy menace. Yet

 STRATEGY

How to Identify Context and Purpose in the Writing of Others

The following questions will help you identify the rhetorical choices a writer is making while asking you to do, or know, or think, or feel a particular way about this subject:

1. **EXAMINE THE CONTEXT:** What personal, political, social, historical, cultural, or experiential circumstances might have influenced the intended message? Why, in the particular situation, would the writer need to establish a particular attitude or tone toward the subject or the reader?

2. **EXAMINE THE PURPOSE:** What does the **writer** want the **reader** to do or know or think about the **subject,** and **why**?

3. **THEN, RELATE THE CONTEXT AND PURPOSE TO THE WRITER'S CHOICES:**

   Consider the Writer's Stance: How does the writer present himself or herself to the reader? Is he or she an expert or a novice? A friend or a mentor? Does the writer challenge or comfort or engage or distance the reader? What is his or her manner of address? Humor? Shared concern? Shared experience? Anecdote?

   Consider How the Writer Regards His or Her Readers: How does the writer regard the reader? What assumptions does he or she make about the audience, their knowledge, their characteristics, their assumptions and biases? What attitude does the writer seem to have about the reader?

   Consider How the Writer Presents His or Her Subject: What is included? What is excluded that might have been included? How are ideas and observations developed? Evidence? Details? Anecdotes? Reasons? Observations? Theories? Appeals to the imagination, emotions, or common sense? Is the subject oversimplified or are relevant complexities included?

   Consider the Writer's Language Choices: What form is it in? How do the parts make up the whole, and how are the parts connected? Are the sentences long or short, complex or simple? Are the words formal or informal, specific or general? Is the writing easy or difficult to understand?

a similar portrait has been accepted and transferred to another group of Semites—the Arabs.

You might suggest several possible purposes and reasons, but each will be something like the following:

Shaheen wants to convince the reader that depicting Arabs as demons is wrong	because	he says it is the same as depicting Jews as demons.

Because Shaheen wrote his essay when the United States was just beginning to experience and attempt to understand the threat of terrorism and because he believed the anti-Arab images were unfair, he chooses to appeal to his readers' sense of fairness by comparing the prejudice against Arabs to the treatment of Jews in an earlier historic period. He thus decided to compare something his readers understood and had strong opinions about with new information about the unknown threat and their responses to it. Fearing that too many citizens would transfer their fear of the unknown to an entire ethnic group, he asks readers to recall their outrage against mistreatment of Jews and recognize that Arabs share a similar heritage. His use of this comparison places the immediate situation into a larger historical context, and his use of the term "demon" for both the Arab and the Jew underlines the comparison. Anti-Arab sentiment, he suggests, is just as offensive as anti-Jewish. By using the comparison, then, Shaheen tries to appeal to his readers' sense of fairness.

As this example demonstrates, a careful analysis of the purpose and context can help you understand the writing of others. The example should also remind you how important the relationship between context and strategy is in your own writing. Your strategy should reflect what you discover from your analysis of the subject, the reader, the purpose, and the context.

■ APPLICATION

Seeing How Writing Reflects Context and Purpose

Read the three excerpted paragraphs by Richard Rodriguez, the Office of the Attorney General, and Marita Sturken, which open their three different responses to the September 11, 2001, attack on the World Trade Center. Using the questions in the strategy box "How to Identify Context and Purpose in the Writing of Others," write a comparison of the paragraphs. Answer the question, "How do the writer's rhetorical decisions demonstrate his or her purpose for writing and understanding the context?"

RICHARD RODRIGUEZ

Vertical City

In truth, I never liked the modernist design of the World Trade Center. Gargantuan, those twin towers were, and expensively sheathed, but they lacked the grace of Manhattan's prewar skyscrapers. Only now, like everyone else, I cannot look at this skyline without immediately seeking the Twin Towers—and missing them. All these weeks later, the first thing I do upon arriving in New York from California—the thing I feel compelled to do—is to come here to lower Manhattan to get as close to the site as I can. I need to pay my respects to the dead, but also to wonder at the loss of such huge human constructions.

OFFICE OF THE ATTORNEY GENERAL

September 11th Victim Compensation Fund of 2001

The Department of Justice, in consultation with the Special Master, is issuing certain procedural rules so the Special Master may commence operations of the program as soon as practicable. In order to allow the Special Master to begin distributing funds, the Department is issuing this rule as an "Interim Final Rule" that will have the force and effect of law immediately upon publication. This rule is designated "interim," however, because the Department is also seeking further comment for a period of 30 days as part of its further review and may expand or adjust aspects of the rule after receiving additional comments.

MARITA STURKEN

Memorializing Absence

It has been said quite often since September 11 that Americans are standing at a juncture of history, that, on that date, the world changed forever into a "before" and an "after." Such proclamations of radical breaks in historical consciousness have happened before, of course. Writing in 1924 about the experience of modernity, Virginia Woolf stated, "on or about December 1910, human character changed." Many years later, Theodor Adorno wrote, "to write poetry after Auschwitz is barbaric," implying that cultural production would never be the same in the wake of the Holocaust. There are many good arguments to reject the current version of the shock of history insofar as it is a particularly American-centric and provincial one, one that awards traumatic events in the

FIGURE 3.3

THE WORLD TRADE CENTER BEFORE
SEPTEMBER 11, 2001.

FIGURE 3.4

THE SAME VIEW ON THE MORNING
OF SEPTEMBER 11.

U.S. more historical weight than those in the rest of the world. Yet, the feeling persists, that this date will be forever understood as one that marks the end of one era and the beginning of another, indeed that September 11, 2001, will be remembered as the beginning of the new world of the 21st century.

WRITING STRATEGICALLY

Writing with a Purpose

When you read for purpose, you determine what the reader has in mind for you. If the writer is successful, for example, at making you laugh, reading for strategy allows you to determine how she succeeded in entertaining you. On the other hand, if a piece of writing doesn't succeed in meeting what you perceive to be the purpose, you can ask, "What choices interfered with the writer's intent?" An editorial that was meant to calm may, instead, anger certain people. What didn't work? A specific anecdote? A comparison? The complexity of the sentences used to convey a simple idea? Perhaps the attitude of the writer insulted and therefore distanced the reader. Seeing a writer's rhetorical choices will help you develop what we call your critical reading ability. Understanding how these choices affect you can help you move beyond "I don't like this" to commenting specifically on how and why something doesn't work. This awareness will also help you make good rhetorical choices in your own writing.

In the last section of this chapter, we showed how the choices of other writers affect readers. In this section of the chapter, we look at how your strategies, as a writer, affect us as readers. When planning, the writer takes inventory of the choices that are available. When drafting, the writer engages in a process of trial and error—generating matches of word with intention. When revising, the writer tests and measures the success of those trials, making choices that are generally informed by an evolving sense of purpose.

Writing in a Context

One question that students frequently ask is, "Should I use the first-person pronoun 'I' in the papers I write in this class?" Asking the question shows that students are thinking about context. What they are asking is "What level of formality is appropriate to this class?" The question is an important one, not only for the writing class but also for every writing situation. Writers shape their writing to follow different sets of conventions or different sets of rules, which depend on the rhetorical situation. The students who ask us whether they should use "I" in their writing are concerned with academic conventions. Of course the answer to the students' question is not a simple one. Certainly, when you are writing in an academic setting, you will need to know what conventions the instructor expects you to understand and use effectively. Sometimes you will be asked to write reflective essays, and in that situation, as you might imagine, not using "I" would be quite awkward. When you are writing formal essays or taking essay examinations, on the other hand, you will probably use the personal pronoun on rare occasions and then only for emphasis, such as in the following paragraph where the writer draws attention to what she considers the major issue by using the phrase "it seems to me":

> In 1975, the Supreme Court found that criminal defendants had the right to self-representation. Writing for the court, Justice Stewart argued that "The Sixth Amendment does not provide merely that a defense shall be made for the accused; it grants to the accused personally the right to make a defense" (*Faretta v. State of California*). With this ruling, the court may have made the courtrooms of our land more open, but it also created administrative problems. In order to receive a fair trial, defendants need legal guidance, and this means that someone will need to spend time helping them. In fact, since 1975, the court has ruled that in some cases, the Faretta decision requires the court to provide assistance for defendants. Because there has been a sharp increase in self-representation, it seems to me that it is time to explore ways to address this problem. One way might be to establish regional clinics that would provide legal advisors and teach workshops.

When you are writing in contexts other than your college classes, you will also need to know the level of formality your readers expect. For example, if you are writing a memo to an entire office, you would probably be somewhat more formal than you would be if you were sending an individual note to one other person in an office. Or, if you were writing the preliminary draft of a committee's study of a problem, you might be less formal than you would be when writing the final report. In the following examples, the student subcommittee is more informal and exploratory in the draft than in the final report.

Sample Student Writing: Committee Report

Draft of the Subcommittee's Study of Students' Impressions

of the Rising Cost of Textbooks

Sarah, Jen, and I polled 75 first-year students about the cost of the books they were required to buy this semester. We asked them about the average price of books for each class and then about how this cost affected their choice of classes. We found that the cost averaged $75.00 per class, an amount that shocked us (we knew it would be high but didn't think it would be that high). What was even worse, though, was how much higher the price was in some classes—as much as $200 in

STRATEGY

How to Match Your Rhetorical Choices to Purpose and Context

The following questions parallel those you use to evaluate the effectiveness of a writer's choices when you are reading someone else's work. When you write, especially when you revise, you have to pretend that you are the reader as well as the writer. You have to ask yourself how your choices will affect another reader.

1. **PURPOSE:** What do I want my reader to do or know or think about my **subject, and why**?

2. **CONTEXT:** What are the influences on me, my audiences, or my subject that might affect the way I communicate my message? What, in the particular situation, requires a particular attitude or tone toward my subject or my reader?

3. **STANCE:** How should I present myself to the reader? Am I an expert or a novice? A friend or a mentor? Do I want to challenge or comfort or engage or distance my reader? What should be my manner of address? Humor? Shared concern? Shared experience? Anecdote? Surprise?

4. **AUDIENCE:** How should I connect with the reader? What will I assume they know, or care about, or feel, or value? What will be my attitude toward them?

5. **SUBJECT:** What will I include? What will I exclude, and why? How will my ideas and observations be developed? Evidence? Details? Anecdotes? Reasons? Observations? Theories? How can I present my subject so that it includes relevant complexities but is not overcomplicated?

6. **LANGUAGE CHOICES:** What form best suits my purpose? How should the parts make up the whole, and how should the parts connect for reader understanding? How should I craft sentences to achieve variety, while matching their purposes and significance with their structure? Long, short, simple, complex? Should my language be more informal or formal, more general or specific, more vivid or concrete?

 ## APPLICATION

Matching Rhetorical Choices to Purpose

Read the Personal Statement that one student wrote as part of an application for admission into a program that trains people to teach special education. After reading the student's draft, use the questions in the strategy box "How to Match Your Rhetorical Choices to Purpose and Context" and write her a letter in which you make suggestions for how she might improve her application.

some classes. Amazing! We were not surprised to find out that more than half of the first-year students told us that, when given the option, they chose the class with the smallest "bottom line." We think this means we need to find some solutions that will allow students to choose classes with considering their wallets.

Final Report of the Subcommittee on Draft of the Subcommittee on Textbook Cost and Class Enrollment: Student Survey

In May of 2001, three members of the Student Senate Bookstore Committee began a study of the effect of the rising cost of textbooks on student enrollment. The subcommittee polled 75 first-year students and found the following:

- The average cost of textbooks in first-year classes was $75.
- The cost per class varied from a high of $200 to a low of $20.
- 60% of the students polled listed textbook price as a determining factor in their choice of class or section.

These findings suggest a problem significant enough to warrant a long-term study of ways to reduce textbook expenses at the college.

Because communicating effectively depends on our ability to recognize and pattern our language use on these expectations, a familiarity with the ways that we shape language to convey personal, public, and academic messages will help us participate in conversations in all of these contexts.

Sample Student Writing: Personal Statement

A Part of Who I Am

Carissa Tomsik

Being around people with special needs is something I have grown up with. My Uncle Mark is severely mentally handicapped. It is unclear as to what the exact diagnosis is for his handicaps because he grew up in a time when society did not try to help, or figure out how to aid people who were labeled "different." With that label came the societal acceptance for them not to succeed. Growing up with my uncle taught me a lot about people who might be considered "different" to society, but who really weren't that "different" after all. My life's circumstances have helped me to be a compassionate person who is dedicated to helping young children feel accepted in society.

It is very difficult to communicate with my Uncle Mark. He only speaks a handful of words clearly and often gets frustrated because he cannot communicate his ideas. This frustration sometimes leads to behavioral issues, which then have to be dealt with. People outside of the immediate family can often not communicate with my uncle. But those of us who are in the family just look into his eyes and listen to his often-jumbled words. Then usually we are able to have a connection with him and understand what he is trying to communicate.

When a person with a handicap is referred to as stupid it is an unacceptable act of ignorance, which sadly seems to be made repeatedly by human kind. Just because someone can't communicate their needs clearly or without frustration does not mean they are any less worthy of societal acceptance. If society would just slow down for one minute and look into the often-knowledgeable eyes of a person with a handicap they would be able to see the vast intelligence that is held within this person.

I am a very compassionate person who understands children of all different levels and capabilities. I make this statement knowing it represents truth, not just an instinctual feeling or goal for my future. Throughout my life I have experienced living with compassion. I not only have had interaction with many different degrees of handicaps, but I have grown up with an amazing and caring Uncle who others simply saw as "weird."

Working with students who have special needs is not something that has to be learned; it is part of who I am. In addition to working with these children, I will be granted the amazing experience to help guide their lives in a positive direction. Working with special needs children is something that I love. I love to see how they are so proud and eager for acceptance because so much of society has discouraged them and deemed them "weird" and "incapable." Being able to instill in a young mind that they can succeed and achieve anything that they put their minds to is incredibly rewarding. I will be an amazing teacher who changes lives, and helps direct others, not only because it is something I have a passion to learn about, but simply because it is who I am.

PERSONAL, PUBLIC, AND ACADEMIC WRITING SITUATIONS

As the examples from the previous section indicate, the choices that are effective in one situation are different from what might be effective in another. In this book, we will invite you to compare written texts in three general categories: **personal, public,** and **academic.** In the chapters, as well as in the casebooks, you will find sample writings representing each of these categories, as well as some that cross the lines between them.

It might help to think about how our day-to-day communication changes with the situations that we are in. A simple, typical greeting can express warmth, disinterest, or even hostility, depending on the words you choose and the physical and vocal emphasis you give them. If you were to share a casual greeting with the person sitting next to you in class, a person sitting next to you on a bus, or a potential employer, you would find yourself using quite different expressions. Why is that? What changes? Despite the apparent similarity of the message, the context is different, and it is a difference you understand well enough to shape different manners of greeting.

When you write in different settings, you will need to go through a similar process of understanding. Sometimes the context will call for you to describe your own individual response and feelings, and as you do so, you will use rather informal language, as the students who wrote the subcommittee's report did in their preliminary draft. Other times the context is more public and requires that you move away from the personal to make a point in a more generalized way in somewhat more structured and formal language, as exemplified in the same group's final report. While you are in college, you will need to learn how academic writing fits between these two contexts, and that is not an easy task.

In some ways, all writing is personal writing because, as many contemporary philosophers and educators believe, we make sense of the world first and foremost through our experiences. And in some ways, all writing is public writing, because when we commit our ideas to a shareable form—paper and ink, visual image, Internet message, publication—they are no longer private. Despite these similarities and overlaps though, we can identify some basic differences in context and stance.

You can recognize personal writing when the subject and the writer seem inseparable. For example, a person might write about baseball in a personal way by making the subject of an essay why baseball is important to the writer.

You can recognize public writing when the writer seems to be speaking in a public forum where everyone has agreed to listen and learn from others through written discourse. A public document about baseball, for example, might call attention to a rule change that would affect the way contracts are structured. What makes academic writing hard to recognize is that it often includes the personal and the public. What makes it academic is that the writer focuses on a subject in order to study or learn about it. For example, an academic writer might document the social or cultural history of baseball through a study of public documents and personal interviews.

In the larger conversation about baseball, all of these can be linked. A writer might read a public document about baseball, and if it raises her awareness and interest, she might be led to her own research study, or she might recall an experience with baseball that impressed her in a way she can explore through reflective writing, or, if the situation called for it, she might take action—political or personal—in response to her learning. In fact, more and more books and articles written by scholars include some element of personal experience from an account of how the writer became interested in the study to a story about the person who inspired the study to a recollection from childhood that relates to the subject of the study.

One of the central assumptions of this book is that being effective when you write depends on your understanding of the rhetorical situation you enter. Knowing the context and purpose helps you decide what you will say and how you will say it. It will also help you decide the basic relationship you establish with your reader, or your stance in relationship to the situation.

Rethinking the shape of the rhetorical triangle helps to show how the different context changes the balance of this relationship so that the focus is more on the writer, the reader, or the message itself. If you conceive of the space within the triangle as the area within which communication occurs, then a piece of writing can bring together the reader, writer, and subject anywhere within that space. Although we have observed that each writing task will mix the personal, public, and academic, we can use the rhetorical triangle to show the major differences in these general tasks. For example, personal writing would bring the reader closer to the writer corner of the triangle because the writer *bends* the subject toward his or her perspective. Public writing would bring the writer closer to the reader corner of the triangle because the writer bends the subject toward the reader, specifically addressing his or her concerns and appealing to the reader to accept a particular role in relation to the subject. Academic writing would require that the writer and reader lean more to the subject corner, because the writer tries to maintain an objective distance and an impersonal stance in relation to the study and asks the reader to do the same.

What Characterizes Personal Writing

Personal writing may begin as an open exploration of a thought or an experience, the purpose of which is simply to record it for later reflection. Writers generally don't go to the trouble of writing something down unless they are trying to make sense of it for themselves or others—unless something about the moment makes it resonate in his or her mind, coming up repeatedly, demanding attention. Most often, those moments appeal to the reader because they have some dramatic element. Something about them changes the reader, or asks that he or she consider a change. The change may be small, just a shift in the way of seeing something, or large, one that seems to change the course of one's life.

Being able to reflect on personal experience as a reader and a writer is an important art both in and out of the academic community. When you read experiences of others who are different from you, it enlarges your own experience. When others read your experiences, they learn both about you and about your way of seeing, which enriches their worldview as well. In either case, reading and writing about personal experience helps you discover why you see things the way you do—how your assumptions and values and experiences influence your vision and judgments.

The following passage from an essay in Casebook 1: The Vote, shows these characteristics.

Emily B. Compton
Why You Should Vote

One vote doesn't matter at all. And I've only got one vote, and it's worth just as much as yours, except in certain senatorial races. But your vote and my vote together exactly equal two votes cast by a couple of our respected elders with way more money, influence, and respect than you and I might think we'll ever see. And if you and I and a few million of our closest friends would just show up, then the parties would be able to take on Great-Uncle Mooch, and maybe, in their spare time, even clean up some of the industrial filth that is poisoning our world.

Although Emily Compton is writing about a public issue, she makes it personal. As she considers the issue, she shifts from a generalization to observations

KEY CONCEPT

Characteristics of Personal Writing

- **A subjective perspective**—the writer's perspective or reaction is a part of the subject. The reader learns about the writer as well as about what the writer is commenting on.
- **An open, exploratory, or flexible form**—the reader discovers the purpose and significance as he or she reads.
- **Descriptive detail**—personal writing engages the reader by including details and images that help the reader experience the situation.
- **Reflection and interpretation**—personal writing explores how and why the experience has significance for the writer and for the reader.

that rely on her own experience, as well as that of her family and friends. She expresses an opinion but does not really enter a public forum in which others will evaluate the strength of her reasons. Nor does she demonstrate her knowledge of the subject matter or provide the kind of evidence that would be expected in an academic setting.

What Characterizes Public Writing

Public writing is often motivated by a desire to make something happen or facilitate change. It is very explicit about its audience and responds to audience expectations. As Aristotle tells us, public discourse can praise or blame, bring past events to bear on present circumstances, or frame public policy. Thus public writing varies dramatically from advertising to legal briefs to political statements to essays promoting a particular cause. It can include, to name just a few genres, newsletters, reports, handbooks, arguments for change, articles and editorials, white papers, public service announcements, and problem-solving analyses. Most recently, public writing has erupted in cyberspace, and everyone with access to a computer is part of the publishing community. It's more important than ever, then, to learn how to recognize the characteristics of public writing and read the messages critically.

When you write with a public voice, how your message affects your reader is most important. For example, when you write a letter of application for a job, your reader will expect that you follow certain conventions of the formal letter. While the letter is about you, it would not do to include personal information irrelevant to your qualifications. Instead, you translate your experience into a form that is expected and welcomed by the employer in order to help that person make a decision to hire you. Likewise, when you write a committee report, you will need to know what your readers expect to see in the report. Although they might be interested in your personal reaction to the issue and the story behind your response, they will probably not want to see that in the report. Instead they will expect you to provide information in a clear and easily understood format.

 KEY CONCEPT

Characteristics of Public Writing

- An authoritative, informed **stance.**
- An **explicit purpose.**
- **A predictable form,** determined by the context in which the writing will be read.
- **Information** selected and arranged to facilitate engagement or comprehension.

The following passage from an essay in Casebook 1 shows these characteristics.

Susan B. Anthony
Women's Right to Vote

It was we, the people; not we, the white male citizens; nor yet we, the male citizens; but we, the whole people, who formed the Union. And we formed it, not to give the blessings of liberty, but to secure them; not to the half of ourselves and the half of our posterity, but to the whole people—women as well as men. And it is a downright mockery to talk to women of their enjoyment of the blessings of liberty while they are denied the use of the only means of securing them provided by this democratic-republican government—the ballot.

Although this writer uses the first person pronoun, we, she does so not to draw attention to her own particular position but rather to identify with the larger group of women concerned with the issue. Unlike the example of personal writing, this paragraph shows a writer moving beyond her own personal experience to generalize about a group. She does more than express her feelings about voting; rather, she gives reasons why she believes women should be given the right to vote.

What Characterizes Academic Writing

Academic writing, or the writing done by people who study at colleges and universities (including both faculty and students), is in some ways much like the writing you find in other public groups. What distinguishes it from other public writing, however, is its explicit focus on research and argument. Because we are writing in an academic community, we are concerned with studying questions that other students and academics have considered important. As we explore those issues, we present our findings in ways that other members of the community will find convincing. This means not only that we use correct grammar and clear and convincing language, but also that we shape our positions clearly and logically so that others might consider and test them and understand how our research led us to those positions.

In Chapter 1, we explained that college communities are made up of smaller groups that join together to study a particular subject, or "discipline." When you take a college class, you enter these communities, and as you do so, you study to gain knowledge of the subject, and you also practice the ways that a particular discipline expresses its knowledge. As English professor David Bartholome has written, "Every time a student sits down to write for us," that student "has to learn to speak our language, to speak as we do, to try on the particular ways of knowing, selecting, evaluating, reporting, concluding, and arguing that define the discourse of a community."

KEY CONCEPT

Characteristics of Academic Writing

- **A focus** on the subject.
- **A general audience** within the writer's discipline.
- **A purpose** that involves answering a specific question at issue.
- **A thesis** that is the writer's answer to the question.
- **The voices of other writers**—generally researched and documented.
- Careful **reasoning and evidence.**

This book will help you understand how to define those different writing practices. We think that all learners who can identify and use the purposes and techniques of a discipline can join its conversations confidently. If you are in a chemistry class, your lab reports will follow a form that allows for easy comparisons and checking of data. If, however, you are involved in a series of experiments toward some end, you will report the results of your work in an academic essay. While each discipline has different forms and conventions that are a part of its shared knowledge, students in many academic disciplines are often called on to compose a form of the academic or scholarly essay.

The following passage from an essay in Casebook 1 illustrates the characteristics of academic writing.

Linda Feldmann
Why the Poll Booths of America Are Empty

To some, low turnout is a sign of satisfaction with government. Indeed, turnout in the US spiked up to 55 percent in 1992, when voters were unhappy with the state of the economy. But the low-turnout-equals-satisfaction argument fails to acknowledge the overwhelming survey evidence of public cynicism and unhappiness with government. In fact, it is older Americans—those with the highest turnout—who are most satisfied with government.

Still, many experts predict turnout this fall could be slightly higher than it was in 1996, when the nation approved of President Clinton's job performance and Republican nominee Bob Dole looked weak. This time around, the race is expected to be one of the closest in the post-WWII era, which could add to turnout.

In addition to giving reasons for voting patterns, this selection considers answers to a question at issue in the field of politics: What are the causes of low voter turnout? The writer suggests some possible answers and provides reasons and evidence that her reader would find persuasive. She also includes the voices of other writers.

The Interdependence of the Personal, Public, Academic

Categorizing writing as personal, public, and academic can help us practice seeing differences in how writers characterize themselves, how they think about their audiences, and how they observe and reflect on their subjects. However, these forms also often overlap and can be used together in a piece of writing as a writer moves in the space of the rhetorical triangle. For example, the personal can influence the public. Let's say that you have been asked to be a student representative on a college committee that will be considering establishing a legal aid clinic. You have been asked because you have volunteered in a public legal aid clinic and consequently will be able to contribute relevant and significant information based on your experience. If, for example, you had difficulty finding information for a client, your experience would suggest that a program using student volunteers should include legal training. Your experience would allow you to give details and information that could help the committee define and clarify their questions about the feasibility of such a program.

The personal, public, and academic often intersect in your college writing. If, as a part of the committee we described above, you were asked to write a report to be submitted to the college president or student or faculty senate, you would draw on the different personal experiences of members of the committee, but you would do so with an academic audience in mind. That would mean that you would identify the problem your group was studying, summarize your conclusions, and give your reasons and the information that led you to draw such conclusions.

A discussion that includes participants' personal experiences does not necessarily use those experiences as evidence for the conclusions to the questions they pose. Sometimes, the stories people tell contribute to helping all group members see their questions in more complex and sophisticated ways. People with stories to tell provide their old information to others. For the others, these stories are new information. The interaction of the old and new compels the group members to redefine the question or add new questions.

We often see public examples of the intersection of the personal, public and academic. A recent *NewsHour with Jim Lehrer* included a discussion of the ongoing Israeli/Palestinian conflict. The participants included two professors from the Mideast currently teaching in U.S. universities, one an Israeli citizen who had served in the Israeli military, the other a Palestinian. Both brought their prior experiences to the discussion of how all parties might seek to solve the conflict. At the same time, they presented academic arguments but in a way that would be accessible to the public audience.

STRATEGY

How to Recognize Personal, Public, and Academic Stances in Writing

1. Examine the focus: Is it primarily on the writer, the reader, or the issue itself?
2. Determine the readers: What expectations do they have about the way the writer will address them?
3. Find the writer's purpose: Is it to suggest a response, support a position, or give information?
4. Describe the form: Is it open and exploratory, strictly conventional, or persuasive?

As this example shows, our experiences may help us clarify and rethink our questions about problems we need to solve. Does it follow that such experiences contribute to the inquiry in all disciplines? We have been arguing that considering our personal experiences is a natural and important part of any exploration of a controversy. When we talk about a problem that has more than one possible solution, we naturally look to our relevant past experiences to begin thinking about the issue.

When people study in a similar area, they tell their stories to each other through sharing the results of their investigations. Whether you are taking a mathematics, biology, literature, or politics class, you have problems to solve that involve you in disputes. You consider competing answers and conflicting evidence. You test your findings against those of others. While each field has a different mode of inquiry, what they have in common is that in each case, their problems are studied by individuals whose past experiences will affect the questions they ask as well as the assumptions they bring to the investigation.

A study in a psychology class might rely on statistical data while one in an anthropology class might examine field research. In either case, the investigators attempt to be as objective as possible, but as humans we know that we are never completely objective, that our past experiences and assumptions shape our interpretations of our findings. To see an everyday example of this phenomenon, just think of the way the two major political parties interpret the significance of public opinion polls. The same set of numbers will allow supporters of the president to claim that he is riding a wave of popularity and his detractors to predict his defeat in the next election. How does this happen? We bring what we might call our "baggage" to our investigations.

Acknowledging this baggage, or recognizing how our experiences affect our assumptions and positions, can help us test our own experiences against those of others, and doing so will allow us to have better and more productive

APPLICATION

Recognizing Personal, Public, and Academic Stances in Writing
Using the questions in the strategy box "How to Recognize Personal, Public, and Academic Stances in Writing," examine the passages written by Anne Hallum, Allan J. Lichtman, and Elaine Tuttle Hansen, experts in three different disciplines—ecology, political science, and literary study. Meeting in small groups, discuss each example and decide whether you think the essay is addressed to an academic audience or a well-educated public. What characteristics helped you decide?

discussions of the problems we share. Consider two very different examples. If you have a particularly difficult problem in a math class, you draw on your past experiences solving other problems that in some way seem related as you attempt to solve the equation. Or, in a constitutional law class, you might be considering possible rulings in a case currently before the Supreme Court. To do so, you would read briefs of previous related cases that might provide precedents for the ruling.

In asking our questions, we look to our prior experiences, and we look to the experiences of others. In each field of study—math, law, or any other area—sets of relevant stories are regularly brought to bear on investigations. Conventions develop that are most effective for telling the stories or solving the problems of a particular field.

In the following excerpt published on the Guatemalan Wildlife, Environment, and Ecology Web page in April 1998, Anne Hallum, professor of political science at Stetson University, explained to Michael A. Arrington, the interviewer, her experience in co-founding an international reforestation agency, the Alliance for International Reforestation (AIR). She tells her story to propose an ecological answer to problems of poverty in Latin America.

ANNE HALLUM

Seeing the Forest FOR the Trees

I went to Guatemala with four students to do research on religion and politics there. It was a Winter Term experience, for which they received college credit, and which changed my life. I fell in love with this country, as many people do who visit Guatemala; but I also felt that I couldn't return unless I was DOING something about the poverty and destruction we saw there. So, one of the students (who had graduated) and I did some brainstorming back in Florida about setting up an NGO (non-governmental organization). We felt that reforestation is vital not only to Guatemalans who are losing their topsoil, rivers, and wildlife, but was also important to people in the U.S. We also felt that we would use a "community-based approach"; NOT a directive from the U.S. planting thousands or millions of trees that would soon die. We wanted to involve Guatemalan villagers from the very beginning of planting each tree seed, so that they would feel invested in the success of each project....We have 23 tree nurseries in 23 villages; plus we've built over 200 fuel-efficient ovens that have cut firewood use in half; plus we've printed two textbooks about the importance of trees for schoolchildren, and another one for adult farmers; we teach classes in 80 classrooms now; we've started a three-year training program—free—for farmers to learn more efficient farming methods that don't destroy the trees or the topsoil; we've planted a few medicinal gardens as well. We've got a staff of six, so AIR is supporting those families as well—and we plant over 150,000 trees a year. Our total budget is only $30,000. The reason AIR's approach works so well is because, as I've said, the villagers work with the tree nurseries from the beginning. They're invested in the success. It's not like a big organization coming in and planting millions of trees that aren't tended to and the majority die. We plant fewer trees, but have very high survival rates.

The following is a "Report on the Racial Impact of the Reception of Ballots Cast in the 2000 Presidential Election in the State of Florida" written by Allan J. Lichtman, a professor in the Department of History at American University. Lichtman explains in his introduction to the report that he "was asked by the United States Commission on Civil Rights to consider whether the rejection of ballots as invalid for the 2000 presidential election in Florida had a disparate impact on the votes cast by African-Americans." His report demonstrates the way he uses the language of social science to share his story of the Florida 2000 election.

ALLAN J. LICHTMAN

Report on the Racial Impact of the Reception of Ballots Cast in the 2000 Presidential Election in the State of Florida

Methodology and Data

1   The database for this study includes county level election returns for the presidential election of 2000 in Florida as well as the numbers by county of ballots cast, undervotes, overvotes, and unrecorded votes. Fifty-four of Florida's 67 counties, encompassing 94 percent of ballots cast in 2000, separately recorded undervotes and overvotes. The database includes identification of voting system by county and county level statistics for a variety of social, economic, and political variables, including race and education. The racial data includes the per-

centage of black registered voters, based on year 2000 voter registration data. The database also included precinct-level data for three of Florida's largest counties: Miami-Dade, Duval, and Palm Beach Counties. This precinct-level data included unrecorded votes, undervotes, overvotes, and voter registration by race, based on 1998 voter registration data.

Summary of Detailed Statistical Analysis

2   In Florida's 2000 election, about 2.9 percent of all ballots cast (about 180,000 ballots out of slightly more than 6 million ballots cast) did not contain a vote that could be counted as a vote for president. The great majority of these invalid ballots were recorded as either overvotes or undervotes, with overvotes outnumbering undervotes by nearly two to one. Counties that separately recorded overvotes and undervotes rejected about 107,000 ballots as overvotes and about 63,000 ballots as undervotes.

3   In the three counties, the rate of rejected ballots by African-Americans ranged from about 10 percent to about 24 percent. For all three counties combined, the rate of rejected ballots averaged about 15 percent—meaning that one out of every seven African-Americans that entered the polling booth in these counties had his or her ballot rejected as invalid. These results closely mirror the county-level findings for the state overall. In these counties, the ballot rejection rate for non-African-Americans ranged from about 3 percent to 6 percent, averaging just under 5 percent. Thus the racial gap was just above 10 percentage points, enough to account for the rejection of more than 20,000 additional African-American ballots in these three counties alone.

4   Part of the problem of ballot rejection for African-Americans in Florida can be solved by requiring the adoption of optical scanning system recorded by precinct for all counties in the state. Based on the 2000 experience, a uniform system of technology, like optical scan systems tabulated at the precinct level, would reduce the level of invalid ballots for both blacks and non-blacks. However, the use of this technology will not eliminate the disparity between the rates at which ballots cast by blacks and whites are rejected. County-level estimates indicate that even in counties using optical scanning methods recorded by precinct, the rejection rate for ballots cast by blacks was still about 5 percent compared to well under 1 percent for non-blacks.

5   Technology alone is not the answer to racial discrepancies in ballot rejection. The results of these analyses demonstrate that technological change must be accompanied in all counties by effective programs of education for voters, for election officials, and for poll workers. Obviously sufficient resources must be devoted to the maintenance of voting technology and steps must be taken to assure clear and comprehensive voter instructions, easily understandable ballots, and adequate resources to assist voters at all polling places.

Elaine Tuttle Hansen begins the Introduction to her book *Chaucer and the Fictions of Gender* by recounting how her interpretation of Chaucer's *Legend of*

Good Women changed in response to an impending rhetorical situation: she was invited to participate in a debate at a national conference about her interpretation of the poem. Anticipating the question that might shape the discussion, she returns to the text to reevaluate her initial interpretation. As she writes the book, she uses the story of her reconsideration of her question and how that allowed her to see the poem in a new light. Because this passage is from the introduction to her book, it does not exhibit all of the characteristics we identified as those we expect from academic writing.

ELAINE TUTTLE HANSEN

Introduction to *Chaucer and the Fictions of Gender*

1   My first reading of the *Legend of Good Women* emphasized an overall design in the narrator's curious treatment of his ten heroines. If her traditional reputation is passionate and aggressive, even wicked in some way (like Cleopatra's, say, or Medea's), he domesticates the heroine's forcefulness and covers up her iniquity; where she is known for innocence and goodness (like Thisbe, Lucrece, or Hypsipyle), he hints at other flaws in her character, devalues her virtues, and punishes her model behavior. At the same time, the narrator reveals from the outset his own interest in the manly world of politics and war....

2   So overt are the biases of the narrator, I decided that readers are prevented from trusting him and obliged instead to see how his selection and treatment of good women ironically define the double bind in which the female in his culture is caught: victimized if she follows the rules of love and lives up to the medieval ideas of the feminine; unworthy, unloved, and unsung if she does not....

3   Not long after completing this reading of the Legends, I was asked to participate in a debate about the poem at a meeting of the New Chaucer Society, and for that purpose I decided to explore more fully the question of how and why the narrator did, as I had observed, impugn men too....The more I looked, the more it seemed that the Legend of Good Women was best thought of as a poem about men, not women, and specifically about two kinds of oddly related men: those who can't seem to help loving women, for one reason or another, and those who can't stop trafficking in stories about women. Part of what makes both types "false men," I began to see, was their feminization (2-3).

READERS, WRITERS, AND RELATIONSHIPS

We began this book by talking about why we define rhetoric as the art of testing ideas with people who share our questions, and explaining how dialogue is an essential part of the testing of ideas. In Chapter 2 we discussed how you might use this new way of talking about rhetoric to strengthen your study of questions you share with others. In this chapter we have explored ways to establish a relationship with other participants in the dialogue about those questions. In the next section of the book, we will develop further these central ideas by looking at different rhetorical situations where you will be applying these central key concepts to special writing tasks. As we do so, we hope that you will see your writing as a way to enter into conversations about ideas that matter to you and problems that you need to solve.

WRITING INVITATIONS

1. Using one of the articles in the casebooks in Part 4, a piece of writing selected by your instructor, or a reading you have discovered and selected, read the piece for purpose and context. Answer the question, "Why is the writer writing this and what does the writer say that makes me think so?" and fill in the blanks in the following sentence:

   The writer's purpose is _____, because the writer _____.

   Then write a two- or three-paragraph paper that begins with that sentence and explains why you filled in the blanks the way you did. Make specific reference to the context, if you know it.

2. Using the same essay or another, analyze the writer's rhetorical strategy. Use the questions in the strategy box "How to Analyze Rhetorical Strategy." Then write two or three paragraphs explaining how effective these choices were in making you wish to do, or know, or think, or feel the way the writer wishes about this subject.

3. To practice finding and using a public voice, find a job description that interests you. Write a letter applying for the job. Then write a letter to a parent or a friend telling them why you'd like to get the job—what it would mean to you personally. Finally, investigate the type of position described, and report what you find—company background, expected salary, number of people in similar positions, job satisfaction, etc.

4. Using the questions in the strategy box "How to Recognize Personal, Public, and Academic Stances in Writing," write a two-page paper in which you compare the stances demonstrated in the following passages by Richard Rodriguez and S. I. Hayakawa. The full text from which this excerpt is taken appears in Casebook 2.

   ### Richard Rodriguez
   ### *Public and Private Language*

   In the early years of my boyhood, my parents coped very well in America. My father had steady work. My mother managed at home. They were nobody's victims. Optimism led them to a house (our home) many blocks from the biggest, whitest houses. It never occurred to my parents that they could live wherever they chose. Nor was the Sacramento of the fifties bent on teaching them a contrary lesson. My mother and father were more annoyed than intimidated by those two or three neighbors who tried initially to make us unwelcome. ('Keep your brats away from my sidewalk!') But despite all they achieved, perhaps because they had so much to achieve, any deep feeling of ease, the confidence of 'belonging' in public was withheld from them both. They regarded the people at work, the faces in crowds, as very distant from us. They were the others, *los gringos*. That term was interchangeable in their speech with another, even more telling, *los americanos*. The full text from which this excerpt is taken appears in Casebook 2.

S. I. Hayakawa
The Case for Official English

The ethnic chauvinism of the present Hispanic leadership is an unhealthy trend in present-day America. It threatens a division perhaps more ominous in the long run than the division between blacks and whites. Blacks and whites have problems enough with each other, to be sure, but they quarrel with each other in one language. Even Malcolm X, in his fiery denunciations of the racial situation in America, wrote excellent and eloquent English. But the present politically ambitious "Hispanic Caucus" looks forward to a destiny for Spanish-speaking Americans separate from that of Anglo-, Italian-, Polish-, Greek-, Lebanese-, Chinese-, and Afro-Americans, and all the rest of us who rejoice in our ethnic diversity, which gives us our richness as a culture, and the English language, which keeps us in communication with each other to create a unique and vibrant culture. (S. I. Hayakawa)

DEVELOPING A WRITING PROJECT

Choose a non-profit agency where you might like to volunteer. Ask the agency to send you materials about their mission. After studying the materials you receive, do the following:

■ Draft a letter you might send in which you tell the director what personal experiences you have had that make you interested in volunteering for the agency. Share your letter with other members of your discussion group. Read each others' letters and suggest ways the writer might strengthen the letter.

■ Write a personal essay describing how your personal experience relates to the mission of the agency.

■ Write two or three paragraphs in which you identify a question at issue related to the agency, one that you might like to explore for an extended essay.

PART 2

Reading and Writing as Dialogues

CHAPTER 4

Summarizing and Responding

Interpretation can be thought of as taking place in two stages (though they will always overlap): a stage where you analyze the author's text, and then a stage where you appraise or evaluate it. It is sometimes useful to think of the first stage as one of understanding, allowing the author to be master for a while, and the second as one of overstanding (a word not in your dictionary), the point where you take charge and ask questions that the author might not even have thought about.

Wayne C. Booth and Marshall W. Gregory

If we have no attitude for our facts, we shall have no predicates for our subjects, no themes for our essays, no points for our remarks, no responsibilities for our actions.

Josephine Miles

When you read a novel, you may begin by reacting with your feelings and imagination before you completely understand what's going on. However, in many academic situations, it is important to fully understand what you are reading before you allow yourself to react and respond. It is helpful to remember the difference between *understanding* and what Booth and Gregory call *overstanding*. Overstanding might also be called "higher order" or "critical" thinking. It involves going beyond understanding to reflecting on how the new information relates to what you already know and have experienced. It involves connecting, comparing, analyzing, evaluating, and extending the ideas. But understanding is not simpler or less important than "overstanding." They are two ways of learning about ideas and issues, and while they can't be clearly separated in most rhetorical situations, we will look at them separately in this chapter in order to help you focus on and strengthen both ways of knowing and learning.

One of the most important conditions for understanding is that you know how to listen well, with an open mind, to a writer's or a speaker's words. Listening to ideas we already agree with is easy; but listening to ideas that are new or different can be challenging.

Ours has been called the information age because so much information is available to us in so many forms. Sometimes it seems as if words and sounds and images are all we produce. Many of the challenges of understanding presented to us by the information age are not new—they just seem more urgent because we are being flooded with words through a deluge of multimedia sources. This can be overwhelming, especially in college classes where you constantly encounter new and complicated ideas expressed in specialized vocabularies and presented in unfamiliar forms. It's important, then, that we all read in a way that makes the best use of our time and intellectual energy.

READING TO UNDERSTAND

How do we read *attentively*, listening closely to what a writer wants us to understand about his or her subject? Reading is a process of meaning-making, like writing. In the same way that writers try to help readers see subjects the way they do, attentive readers are attempting to see subjects the way writers want them to. When we read to understand, we are receiving meaning about the subject through the language of the writer.

When we read to understand, we think both about what the reader is saying and about our reactions to his or her statements. Both of these perspectives are necessary to the task of attentive reading, but it is important to tell them apart. Sometimes readers misunderstand what they read because their strong reactions to the message cause them to read inaccurately. Sometimes readers misunderstand because they aren't engaged at all with what a writer is saying, which makes it difficult for them to stay focused on the message. To make sense of our reading, we must try to listen carefully to what the writer is saying, and then we can respond more thoughtfully and usefully to the information in terms of our own knowledge and experience. If we think as we read, composing and revising our understanding as we go, and if the writing is good, we may come closer to a meeting of minds with the writer.

As readers, you have certainly benefited from graphic summaries of information—charts, graphs, tables, and pictures that represent complex ideas or relationships among ideas. Many readers have also found that representing ideas with a visual diagram, a form of graphic summary, helps them listen responsibly and with an open mind. Figure 4.1 presents a model of a graphic summary.

Many factors other than reader error can influence your understanding as a reader. Maybe you are not a part of the audience the writer had in mind. Maybe the writer seems to be writing to experts in the subject, and you need a basic introduction to the subject; or maybe he or she is writing for beginners when you need more specialized or complete answers. Maybe you have never seen the form of the writing before, so it seems disorganized or strange. Maybe

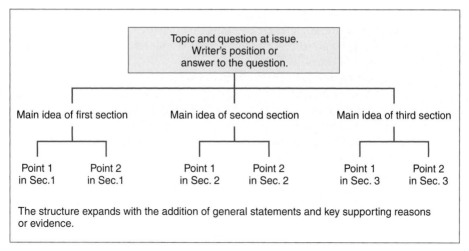

FIGURE 4.1   MODEL OF A GRAPHIC SUMMARY

the writer is making assumptions about your beliefs or values that are inaccurate, so you have no common ground on which to share meaning. All of these factors can get in the way of understanding. But knowing as much as you can about rhetorical strategies and rhetorical situations will strengthen your ability to "hear" a writer talking to you, even when you feel resistance to the ideas that are presented.

Of course, understanding the choices a writer makes within a particular rhetorical situation is a constant challenge for a reader. If words had only one meaning, and if we had enough words to use different ones for every possible situation, and if we had the time and patience to master such a system of symbols, we might hope to perfect our art. But we would never know if we had succeeded. Why? We can't get inside a writer's head, so we will never know if what we understand is what he or she intended. In the same way, because writers can't get inside the heads of readers, they can only hope to choose the very best language elements to match strategy with situation.

And that isn't the end of the complications. As we said earlier, because we are human readers with emotions and values and beliefs as well as intellect, we bring our own experiences, backgrounds, and personalities to our reading, which explains why the same writing is understood in different ways by different readers.

Well then, if understanding can't be perfected, why should we bother to read, much less read attentively? Because if we care about learning from each other, we need to consider the ways messages are transmitted. We would like you to understand reading as a dialogue between at least two people, you and a writer. The literary critic and rhetorician Wayne Booth encourages us to think of authors as different kinds of friends. Most of us have friends who are our companions, but we also have friends who are mentors or teachers, friends who challenge us or comfort us, friends who set us straight when we are confused or offer complexity when we are thinking in terms too simple. We can vary our reading strategies according to the purpose of the reading material, but also according to our purposes for reading.

Attentive readers listen to the writer's voice, or attitude, to identify what is at issue and what the writer's assumptions are. Attentive readers observe the language and structure of a text, noting the way the ideas are expressed, developed, and connected. Attentive readers pay attention to their own responses, positive or negative, and inquire about them, asking what features in the work or what factors in their personal lives or values might have generated the responses. When readers do all these things carefully, they are making the most of their conversation with the writer. The process of reading strategically to connect with others through ideas can help us move beyond first impressions or preconceived notions to thoughtful, reasonable understandings and positions.

Reading makes more sense if you can imagine that a real person is talking to you about something he or she cares about and wants to share. To help you listen to a writer, try asking and answering the questions in the "How to Read for Understanding" strategy box.

 ## STRATEGY

How to Read for Understanding

Part I: To read for understanding, read carefully, take notes on each paragraph, and ask yourself these questions:

1. What is the topic of this piece of writing? State it as a word or a phrase.
2. What question about the topic does the writer address?
3. What position does the writer take concerning the question? Or, what answer does the writer propose to the question?
4. How is the writing structured? What are the main sections?
5. What reasons does the writer offer in support of his or her answer? Or, what general statements does the writer make in answering the question?
6. What key support or evidence does the writer provide?

Part II: The Graphic Summary

A graphic summary depicts visually the structure and relationship of the key ideas in any piece of writing. Graphic summaries are often used in reports and articles in many disciplines and professions.

APPLICATION

Taking Notes to Understand

Read the essay by Eileen Parks, "Who Cares about the Youth Vote." Take notes on her topic, her question, her answer, and her support.

EILEEN PARKS

Who Cares About the Youth Vote?

1   Who can forget Bill Clinton's pandering to the youth voter during his 1992 bid for the presidency—playing his saxophone on Arsenio Hall and doing an MTV Rock the Vote special, in which he fearlessly answered the question, "Boxers or briefs?" In these attempts to capture the youth vote, the future president seemed young, somewhat hip, and decidedly different than any candidate we had ever seen before. And all that courting had big results. That November the number of 18- to 30-year-olds who actually showed up to vote on election day went up for the first time in recorded voting history, climbing 20 percent to create a 43 percent turnout.

2   But by 1996, the numbers were down again—it was an incumbent year for Clinton, and Dole hardly reached out at all. So far this cycle we've seen George W. Bush on Letterman and Leno, but an all out commitment to reach the 18–30 voter hasn't materialized among either of the major candidates now heading for the general election. Indeed, Senator McCain was the only candidate with a full-time paid youth advisor on his campaign staff. His and Senator Bradley's campaigns were reinvigorating the American voter, creating higher public interest and involvement. Now it's down to two men and, apparently, business as usual.

3   *Would 'Someone Else' Please Step Forward?* In a Shewire/Snowball poll informally conducted at our site, results were feeble for all candidates before the Super Tuesday primary. The results for Shewire's poll question, "If the election were held today, who would you vote for?" had "Someone Else" in the lead, with Al Gore a close second.

4   Figuring it couldn't be as obvious as cynicism, I sought out John Dervin of Youth Vote 2000. "Neither party has much relevance to youth voters," says John. "This election so far is all about personality and the mechanics of politics. That's just noise to young people." Dervin points out that although this 22 million–strong demographic has millions of marketing dollars spent trying to capture their dollars and their loyalty, very little resources are expended trying to get their vote. "It's really a vicious 'chicken-and-egg' style cycle," says Dervin.

FIGURE 4.2

MTV ROCK THE VOTE POSTER

"This group of people has low voter turnout." Consequently, there are very little campaign resources directed at trying to get the youth vote for this coming general election. And not getting a targeted message from the candidates results in low turnout, which perpetuates the cycle, Dervin explains.

5   As for the general election, Julia Cohen, executive director of Youth Vote 2000, says it's still too early to forecast this year's voter turnout. "It's going to be a long, slow spring and summer heading up to election," she says. "I'm just not sure how a Gore/Bush election will go about attracting more people and keep them engaged."

6   *Alive and Kicking—Just Not Voting* Alison Byrne Fields from Rock the Vote says her organization's goal is to get young voters to understand that voting doesn't occur in a vacuum, it's part of a set of actions. "We help young people understand that actions, whether its running a 'zine, organizing within your community, or attending a town council meeting, are essential actions to take while living in a democracy." She says that low numbers at the polls aren't evidence of a lack of political engagement. One need look no further than the footage from the World Trade Organization's summit protests for evidence of youth engagement. During the days of tumultuous protests, young people marched alongside people from every age group to voice their opposition to the WTO. And Dervin points out that volunteerism among this age group is at an all-time high.

7   In a national youth survey conducted last September by 20/20 Vision, 93 percent of respondents said "volunteering locally to help people directly" is an effective way to make change. Clearly, this is a group willing to get involved, especially at a community level. Building on that information, Youth Vote 2000 aims to build on its 50 organizations and coalitions by bringing youth together at a grass roots level, drawing them closer to national politics, and adding volume to their political voice. These voters are concerned with issues of education, crime and violence, jobs, and the future of social security, not tax cuts and defense spending.

8   But Byrne Fields puts it best: the disconnect between the candidates and young adults is in the way candidates address the issues. "Both candidates have youth advisors; I just don't think they are doing a very good job. When they address issues like crime and education, they usually direct the message towards the parents," she says. "Even the obligatory speeches at universities are merely a backdrop for the candidates to address a national audience. The political arena hasn't figured out how to market themselves to a generation of people that have instigated some of the savviest marketing ploys ever." In the end, she likens the situation to a school dance, with the youth vote as a wallflower, hoping to get asked to dance. "It's really kind of sad how they aren't being brought together. I don't want to condescend to young people when I say this, but it doesn't take much to bring young people together and get them involved." So to all the wall flowers out there: Shall we dance?

WRITING A SUMMARY: LISTENING TO THE WRITER

Summary writing helps us to hear, understand, and remember what a writer has to say. A summary is a restatement, in your own words, of the key ideas of a text. It's a condensation of the whole—shorter, but with all the essential ingredients. To address the rhetorical situation of the summary, imagine yourself writing your summary to the author of the text you are summarizing. Imagine the author reading your words to see if you have really understood what the text was trying to convey. Persuade the author of the text that you have listened attentively and respectfully for his or her purpose and main ideas.

You may be asked to write summaries for many reasons. In professional settings, reports are often condensed into summary form for easier access and distribution. On the Internet, summaries of articles and books are often provided to help consumers and researchers decide whether the information they need is likely to be included. In professional journals, summaries often precede lengthy, complex material as aids to readers. One of the best reasons for you to know how to write summaries, though, is because they help you understand, use, and remember information. When you write a summary, you make information your own by transforming an author's ideas into your own words. You can then incorporate references to the material into research essays or recall the information for tests.

Summaries include the key generalizations of a text, usually in the order of the original, but sometimes rearranged for coherence or emphasis. They do not include commentary, responses, interpretations, or anything else that was not in the original work. Good summaries have several of the qualities of any good writing: the purpose is clear, the ideas connect to the purpose and to each other, the development is sufficient, the sequence is apparent, the paragraphs are focused and coherent, and the sentences, vocabulary, and conventions are clear and correct.

Sound simple? As the information and ideas you encounter become more complex, so does the task of summarizing. Sometimes the general statements are not at the beginnings and ends of paragraphs, where you'd expect them. Sometimes they are divided—parts show up in two places, and you have to put them together in your own words. Sometimes writers leave out their assumptions altogether, expecting the reader to infer them. These characteristics do not mean the writing is bad—complexity is necessary in much writing. These kinds of complexity, however, make finding appropriate words to restate the ideas and their relationships intellectually challenging. That is why we suggested that you keep reading notes paragraph-by-paragraph, so that you can focus on the purpose of smaller units of meaning. It may also help to think and compose out loud. Tell a friend—or imagine telling a friend—what a writer is saying; this can help you gain independence from the original text while you record the ideas accurately.

 # KEY CONCEPT

Qualities of a Good Summary

Good summaries will be characterized by the following qualities:

- **CONCISENESS:** Summaries are significantly shorter than the original work. They avoid repetition and unnecessary words.

- **COMPLETENESS:** Although summaries may also include an example essential to the reader's understanding of the original, they always include the general statements and key ideas necessary to the development of the writer's purpose.

- **OBJECTIVITY:** Summaries maintain an emotional distance from the original work. Writers of summaries focus on the original author's ideas rather than on their reactions to those ideas.

- **ACCURACY:** Summaries represent the writer's ideas as correctly and precisely as possible, within the constraints of conciseness.

- **COHERENCE:** The summary must stand on its own as a unified, focused paragraph. Sentences must be connected in ways that represent the relationships among the ideas in the original work.

STRATEGY

How to Write A Summary

1. **PLAN** your summary by reading a text to identify the writer's topic, question, and purpose—what does he or she want you to do, know, think, or feel about the topic, and why? Note how each paragraph helps to answer those questions. Then reread the text, identifying key points by underlining them.

2. **Draft** a summary combining your notes on the writer's purpose, position, or answer with the key reasons and support you have identified.

3. **Revise** the summary for the qualities listed in the key concepts box "Qualities of a Good Summary," making sure to recheck the original text where necessary.

Student Samples: Summaries

The following summaries were written by students. As you read them, think about how they do or do not meet the criteria for a good summary that are listed in the "How to Write a Summary" strategy box.

1. Eileen Parks' essay addresses the topic of youth voting in America and in the 2000 Presidential election. During the 1992 election, President Clinton made an all-out effort to capture the youth vote; this worked with an extra 20% of the youth electorate turning out to vote. In 1996, the candidates paid little attention to this demographic and the numbers dropped. During the 2000 primary, the two major candidates once again overlooked the 18–30 year old electorate. A pre-election poll showed that many youth voters would vote for the other candidate if Gore were in second place. The problem with capturing the youth vote is the cycle in which candidates pay little attention to the 18–30 year old electorate to become even more disinterested, perpetuating the sequence; it's a "chicken-and-egg" cycle. In such a boring election, it's even hard to predict the turnout of the total population. The youth voters have been very active in the community and country over the past years, but they still do not turn out in the polls. What Rock the Vote is trying to do is get this group interested in our nation's politics to add volume to their political opinions. In the end, the political parties will have to make a concerted effort to present the issues to the youth electorate in ways that will spark their interest and bring them to the polls.

Mike Slatkin

2. In 1992, Bill Clinton captured the youth vote by appearing on MTV's Rock the Vote, and playing his saxophone on Arsenio Hall. This

resulted in Bill Clinton's young, hip image, and a 20% increase in voters from the age of 18 to 30. Today in 2000, the presidential race has returned to its usual characteristics. Candidates are appealing more to adult voters, and the race has become about personality and "the mechanics of politics." This will probably result in a low amount of youth voters, because this dry race gives the impression that voting does not matter. Parks does not say that the youth are apathetic about becoming involved and making a difference in their world, in fact, the youth show exactly the opposite. Youths are volunteering at a grass roots level at an all time high, and are protesting at the WTO conference. Youths are actively involved in the political process just at the grass roots level, and they want to be involved in the higher realms of politics, but no political campaign is geared toward youths in order to capture their attention.

Maria Devaney

3. Eileen Parks addresses the voting situation of youth in her article "Who Cares About the Youth Vote" and how in the recent years, candidates for the presidency have addressed the situation from various angles. First, Bill Clinton took the hip and different approach by appearing on MTV and Arsenio Hall and answering personal questions. By his involvement, he increased the vote to a 43% turnout of 18 to 30 year olds. But the rise in votes was only temporary and in his second election it had declined. This year's election was not looking for the target youth group anymore; Bush and Gore were once again back to the plain-Jane attempts at the presidency. John Dervin of Youth Vote 2000 explains that Bush and Gore were based on personality and politics, definitely not aimed at the youth vote. This is a vicious cycle, because an insignificant turnout of young voters causes candidates to spend little time and money campaigning for their votes. Furthermore, Alison Byrne Fields from Rock the Vote claims that volunteering at organizations within the community increases the numbers of voters at the polls. Fields also explains that the candidates tend to address the youth's parents and not the youth, completely missing the point of connecting with the younger generations. Overall, this piece explains that political campaigns still don't know how to market to the younger generations.

John Riles

Read the following essay and identify Goodman's topic, question, and purpose.

ELLEN GOODMAN

Reviving the Habit of Voting

1   And now we come to that wonderful moment in the election year when all eyes turn to the ballot box and find it half empty. This year special attention is going to that near-oxymoron, the youth vote. In 1996 only 28 percent of 18- to 24-year-olds voted. This year they may under do themselves.

2   Questions about young voters have less to do with Gore and Bush than with chickens and eggs. Which came first?

3   Chicken and Egg One. Do young Americans not vote because the candidates ignore them, or do candidates ignore them because they don't vote? It's no coincidence that the issues being raised are Social Security and prescription drugs. Who's chicken?

4   Chicken and Egg Two. Do young voters refuse to choose because they don't know enough, or do they not learn more because they have no intention of voting? A disheartening MTV poll showed that a quarter of 18- to 24-year-olds couldn't name both presidential candidates and 70 percent couldn't name the veeps. Who laid the egg?

5   Chicken and Egg Three. Are they apathetic because they are alienated from politics, or alienated because they are apathetic? College students volunteer and work for change one on one and in the private sector, not en masse or in politics. Anyone for an omelet?

6   Now, I am not into breaking eggs, wringing chicken necks, or bashing youth, although some of the reasons coming from Generation-Y-Vote are enough to turn my roots gray. Try these two from North Carolina students: "It doesn't relate to me" and "I think they're both crackheads." The real problem is how to break what one pollster called a "cycle of mutual neglect."

7   Even groups targeting the problem, like Rock the Vote —have you seen their tag line, "Piss off a Politician. Vote"?—can't seem to slow the downward spiral. Maybe you can lead a young person to register at the World Wrestling Federation theme restaurant in Times Square, but you can't make him vote.

8   There are all kinds of theories about the incredible shrinking voter. Curtis Gans at the Committee for the Study of the American Electorate does a six-minute rap on the erosion of big issues like Vietnam or civil rights, on political disillusionment from Nixon to Clinton, on a breakdown in community and the proliferation of media. The end result, he says, is that voting has become the specialty of policy junkies and ideological zealots.

9   Tom Patterson of the Vanishing Voter Project adds that interest in news and interest in politics go together. He is looking at what happens at home. The "pre-cable" generation grew up with the evening news on televi-sion and around the dinner table. The post-cable generation of under-30s "hasn't gotten the news habit." "Unless you follow what's going on," he says, "politics is like going to a football game for the first time if you are European."

10   Older voters, Gans says, are "the last upholders of the religion of civic duty." Civic duty? Consider the recent death notice of Rhode Island great-grand-mother Mary Hallowell: "In lieu of flowers, please vote for Al Gore."

11   In any case, a 65-year-old American is more than twice as likely to vote as a 25-year-old. There's no quick fix for a massive change unless there's some national disaster. No one wants that kind of wake-up call.

12   But if the researchers are right, if politics was once a family affair and if, among other things, the older generation has failed to pass on the civic religion, maybe there's another way to intervene in this spiral of mutual neglect.

13   If older Americans are twice as likely to vote as young, you do the math. A lot of those non-voters are the adult children of voters. Remember Take Your Daughter to Work Day? What about Take Your Daughter or Son to the Polls Day? Take anyone's son or daughter. Take anyone over 18.

14   This may sound like some hopelessly retro Frank Capra movie. It's more sophisticated to sit around talking about the chicken and the egg of disconnection. But one of the things we know is that voting is a habit. Anyone who votes a couple of times will keep doing it. They'll get involved. Anyone who skips the first couple of national cycles probably won't ever get to the polls.

15   In this civic religion, the one who never gets to the booth is the rotten egg.

 APPLICATION

Writing a Summary

Write a summary of the essay by Ellen Goodman using the strategies in the "How to Write a Summary" strategy box. Revise your summary, and then, in a conversation with other readers and writers, evaluate it based on the key concepts box "Qualities of a Good Summary."

Reading for the Writer's Assumptions

Assumptions have to do with the way we see the world, human nature, right and wrong, what is always true or what is never true. For example, you may believe that even the president of the United States should have a private life. Or you may believe that political leaders assume a responsibility to exemplify moral behavior even in their personal lives. These assumptions could influence the way you vote. You may assume that the nature of modern politics is such that the individual vote is irrelevant. Or you may believe that in a democracy, the effects of political decision-making are directly attributable to the actions and decisions of the voter participants. These assumptions will influence your decision about whether to vote at all.

When you read something that addresses a question at issue, you not only need to identify the author's question and answer, but you also need to be aware of and identify the author's assumptions, because identifying the assumptions underlying the author's ideas will help you summarize completely, accurately, and objectively.

Sometimes it is easier to identify assumptions that are different from your own, because you will have a sense that something is unacceptable in the presentation. When a writer makes assumptions that you agree with, it is difficult to perceive them as anything other than "true" or "right," without considering

STRATEGY

How to Read for Assumptions

To identify an author's assumptions:

1. First look for explicit statements of belief or value. (These statements are often accompanied by the word "should.")

2. Then look at his or her general statements, and ask yourself, "What do I need to believe in order to accept these statements as correct?"

 APPLICATION

Reading for Assumptions

Ellen Goodman's essay presumes certain beliefs about voting. To discover them, first look for clues in the writing itself, and then think about what beliefs and values underlie her arguments.

1. What assumptions or beliefs are stated or implied in the following excerpts?
   "One of the things we know is that voting is a habit."
   "The end result, he says, is that voting has become the specialty of policy junkies and ideological zealots."
   "In this civic religion, the one who never gets to the booth is the rotten egg."

2. Reread the summary you wrote on Goodman's essay. Would you make any revisions to the summary for completeness, accuracy, and objectivity based on your analysis of her assumptions?

other alternative positions. So, to read responsibly, it is important to see not just what a writer is saying, but also what beliefs underlie his or her statements.

After a local Fourth of July celebration, a community expressed a wide range of reactions when the singer who was invited by the organizing committee to sing "The Star Spangled Banner" chose to sing half the lyrics in English, and half in Spanish. Letters appeared immediately in the *Yakima Herald-Republic*, and each demonstrates how personal experiences, values, and backgrounds influence the way the event was interpreted. Although some wanted to see this as an issue with only two sides, "pro" or "con," each letter writer's reaction is grounded in different experiences and emotions. Each reaction is unique.

Letters to the Editor of the *Yakima Herald-Republic*

To the editor:

1   We attended a portion of the Fourth of July festivities at our Central Washington Fairgrounds this year. This was a first for us despite being long-time Yakima residents. The fireworks display was especially impressive and we enjoyed the show.

2   I am curious, however, if I am the only Yakima resident and citizen of these United States of America who objected to the national anthem of our great country being partially sung in a foreign language. I am more than aware of the changes in our city, our state, and our society as a whole.

3   However, after more than half a century of hearing and singing the anthem of my country in English, I was upset to hear the lyrics sung in Spanish. It seems that part of what coming to a foreign country to live should be is to learn the language, understand and obey the laws of the land, and become part of the citizenry that makes up a united country.

                                                            Greg Smith

To the editor:

1   The ugly head of racism rises yet once again in Yakima. I refer to the vitriolic letters of July 8, decrying the singing of the national anthem on the Fourth of July in both English and Spanish. Around the world, multilingualism is valued by the majority of peoples. As a nation, we are in the minority when we embrace monolingualism. I thank Krista Bodeen for her sane letter (July 9) of inclusion and diversity and love. It reminded me of the poem by Edwin Markham:

2   "He drew a circle that shut me out—Heretic, rebel, a thing to flout. But love and I had the wit to win: We drew a circle that took him in!"

                                                    Deborah Severtson-Coffin

To the editor:

1   I am writing to express my disgust over the national anthem fiasco on the Fourth of July. I believe it shows great disrespect to sing the "Star Spangled Banner" in any language other than English. If the organizers of the Fourth of July celebration believed it would bring our community together, they were wrong. As a member of the U.S. Navy band, I played the national anthems of many foreign countries, oftentimes changing the lyrics to another language just because I couldn't understand them.

2   If the people who do not understand English cannot take three minutes to listen to a song that is (or should be) sacred to Americans and thank their lucky stars their children do not go to a school where the walls are made of cardboard, then maybe they should not attend a Fourth of July celebration.

La Bandera de Estrellas
Amanece: ¿no veis,
a la luz de la aurora . . .

FIGURE 4.3

"THE STAR SPANGLED BANNER,"
IN SPANISH

I bet the Mexican national anthem is never sung in English during a Cinco de Mayo festival.

3   I hope I never hear such a sacrilege again.

Melissa Preiser
USN, Retired

To the editor:

1   The argument about the national anthem being sung only in English is just plain racist. Many things that we use in our culture have been translated for our language, and the national anthem should not be so precious that it can't be shared with everyone in their own languages. Many of you forget how many languages and cultures we have damaged or diminished in the Anglo-Saxon small-minded thinking that everyone should bend to a single way. Native Americans, African Americans and now Mexican Americans can give witnessed accounts to just that.

2   Nothing is so sacred that it cannot be shared in another language. If this weren't true, then we could only read the Bible in Hebrew and Latin, we could only sing "Silent Night" in German, and we would not understand the Magna Carta that was written in an English language that was far different from what we speak today.

3   Follow everyone's constitutional First Amendment rights of free speech. Our founding fathers did not state what language was required to express ourselves.

Ellie Lambert

APPLICATION

Identifying Assumptions

After you have read the letters to the editor of the *Yakima Herald-Republic*, discuss them with other readers. In complete sentences that include the word "should," express the assumptions and values reflected in each letter. Then write your own letter to the editor on this issue, including your own assumptions in the letter.

READING TO RESPOND

We began this chapter by making a distinction between understanding, or listening to the message the writer presents, and overstanding, or reflecting on and responding to how the new information relates to your former knowledge. Your response begins with your understanding but does not end there. You will need to find connections between your new knowledge, or what you just learned from your reading, and your old knowledge, including your prior understanding and experiences. Responding to new knowledge is a way to practice taking personal responsibility, because most important questions that we face as community members, as citizens, as human beings, are at issue until we answer them for ourselves and take responsibility for those answers. When we read to respond to the text, we are conversing with the writer about the subject, answering the writer's ideas with our own.

Sometimes we agree or disagree immediately with the ideas in the writing of others. Other times, however, our first response may be confusion. Often when we read, we find ourselves puzzled by something the writer says or by an example the writer uses. Our confusion may make it difficult to understand the writer's message. Some readers are embarrassed by their confusion, because they don't realize that all readers find themselves confused at times. As our reading improves, we discover that how we deal with these puzzling moments can actually help us make sense of and identify our responses to a piece of writing.

As reading for understanding requires you to listen well, reading to respond requires you to ask good questions of the text. We have found that students are often in the habit of taking reading notes that *either* record the main ideas *or* respond to those ideas, but not both. To help you reflect on your reading, you might use what one writing theorist, Ann Berthoff, calls a "Double Entry Notebook." Berthoff has found that the habit of dividing recording from responding encourages readers to be both attentive and reflective. She recommends, rather than being limited to the space in the margin, that we keep our responses in a notebook. On the left side, you can record direct quotations and generalizations. On the right side, you can comment on and ask yourself questions about your notes (Figure 4.4).

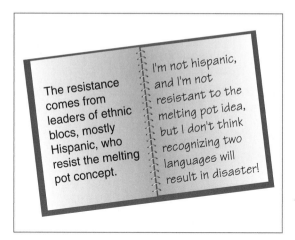

FIGURE 4.4

AN EXAMPLE OF A DOUBLE
ENTRY NOTEBOOK

Dividing recording from responding helps readers remember to engage with their reading in both ways. To read actively is to engage with the writer's ideas. You don't have to use this page-division style of note-taking—you may already have a system of recording responses to your reading that works for you. No matter how you keep your notes, the important strategy is to ask yourself questions about your reading so that you can *make your own sense* as you read.

What questions should you ask? Many will occur to you spontaneously, but when the reading is difficult or challenging, it helps to have strategic questions in mind. What in your knowledge and experience is contradicted or modified by what you're reading? What does the reading remind you of? What other perspectives are possible? Use these questions to identify and explore your response to what a writer is saying.

Such an exploration is more than an emotional reaction. The quality and depth of an answer to a question at issue depends on the variety and quality of information, experience, and points of view brought to bear on the question. In college classes, you have diverse and thoughtful communities available to you—the instructors and students you share classes with, and the wealth of voices that live in the books in the library and on the Internet. We want you to think about reading and writing in college as invitations into ongoing conversations about subjects that challenge you personally and intellectually. Writing informed responses and sharing them with others in your community is a good way to begin those discussions.

Asking and reflecting on possible answers to the questions in the "Reading to Respond" strategy box can help you see how the new knowledge validates, challenges, modifies, or extends your previous understanding. When you read responsively, you read actively, because you are acting on the information rather than simply recording it. Reading actively helps you contribute productively to conversations about whatever is at issue, helps you remember what you've read, and helps you use the information for your own purposes in addressing issues of your own.

STRATEGY

Reading to Respond

To help you respond actively as you read, try using these generic questions to help you reflect on specific responses.

1. What relates to what? (Reflect on how the reading connects to what you already know.)
   What does it remind me of?
   What does it connect to?
   What else does it seem to explain?

2. What conflicts does it raise? (Reflect on how the reading contradicts or challenges what you already know, or how it seems to create unaddressed conflicts.)
   What puzzles me?
   Are there contradictions in the reading?

3. What changes? (Reflect on how the reading moves your knowledge or thinking to a different level.)
   How has my mind been changed by this reading?
   How do the ideas change as the writing develops?

4. So what? (Reflect on how the reading is significant to your understanding of yourself, your communities, or your world.)

5. What's important about this to me?

6. To others?

As you read the following essays, use the generic questions to focus your response.

GUY WRIGHT

U.S. English

1   At last we have a national organization to combat the misnamed bilingual movement. U.S. English, nonprofit and tax-deductible, has opened shop at 1424 16th St. N.W., Washington, D.C. 20036, and welcomes to its membership "all who agree that English is and must remain the only official language of the people of the United States."

2   Or, to put it another way, it will try to speak for those who don't want to see this English-speaking nation turned into a poly-lingual Babel.

3   Former Senator S. I. Hayakawa, who fought this battle almost alone while in Congress, is honorary chairman of U.S. English.

4   Chairman is Dr. John Tanton, a Michigan physician whose years of concern about population trends and immigration—he founded the Federation for

American Immigration Reform—led him to embrace this kindred cause. "With an organizational structure in place, we may at last be able to gain some ground," he said.

5   It is none too soon. Although there is virtually no public support for the proposition that this country should conduct its affairs in foreign languages for the convenience of those who don't want to learn English, the ethnic leaders pressing that demand are highly organized and single-minded, and they have won every skirmish so far against the disorganized opposition of a general public with many other worries.

6   Until a few years ago there was no problem. It was taken for granted that everyone who wanted to share in the benefits of American citizenship should learn English. Even today most immigrants realize the value of knowing English and are eager to learn—witness the packed newcomer classes.

7   The resistance comes from leaders of ethnic blocs, mostly Hispanic, who reject the melting-pot concept, resist assimilation as a betrayal of their ancestral culture, and demand government funding to maintain their ethnic institutions.

8   We have seen the fruit of their victories. Laws now require multilingual ballots and voting aids, and tax money pays for voter registration campaigns aimed solely at those who will vote in a foreign language.

9   As for bilingual education, it has fallen into the hands of people less interested in building a bridge to help immigrant children learn English than in building a bridgehead within the school system for foreign-language pressure groups.

10   This anti-assimilation movement (a more accurate name than bilingualism) comes at a time when the United States is receiving the largest wave of immigration in its history. This influx strains our facilities for assimilation and provides fertile ground for those who would like to turn language minorities into permanent power blocs.

11   To combat these forces, U.S. English offers this program:

- Adopt a constitutional amendment to establish English as the official language of the United States.
- Repeal laws mandating multilingual ballots and voting materials.
- Restrict government funding for bilingual education to short-term transition programs only.
- Control immigration so that it does not reinforce trends toward language segregation.

12   U.S. English is no refuge for red-necked chauvinists. Among its guiding principles, it says: "The study of foreign languages should be encouraged," and "the rights of individuals and groups to use other languages must be respected."

13   But it also says: "In a pluralistic nation such as ours, government should foster the similarities that unite us, rather than the differences that separate us."

14   Amen.

APPLICATION

Responding in Writing

Many people have reactions to what they read but often do not think critically beyond their initial reactions. Respond in writing to "U.S. English" by Guy Wright. Using the generic questions in the "Reading to Respond" strategy box, try to extend, complicate, and elaborate on your notes and questions.

WRITING A RESPONSE ESSAY: CONVERSING WITH THE WRITER

We began this chapter with a quotation from Josephine Miles, who argues that having an attitude toward our facts is a prerequisite to taking responsibility for our actions. If writing summaries is a way to find the "facts" about an author's work, then writing a response is expressing an attitude toward those facts, *responding* to them or investigating them further through informed *inquiry*. You position yourself in relation to the ideas, and when you share your ideas, you open yourself up to responses from others.

Writing summaries allows you to practice the fine art of distancing yourself from your reading. Writing responses allows you to release some of the enthusiasm or resistance that motivates you to care about your reading. Both activities are important to our understanding of the works we read. John Gage, a professor of rhetoric, wrote that we come up with good ideas "in response to a genuine conflict of thought." He says that ideas "emerge from exposure to the thinking of others." That explains why good conversations about ideas naturally occur when people are gathered together around a dinner table or at a coffee bar. (It may also explain the popularity of radio and television call-in shows.)

When you write a summary, your goal is primarily to learn about the writer's perspective on a subject. When writing a response, you learn not just about the writer's perspective, but also about your own. Written responses are usually informal explorations of the questions you have about the new information you are learning by reading the work. They explore how the new information makes you reconsider your previous ideas and experiences.

One of the best ways to reconsider your prior knowledge is to discuss your responses with others. Discussions of shared questions and concerns involve multiple points of view, and our written responses are a way of participating in this examination of relationship and difference. In any case, the experience of interacting with and responding to other points of view enriches both reader and writer—both are changed by the experience. This is a good thing. Intellectual and personal growth occurs when we change, reassess our assumptions, and reconsider our opinions. Seeing the ways our responses differ from those of others encourages us to consider the reasons for our differences.

KEY CONCEPT

Qualities of Good Response Essays

- **Thoughtfulness:** Though a response essay will be based on the issues and ideas raised in your reading, it should focus on your own reflections, explorations, and responses.
- **Accuracy:** When you refer to the ideas of the writer, the references should be accurately and fairly represented.
- **Coherence:** Each point made in a response essay should relate specifically to the reading and be supported by information from your own experiences.
- **Unity:** Although the points made in a response essay may be of various types, readers should be able to summarize the essay—that is, they should be able to relate the several main points of the essay to each other and communicate them in a single assertion.

Good response papers will be informed and guided by your own purpose: to express your unique reactions and ideas based on your knowledge and experience to others so that they will have a fuller understanding *both of you and of the issue.* But because you are writing these responses to share with other readers of the work, you will need to incorporate relevant ideas, sufficient development, an apparent and appropriate sequence, coherent and focused paragraphs, and correct, clear sentences, vocabulary, and conventions. As you write responses, consider the attributes listed in the key concept box "Qualities of Good Response Essays."

Sample Student Writing: Response Essay

This essay was written by a student writer in response to Ellen Goodman's column, "Reviving the Habit of Voting." Read it carefully, keeping in mind the qualities of a good response essay.

Reviving Respect for the Voter

Chris Timmerman

Ellen Goodman is not the only writer to have described the problem this last election season: young people apparently don't vote in the numbers that they ought to. Goodman does explore reasons why this might be the case, but she concludes by suggesting that the aging, habitual voters out there take youngsters by the hand and lead them to the voting box on election day.

Maybe her assertion that voting is partly habit—like flossing or cleaning the furnace filter at appropriate times—is correct. After all, I am of voting age, and considered young. I paid attention to the political discussions during the election season. I talked with friends over coffee, on other occasions over beer, about what the candidates seemed to be for and against. And, I confess it here, I didn't vote.

However, it's difficult to be chastised in print for my failure. Goodman chides us non-voters with Oscar-award-show language: "And now we come to that wonderful moment...special attention is going to..." Going to whom? "That near oxymoron, the youth vote." I do know the difference between a moron and an oxymoron, but still, it's an insult.

I agree with Goodman that the young voter may not be in an employment or taxation or health situation yet that will put Social Security or prescription drugs at the top of our priority list. On the other hand, whose job is it to point out that although we may not be getting Social Security checks, we are the ones who contribute a portion of our entry-level or minimum wage salaries to the comfortable retirement of our elders? Whose job is it to translate the implications of various Social Security proposals for the generation who pay for them?

I also agree, in theory, that a seeming erosion of the kinds of big issues that attracted youth attention in the past—Vietnam, civil rights—may result in reduced involvement. But the campaigns of Nader and to some extent McCain showed that the big issues exist in the real world, but not in the political world. We don't get to vote on them, because the major party candidates don't talk about them.

Goodman notes that 28% of 18–24 year olds voted in 1996, a statistic meant to shock us. But that percentage represents that nearly one out of three registered youth voters made it to their precincts. Given that only one out of two registered voters participated across all age groups, the youth statistic isn't as much shocking as it is interesting. If the ballot box is half empty, then the youth are only marginally more responsible for that statistic than is the general population.

Why might we be a little less visible in this particular form of democratic participation? I suppose the answers are as numerous as the numbers of voters, but since Goodman can speculate, I give myself permission to do the same. Is it because those of us enrolled in school are overwhelmed already? Like other voters, we work and take care of families, but we also go to class, study, research, do internships, projects, performances, and volunteer for community service. Sometimes we protest, write, or video-tape what's going on in the world. And let's remember—we absolutely own the Internet, where political dialogue flourishes. Voting is one means of being a good citizen, but it is not the only one, and sometimes the particular moment may pass us by.

I can attest that youth voters are not apathetic or alienated. Those who, like me, are trying to fit a liberal education into our lives are learners and critical thinkers. These very abilities might cause some of us to believe that voting is just one form of democratic action, but possibly one of the least effective because the candidates' positions and issues are so similar. Oddly, the candidates pitch issues and ideas in ways that seem to assume voters are selfish and self-interested. Young people are often assumed to be selfish and self-interested. But in my experience, one reason some young people don't vote is because they're not disaffected enough yet to limit their motivation to self-interest. They're not even invested in the economic culture enough to determine what their self-interest would be.

Goodman expresses her dismay at the "downward spiral" of the youth vote by saying "Maybe you can lead a young person to register at the World Wrestling Federation theme restaurant in Times Square, but you can't make him vote." Maybe, instead, young voters actually know what the difference should be between a presidential election and entertainment, and maybe the media and the major parties have forgotten the difference, and maybe the theme restaurant is better at what it does than the parties are at what they should do. If student comments about elections turn Goodman's roots gray, then where are her ideas about how politics *can* engage youth?

Goodman is right that voting is a habit developed, a value learned. Let the employers of youth allow some flexibility on voting day. Let the professors of youth allow time and opportunity for people to interpret political proposals in terms of their impact on and implications for the younger generations of voters. But I would add that politicians and political parties have much more work to do than a young voter's parents if more of us are to develop the voting habit. Nearly all political issues impact young citizens. The candidates and their "handlers" have to connect with younger, savvy advisors who will help them understand the concerns they might address and the actions they might propose.

Young voters will vote when politicians accept and address and respect them as an audience and as a constituency. There are so many stereotypes out there about people my age that we spend more of our time arguing against our image than arguing about our real concerns. Goodman herself, in addressing our parents rather than us, ignores us, suggesting that we need hand-holding rather than respect. Why did I not vote? In the end, I had no compelling reason to cast a vote for either major party candidate, and the alternates had no chance of success. I'm not justifying my actions; I'm just saying that my own particular failure to vote was in some way the result of too much thinking, not too little. We listen to people who respect us; and for all my listening, I got no respect.

The following article is on the topic of the "English Only" movement, as was the piece by Guy Wright that appears earlier in the chapter. As you read, listen attentively to the writer, and read actively: respond and inquire, reflecting on and developing your own ideas on the question at issue.

EDITORIAL IN THE *DENVER POST*, JANUARY 6, 1987

Legislating Language

1   At first glance, the "English Only" bill to be put before the Colorado legislature this month looks like a celebration of the obvious. To declare that English is "the official language of the state of Colorado," as the one-sentence bill proposes, would seem akin to proclaiming the Denver Broncos

■ STRATEGY

How to Write Response Essays

PLAN YOUR ESSAY   Begin by doing the kind of active reading we have described in this chapter. Read for the issue, the assumptions, and the purpose; distinguish the general ideas from the specific support; reflect on your reading by asking questions that explore the connections between the work and your prior knowledge and experience.

DRAFT YOUR ESSAY   Written responses to readings will have four main components:

1. An **introduction** that raises the issue or identifies your question about the writing in your own way. You may begin with the issue that was the focus of the writer's work or you might begin with your personal response to reading the writer's work. You might describe an experience or an idea that illustrates your perspective. Doing so will personalize the issue.

2. A **summary** of the points you agree and disagree with in the reading. You may do this in a paragraph that simply highlights similarities and differences.

3. **Your own assertions** about the ideas and issues in the reading, sup- ported by **your own arguments** and evidence, which agree or disagree with specific points in the reading. This should extend the summary of similarities and differences.

4. A **concluding statement** that relates your main points to each other and gives a sense of unity to the whole essay.

As you become more accomplished, you will find that the four compo- nents won't necessarily be written separately, much less in numerical order. But a complete response will include all four. The introduction lets your reader know why you will talk about what you will talk about, and it creates interest. The summary lets your reader know that you really have listened to the writer and so you, in turn, deserve to be listened to. The rest of the essay will accomplish any of the following purposes:

- To express your reactions based on your knowledge and experience.
- To explain the limits or implications of the reading.
- To inform other readers about the significance of the writer's work.
- To extend or apply the meaning of the work.

REVISE YOUR ESSAY   Revise the essay, making sure to recheck the original where necessary. We said before that responses are explorations, and while they are often written primarily for the person writing the response, they should be shared with other readers of the text. As writers read and comment on each other's responses, everyone's learning is enriched. Revising for other readers ensures that your thoughts will be clear and your expression of them readable.

the city's official football team. It's such a dominant force that it hardly needs an imprimatur.

2   But many supporters of the "official language" concept aren't really concerned about English per se. They're worried about the flood of immigration from Latin America, and the threat this may pose to the nation's cultural integrity. Specifically, they fear that the growth of Hispanic ghettos in cities like Los Angeles and Miami—where Spanish-speaking aliens may live for years without ever learning English—eventually may fracture the body politic in the same way that French speakers in Quebec have weakened the sense of national unity in Canada. In addition, concerned politicians like Governor Dick Lamm have argued that immigrants who fail to learn English and assimilate in the society are a "social time-bomb," composed of millions of ill-educated, poverty-stricken, and alienated foreigners on American soil.

3   It seems to us that one self-evident fact of life in the U.S.—to get ahead, you have to be fluent in English—should give anyone a pretty strong incentive to learn the language. But even if today's immigrants don't turn out to realize this, as previous generations of newcomers have, will an "English only" rule do the trick? Most likely not. If anything, scrapping the bilingual approach will make it even harder for the hordes of new arrivals to assimilate. One way of picking up the mother tongue, after all, is to see Spanish and English side by side—on everything from ballots to utility bills.

4   More important, the strident rhetoric of the "official language" folks conveys a discouraging air of cultural arrogance that can easily be interpreted as racism by those for whom English is a second language. By inviting the state to say "shut up"—presumably in a foreign language, so it can be understood—to anyone who walks in the door speaking a foreign language, it offers a phony solution to an exaggerated problem.

5   In a year when there are so many constructive challenges facing lawmakers, this divisive legislation would only waste valuable time and create needless tension. The legislature should give this ill-conceived bill a deaf ear.

■ APPLICATION

Writing a Response Essay

After you have read the *Denver Post* editorial "Legislating Language" and have taken notes on your questions and responses, write a response essay based on the information in the "Qualities of Good Response Essays" key concept box and "How to Write Response Essays" strategy box. Share your essays with others, comparing your responses and evaluating the essays based on the qualities of good response essays.

READING, WRITING, AND RESPECT

When you summarize and respond to the writing of others, imagine that the writers are people you know and whose opinion you care about. Practice responding to them with honesty, but also with respect, demonstrating both that you understand their interests and concerns and that you want them to understand yours. In this way, you write as though your words are actions, which in fact they are.

In this chapter we began by making a distinction between understanding, or listening to the message the writer presents, and overstanding, or reflecting on how the new information relates to your former knowledge. As you read the writers we have included in this text, you will be both understanding and overstanding. Your response begins with your understanding but does not end there. You will extend your learning by finding connections between the writer's position and your previous experiences with the questions and issues the writer is addressing. Responding to the writer's perspective is a way to begin taking responsibility for your own answers to questions not answerable by verifiable facts alone, because most important questions that we face as community members, as citizens, as human beings, are at issue until we answer them for ourselves and take responsibility for those answers.

WRITING INVITATIONS

1. Choose a selection from one of the Casebooks for practicing the note-taking and summarizing strategies introduced in this chapter, and write a summary based on your reading. If your class regularly divides into discussion groups for reading and writing exercises, your group may decide to write summaries of the same or different selections for comparison and evaluation.

2. Choose a selection from one of the Casebooks for practicing the note-taking and responding strategies introduced in this chapter, and write a response essay based on your reading. If your class regularly divides into discussion groups for reading and writing exercises, your group may decide to write responses to the same or different selections for comparison and evaluation.

3. Write a summary of and a response to the same article from one of the Casebooks, an article selected by your instructor, one you've identified yourself, or one chosen by your reading and writing group.

DEVELOPING A WRITING PROJECT

Identify a topic for research and development. Find at least two articles that address your topic. Summarize and respond to each, and then write a statement for your instructor identifying what specific question you would like to investigate during the course of the class, and why that question is significant for you.

CHAPTER 5

Analyzing

My mind rebels at stagnation. Give me problems, give me
work, give me the most abstruse cryptogram, or the most
intricate analysis, and I am in my own proper atmosphere. I
can dispense then with artificial stimulants. But I abhor the dull
routine of existence. I crave for mental exaltation.

Arthur Conan Doyle

To analyze something, to "really see it," we have to break it
down and then intensely examine all of its component parts.
Only then can we really begin to understand how it works,
what it means, whether it floats….When we analyze
something, we observe it, study it, walk around it and see it
from different angles to discover what new conclusions can be
drawn about it.

Stacy Tartar Esch

CRITICAL LITERACY: READING AND WRITING RHETORICALLY

To read and write rhetorically is to be conscious of the effects of the signs and symbols we are using. It is absolutely essential to develop a critical consciousness of the way words and images are being used to influence us, and it is equally essential to use words and images consciously and responsibly as we communicate with others. To the extent that we are conscious of the effects of words when we comprehend them or use them to compose, we are considered critically literate.

In Chapter 1 we observed that most people think of rhetoric as using words and images consciously in a deceptive, manipulative process. We have heard politicians refer to the words of their competitors as "all rhetoric," suggesting that the words may sound good but have no substance. The point of this chapter is to demonstrate how rhetoric can be strategic in a good way; that is, good writers choose words and images purposefully to help listeners or readers understand them the way they want to be understood. As writers make their choices, rhetoric can be used to manipulate or persuade, to deceive or to reveal truth. We want you to know, first, that people who use words to manipulate can only succeed if you don't understand what they are up to, and second, that using words effectively to convey your ideas in a responsible way is an art that you can learn.

Communication vs. Manipulation

One field that relies on artful crafting of language and image, often in the manipulative sense, is the field of advertising. Advertisers make their living by using words strategically. Because companies and organizations hire them to persuade people to buy their products or join their causes, advertisers target a particular audience of potential consumers. They then craft ads that appeal to that group. The crafting does not need to be elaborate; in fact, often it is not. What is important is that the ad be designed with a particular audience in mind. For example, when a car company campaign began with the line "It's not your father's Oldsmobile," it was clear that the campaign was appealing to young consumers.

Most people are familiar with the "Marlboro Man," one of the most successful advertising campaigns in history. The ads typically feature a cowboy or two, close up or at a distance, smoking filter cigarettes. Is the ad designed to appeal to cowboys? Not likely. Cowboys are not the people most likely to buy the magazines featuring the ads; they are also not known for smoking filter cigarettes that come in little foil-lined packages. The audience is much more likely to include the executive in the office high-rise wishing he were virile and strong, out there on the open land, riding against the sunset sky. The ad appeals to our desire for pleasure, to our imaginations and emotions, but not to reason.

The California Department of Health Services seems to have relied on the familiarity of the Marlboro Man to turn the message around. They produced a public service advertisement (see Figure 5.1) featuring two cowboys out on the range, also riding into the sunset. One says to the other, "I miss my lung, Bob." Now the question becomes, is the pleasure worth the cost?

The original Marlboro Man ad suggests that if we smoke Marlboros, we will be as strong and independent as the people featured in the ad. That is manipulative, because there is obviously no reasonable support for that claim, and despite the addition of a Surgeon General's warning in the corner, the ad presents a deceptive message about the truth of the health effects of smoking. The California Public Health Department advertisement also targets the smoking public. It also relies on the audience to respond imaginatively and emotionally, because here, too, there is no presentation of information—just image. But this time the emotional appeal is communicative rather than manipulative, because it calls attention to an important truth about smoking and public health. A secondary message of the ad is that we should all be critically aware

FIGURE 5.1   CALIFORNIA DEPARTMENT OF HEALTH SERVICES ANTI-SMOKING AD

of the messages being offered to us through the media so that we can recognize the difference between manipulation and communication.

The writings of Paulo Freire, Kenneth Burke, and Wayne Booth suggest ways of reading that demand careful and respectful attention to a writer's message. Freire was a Brazilian educator who believed that citizens should participate responsibly in their communities, whether local, national, or international, and he saw reading and making sense of reading as a central activity for such participation. He argued that all human beings have the capacity to solve problems they encounter, whether they are concerned with how to find the most productive way to till the soil or how to read a complicated text. Kenneth Burke was a poet and novelist and writer of works on rhetoric, philosophy, literary theory, and music. He believed that learning rhetoric prepared us to negotiate differences in the inherently divisive world of humans. Wayne Booth sees rhetoric as a way for humans to explore answers to questions that matter to them.

At the heart of these three theories is dialogue, both between the reader and the writer and among readers, about the ideas the writer presents. The reader tries to understand and challenge a writer's ideas by attending carefully to the ways they are presented. While Freire did not call his methodology rhetorical analysis, his process of reading parallels the process described by Burke and Booth. In this chapter we will demonstrate ways of using rhetorical reading to make sense of a written work and to see how our reading may affect our beliefs and actions.

The Choices Writers Make

In Chapter 3 we introduced you, as practicing writers, to the concept of **rhetorical strategy,** the kinds of artful, purposeful choices a writer makes in the process of achieving effective communication with an audience. In this chapter we want to return to a focus on rhetorical strategy but from a somewhat different perspective. While we will again be talking about purposes, contexts, and choices, now we will be practicing reading attentively the writing of others to determine how, and to what extent, their choices support and enhance their purposes. We want to explore the effects of rhetorical choices on readers.

Strategy is a word historically associated with war and business, but it has come to be used in a more general sense to mean a calculated method of achieving an objective. Strategy is an appropriate synonym for rhetorical choices because when we choose words artfully, we do so in a calculated way so that readers will listen, understand, and be persuaded by our writing. In the worst sense, strategic choice is manipulative; in the best, it is informative or inspirational. We resent being tricked into believing something we would rather not believe in one case; we value the occasions when a writer's words communicate new knowledge or inspire us to take actions we find worthy.

Examining a piece of writing rhetorically means looking at more than its explicit message. To analyze the rhetoric of an essay or article means to look at how its author attempts to shape readers' responses to its message. The first step in this kind of analysis is to determine the writer's question at issue.

The Writer's Question

One way to observe rhetorical strategy is to see what question the writer seems to be answering and what kind of question it is. Rhetoricians during the late Greek and early Roman period suggested identifying what are called **stasis questions.** *Stasis* is a Greek word that meant strife and referred to the point at issue in any dispute. Stasis questions provided a way of analyzing the complexity of a problem. Writers or speakers would begin their study of an issue by deciding what kind of question they needed to ask about the problem they wished to solve. By doing so, they could determine the major points of disagreement concerning the issue. Though there is a long list of questions a writer could ask, most questions will fall into five major categories. See the key concept box "Categories of Questions at Issue."

 KEY CONCEPT

Categories of Questions at Issue

- Questions of **fact**
- Questions of **definition**
- Questions of **circumstance**
- Questions of **policy**
- Questions of **value**

One place we find people explicitly using stasis questions today is in the field of law. When lawyers defend clients, they begin with stasis questions as they decide how they will argue the case. As they construct their defense, they need to determine the central issue. Is the question whether the client is innocent, or whether the event actually occurred? Was the accuser someone who didn't like the defendant and consequently falsely accused him or her? In this case, the attorney would be arguing about a **question of fact,** or whether the accused committed the crime.

On the other hand, the attorney might know that the client did the deed, but might believe that the action was not criminal. In other words, the attorney might argue that the act did not fit the definition of a criminal act. The attorney might then consider the question at issue in the case one of **definition.** If he argued rather that his client committed a crime in self-defense or was in a state of emotional distress when acting, the question would be one of **circumstance.**

If the attorney knew that the client had committed the act and was fairly certain that a jury might not accept any of the arguments of definition or circumstance, he might build a case for lenient treatment because of potential outcomes of a guilty verdict. If so, the attorney would be arguing a **policy question**—what kind of sentence the client should receive. On the other hand, in some cases the attorney might acknowledge the client's guilt but wish to argue that, while the act was technically against the law, the client was acting according to a law of conscience—if the client committed an act of civil disobedience, for example. The attorney might in such a case consider a **question of value** at issue.

When politicians write speeches they go through a similar process. As we listened to Democratic presidential candidate Al Gore's concession speech after the long, complicated wait for the outcome of the 2000 presidential election, we might have asked what kinds of questions he was answering. The rhetorical situation for that speech was unique and complex. The morning after the election, Gore called George Bush and conceded the election. However, questions about voting results in Florida emerged, and that state, as it turned out, controlled the deciding votes in the electoral count. Gore called Bush again, rescinding his concession. In the days before the speech, the American public was wondering, "Will he concede?" His speech could be read primarily as an answer to a **question of fact:** "Am I conceding?" Secondarily, though, he also is answering a **policy question** about what should be done. The Supreme Court had just ruled that the deadline imposed by the Florida legislature would stand. After the ruling, the vice president had to decide what course of action to take. Should he continue the dispute by supporting the challenges to the election that many of his supporters were preparing? Or should he accept the ruling of the Supreme Court as the definitive word? In the speech, he gives his reasons for his decision, and thus his speech provides his answer to the question.

AL GORE

Concession Speech, 2000 Presidential Election

1   Good evening.

2   Just moments ago, I spoke with George W. Bush and congratulated him on becoming the 43rd president of the United States, and I promised him that I wouldn't call him back this time.

3   I offered to meet with him as soon as possible so that we can start to heal the divisions of the campaign and the contest through which we just passed.

3   Almost a century and a half ago, Senator Stephen Douglas told Abraham Lincoln, who had just defeated him for the presidency, "Partisan feeling must yield to patriotism. I'm with you, Mr. President, and God bless you."

4   Well, in that same spirit, I say to President-elect Bush that what remains of partisan rancor must now be put aside, and may God bless his stewardship of this country.

5   Neither he nor I anticipated this long and difficult road. Certainly neither of us wanted it to happen. Yet it came, and now it has ended, resolved, as it must be resolved, through the honored institutions of our democracy.

6   Over the library of one of our great law schools is inscribed the motto, "Not under man but under God and law." That's the ruling principle of American freedom, the source of our democratic liberties. I've tried to make it my guide throughout this contest as it has guided America's deliberations of all the complex issues of the past five weeks.

7   Now the U.S. Supreme Court has spoken. Let there be no doubt, while I strongly disagree with the court's decision, I accept it. I accept the finality of this outcome which will be ratified next Monday in the Electoral College. And tonight, for the sake of our unity of the people and the strength of our democracy, I offer my concession.

8   I also accept my responsibility, which I will discharge unconditionally, to honor the new president elect and do everything possible to help him bring Americans together in fulfillment of the great vision that our Declaration of Independence defines and that our Constitution affirms and defends.

9   Let me say how grateful I am to all those who supported me and supported the cause for which we have fought. Tipper and I feel a deep gratitude to Joe and Hadassah Lieberman, who brought passion and high purpose to our partnership and opened new doors, not just for our campaign but for our country.

10   This has been an extraordinary election. But in one of God's unforeseen paths, this belatedly broken impasse can point us all to a new common ground, for its very closeness can serve to remind us that we are one people with a shared history and a shared destiny.

11   Indeed, that history gives us many examples of contests as hotly debated, as fiercely fought, with their own challenges to the popular will.

12   Other disputes have dragged on for weeks before reaching resolution. And each time, both the victor and the vanquished have accepted the result peacefully and in the spirit of reconciliation.

13   So let it be with us.

14   I know that many of my supporters are disappointed. I am too. But our disappointment must be overcome by our love of country.

15   And I say to our fellow members of the world community, let no one see this contest as a sign of American weakness. The strength of American democracy is shown most clearly through the difficulties it can overcome.

16   Some have expressed concern that the unusual nature of this election might hamper the next president in the conduct of his office. I do not believe it need be so.

17   President-elect Bush inherits a nation whose citizens will be ready to assist him in the conduct of his large responsibilities.

18   I personally will be at his disposal, and I call on all Americans—I particularly urge all who stood with us to unite behind our next president. This is America. Just as we fight hard when the stakes are high, we close ranks and come together when the contest is done.

19   And while there will be time enough to debate our continuing differences, now is the time to recognize that that which unites us is greater than that which divides us.

20   While we yet hold and do not yield our opposing beliefs, there is a higher duty than the one we owe to political party. This is America and we put country before party. We will stand together behind our new president.

21   As for what I'll do next, I don't know the answer to that one yet. Like many of you, I'm looking forward to spending the holidays with family and old friends. I know I'll spend time in Tennessee and mend some fences, literally and figuratively.

22   Some have asked whether I have any regrets and I do have one regret: that I didn't get the chance to stay and fight for the American people over the next four years, especially for those who need burdens lifted and barriers removed, especially for those who feel their voices have not been heard. I heard you and I will not forget.

23   I've seen America in this campaign and I like what I see. It's worth fighting for and that's a fight I'll never stop.

24   As for the battle that ends tonight, I do believe as my father once said, that no matter how hard the loss, defeat might serve as well as victory to shape the soul and let the glory out.

25   So for me this campaign ends as it began: with the love of Tipper and our family; with faith in God and in the country I have been so proud to serve, from Vietnam to the vice presidency; and with gratitude to our truly tireless campaign staff and volunteers, including all those who worked so hard in Florida for the last 36 days.

26   Now the political struggle is over and we turn again to the unending struggle for the common good of all Americans and for those multitudes around the world who look to us for leadership in the cause of freedom.

27   In the words of our great hymn, "America, America": "Let us crown thy good with brotherhood, from sea to shining sea."

28   And now, my friends, in a phrase I once addressed to others, it's time for me to go.

29   Thank you and good night, and God bless America.

We can find further examples of how writing answers a question at issue by looking at some of the writings included in Casebook 1: The Vote. We could argue that Jefferson's Declaration of Independence answers a question of circumstance such as "Why are the colonies justified in becoming a free and independent country?" We could see Martin Luther King's "I Have a Dream" speech at least in part as an answer to a question of policy: "What ought people to do if they believe in the equality of the races?"

As you think about how these various examples demonstrate the ways that identifying questions helps determine the writer's purpose, you may notice that for each of these examples, you could argue that the writer is answering more questions than one. In fact, essays and speeches often include several questions that would lead to different lines of argument; the longer and more complicated the piece, the more questions it addresses and, as a result, the more lines of argument it develops.

To think critically about your reading, use the techniques listed in the strategy box "How to Read for the Question at Issue."

The Writer's Purpose

The writer's purpose is his or her answer to the question at issue, but as you have seen already, purpose means much more than that. If you tell a group of friends a joke, for example, you wish to amuse them, but you may also want to relieve the tension of the moment, or want them to know how clever you are or how well you can tell an amusing story or that you are comfortable in their presence. Listeners don't always know your reasons, but the point is that a purpose can be complex.

STRATEGY

How to Read for the Question at Issue

1. Consider how the writing addresses as its main question one of the categories of questions in the key concept box "Categories of Questions at Issue."

2. Phrase the specific, main question the writing is addressing.

3. Identify subordinate questions the writing answers in the process of addressing the main question.

APPLICATION

Reading for Questions at Issue

Read the following paragraphs and discuss what kind of question each seems to be addressing. How might the details of the paragraph differ if the writer were addressing a different kind of question?

Introducing the China Ruling Party
Thomas L. Friedman
The New York Times *Editorial, August 11, 2001*

Beijing—The world has grown so used to all the contradictions in China these days that "the mother of all Chinese contradictions"—the July 1 decision by President Jiang Zemin to allow capitalists to join the Chinese Communist Party—barely got a shrug. It deserved more.

Is There No Choice?
Anthony Lewis
The New York Times *Editorial, August 4, 2001*

Boston—The government of Israel and its supporters abroad put all the blame for the terrible present violence on the Palestinians. Over the years since Oslo, it is said, they have repeatedly violated the agreements. In the last failed negotiations, Yasir Arafat walked away from generous offers. Palestinians really do not accept a two-state solution; they want to destroy Israel.

Not Such a Hero at Home
Washington Post *Editorial, August 20, 2001*

Outside his own country, South Korean President Kim Dae Jung enjoys a reputation as a lion-hearted defender of human rights. He courageously protested decades of military rule, at times risking his life. As president, he won the Nobel Peace Prize for his overtures to Communist North Korea. But his domestic record is mixed in a way that might surprise Mr. Kim's overseas admirers. The latest manifestation of that came in the arrests of two top executives of newspapers that have sharply criticized the Kim administration.

Sometimes a writer's purpose may be as simple as to explore an idea and ask someone to consider his or her way of looking at the issue. Other times it may be to make us see the issue in the way the writer does. Occasionally, it may be just to vent and hope that people who agree will feel vindicated by reading the piece. Often letters to the editor have this purpose. Whatever the writer's purpose, we need to try to identify it fully. Why is this so important? One reason is that a writer's purpose may be to make us think or believe a certain way without giving us good reasons for doing so. In other words, we need to learn to recognize a writer's strategies so that we can judge the validity and strength of an argument rather than be swayed by appeals that play on our emotions and value systems.

How can we determine a writer's purpose? One way is by listening when the writer explains what he or she plans to do. Often a statement to this effect comes at the beginning of a piece of writing. The statement may be in the form of a sentence that begins as clearly as "In this essay I will be arguing" or more subtly as when Thomas Jefferson begins the Declaration of Independence with "The unanimous Declaration of the thirteen united states of America" and by doing so lets the reader know the primary purpose to be the act of declaring.

Another way to find a writer's purpose is to identify the writer's assumptions. Some writers make their assumptions clear and explicit. Thomas Jefferson says "We hold these truths to be self evident," and then lists those truths. When we try to determine his purposes beyond the simple declaring of the independent status of the colonies, we must ask ourselves why he would begin by telling readers his assumptions. Choosing to begin with what he calls truths tells the reader that the action is based on a common belief system. We thus conclude that one purpose Jefferson has is to show readers who accept the value system he outlines that the act of declaring the colonies' independence is fair and reasonable.

We also determine purpose by examining the examples the writer uses. After listing the truths he thinks his readers also accept, Jefferson goes on to show the extent to which the king of Great Britain has violated the rights associated with those truths. He then asserts that the colonists have asked that their rights be granted. From these examples, we assume that his purpose is to convince a reasonable reader that the colonists' actions are not only reasonable but also necessary because they tried less extreme methods before declaring independence.

Purpose is also suggested by the audience the writer addresses. When you read Jefferson's Declaration, you may not know whom he was addressing, but you can make certain assumptions about his audience if you look carefully at references to potential readers. Throughout the Declaration, he uses the pronoun "we" and calls the action unanimous. You might conclude from this

---

 STRATEGY

How to Read for the Writer's Purpose

1. Read attentively when the writer explains what he or she intends to do.
2. Identify the writer's assumptions in order to see what he or she expects us to believe.
3. Identify the writer's examples to consider what they suggest about the purpose.
4. Identify the writer's audiences to understand what ideas and characteristics the writer imagines that they share, and how those ideas and characteristics are significant for the members of each audience.

APPLICATION

Reading for the Writer's Purpose

Read the following opening paragraphs to editorials and write a sentence that summarizes what you think the writer's purpose is. What makes you think so?

Put Some Polish on Government Service
Joseph S. Nye Jr.
Washington Post, August 20, 2001

President Bush plans to focus this fall on education and values. A good place to start is the problem of attracting young people into public service. In 1980 three-quarters of the young Americans graduating from Harvard's John F. Kennedy School of Government went to work for government. Today, only a third do. The numbers are similar at other schools of public affairs.

You Can Use God to Justify Anything
Robert Scheer
Los Angeles Times, August 21, 2001

This has not been a good season for God. From the blowing up of innocents in a Jerusalem pizzeria to the limiting of stem cell research in the United States, the moral authority of the deity has been invoked to support actions that are at best contradictory and at worst murderous.

Don't Exploit Workers
Denver Post, August 21, 2001

The plight of 25 Mexican workers at a Lyons flagstone quarry underscores the need for federal, state and local officials to make certain that laborers who are here legally aren't exploited.

Hyperactive Advertising
Denver Post, August 21, 2001

Should drug companies advertise controlled substances like the behavior-altering Ritalin in print and on television? We think the answer, for reasons outlined shortly, is no. The fact is, however, that drug companies are paying for such advertising in the hope, we presume, that greater sales will result.

choice that one of his audiences includes the colonists and that his purpose is to unite them behind the document. But they don't seem to be the only audience. At the end of the document, he appeals to the "supreme Judge of the world" to rule on the correctness of their action so that they might be recognized as a sovereign state. From this section, you might conclude that he also wishes to address a world community of sovereign states that need to acknowledge the United States' rights to participate fully as an independent state.

Rhetorical Context

Issues do not exist in a vacuum; rather, they are actions, problems, and events that happen in a setting or within certain circumstances. This setting or circumstance is what we call the context, or the scene in which action takes place. In the diagram of the rhetorical situation that we included in Chapter 1, context is represented by the circle surrounding the triangle. The context may include the events that caused or influenced the action, the cultural backgrounds, belief systems, identity, and desires of the people involved in the action, and the attitudes of those who are either involved in the problem, observing the event, or affected by its outcome. It also may include larger historical or political history and consequence.

Reading Gore's speech, you might consider what events had immediately preceded it—the election of 2000. What was the context for the speech? The outcome of the 2000 election had been in doubt for five weeks because of problems with the vote count in the state of Florida. During that time each side expressed great anger at the other. Supporters of both candidates protested the procedure, and attorneys and political leaders from both camps appeared on television news shows to argue their cases before the American public. Finally, the Supreme Court of the United States ruled that the hand recount of the votes in Florida could not resume and that the Florida Secretary of State could certify the electors named to support George W. Bush. The following day, Al Gore went on television during prime time to concede.

Gore could have spoken one simple sentence, "I offer my concession." However, while that would have been adequate for the message, it would not have been enough for the context. But the context included a larger historical event. Al Gore was the first presidential candidate required to concede an election because of a Supreme Court ruling on its outcome. The circumstances then required him to speak about the historical moment and to concede in such a way that might reunite a divided country.

In addition, he had personal ambition. The Democratic Party was also a part of the context. He wished to be considered the leader of the Democratic Party while George W. Bush was in the White House. And so, he needed to

 KEY CONCEPT

Rhetorical Context

- The rhetorical context is the setting or set of circumstances in which communication occurs.
- The setting can include elements of time, place, and culture.
- The circumstances can include issues related to the identities, attitudes, values, actions, backgrounds, messages, and behaviors of participants.

sound like a strong leader, someone who believed he should have acceded to the presidency but was able to concede graciously. He needed to show that he was doing so for the good of the country but also to remind the American public in general and the Democratic leadership in Washington that his values were those they supported.

If you look at the Declaration of Independence in terms of the context in which it was written, you may approach the questions about this document we asked earlier in different ways. Thomas Jefferson began by identifying the assumptions on which he would build his argument. The fact that the colonists had just fought a country they saw as imperialistic and unyielding may have affected his decision. In addition, another major country, France, was going

STRATEGY

How to Analyze Context in the Writing of Others

To analyze rhetorical context, try to imagine all that you can about the circumstances under which the writer worked to express her or his ideas, and compare them to your own circumstances as a reader. Ask:

1. **WHERE WAS IT ORIGINALLY PUBLISHED?** Where did it first appear, and thus, who would be likely to read it?

2. **WHO WROTE IT?** What is the occupation, expertise, personal background, or political leanings of the writer?

3. **WHY AND FOR WHOM WAS IT ORIGINALLY WRITTEN?** What are the circumstances, occupations, levels of expertise, personal backgrounds, and political biases of the intended audience?

4. **WHEN WAS IT ORIGINALLY PUBLISHED?** What was the occasion for which or circumstances in which it was written or published, and how are present circumstances different?

APPLICATION

Analyzing Rhetorical Context as a Writer

Identify a current issue at your college or in your community. For example, your college might be considering whether to change general education requirements or to build a new dormitory. Your community might be discussing whether to build a light rail system or to change laws regarding the ownership of weapons. Write a one-page analysis of the context that would determine the decisions a writer might make in writing about the issue.

through revolutionary changes, and political philosophers were writing eloquently about human rights.

All writing occurs within a context, whether political and public or private and local. This context determines who is reading the piece, what the writer's purpose will be, and how the writer will plan and write the piece. It also affects how readers read the piece.

Rhetorical Appeals

Writers must consider ways to appeal to their targeted audiences as they construct their arguments. Experienced writers know that readers respond not only with their minds, that is, to the explicit reasoning of the message, but also with their hearts, to the values and emotions the message elicits. Think, for example, about how reading a textbook or news story in your local newspaper that merely gives you information feels different from reading the letters to the editor or, for that matter, a letter from a friend.

When writers want their readers simply to accept the information and reasoning they present as valid, they include very little obvious appeal to the readers' value systems or emotions. In contrast, a column from the editorial page may delight or annoy readers by appealing to what readers believe to be morally appropriate or appalling or find touching, amusing, horrifying, or sad. Reporters need to write news stories in as objective a manner as possible, but in other situations, knowing how to appeal to values and emotions often separates the truly great writers from the merely good ones.

 KEY CONCEPT

Rhetorical Appeals

- ***Ethos*, or the ethical appeal,** relies on the character of the speaker and appeals to readers' value systems.

  Writers are using ethical appeals when they show good sense or practical wisdom, when they are knowledgeable about the subject matter, when they demonstrate their value system, and when they exhibit good will toward their readers.

- ***Pathos*, or the emotional appeal,** relies on the feelings of readers and therefore appeals to their emotions.

  Writers are using emotional appeals when they include examples that arouse such feelings as pity or fear in their readers.

- ***Logos*, or the logical appeal,** appeals to readers' intellect.

  Writers are using logical appeals when they provide information that functions as support and show how that evidence leads to the writer's conclusion, and when they give reasons to accept conclusions that follow from generally held premises.

STRATEGY

How to Use Rhetorical Appeals

1. **To APPEAL ETHICALLY:** Identify for readers the beliefs and values they (should) share with you, the writer, and then show how your argument is connected to those values and beliefs. If you share with your readers a belief that historical heros have lessons to teach us about the present, cite their words in your presentation. Argue that your position is the "right" one.

2. **To APPEAL EMOTIONALLY:** Identify the emotions readers need to feel in order to be receptive to your message, and use strategies that will engage those emotions. If readers need to feel a connection with family, put a family group in the picture for a Kodak camera advertisement. If readers need to identify with the citizens of another country in order to listen to your arguments against economic sanctions, describe them as "fellow humans in a war against poverty," not as "faceless heathens bent on the destruction of the world order." Emotional arguments are useful when you want to illustrate a truth or present ideas in a way that draws on our basic instincts for understanding. They are often frowned on by academic audiences, however, for the way in which they are sometimes used to undermine or subvert truth through deception or the distortion of facts, undermining logic and reason so that misunderstanding, rather than understanding, is the result.

3. **To APPEAL LOGICALLY:** Rely on reasons supported by evidence, and use logical relationships such as cause or comparison to support your positions. Logical appeals are the basis of most academic writing.

The strategies that good writers rely on to appeal to values, logic or intellect, and emotions are what Aristotle called the three major sources of persuasion in the art of rhetoric. Today, we call them the ethical, logical, and emotional appeals.

All three appeals give the reader reasons to accept the writer's argument. Sometimes we decide that an argument makes sense to us because we identify with its emotions; other times its values make sense, or its line of reasoning seems compelling. Most often we are convinced by a combination of the three appeals. However we decide, when we read an argument, we are always responding to appeals. The rhetorician Wayne Booth suggests that we make such decisions in an active process he calls granting assent. Another way to put this is that we say "yes." We choose to say yes when we find the appeals convincing enough that we believe the writer has earned the conclusion he or she draws. Because our responses to an argument are dependent on the ways we respond to the appeals a writer makes, learning to identify those appeals will make us better and more responsible readers.

APPLICATION

Identifying Rhetorical Appeals

Each of the following sentences comes from "What Should Not Be Aloud" (*Washington Post*, August 21, 2001), an article by Evan Gahr on keeping private conversations out of the workplace. For each sentence, decide whether the writer is appealing primarily to your values, emotions, or reasoning.

1. Whatever happened to being discreet?

2. Sure, everybody is complaining about the loud, obnoxious cell-phone calls that have become commonplace in restaurants and on commuter trains.

3. A cell-phone user, however, is usually a stranger who maintains a certain amount of anonymity—once the dinner or train ride is over, he won't be inflicting his personal woes on us ever again.

4. In a country that claims to value privacy, why do so many office workers sound indistinguishable from Jerry Springer's guests the moment they pick up the phone?

5. I'm a child of the '60s.

ELEMENTS OF RHETORICAL ANALYSIS

To construct messages that communicate effectively with readers or listeners through strategic decisions based on questions at issue, clear purpose, attention to context, and rhetorical appeals, writers choose the materials of their craft. The common materials are diction, syntax, example, persona, and structure. To see how rhetorical choices appeal to readers, let's look at each appeal by examining the rhetorical choices made by three of the writers of essays from the first casebook: Thomas Jefferson, Martin Luther King, and George Will. While each writer makes use of all three appeals, we want to examine Jefferson's writing for its appeal to values, King's for its appeal to emotions, and Will's for its appeal to reason.

Diction and Appeal

Perhaps the most obvious way writers appeal to their readers is by the words they choose, or their **diction.** Whether abstract or concrete, vivid or nondescript, active or passive, words work to shape readers' responses to the writer's message. If we compare the choice of words in the writings of Thomas Jefferson, Martin Luther King, and George Will, we see quite a difference in the ways they appeal to readers.

In the opening section of the Declaration of Independence, for example, Jefferson chooses nouns that refer to abstract concepts: *truths, rights, foundation,*

principles, prudence. After listing the ways in which the king of England has violated these principles, he characterizes the violations as *oppressions* and contrasts them with the principles represented by the terms *justice, consanguinity*
(a close relationship because of common ancestry), and *honor.* The violations
are each suggested by verbs ending in an "ed," "en," or "ing," as in *refused,*
forbidden, imposing, or *depriving.* We call such verbs participles. A participle
shows continuing action in the present or completed action in the past. Jefferson's choice of this verb form emphasizes the regular and repeated abuse of the
colonists. Such diction defines the values his document celebrates and those it
challenges. It is therefore a kind of ethical appeal.

In contrast to Jefferson's use of abstract nouns, Martin Luther King's language includes many modifiers in the form of adverbs and adjectives to illustrate the situation of African Americans in the 1960s. By doing so, he appeals
to readers' emotions—a pathetic appeal. While there are examples throughout
King's speech, a few illustrate the strategy. His reliance on modifiers can be seen
in an adverb plus adjective combination such as *sadly crippled* and in adjective
plus noun combinations as in the phrases *withering injustice, joyous daybreak,*
fierce urgency, and *dark and desolate valley.* Such modifiers direct readers to add
an emotional dimension to the nouns they accompany.

Similarly, King's metaphors evoke vivid images of slavery and its descen-
dent injustice. He illustrates the injustice of slavery with striking comparisons

FIGURE 5.2

*The Rev. Martin Luther King Jr.
acknowledges the crowd at the Lincoln Memorial for his "I Have a
Dream" speech during a march on
Washington, D.C., on August 28,
1963. About 250,000 people
attended the march to urge support
for impending civil rights legislation.*

such as *manacles of segregation and the chains of discrimination* and *a lonely island of poverty*. He also contrasts the symbolic *long night of captivity* with the *joyous daybreak* of a bright day of brotherhood. *This sweltering summer of discontent* is in contrast to the potential *autumn of freedom and equality*. Like the modifiers, his metaphoric language evokes the sorrow, pain, and suffering of injustice and the exultation of freedom and warmth of brotherhood. In other words, King's language provides a powerful emotional argument for supporting the civil rights movement.

George Will, on the other hand, tries to avoid such emotive language. Instead he wishes his readers to respond to logical appeals. Presenting an argument supporting the Electoral College and refuting the critics' attack, he chooses language that contrasts what he wishes readers to see as his careful analysis with what he considers the emotional overreaction of some politicians and political commentators. He uses few adjectives because adjectives might make his appeal appear less objective. Rather than use the language of emotions, he relies on numbers that give what appear to be reliable historical and current statistical data.

Because his argument critiques a proposal, his verbs suggest consequence—what would happen were the Electoral College abolished, which he considers the wrongheaded position of the critics. He contrasts his own analysis of the Electoral College with that of the critics by shifting between verb tenses—*future* possibilities vs. *present* realities. He associates the results of abolishing the

---

■ STRATEGY

How to Observe the Effects of Diction

Observing the effects of diction involves two skills: identifying the types of words and phrases, and speculating about their connection to the purpose of the writing. If you need help identifying the types of words and phrases, Chapter 13: Editing Effectively will help you.

1. Observe the **nouns:** Are they more concrete or abstract? Vivid or general? Does the writer use jargon or clichés?

2. Observe the **pronouns:** When are first person, second person, and third person pronouns used? Are there patterns?

3. Observe the **verbs:** Where are particular tenses used: past, present, future? Are there patterns in their use? Do the verbs tend to be active or passive? Are participles often used?

4. Observe the **modifiers:** Are there many or few? Do they engage the reader's emotions, or are they neutral? Are they metaphors or meant to be taken literally?

5. Do you see **patterns** that seem significant? Do you see specific words and phrases that call attention to themselves as distinct from the patterns? How does the diction support the writer's purpose?

APPLICATION

Observing the Effects of Diction

Reread Vice President Al Gore's concession speech (pages 119–121) and take notice of his patterns of word choice. What pronouns does he use? What words does he use that define his audience, and how do they appeal for a sense of community? What words does he use that convey attitudes or actions he expects? When does he use active verbs, and when does he use passive verbs; is there a pattern in his choices? What kinds of appeals is he making with these language choices? Why do you think so?

Electoral College with the verbs *would incite, might become, could get elected* but the present system with *shapes, buttresses,* and *pulls.* In each case, the verb associated with the present system is not only more positive in connotation but also stronger. His choice of verbs illustrates his point that "Serious people take seriously probabilities, not mere possibilities." Even the verb in this sentence makes the point—rather than saying *should take,* he says, *take.*

Syntax and Appeal

In addition to choosing words that appeal to readers' values, emotions, and reasoning, writers make choices of particular sentence structures, or **syntax.** At a very basic level, most writers know that they must vary their syntax to maintain their readers' attention. Good writers also attend to the rhythm and stress of their sentences as they construct arguments. To see ways writers make appeals by varying syntax, we can return to our three writers.

Thomas Jefferson, writing in the 18th century, uses a sentence style rather different from that of a 21st-century statesman. Unlike a president, senator, or governor of today, he uses complicated sentences with many dependent clauses and modifying phrases. While we could say that his style is in part a product of his time, it is also very consciously crafted for effect. To see how he appeals to readers' values by varying his syntax, read the Declaration's first sentence aloud and listen carefully to the rhythm of your voice:

> When in the Course of human events, it becomes necessary for one people to dissolve the political bands which have connected them with another, and to assume among the powers of the earth, the separate and equal station to which the Laws of Nature and of Nature's God entitle them, a decent respect to the opinions of mankind requires that they should declare the causes which impel them to the separation.

As you read and heard this opening section, you probably noticed the rather slow and stately pace. This rhythm and the syntax work together to appeal to readers' values by underscoring a message that is also serious and stately. We know that the material the writer is discussing warrants serious consideration: to dissolve political bands, to assume their entitled station which is separate and equal.

In addition to establishing this cadence, Jefferson shapes the structure of his sentences to emphasize the weight of his argument. The first sentence ends with its main clause. The end position of a sentence is arguably the strongest and carries the most weight, particularly when the earlier sections clearly lead the reader to wait for and anticipate the main point. This kind of structure builds tension while the listener is held in suspense. When we read the sentence, we await the final point, and when we arrive at the main clause, our attention is drawn to the subject of that clause: "a decent respect to the opinions of mankind." After hearing about the actions the colonists are taking, we now are given the reason, which is Jefferson's ethical stance. In other words, Jefferson and the colonists are decent and respectful and have only taken action because the actions of the king of England have compelled them to rebel.

Martin Luther King's speech also appeals to the values of its listeners; it is also one of the best-known modern examples of the way a writer may use sentence structure to appeal to a reader's emotions. Using repetition the way it is often used in a sermon, King draws the listener in by building emotional intensity. The device he uses is so noticeable that most readers know the speech by the repeated phrase: the speech is commonly called the "I Have a Dream" speech.

Like Jefferson, King uses repetition to define a central idea, but while Jefferson's usage draws attention to his values, King's repeated phrases build emotional intensity. After delineating and describing the treatment of African Americans in the 1960s in the first half of the speech, he uses a series of sentences that begin with the same opening, "I have a dream." Each instance of this opening is followed by a clause that gives the different ways of defining the dream: that one day this nation will rise up, that one day the state of Alabama will be transformed,

---

 STRATEGY

How to Observe the Effects of Syntax

If you need assistance observing the basic types and patterns of sentences, see Chapter 13: Editing Effectively.

1. Observe sentence **types:** simple, compound, complex, compound/complex; are the types varied, or repeated?
2. Observe sentence **lengths:** are they varied or repeated?
3. Observe **specific strategies:** is there repetition in content or structure?
4. Observe the **order of elements:** does the main clause come at the beginning, in the middle, or at the end?
5. Do you see **patterns** that seem significant? Do you see sentences that call attention to themselves as distinct from the patterns? How does the syntax support the writer's purpose?

APPLICATION

Observing the Effects of Syntax

Read the following two paragraphs from Gore's concession speech. In what ways do you think his syntax appeals to the reader? Are the appeals in the two paragraphs different? Why do you think they are, or are not?

> Over the library of one of our great law schools is inscribed the motto, "not under man but under God and law." That's the ruling principle of American freedom, the source of our democratic liberties. I've tried to make it my guide throughout this contest as it has guided America's deliberations of all the complex issues of the past five weeks.
>
> So for me this campaign ends as it began: with the love of Tipper and our family; with faith in God and in the country I have been so proud to serve, from Vietnam to the vice presidency; and with gratitude to our truly tireless campaign staff and volunteers, including all those who worked so hard in Florida for the last 36 days.

etc. Each of these sentences begins the same way but ends differently. This strategy draws the reader's attention to the variations in the endings of the sentences in the series. King uses the device in a masterful way as he weaves an ethical appeal with an emotional one. While he suggests that his dream will enact the values America was founded on, he also gradually builds emotional intensity with the repeated opening and the ever-lengthening clauses that define the dream.

George Will's syntactic choices are quite different from either Jefferson's or King's. He uses simple, direct prose, making his appeal appear to be to the mind, not to the emotions. When he appeals to the values and emotions of his readers, he does so in very subtle ways, through a more obvious appeal to their reasoning. It could be argued that he masks his emotional and ethical appeals so that readers will see his position as reasonable in contrast to the emotional arguments of his opposition. He contrasts his words with the emotional language he says comes from the "simple-minded majoritarianism."

One example shows how Will uses a syntactic device without drawing attention to its structure, and by doing so makes his argument seem more one of reason than emotional appeal. Will chooses a structure of repetition, but not a noticeable one. He uses parallel structure. Toward the end of the article, he begins two paragraphs with the following sentences:

> Some Electoral College abolitionists argue that a candidate could get elected with just 27 percent of the popular vote—by winning the 11 largest states by just one vote in each, and not getting a single popular vote anywhere else.
>
> Critics of the Electoral College say it makes some people's votes more powerful than others.

Despite the difference in length and development, these two sentences have the same basic form: subject, verb, direct object. This structure summarizes the opposition's argument so that Will might dispute it with his response and evidence. Unlike King, who repeats the same opening clause, Will simply repeats the same structure. His choice does not draw attention to its parallelism because to do so would make it seem too crafted and therefore too emotional an appeal. Rather, he wishes to make his argument appear to be based simply on reason.

Examples and Appeal

Another way writers support their arguments is through the use of **examples.** Examples provide the evidence for the audience to consider as they weigh the strength of the writer's claim. Yet, while seemingly developing the logic of the argument, examples also may appeal to the emotions or value system of the listener. Like the language a writer chooses, the examples give the reader reasons for granting assent. Examples are a way of giving evidence that the reader would find compelling.

Jefferson's examples are more than mere illustrations of a central idea. Jefferson lists the king's repeated and continual abuses to contrast negative examples with the value system he believes his readers share. After asserting that all men have rights, he provides a list of the ways in which the king of England has denied the rights of the colonists. By using this strategy, he supports the position that the people have the right to alter or abolish any government that denies such rights.

Like Jefferson, Martin Luther King appeals to the readers' value system, and yet we can see how his examples appeal more overtly to the readers' emotions. Often implied by metaphor, King's examples evoke the inhumanity of the treatment of African Americans, during the era of segregation as well as that of slavery. And yet, one might argue, Jefferson was dealing with abuses as well; so what makes King's examples an appeal more to emotions and Jefferson's more to values? Jefferson's subject was the abuser, the man who was violating the rights of others, while King's subject is the victim of such abuse.

 STRATEGY

How to Observe the Effects of Examples

1. Identify examples used to support general statements.
2. Explore how the examples appeal to the reader's values, emotions, and reasoning. In order to help you think about the effects of particular examples, try imagining other ways the writer might have supported a particular point.
3. Generalize about how the selections of examples contributed to and supported the writer's purpose.

APPLICATION

Observing the Effects of Examples

We have begun for you an analysis of the way examples are used in three readings in Casebook 1. Pick one of the three readings, by Jefferson, King, or Will, and extend the list of examples, stating what point each supports. Then speculate about how the writer uses examples to support his main purpose.

Putting the Negro as the subject or object of each example forces readers to consider the abuse as an attack on a real person as well as the race—the "Negro" in the singular but representing all members of the race. Considering the victim rather than the abuser gives greater emotional weight to the example.

George Will chooses examples that act as factual evidence for his claims. He often uses numbers to support his argument. To counter the concerns of critics that presidential candidates who won the popular vote might win the electoral vote, Will provides the following response: in 50 of 53 elections for over 200 years, in 94 percent of elections, the man who won the popular vote also won the election. As we read his argument, we consider whether this example and the ones that follow fairly represent the history of the Electoral College.

Structure and Appeal

In addition to diction, syntax, and examples, the **structure** or organization of the entire piece appeals to readers' values, emotions, and reasoning. To analyze how structure supports a purpose, readers must first be able to see an overall design in the structure, and then be able to connect the writer's choices with his or her purpose.

All three of the pieces we have been looking at have structures that demonstrate a line of argument, and therefore appeal to the reasoning of readers and listeners, but each of the three demonstrates a somewhat different appeal with the particular structure the writer chooses.

Jefferson sets up a structure that makes its line of reasoning very easy to follow. He begins by clearly stating a principle he assumes all readers will share—that when any group of people declare their independence from their monarch, they must explain their reasons openly. He then gives an overview of the parts of his general argument: that humans have innate rights; when such innate rights are violated by their monarch, they have the right to seek independence from that monarch; that their monarch violated their innate rights; and finally that the colonists have the right to declare their independence. In the rest of the Declaration, Jefferson presents evidence that the monarch violated their rights, that they petitioned him to end such violations, and when he refused, they therefore declared their independence. By following a clear line

KEY CONCEPT

Principles of Structure

There are no formulas for structuring most complex writing. The form a writing takes will depend on the content the writer needs to convey. The following principles of structure, however, describe what writers may choose to do in order to support their overall purposes or specific points within an overall design.

- A question followed by an exploration of possible answers, to emphasize the one the writer sees as most acceptable.
- A line of argument: a claim followed by support (evidence and reasoning) to establish, extend, or promote a general principle that the audience holds.
- A line of argument: a claim followed by counterarguments supported by evidence and reasoning to distance oneself from a general principle the audience might hold.
- Comparison to emphasize similarities; contrast to emphasize differences.
- A cause followed by effects to project future consequences.
- An observation or phenomenon followed by causes to establish past reasons for present effects.
- A definition to clarify a difficult, ambiguous, or essential concept.
- A system of classification to sort information into specific sets for clearer understanding.
- A sequence of details to help the reader imagine specific circumstances, real or imaginary.
- A narrative sequence to present a process or a series of events.

of reasoning, this structure demonstrates the ethical dimension of the colonists' action and thus appeals to the readers' values.

Martin Luther King's speech, while also clearly developing a line of reasoning, does not highlight the development quite so overtly. Instead, his argument seems to unfold. He begins by establishing a shared principle, noting that when Lincoln signed the Emancipation Proclamation, it seemed that doing so would end the injustice to those who had lived years in slavery. Then he presents an observation that becomes a counterargument to the first agreement, that one hundred years later, injustice, now in the form of segregation, still exists. He then issues a call to recognize the promise made to African Americans, their determination to demand that the promise be fulfilled, and the urgency of the demand for the good of the country.

The development of this section leads to the "I have a dream" section, which gives a chronological narrative of a hypothetical civil rights movement and by doing so functions as an exploration of the consequences of integration. The final paragraph then ends the chronology by suggesting the aftermath of such a movement in which Lincoln's goal will be met in a true end to injustice.

The speech's line of reasoning shows its emotional contours. Rather than previewing his point, King makes the listener experience it. The gradual unfolding of the argument makes us identify and move through the speech with immediacy. We stand with King in front of Lincoln's statue and look out on the listeners who have not received the promise made them. We hear the voice of urgency in the repeated "I have a dream," and in the imagery of darkness and heat and its contrast in light and cool relief. We lean closer as he repeats the word *together*, feel uplifted with the sound of freedom ringing, then return emotionally to the steps of the Lincoln Memorial to join in the final call for freedom.

Will's structure makes his appeal to reasoning less overt than Jefferson's and the underlying emotional appeal subtler than King's. Will begins by considering a question without explicitly identifying what the question is. He does so by stating the opposition's position he intends to disprove—that the Electoral College is unwise. By pointing out what others are arguing, he makes the reader wonder about the problem, and so his article gradually argues that no problem exists.

The article begins and ends with his refutation of the opponents' arguments. In the central section, he provides a series of reasons the Electoral College works well. He shapes the central section by contrasting the opponent's objections to the Electoral College with his reply. He refutes the critics by taking up each objection, then giving his response and supporting evidence for his position. In his support of what he considers to be the Electoral College's strengths, he develops each point by stating it, then explaining his reasoning and offering a few examples to illustrate his point. He ends with a direct appeal to the reasoning of his readers—if one were to extend the reasoning used by those who oppose the Electoral College, one would have to favor abolishing the Senate as well.

In each of the three readings, then, we see examples of the ways the writer shaped his material to appeal to readers, either through focus, buildup of emotion, or gradual development of argument.

 ## STRATEGY

How to Observe the Effects of Structure

1. Read a text, observing and describing the overall design. What comes first? Second? Third? Tie the overall design to the writer's purpose.

2. List the key points or sections. Using the list in the key concept box "Principles of Structure" (page 137), identify where possible the principle guiding the structure of specific sections or the order of sections. Tie the sequence of sections to the writer's purpose.

APPLICATION

Observing the Effects of Structure

Return to Vice President Gore's speech. Describe the overall design. How does he begin, develop, and end his remarks? Then list the key points or sections. Using the "Principles of Structure" key concept box (page 137), identify the principles guiding specific sections. Connect the structure to Gore's purpose.

Persona and Appeal

Every written text has a **persona.** All writers present their subjects to their readers, but they also present themselves. Each time we write, the specific rhetorical situation will require that we analyze how to best present ourselves to make it likely that our readers will hear us the way we want to be heard.

One observation we make about persona is what **voice** the writer is using. If the writing is presented from a first person perspective, the writer tells his or her own story using the pronouns *I* and *we*. If the writing is from a second person perspective, the writer addresses the reader directly using the pronoun *you*. If presented from a third person perspective, the writer describes what happened, happens, or is happening to others, using the pronouns *he*, *she*, and *they*, or observes objectively without needing to refer to participants at all. Often, as in the case of this book, the voice shifts with the purpose. Are we describing what *we*, as writers or as teachers, do or think or observe? Are we suggesting that *you* try an idea which has worked for others? Are we conveying a concept, or a story about others?

Other observations we make about voice have to do with the formality or informality of the language, the attitude of the writer toward the subject (positive, negative, neutral), the attitude of the writer toward the audience (familiar, confrontational, superior, engaging, apologetic), and the manner of address (serious, humorous, ironic, sarcastic, direct, roundabout). Together, these considerations are called **tone.** When you speak, you express attitudes as well as explicit meaning. Using gestures and inflections (how your voice rises and falls), you can ask the person next to you to "Move over" while also communicating irritation, affection, or bored indifference. When you say, "That film was one of the best I've ever seen," your intonation will tell people if you really mean it or if you mean exactly the opposite. Writers use signals and strategies in writing to convey the same attitudes. When we write, we want to convey our attitudes to our readers without offending or confusing them.

It is helpful to see the persona of a piece of writing as a character or a role adopted by the writer for the purposes of communicating a particular message. The word *persona* first referred to a mask worn by actors in plays in ancient

Greece. As with any other rhetorical strategy, the persona may be used to deceive and manipulate, or reveal and communicate.

Writers communicate persona in many ways, the most obvious of which is the choice of words that convey meaning beyond the dictionary definitions. For example, if a writer describes a person as *extraordinary*, it's a compliment to the person and to the writer, because the writer is presenting a self-image of someone qualified to judge what is extraordinary. If the same person is described as *weird*, the dictionary definition of which often includes the word *extraordinary*, the choice reflects negatively on the person and also conveys a tone of informality. In either case, the persona is designed to appeal to readers either by establishing authority or credibility (ethical appeal), or by moving readers to share a particular feeling (emotional appeal).

The author may create a self-image of an open-minded and informed person, a wry and self-satisfied observer, or an arrogant blowhard. He or she may inspire us to listen, cajole us into participating in a hearty laugh, or engage us into imagining ourselves as co-conspirators in a mystery. But in all cases, we, as readers, will listen to those who seem to respect readers' intelligence and good will more easily than we will listen to those who disrespect us.

Although the subjects of each of the pieces of writing we have been examining in this chapter are related, the persona created by each writer is different.

In the Declaration of Independence, Jefferson begins with a third person perspective, establishing a principle which, he assumes, will define his audience: those who accept the principle. Rather than asking his audience to affiliate with him, with the newly conceptualized United States of America, or with any specific group of vocal protesters against the king's pronouncements, he speaks from the authority of the "Laws of Nature and Nature's God." His attitude toward his audience is one of respect: he recognizes that political allegiance is not easily shifted, so he appeals, instead, to their notions of justice and freedom that originate beyond national affiliation.

 KEY CONCEPT

Persona

The persona of a piece of writing includes:

- **Voice:** the perspective or point of view. In first person, the writer recounts his or her own experience or observations. In second person, the writer appeals directly to the readers. In third person, the writer adopts an objective perspective on the subject.
- **Tone:** the level of formality or informality of the writing, the writer's attitude toward the subject, and the writer's attitude toward the readers.

After the audience is defined, Jefferson shifts immediately to a first person "We," the victims of a list of atrocities, as distinct from the repeated "He," the perpetrator of those atrocities. Although appealing to his listeners as a rational man, Jefferson chooses words that reinforce the unity of the victims and that underscore the horror of the grievances against them. Simultaneously, Jefferson is adopting a persona that is speaking to the world community for the "people" and speaking to the people, inciting them emotionally to respond to the declaration of their own independence.

Martin Luther King's persona is complex and fascinating. He, too, begins with an appeal to shared principles. He calls on the powerful and historically significant words of the Declaration of Independence and the Constitution, recognizing that no one who identifies as an American can refute those principles. So his initial persona is that of the American, spokesperson for American values and ideals. The circle of his audience includes all those who share those beliefs. Then, somewhat curiously, he refers to "the Negro," as if he is inside the circle trying to extend it to include black Americans, while at the same time, as a black man, being outside the circle himself. This unusual split in his persona has the effect of making ambivalent white members of the audience uncomfortable with their situation—an emotional discomfort that may move them to rectify the situation.

 ## STRATEGY

How to Observe the Effects of Persona

The writer's persona is intended to influence how we regard him or her and how we see our own roles as readers. The writer's choices in shaping the persona will influence how the message is heard and comprehended.

1. Note the point of view: first person, second person, or third person. Speculate about how the point of view supports the writer's purpose. If the point of view shifts, speculate about how the changes signal a change in attitude or perspective toward subject or writer.

2. Note language choices that signal a specific attitude or bias toward reader or subject. How do they relate to the writer's purpose?

3. Note language choices that signal characteristics of the writer's stance.

   Is the language more formal or informal?

   Is the writer's attitude more negative or positive?

   Is the perspective balanced, or does the writer rely on understatement or overstatement to make and support key points?

   Is there evidence of irony or sarcasm?

APPLICATION

Observing the Effects of Persona

Once more, review Vice President Gore's speech to observe his conscious attempts to create a persona. Using the points listed in the "How to Observe the Effects of Persona" strategy box, take notes on the language choices that indicate point of view, attitudes and biases, and characteristics of the writer's stance. Then write a paragraph describing, in terms of Gore's question and purpose, how he wants to present himself, how he regards his audience, and how he wants his audience to regard his subject. Make specific references to the speech.

One part of King's persona is constructed as a rescuer of the white community, to emancipate them from their life of crime and destruction. King describes the Negro people as having been given a "bad check" by America. He also warns against the "tranquilizing drug" of gradualism. So having appealed to the politically sacred values of America, his metaphors reflect on those unwilling to move from a state of inertia to a state of action as petty criminals and drug users. He contrasts the "dark and desolate valley of segregation" with the "sunlit path of racial justice," inviting Americans to save themselves by saving black Americans from their oppression.

When he uses "we" to describe African Americans, he speaks with the other part of the persona, referring to "my people" and complimenting the "marvelous new militancy." But he also speaks as a rescuer of the black community, warning that "we must not be guilty of wrongful deeds" and, in effect, holding both communities accountable to the same values. In the most famous part of the speech, when he proclaims his vision, he speaks from the first person, but in that first person he has encircled both the black and white communities. When he says "I have a dream," it is clear that realizing the dream of "life, liberty, and the pursuit of happiness" will necessitate uniting the two parts of his persona, and metaphorically uniting the divided races.

George Will's purpose and persona are less complex because of the nature and context of his writing. Will consciously constructs the persona of an intelligent, reasonable, and erudite commentator. He relies on rational persuasion through the use of statistics and facts. On the other hand, his perspective is not altogether balanced, as is clear in his description of anyone who disagrees with him as a "political hypochondriac" and their ideas as "simple-minded majoritarianism." His voice is somewhat pedantic, meaning that his attitude toward his audience is one of superiority. If you read the essay and agree with him, you accept his expertise and your role as learner. If you read it and disagree with him, you might find his persona disrespectful and self-righteous.

WRITING A RHETORICAL ANALYSIS

We do not intend to suggest that Jefferson's Declaration of Independence is a purely ethical argument, King's a purely emotional one, or Will's a purely logical one. Each includes all three appeals. Jefferson's list of the king's violations of the rights of the colonists, for example, gives good reasons for the colonies to become a sovereign state and is a solid logical argument. King's metaphors express an ethical position he assumes his readers share in addition to appealing to their emotions. Will's characterization of critics of the Electoral College as *hypochondriacs* or *simple-minded* or *abolitionists* evokes an emotional response to extremist positions.

How does the reader decide whether to grant assent to such arguments? Does the reader dismiss an emotional appeal, for example, because it is not merely "logical"? Of course not. But by seeing the way the writer appeals to the reader's value system, emotions, and reasoning, we may judge whether such an appeal is justified. We do not find Jefferson's argument compelling simply because the king of England acted in a particular way, but because we believe his actions abused a value system we revere. We do not applaud King's "Dream" speech because his argument logically supports the civil rights movement, but because our hearts tell us that the treatment of African Americans both violates their basic human dignity and is detrimental to their welfare. The degree to which we agree with George Will depends both on whether we believe he has constructed a logical argument with factual evidence, as well as on whether we consider that evidence to be a valid representation of the history of the Electoral College.

When we engage in this kind of critical reading, we analyze the rhetorical choices the writer has made by identifying the appeals he or she is making. If we write about our observations, the result is a rhetorical analysis. Sometimes we engage in this kind of analysis when we look at the ways advertisers use the classical appeals to tempt us to buy their products. For example, in that commercial for the Oldsmobile automobile which included the line, "It's not your father's Oldsmobile," the advertiser was appealing to the *emotions* of young adults who did not want to identify with an outdated, old-fashioned, stodgy way of being an adult. When the army advertises itself with Uncle Sam pointing at the observer and saying, "The army wants you," the advertiser is appealing to the value system of young patriotic Americans, as well as to their desire to be wanted and needed.

A good exercise to practice reading in this way is to write an extended rhetorical analysis. A rhetorical analysis allows the reader to examine the diction, syntax, examples, structure, and persona to see how they are operating as strategies, yet it does not attempt to account for each and every rhetorical choice the writer has made. Rather, when we write rhetorical analyses, we do so to study the ways in which particular rhetorical choices make particular appeals to the reader. So, for example, you might write a rhetorical analysis showing that Martin Luther King's "I Have a Dream" speech uses syntactic choices to weave together an ethical and emotional appeal.

KEY CONCEPT

Qualities of an Effective Rhetorical Analysis

- It identifies the writer's question at issue and purpose, clearly but without oversimplifying the issues raised.
- It observes strategies of diction, syntax, examples, structure, and persona, tying them to the writer's purpose by describing how they appeal to the writer's logic, emotions, and values.
- It draws a conclusion about the degree to which the strategies effectively support the writer's purpose.

Although our examples for analysis in this chapter have been drawn from casebook readings on citizenship and voting, all writing can be analyzed using the strategies in this chapter. Read the following essay, a descriptive non-fiction narrative very different from public, political speech, for the kinds of rhetorical choices Dillard makes to support her purpose.

ANNIE DILLARD

Stalking Muskrats

1   Learning to stalk muskrats took me several years.

2   I've always known there were muskrats in the creek. Sometimes when I drove late at night my headlights' beam on the water would catch the broad lines of ripples made by a swimming muskrat, a bow wave, converging across the water at the raised dark vee of its head. I would stop the car and get out: nothing. They eat corn and tomatoes from my neighbors' gardens, too, by night, so that my neighbors were always telling me that the creek was full of them. Around here, people call them "mushrats"; Thoreau called them "Musquashes." They are not of course rats at all (let alone squashes). They are more like diminutive beavers, and, like beavers, they exude a scented oil from musk glands under the base of the tail—hence the name. I had read in several respectable sources that muskrats are so wary they are almost impossible to observe. One expert who made a full-time study of larger populations, mainly by examining "sign" and performing autopsies on corpses, said he often went for weeks at a time without seeing a single living muskrat.

3   One hot evening three years ago, I was standing more or less *in* a bush. I was stock-still, looking deep into Tinker Creek from a spot on the bank opposite the house, watching a group of bluegills stare and hang motionless near the bottom of a deep, sunlit pool. I was focused for depth. I had long since lost myself, lost the creek, the day, lost everything but still, amber depth. All at once I

couldn't see. And then I could: a young muskrat had appeared on top of the water, floating on its back. Its forelegs were folded languorously across its chest; the sun shone on its upturned belly. Its youthfulness and rodent grin, coupled with its ridiculous method of locomotion, which consisted of a lazy wag of the tail assisted by an occasional dabble of a webbed hind foot, made it an enchanting picture of decadence, dissipation, and summer sloth. I forgot all about the fish.

4   But in my surprise at having the light come on so suddenly, and at having my consciousness returned to me all at once and bearing an inverted muskrat, I must have moved and betrayed myself. The kit—for I know now it was just a young kit—righted itself so that only its head was visible above water, and swam downstream, away from me. I extricated myself from the bush and foolishly pursued it. It dove sleekly, reemerged, and glided for the opposite bank. I ran along the bankside brush, trying to keep it in sight. It kept casting an alarmed look over its shoulder at me. Once again it dove, under a floating mat of brush lodged in the bank, and disappeared. I never saw it again. (Nor have I ever, despite all the muskrats I have seen, again seen a muskrat floating on its back.) But I did not know muskrats then; I waited panting, and watched the shadowed bank. Now I know that I cannot outwait a muskrat who knows I am there. The most I can do is get "there" quietly, while it is still in its hole, so that it never knows, and wait there until it emerges. But then all I knew was that I wanted to see more muskrats.

5   I began to look for them day and night. Sometimes I would see ripples suddenly start beating from the creek's side, but as I crouched to watch, the ripples would die. Now I know what this means, and have learned to stand perfectly still to make out the muskrat's small, pointed face hidden under overhanging bank vegetation, watching me. That summer I haunted the bridges, I walked up creeks and down, but no muskrats ever appeared. You must just have to be there, I thought. You must have to spend the rest of your life standing in bushes. It was a once-in-a-lifetime thing and you've had your once.

6   Then one night I saw another, and my life changed. After that I knew where they were in numbers, and I knew when to look. It was late dusk. I was driving home from a visit with friends. Just on the off chance I parked quietly by the creek, walked out on the narrow bridge over the shallows, and looked upstream. Someday, I had been telling myself for weeks, someday a muskrat is going to swim right through that channel in the cattails, and I am going to see it. That is precisely what happened. I looked up the channel for a muskrat, and there it came, swimming right toward me. Knock; seek; ask. It seemed to swim with a side-to-side, sculling motion of its vertically flattened tail. It looked bigger than the upside down muskrat, and its face more reddish. In its mouth it clasped a twig of a tulip tree. One thing amazed me: it swam right down the middle of the creek. I thought it would hide in the rush along the edge; instead, it plied the waters as obviously as an aquaplane. I could just look and look.

7   But I was standing on the bridge, not sitting, and it saw me. It changed its course, veered towards the bank, and disappeared behind an indentation in the rushy shoreline. I felt a rush of such pure energy I thought I would not need to breathe for days.

8   The innocence of mine is mostly gone now, although I felt almost the same pure rush last night. I have seen many muskrats since I learned to look for them in that part of the creek. But still I seek them out in the cool of the evening, and still I hold my breath when rising ripples surge from under the creek's bank. The great hurrah about wild animals is that they exist at all, and the greater hurrah is the actual moment of seeing them. Because they have a nice dignity, and prefer to have nothing to do with me, not even as the simple objects of my vision. They show me by their very wariness what a prize it is simply to open my eyes and behold.

Sample Student Writing: Rhetorical Analysis Essay

This essay analyzes the rhetoric of Annie Dillard's essay. As you read it, note where the writer addresses Dillard's use of diction, syntax, examples, persona, and structure.

Annie Dillard's "Stalking Muskrats"

Andrea Fisher

Annie Dillard's description of her search for the wild muskrat asks us to contemplate the question "Why bother to stalk muskrats?" The title itself invites readers to ask why one would stalk (an ominous-sounding verb) a muskrat (an odious-sounding animal). But she persuades us to follow her into the wild because she convinces us that she will reveal something of significance to us, and she does, because the persona she creates, as well as her structure, her language, her syntax, and her examples all appeal to us to look hard for the significance of her experience, as she has to look hard to find muskrats.

The piece begins with an introduction that relies on all three forms of appeal, ethos, logos, and pathos, to persuade us to stalk the answer to her question as she stalks the muskrats. Following the introduction is an extended example, a narrative describing two brief muskrat sightings, that demonstrates how one should search. After her narrative, she concludes with a passage of reflection in which she offers her answer to her question.

She begins by appealing to us through our reason and emotion. Her persona is of a knowledgeable, keen observer, and she appeals to her readers to be the same. The first sentence stands alone, simple in structure, but mysterious in meaning: "Learning to stalk muskrats took me several years." The emotion it appeals to is curiosity: why would someone spend several years stalking muskrats? We reason that no one would spend years learning to do something worthless. We know from the simplicity of that first sentence that it is a task possible to fulfill, and one worth the work. In the second sentence, she says "I've always known there were muskrats in the creek," establishing her authority on the subject. The third sentence appeals to us imaginatively and emotionally through its length and complex structure. The subjects of the clauses gradually narrow our focus from the whole scene including the speaker, to what is visible in the car's headlights, to the bow wave made by a swimming muskrat, to the "dark vee of its head." The syntax focuses our vision so that we are looking specifically where the writer wants us to, at the muskrat.

The fourth sentence is short: "I would stop the car and get out: nothing." It imaginatively joins us with the writer; our disappointment blends with hers in the word "nothing." This word creates in the reader the desire to see *something*, to succeed at the task of seeing the muskrat.

The fifth sentence appeals to us through reason. We are given evidence of and testimony about the muskrat: "They eat corn and tomatoes from my neighbor's gardens, too, by night, so that my neighbors were always telling me that the creek was full of them." The sixth sentence adds the authority of historical reference to that of local knowledge: "Around here, people call them 'mushrats'; Thoreau called them 'Musquashes.'" Then, to establish again her own credibility and expertise, she adds, "They are not, of course, rats at all (let alone squashes). They are more like diminutive beavers, and, like beavers, they exude a scented oil from musk glands under the base of the tail— hence the name." Returning to reason through testimony, and at the same time engaging us emotionally, she adds that she "had read in several respectable sources that muskrats are so wary they are almost impossible to observe." We are made to understand that respectable scholars are engaged in this work; we are also made to understand that the experience is a rare one and thus worth the work involved, so by the close of the paragraph, we have fully identified with her and are ready to hear her story.

The second full paragraph signals a story is beginning with a familiar structure that puts the reader in the setting: "One hot evening three years ago, I was standing more or less *in* a bush." The diction of the next few sentences brings us deeper into her way of seeing. She is "stock-still," "looking deep, "watching," as bluegills "stare and hang motionless." Then she explains the way of seeing as "focused for depth." The syntax of the next sentence uses repetition to focus our own vision deeply, shutting out the day: "I had long since lost myself, lost the creek, the day, lost everything but the still, amber depth." The strategy works so well that when she says, "All at once I couldn't see," neither can we, until the muskrat appears. We are taught to know that in order to see a muskrat, we have to close off everything else and be completely still. Now we identify not with the writer and her search, but with the muskrat itself. And what does the muskrat look like? Like a lazy, happy, human. "It's forelegs are folded languorously across its chest"; it sports a "rodent grin"; its tail moves in a "lazy wag" and its hind foot "dabbles." These words are all chosen carefully to help us see the muskrat in human terms and encourage our connection with it. When at the end of this paragraph Dillard adds "I forgot all about the fish," we have too, illustrating the effectiveness of her language choices.

And then the moment is over. The muskrat is gone. In the next two paragraphs, the search continues, without success. "But," Dillard adds, "I did not know muskrats then," cuing the reader that she will, with continued effort, come to know them. Describing her developing knowledge, she tells us she has "learned to stand perfectly still." To keep us with her, there is an abrupt shift in the pronouns at the end of this section from first person "I's" to second person "you's." "You must have to spend the rest of your life standing in bushes. It was a once-in-a-lifetime thing and you've had your once." Expressing that frustration and regret as her own experience would have excluded us. Shifting to "you" allows us to share the frustration, and thus the motivation to finally succeed.

The conclusion of the narrative begins with the sentence "Then one night I saw another, and my life changed." Her life has changed, and our lives, implicitly, are about to change. She sees another, and through her vivid descriptive words, so do we. Her great discovery in seeing another is that it did not hide. It swam "right down the middle of the creek," and gave her a "rush of pure energy," an experience that this essay is designed to motivate us to want to repeat.

The significance of her discovery is the subject of her concluding paragraph. The answer to the question "Why stalk muskrats?" is answered directly: "Because they have a nice dignity, and prefer nothing to do with me, not even as the simple objects of my vision." The argument she has constructed through careful rhetorical choices, and that she now expresses directly, is that it is important for us to learn to observe that which exists in the world without reference to humans, without dependence on us, to remind us that we are not the center of all existence. To help us remember that lesson about our humanity, Dillard reminds us "what a prize it is simply to open [our] eyes and behold."

THE QUESTION OF STYLE

Some student writers unaccustomed to receiving responses from other readers often chafe at questions about their writing. Sometimes we hear "You just don't like my style." These students think of rhetorical style in the same way they think about style in fashion. We wear clothes to present ourselves to the world in a way that reinforces who we are and how we want others to relate to us. As you learned when reading and writing about the concept of persona, writers also write to project a certain stance and attitudes toward their subject and their readers. But in rhetoric, style is the synthesis of *all* of the elements—diction, syntax, examples, structure, *and* persona—in response to a situation.

We may recognize a characteristic style on the part of our favorite writers, because even though the subjects of their works may change, their way of seeing the world and their way of addressing an audience become stable as they work to express their way of seeing through various situations. In all cases, though, style includes all of a writer's language choices made to support a particular purpose, not just those that relate to a writer's persona.

In the study of rhetoric and literature, scholars have assigned names to particular styles of expression that characterize whole periods of history. Each period, for example the Renaissance or the Victorian, is associated with particular language conventions, though within each period there are as many variants of the style as there are writers. The appearance of a characteristic style results partly from the fact that, in each artistic era, writers test the powers and limits of their rhetorical choices and extend those choices to include new strategies. As they do so, they learn from each other. Another reason for the appearance of stylistic conventions in historical periods is because each era is characterized by cultural, political, and social forces that become a part of the context for the writing. So, even though we can talk about the style of a period or the style of a particular writer, style is constructed through rhetorical strategies that respond to specific situations. If strategies don't match situations, the style is ineffective. When the strategies do match the situations, the writing is successful.

Therefore, successful writers are critical readers and critical writers. They develop an awareness of rhetorical strategy and situation, and they understand that through the process of writing and revision, they can increase the probability of successfully achieving their rhetorical purposes.

WRITING INVITATIONS

1. Using your notes from the application boxes "Observing the Effects of Diction," "Observing the Effects of Syntax," "Observing the Effects of Structure," and "Observing the Effects of Persona," develop a rhetorical analysis of Vice President Al Gore's speech. Make sure your analysis identifies the writer's question and purpose; observes strategies of diction, syntax, example, structure, and persona, tying them to the writer's purpose by describing how they appeal to the readers' logic, emotions, and values; and draws a conclusion about to what extent the writer's strategies effectively support his purpose.

2. On the editorial page of your local newspaper, find at least two letters to the editor that address the same issue. Identify the appeals the writers are using and write a short essay in which you evaluate the effectiveness of the writer's appeals.

3. On the editorial page of your local newspaper, read one of the editorial columns. Identify the strategies the writer is using to convince readers to accept the writer's position. Write a short rhetorical analysis of the column.

4. Political commentators on television spent the hours before Vice President Gore's concession speech reminding viewers of how significant this speech would be, what an opportunity Gore had to create a positive impression, and not only to say something important and historic but to say it well. The discussion continued in the days following the speech. After looking at the following editorial from *New York Times* columnist Thomas L. Friedman, write a

brief essay in which you explain whether you agree or disagree with Friedman's evaluation of Gore's purpose.

Thomas L. Friedman
Medal of Honor

December 15, 2000

When Al Gore was in Vietnam he never saw much combat. Throughout his presidential campaign, though, he insisted he wanted to "fight" for every American. Well, Wednesday night, in his concession speech, Mr. Gore took a bullet for the country.

The shot was fired at the heart of the nation by the five conservative justices of the U.S. Supreme Court, with their politically inspired ruling that installed George W. Bush as president. The five justices essentially said that it was more important that Florida meet its self-imposed deadline of Dec. 12 for choosing a slate of electors than for the Florida Supreme Court to try to come up with a fair and uniform way to ensure that every possible vote in Florida was counted and still meet the real federal deadline, for the nationwide Electoral College vote on Dec. 18. The five conservative justices essentially ruled that the sanctity of dates, even meaningless ones, mattered more than the sanctity of votes, even meaningful ones. The Rehnquist court now has its legacy: "In calendars we trust."

You don't need an inside source to realize that the five conservative justices were acting as the last in a team of Republican Party elders who helped drag Governor Bush across the finish line. You just needed to read the withering dissents of Justices Breyer, Ginsburg, Souter and Stevens, who told the country exactly what their five colleagues were up to acting without legal principle or logic and thereby inflicting a wound, said Justice Breyer, "that may harm not just the court, but the nation." Or, as the Harvard moral philosopher Michael Sandel put it: "Not only did the court fail to produce any compelling argument of principle to justify its ruling. But, on top of that, the conservative majority contradicted its long-held insistence on protecting states' rights against federal interference. That's why this ruling looks more like partisanship than principle. And that's why many will conclude that the five conservative justices voted twice for president once in November and once in December."

Which brings us back to Mr. Gore and his concession speech. It was the equivalent of taking a bullet for the country, because the rule of law is most reinforced when even though it may have been imposed wrongly or with bias the recipient of the judgment accepts it, and the system behind it, as final and legitimate. Only in that way, only when we reaffirm our fidelity to the legal system even though it rules against us, can the system endure, improve and learn from its mistakes. And that was exactly what Mr. Gore understood, bowing out with grace because, as he put it, "This is America, and we put country before party."

If Chinese or Russian spies are looking for the most valuable secret they can steal in Washington, here's a free tip: Steal Al Gore's speech. For in a few brief pages it contains the real secret to America's sauce. That secret is not Wall Street and it's not Silicon Valley, it's not the Air Force and it's not the Navy, it's not the free press and it's not the free market, it is the enduring rule of law and institutions that underlie them all, and that allows each to flourish no matter who is in power.

One can only hope that Mr. Bush also understands that the ultimate strength of America and the impact it has on the world does not come from all the military systems he plans to expand (though they too are important), or from Intel's latest microchip. It comes from this remarkable system of laws and institutions we have inherited, a system, they say, that was designed by geniuses so it could be run by idiots.

Mr. Bush will soon discover that preserving this system is critical not only for America, it is critical for the world. America today is the Michael Jordan of geopolitics. Many envy the institutions and economy that ensure our dominance; others deeply resent us for the same. But all are watching our example and all understand, at some level, that the stability of the world today rests on the ability of our system and economy to endure.

Al Gore reinforced that system by his graceful concession; Mr. Bush will have to reinforce it by his presidency. Now that the campaign is over, and the system has determined the winner, no one should root for his failure. Because, as Al Gore would say, "This is America," and it's the only one we've got.

DEVELOPING A WRITING PROJECT

1. Having identified and selected several pieces of writing on the same issue for an extended research project, read each piece to identify its question, purpose, and rhetorical context.

2. Select your most important and relevant sources, and analyze the ways in which the writers' choices support or, in some cases, undermine their messages. Be sure to tie strategies to specific forms of appeal.

3. Reflect on and record the results of your critical reading. How do your observations affect the ways you may or may not use particular sources in your research project?

CHAPTER 6

Researching
a Question

We are inundated with information, most of it packaged to suit someone else's commercial or political self-interest. More than ever, society needs people with critical minds, people who can look at research, ask their own questions, and find their own answers. Only when you have experienced the uncertain and often messy process of doing your own research can you intelligently evaluate the research of others.

Wayne C. Booth, Gregory G. Colomb, and Joseph M. Williams

RESEARCH AND THE RHETORICAL SITUATION

We do research to find out more about an issue we care about. A woman who wants to make the lasagna her grandmother made might consult a number of cookbooks or an Italian cooking Web page. She may need to consult several different sources before finding a recipe that looks like it might be close to the one she remembers. A high school senior who is trying to decide where to go to college might look in published guides to colleges or might write schools that interest him and ask for catalogues or might look at college Web pages to see what kinds of programs they offer. A consumer who is thinking about buying a car and wondering about the best prices, values, and safety records of various models might read *Car and Driver* magazine and *Consumer Reports*.

Each of these examples shows someone conducting research. Whether we are looking up recipes, studying college catalogues, or browsing old *Car and Driver* magazines, we begin with a question: "How can I make my grandmother's lasagna?" "Which college looks best for me?" "Should I buy the Honda, Ford, or Chevrolet?" This may not seem like what we do when we write a research paper for a class, but the connection between this kind of careful investigation and academic research can be seen in the response we often make when we hear about someone who has made an informed decision: we say "She really did her homework before she made her decision."

KEY CONCEPT

Research

- **Research** is an exploration into a subject we need to know more about.
- Our sources of information may be found in the library, on the Internet, or in our real-world observations, but in all cases, when we research, we are interacting with—conversing with—others regarding a question we share.

As a writer, your job is to help your readers see your subject the way you do. One of the questions you must answer, then, is "Why should my readers listen to me?" Unless you are already a recognized expert in the subject, you will need to establish your credibility as a reliable observer by (1) carefully investigating as many perspectives on the issue as possible by listening to others who have addressed your subject, and (2) presenting your exploration in a balanced, reasonable way.

Research, then, may be a necessary part of your writing process, both to make sure that you know what you are talking about, and to help establish your stance and believability as a writer. In terms of the rhetorical triangle, you will be strengthening your knowledge of the *subject* and your stance as a *writer* in order to help your *reader* see your subject the way you do.

Researching is not an activity limited to the classroom, nor is it just an exercise professors assign so that students might demonstrate their library skills. Your research may take you to the library, the Internet, the laboratory or clinic, or what we call the "field"—sites of research in real-world settings. Research is something we do whenever we have a problem that requires us to know more. It is what we do when we need to have more information about a question that concerns us, when we need to make informed decisions, when we need to make a case for a proposal. Our research process depends on our analysis of the rhetorical situation. In other words, we need to know what is at issue, why, for whom, and to what audience we will address the findings of our research. In the rest of this chapter we will be looking at this process. Before doing so, though, let's look at the relationship between this public research process and the kinds of research opportunities you may have in your college classes.

Research and the College Curriculum

Research is a central part of the college curriculum. You may not have thought of your academic classes as investigations of questions, but every class you take will address central questions. Introductory classes generally address "what" and "how" questions. What is the field of anthropology or art history or biology or chemistry? How do anthropologists or art historians or biologists or chemists look at their subject matter?

In addition to addressing these basic, introductory questions, each discipline is built on certain foundational questions at issue, such as determining the best explanation for a particular phenomenon. Scholars disagree about these questions, and thus each discipline is characterized by ongoing conversations in which experts discuss and debate various answers. When they write their answers to such questions, they enter conversations with other scholars who are interested in the issues but have different answers to the questions.

Among the many issues professors discuss, some are as broad as the following: English professors may debate which classes ought to be required of all students; historians may disagree about whether students need a course in western civilization; philosophers may debate the merits of a required logic class. Others are narrower: an English professor may wonder why Chaucer used so much legal language in his works, or a sociologist may consider the effects of divorce on the social interaction of children, or a biologist may wonder how pollution in a particular river is affecting the fish population.

 # KEY CONCEPT

Academic Disciplines as Research Communities

- Each college **class** you take will focus on general and specific questions about an area of study, or discipline, such as history, biology, or business. The class, through shared exploration and inquiry, is a specific research community.
- Each **discipline** is characterized by shared questions at issue that provide focuses for the conversations of that discipline. The discipline, through shared exploration and inquiry, functions as an ongoing research community. When you enter a discipline as a major or a minor, you join that conversation. It is your responsibility, then, to find out what other participants have said and are saying, so that you can contribute productively and successfully in the conversation.

 # STRATEGY

Participating in Classroom Research Communities

1. In each class that you take, listen for and keep a list of the general and the specific questions at issue that characterize a field of study.
2. Try to identify questions that engage you, that motivate you to investigate further. (If you have not yet selected a major field of study, thinking about the key questions addressed in the classes you take can help you consider your strongest interests.)

When you join a department as a major or a minor, you have entered a community where people discuss their fundamental differences on questions at issue, whether in the classroom or among experts in specific disciplines. You are now a part of that conversation. This can be an exciting adventure because

■ APPLICATION

Identifying Questions in Academic Courses

Read the following course descriptions and write at least one question the course will be answering:

ORGANIC CHEMISTRY:	This is an introductory level laboratory course that teaches the basic techniques used in organic chemistry as well as the theories behind them.
POLITICAL SCIENCE:	Students will leave this course with a broad understanding of government and politics in the United States. More specifically, students who complete this course will be able to describe theories and concepts of democratic government, the foundations of the United States political system, the protection and extension of civil liberties and civil rights, and the linkages between people and government and the policy making process.
ENGLISH GRAMMAR:	A study of the system of grammatical conventions shared by American speakers and writers of the English language and a consideration of the current concern for correctness in speech and writing.
HISTORY OF RHETORIC:	This course is a study of the history and theory of rhetoric from ancient Greece to the 20th century. A chronological survey, the class will begin by examining the earliest attempts to systematize rhetoric, and then will explore the effects of cultural, political, and intellectual changes in the assumptions underlying competing systems of rhetoric.
CHAUCER'S *CANTERBURY TALES*:	A close study of Chaucer's *Canterbury Tales* and the historical and philosophical context within which Chaucer wrote. In addition to reading the tales, we will be discussing major critical studies of Chaucer's work and some medieval documents that provide background available to Chaucer and his first audience.

at the heart of academic inquiry is the belief that our knowledge grows when we are willing to question and test our assumptions and approaches in discussions with other people who share our interests.

The tradition of education as an ongoing conversation is as old as education itself. From Plato's dialogues to modern-day scientific debates about the most effective way to cure diseases, scholarship has developed, changed, and grown because experts disagreed and were willing to discuss their differences. As we study and attempt to answer questions in our disciplines or in our classrooms or in public forums, we will consider how our answers differ from those of others who have studied the same questions. And those are the people we address when we explain our positions.

IDENTIFYING RESEARCH QUESTIONS

How do you identify the questions you will study in your classes? Sometimes your instructor will assign the questions, but other times you will need to identify the question for yourself. Before you can begin your own research projects, you need to recognize how what you do will be part of a larger conversation. Whether you are doing research about an issue in your community or for a class, you need to know your question and what others have thought and said about it. This means you need to see how the conversations you have—either through reading or direct interaction with others—raise, address, and explore questions.

Reading for Research Questions

One of our students once said, "I read for answers, but all I find are questions. I'm just not getting it." What this student didn't realize was that she was beginning in the exact place we wanted her to begin. When you read, you are engaging in a kind of conversation with the writer. While you may not be talking back directly, you are noticing the questions writers or speakers raise, considering the arguments and evidence they give you, and silently agreeing or disagreeing or thinking about your own questions about what they are saying. Reading to see those questions will help you follow the writer's argument and also see how such questions might be starting places for your own inquiry process.

Seeing the question addressed by a writer is an important starting point for understanding the writer's argument, but we need to go further to see the writer's position and how that position shows the writer addressing a reader. We need to read in a way that makes us more actively engaged in the conversation with the writer. To improve your listening and responding to the ideas raised, you can read with a pen or pencil in hand and make notes in the margin. Whenever you notice a question the writer addresses, make a note saying "significant question" or "important question." Sometimes you may notice that the writer is taking a position that seems different from what others have said. The author might tell you this directly, or indicate that a difference of opinion exists by adding a footnote that summarizes what others have said about the issue. When you notice such differences, make a marginal note that you have identified a controversial point. Or you may simply have questions of your own about something the writer has said. Write your questions in the margin. All of these questions are ones that you might pursue through your own research.

The following opening paragraph is from an essay included in Casebook 2: English Only. It is by S. I. Hayakawa, who was a U.S. senator from 1977 to 1983. Before becoming a senator he was a professor of semantics. When he was a senator, he sponsored an amendment to make English the official language of the United States. He also founded an organization supporting such legislation.

The Case for Official English

S. I. Hayakawa

What is it that has made a society out of the hodgepodge of nationalities, races, and colors represented in the immigrant hordes that people our nation? It is language, of course, that has made communication among all these elements possible. It is with a common language that we have dissolved distrust and fear. It is with language that we have drawn up the understandings and agreements and social contracts that make a society possible.

> Identifies his central question— what makes a society? More specifically, what makes the United States a society? Are we one society? Is that our goal?
>
> Is this correct? Is shared language what forms society? Are there other answers?
>
> How do we know this? Is there evidence to show this?
>
> My question: Having to translate documents is a problem, but would other experts agree that we must have a single language to "make a society possible"?

■ APPLICATION

Reading for Research Questions

After reading S. I. Hayakawa's paragraph about the English Only issue and the reader's comments, choose the opening paragraph from a different essay in Casebook 2. Make your own comments in the margin or in your reader's notebook. Identify the questions the writer addresses or the questions you have about the material.

STRATEGY

How to Read for Research Questions

Read critically, with pen or pencil in hand, noting questions in the margins or in your reading notebook.

1. Identify the key questions the writer raises.
2. Identify questions the writing raises for you. How does the writer's position differ from yours or from the positions of other writers.

Both kinds of questions are beginning points for your own research.

After reading what someone else has to say about a question, a reader might want to enter the conversation. For example, you might decide, after reading "The Case for Official English," that Hayakawa has or has not given you sufficient reasons for accepting his argument that English should be the official language of the United States.

In addition to addressing the same question another writer has discussed, you may find that you want to explore the issue but from a different perspective. As you read an essay, you may wonder whether there are other related questions that might lead to different answers or different perspectives. For example, after reading Hayakawa's essay, you might decide that your question is not whether a law should be passed making English the official language of the country, but rather how American attitudes toward language differ from attitudes toward language in places where many languages are spoken. You may want to investigate whether England has an English Only debate going on, or France a French Only, or Germany a German Only.

Discovering Questions Through Discourse

Another way to identify questions you might wish to explore is by discussing readings and the issues they raise with other people who care about the same questions and share a way of discussing their questions. Such a group is called a discourse community, another name for a rhetorical community. Discourse is another word for conversation, and so a discourse community is a group of people participating in an ongoing conversation about shared issues. They are interested in the same questions and share a way of talking about those interests. Although Hayakawa and other writers represented in Casebook 2 disagree about multilingualism, they are members of a discourse community. They all care about issues of language politics. They speak the same language and use similar approaches to explore the questions they share.

STRATEGY

How to Explore Questions with Discourse Communities

As you discuss issues in discourse communities, you might use the following questions to help you decide what is at issue for the group.

1. What problems do we share?
2. Why do we find these problems significant?
3. What do we know about the problem or question?
4. Who else has a stake in answering the question?
5. What positions might these stakeholders have?
6. Where might the stakeholders agree?
7. How might the stakeholders disagree?
8. What reasons would the stakeholders give for their positions?
9. How will we approach solving the problems we share?
10. What language conventions do we share?

 ## APPLICATION

Exploring Questions with Discourse Communities

With your writing group, focus on issues that face you as college students. Using the questions listed in the previous strategy, try to identify at least three questions you share that might be investigated by your group. List possible answers to each question and discuss them in terms of their strengths and weaknesses. Then develop a strategy for investigating the issue further through research. What information will be needed? Where might you get the information you need?

Discourse communities may be organized around personal issues with friends or family, community issues—on campus, in a dorm, off campus, in a neighborhood—or academic issues—in classrooms, at academic meetings and conferences, and in book groups or the pages of academic journals.

CONDUCTING RESEARCH

We have been arguing that one of the most difficult parts of the inquiry process is deciding what questions are worthy of an extended study. But research papers should not be mere exercises. Good research begins with a question worthy of the effort and time that will be spent on the process. One test of a worthy question is whether others share it. After we identify a question, we should investigate whether we agree or disagree with other people who care about the issue and why we do so.

Preliminary research, or the initial stage of research, is very open ended, but you have two questions to answer. (1) Is my question viable? Is the question still open, or is there an available and uncontested answer already established? (2) Are there resources available that will help me develop an answer to my question in the time available?

You might want to test your question by discussing the issue with others who are interested or knowledgeable about the subject. You will also need to read what others have said about the issue. A good place to begin is with the books or essays you are reading in your class. These books will include bibliographies of the works the author consulted. Bibliographies are rich resources for your own study. You can use them to make a list of the works that might help you learn more about your question.

Go to your college library; find the sections of books and periodicals related to your question and browse the shelves for key terms and related issues. In this early stage, you do not need to read for information, but merely to find what resources are available and where else you might look. Having identified key terms and related issues, you can do Internet searches for available resources online and in your library.

Primary research involves looking at what we might call raw material rather than at someone's interpretation of that information. The kinds of material you are examining will depend on the question you are addressing. Doing primary research may include a close analysis of the books and essays you read in your class, but it may also involve what we call field work, or conducting your own polls or interviews, and reading original documents that pertain to your question. Or it may involve laboratory or clinical observations of experimental procedures. You might visit sites that would provide information about your question. You might go to law libraries and read court cases or to government libraries to read documents or to libraries that have collections of other kinds of original documents. Each academic discipline develops its own accepted methodologies for primary research, and you will have opportunities to practice them in the context of your college courses.

Secondary research relies on the scholarship of others, on scholars' interpretations of the primary material or data. Whatever discipline you are studying, it is helpful to know some basic strategies for investigating secondary source material available to all of us through our libraries and the Internet. In these materials we witness the ongoing conversations of academic and discourse communities on questions they share.

It is not possible for us to know which of the hundreds of helpful print and digital resources your library may subscribe to, but all academic libraries make lists of resources available to student researchers. Our purposes here are simply (1) to encourage you to recognize your responsibility as a part of an academic community to know what others are saying on a subject you are investigating, and (2) to encourage you to explore the resources your college has made available to you.

Identifying Library Sources

If you understand how to use a library's resources, investigating a question that interests you is like solving a puzzle. You find one piece that leads you to another; and after you have all the pieces you need, you put them together in a shape that makes sense.

One person you should get to know is the reference librarian at your college library. Reference librarians know their libraries well and can help you learn to use the available search tools. They can also help you design a research plan.

The materials available to you may be in your library or located elsewhere. Get to know your library catalogue, which is probably online. It will allow you to find all material owned by your library, including books, magazines, journals, documents, media productions, and other catalogued materials. Your library will also have a means for you to investigate resources not owned by your library. Through interlibrary loan, you may order books and articles from other libraries. Depending on the area in which you live and how far away the lending library is, interlibrary loan can take anywhere from two days to two weeks. In addition to providing interlibrary loan, your college library may be part of a statewide system that links all college and university libraries and can have materials delivered within two days. For example, at Central Washington University, the library catalog is called Cattrax and is available online. The Northwest interlibrary loan system is called the Orbis system, and includes the libraries of all the state universities in Washington and Oregon. The catalogs of

 KEY CONCEPT

The Purposes of Research
Reading the writing of experienced and knowledgeable scholars can help us:

- **Explore** the range of possibilities and variety of questions asked by expert readers.
- **Consider** ways critical dialogues help us find interesting and complicated answers to our questions.
- **Discover** new questions that emerge as we observe the conversations among scholars.
- **Develop** ways of integrating scholarship into our own essays.

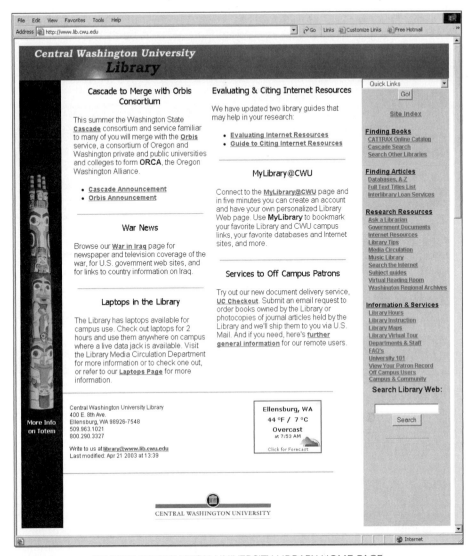

FIGURE 6.1   CENTRAL WASHINGTON UNIVERSITY LIBRARY HOME PAGE

other regional, national, and international libraries are accessible through the same Web page. The Internet has transformed our ability to access information efficiently and effectively, and reference librarians can help us utilize the new tools in the most productive ways.

Search tools other than catalogs are equally and sometimes more valuable. Your reference librarian can direct you to bibliographies, or lists of writings relating to a particular subject, author, or period. Bibliographies may be on the

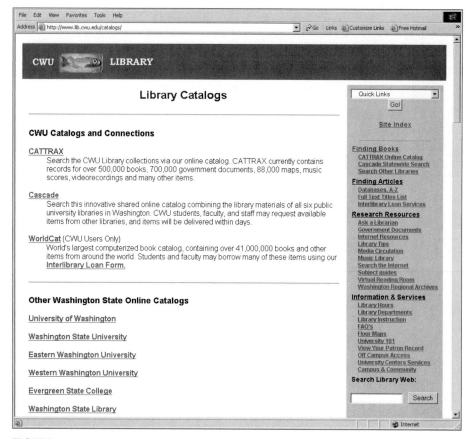

FIGURE 6.2   CENTRAL WASHINGTON UNIVERSITY ONLINE CATALOG

shelf as a book or computerized as a database. In whatever form, these bibliographic resources will help you find the materials you need. Examples of major
reference works include the *Art Index* for art history, *Historical Abstracts* for history, *Anthropological Index Online* for anthropology, the *Social Sciences Index*
for politics, sociology, and other social sciences, and the *Humanities Index* and
MLA International Bibliography for English.

Identifying Internet Sources

The Internet has greatly expanded research possibilities, but it has also complicated the research process. Knowing how to use subject or key word searches
can help you do a kind of computer "shelf browsing." You may either use search
engines or electronic databases for these preliminary searches. New search
engines seem to turn up all the time. Two fairly well known ones are Altavista

STRATEGY

Know Your Library

Every college library is different, but each will include many of the following areas.

CIRCULATION:	Where you check out and return books.
CATALOG:	Information about the library's holdings is usually accessible through a bank of computers near the library entrances. Most libraries also still house rows of card boxes that specify key information about sources organized by subject, author, or title.
REFERENCE:	Where you find general resources such as encyclopedias, dictionaries, atlases, indexes, and bibliographies. These materials are usually non-circulating. Reference librarians will help you with most research questions.
RESERVE:	Where college faculty and staff put materials they want to make available to students on a temporary basis.
THE STACKS:	Areas of bookcases that house the collections, organized by the Library of Congress circulation system, which is usually posted in several locations.
PERIODICALS:	Where you will find magazines, journals, and newspapers.
GOVERNMENT DOCUMENTS:	These are often shelved separately from the general collection because of their complexity. Specially trained reference librarians can help you access and use these materials.
OTHER AREAS:	Additional materials are available through interlibrary loan (books and articles from other libraries) and on microfilm; non-print media such as films, CDs, and videos are available in Media Centers; rare books, new books, and books in braille and on tape are often housed in separate collections; study support is often available through carrels, group study rooms, photocopy services, and computer labs.

and Google. Electronic databases are resources you will find on your college library's home page. Some, like EBSCOHost, are subscription databases that cover a wide range of academic subjects and published materials. Others focus on specific disciplines.

APPLICATION

Library Orientation

In teams or independently, do one or both of the following activities to orient yourself to your library's collections and services.

1. Draw a map of your library's floor plan, identifying the key areas listed in the "Know Your Library"strategy box.

2. Each area of a library has particular policies related to its use and function. Explore each area, identifying and listing policies relevant to the services.

Note: If your library's Web site is as comprehensive as the one for Central Washington University shown in Figure 6.1, both of these steps will have already been done for you. Take the time to explore, both virtually and in person, the various and useful resources provided for you by your library professionals.

General Search Engines Through the Internet

Alta Vista

Excite

Google

GoTo

Look Smart

Netscape Search

Electronic Databases Accessed Through Most College Library Systems.

Your reference librarian can help you identify other electronic resources for your particular search, but these will give you a place to begin.

Periodical Abstracts: This database includes articles found in general and academic journals after 1986. This is where you would find articles about current affairs in business, economics, literature, religion, psychology, gender, and cultural issues. It includes some full-text articles.

Expanded Academic ASAP: This database lists general and scholarly articles in the humanities, social sciences, and general sciences. It also includes many full-text articles.

EBSCOHost: This subscription database covers a wide range of academic subjects. Features full text for selected journals, abstracts and indexing for over 3,100 scholarly journals, and coverage of the *Wall Street Journal, New York Times,* and *Christian Science Monitor.*

Disciplinary Databases

Art Index: For art and art history

General BusinessFile: For business and economics

EconLIT: For business and economics

ERIC: For education

Historical Abstracts: For history

RILM: For music

Academic Universe from Lexis/Nexis: For newspapers in America and other countries

Worldwide Political Science Abstracts: For political science

PsycINFO: For psychology

Sociology Abstracts: For sociology

To use search engines and databases, you will need to understand a very simple concept with a complicated name: Boolean logic. The concept is this: you begin your search with key words that relate to your question. When you enter these terms on the search line of the search engine, the engine searches a database and responds with a list of all entries that include your key term. Let's say you become interested in the "English Only" question after reading the essays in Casebook 2. You begin your search by identifying key words. Because "English Only" is a phrase, you will need to put quotation marks around it so that the search engine recognizes it as only one key term. A search using "English Only" as your search term will result in over 200,000 sources. This would not help you very much in finding possible sources. You realize that you need to narrow the scope of your search.

Boolean logic allows you to combine key words, concepts, and terms to broaden, narrow, or limit the scope of your search. The way to do so is by combining keywords with the conjunctions *or*, *and*, and *not*. *Or* allows you to broaden a search; *and* allows you to narrow your search, and *not* allows you limit your search.

If you enter two or more words joined by *or*, the search engine will give you all entries for each word. If you link two or more words with *and*, the search engine will find only records that include *all* the words you have listed in their title. Using the Excite search engine, for example, you will find over 100,000 Web sites if you search with "English Only" *or* "Bilingualism," and under 2,000 sites if you search with "English Only" *and* "Bilingualism."

If you wish to narrow your search by excluding elements you do not wish to see, you may link two terms with *not*. Doing so allows you to find all records that include the first term but not the second. If you decided that you wanted to study bilingualism but were not interested in the English Only debate, you could exclude all references to "English Only" by joining the two terms with *not*. Searching with "Bilingualism" *not* "English Only" would give you about 80 Web sites.

KEY CONCEPT

Conducting Research

Good researchers will know how to access information from the following sources:

- Reference librarians.
- Knowledgeable people: Academic instructors or non-academic professionals.
- Reference works, including encyclopedias, almanacs, indexes, yearbooks, handbooks, and directories for general topic information.
- Browsing the stacks to get leads, a general sense of alternate perspectives, available resources, and key names in the conversation.
- Indexes to periodicals (journals and magazines) in print.
- Library card catalog or online catalog: key term and subject searches.
- Online catalogs of other collections.
- Internet searches, using search engines and Boolean logic, including truncation, when helpful, for focusing and limiting inquiry.
- Electronic indexes and databases available through your library and online.
- Abstracts and bibliographies for information about specific sources.
- Government documents through your library and the Internet.
- Interlibrary loan, for resources held at regional libraries accessible through your own.
- Non-print media sources, including videotapes, CDs, DVDs, audiotapes, etc.
- Field materials, including interviews, surveys, questionnaires, observation reports, lecture notes, and other non-library materials.

Some search engines allow you to use what is called truncation. Truncation allows you to search for all forms of a word. For example, you could search using the term *bilingual* and receive information on all sites using *bilingual* or *bilingualism* in the title.

Before trying to use Boolean logic with search engines, check to see what search methods are in operation on the engine you are using. You will find this information by clicking on the search tips link on the search page or help icon.

Let's look at one student's search. This student was interested in the English Only debate in the Los Angeles area, so he began his search by entering "English Only" and "Los Angeles" on the search line of Google. This resulted in over 700,000 entries. Realizing that he could never look at all those entries, he decided to search with the term "bilingualism," which resulted in over 50,000 sources. Still too many, he thought. He decided to narrow the search by combining two terms. He entered "bilingualism" and "Los Angeles": 4,000 entries. Better, but still unwieldy. After thinking about what question he was exploring, he decided that he was concerned with bilingualism in the schools of Los Ange-les. So he added education as a fourth term. Now he had about 843 entries.

From this preliminary search, he discovered that the issue he was studying was fairly broad and quite controversial. This told him that he needed to con-sider just one aspect of the question. As he browsed the titles of some of these entries, he discovered that many seemed to address the issue of civil liberties. It seemed that his question about whether bilingual education ought to be offered had a great deal to do with the civil liberties of those involved. Adding "civil lib-erties" to his search gave him only about 40 entries. Not only did he have a man-ageable number of entries to examine, but his search led him to a question that addressed his original concerns: To what extent is bilingual education a civil lib-erty and why might the English Only advocates disagree that it is?

EVALUATING SOURCES

Finding information is just the first step in responsible research. You must also know how to evaluate the reliability and usefulness of the information you find. The critical questions you can ask to judge the appropriateness of books, peri-odical articles, multimedia titles, or Web pages are similar; however, different tools are available for judging print and Web sources.

Evaluating Print Sources

Even preliminary research will require that you consider the validity of the information you read. Your instructors will be the best resources for finding the appropriate publishers and journals in their fields of study, but it will help you to know that books published by university presses and journals produced by universities include scholarship that has been judged by peers in the field and, as a result, will be considered authoritative.

As you become more proficient in research, you will take more responsi-bility for judging the quality of the work you read. You will need to find out who the author is, whether he or she is an authority on the subject, where the piece was published, and when. Whether you should use a book or article that is recent or older depends a great deal on the subject you are studying. In any case, you should include some of the most current research on the question, if only to read what experts are currently saying about the issue.

You may also need to determine whether the material is accurate. In part, finding out whether the author is an authority on the subject helps you deter-mine accuracy, but you will also need to compare the answers provided by one author with those of others. As you do, ask yourself whether the author has given you good reasons for believing the position presented and good evidence for those reasons. If the author's position differs greatly from that of others, try to account for the differences. For example, what assumptions does the writer seem to have about the question? How do the writer's prior assumptions affect his or her position?

In other words, to judge a book or article, you need to read carefully, recognize the argument the author presents, and judge the reasons he or she gives for that argument. You will also need to find out about the book publishing company or editorial position of the magazine or journal. If the book is not published by a university press, you may need to find out whether the publisher is recognized as having some authority in the field of study. One way to do so is to use the Internet. You may be able to find the publishing company's home page and read a description of the company and its philosophy, mission statement, or editorial policies. You can also read book reviews that evaluate the argument of the book. To find out about a magazine or journal, read the description given on the inside cover. Or a guide to periodicals such as Ulrichsweb.com will give descriptions that indicate the editorial perspective of the articles.

 ## STRATEGY

How to Evaluate Print Sources

Use the guidelines below to evaluate print materials relevant to your research subject.

1. **Is it credible?** Who is the author, and what authority does he or she bring to the subject? What credentials, training, or affiliations suggest credible expertise? Who is the publisher? Reference librarians can help you identify the important publishers of reputable books and periodicals relevant to your research. Academic and trade presses often specialize in particular areas.

2. **Is it relevant to your question?** For a book, check the preface, the table of contents and other introductory materials to see whether it is too general or too specific for your needs. If articles are preceded by abstracts or summaries, read them to determine the article's focus and coverage. For articles without abstracts, skim first and last lines of paragraphs to get an overview of the sequence of ideas.

3. **Is it current?** Note the publication date. For some fields and questions, currency isn't an issue. For many research projects, though, it is important to join the present conversation rather than revisit what was discussed in the past.

4. **Is it accurate?** If the perspective or the facts seem to differ significantly from those of other writers on the subject, try to determine whether the reasons for the differences include an authorial bias that complicates the credibility of the publication.

5. **Are the ideas clearly presented and appropriately supported?** Are general statements followed by illustrations or examples? Are claims supported by reasons? Is the discussion balanced?

APPLICATION

Reviewing Sources for Relevance

Read the following descriptions of book publishing houses and journals. For each one, write a sentence or two describing what perspective it might have on the English Only issue.

1. A book published on bilingualism by the Pioneer Institute for Public Policy Research: "Pioneer Institute is Massachusetts' leading public policy think tank. Underlying our work is a commitment to individual freedom and responsibility, limited and accountable government, and the application of free market principles to state and local policy issues."

2. An essay about a California bill requiring English Only education, published in the *National Review*: "This is the standard to which all other conservative journals should be held....In addition to pointedly right wing editorials, each issue features a number of short articles on items of current interest, a longer feature article, and reviews of the arts."

3. An article assessing the effectiveness of bilingual programs published in *Hispanic Journal of Behavioral Sciences*: "Distinguished experts from diverse fields of study present scholarly articles that keep you up-to-date with the latest behavioral research on a wide variety of Hispanic concerns, including cultural assimilation, immigration barriers, intergroup relations, employment discrimination, substance abuse, AIDS prevention, family dynamics, and minority poverty."

Evaluating Web Sites

When you find Web sites that relate to your issue, you will need to evaluate them for their usefulness. While you must apply the same kinds of evaluative questions to books and articles, Web pages require very careful scrutiny. Some Web sites are constructed by twelve-year-old computer hobbyists. These children may be experts on how to construct a Web page, but they may not necessarily be experts on the question you are studying.

After you have found a Web site that includes essays and information relating to the issue you are studying, you will need to determine who built the site. Is the person an expert in the field? How can you find out? The person may give a brief biography that establishes his or her credentials. Read the biography carefully. If it includes the person's affiliation, go to the Web page for that organization and find out more about it.

Let's return to the student who used the Web to begin his study of bilingualism. After his preliminary search, he looked at the following listing: "Language

Policy—English Only." At the site he found only the transcript of a speech entitled "Surviving the English Only Assault: Public Attitudes and the Future of
Language Education" by James Crawford. At the end of the transcript, a note
explained that this was a speech given by James Crawford to the Michigan
Teachers of English to Speakers of Other Languages. Below the note was a link
to James Crawford's home page. On Crawford's home page, he found the following biography:

> I am an independent writer and lecturer—formerly the Washington
> editor of *Education Week*—who specializes in the politics of language.
> Since 1985, I have been reporting on the English Only movement, Eng-
> lish Plus, bilingual education, efforts to save endangered languages,
> and language rights in the U.S.A.

Our student also found a list of Crawford's publications, including four
books published by Multilingual Matters, Bilingual Educational Services, Addison-Wesley, and the University of Chicago Press. He knew that the University
of Chicago Press is a scholarly press but didn't recognize the other presses. A
search for Multilingual Matters led him to the publisher's Web page and with
the following description:

> Multilingual Matters is an international publisher specializing in books
> and journals on all aspects of multilingual and multicultural educa-
> tion, including second language learning. Under its related imprint,
> Channel View Publications, it also publishes material on environ-
> mental education and tourism.

The Web page also included a brief history of the company that explained
that the company distributes academic journals but is a family-run operation.
That the company was a family business and linked interests as diverse as
tourism and second language learning seemed unusual; this information might
make our student wary of using their materials even though some of their publications are written by academics.

When he conducted a search of Bilingual Educational Services, he found
it to be associated with the National Clearinghouse for Bilingual Education, an
organization funded by the U.S. Department of Education's Office of Bilingual
Education and Minority Languages Affairs (OBEMLA) "to collect, analyze, and
disseminate information relating to the effective education of linguistically and
culturally diverse learners in the U.S." He assumed that publishing a book with
Bilingual Education shows that Crawford is considered an expert by other
experts in the field.

The Web site also listed a number of recent articles and speeches James
Crawford has given. Looking carefully at Crawford's publications, the student
discovered that they are all in journals devoted to the support of bilingual education. He guessed what position Crawford would take but decided that because
Crawford has written extensively on the issue for many years and is considered
an expert, he should read what he has to say. He decided to read to find out reasons Crawford gives for his position.

STRATEGY

How to Evaluate Web Sources

The following critical questions will help you assess the reliability and usefulness of your Web sources.

1. **WHAT DOES THE URL ADDRESS TELL YOU?** Is the site someone's personal Web page? Does the domain name indicate that the site is affiliated with a business (.com), an educational institution (.edu), a government agency (.gov), or an organization (.org)?

2. **WHO IS RESPONSIBLE FOR THE PAGE?** Is it an individual, an organization, an agency? Who is accountable for its contents? Can that person or group reasonably claim authority or expertise on the question? Note: Anonymous information is not credible. Don't use it.

3. **WHEN WAS THE PAGE PUBLISHED?** Is it current enough for your purposes? Note: Undated factual or statistical information is not credible. Don't use it.

4. **IS THE INFORMATION RELIABLE?** Are claims and evidence documented with references or links to other reputable sites? If the information is reproduced from another source, is it accurate and complete, and has it been reproduced with appropriate copyright permission?

5. **IS IT PART OF A LARGER DIALOGUE OR CONVERSATION ON THE QUESTION AT ISSUE?** Try searching for the name of the author or organization on the Web to see if others refer to the site and to determine if those responsible for the site are regarded with respect. Try copying the Web address into a search tool to find out if others refer to the site.

6. **IS THE SITE THE BEST SOURCE FOR THE KIND OF INFORMATION INCLUDED?** Generally print sources are regarded as more reliable, even though a tremendous collection of useful information is finding its way onto the Web.

Creating a Bibliography

As you evaluate and select relevant and trustworthy sources, you need to begin to keep records of your search so that you can refer to your sources as your project develops. In order to be credible as a researcher and writer, you need to persuade your audience that you have conducted an appropriately thorough job of investigating available resources. In preparation for a writing project that requires research, develop the essential routine of keeping track of your research through a *working bibliography*. The working bibliography is a list of all the resources you plan to use in your project.

When you create your working bibliography, you should do so in the style most relevant to the area of study. Many disciplines of study have their own documentation styles. Two are presented in the Documentation Appendix at the end of this book, the Modern Language Association Style (MLA) and the American Psychological Association Style (APA). In college, your instructors may provide you with samples of and directions for other styles.

STRATEGY

How to Track Your Research with a Working Bibliography

Use one of the two methods for tracking sources: note cards or computer. Note cards can be easily manipulated, shuffled, or diplayed spatially. Because of the availability of laptop computers, a word-processed list may be easier for people who type faster than they write by hand. (If you are using a computer, note that computer software programs such as EndNote and Bibliocite can arrange the publication information listed in the next step into a specific bibliographic style when you integrate your research into a writing project.)

For each source, make sure that you list all relevant documentation information from the following list, in the style that you intend to use for your writing project (MLA, APA):

- source author or editor.
- title of article or chapter.
- title of periodical or book
- publisher location and name
- For Internet sources, note the URL or Web address and date accessed, and where relevant, include the organizational affiliation.

For each source, add brief summary information, including key ideas and how you think the ideas from the source connect to your own inquiry. Also note any biases or assumptions that may be siginificant to your inquiry.

 ## APPLICATION

Composing a Working Bibliography

Read the letters to the editor of your town's newspaper, then choose one local issue many letters are addressing. Identify the key terms that relate to the question. Using as many of the sources identified in the "Conducting Research" key concept box (page 168) as possible, make a list of at least ten potentially relevant sources, including all essential bibliographic information in a consistant style. Then write a one-page description of your search including (1) a definition of the issue, (2) working bibliography entries of your sources, and (3) a specific question you could pursue as a research project.

WRITING THE RESEARCH PROPOSAL

Often we begin a research project with a hypothetical answer to our question, and then we do initial reading to help us understand the problem. As we increase our knowledge of the issue and others' positions, we may reassess our original ideas. This is not a bad thing. As we conduct inquiries, we educate ourselves about a subject, and changing our minds means that we are willing to consider different answers when our new knowledge offers us new ideas and reasons for believing them.

Sometimes after preliminary information gathering, you may find that while you have not changed your mind, you no longer have a strong opinion. Is your question still worth studying? Absolutely. Conducting research is a way of opening up a question and seeing its complexities. Often our first answers do not account for the complexity of the issue. So how might you go about rethinking your position and refocusing your search? See the list of questions in the strategy box "How to Focus Your Research Question."

As you explore your answers to these questions, you may redefine the question, narrow it, or consider whether you have something new to offer to the discussion. Doing so will help you design a research plan.

A research proposal is a systematically organized plan for a research project. Research proposals are used for all kinds of writing projects that require more

 ## STRATEGY

How to Focus Your Research Question

Examine your working bibliography to explore the following questions.

1. What key terms do my sources share?
2. Do my sources use the terms differently?
3. How have my sources seen the question differently?
4. What assumptions do the sources have about the question?
5. How do my sources agree? Disagree? Which do I find more convincing? Why?
6. What part of the question have sources not answered to my satisfaction?
7. Is there a smaller part of the issue that I might explore in greater depth?
8. Why is this question important to me?

 ## KEY CONCEPT

The Research Proposal

Research proposal: a systematic plan for completing a research project. Purposes:

- to organize your thinking
- to invite response, evaluation, and suggestions from others
- to test the viability of a research project

STRATEGY

How to Write a Research Proposal

There is no standard format for a research proposal; the structure will depend on the type of research question, the audience for the project, and the preferences and expectations of those requesting the proposal. However, most proposals require the following sections.

1. **INTRODUCTION:** Includes your research question, how you arrived at your question, and why you think it is significant. A good question has multiple possible answers. It will bring you into a conversation with other researchers who are writing and thinking about your question. Explain how you came to identify your question (in your reading, a class, discussions, and other sources), and describe why it is a question worth answering. Your answer to the question "Why am I researching this subject" should be more than "It interests me." What do you hope to learn from it? What value might it have for others? What behavior, decisions, or actions might be impacted by the answer?

2. **WORKING HYPOTHESIS:** Include possible answers to your question, and end with what seems most credible and reasonable *at this point in your research*. You will generally not be looking for the "right" answer but for the one answer or combination of answers that offers the best evidence or fullest explanation or most convincing arguments.

3. **WORKING BIBLIOGRAPHY:** List your most promising preliminary sources, using the documentation format (MLA, APA) appropriate for your project, and include your summary notes on key ideas and their connection to your inquiry.

4. **RESEARCH STRATEGY:** Your research strategy has two parts:

   What do I need to know? A list of the questions you will need to answer, key ideas or concepts you will need to define, and assumptions or biases you will need to question in order to complete your project.

   Where will I look for answers? A description of how you will go about getting the information you need: what sources you will consult, what leads you have, what difficulties may present themselves.

information than you currently have. Knowing how to do a research proposal will help you prepare and complete research projects in college, but you will also find the skills useful in the workplace, for example if you need to apply for grants and support from corporations and agencies, or establish timelines in situations requiring project development, or prepare a book proposal.

Writing a research proposal helps you organize your thinking prior to moving forward on a project, and the proposal allows others to evaluate your plans and make suggestions early in the project's development. Completing a proposal also forces you to consider thoroughly the value of a project before you have invested a lot of time in it—it's disheartening for student writers to spend several weeks reading and taking notes on a question, only to discover that to answer the question will require information that is not available in the time that they have.

■ **APPLICATION**

Writing a Research Proposal

You may want to embark on your own research project, but if you first want to make sure that you understand exactly what is meant by a research proposal, practice the process by sharing the work on a group proposal. Using the collection of materials in one of the casebooks, practice composing the four components of a research proposal.

1. Divide the readings among the members of the group.
2. Meet together, and share your reading. Identify potential research questions, and focus on one. Then identify a Working Hypothesis. Write your proposal's Introduction and Working Hypothesis sections.
3. Divide the sources in the Working Hypothesis among the members of your group. Individually, prepare entries for the Working Bibliography, being very careful to use appropriate documentation guidelines, referring to as many of the casebook sources as are relevant, and noting their significance to your question.
4. Meet a second time, compile your entries, discuss possible research plans, and write the Research Strategy.
5. Submit the group research proposal to your instructor.

In the following research proposals, two students present their plans for research projects. The first uses APA documentation; the second, MLA.

Sample Student Writing: Research Proposal, APA Documentation

■ ▬ ▬

Research Proposal: Homelessness

Lucille Burrows

Introduction

The research topic I have chosen for Writing 123 is focused on our mental health system, what services are provided in Bend, and what services are needed. The research question I wish to answer is this. Homelessness among the chronically mentally ill is a community problem in Bend as well as elsewhere in the United States: As a community, how can we address this problem? I have chosen this topic partly as a result of my interest developed from my psychology professor last term. She mentioned in class that there are some chronically mentally ill (schizophrenic) people who live in Juniper Park.

Additionally, I recently viewed a program on *60 Minutes* that profiled a community in Geel, Belgium, that has a unique way to care for the mentally ill in their community. I was intrigued by the total community commitment and support of the mentally ill. In Geel, Belgium, you never see someone sleeping on the street. I wanted to further investigate their system for caring for the mentally ill and see if their methods could be duplicated in other communities, such as in the United States. If some of the methods used in Geel, Belgium, could be used elsewhere, as in Bend, this might have significant implications for the services we can provide in Bend. As a community, we have a responsibility to care for those who are unable to care for themselves. I do not feel it is acceptable to have the chronically mentally ill living in our community parks or on the streets. I think some of our social problems are just accepted as part of living in a community, and perhaps they are not addressed as they should be.

In my preliminary research, I discovered a model program that was started in Long Beach, California, as a result of the frustration and dissatisfaction of family members of the mentally ill, as well as professionals and business people who had an interest in improving the mental health system. As a result, the Village Integrated Service Agency in Long Beach, California, has received a growing amount of attention and commendation as a model mental health program. It incorporates a number of innovative approaches that may be valuable in effecting widespread system change.

Working Hypothesis

Homelessness is a problem not only in Bend, but in large, economically sound communities as well. It is a problem that must be addressed as a community to have a working, caring system to provide for the mentally ill who are homeless. Viable solutions include having one or more community homes to provide for these homeless individuals, having a foster care system that supplements a community home and having people receiving these services treated with "respect, dignity and without labeling or discrimination of any type" (CareLink, 2002).

Working Bibliography

I intend to use the American Psychological Association (APA) documentation system for this research topic because it is generally used for research in the social sciences.

Preliminary Sources:

Anthony, W. A. (2001). Vision for psychiatric rehabilitation research. *Psychiatric Rehabilitation Journal, 25*, 1. Note: Expanding the vision for recovery of severe mental illness and its effect on the research agenda in mental health.

Baxter, E. (1997). An alternative approach to recovery—St. Dimpna. http://www.mentalhealthconsumers.org/connet/cnn/9711/ alternative.htm. Retrieved 4 Apr 2002. Note: A specific community addresses the problem in a unique way.

Fallot, R. D. (2001). Spirituality and religion in psychiatric rehabilitation and recovery from mental illness. *International Review of Psychiatry, 13*, 110. Note: This source is very interesting. The spiritual aspects of rehabilitation are addressed and should be taken into account in structuring solutions.

Principles of psychiatric rehabilitation. CareLink (no date). http://www.carelink-svs.org/psychrehab.htm. Retrieved 12 Apr 2002. Note: A list of governing principles on the rights of the mentally disabled and the responsibilities of community care.

Ragins, M. History and overview of the village. *The Village Integrated Service Agency*. http://www.villageisa.org/Ragin"s%20Papers/ Hist.%20&%20Oveview. Retrieved 4 Apr 2002. Note: Specific example of a care facility that works and how it came into existence.

Ragins, M. (2000). A personal worldwide perspective of psychiatric rehabilitation. *The Village Integrated Service Agency*. http://www.village-isa.org/Ragin's%20Papers/ worldwide_perspective.htm. Retrieved 4 Apr 2002. Note: A worldwide perspective of rehabilitation by Dr. Ragins, based on his own visits to various countries and personal observations on how other countries care for the mentally ill. Site sponsored by the Mental Health Organization of Los Angeles County.

Shern, D. L., Tsemberis, S., Anthony, W., Lovell, A. M., Richmond, L., Felton, C. J., Winarski, J., & Cohen, M. (2000). Serving street-dwelling individuals with psychiatric disabilities: Outcomes of a psychiatric rehabilitation clinical trial. *American Journal of Public Health, 90*, 1873. Note: Empirical research on specific treatment options. What works?

Spaniol, L., et al. *The role of the family in psychiatric rehabilitation.* (Book requested through interlibrary loan 4/12/02)

Spaniol, L., et al. *Introduction to psychiatric rehabilitation.* (Book requested through interlibrary loan 4/12/02)

Research Strategy Description

A. What do I need to know?

Assumptions

In the United States you see many homeless people. In Bend we have homelessness. My psychology professor stated there are some schizophrenic people living in Juniper Park. Our mental health system fails to care for the chronically mentally ill.

Research Questions

Is our mental health system adequate? What services are provided in Bend? Why are the chronically mentally ill homeless? What services are needed in Bend?

Assumptions

There is a different approach for the care of the mentally ill in Geel, Belgium. You never see a person sleeping on the street there. They seem to have a successful way to care for the mentally ill.

Research Questions

How do the people in Geel, Belgium, care for the mentally ill? What accounts for the success of their methods? Would this model be transferable to other places, i.e., cities in the United States? Bend? If not, why not?

Assumptions

The Village Integrated Service Agency in Long Beach, California, has received a growing amount of attention and commendation as a model mental health program. It incorporates a number of innovative approaches that may be valuable in effecting widespread system change. Dr. Mark Ragins, who is involved with the Village Integrated Service Agency, visited Geel, Belgium, and observed their system of care for the mentally ill in his process of gaining a worldwide perspective of psychiatric rehabilitation.

Research Questions

What is the Village Integrated Service Agency? How did it get started and why? What is it doing differently and what is successful, not successful? Would this approach work elsewhere? In Bend?

B. Where will I look for answers?

I used Ebsco Host database for a Web search of key terms: mental health; mental illness; psychiatric rehabilitation, Geel, Belgium. I have also searched Google.com. I have found useful journal articles relating to my topic, including an article in the *Psychiatric Rehabilitation Journal*, Summer 2000, outlining and describing the Denver approach which combines "the best rehabilitation models and influences into one system of rehabilitation services." Additionally, I discovered information about The Village Integrated Service Agency in Long Beach, California, which incorporates a number of innovative approaches in care for the mentally ill.

I asked the librarian at the Central Oregon Community College library for sources of information about services provided in Bend. She directed me to the appropriate Web site and the new Deschutes County Mental Health office located at 2577 NE Courtney in Bend to obtain information on what services are currently available in Bend. I visited the new office in Bend and obtained a pamphlet of information describing the services currently provided.

I have requested two books through interlibrary loan, *Introduction to Psychiatric Rehabilitation* and *The Role of the Family in Psychiatric Rehabilitation*, which I hope will offer some valuable insight into how the family and community can integrate care for the mentally ill.

Additionally, I have ordered a transcript of the *60 Minutes* program concerning the unique care the community of Geel, Belgium, provides for the mentally ill. Viewing this program provided me with a new awareness and heightened interest to investigate this topic further.

Sample Student Writing: Research Proposal, MLA Documentation

Research Proposal: Orca Population Decline

Charlotte Bemis

Introduction

This past summer, I worked on a whale-watching boat called the Glacier Spirit. I worked with researchers and wildlife guides taking groups out to see the beautiful orca whales in their Puget Sound habitat. In my job, I learned to love the orcas, and I learned that the population of the Southern Resident Community of orca whales, their range extending from lower Puget Sound through British Columbia, is declining at an alarming rate. My research question is, "What is causing this decline, and what can be done to correct it?"

What also got me interested was the flurry of interest recently in Keiko, the orca that was a captive who was featured in the "Free Willy" films. Huge amounts of money have gone into trying to introduce him back into the wild, which may mean that our society has acknowledged the importance of protecting the orca as a species.

Working Hypothesis

At this point, I don't know all of the causes for the decline, but some seem more easily addressed than others. Certainly in my job and from my initial research I learned that there are issues of human interference, disease, and toxins in the environment. Several sources have also referred to the Endangered Species Act as one means of protecting orcas; in fact, my visit to the Whale Museum on San Juan Island was very informative, and from the perspective of the staff there, listing orcas as an endangered species is an important step in turning the decline around.

My hypothesis at this point is: Because the orca population is declining, and because their problems have been at least partially created by humans, it is our responsibility to try to correct the decline by listing the orcas as an endangered species.

Working Bibliography

I intend to use MLA documentation style in my research project. These are the sources I have consulted so far.

Beacham, Walter, ed. <u>The World Wildlife Fund Guide to Extinct Species of</u> <u>Modern Times</u>. Osprey, Fl: Beacham Publishing, 1977. This guide helped me understand what circumstances warrant inclusion in the federal list of endangered species, and what protection such a listing provides.

Cahape, Beth. "What's Killing our Orcas?" <u>The Port Townsend Leader</u>. 22 Sept. 1999: B1 + . This article explores from the perspective of an active on-site researcher the possible causes of the decline in orcas.

Ford, John K. B., Graeme M. Ellis, and Kenneth C. Balcomb. <u>Killer</u> <u>Whales: The Natural History and Genealogy of Orcinus Orca in</u> <u>British Columbia and Washington</u>. Vancouver: University of British Columbia Press, 2000. Information on whale history, whale watching, behaviors, feeding habits, and family groups, accompanied by great pictures of all the north coast pods.

Flaherty, Chuck, and David G. Gordon. <u>Field Guide to the Orca</u>. Sasquatch Field Guide Series. Seattle: Sasquatch Books, 1990. A practical guide showing how to observe orcas, their lifecycles, and a record of recent sightings.

McNeil, Andrew. Personal interview. 26 Nov. 1999.

The Whale Museum, San Juan Island. Pacific Northwest Orca Population Declining. 23 Nov. 1999 http://www.whale_museum.org/Press/declining.htm. This museum is an amazing resource for specific information on the orcas themselves, especially the families and the threats.

———. Issues. 23 Nov. 1999 http://www.. Specifically about the effects of environmental pollutants on the whale population.

Research Strategy

A. What do I need to know?

There are several separate questions I need to pursue in order to thoroughly answer my question.

What are the specific causes of the decline?

What is the status of the present population?

What connections can I make between these pods and the
ecosystem and food chain, i.e., why should this matter to the
general population?

In what ways has human interference contributed to the
ecosystem of the area?

How did the era of captivity affect the populations, i.e., the Sea
World influence?

How dire is the situation? Might they become extinct? Under what
conditions?

Why should we interfere? Isn't this a natural process? (My
assumption is that what humans break, they have a
responsibility to fix, but not everyone assumes that.)

To what extent would it solve anything to list orcas as endangered
species?

Are there other solutions?

What would be the costs of various solutions? There's always the
"jobs vs. nature" debate.

B. How will I find out?

First, I will revisit the whale museum when I have a more specific
research direction. The reference librarians there are very helpful, and
the information is very specific. I will also talk more formally, with
specific questions, to the researchers from the Glacier Spirit. I will get
a copy of the original language of the Endangered Species Act of 1973
to see if my assumption is correct that a listing would help the orcas.

RESEARCH AS LEARNING: CONNECTING OLD IDEAS WITH NEW KNOWLEDGE

As you read the materials you have chosen for your research, you will begin to
make generalizations that connect the new information with the old information
you had before your search began. For example, let's say that you were studying
the "English Only" question. You read in the census data from the Census 2000
Supplementary Survey reported in August 2001 that nearly one-fifth of school-
age children speak a language other than English in their homes and that two-
thirds of children age 5 to 17 who speak English at school but Spanish at home
believed that they spoke English very well, whereas only 50 percent of those 18 to
64 who spoke Spanish at home believed that they spoke English well.

Considering how that information affects your position on bilingual education, you learn that people interested in bilingual education draw different conclusions from this data. For example, Lisa Navarette of the National Council of La Raza, an Hispanic advocacy group, says, "The new numbers offer more evidence of the diverse makeup of American youngsters and show the need to expand bilingual education programs" and that "the survey also helps to dispel the notion that children who speak Spanish at home have difficulty conversing in English." In contrast, a critic of bilingual education wondered why more school-age children who speak Spanish did not rate themselves as speaking English very well. "The figures should be closer to 100 percent," said Ron Unz, chairman of the Palo Alto, California-based English for the Children, who successfully pushed a California ballot question in 1998 dismantling the state's bilingual education program. "If the schools are failing to teach English, that's a crime" ("New census survey shows increase in non-English speakers." Genaro C. Armas, *Associated Press*, August 5, 2001).

You might look at the figures and the two opposing positions and wonder whether there might be a way to read the data in a less politically and emotionally charged way. It is impressive that two-thirds of all Spanish-speaking children believe that they are acquiring English skills, particularly given that Spanish is the language of their heritage. And yet, they live in a culture where English is the language of popular culture, in which young children would hear English song lyrics, television shows, and radio broadcasts. Is it the case that because children adapt easily and learn language quickly, they don't need bilingual education? Is it the case that bilingual education programs are succeeding or failing to teach English?

When we analyze information, we rely on the assumptions we believe we share with our community. As you consider the data the survey reported, you are connecting the various parts of the survey (your new information) with those assumptions (your old information). You may assume that children are proud of their national heritage, but you may also assume that they identify with and learn from popular culture. You may assume that children are quick learners, but you may also question the assumption that having two-thirds of a group rate themselves highly on their language skills represents a failure.

As you explore your response to the new information, you will be making generalizations about the issue. Does this new information lead you to generalizations closer to those of Lisa Navarette or Ron Unz or somewhere between? As you consider the conclusions that make sense to you, you are beginning to shape an argument because you are thinking about the reasons for your conclusion, the assumptions that account for those reasons, and the evidence that supports those reasons. In the following chapters we will be looking more closely at how we construct good writing projects, many of which will require formal research. Before you begin any essay, however, you need to have explored your question by responding, listening to others, and finding the information that will allow you to draw informed conclusions.

Whether you are finding more information for your own personal use, for a paper you are writing in one of your classes, or for a public issue you hope to help solve, you need to know the kinds of resources available to you and how to use them. Beginning with a clear sense of what question you will be exploring will ensure that your search has focus and purpose. Then knowing the many options available to you—whether in your college library, on the Internet, or through direct interaction with experts or public document offices—will open your search to rich and varied sources of information.

WRITING INVITATIONS

1. Write a narrative that describes your process of completing a research project you have conducted at some time in your life. Explain what made the project a success or failure.

2. If you have chosen a major, identify what you see as the key questions that characterize the research in the subject area. To develop your observations, look at the department's mission statement, interview faculty members, and talk to other students. If you have not chosen a major, investigate and report on the key questions of at least three different fields of study.

3. Read Deborah Tannen's "Can We Talk?" and Robin Turner's "Male Logic and Women's Intuition" in Casebook 3: He Said/She Said. Identify the key questions each writer raises. Then identify questions the writing raises for you. How does each writer's position differ from yours or from the positions of other writers?

4. Think about one of the communities you belong to outside of school: occupational, recreational, or even personal (friends or relatives). Investigate and describe the questions that the members of this "discourse community" hold in common. Talk with other members about what questions you share and why the questions are important to the members.

5. Visit your library to test the potential of a question at issue that has emerged in one of your classes. Try, in one hour, to locate at least five sources relevant to the question in five different areas of the library. Then, on your own, read and evaluate each source according to the criteria in the strategy boxes "How to Evaluate Print Sources" and "How to Evaluate Web Sources." To what extent is the source material credible, relevant, current, accurate, and clear?

6. After completing Writing Invitation 5, write a two-page inquiry paper in which you consider possible answers to the question and how your preliminary research has influenced your thinking about the question. Exchange papers with another person in the class, then write a one-page response to your classmate's inquiry paper.

DEVELOPING A WRITING PROJECT

Focusing on an issue of personal interest or one that has emerged from your study in other classes, use the strategies in this chapter to write a fully developed research proposal on a subject you intend to develop further. Include the four components of a research proposal listed and explained in the strategy box "How to Write a Research Proposal" (page 175).

CHAPTER 7

Synthesizing Ideas

To exist, humanly, is to name the world, to change it. Once named, the world in its turn reappears to the namers as a problem and requires of them a new naming. Men are not built in silence, but in word, in work, in action-reflection.

Paolo Freire

Everything should be made as simple as possible, but not simpler.

Albert Einstein

CONSIDERING MULTIPLE PERSPECTIVES

One of the great virtues of a college education is that it offers so many opportunities to look at ideas and situations in multiple, sometimes conflicting ways. This can be exciting; it can be confusing; it can even be embarrassing to discover that others may not necessarily share your perceptions, your knowledge, or your experience. One of the best ways to check the validity of your assumptions and biases is by engaging in dialogue with others, and college classrooms are natural sites for you to express your ways of thinking and compare them with those of others. Of course, the classroom is not the only place you will grow intellectually and ethically by seeing through others' eyes. As you read the writings of others, you will be considering alternate perspectives. The ability to make sense of multiple perspectives is a life skill: it helps you resolve conflicts and make decisions in the workplace, in your communities, and in your families.

Recently, at a forum on issues of "masculinity" sponsored by a university center dedicated to investigating the complications of gender and power, the following exchange took place among faculty participants. They were discussing

FIGURE 7.1

CHARLES BARKLEY, HALL OF FAME
NATIONAL BASKETBALL ASSOCIATION
PLAYER

ways in which masculinity and violence are culturally linked when the discussion took a surprising turn:

> Participant 1: "For example, a few years ago in an NBA game, Charles Barkley was called for a foul, and he pointed a finger at the ref, shaped his hand like a gun, and pretended to pull the trigger. Then, at home, our little boy 'shot' his mom the same way, and she said, 'Where did he learn that,' and I said, 'from Charles Barkley.' I think Barkley's action was threatening. It's not like the old days with John Wayne movies or something."
>
> Participant 2: "What are you talking about? How is it different from John Wayne movies?"
>
> Participant 1: "Well, John Wayne wasn't really shooting people."
>
> Participant 2: "Yes he was! They happened to be Indians!"

They were talking about men, violence, and power, and then suddenly they were talking about race. Is that off the subject? Certainly not. Both of these speakers were white, but one recognized that cultural assumptions and biases may have influenced the other's sense of what was a threat and what was not. The first speaker probably meant that John Wayne was playing a fictional role, killing fictional Indians. The second speaker assumed, though, that in both situations the participants were playing roles, and saw a possible bias against a black man threatening a white man versus a white man threatening a Native

American man. Acceptable and unacceptable portrayals of violence may have had to do with the actions of real people rather than fictional characters, but it also had to do with who might be wielding the pretend gun. After this interchange, the discussion continued in a more complicated, less comfortable way. The members of the discussion dealt with the fact that what we permit or excuse or condemn has to do not just with preconceived notions of what is masculine but also with what constitutes a threat. Although this made the conversation less comfortable, seeing multiple perspectives made everyone learn more about campus problems.

Making ourselves consider multiple perspectives isn't easy. Sometimes we want to avoid the complexity, as do the individuals speaking in the following examples:

> "I thought I was going to write about my experience at the Animal Shelter and my ideas about animal rights, but as I read more, I started to change my mind, so I wrote about something else I felt certain about."

> "My professor wants us to write about whether Oliver North's actions in Latin America were ethical. How would I know? I wasn't there."

Do these remarks sound familiar? The first student didn't think that she could write about a subject unless she was certain about her position; she may not have known how helpful it might be to write *conditionally* about animal rights, exploring the possible positions and examining the complexities involved in the issue. The second student may just have been venting his frustration over an assignment, but he also may not have known how to go about studying issues that can't be decided by fact or direct observation.

Thinking is hard work. In this complicated, multinational, multidisciplinary, multicultural world, we are often confronted with issues that have more than one possible answer, issues that may involve ethical or philosophical dilemmas or that may have implications for a future we can only imagine. We may not always have the opportunity or time to resolve questions that engage us, so sometimes we turn away from the problem or leave the problem-solving to others. But it is empowering to know how to make sense of complex issues when we want or need to grapple with them. We need to know how to identify the question, how to name the alternative answers, how to see the relationships among those answers, and how to find words to express, as simply as possible, the complexity of an issue.

SYNTHESIZING SOURCES

As you study issues, you will find yourself reading essays and books that present very different perspectives. Doing so can sometimes be overwhelming. You will agree with some positions and disagree with others. However you respond, you will need to keep a record of the varying positions, and one way to do so is by writing a synthesis.

KEY CONCEPT

A Synthesis

A synthesis is an exploration of a question at issue that

1. Includes diverse views on a subject.
2. Organizes them to show the relationships and differences among them.
3. Expresses information on a complex issue as an organized, accurate record of alternate perspectives for the purpose of explanation.

Synthesis as Inquiry

What situation might call for a synthesis? As we suggested above, a synthesis is a way in which you may come to grips with information that is varied in purpose and perspective. You will write syntheses for yourself, for work, or for college classes in order to learn and to share your learning with others. Your job as a writer of a synthesis is to organize, categorize, and express information on a complex issue in order to present it accurately and clearly for yourself, as a record of the competing ideas, or for others who share your concern.

In this chapter, you will not be taking a position on an issue. Because the ability to listen carefully and respectfully to alternative views is so important to critical thinking, we will ask you to practice suspending your opinion while you reflect on the perspectives of others. We will ask you, too, to construct statements that express the complexities of an issue in ways that will clarify, but not decide, the issue for others. You engaged in this kind of activity if you tried writing an inquiry paper, which we discussed in Chapter 2.

A synthesis is like an inquiry paper because the writer writes one not to answer a question, but rather to explore various answers to a question. Writing a synthesis differs from writing an inquiry paper in that you are not simply exploring different answers you might propose, but instead you are exploring actual answers others have proposed. As you consider these answers, you will learn more about the question.

This ability—to complicate an issue in order to make sense of it—relies on your willingness to hear what other writers are saying and assuming. This means that you will have to suspend your desire to name your position before beginning your inquiry. You may have been asked in some previous class to write a "pro or con" paper, for which you were required to take a stand for or against a position and defend it. Writing the "pro-con" paper requires that you find the evidence that supports a particular position and arrange it into an "unassailable" argument. Do you hear the images at work here? "Take a stand," "defend," supporting a "position," "unassailable." This way of seeing presents writing as an effort to "win" an argument the way you might win a battle or hold a fort against attack. While this kind of debate-style writing and reasoning can be exciting, taking a position on a question before studying it thoroughly, or seeing it simply as on one side or the other, may lead a writer to oversimplify the situation, accidentally or on purpose, in order to strengthen the case. Alternative positions on an issue aren't necessarily "enemies," and winning isn't always the goal of writing. Sometimes we just want to make sense of the possibilities.

In Chapters 5 and 6, you observed the writer's purpose and the strategies he or she uses to achieve that purpose. In this chapter, you will be reading with your own purpose in mind, but your purpose will not be to construct your own argument; instead, your purpose will be to answer the question you have identified. It is important to find and read selections that offer information and ideas relevant to your question, not just ones that are supportive of a predetermined answer.

Reading and Writing to Synthesize

The kind of writing we will ask you to do in this chapter relies on your ability to analyze your reading: you will not only need to analyze the strategies of other writers, but you will also need to analyze and categorize the positions they take. To do so, you will need to *synthesize*, or connect and relate the positions in order to see the whole web of intersecting ideas. In college and in the professional world, people are often asked to write syntheses—of problems and solutions, of debates on issues, of responses to ideas, of resources and plans.

Syntheses have become an important part of research in all fields. Often called "white papers," these kinds of syntheses provide background information to government, business, and university groups responsible for making policies and decisions. These groups depend on the accuracy and thoroughness of such reports to educate them about the issues they are addressing. For example, a member of Congress voting on a bill to allow oil drilling in the Arctic National Wildlife Refuge in Alaska would need information about the potential oil resources in the area, national fuel needs, and the potential effects on the eco-systems in the region. While considering the issue, the Congressperson would read white papers written by experts in the various fields. These papers would present thorough, unbiased reports of the most current information on the issue.

Often businesses and non-profit organizations list white papers on their Web sites. Designed to educate and inform, these papers are rich resources of information but may provide only one side of an issue. This does not mean that the report is biased but merely that it is considering one particular aspect of the question, such as "What might be the environmental effect of oil drilling in the Wildlife Refuge?" or "How much oil might be pumped from the region?" or "What would be the costs of pumping oil from the region?" Each report would provide a different perspective on the issue, but each would also synthesize different perspectives on the narrower question.

Like white papers, syntheses play an important role in college research projects. As you research an issue, sometimes you will need to rely on the syntheses of others, and other times you will write your own synthesis. In either case, knowing what goes into a synthesis will improve your use of syntheses, whether they are your own compilations of information or published reports written by experts in the field you are studying.

PLANNING AND WRITING A SYNTHESIS

Because a synthesis paper is one that collects and arranges multiple perspectives on an issue, it functions as a kind of research report. Its purpose is to provide information in a clear and accessible document. To make the information accessible you will need to present it in a clear, accurate, and understandable format. When you write a synthesis that reflects what you've learned from your discussions, your readings, and your reflection, you can create a new way of looking at a subject, leading your readers to a clearer understanding.

We are presenting these actions as stages in a process, but you should know that most people do not write by following the stages as if they were a formula for successful writing. You may use them to draft, but as you revise, you will need to consider your audience's needs, the complications of your subject, and your role as the facilitator of a dialogue among various "author/speakers" on your subject. In the rest of this chapter, we will consider ways to use these elements to write and revise a synthesis.

 STRATEGY

How to Plan and Write a Synthesis

Considering the following elements may help you write a synthesis:

1. Find a question at issue, one with multiple possible answers.
2. Read writers who answer your question differently. (Remember: These writers will be writing to answer their own key questions, which may or may not be yours. They may simply address your question in the context of answering their own.) Take notes on their answers.
3. Form and sequence generalizations that are alternative answers to your question.
4. Craft your thesis statement.
5. Use reader cues.
6. Integrate ideas.
7. Avoid plagiarism: cite your sources.
8. Read for sense.

Find a Question

We have argued throughout this book that nearly every piece of writing is an answer to one or more questions. Therefore, one of the essential skills of critical reading is being able to identify the questions a writer is answering. In Casebook 1: The Vote, each article and document raises a central question that the remainder of the work answers. For example, the Declaration of Independence asks whether the current political circumstances justify the colonists' action to abolish the government allegiance and replace it with another. The article by Linda Feldmann, "Why the Poll Booths of America Are Empty," asks whether American democracy is broken, or simply changing. Rob Richie and Steven Hill, in "The Dinosaur in the Living Room," ask how we can pull out of what they call our political depression.

To synthesize some of the ideas expressed in these essays that refer to voting, though, you will need to begin your own inquiry by identifying your own question, your own way of connecting the various positions raised in the readings. So, read the essays for the questions they address, and then ask "What question does this raise for me?" Moving from the writer's question to your own will help you find the connections among the various essays you read.

To illustrate how this works, review this list of questions that students generated as they read the articles in Casebook 1:

What is democracy?

What is the relationship of voting to democracy?

Is voting a right, a freedom, a responsibility, an illusion?

Is the right not to vote as valid as the right to vote?

Is low voter turnout a problem, or not?

What is the relationship between voting and civil rights?

Have our assumptions about the vote changed over two centuries? If so, how?

Why is voting included as a universal human right?

Why would someone vote?

Why would someone not vote?

Why should someone vote?

—Why should someone not vote?

What constraints or limits have been placed on voting over the history of U.S. democracy?

What's a flag-waver?

Why is America's voter turnout lower than in other democratic countries?

Why are people cynical about politics?

How does age relate to voting?

Who doesn't vote, and why?

What is being done, or could be done, to reverse the decline in voter turnout?

What are the effects of the two-party system on voting?

Should there be a law requiring people to vote?

What are the benefits and limitations of the American Electoral College system?

Do any of these questions engage you? Many of you might not come to the subject of "voting" already engaged in the issue. "I have to be interested in something to write about it," you might say. But nearly all people, once they discover questions at issue through reading and discussion, have something to say on the subject. Why is that? We think it's because we come up with good ideas in response to a genuine conflict of thought.

Read Attentively and Take Notes

In order to synthesize ideas on an issue presented in readings, you will need to do more than simply identify the questions each selection addresses. You will need to examine the position each writer takes and note the reasons and evidence used to support that position.

As you read, make a list of the answers the writer suggests and the specific details the writer provides. It may help to make marginal notes that identify the writer's main points, and then number the details that support each point. After reading and annotating all the essays, look for the places where writers are addressing similar questions, and note whether the answers, reasons, and support are the same, similar, or different.

 APPLICATION

Finding Your Question

After reading the essays in Casebook 1: The Vote, meet in small groups to discuss the questions the essays raise, addressing the following questions:

1. Which questions are intriguing to you?

2. Which generate specific answers for you?

3. Which seem easy to answer?

4. Which seem difficult?

5. Which readings come to mind in relation to each question?

At the end of the discussion, choose one question that interests you and write a paragraph in which you explore your interest in the question.

FIGURE 7.2

Nelson Mandela votes in the first South African election to include black voters. He is elected South Africa's first black president.

Sample Student Writing: Reading Notes from Casebook 1: The Vote

The following reading notes from articles in Casebook 1 were taken in the process of researching one of the example questions, "Is low voter turnout a problem, or not?" It is important to observe that there are quite a few notes: good writers will examine a lot of material in order to ensure that they have adequate information to clearly and accurately synthesize the perspectives.

Student Reflections

Declaration of Independence

[A]ll men are created equal, that they are endowed by their Creator with certain unalienable Rights, that among these are Life, Liberty and the pursuit of Happiness—That to secure these rights, Governments are instituted among Men, deriving their just powers from the consent of the governed,—That whenever any Form of Government becomes destructive of

Voting is a responsibility assigned to us in the Declaration.

these ends, it is the Right of the People to alter or to abolish it, and to institute new Government…

Martin Luther King, "I Have a Dream"

We can never be satisfied as long as a Negro in Mississippi cannot vote and a Negro in New York believes he has nothing for which to vote. No, no, we are not satisfied, and we will not be satisfied until justice rolls down like waters and righteousness like a mighty stream.

Voting must be important—people have fought hard for the right.

Susan B. Anthony, "Women's Right to Vote"

And it is a downright mockery to talk to women of their enjoyment of the blessings of liberty while they are denied the use of the only means of securing them provided by this democratic-republican government—the ballot.

The right to vote is a means of securing the blessings of liberty.

is a necessary

Richard Rose, "Evaluating Election Turnout"

Non-totalitarian societies, by definition, value what Sir Isaiah Berlin (1969) has described as "freedom from the state." Political participation need not be mandatory, and freedom usually includes the right not to vote.

We also have the right not to vote.

To be effective, a boycott must be organized. It can be backed up by patrolling outside polling stations on election day, so that anyone who turns out to vote has to publicly break ranks with the boycott. In Northern Ireland, there was an organized boycott of the 1973 referendum on whether Northern Ireland should remain part of the United Kingdom.

People can refrain from voting for political reasons.

The abnormally low turnout in the United States reflects archaic registration laws and, to a lesser extent, a history of effectively disenfranchising most blacks and many whites in the South.

Low turnout reflects historical exclusion of certain groups.

Linda Feldmann, "Why the Poll Booths of America Are Empty"

Indeed, while the United States often holds itself up as a model of democracy, it has chronically produced one of the lowest voter participation rates in the Western world since World War II. It hardly seems what the Founding Fathers had in mind 224 years ago when they set forth a blueprint for a new kind of representative government, one deriving just powers from the consent of the governed.

Is voting a measure of the health of a democracy?

Since 1960, when modern-day U.S. presidential voting peaked at 63 percent, turnout has declined by 14 percent, to less than half the voting-age population.

If fewer than half of eligible voters actually participate, can the election actually be called democratic?

Mark Mills cares passionately about community issues. He calls local officials and writes letters to the editor about everything from school spending to local tax rates. Yet he rarely votes. Currently, he's not even registered.

However, maybe voting is not the only way to participate in a democracy.

Some appear so intimidated by the complexity of the issues involved that they don't vote, almost out of respect for democracy.

"But, in fact, the two phenomena may be unrelated," says Ruy Teixeira, author of two books on voter turnout. Turnout now is not catastrophically lower than it was in 1960—63 percent—when government was viewed as more responsive, he says.

Maybe our low turnout isn't all that big a problem, when seen in a historical context...

He also notes that turnout in most other major democracies has been dropping as well. Switzerland, the only country in the

or in the context of other democracies.

Organization for Economic Cooperation and Development with lower turnout than the U.S., has declined by 39 percentage points since the 1950s. Only two countries have seen an increase: Denmark and Sweden.

To some, low turnout is a sign of satisfaction with government. Indeed, turnout in the U.S. spiked up to 55 percent in 1992, when voters were unhappy with the state of the economy.

Low turnout may even be a sign of voter satisfaction!

Taipanonline, "Why People Don't Vote"

As for the 49% voter turnout, I say: Big deal!

Low voter turnout not a problem.

Anthony Downs's An Economic Theory of Democracy—published in 1957—became the most cited book in the discipline of political science. Why would an economist's dissertation be so widely cited and read? Simple. An Economic Theory of Democracy explains...why people vote...or don't vote in a democracy.

Anthony Downs believes we don't vote because we'd rather receive the benefit without the cost of researching the issues.

According to Downs, people who do not vote, don't vote on the basis of a rational, economic decision. The pin that holds Downs's theory together is the economic phenomena known as the "free rider." In a free rider, a person receives a benefit without absorbing the cost of receiving the benefit.

A person who wants to make a "rational decision" in a vote would absorb substantial costs. Namely, reading "everything" about the issues and candidates...attending debates, etc. After reading everything, a fully informed person could then vote rationally.

"Interview with David Pryor"

Surveys indicate that young people do not feel that government and politicians are the best way of implementing change. Students are very active about volunteering and giving back to their community and country.

Young people prefer to participate democratically in other ways.

Candidates focus on the issues that affect voters and if young people don't vote, politicians will pay very little attention. Politicians go where the voters are and right now voters are not represented by the younger generation.

Young people don't vote because the issues don't relate to them.

In a national survey of college undergraduates conducted by the Institute of Politics, 85% of college student prefer community volunteerism to political involvement to solve issues in their community and 60% prefer it to solve important issues facing the country.

Statistics on youth participation in community volunteerism as a way to solve issues.

Rob Richie and Steven Hill, "The Dinosaur in the Living Room"

Let's take Virginia. Turnout in the 1997 governor's race among registered voters was 48%—as opposed to 67% and 61% in the state's last two gubernatorial elections. And that doesn't even count eligible voters who never registered. Turnout among all eligible adult Virginians was an abysmal 34%.

Statistics on just how low participation has been in Virginia and Florida.

But Virginians can take heart. Their turnout was better than Broward County, Florida, where a mere 7% of registered voters made their way to the polls.

State and local elections draw even fewer participants. How low can it go, and still be called an election??

Detroit's mayoral primary turnout was 17% of registered voters; in Charlotte's primary, it was 6%.

> General election turnout was under 40% of
> registered voters in Miami and New York City
> and under 30% in Boston and San Francisco.

Form and Sequence Answers to Your Question

Whenever you write, you learn because you find new, individual ways to join and connect ideas in order to make sense of a subject. If you write with the intention of sharing what you have learned with others, you are joining a conversation. One way to think about college is as a big collection of conversations that you can listen in on and, when you are ready, contribute to through writing. One rhetorician, Kenneth Burke, described such conversations this way:

> You come late. When you arrive, others have long preceded you, and they are engaged in a heated discussion, a discussion too heated for them to pause and tell you exactly what it is about. In fact, the discussion had already begun long before any of them got there, so that no one present is qualified to retrace for you all the steps that had gone before. You listen for a while, until you decide that you have caught the tenor of the argument; then you put in your oar.

Imagine coming into that room, maybe a political science classroom, in which the students are discussing voting. Maybe someone in the room admits to being a non-voter, which makes the others criticize her. Others consider their reasons for voting, and the discussion becomes quite lively. Having read the

---

■ APPLICATION

Reading Attentively and Taking Notes

Review the student-generated list in the "Find a Question" section (pages 193–194) and pick a question other than "Is low voter turnout a problem, or not?" Read the articles in Casebook 1: The Vote, and take notes from the readings related to your question. As you read the essays, make marginal notes:

1. Note places where the writer answers your question.
2. Mark and number the examples the writer uses to support each position.
3. In a notebook or computer file:
   - For each reading, in your own words, list the positions the writer takes that seem to answer the question.
   - Under each position, list the details that support it.
   - Note similarities and differences in the answers each writer presents.

articles in Casebook 1, having thus "listened in" on the conversation related to voting, would you be more prepared to put in your oar? Such conversations are central to the discourse of college communities because all issues in college classes, all issues in the larger community, thrive on the thoughtful, informed discussion of reasons and evidence.

This chapter is about listening, without judgment, to the various ideas people may articulate on a subject at issue. As you may discover, that can be much more difficult than just adding to the conversation, just "giving your opinion." To synthesize the ideas of others, imagine yourself in Burke's room. You've been there a while, listening in, and an acquaintance who has just arrived whispers to you, "What's this all about, anyway?" If you are inclined to be helpful, you will try to describe, simply but without oversimplifying, the "key points" of the discussion. These will be stated as generalizations.

Student writers are sometimes frustrated by the fact that their teachers can't present the process of organizing and sequencing generalizations as a set of fool-proof directions. But rarely do readings on a similar subject yield easily to syn-thesis, because their purposes differ from yours. The same list of notes in two writers' hands will arrange themselves into two different expressions, with dif-ferent sets of relationships, different webs of meaning. People use various strate-gies to make this creative process happen. For example, some writers draw "maps" of their ideas, connecting their points spatially rather than in a linear fashion (as in an outline). An art student might use color and line drawings to shape a syn-thesis; a business student might draw a flowchart. One philosophy student we know doesn't use writing in his planning process at all; he can hold the arrange-ment of thoughts in his head and rearrange them at the same time, writing only when he is ready to draft. However, at the very least, it is essential to be able to generalize about what you discover in your reading in order to establish a basis for connecting the ideas in your writing. The generalizations will become "turn-ing points," or organizers—they will help you find the shape of your content.

■ APPLICATION

Forming and Sequencing Answers to Your Question

The student writer who chose to examine the question, "Is voter turnout a problem, or not?" based on the readings in Casebook 1 wrote the following list of general statements she had noted in her reading. She arrived at these generalizations by reviewing her reading notes and reflecting on how they connect to and answer her question.

- Voter turnout is shockingly low.
- The Declaration of Independence seems to assume that active consent through voting is one of the requirements for democracy to exist.

continued

- Other historical figures document how significant voting rights have been in the struggle for equality as a measure of the health of a democracy.
- If voter turnout is a problem now, the evidence shows that it has always been one and will continue to be one, because we have not yet found ways to ensure free and full participation.
- Voting rights have always been restricted—first to propertied white men, then slowly extended to men without property, blacks and women.
- But some argue that the Voting Rights Act, in place for 30 years, has still not ensured free and full participation.
- Electoral College system discourages and disenfranchises some.
- Poll corruption still disenfranchises some, as in the Florida presidential elections in 2000.
- It's pointless for people to vote Republican or Democrat whose needs are not taken into account in the decision-making or the distribution of resources.

1. Discuss how each generalization in the list above might be supported. What kind of information would be useful? What kinds of reasons and appeals might be employed? Which articles will the writer refer to as she supports each point?

2. Seeing the generalizations in the works you read will help you make the connections between the question you find compelling and the perspectives the various writers present. Doing so will also help you find the similarities and differences in their perspectives. Read several articles from Casebook 1 related to one question you have chosen to explore. Take notes, and after reviewing your notes:

   List the key points made by the various authors.

   Compare the key points in terms of similarities and differences, noting, for example, where they address similar or competing views, or where their evidence is complementary or competing.

   Combine the key points into general answers to your question, and align your notes about each writer's key points with one of the general answers.

   Write a thesis statement of your own that summarizes the possible answers to your question.

   Use your thesis statement to help you sequence your key points into an effective order.

Identify Your Thesis Statement

Even though you are not writing an argument essay in which you are presenting and supporting a position of your own on the question, you will need to have a thesis statement for your synthesis. For example, if you are addressing the question "Is voting a right, a freedom, a responsibility, a pointless exercise?" and the most prevalent answer you find in the articles you read is "Voting is a responsi-

■ **APPLICATION**

Composing Thesis Statements

Pick three of the student-generated questions listed in the "Find a Question" section (pages 193–194) or identify three of your own on a subject you are researching. Having explored several readings on your subject, write at least two alternative thesis statements for a prospective paper. Each thesis should include (1) a statement that summarizes the possible answers to the question, (2) a statement that identifies the most common or commonly accepted answer, and (3) a reason or reasons that support the answer.

bility," you will need to give a reason why the writers believe that position. In other words, you need to explain what it is about voting that makes it a responsibility. So, you might argue, "Although there are many different perspectives on the value of voting, most of the writers I have read see voting as a responsibility because they believe that it is the only way citizens maintain the democratic system."

Use Reader Cues for Coherence

Your thesis statement is the key to the map of the territory you are describing. But you will have to use other signposts and signals along the way. In the following two paragraphs from the sample student essay included later in this chapter, several kinds of signposts have been marked. They include guide sentences, repeated key words—or synonyms for those words, or pronouns that refer to them—and transition words. Guide sentences let the reader know how the information in the new paragraph relates to what has come before. Repeated key words lead the reader from old information to new information while keeping the reader's attention on the subject. Transition words like "however," "for example," "although," and "on the other hand" tell the reader how to regard the information that is coming up. "For example," for example, tells the reader that the next sentence will present a particular instance of the general idea that has just been stated; "on the other hand," on the other hand, tells us to contrast what we are about to hear with what came before. All three kinds of signposts make the writing easy to read and follow. In the following example the guide sentences are in italics, the key words, synonyms, and pronouns that refer to them are in boldface, and the transition words are underlined:

> *However, perhaps voting is not the only, or even the most necessary, **measure** of **democratic health.*** There are other ways to **assess political involvement.** Although the "**youth**" age category (however it's defined) is often cited for **their** low turnout, David Pryor suggests that "**young people** do not feel that government and politicians are the best **way of implementing change.** For example, **students** are very active about **volunteering**

and giving back to their community and country." In fact, he says, "85% of **college students** prefer **community volunteerism** to **political involvement** to solve issues in their community and 60% prefer it to solve important issues facing the country." (Office of Communications)

This notion that there are multiple ways to **promote the health of a democracy** is *not* just a **youth** phenomenon. Mark Mills is a good example. He "cares passionately about community issues. He calls local officials and writes letters to the editor about everything from school spending to local tax rates. Yet he rarely votes. Currently, he's not even registered." (Feldmann). But he is an activist: he makes an impact directly rather than voting for someone else to act.

■ APPLICATION

Using Reader Cues

Find the guide sentences, repeated words and phrases (or their equivalents), and transition words in the following paragraphs. Copy the paragraphs, and invent a system for marking each type of reader cue. Compare your markings with those of your classmates. Did you find the same cues? Did you interpret the writer's cues differently?

Turnout is a ratio, determined not only by the number of people who vote but also by the number of people legally eligible and registered to vote. The number of people legally eligible to vote was traditionally a small—and exclusively male—portion of the adult population. When there is a big difference between the total adult population and the number eligible to vote, turnout can at the same time be high as a percentage of eligible voters and low as a percentage of the population.

In the transition from oligarchic or proto-democratic to democratic elections, the turnout of the eligible electorate did expand; in more than a dozen European countries it already averaged 50% in 1875, and rose to 83% in 1975. By contrast, the proportion of the adult population turning out to vote changed radically. In 1875 it was less than 8%; it had doubled by 1900, but even that meant only one in six. Not until the 1920s did a majority of adults normally vote in a country's national election. Only after the Second World War did 75–80% of a European nation's adults normally vote, thus completing the transformation of oligarchic political systems into participative democracies.

The gap between turnout as a percentage of eligible electors and as a percentage of the adult (voting age) population was only closed by the adoption of universal suffrage; but in most countries that are today established democracies, this goal was only achieved by a gradual evolutionary process. To begin with, the franchise was initially restricted to a small percentage of males; then most or all men were given the right to vote; and finally women gained the right to vote as well.

Integrate Ideas: Summary, Paraphrase, and Quotation

In this chapter, we have demonstrated how some of the articles you read in Casebook 1 could be blended into a synthesis that would explain possible points of view on a question at issue. For other issues you study, you will be finding sources of your own through library, online, and community research. When you have collected resources, you can make notes relevant to your questions, and in addition to using quotations, you may also paraphrase or summarize important ideas. It helps to remember that, when you synthesize, you are accounting for different voices in an ongoing conversation. You want to make sure that you represent those other people accurately and clearly, because in doing so you give them the same kind of respect that you want from *your* audience. Most academic writers make sense of source material by using a combination of summary, paraphrase, and quotation to integrate the ideas of others into their own statement of meaning.

As is the case in our sample essay below, you will probably not use all of the notes you collect when you write your essay. You will be selecting the best statements, arranging them into coherent sequences, and integrating them into clear, connected sentences. The result will be an essay with a purpose and a sense of unity, not just a series of other people's ideas. Source material should not dominate your ideas or take over your paper; your ideas should always control the direction and shape of the writing.

The following sample synthesis is based on the readings from Casebook 1 and the notes that were reproduced earlier in this chapter in response to the question: "Is low voter turnout a problem, or not?" Read critically, underlining the generalizations and noting how each generalization is developed and supported. What did this writer learn from the readings?

Sample Student Writing: Synthesis, MLA Documentation Style

Voter Turnout: Is "Active Consent" Essential to Democracy?

Paula Johnson

Our Declaration of Independence asserts that it is not only our "right" but our "duty" to participate in the institution and alteration of our democratic governance structures. The signers of the Declaration established the assumptions that "all men are created equal, that they are endowed by their Creator with certain unalienable Rights, that among these are Life, Liberty and the pursuit of Happiness," and then they assign us, as citizens, the responsibility for insisting that our government protect these rights: "whenever any Form of Government becomes destructive of these ends, it is the Right of the People to alter or abolish it, and to institute new Government...."

According to Feldmann, the United States, seen as the archetype for democratic government throughout the world, has "chronically produced one of the lowest voter participation rates in the Western world." Richie and Hill note that "Bill Clinton was re-elected with the support of fewer than one in four eligible voters," a fact that raises the question "At what point does a democracy cease to be democratically governed?" Feldmann agrees, reflecting that "It hardly seems what the Founding Fathers had in mind 224 years ago when they set forth a blueprint for a new kind of representative government, one deriving 'just powers from the consent of the governed.'"

How bad is the record of voter turnout? Turnout for the presidential elections peaked in 1960 at 63%; in 1996, voter turnout was 49%; fewer than half of eligible voters participated (Feldmann). According to Richie and Hill, the general elections drew 30% of voters in Boston and San Francisco. They also documented some shocking percentages in local elections: In the 1997 governor's race in Virginia, registered voter turnout was 48%; if eligible but unregistered voters are counted, participation was 34%; the Broward County, Florida, elections that year drew 7% of registered voters, and Charlotte's primary election drew 6%. Does low voter turnout indicate that American democracy is at risk? Is voter turnout a fair measure of the health of our democracy?

Many would say yes, if we are to honor not just the words of the Declaration of Independence and the Constitution but also the efforts of leaders whose lives were dedicated to the protection of civil rights and women's rights, including the right to vote. Martin Luther King, in his speech "I Have a Dream," asserted that the right to vote must be extended to all citizens of the United States, because it is an essential component of freedom: "We can never be satisfied as long as a Negro in Mississippi cannot vote and a Negro in New York believes he has nothing for which to vote." Susan B. Anthony, justifying her illegal act of voting in 1872, asserted that the vote secures the blessings of liberty: "And it is a downright mockery to talk to women of their enjoyment of the blessings of liberty while they are denied the use of the only means of securing them provided by this democratic-republican government—the ballot" (152). Certainly, with this cultural heritage of assumptions regarding the significance of the vote to the concept of democracy, it is easy to understand how voter turnout can be seen as a thermometer of democratic health.

However, perhaps voting is not the only, or even the most necessary, measure of democratic health. There are other ways to assess political involvement. Although the "youth" age category (however it's defined) is often cited for their low turnout, David Pryor suggests that "young people do not feel that government and politicians are the best way of implementing change. For example, students are very active about volunteering and giving back to their community and country." In fact, he says, "85% of college students prefer community volunteerism to political involvement to solve issues in their community and 60% prefer it to solve important issues facing the country" ("One Expert's").

This notion that there are multiple ways to promote the health of a democracy is not just a youth phenomenon. Mark Mills is a good example. He "cares passionately about community issues. He calls local officials and writes letters to the editor about everything from school spending to local tax rates. Yet he rarely votes. Currently, he's not even registered" (Feldmann). But he is an activist: he makes an impact directly rather than voting for someone else to act.

Furthermore, his choice not to vote may relate to a key part of the American character. We want to be free to choose—to vote, or *not* to vote. As Rose notes, "Non-totalitarian societies, by definition, value what Sir Isaiah Berlin has described as 'freedom from the state.' Political participation need not be mandatory, and freedom usually includes the right not to vote." Americans resist following the lead of countries like Australia and Belgium, which have instituted laws making voting mandatory.

Why would people free to vote choose not to? Rose suggests that "The abnormally low turnout in the United States reflects archaic registration laws and, to a lesser extent, a history of effectively disenfranchising most blacks and many whites in the South." Some people are "so intimidated by the complexity of the issues involved that they don't vote almost out of respect for democracy" (Feldmann). After all, it can be a lot of work to prepare to vote responsibly, "namely, reading 'everything' about the issues and candidates...attending debates, etc. After reading everything, a fully informed person could then vote rationally"("Why People Don't"). Citing Anthony Downs' book <u>An Economic Theory of Democracy</u>, a Taipanonline editorial calls those who choose not to vote "free riders." "In a free rider, a person receives a benefit without absorbing the cost of receiving the benefit," a phenomenon described as "big deal." Finally, a decision not to vote made in the context of an organized boycott can be a political act with significant consequences, as when Northern Ireland's 1973 referendum on continued alliance with the United Kingdom precipitated a boycott by Catholics (Rose). Perhaps a democracy is healthier when only those who have bothered to read and reflect take responsibility for governance.

In fact, this may be the way American democracy has functioned—durably, if not perfectly—for a long time. Ruy Teixeira makes this argument, which is cited in Feldmann:

> Turnout now is not catastrophically lower than it
> was in 1960—63 percent—when government was
> viewed as more responsive....He also notes that turnout
> in most other major democracies has been dropping as
> well. Switzerland, the only country in the Organization
> for Economic Cooperation and Development with lower
> voter turnout than the US, has declined by 39
> percentage points since the 1950s.

Feldmann notes that low turnout may even be seen as a "sign of satisfaction with government." From that perspective, silence may be a form of consent—not active, but passive.

Despite the inclination of many to see low voter turnout as an indication that our democracy is ailing, it is a limited and confusing measure at best, because voting is not the only way to participate in a democracy and because non-voters may be expressing their satisfaction, or unpreparedness, or general lack of support, all of which are political messages. Certainly community activism helps to keep democracy healthy, and just as certainly, working to increase the participation of voters who are unprepared to make rational, informed decisions isn't necessarily beneficial to good governance. Nonetheless, our form of governance is based on the notion that all voices are necessary if a democracy is to be representative, and our vote is our voice. Attending to this discussion of the implications of voter turnout is one way to make sure our society continues to require government by our consent, a condition of democracy that we value highly.

Works Cited

Anthony, Susan B. "Constitutional Argument." <u>Elizabeth Cady Stanton/Susan B. Anthony: Correspondence, Writings, Speeches</u>. Ed. Ellen Carol DuBois. New York: Schocken Books, 1981.

Feldmann, Linda. "Why the Poll Booths of America Are Empty." 3 October 2000. <u>Christian Science Monitor Online</u>. 3 October 2001. <http://www.csmonitor.com/durable/2000/10/03/fp1s2-csm.shtml>.

United States. National Archives and Records Administration. Second Continental Congress. "The Declaration of Independence." Philadelphia, PA: 1776. 7 October 2001. <http://www.nara.gov/exhall/charters/declaration/declaration.html>.

"One Expert's Opinion on Election 2000: David Pryor Looks at the Youth Vote." Office of Communications and Public Affairs, Kennedy School of Government at Harvard University. 12 October 2001. <http://www.ksg.harvard.edu/news/experts/pryoryouthvote.htm>.

Ritchie, Rob, and Steven Hill. "The Dinosaur in the Living Room." The Center for Voting and Democracy. 1999. 14 October 2001. <http://www.fairvote.org/aboutus/index.html>.

Rose, Richard. "Evaluating Election Turnout." The Center for Voting and Democracy. 2000. 7 October 2001. <http://www.fairvote.org/aboutus/index.html>.

Ryan, Halford Ross. <u>Rhetoric from Roosevelt to Reagan: A Collection of Speeches and Critical Essays</u>. Prospect Heights: Waveland, 1983.

"Why People Don't Vote." Taipanonline. 10 October 2001. <http://www.taipanonline.com>.

Summarizing in an Essay

Sometimes a source presents an idea that you would like to include, but the original expression of that idea is too long or complex for your purposes—including it fully would take over the balanced presentation you want to make. Summarizing the idea—presenting just the key points in an abbreviated (but accurate) form—can help you integrate the idea smoothly and effectively.

You should use summary judiciously, because too much summary will make your paper sound as if you have done no more than repeat other people. Summarizing may also make the writing too general to be interesting. The length and specificity of a summary varies with your purpose: an entire article may be summarized in a key sentence or in a few paragraphs, depending on your need. Keep your purpose clearly in mind, but be careful not to change the intention of the source material.

Original source material:

> The freedom not to vote can be used by political opponents of a ballot to organize a boycott of voting. The purpose of an electoral boycott is for non-voters to show that the choice offered or the expected outcome is unacceptable to them; they thus reduce the legitimacy of the result. Contrary to Burnham's (1987: 99) assertion, "if you don't vote, you don't count," boycotters make withdrawing from participation a means of voicing their rejection of a ballot that they expect not to win (cf. Hirschman, 1970). In the closing days of the Soviet Union, when Moscow sought to bolster its legitimacy by organizing a pan-Soviet referendum, six republics officially boycotted the ballot and substituted their own questions on relations with Moscow.
>
> To be effective, a boycott must be organized. It can be backed up by patrolling outside polling stations on election day, so that anyone who turns out to vote has to publicly break ranks with the boycott. In Northern Ireland, there was an organized boycott of the 1973 referendum on whether Northern Ireland should remain part of the United Kingdom. Since voting on this issue follows communal religious lines, the Protestant majority was sure to carry the issue and keep Northern Ireland in the United Kingdom; to deny legitimacy to this outcome all Catholic political forces recommended boycotting the referendum. Among those who did vote, 98.9% favoured keeping Northern Ireland within the United Kingdom. But turnout was only 58.1% of the electorate, almost the same as the non-Catholic portion of the Ulster population. Catholic political leaders argued that they were not bound by the outcome because they had boycotted the ballot." (Rose)

As summarized in the sample synthesis:

> Finally, a decision not to vote made in the context of an organized boycott can be a political act with significant consequences, as when

Northern Ireland's 1973 referendum on continued alliance with the United Kingdom precipitated a boycott by Catholics.

Paraphrasing in an Essay

Paraphrasing is saying what someone else said, but in *your own words*. Paraphrasing allows you to share with your readers ideas you find compelling or necessary to your explanation. It is very like summarizing, but when you summarize, you condense a long passage, presenting only the key ideas in an order that suits your purpose, whereas when you paraphrase, you present all of the points in a short passage in the original order. In an essay about whether low voter turnout is a problem, you might get by with a one-sentence summary of Anthony Downs's idea of the "free rider," as explored in the Taipanonline article in Casebook 1. But if you are writing an essay about voter behavior, you may need to present a more specifically developed account of his idea, and for that you would need paraphrase. The Taipanonline article incorporates a paraphrase of an idea from Downs's *An Economic Theory of Democracy*:

> According to Downs, people who do not vote, don't vote on the basis of a rational, economic decision. The pin that holds Downs's theory together is the economic phenomenon known as the "free rider." In a free rider, a person receives a benefit without absorbing the cost of receiving the benefit. For example, let's say my neighborhood is collecting funds for a parade. My neighborhood is fairly large, so I know they'll get enough (without my money) to pay for the parade. Why would I contribute money (a cost) to enjoy a parade (a benefit) that I can watch regardless if I pay or don't pay? Strictly speaking, a person acting rationally wants to maximize benefits at a minimal cost…at no cost if possible.
>
> Well, as Downs argues, the same logic applies to voting. A person who wants to make a "rational decision" in a vote would absorb substantial costs. Namely, reading "everything" about the issues and candidates…attending debates, etc. After reading everything, a fully informed person could then vote rationally. But why do that? Especially when polls tell you who will most likely win. For instance, in October, Clinton held a strong 15-point lead. So why would a Clinton supporter—acting rationally—go to the polls knowing his vote really wouldn't make a difference? He'll receive the benefit without absorbing the cost of voting. Well, the answer is: Some people have different values when it comes to democracy. They view voting as their civic duty…regardless of the outcome. That's perfectly valid. But so is the person who doesn't vote.

Paraphrasing makes it possible to introduce the ideas of others naturally into your writing. But doing this can be difficult. One strategy used by writers is to read the original, then set it aside and imagine rephrasing the material to explain it to a friend. This can help you find ways to translate the ideas into your own voice and style.

When you use paraphrase, you must take care to be accurate. Paraphrasing is used to explain ideas to readers, but it is also a way to let them know that you have read responsibly, "done your homework," that you know what you are talking about. Read attentively. Be careful not to manipulate your reading to suit your own preconceived ideas.

Quoting in an Essay

Quotation is the most direct way to integrate the ideas of others into your writing. When you quote, you use the exact words of the source enclosed in quotation marks. Quoting exact words is easier than summarizing or paraphrasing them, but integrating the words of others into your own sentences and paragraphs smoothly and effectively can be difficult. Therefore good writers use quotation judiciously and for specific purposes.

Paraphrase and summary are preferable to quotation because they cause less interruption to the flow of the writing, but quotation is preferable when:

- The original words are more vivid and effective than any paraphrase. In this case, figurative language or well-crafted sentences can enhance the quality of your own work.

- You want to take exception to the original idea. When you want to distance yourself from another person's idea, using the writer's exact words helps you seem like a knowledgeable and credible critic.

- The authority of a particular source enhances your own. Introducing the words of a known expert helps you strongly support your ideas.

- The idea from the source is central to or critical to your reasoning, in which case using exact words lends a sense of precision and immediacy to your writing.

- An accurate understanding of your writing requires technical specificity— no other words will accurately represent the necessary ideas adequately, as in policy statements or laws.

The writer of the synthesis on voting demonstrated the two main ways you may introduce quotations from sources into written discussions. First, you can quote directly, separating the words of a source from your own statements within the context of a paragraph or sentence:

> In fact, this may be the way American democracy has
>
> functioned—durably, if not perfectly—for a long time. Ruy Teixeira
>
> makes this argument, which is cited in Feldmann:
>
>> Turnout now is not catastrophically lower than it
>>
>> was in 1960—63 percent—when government was
>>
>> viewed as more responsive....He also notes that turnout
>>
>> in most other major democracies has been dropping as

> well. Switzerland, the only country in the Organization
> for Economic Cooperation and Development with lower
> voter turnout than the US, has declined by 39
> percentage points since the 1950s.

Second, you may integrate quotations into your own sentences, using either the complete source sentence or only the part that you need:

> According to Feldmann, the United States, seen as the archetype for
> democratic government throughout the world, has "chronically produced
> one of the lowest voter participation rates in the Western world." Richie
> and Hill note that "Bill Clinton was re-elected with the support of fewer
> than one in four eligible voters," a fact that raises the question "At what
> point does a democracy cease to be democratically governed?"

Quoting isn't as easy as it may look. As a writer, you must clearly indicate where the words of your sources begin and end, you must quote accurately, and you must blend the voices of your sources smoothly into your own sentences and paragraphs so that your writing is readable. Fortunately for all of us, writers have developed a set of conventions for signaling and blending that will help us write about the words of others in effective ways.

- Surround exact words with double quotation marks: "Everything he told us," she argued, "was false."
- When you are using a quotation that contains a quotation, use single quotation marks for the inside quotation: "Everything he told us," she argued, "was false. I didn't believe him, even though he constantly shouted 'I've never lied, and I'm not lying now.'"
- When a complete sentence will be followed by a quotation, use a colon to separate your words from the source's: The juror's decision on the case was based heavily on the fact that she did not find the witness to be credible: "Everything he told us was false."
- Even though you often see quotations integrated into sentences preceded by commas, actually, the grammar of your sentence will determine whether you use a comma or not: The juror proclaimed, "Everything he told us was false." The juror explained that "the jury had to disregard the testimony."
- You may delete words from a quotation if you indicate to the reader that you have done so, and as long as you do not manipulate the original meaning. This can help your writing be more economical and forceful. To omit words, use the ellipsis, a series of *three* spaced dots (...). "Everything he told us," she argued, "was false...even though he constantly shouted 'I've never lied, and I'm not lying now.'" If the deleted portion comes at the end of the sentence, the three dots are preceded by a period: "Everything he told us," she argued, "was false. I didn't believe him. ..."

- You may also change or add things to a quotation, but again, you must indicate to the reader that you have done so, and this must be done without manipulating the original meaning, only to blend the ideas more effectively into your own sentences. Brackets are used to indicate change. You may correct an error in a quotation, replace a pronoun with its antecedent, or substitute a confusing word or phrase with a synonym that is more familiar: "Everything [Mr. Plum, the accused] told us [the jurors] was false."

- Punctuation: All commas and periods are placed inside the end quotation marks. All semicolons and colons are placed outside the end quotation marks. But exclamation marks and question marks may go inside or outside. If the quotation itself is a question or an exclamation, put the punctuation inside: The juror asked, "Is the witness reliable?" If you, the writer, are asking or exclaiming, put the punctuation outside: Will the jury consider the fact that "Everything he told us was false"? (It makes sense when you think about it as attributing both ideas and attitudes to the appropriate thinker!)

Avoid Plagiarism: Cite Your Sources

Plagiarism is using someone else's words or ideas without giving them credit. Plagiarism disrespects the people you are learning from, and it misrepresents your own learning process. It is quite unnecessary: there is no requirement that all the ideas in an academic essay be original. But there is an expectation that a writer will have gone through the mental process of relating and shaping, and contributing to, the ideas of others in a way that composes the writer's unique "sense" of things.

Sometimes plagiarism is simply theft, as in situations where people try to get college credit for NOT thinking or learning by purchasing or simply copying the work of others and submitting it as their own. Other times, though, people inadvertently plagiarize because they do not understand how to use source material properly. For example, some people think they need to cite a source only when they quote exact words, but summaries and paraphrases from sources must also be credited. Sometimes, too, careless note-taking, especially the omission of quotation marks around exact words, may result in plagiarism. Or a source may be so compelling to you that arguments or evidence you borrow from others may seem, as you draft and redraft, to have become your own. But you must be socially and ethically responsible—introduce your sources to your readers, just as if they had entered a conversation in which you were already speaking with your sources and it was up to you to make introductions.

To avoid plagiarism, remember to cite your sources carefully and fully. Use quotation marks correctly. Examine the casebook articles and the sample synthesis in this chapter for ways that writers can give credit to their sources.

The best textual representation of the title of our book is in the procedures for citing and documenting source material. When you look at pages of writing that include references to other sources, you can see in the parentheses, in the names or dates or page numbers, a conversation taking place among readers and writers. *Minds meet* in the connections among sentences and paragraphs. The procedures, precise as they are, represent no more than the rules of polite conversation in print.

When you refer on paper to someone else's idea, you can't nod your head or point in their direction, so you cite their work in the context of your words. You might be referring to their authority on an issue; you might be citing them to disagree with them, or because they explained an idea better than you believe you can; you might want to use what they said as an example of something you want to argue. In any case, they must be physically included in the conversation—to do otherwise is to insult and disrespect the other people whose voices have mattered in your search for understanding.

There are two reasons that writers might be tempted to be less responsible than necessary in giving credit to others for their words and ideas. First, when you are writing for class, it's easy to be tempted into thinking the writing doesn't matter because only the teacher will read it. To borrow others' ideas, in that case, is just that—borrowing. You aren't really using them for your own purposes. That's a problem because in all cases your writing should be valuable for *you*; it should represent authentic learning, regardless of the topic or situation. Borrowing words and ideas is also a form of theft. What if you attended a gathering to listen to a writer read one of her short stories, and you realized that the story had the precise plot outline of a movie you'd seen? Wouldn't you be insulted, even though the story line didn't belong to you? It's called plagiarism: failing to document the use of someone else's words or ideas, presenting them as your own.

Second, some writers seem to think that if they can't say anything original, they shouldn't bother to write, so sometimes they think that failing to give credit to others makes them look more original than they are. Please don't believe that. As we have said elsewhere in this book, we are all members of communities interested in shared questions. Let's take advantage of our mutual intelligence and energy. When we write in a learning or problem-solving or decision-making situation, we *should* do our homework, find out what others have learned or tried, and take that knowledge into account in our own critical thinking process. That's the smart thing to do. The way we select, arrange, relate, prioritize, and value the ideas of others to reach our own conclusions—that is our creative act.

As we explained in Chapter 6, disciplines of study have their own documentation styles. We use two in this book: the Modern Language Association (MLA) style and the American Psychological Association (APA) style. Guidelines for using these styles are presented in the Documentation Appendix. A basic familiarity with the reasoning behind and the strategies for MLA and APA styles should help you understand the rationale behind other forms. Several of the articles in the casebooks include documented source material, but for examples of applications of MLA and APA styles, see:

MLA: "Real Men Don't: Anti-Male Bias in English," by Eugene R. August, Casebook 3.

APA: "Gender Issues in Online Communications," by Lisa J. King, Casebook 3.

Read for Sense

Each time you put ideas together, they interact with each other. One complicates or clarifies another. As writers, we will make adjustments *constantly* as we draft, thinking and rethinking our ideas. However, it is always a good idea, after your ideas are aligned, to take some time away from your writing before you read it again, *as if you were seeing your ideas for the first time.* Check to see that your thesis statement accurately reflects the ideas represented in your essay without oversimplifying them. Check to see that each paragraph contributes to the paper's purpose and that each sentence contributes to each paragraph's development. Check to see that each supporting idea that originated with a source is accurately presented and that credit is given to the source. Finally, check your paragraphs, sentences, words, punctuation, and mechanics for clarity and effectiveness.

THE PRACTICAL VALUE OF SYNTHESIS

The synthesis is an amazingly valuable tool for several reasons. First, through synthesis, you can accommodate new ideas and *make them your own* by finding ways to make sense of them in relation to each other. Second, in this age of technology when more information is available to all of us than we can take in, the ability to discover questions, find relationships, and clearly and effectively connect ideas is an essential survival skill. Third, the emerging society is global: multinational, multidisciplinary, multicultural. We not only need to be able to see from several perspectives, but we also need to be able to find common ground among them if problems are to be solved.

In this chapter, we have asked you to suspend your judgment on an issue long enough to take into account what others think, feel, know, and believe. When people choose to vote or not to vote, they sometimes do so based on the degree to which they understand the issues they are being asked to decide. Practicing writing syntheses develops your ability to think through issues to clarify them for yourself, making them, as Einstein says, "as simple as possible, but not simpler." Thinking this way makes you feel confident that your ideas are grounded, fully considered, more than just your "own opinion"—a feeling of confidence that is part of what characterizes the educated person.

WRITING INVITATIONS

1. Read the articles on the topic of the English Only movement in Casebook 2. In groups or individually, compile a list of questions that are asked (directly or indirectly) or answered in various ways. Pick a question. Reread the most relevant articles for perspectives on the question and for possible answers, and take notes using quotation, paraphrase, and summary. Make a list of the answers to your

question that are presented in the reading. Then write a synthesis essay that combines the various perspectives into a clear, coherent statement regarding the strengths and weaknesses of possible answers to your question.

2. Interview a professor in another class you are taking about questions in his or her field of expertise that are currently being debated. Ask for the titles of available articles and books that relate to the question. Read them carefully and write a synthesis of possible answers.

3. Pay attention to news reports of a surprising event that provokes a strong public reaction, and carefully read different accounts from several sources for reasons why the event might have occurred. Note the names of experts who have opinions, and follow up on them at the library or on the Internet. In an essay, synthesize the perspectives in order to create a fuller, more complex picture of the event.

4. With classmates, brainstorm a list of events that have occurred in politics, music, film, technology, or another cultural area in the past year. Then write a synthesis that characterizes the trends or events of the year in a particular way, e.g., "The Gentrification of Heavy Metal," or "Discussions of Morals Return to Politics."

5. Reread the synthesis essay "Voter Turnout: Is 'Active Consent' Necessary to Democracy?" Evaluate its effectiveness by doing the following:

Find the statement that unifies the observations in the rest of the essay.

Find the guide sentences, repeated words and phrases (or their equivalents), and transition words in each paragraph. Are there places where reader cues are missing? Are there places where better reader cues could be substituted for clarity and effectiveness?

DEVELOPING A WRITING PROJECT

Return to the research proposal you wrote at the end of Chapter 6. Choose at least three readings from your working bibliography that represent different positions on the question you plan to address in your proposed research project. Using the strategies for synthesizing information, plan and draft a paper that synthesizes the multiple perspectives presented in the readings.

CHAPTER 8

Taking a Position: The Academic Argument

The opposite of a correct statement is a false statement.
But the opposite of a profound truth may well be another
profound truth.

Niels Bohr

If the aim of argumentation is always to act effectively on
minds, in order to make a judgment of its value we must not
lose sight of the quality of the minds which the argument has
succeeded in convincing.

Chaim Perelman and L. Olbrechts-Tyteca

ARGUMENT AND THE RHETORICAL TRIANGLE

The quotations above identify two of the central points we wish to make about arguing. First, you must see the position you wish to argue as one of two or more competing answers to a problem: as Niels Bohr says, we may have two opposing "truths." Second, arguments are addressed to readers, or listeners, who are interested in and knowledgeable about the question at issue. Both of these observations should remind you of discussions of the rhetorical triangle you have read throughout this book because you depend on your analysis of the rhetorical situation as you present answers to a question to others who share your concern and bring their understanding of the issue to the discussion.

Much of the writing we have discussed to this point has asked you to explore, respond, or account for the positions of other writers. As you have done so, you have identified the questions these writers have addressed and the ways they have supported their answers to those questions. As you responded and began researching issues, however, you began the process of taking a position of your own about a question at issue. This process involves seeing what question is at issue, exploring that question, studying what has been written about it, judging the positions that others have taken in light of your own analy-

KEY CONCEPT

The Academic Argument

An **academic argument** includes:

- A **position** on a question at issue.
- **Reasons** for the position.
- **Evidence** that supports the reasoning.
- A consideration of **other possible answers.**
- A **structure** that makes the argument compelling to knowledgeable, interested readers.

sis, and answering the question for yourself. This is not an easy task, but it is a challenging, exciting, and empowering one.

Writing an argument that is convincing will require that you do research to find appropriate evidence. In Chapters 6 and 7, we talked more about doing research; in this chapter we will be focusing more specifically on what it means to construct an essay that relies on that research to present and support an argument.

Learning to write arguments well is an important skill. In addition to preparing you to write the kinds of essays your instructors will assign in your college classes, this process will help you write letters to friends or relatives in which you justify a decision you have made or ask for advice or financial assistance. It will provide you the reasoning ability to compose effective letters to the editor of your local newspaper or your senator about community and national issues. It will also teach you skills that you will need if you wish to correspond with companies about products or services you have received. Before we discuss those contexts and others like them, though, we will begin by considering what should be an immediate concern for you as a student, and that is how to write the academic essay.

Argument and Your Stance

When instructors assign academic essays, they expect well-argued answers to significant questions at issue in the class. The question, they will say, must be a good one, the answer probable, the reasons compelling and well-supported, and the evidence appropriate and clearly illustrating the reasons. How can we help you do this well?

It may seem that such assignments simply test and evaluate your knowledge of the material of the class, and while that is certainly one part of any assignment, instructors assign essays that will enable you to be a part of the academic community. They hope you will engage in an inquiry so interesting that you have a real investment in the class. To have such an investment, you need to believe not only that the question is important, but also that you can write with some authority so that others who are interested will listen and take your opinions seriously. This means that you will need to determine your stance, or your position on the issue. In other words, an essay assignment is your opportunity to make the materials of the class your own. You do this by listening to all the positions presented in lectures, readings, and class discussions, then finding one issue in particular that you would like to study at greater length, or sometimes by responding in your own way to a question that the instructor has asked you to consider. The question should be one the class has explored, one that no one has definitively answered, or one with more than one possible answer that a community of experts in the field would consider reasonable.

Because an academic essay explores a question that has more than one possible answer, it requires you to investigate the problem from many different perspectives. Sometimes this inquiry will only require you to read a text very closely; other times you will need to read additional material. In any case, you will be studying many different aspects of the question and doing so in an open-minded way. As you study the question and read materials, you will be analyzing, sorting, judging, and considering different possible answers to your question—your answers and those of others. You will also be evaluating the material that will help you find reasons for those answers and judge their quality, and you will be determining how a reader or listener will judge their quality. Everything you do as you study the issue and plan your paper depends on your question and your knowledge of the relevant information, but your decisions also depend on what others think, say, and have said about the question and how you might discuss it with those people.

So, where might you begin? The strategy box "How to Write an Academic Argument" lists the basic steps.

 STRATEGY

How to Write an Academic Argument

Writing an academic paper requires you to think critically about a problem. To think critically, you will need to:

1. Develop a thesis statement.
2. Test the reasonableness of your thesis statement.
3. Use evidence to develop your argument.
4. Use reasoning to develop your argument.
5. Acknowledge honestly the value of alternate positions.
6. Shape your argument to support your position as the best alternative.
7. Read and revise for coherence.

DEVELOPING A THESIS STATEMENT

The first challenge in writing an academic paper is developing a thesis statement.

Begin with Good Questions

By now you know that we begin an inquiry because we have a question we wish to answer, and that we start with questions that are real ones. By real questions, we mean ones that we do not already have an answer for, or if we have an answer, it is a tentative or conditional one.

Why is it important that the question be a real one? If you begin with a position you already hold then do research that will support your original position, it is unlikely that you will look at the information you gather in an unbiased way. For example, if you begin a study believing that requiring businesses to pay a greater percentage of their employees' health care premiums will unfairly discriminate against small businesses, you are unlikely to consider whether there might be reasons for small businesses to pay their employees' insurance. On the other hand, if you begin your study in an open-minded way, willing to entertain various possible answers or willing to change your mind, you are attempting to find an answer to a question that you have not already answered. One way to make your question more open is to ask it in a way that does not require a yes or no answer. Instead of asking whether proposed health care legislation will unfairly discriminate against small businesses—in which case your answer will be either "Yes, it will" or "No, it won't"—you might ask what effects will result from the proposed law.

Beginning with an open question is important to any study because although all of us bring previous beliefs, prejudices, and assumptions to any study, being willing to change our minds makes it much more possible to conduct a true inquiry. As we explained earlier, identifying these prior beliefs is an important part of our initial exploration. We begin an open inquiry by identifying these previous beliefs and what other people who have different answers

KEY CONCEPT

A Thesis Statement

A **thesis statement** includes two parts:

1. Your **position** on the issue you are exploring. Your position will be an answer to the question you are exploring.

2. A **reason** for your position. Your reason should provide your reader a justification for considering your answer a valid one.

might say in response so that we might consider all plausible answers and the reasons for believing them. We consider what we already know about the issue and what more we need to learn to come up with a better answer to the question, and we consider the implications of various answers.

The question you study for an academic essay also needs to be an issue in the field you are studying. You are entering into a conversation whenever you write an argument, and entering a conversation means that you need to consider what concerns you share with others in the community. As you listen in discussions or to a lecture or read assigned material, you will notice that people disagree on why some events happened or how something might be interpreted. One way to identify issues that might lead to interesting and productive studies is to keep a record in your class notebook of controversies that the professor identifies for you or that you identify yourself as you read. Or, when you have questions about the material of a class, you may notice whether your question is one that the books and articles address. If they do, the question is at issue; if they don't, you will need to ask your instructor whether the question is one that is worthy of study.

Another way to identify questions at issue in the courses you take is to read the introductions to essays or chapters in the assigned books. Academic writing typically begins with the issue the author is addressing and why it is significant and controversial. This does not mean that the writer begins with a simple statement of the question but rather that he or she focuses the reader's attention on the issue.

■ APPLICATION

Beginning with Good Questions

Read and evaluate the following questions. Do you think they are good places to begin a study? Why or why not? If not, how might you reword each question so that it might lead to a productive inquiry?

1. What is the difference between the ways that men and women communicate?
2. Should all citizens vote?
3. Do laws requiring English to be the language of instruction in public schools lead to a loss of ethnic diversity in our society?
4. Why don't people vote?
5. Are the differences between the ways men and women communicate inherent or learned?

Analyze Your Question

Having spent some time exploring your early responses to questions, you will move on to a more analytical part of your study. We have discussed analysis a number of times before—we have analyzed rhetorical situations and authors' rhetorical choices, and we have looked carefully at ways writers begin their essays and the ways the details they include reveal their assumptions. When you begin an academic study, you will be using a similar process, but now your focus is on your own question and its implications.

It may seem an obvious point, but you need information to answer a question. It is far too easy when writing a thesis statement to record your initial reaction or simply repeat what you have heard others say. To avoid such a response, you need to see your question as one that obligates you to consider information that would help you answer it in a more complex and responsible way.

Most of us participate frequently in discussions that require us to consider the experiences and opinions of others. We hear a news report and state our approval or disapproval of the commentator's position, or we leave a class and comment on how fair or unfair an assignment is, or we express our enthusiasm or disgust for a movie we have seen. Typically, we do so when we are in the company of others who then either agree or disagree with our opinions. When this happens, the discussion that follows requires us to think about what information and evidence we have for our opinions and why our positions differ from other people's.

When you are writing papers, your initial inquiries should be as natural as these everyday conversations. And yet, students rarely think of them that way. Writing a paper about a question that truly interests you can be an exciting and satisfying—though not necessarily easy—experience. When you begin with a real question, examine details that tell you more about the question, and know that others have different opinions about possible answers to the question, you will find that you enjoy discussing those differences, whether you do so in face-to-face conversations or on paper

Where to begin your analysis of your question? You might begin by writing an exploration of the question. As you do so, you will find yourself repeating certain terms and ideas, and so a place to begin your analysis is with the key terms you choose. These terms are the words that suggest the shape and direction of your study. Finding these key terms will help you determine what further research you need to fill in gaps in your knowledge.

In the following example, a student began exploring the problem of the rising cost of textbooks in the student bookstore. We have marked sets of repeated or related words with italics, bold font, and underlining. As the markings indicate, this student is concerned with not only the cost of the textbooks but how that cost affects a student's motivation to make the effort to return to school. The words that are underlined have to do with the costs, the subject of her exploration. The words in bold font concern her emotional response to having to pay so much for books. This response is the result of the costs. The word *form* is in italics because she repeats it several times, yet you will notice that forms or other entry issues disappear after the opening section of the paper.

Sample Student Writing: Exploration

The Problem of Textbook Prices

Lisa Dell Vandever

When I was 18 years old, I made a poor attempt to inquire about admission to a local college. I remember being handed what I believed to be an enormous stack of *forms* and told to fill all of them out. I slipped over to the library with every intention to do as asked, but after a few moments of consideration I tossed the *forms* in the trash. I was in no way **prepared** or **motivated** enough to attend college.

A few years later I found I was more **prepared** and **motivated**, thanks mostly in part to the "dress-right-dress" mentality of the Army. After being stationed in Seoul, South Korea, I found myself faced with a unique opportunity: tuition assistance. This meant that the Army paid 75% of my tuition and I paid 25% and the <u>cost</u> of books. Since I was in Korea I had few expenses so this opportunity fit well into my budget. Although I was limited to the amount of classes I could take, I was very **enthusiastic** about the challenges college offered me. While in the Army I was able to accumulate 21 transferable semester hours.

After my discharge from the Army I was still **motivated** and wanted very much to finish my degree. I had contributed my required <u>$1200</u> to the Montgomery GI Bill and knew that the opportunity to return to college was there. Most people falsely believe that the GI Bill pays for all of a veteran's education. Wrong! I was appalled to find out that the GI Bill would only pay me <u>$536</u> a month to supplement my <u>income</u> while I attended school. Since I was no longer considered a dependent and I had accumulated some <u>debt</u>, which added to my other day-to-day <u>living expenses</u>, my opportunity no longer looked so **appealing**. Again I found myself handed an enormous stack of *forms* and asked to fill them out. This time I was prepared and did not throw them in the trash. I had been working two jobs before the fall term started and was frightened by the fact that I still did not have enough money to purchase books, pay the electric bill, and buy groceries. Embarrassed but **motivated**, I went to the student financial office and begged for an advance on my loans. It would be another 8 weeks before my monthly GI Bill payments would kick in and I was feeling very desperate.

I have never understood the high cost of textbooks. I have worked in and managed a few bookstores while I have trudged my way through college and cannot comprehend why there is such a huge difference in prices. Even today, after two more colleges and much more knowledge on the college admission process, I still find myself robbing Peter to pay Paul when it comes to my textbooks. I am often **angry** and **frustrated** with the "powers-that-be" in academia. There are quite a few of us that are **willing** and **motivated** to continue our education, but that one major speed bump (textbook prices) often leaves us tapped out. In my experience I have found that loans, grants, and stipends don't usually kick in until after the term has started, and so it is senseless to rely on them as an immediate source for textbook purchasing.

I have been in and out of college for the last eleven years and if all goes well, I will only have another three to go before I get my bachelor's degree. I often work up to three jobs at a time in order to pay for another year of tuition and books. I hate to **complain** but I am **tired**, physically and emotionally. Fall term is nearing and I have two more textbooks to purchase, one $75 and the other $15. It may not sound like much, but my auto insurance just went up and my dog needs an eye operation. Now I get to decide who is Peter and who is Paul.

Writing an exploration such as this one will help you identify the question you wish to explore. Noting her key terms should help this student recognize that her major concern is how the cost of textbooks affects students who are on a limited income.

When you identify your key terms, you also may find that your original question is not the one you are really interested in exploring. You might find yourself saying, "Is that what I really want to ask?" Or "Somehow that isn't quite what I wanted to know." The student who was concerned with the price of textbooks began her research by considering ways to deal with the rising cost

APPLICATION

Analyzing Questions

Read the sample student exploration titled "Gridlock," about traffic congestion in the city of Denver, Colorado. As you read it, mark key terms and then
identify at least one question this student might wish to address in an argument essay. What kind of question is it (fact; definition; circumstance or
cause and effect; policy; value)?

of textbooks, but after exploring her response, she might have realized that she
was far more interested in how students on a limited income deal with the
problem. When this happens you may need to reword your question. One way
to do so is to determine what kind of question you wish to address. Using the
stasis questions we discussed in Chapter 5 can help you do this. You will recall
that we listed five major questions:

1. Questions of **fact:** Is it true? Did it happen?
2. Questions of **definition:** What is it?
3. Questions of **circumstance** or **cause and effect:** What will result from it?
   Why did it happen?
4. Questions of **policy:** What should be done about it?
5. Questions of **value:** Is it good or bad?

The student whose exploration we just examined shifted her question from
one of policy—What should be done about the high cost of textbooks—to one
of cause and effect—How will textbook costs affect students on a limited income.

Sample Student Writing: Exploration

The following paper was written as an exploration of the problem of traffic
congestion in Denver, Colorado.

Gridlock

Mattie McDowell

Last month, my roommate asked me to drive her to the airport so

that she could fly to Pittsburgh for a friend's wedding. Her flight was

leaving at 5 o'clock so we decided we should leave campus by 3. We

thought an hour should give us enough time to get to the airport so that she would be able to check in an hour before her flight. When we took the on-ramp to I-25, it was ten minutes before 3. A breeze, I thought. But I had never driven to the airport in the afternoon. When I arrived for school in September, it was early morning and I didn't notice the traffic. We reached the exit to I-70 by 3:15. Okay, I thought, this is going to be fine. I started to relax, but only moments later, I hit it. Gridlock. The traffic just stopped then inched forward. 3:20. 3:25. 3:30. I was starting to sweat. My roommate kept assuring me that everything was fine, but by 3:40, I could begin to hear the panic in her voice. We were stuck in gridlock for 40 minutes. When we got to the airport, she jumped out of the car and ran for her flight. She made it, but what a royal pain. If this can happen at 3 on a weekday afternoon, what must it be like at 5? I'd always heard that Denver's traffic was terrible but I've never been caught in the middle of it. So I started thinking: What's the problem? Why can't a city that has lots of money and pretty good public services and a great climate find a solution to the problem of gridlock?

I grew up in Cleveland. It's kind of a poor city and has pretty nasty weather. But you can get to the airport using public transportation and you can be there in less than an hour, even if you are coming from the other side of the city! The rapid transit, which is what they call their light rail in Cleveland, isn't as good as the subway in New York or the "L" in Chicago, but still, it's something.

I know Denver has busses, but I never take them. Everyone tells me that you have to wait 30 minutes for a bus sometimes, and if you want to take a bus to the airport, you have to go all the way downtown on one bus then take another to the airport. If you have to wait for almost 30 minutes here then wait again downtown and still get stuck in traffic on the freeway when you get on the airport bus, that sounds like it would be even worse.

Why doesn't Denver have light rail to the airport? The west seems like a great place for railroads. I remember reading lots of stories about people taking the train west. So there must be tracks. I guess there are a couple of small routes in the city, one near downtown and one from downtown directly south. And someone told me that they're going to build another line south, but that seems pretty weird. I mean I know that traffic is pretty heavy going south because lots of people live in the southern suburbs, and there's gridlock there too. But a fast and easy way to get to the airport, which is northeast of the city, seems really important.

I heard that there was a vote on a ballot measure that would have added an east-west light rail line. It's hard for me to figure out why anyone would vote against a train to the airport. Maybe they think it would be too expensive or that people wouldn't use it or maybe that some other projects are more important. Some of my friends who are from the west tell me that people love their cars today the way cowboys loved their horses in the old days. Guess I need to see whether light rail has been on the ballot in the area and I could read letters written to the editors of the local newspapers.

I think this is a pretty important problem and should be interesting to study.

Write Your Answer as a Thesis Statement

In our everyday conversations we answer questions by saying things like, "I can't go out tonight because I have a paper to write." When you do so, you are answering the question "Why can't you go out" by implying that when you have an important assignment, you can't take the time off to socialize. Or you say, "The university needs to build a new parking lot because it has so many commuters" in answer to a question like "Why should the university build a new parking lot?" When you do so, you suggest that a school with a great number of commuters must have sufficient parking. In both these instances, you state a position (or make an assertion or claim), give a reason, and assume that your listener agrees with the assumption behind your reasoning. What you have done informally is construct a line of argument, or what we call an enthymeme. *Enthymeme* is a word that the philosopher Aristotle used for rhetorical arguments, or arguments appropriate in situations where we consider the merits of more than one good answer. An enthymeme represents a way of demonstrating the reasoning behind a position. The word means something like "to the heart," so we might say that when we argue about a controversial issue, we need to argue in a way that asks readers to take our reasoning to heart, to consider it well.

We use enthymematic reasoning to shape arguments by finding a place to begin that readers will accept. This place may be an assumption about an issue, an attitude toward the subject, or shared values concerning the issue. This assumption or attitude will help you construct an argument that gives readers good reasons for accepting your conclusion. In other words, when your readers identify an assumption or values they share with you, they will be more sympathetic to your reasoning.

When you identify the enthymeme that represents the heart of your argument, you have begun developing what we may now call a thesis statement. You may have heard the term *thesis* used to name the sentence that ties a paper together, your statement of purpose. Thesis statements can serve that function when papers are straightforward enough to follow entirely from one position and one or more main reasons. But as your ideas become more complicated, you may find that you need to incorporate several related ideas into the development of a paper with a single, unifying purpose. This makes it important to understand the components of a thesis statement.

We use the classical term enthymeme for this process because the kind of thesis statement we are asking you to write includes your position and reason. The student writing on textbook costs might argue: "High textbook prices may decrease the enrollment of low-income students because such costs lead to those students feeling anger and frustration at the institution." The first clause represents her assertion, and the second clause gives her reason for believing it. Implied in the argument is that when low-income students feel anger and frustration at the institution, they are less likely to enroll.

Before trying to construct your own thesis statements, look at the following examples. Each thesis statement includes an assertion and a reason.

The accused are not guilty because they did not commit the act.

The accused are not guilty because they were following international law.

The assertion and reason for believing it are stated as two clauses. Each clause names a **subject** and then makes an assertion about the subject, called

KEY CONCEPT

The Enthymeme

An **enthymeme** is an argument that includes a position on a question at issue and reasons for accepting the position. The enthymeme connects the position and reasons by identifying assumptions or values shared by the writer and the audience.

the **predicate.** The subject of the thesis is "the accused," and what the attorney wants to argue is (1) that the accused is not guilty or deserves lenient treatment, and (2) the reason the attorney wishes the jury to accept that position.

Both the position and the reason give information about the same subject ("they" refers to "the accused"). In everyday conversations, few of us state our opinions in this formal way, repeating the subject in both our assertion and reason. Rarely do you hear someone say something in conversation like "A light rail line to the airport is necessary because light rail would provide fast and efficient transportation." Yet, while we rarely speak this way, restating arguments in such a focused way allows us to see the reasoning process clearly.

Identify the Assumption Behind Your Reason

Writing our position in the form of a thesis statement helps us to see whether our reasoning makes sense because it allows us to discover the assumption which links our position with our reasons. It also shows us how those assumptions control our line of reasoning. If we can identify our assumptions, we can decide whether the argument might be convincing to the people listening or reading it, because they will only accept arguments based on shared assumptions. As we said in Chapter 4, between the position and the reason is a link—an assumption—that readers must share with writers if there is to be a meeting of minds. In the example "The accused are not guilty because they did not commit the act," we assume whoever hears the argument will agree that someone who has not committed an act should not be found guilty of doing so.

 APPLICATION

Writing Answers as Thesis Statements

Read the following thesis statements, then identify the assertion and the reason for believing it. Underline the assertion once and the reason twice. Then find the subject of each clause of the thesis statement. Are the subjects of the assertion and the reason the same? If not, reword them so that they are.

1. The light rail system should not be built because people are opposed to raising sale taxes.
2. The light rail system must rely on increased taxes because it will be efficient only if rates are kept low.
3. The college bookstore should offer a discount to low-income students because they are living on a limited income.
4. Low-income students should have a discount card to use at the college bookstore because they are living on a limited income.

One way to find assumptions is to diagram thesis statements so that the subject of both the assertion and the reason are the same, as we did in the examples listed above. The assumption then shows the relationship between the assertion and the reason, as we see in the following example.

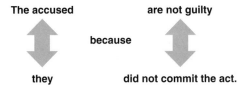

The accused   **are not guilty**

because

they   **did not commit the act.**

Assumption: Someone who did not
commit the act is not guilty.

In this example, the subject of the assertion ("the accused") and the subject of the reason ("they") refer to the same people. The two claims the lawyer makes about the subject, that they are not guilty, and that they did not commit the act, are related by the assumption that someone who did not commit the act is not guilty.

Usually, we make observations that hide the claims they imply. In fact we rarely speak in neat, carefully linked thesis statements like the ones we have been discussing. In everyday conversations, we make claims and imply reasons, but we can translate these implied arguments into enthymemes that allow us to find the claims, reasons, and assumptions. Both authors of this book are English teachers and have often heard people say that they will have to watch their grammar when they are speaking with us. Without directly saying so, these people are suggesting the following lines of argument about us:

(Assertion) You will judge me according to the grammar I use

because

(Reason) you are an English teacher.

A diagram of the position and reason would look like this:

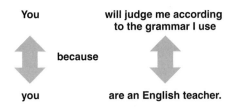

You   **will judge me according
to the grammar I use**

because

you   **are an English teacher.**

Assumption: All English teachers judge others
according to the grammar people use.

When you diagram thesis sentences so that the subject of both the claim and the reason are the same, you can see how the predicates are related. The underlying assumption reveals the relationship between the two parts. When people say they will have to watch their grammar when they speak to us, they assume that we agree with their idea of what all English teachers are like, and therefore will agree that they should watch their grammar when they talk to us. (By the way, we don't agree with the assumption!)

When we write thesis statements in such a simple and straightforward manner, we should be able to see what assumptions they imply, and yet, as the last example showed, arguments are often expressed in less direct ways. Restating them as sentences with the position and the reason having the same subject allows us to decipher implied positions and discover the assumptions beneath them. For practice, complete the exercise in the "Finding Assumptions" application box.

What did you notice when you found the assumptions behind the arguments in the "Finding Assumptions" application exercise? Were the assumptions ones that you accepted? Often we discover that seeing the assumption allows us to test how strong or convincing an argument might be. For example, not all listeners would agree with the argument in number 5, that professors who have advanced knowledge of a field ought to lecture more. Some people think that knowing a field well might allow a professor to plan classes that would lead students to find information and answers for themselves, that doing so may teach the field better than relying only on lecturing.

 APPLICATION

Finding Assumptions

Read the following lines of argument, which have been written with the subject of the assertion and the reason being the same. Identify the predicates of the two clauses. Draw a diagram that shows the relationship between the two predicates and express that relationship as an assumption that links the predicates.

1. The school parking policy is a problem because it has too few passes for the number of commuters.

2. All citizens ought to vote because they have a vested interest in the public policies on the ballot.

3. The college ought to build a new science building because it is attracting so many students who wish to major in biology, chemistry, and astronomy.

4. Students ought to take an advanced writing course in their majors because they need to learn the language conventions of their discipline.

5. My history professor should lecture more because he has the advanced knowledge of the field.

You also may have noticed that the assertion, or thesis, is an answer to a question. The argument in number 3, for example, answers the question "Why should the college build a new science building?" We have said before that we write essays in response to questions that we are interested in exploring, and that we attempt to answer these questions by engaging in some kind of study, either extensive research or simply careful analysis. The argument essay is our answer after we have completed our study.

TESTING YOUR THESIS STATEMENT

Testing how reasonable your thesis is happens in an ongoing, developmental way as you reflect on your personal experience, the experiences of others who have spoken or written about your question, and the information you have acquired from your research. This kind of reflection should make you look at the question from another point of view, and doing so will help you see the complexity of the issue.

Discuss Your Thesis with Others Interested in the Issue

As you probably know, one of the best ways to clarify your ideas is to talk with others. Seeing an issue through someone else's eyes, either through direct discussion or through reading an argument that differs from your own, forces you to consider other possible answers and, in addition, other aspects of the question you might not have considered in your initial response.

Sometimes writers in college forget how helpful, even essential, this interaction can be. The student who was studying the light rail system in Denver, for example, might look at articles published in the local paper

 STRATEGY

How to Test the Reasoning of Your Thesis Statement

As you examine your thesis statement, ask yourself the following questions:

1. Does your position answer a question at issue?
2. Is it stated as a complete clause?
3. Have you given your reason as a because clause that has the same subject as your position?
4. Does the relationship between your position and reason imply an assumption that you think your reader also knows or believes?

about the question. If she does so, she might find articles that argue that the transit system could not be extended without changing the system's taxing district, or that an extended system would require a significant sales tax increase, or that the governor of the state opposes putting the proposal on the state's ballot because he opposes all tax increases, or that without raising taxes, the transit fares will drive riders away. Such arguments should make this student return to her original exploratory essay to decide whether she still supports extending the light rail system and, if so, how she might present an argument that would address the concerns of those who oppose such a change.

Engaging in dialogue with someone who challenges your position will help you judge the strengths of your inquiry process. There are many ways to engage in such dialogue. You may do so in out-of-class meetings or in the classroom in writing groups or thesis workshops. You may also write responses to each other's papers. However you proceed, your objective is to engage in discussion about the ideas raised by the writer. If you disagree, explore your differences by identifying the question you have answered, by defining your key terms, by acknowledging your assumptions, and by looking at evidence you have collected. In this stage of the critical reasoning process, the key is to keep an open mind. Test your prior knowledge against what you have learned, and change your question and your inquiry to reflect your learning.

An important way to test the strength of your reasoning is by determining whether it would be acceptable to a dissenting audience. If you are working in a group setting, this assessment is fairly easy. You can simply ask those who disagree with your conclusion whether they would accept your assumption. If you are working alone, you will have to imagine your opposition. If you determine that you have an assumption your audience does not share, you will have to reshape your thesis so that it depends on an assumption that your audience will accept, or determine how you will address and support the assumption in the context of your argument.

SUPPORTING YOUR THESIS STATEMENT

You support your thesis statement through the reasoning you offer your readers and through the evidence you provide for your argument.

Support Your Thesis with Reasoning

There are two major kinds of reasoning: induction and deduction. When you use an inductive reasoning process, you draw general conclusions from an examination of specific incidents. If, for example, you wanted to find out whether a light rail system from downtown Denver to the airport would solve some of the city's traffic problems, you might examine a few other cities of comparable size that have such light rail systems. If you discover that in each case the traffic to the airport decreases significantly, you might generalize that building a light rail system to airports decreases traffic gridlock in medium to large cities.

The tests we typically use to determine whether an inductive study is reasonable are "Have you looked at enough examples?" and "Are the examples representative of the material you are examining?" In this case you would probably conclude that you looked at enough examples, but you might wonder whether your sample was representative. To answer this question, you would need to determine whether the cities you compared had similar traffic problems, reliance on cars as the major mode of transportation, and so forth. There are no special rules for how many or how representative your examples are when you write academic essays. Your guide will always be whether you think your reader will find the numbers and kinds of examples compelling and persuasive.

Unlike inductive reasoning, deductive arguments move from the general to the specific. If you begin with a generally held belief to a specific case, you are arguing deductively. To return to the traffic problem, you might begin with a study conducted by a major research institute that indicates light rail systems are cost-effective ways to reduce traffic problems in major cities. You could use this generalization to argue that a light rail system would be a cost-effective way for a major city like Denver to reduce its traffic problem. While this may be a reasonable argument, it will be effective only if the reader agrees that the institution conducts valid studies, that there is a traffic problem in Denver that needs solving, and that Denver is a major city.

Support Your Argument with Evidence

Just as you consider who will be reading your essay as you choose the reasons you give for your position, you also must think about your reader as you decide what evidence will support your argument. When you are writing an academic essay, you will be relying on the careful and responsible research you have conducted. This is essential because you are now writing for an

 KEY CONCEPT

Evidence

Evidence is the support you give for the claims you make when you take positions. It may include facts, studies, and the opinions of authorities.

expert audience. Your argument will be demonstrating your knowledge of the material as you contribute to the ongoing conversation in your discourse community.

The most difficult part of writing an academic essay is balancing your own stance with the information you have gathered from your research. You may have had the experience of writing a research paper that was nothing but a report on "the state of the research on an issue." This is an important stage of the research process and one we discussed when we talked about synthesis papers in Chapter 7. When you write an academic essay, however, you need to go beyond this report, to make the material your own. You need to present your own opinion but demonstrate that it is an informed opinion and thus one that is worthy of consideration by others in the field.

When you are considering what evidence to offer as support for your argument, review the questions in the strategy box "How to Test Evidence."

 ## STRATEGY

How to Test Evidence

Before choosing what evidence you will use, ask yourself whether it is:

- **Relevant:** Is it directly related to the claim it is supporting?
- **Credible:** Would experts in the field recognize it as evidence?
- **Timely:** Does it represent the most recent thinking on the question?
- **Reliable:** Is it from a source that has been credible in the past?
- **Unbiased:** Does it fairly access the information generally accepted in the field?
- **Consistent:** Does it support the information generally accepted in the field? If it doesn't, does it provide justification for the difference?

 ## APPLICATION

Testing Evidence

Read Mattie McDowell's draft argument essay, "An Answer to Gridlock." Use the questions in the "How to Test Evidence" strategy box to discuss whether this essay would be an effective argument for an audience of taxpayers in the city of Denver.

Sample Student Writing: Draft of an Argument Essay, MLA Documentation Style

The following essay was written by the student who wrote the exploratory essay on Denver gridlock.

▬▬▬

An Answer to Gridlock

Mattie McDowell

The Denver International Airport, DIA, is located about 35 minutes from downtown. To get there, people in Denver must travel by car, taxi, limousine, or bus. Drivers enter the airport on a 10-mile highway, accessible by only two major highways. Every day from 5 a.m. until early evening, the roads leading to this airport highway are heavily used. In rush hours—weekdays from 6 a.m. until 9:30 and 3:30 p.m. until 7—they become like long parking lots. Cars creep along at five to ten miles an hour, their drivers hot behind the wheel and under their collars. In other major cities such as New York, Boston, Chicago, San Francisco, even Cleveland, residents may hop on a train that whisks them to the airport out of traffic and the headaches associated with gridlock. But Denver, a city with a population over half a million and an airport with about 1,300 flights daily (Denver), has no light rail line to the airport. And, despite the gridlock, the state has repeatedly refused to build such a line. Currently, though, a new proposal shows promise. What will it take to convince the voters in the area and their representatives in the State Congress and Regional Transportation Board that the time has come to break up the gridlock?

In 1994, Denver built its first light rail line, called the Central Corridor Light Rail System (Regional). It ran through downtown and approximately 15 blocks north and about 4 miles south. In 2000, the original line was extended 10 miles to the southeastern suburbs and in 2001 a new line in the downtown area was added. The new southeastern corridor has been a great success. According to Cal Marsella, General Manager of the Regional Transportation District, "When planned, that portion of the light-rail system was projected to provide 8,400 rides per weekday. It opened with more than 14,000 riders per day and now averages some 17,000 riders per day. On the entire light-rail system, which now includes the Southwest line and the original Central Corridor line, we are carrying nearly 35,000 riders per day" (Marsella).

Despite the success of the new lines, a new proposal called FasTracks for extending the light rail system is not receiving the public support one might expect. Today, the Regional Transit District is asking for an increase in sales tax for six new lines that would cost about $4.7 million. This would mean a tax of 4 cents on each $10 purchase, making the transportation tax 1 percent, "a penny on every dollar's purchase" (Leib "RTD"). But the measure probably won't be on the November ballot. According to Marsella, "The Regional Transportation District is considering a delay for a FasTracks vote because a private poll shows the ballot measure might have trouble passing as one of the few items on the November 2003 ballot" (qtd. in Leib "Public"). It seems that the city is in the same place it was in 1997 when voters defeated a tax hike for an expansion of the system. At that time, the arguments against the extension were that the tax was too high and the new lines would not "necessarily reduce traffic" (Young).

Voters need to weigh a one-percent tax for transportation against the efficiency of a light rail system. To be efficient, the system must be less expensive and faster than driving. If it is, then people will use the system.

Today the evidence is strong that people are riding the new lines. It's hard to argue against 35,000 riders a day on one line. They do so, presumably because the light rail ride takes almost half as long during rush hour as the car commute would take (Marsella). If the time saving is the same to the airport, what today may take a driver up to an hour during rush hour on the highway would take no longer than 30 minutes.

Another reason people may be using the southeastern line to commute may be because parking downtown now costs at least $1.50 an hour ("Hair"), compared to a $5.00 round trip ticket on light rail, or $70.00 monthly pass. Parking at DIA now costs $2.00 an hour or, in the economy lot, $7.00 a day. That's at least a $2.00 savings for every trip.

Perhaps the voters need to take a second look. A system that saves time and money and costs less than a quart of milk every time we go shopping might not only save the time and money but also the headaches of sitting on the highway wondering whether you will make your flight.

Works Cited

Denver International Airport Page. 9 July 2002
    <http://www.cuug.ab.ca:8001/~busew/dia.html>.

"Hair of the Dog." The Denver Post Online. 19 May 2002
    <http://www.denverpost.com>.

Leib, Jeffrey. "Public May Lack Appetite for New Rail in '03, Poll Says."
    The Denver Post Online. 8 July 2002
    <http://www.denverpost.com>.

———. "RTD Sales Tax Vote May Be Pushed to '04." The Denver Post
    Online. 8 July 2002 <http://www.denverpost.com>.

Marsella, Cal. "FasTracks? Why Now?" The Denver Post Online. 24
    February 2002 <http://www.denverpost.com>.

Regional Transportation District Home Page. 9 July 2002
    <http://www.rtd-denver.com/>.

Young, Ricky. "Campaign Near Road's End: Foes Air Drive-Time Radio
    Spots." The Denver Post Online. 31 October 1997
    <http://www.denverpost.com>.

CONSTRUCTING YOUR ARGUMENT ESSAY

An important part of using evidence is explaining how the evidence supports your argument. All too often students will include information or quotations from experts in an argument essay without any explanation of the connection between the evidence and the claim it is supporting. These connections do not have to be lengthy but they are necessary if you wish your reader to follow your reasoning.

Other elements of constructing your argument essay include acknowledging other positions on the question, shaping your argument, and reviewing your essay for coherence.

Acknowledge Honestly the Value of Alternate Positions

Throughout this chapter, we have been saying that the rhetorical situation affects all the decisions we make as we begin a study, that we share questions with others, that we need to consider the different positions others hold and compare them with our own, that we will shape our argument in a way that takes into account these other positions by finding shared assumptions.

It is also the case that our consideration of others' positions will affect the inquiry we conduct. We are not out searching for information that will contradict others. Instead, we are thinking about the kinds of arguments we use to compel others to consider our lines of reasoning.

You begin your initial exploration by considering your own response: what you know, what you think, what experiences you have had, what you have heard. Let's say that you are studying the Electoral College. You decide that your initial question is a policy one—whether a constitutional amendment ought to be passed that would modify or abolish the Electoral College. Whether you argue any one of three positions—that it ought to be abolished or retained or modified—you need to consider the responses of others. What value judgments would others bring to the discussion? What emotional judgments? What reasons would they consider valid? Your answer to these questions would probably help shape the inquiry.

As you examine the possible value systems evoked by people who wish to retain the Electoral College, you discover that they value the Constitution and find the American system of checks and balances to be not only effective but also representative of a great experiment in democracy and republicanism. Such people believe that the Constitution should be amended only in extreme cases of constitutional crisis. Discovering this attitude might lead you to a study of whether the problems in the 2000 presidential election represent a constitutional crisis, an exploration leading to a logical appeal. On the other hand, it might lead you to a study of the value of the great experiment and how the Electoral College represents the unique system of checks and balances, an exploration that might lead you to an ethical and probably an emotional appeal. In any case, knowing the value system and emotional responses of people interested in the question can be just as productive for your research as knowing what kinds of reasoning process they might accept.

When you construct arguments, you take on a certain responsibility. To argue is not to manipulate or pull the wool over someone's eyes. Rather, it is to give your audience good reasons to consider your position. Arguing this way differs significantly from the manipulation of political or commercial advertising or the spin of news shows' "talking heads" who tell us how to interpret current events. Such commercials, advertisements, and political statements include little proof. Often advertisers simply assert positions. A political ad may claim that a candidate ought to be elected because she has a plan for protecting Social Security, without explaining the plan or why it would be a good one. A commercial may imply that a particular perfume may attract suitors. An advertisement may suggest that buying a particular brand of car may demonstrate its driver's virility. In each of these cases, the ad leaves the reasons and the support unstated.

Sometimes, however, these manipulative campaigns may seem to be giving good reasons by bombarding the viewer or listener with information. Three out of four dentists recommend a particular toothpaste; a recent study at a major research institution found that elementary students' test scores fell in the previous year; a prominent scientist recommends a diet plan. Statistics, studies, and experts' testimonials give the appearance of reasonable documentation, but again, the advertisers often omit explanations of their evidence.

In academic writing we attempt to present arguments that will participate in open inquiry with others rather than close down discussion by providing final and ostensibly irrefutable answers. Our objective is to add to the larger discussion, of a literary work, or historical event, or political issue, or business decision. Agreeing that we share this goal should encourage us to do the best possible job that we can of giving good reasons for others to listen to our arguments.

Shape Your Argument to Support Your Position

You probably have been writing all along as we discussed the various parts of planning your paper. What you are ready to do now is begin to shape all of that material into a clear, coherent, well-supported statement of your position, one that will earn your voice a place in the discussion of the issue. Where do you begin?

One way to think about how to shape a paper is take your reader though your own process of inquiry. In other words, you began with a question or a problem that you thought was important enough to study. You could begin your essay by identifying the question or problem, explaining it, and showing why you think it is important enough to consider or explore. You will also need to define any terms that are important to your argument.

Your assumptions about the issue might be a good place to move next. Whether or not you tell your reader what answer you found at the end of your study will depend on the rhetorical situation. If you are writing an essay for a class, you may need to state your position at the outset so that the reader may evaluate every stage of your developing argument. If you are writing to readers who will disagree with your position and you wish to take them gradually though your argument in a way that asks them to evaluate each new move separately, you might wait to the end and state your position as the conclusion you draw as a result of the inquiry. Editorials on controversial issues often use this structure.

However you decide to structure the opening of your essay, the middle section will develop the reason for your position. In this section, you will need to demonstrate how what you have learned and discovered should lead your reader to draw the conclusion you have drawn. This is what we call your *burden of proof*. Before continuing, we should remind you that by proof we do not mean showing that your position is correct but rather giving reasonable support for your position. Aristotle claims that there are three ways to convince an audience: by showing that you are using good reasoning, that you understand human character, and that you understand human emotions.

The end of your essay is your conclusion or position. In this final section, you will be showing why your conclusion follows from your reasoning.

One way to plan the essay is to keep a notebook in which you explore your research and the evolution of your thinking about the argument you will be constructing. The following example is from the notebook of the student who wrote the exploratory paper and draft argument essay on Denver gridlock.

Sample Student Writing: Notebook Entries

Reflection on my Exploratory Paper: "Gridlock"

Mattie McDowell

I wrote my Exploratory Paper after a very bad experience with Denver traffic. Since then I've noticed that the traffic on the freeways is terrible. I've been driving on them more and listening to others who do so. I don't know much about the issue yet but am beginning to notice that the local paper has editorials and news stories that mention the controversies surrounding the traffic problems and light rail. As I've talked to friends who live in Denver, I've learned that people in the west love their cars and are not used to the idea of public transportation. That the west has lots of land and so the city is quite spread out making it difficult to have effective public transportation. I've also learned that the state has an amendment in the constitution called the Taxpayers' Bill of Rights (TABOR) that puts a limit on state taxes. This limit affects governmentally supported systems like public schools and projects like light rail. Before I write my thesis statement, I need to find out how the light rail system is funded now, whether people are using it, and why some people oppose it.

Tentative Thesis for First Thesis Workshop

Extending Denver's light rail system along freeway routes would improve the traffic congestion because it would reduce the number of cars traveling on the freeway.

Assumption: Reducing the number of cars traveling on the freeways would improve the traffic congestion.

Reflection

What are my key terms and what information do I need for the paper?

In my first thesis statement, my key terms are "light rail," "freeway routes," "traffic congestion," "number of cars on the freeway." Traffic congestion and number of cars on the freeway sound like they refer to the same problem. I wonder whether I'm saying anything new in my because clause—am I just saying that reducing traffic congestion will reduce traffic congestion? If I am, I'm not really making an argument.

I was surprised to hear some people from Denver object to my thesis. They agreed that the traffic is terrible on the highway to the airport, but didn't think that light rail would help. They said people wouldn't use light rail when they go to the airport, or not enough people. They argued that people who don't use the light rail would object to having their taxes raised to pay for extending it, and they said that the state needs a better highway system. If I want to convince them that light rail is the answer to the problem, I'll need to convince them that people will ride the airport line. People here won't agree to more taxes unless they are convinced that the reason makes sense. I guess I need to look at other cities that extended their light rail and at rider-ship in those cites. And I need to look at cities I could use for comparison.

The Inquiry Using Key Terms

When I began doing research, I began with a Web search using "Denver" and "light rail" as my key terms. From the Denver Regional Transit District page, I learned that Denver built its first light rail tracks in 1994 but that the system has been expanded and plans for further expansion are underway. I also found a Web page called Urban Transport Fact Book from a group called the Public Purpose that reported the 1997 defeat of a transit sales tax to build 100 miles of light rail. This makes me wonder who the opponents were and what arguments they used to defeat the measure.

So I decided to search the local newspapers archives for information about the election. An editorial published in the Denver Post prior to the vote reported that opponents to the sales tax increase for light rail argued that it would be too heavy a tax and would not "necessarily reduce traffic" (Ricky Young, "Campaign Near Road's End: Foes Air Drive-Time Radio Spots," October 31, 1997). In 2002, the Regional Transit District is asking for an increase in sales tax for six new lines that would cost about $4.7 million. This would mean a tax of 4 cents on each $10 purchase, making the transportation tax 1 percent, "a penny on every dollar's purchase" (Jeffrey Leib, "RTD Sales Tax Vote May Be Pushed to '04," *The Denver Post*, July 8, 2002).

From my general search for information using "light rail" as my search term, I discovered the Web page of the Light Rail Transit Association, which has a wealth of information including the history and evolution of light rail and a complete listing of Light Rail, Light Railway, Tramway and Metro systems throughout the World. This helped me find cities that I might use for comparison. Baltimore, Dallas, Sacramento, and St. Louis, Missouri seem like possibilities.

From the linked page that defines light rail, I found the benefits to be that light rail doesn't pollute, is faster than the car, and is cheaper than the automobile. But it sounds like the system has to be a good one for there to be these benefits. So I'm back to how do you convince people that such a system would be worth the money? From the fact sheet section, I learned that Sacramento's light rail usage increased from 6,000 in 1987 to 28,500 per day in 2001. Because it is a western city where people love and use their cars, I may want to use Sacramento for comparison.

I used the key terms "Sacramento, California" and "light rail" and found the Web page for the Sacramento Regional Transit System that includes the city's light rail system—this gave me a wealth of information! Like Denver, Sacramento is considering adding light rail to their airport. The STS identifies the following objectives for the new line: to improve corridor mobility, to improve air quality, to find cost effective solutions for transportation problems in corridor, to encourage patterns of smart growth, and to provide solutions that are consistent with other planning efforts.

As I looked for essays about the successes and problems associated with light rail, I found an essay from the Denver Business Journal that reported that the "new Southwest rail line is carrying up to 14,000 people on weekdays—66 percent above the original projections of 8,400." (Copyright 2001 American City Business Journals Inc.). So it sounds like people in Denver are riding the new line. I'm sure I can use that information. I still think light rail to the airport makes sense.

From what I'm reading, it seems that cities like Denver move slowly on projects like light rail. The system is gradually being developed, but voters will support increases to their taxes only when they are sure that the project to be funded will be efficient and effective. That means that people will ride the line and so the system will make enough money that taxpayers don't have to subsidize fares. Because I'm mainly concerned about adding a rail line to the airport, I guess I need to show the efficiency of that line, in other words, that people would ride it.

New Thesis

Adding an airport light rail line would provide efficient transportation to the airport because it would be fast and reasonably priced.

Assumption: A fast and reasonably priced transportation system would be efficient.

Idea Outline:

Introduction

1. Gridlock on the way to the airport
2. Denver's history of light rail

   the votes

   the arguments on both sides
3. My assumption: Denver voters agree that they want a fast and reasonably priced transportation because it would be efficient.

Development of My Argument

1. The airport line

   What would the line be

   How much would the line cost

   Who would pay for it
2. Compared to current system
3. Time to the airport taking light rail compared to in the car
4. Cost of light rail pass compared to driving and parking

Conclusion

The proposed airport light rail line would provide efficient transportation because it would be fast and reasonable priced. And the implications are that Denver voters should support a tax increase to finance the new line.

Read and Revise for Coherence

The final stage in writing your academic argument is to read it carefully and decide how you might revise it. Although you have been rethinking and revising your argument the entire time you have been working on it, you should take the opportunity to read a draft of your argument as if you were the targeted audience. This is not an easy exercise. It is difficult to get the proper distance from your paper to see it as another reader might. One way to do so is by giving yourself some time between the first draft and the final version. A few days after writing you may be able to see where you have not explained your position well enough, where you have omitted the connections necessary to follow your line of reasoning. Reading your draft aloud may also help you find places that you need to revise.

Another way to test to see whether your reasoning is clear and coherent is by having someone else read your draft. If you have a writing center at your college, you could take it or email it to a writing center tutor, then meet with that person to discuss where the tutor is missing the connections or needs more information or further explanations. For further suggestions for revision, see Chapter 12: Revising Effectively.

Sample Student Writing: Academic Argument, APA Documentation Style

We end with an argument essay that a student planned, wrote, and revised. As you read the essay, think about the argument he is constructing and how effectively he has used reasoning and evidence.

Educational Vouchers: The Solution

to the Problems in Public Education?

Peter Briggs

By all accounts, our public education system is in trouble, and of the many proposed solutions, educational vouchers have recently gained popularity as a way to address the problems seen within our current system. Vouchers were originally proposed as a way to create a free market system, breaking the stranglehold of government on the educational world. However, the implementation of a tax-funded voucher system would significantly harm the public schools and would not achieve the desired outcome of overall educational improvement.

The concept of giving a voucher to students that could then be used to pay for any school of their choosing is not a recent idea. As Kirkpatric says, "The proposal, though not the name, is literally older than the United States, first appearing in Adam Smith's *Wealth of Nations* in 1776, and even more specifically in Tom Paine's *The Rights of Man* in 1792" (Kirkpatric, 1990, p. 1). While many of those who propose ideal societies have toyed with the voucher idea, its primary appeal seems to be as a way to create a free-market system of education. Tannenbaum holds that "The original supporters of the idea focused on the concept of competition, which would supposedly improve educational offerings, and the mechanisms of the free market, which would destroy the government monopoly on schools" (1995, p. 7).

More recently, vouchers have captured the public interest in Washington State as a way to solve some of the problems with the current system of education, problems acknowledged by many but which also have complex causes. "Education experts claim that the deterioration in educational quality is caused by several factors including the subpar performance of schools, urban blight, drugs, the prevalence of television, the abject failure of national leadership, and the erosion of the family" (Hakim & Seidenstat, & Bowman, 1994, p. 3). What is more, our country now seems to expect the public schools to address these social and cultural issues in the classroom. In essence, "the schools are expected to babysit children of working parents, to eliminate the roots of racism, to prevent drug use, to teach children to become responsible parents, and to perform a dozen other tasks that were earlier considered the responsibility of the family and church" (Hanus & Cookson, 1996, p.5). And yet, disregarding how complex the task has become, many charge the public schools with failure. Kirkpatric sees the interest in a voucher system not as a desire for a solution but as an emotional response to this sense of dissatisfaction with the current system: "Many supporters of vouchers seen not so much to be really committed to educational choice and/or student welfare as they seem to be motivated by anti-teacher and anti-public school feelings or by an interest to get money for their own projects" (1990, p. 165). The public dissatisfaction can be noted when one considers the recent increases in the number of students being home-schooled. In addition, many school districts across Washington State are having difficulty finding public support to pass the local property tax levies that substantially support their needs.

Stemming from the recent dissatisfaction in the educational system, the public support for a voucher program in Washington and across the nation has grown, as evidenced by an increase in voucher-focused legislative proposals and court cases that seek voucher-type options. There is danger, however, in too quickly accepting a particular path to school improvement without carefully considering whether the proposal would achieve the desired outcome of general educational improvement.

One assumption underlying the voucher movement is that a truly competitive free-market environment improves quality in all cases. Would this assumption hold, if a voucher system encouraged competition with the public schools? In an editorial in the *Bremerton Sun*, Maggie Gallagher claims that forcibly breaking up monopolies creates competition, which leads to better products and/or innovation at less cost. She makes a comparison of the governmental involvement in the Microsoft anti-trust case to the public school's monopolization of tax dollars and students. Ideally, allowing students to choose schools would motivate continuous improvement, causing all schools to produce quality results in order to keep enrollments viable. However, the voucher system does not prepare public schools to compete adequately with private and parochial schools; furthermore, the competing schools could potentially promote widely varying educational goals, and the choices would therefore be based primarily on the type of school rather than on the quality of the learning.

One of the most significant deterrents of a supposed free-market educational system is a result of how the funding would be redistributed. "We have a real fight on our hands. These vouchers are literally taking dollars away from our public schools," says Karen Gutloff, a National Education Association member and activist against legislation which gives public tax dollars to private schools (Gutloff, 1999, p. 8). According to the recent *NEA Today*, the voucher program in Milwaukee is shifting a total of $25 million a year away from public schools (1999, p. 9). Instead of leveling the playing field to yield a truly free market economy, these cuts in tax funding damage the public schools to the point that they are unable to compete with privately funded schools which gain supplemental funding from voucher/tax money.

Funding is not the only area where the voucher program hinders the public schools while aiding the private. Because the private schools are able to choose their students, there is a good chance that they will accept the excellent students, thereby "skimming the cream" from the public schools, further complicating the public school efforts to demonstrate improvement. "Private schools have the right to reject or accept any student, regardless of whether the student holds a voucher. Private school officials often choose the so-called 'desirable' students and leave those they would find more difficult to educate for the public schools" (Gutloff, 1999, p. 9). Supporters of the vouchers claim that equal opportunity for all social classes is a better ideal to strive for than equality through integration. Further, they point out that the current area-division, or "neighborhood" organization of schools creates just as much socioeconomic division as the voucher system would. However, it seems as though the public system is and should be able to serve all, gifted and challenged, from upper and lower economic classes. Diana Herrera, a teacher and NEA member in Texas, believes that "As public school educators, we need to meet the needs of all students, from those with low abilities to the gifted. If a child is in special education, private schools won't meet the child's needs" (1999, p. 8). What is more, if the voucher system is adjusted to include a truly equal opportunity for all, many private schools would balk at the idea. According to a U.S. Department of Education report published in 1998, "46 percent of private schools would not accept the vouchers if they had to accept students randomly. Even more, 68 percent, would not accept vouchers if they had to accept special-needs students" (1999, p. 9).

Even if the best students remained in the public education system, voucher systems would still negatively impact students from lower-income families. The NEA claims that "some low-income families may benefit from vouchers, but the vast majority of poor people depend on public schools. These schools have fewer resources if taxpayer dollars are sidetracked into private tuition," (1999, p. 9). Though some claim that an educational voucher system would make it possible for those who can't pay tuition to attend a private school, opponents of the vouchers are afraid that those most negatively affected by the voucher system would be the members of racial and social class groups already suffering from prejudice and inequity (Tannenbaum, 1995, p. 8).

These complications of implementing a voucher system are not just speculation, because we can see what is happening in areas currently under a voucher program. Findings from voucher programs in California and Milwaukee are showing that the quality of learning is not necessarily improving. "Voucher students' test scores in reading and math have stayed on a par with those of students in Milwaukee public schools. ... As a result the Center [for Advancement of Public Education] continues to argue that vouchers are the wrong answer. ..." (DiLorenzo, 1997, p. 38). Furthermore, according to the NEA, official studies of the voucher plans in Cleveland and Milwaukee conclude that vouchers don't improve overall student achievement (Gutloff, 1999, p. 9).

If it is true that the voucher system does not improve the overall education of the students and has such negative effects on public schools, students from low income families and students with special needs, what alternatives might better address the existing problems? Rather than undermine the existing system, it seems more rational to attempt to improve and enhance what we have, focusing repairs specifically on problem areas, and it appears that there is support for such an effort. National Public Radio pollsters randomly phoned 1442 people nationwide and found that "75 percent of Americans would be willing to pay an additional $200 in taxes to improve their public schools, while 55 percent would be willing to pay an additional $500" (1999, p. 9). While these figures may seem difficult to reconcile with the recent decline in levy support, they do suggest that there is still enough support for public education to attempt to find ways to improve the existing system.

Much educational research has focused on possibilities for focused improvement. For example, "The recent research of Chubb and Moe has emphasized the importance of the organizational features of schools for explaining academic performance. ... They found that the characteristics of an effective school include strong leadership by the principal, clear goals, strong academic programs, teacher professionalism, shared influence, and staff harmony" (Hanus & Cookson, 1996, p. 72).

Research is also examining how education is impeded by governmental bureaucracy. Because school boards must adhere to multiple levels of regulations and policies, the process of educational decision-making can be slow.

> One of the most serious obstacles to the development of policies that would bring about [beneficial] characteristics is excessive bureaucracy, a danger to which all institutions are prey but which seems to be particularly endemic to governmental organizations. [Chubb and Moe's] recommended cures for this ill are to increase the autonomy of the individual school, reduce the size of schools, and reduce or abolish the close supervision by school boards.
> (Gutloff, 1996, p. 73)

Not only would smaller schools be academically efficient, but they would also be financially efficient. The NEA states that "for the same money that Milwaukee spends on vouchers for 6500 students, the district could put 13,000 students in smaller classes—with better academic results" (Gutloff, 1999, p. 9).

Though the current organization of community members on a school board may need adjusting, it is essential for the public to remain involved in the public school system. Eliminating the presence of community members who participate in directing the public schools would most likely cause the general public to be less supportive of the system. When the communities have a sense of ownership in the schools, they are more likely to work toward improving the quality of education.

Therefore it is important to find solutions that reduce the bureaucracy and increase school autonomy while increasing public participation and ownership. Some schools have already attempted such changes. The Selah, Washington School District has been on the cutting edge of educational problem solving. They have worked to create a smaller, more intimate school atmosphere while maintaining the high standards required by the state.

> What grew from [parent/teacher meetings] are 'schools within a school' to break up the large elementaries and now the new intermediate school, multiple teaching techniques to meet the students' learning needs, and more inservice and planning time for teachers.
>
> The district created a 'benchmark band' system where students in kindergarten through fourth grade are in benchmark one, those in grades five through seven are in benchmark two, and those in eight through twelve are in benchmark three. The district even reconfigured their school buildings to match the benchmarks and gave teachers in the same teams time to work together.
>
> Within the benchmark bands, smaller learning communities are formed into 'teams.' Depending on the school, a team consists of 12 to 15 teachers who share the same 350 to 450 students, and those students will stay with the same team until they progress to the next

> benchmark. Those same teachers also work and plan
> together. For example, instead of a school of 900
> students at the new intermediate building, there are
> three schools of 300. (Pohlig, 1999, p. 7A)

The results of the changes in Selah are still new, but the outlook is good. Test scores have consistently improved. The "schools within a school" structure has reduced the teacher/administrator ratio. The largest hurdle they face now is not the changes themselves but the pace of change. While many strongly support the rapid advances and efforts of the school district, others feel that there have been too many changes made too quickly. Kathy Lambert, a Selah kindergarten teacher, feels that the rapid changes are putting pressure on students, parents, and teachers. What is more, she feels that parents should have been more involved in the reform process to increase the sense of community ownership (Pohlig, 1999, p. 7A).

Though the educational voucher system has emerged as a potential solution to a shared sense of the problems faced by public education, its implementation could cripple the public system and compromise the goal of overall educational improvement. Whatever solution does evolve in response to educational needs, it should capitalize on the research already conducted and the progress already made. Rather than discard public education as we know it, we should attempt to improve it, care for it, recognize its responsibilities and limits. Whether we choose reforms like those of the Selah School District or attempt to find other locally-appropriate solutions, it is important to involve the public and educators in reform decision making. Such solutions would ideally bind parents, teachers, and students in a unified quest to better our educational system for all.

References

DiLorenzo, Andrea. (1997). Views from Washington. *Devolution: Implications for education finance*, Washington DC: National Education Association Research Division.

Gallagher, Maggie. (1999, November 26). Go After a real monopoly [Editorial]. *The Bremerton Sun*, p. C3.

Gutloff, Karen. (1999, November). Talking turkey. *NEA Today*, 8–9.

Hakim, S., Seidenstat, P., Bowman G.W. (Eds.). (1994). *Privatizing education and educational choice: Concepts, plans, and experiences*. Westport, Connecticut: Praeger.

Hanus, J.J., Cookson, P. W. Jr. (1996). *Choosing schools: Vouchers and American education*. Washington D.C.: American University Press.

Kirkpatrick, David W. (1990). *Choice in schooling: A case for tuition vouchers*. Chicago: Loyola University Press.

McGroarty, Daniel. (1996). *Break these chains: The battle for school choice*. Rocklin, Calif: Prima Publishing.

LaNoue, George R. (Ed.). (1972). *Educational vouchers: Concepts and controversies*. New York: Teachers College Press.

Pohlig, Colleen. (1999, November 22). *Too much Too fast?* Yakima Herald-Republic, p. A1, A7.

Tannenbaum, Margaret D. (1995). *Concepts and issues in school choice*. Lewiston: Edwil Mellen Press.

ARGUING IN OTHER CONTEXTS

We have discussed ways to identify the questions you will be addressing in your academic essays, the approach you will be taking, and the position you will test and develop. We have also talked about ways to analyze and study the materials that will help you rethink your answer to the question and how to consider responsibly other possible answers to the question. We have also explored ways to find the thesis statements that represent the line of reasoning you might follow in developing your positions. Finally, we have talked about ways to develop the positions, through inductive and deductive arguments, and ways to shape the structures that develop from thesis statements. The approach we have suggested for academic essays also applies to the arguments you will construct in non-academic contexts. For example, if you wish to write your parents a letter in which you explain why choosing a particular major is a responsible decision, you might use the same critical reasoning process to construct an enthymeme that would begin with an assumption your parents would share, such as:

> Studying history will prepare me for any job that requires me to confront and manage change because studying history gives me experience in analyzing the social, economic, political, intellectual, and technological changes that occur over the whole of recorded time.

This would be an effective argument if your parents agree that experience in analyzing the social, economic, political, intellectual, and technological changes that occur over the whole of recorded time will prepare you for any job that requires you to confront and manage change.

If you wish to enter the discuss of an issue in your community, you could write a letter to the editor of your local newspaper, in which you might argue:

> The Supreme Court's school voucher decision will offer better education to the children of poor families because it will give them the means to enroll in private schools.

This would be an effective argument if your readers agree that having the means to enroll in private schools will offer better education to the children of poor families.

You might use this process to shape an argument asking a company to refund your purchase of a flawed product, as in the following:

> The Electronics Today store should refund the purchase price of my Dell Computer because the store sold a computer that began malfunctioning within two weeks of the purchase.

This would be an effective appeal if the store has a refund policy for damaged products.

It isn't easy to construct and write arguments that allow us to enter into conversations about issues that matter to us, but it is challenging and exciting. As we explore the issues and listen to others and put our "two cents" in, we participate in larger discussions and take responsibility for our own beliefs and knowledge.

WRITING INVITATIONS

1. Read through the editorial page of your local newspaper or campus newspaper. Are there any issues raised that you have experience with? Write a few paragraphs in which you explore your responses to the question. Based on your paragraphs, identify a question you would like to explore. How does your initial answer to the question differ from others' answers? Why is the question important? What do you need to know to write a responsible, supported essay? Write a proposal in which you explain how you will go about studying the issue.

2. After exploring and analyzing a question you find compelling, write a paragraph explaining how someone who disagrees with you would answer the question. What assumptions might you share with this person? Construct a thesis statement that begins with an assumption you would share with a dissenting reader. Write a paragraph explaining how beginning with a shared assumption changes the way you think about your position.

3. Return to an exploratory paper you have written and identify the potential thesis for an argument addressing the question that the paper explored. Using the information you will need to construct a compelling argument, write a three to five page argument essay.

4. Identify a question that a professor in another class has discussed that you would like to explore in greater depth. After identifying your responses, state the question clearly. What kind of question is it? Are there key terms you must define? What material from the class will help you justify your position? Construct a thesis statement that begins with an assumption you share with the professor but with new information that allows you to draw a different conclusion. Write a three to four page essay in which you justify your position.

5. Choose an essay from one of the casebooks. After reading it, answer the following questions and do the writing indicated.

What is the topic of the essay? State it as a word or phrase.

What question about the topic does the writer address?

What is at issue about the topic? How do you know?

What position does the writer take concerning the question? Or what answer does the writer propose to the question? State it in a sentence with the topic as the sentence's subject. What different answers might other writers propose?

What major reason does the writer offer the reader to accept the writer's answer? State it in a sentence with the topic as the sentence's subject.

Restate the writer's position as a two-part thesis statement with the writer's position as the first clause and the reason as a because clause.

What evidence does the writer give as support of the thesis?

How convinced are you by the argument? Why?

DEVELOPING A WRITING PROJECT

In previous chapters, you have been invited to read, summarize, respond to, research, and synthesize multiple views on a question at issue. This chapter prepares you to move from an understanding of alternative answers to taking a reasoned position on the question, with confidence that your position is the best of the available alternatives. To continue developing your writing project, return to your research. Examine the positions and reasoning in your source material, and as you do so, begin to structure your own reasoning. Identify your thesis, or your position and the reasons for your position. Test your reasons by examining your assumptions. Support your position with reasoning and evidence. As a part of your exploration of the question, present honest appraisals of alternate positions. Then, with your position, your reasons, your evidence, and your exploration of alternatives as your resources, draft an academic argument that is shaped to support your position.

CHAPTER 9

Interpreting Literature

When an acquaintance greets me on the street by removing his hat, what I see from a formal point of view is nothing but the change of certain details within a configuration forming part of the general pattern of colour, lines and volumes which constitutes my world of vision. When I identify, as I automatically do, this configuration as an object (gentleman), and the change of detail as an event (hat-removing), I have already overstepped the limits of purely formal perception and entered a first sphere of subject matter or meaning.

Erwin Panofsky

Writing, like dreams, confronts, pushes you up against the evasions, self-deceptions, investments in opinions and interpretations, the clutter that blinds, that disguises that underlying, all-encompassing design.

Toni Cade Bambara

INTERPRETATION

Erwin Panofsky has sometimes been called the father of modern art history, a discipline that relies on interpretative skills to find meaning in works of art. As his observations indicate, interpretation is a natural activity we engage in every day. Whether we are trying to figure out what a friend meant when he took off his hat or trying to understand an image in a painting, we are attempting to make meaning from an ambiguous event or moment or image. From infancy, we engage in interpretive acts. When the toddler sees a frown on her parent's face, she learns to interpret it as disapproval. When a child sees a man and a woman holding hands and wearing wedding bands, he may assume he is looking at a happily married couple. When an adolescent listens to the lyrics of a popular song that describe magical and surreal visions, he may take for granted that the song is about drugs. When a student in a literature class reads a poem that includes a shepherd protecting his sheep, she may wonder whether she is reading religious allegory. When a student in a writing class receives a grade that surprises or confuses him, he may think that the instructor didn't like him. Each of these actions involves interpretation.

Although interpretation is a natural process, sometimes our interpretations go awry. We misunderstand the words or actions of others because we jump to conclusions too quickly or base our conclusions about their meanings on faulty generalizations. Such misunderstandings can lead to strife in personal relationships; all too often arguments among friends result from a misunderstanding. Misunderstandings may also lead to difficulty in college classrooms; the misinterpretation of an exam question can lead students to write an unacceptable response. In the public arena, misunderstandings can have global effects. A world leader's misinterpretation of a word or language convention could lead to diplomatic disaster.

Fortunately, interpretation is both natural and learned. Although you have been engaging in interpretation all your life, you can learn to improve the process. You can improve your interpretive skills by identifying the components of the interpretive process and by practicing it through shared inquiry about questions that require interpretation. And so, in this chapter we will focus on the interpretive process by examining together works that demand more advanced interpretive methods for their audiences' understanding.

The Process of Interpretation

To illustrate the way people engage in interpretation, let's consider an imaginary discussion of a literary text. The following description of such a conversation is from Gerald Graff's book *Beyond the Culture Wars*. The text under

KEY CONCEPT

Interpretation

To interpret is to clarify meaning. An interpretation of an artistic work, whether a film, play, novel, poem, or painting, involves the following:

- Interpretations represent the interpreter's understanding of the work.
- Interpretation requires analysis.
- Interpretation involves drawing conclusions about specific details based on shared assumptions.
- Interpretation is addressed to readers who are interested in the work being interpreted and thus includes reasons for conclusions.

discussion is Matthew Arnold's famous poem "Dover Beach." So that you may follow the discussion, we begin with the poem.

MATTHEW ARNOLD
Dover Beach

The sea is calm tonight.
The tide is full, the moon lies fair
Upon the straits; on the French coast the light
Gleams and is gone; the cliffs of England stand,
Glimmering and vast, out in the tranquil bay.
Come to the window, sweet is the night air!
Only, from the long line of spray
Where the sea meets the moon-blanch'd land,
Listen! you hear the grating roar
Of pebbles which the waves draw back, and fling,
At their return, up the high strand,
Begin, and cease, and then again begin,
With tremulous cadence slow, and bring
The eternal note of sadness in.

FIGURE 9.1   DOVER BEACH

Sophocles long ago
Heard it on the Aegean, and it brought
Into his mind the turbid ebb and flow
Of human misery; we
Find also in the sound a thought,
Hearing it by this distant northern sea.

The Sea of Faith
Was once, too, at the full, and round earth's shore
Lay like the folds of a bright girdle furl'd.
But now I only hear
Its melancholy, long, withdrawing roar,
Retreating, to the breath
Of the night-wind, down the vast edges drear
And naked shingles of the world.

Ah, love, let us be true
To one another! for the world, which seems
To lie before us like a land of dreams,
So various, so beautiful, so new,
Hath really neither joy, nor love, nor light,
Nor certitude, nor peace, nor help for pain;
And we are here as on a darkling plain
Swept with confused alarms of struggle and flight,
Where ignorant armies clash by night.

GERALD GRAFF

Debate the Canon in Class

1   In the faculty lounge the other day, a dispute arose between a couple of my colleagues that typifies the warfare currently agitating the educational world. It began when one of our older male professors complained that he had just come from teaching Matthew Arnold's "Dover Beach" and had been appalled to discover that the poem was virtually incomprehensible to his class. Why, can you believe it, said the older male professor (let us call him OMP for short), my students were at a loss as to what to make of Arnold's famous concluding lines, which he proceeded to recite with slightly self-mocking grandiloquence:

Ah, love, let us be true
To one another! For the world, which seems
To lie before us like a land of dreams,
So various, so beautiful, so new,

> Hath really neither joy, nor love, nor light,
> Nor certitude, nor peace, nor help for pain;
> And we are here as on a darkling plain
> Swept with confused alarms of struggle and flight
> Where ignorant armies clash by night.

My other colleague, a young woman who has just recently joined our department (let us call her YFP), replied that she could appreciate the students' reaction. She recalled that she had been forced to study "Dover Beach" in high school and had consequently formed a dislike for poetry that had taken her years to overcome. Why teach "Dover Beach" anyway? YFP asked.

2   Furiously stirring his Coffee-mate, OMP replied that in *his* humble opinion—reactionary though he supposed it now was—"Dover Beach" was one of the great masterpieces of the Western tradition, a work that, until recently at least, every seriously educated person took for granted as part of the cultural heritage. YFP retorted that while it might be so, it was not altogether to the credit of the cultural heritage. Take those lines addressed to the woman by the speaker, she said: "Ah love, let us be true / To one another...," and so on. In other words, protect and console me, my dear—as we know it's the function of your naturally more spiritual sex to do—from the "struggle and flight" of politics and history that we men have regrettably been assigned the unpleasant duty of dealing with. YFP added that she would have a hard time finding a better example of what feminists mean when they speak of the ideological construction of the feminine as by nature private and domestic and therefore justly disqualified from sharing male power. Here, however, she paused and corrected herself: "Actually," she said, "we *should* teach 'Dover Beach.' We should teach it as the example of phallocentric discourse that it is."

3   OMP responded that YFP seemed to be treating "Dover Beach" as if it were a piece of political propaganda rather than a work of art. To take Arnold's poem as if it were a species of "phallocentric discourse," whatever that is, misses the whole point of poetry, OMP said, which is to rise above such local and transitory problems by transmuting them into universal structures of language and image. Arnold's poem is no more about gender politics, declared OMP, than *Macbeth* is about the Stuart monarchical succession.

4   But *Macbeth* is about the Stuart monarchical succession, retorted YFP—or so its original audience may well have thought. It's about gender politics too—why else does Lady Macbeth need to "unsex" herself before she can participate in murdering Duncan? Not to mention all the business about men born of women and from their mother's womb untimely ripped. The fact is, Professor OMP, that what you presume to be the universal human experience in Arnold and Shakespeare is male experience presented as if it were universal. You don't need to notice the politics of sexuality because for you patriarchy is the normal state of affairs. You can afford to ignore the sexual politics of literature, or so "transmute" them, as you put it, onto a universal plane, but that's a luxury I don't enjoy.

THE INTERPRETIVE ESSAY

An interpretive essay is one that addresses the question *what does this mean?* Being able to determine what something means is essential in personal interaction, academic conversations, and public discourse. The dispute between the OMP and YFP involves their personal readings of "Dover Beach" and shows the way literary arguments sometimes are not unlike everyday conflicts. In fact, Gerald Graff's hypothetical discussion parallels a scene in the popular television show *West Wing*. When a male speechwriter comments on a female attorney's backless dress, his secretary thinks his comment is demeaning. The female attorney thinks the comment is a compliment indicating that the male speechwriter respected her enough to be playful.

Like Graff's OMP and YFP, the two interpreters in the *West Wing* scene were trying to find the intended meaning of a message. What distinguishes the hypothetical conversation about the poem "Dover Beach" from the *West Wing* scene is the language of literary criticism. Does this make the OMP and YFP better interpreters than the characters in the television show? Not necessarily—in fact, the professors' comments lack some of the important elements of good interpretation as much as the television characters' do, but we'll come back to that.

As the previous examples show, we need to hear and understand what our friends and colleagues are saying if we want to learn from such conversations. We also need to determine the meanings of the materials we study to make sense of our search for knowledge and understanding. Writing interpretive essays can help you reflect on what you know, think, and believe, and thus make decisions in a world where facts aren't always sufficient. By sharing your interpretations, you may look beyond your own perceptions to see in new ways in order to make reasoned judgments.

Of course, as the two examples show, this isn't always easy. All too often we stake out positions and refuse to consider other opinions either because we think the other person is wrong or because we think "everyone is entitled to his or her own opinion." When we do this, we are shutting down the inquiry process by refusing to test our own positions. Seeing interpretation as an inquiry into shared questions can help us avoid this trap and, more importantly, can help us shape a richer reading of the work or controversial situation.

Analyzing Literary Works

Analyzing involves seeing how something works, is put together, or is structured. You have been using skills of analysis throughout this book, and in fact you rely on them every day. When you read the instructions for a piece of electronic equipment, try to understand an assignment, or even watch a sports event, you almost intuitively analyze the parts of the instructions, assignment, or event and how they are organized. When you attempt to understand an artistic work, you will need to use a similar process. In order to analyze effectively, it may be necessary to become more conscious of the process you are using. We will suggest several ways to begin that may help you improve your skills of analysis.

STRATEGY

How to Write an Interpretive Essay

Writing an interpretive essay will require you to do the following:

1. Conduct analysis that will lead to a question you wish to answer.
2. Determine what question your paper will answer.
3. Research the question.
4. Construct a thesis statement.
5. Shape the interpretation.

Analysis simply means taking something apart and looking at the various parts and how those part work together to make a whole. This definition makes the process sound much easier than it is, of course. Examining the choices a writer makes requires sensitivity. The first step in analysis is observing the details of the work. When we examine literary works, we look at words, structures, and literary conventions.

As you read or observe a work, consider the artist's choices by asking yourself the following questions:

1. **What works against what?** This question helps you identify and name conflicts. The conflicts may be between or among people, feelings, experiences, competing perspectives, forms of evidence, values, loyalties, priorities, or expectations. They may also be between your past knowledge and your present awareness.

2. **What relates to what?** This question helps you look for connections and relationships between and among things: for example, how your past experience relates to your present self; how one circumstance or situation predicts, causes, or leads to another; how your knowledge relates to the knowledge of others; or how the time, setting, or cultural context of an event or idea relates to your interpretation of its meaning.

3. **What changes?** This question helps you reflect on what differences you can observe as a literary work progresses from beginning to end, or over the course of time, or between experiences, or between time periods or places. You can ask how you were changed, or how something or someone in the work changed, in response to an event or series of events.

4. **So what?** This question helps you reflect on how your analysis may lead to your interpretation, or reflect on the significance of the artist's choices and how that relates to your understanding of yourself or your world.

As the questions above suggest, interpretation relies on knowledge. If you can't understand the words of a poem or short story or novel, or you don't understand the references the writer makes, or you can't follow the action the words imply, you will not be able to discuss its meaning. The way we improve our knowledge of puzzling situations is through analysis.

Analyzing Literary Conventions

Entire books are written on the many literary conventions you might find in any given work. As a place to begin, we suggest that you examine four major questions that can help you identify and name the writer's literary choices and then use that analysis to suggest answers to your interpretive question. The four questions are:

1. What kind of language does the author use?
2. What choices of shape, form, and order does the author make?
3. Who are the participants?
4. What is the setting of the work?

Language

When you examine the language of a literary work, you will consider the way words convey meaning, the way language creates sounds and images, rhythm, and ideas. You will look at how the writer uses abstract and concrete language, metaphor, rhyme, meter, and figurative language. Because language is conventional, if we are decoding a puzzling comment, we need not only to break the message down into its words, phrases, and clauses, but also to look at what those language conventions mean in the particular context.

Our language conventions are ones we share in a particular culture and particular time. For example, in "Dover Beach" Arnold uses the word *turbid*. In order to understand the line, you must know what the word means and, in addition, whether it would have had a special meaning in the middle of the 19th century when Arnold wrote the poem. To find out, you can look in the *Oxford English Dictionary*, a twenty volume resource dictionary that your library should have in print edition and may have on CD-ROM or online. The OED will give you definitions of most of the words in the English language and how those words were used in different historical periods. If you look for the word *turbid* in the OED, you will find several definitions. After each definition, the entry has examples that represent the ways the word was used in works at different times in history.

The entry indicates that the word means first "Of liquid, thick or opaque with suspended matter, not clear: cloud, muddy" (OED). Knowing this will help you understand the line better: the ebb and flow of the Aegean Sea may literally be muddy. But Arnold refers to the ebb and flow of human misery. The second OED definition also helps you understand the meaning of the line. This definition is figurative: "Characterized by or producing confusion or obscurity of thought, feeling, etc; mutually confused, perplexed, muddled, disturbed, troubled." Reading both definitions and noting that both usages were current in the 19th century, we can assume that Arnold uses the muddy image to suggest how troubled and disordered life can be.

Shape

From our earliest experiences of hearing or reading literature, we learn that the way a work is shaped affects the way we understand it. When you hear a story begin with the words "Once upon a time," you expect an imaginative narrative, one that will ask you to suspend your expectations that logic will control the events. Looking at the choices of form and order will lead you to terms associated with the design of the work, or the way the parts work together as a whole. You may notice that poets shape their works by means of stanza, rhyme scheme, or larger structural units such as stanzas linked together as groups, and the shape of sonnets differs from the shape of other forms of poetry such as ballads. You may notice that fiction writers may tell a story chronologically or may break the development with flashbacks, that some plots are repetitive and others follow logically. You may notice the characteristics of what we call genres: folktales, poetry, fiction, essays, novels, and plays.

Arnold has organized his poem into four groups of lines called stanzas. In the first stanza the poet associates the grating roar of pebbles with the eternal note of sadness, in the second he speaks of the ebb and flow of human misery, and in the third he claims that the Sea of Faith has been replaced by a melancholy withdrawing roar. These three observations lead the narrator to ask his love to join him in a vow of faithfulness that will offset the uncertainty of the world, which is like a darkling plain.

Participants

An examination of the participants will distinguish the various voices of the work—the voices of the narrator and the characters. In a poem you will need to determine who the speaker is and whether you should consider his or her viewpoint that of the author. In a fictional work you will ask who tells the story and how, whether we are to consider the narrator trustworthy or limited in some way. You will also need to consider who the characters are, how they speak and interact, whether they change or grow, and what the narrator or other characters say about them.

In "Dover Beach," the narrator speaks directly to another person: he comments on the sadness in the scene before them as he and his companion look out upon what some might consider a beautiful scene. The poem is a monologue, that is, only one speaker speaks and the other is silent. The speaker seems to be arguing that the sounds and sights before them can be compared to a loss of faith.

Setting

When you examine the setting, you will ask how the work's location influences the actions, behaviors, and events within the work. Or you might ask how the scene evokes a particular response or gives you important information about attitudes the writer supports or critiques. The setting includes the place in which the work occurs, but also its historical period and social situation. A longer literary work may include several different settings.

"Dover Beach" is set on the southeast coast of England, in a room with a window that looks out upon the sea. The time is night, the weather is calm, and the moonlight illuminates the sea. The action of the poem occurs in the mid-19th century, during a period when advances in science were causing many intellectuals to question their religious faith. The poem was written about fifteen years before Charles Darwin published his theory of human evolution in *The Origin of Species*. In addition to a specific historical time, the setting also includes the narrator's imaginative interpretation of the view he sees from their window—the world as a dark battlefield full of sounds of sadness, misery, and melancholy, where armies clash in the night.

These four questions are only a beginning. As you study literature or any artistic work, you will add more specialized terminology to your analysis. But these four will give you a starting place to conduct your own examination of a literary text and to read the interpretations of others. Sharing the language of literary conventions is one place to begin finding the common ground necessary for arguing interpretation.

If the OMP and YFP were to identify the poetic characteristics of "Dover Beach," they would probably discover that they agree more than they realize. Both would recognize Arnold's use of visual and auditory imagery; they would see the way he contrasts light and dark imagery and how he associates the light imagery with beauty while he connects the dark with melancholy. They would both identify "Sea of Faith," "naked shingles," and "darkling plain" as examples of figurative language. And they would agree that Arnold uses end rhyme but not in any recognizable, nameable pattern such as "sonnet form." So, despite the differences in their critical approaches, the OMP and YFP share a knowledge and set of definitions of poetic conventions.

Analyzing Literature as Act

A literary work is more than its words and shape. Literature is not static. When we read, we see more than form; we respond to a dynamic act. Even in the least narrative literary work, something is happening, something that we are overhearing or observing, something we can talk about as a kind of dramatic act.

The rhetorician Kenneth Burke proposes a method of analysis that may help explore the complexity of the literary work. He begins his book *A Grammar of Motives* with the following question: *What is involved, when we say what people are doing and why they are doing it?* Whether we are examining a legal case, a literary work, a political or scientific text, or the news or gossip, Burke claims that we may talk about the discourse as an act that has five components:

The **act,** which names what happened.

The **scene,** the situation in which the act occurs.

The **agent,** the person who performs the act.

The **agency,** how the act was performed.

The **purpose,** the reasons for the act.

If you look at "Dover Beach" using these five terms, you will find something like the following:

Act: Someone stands at a window looking at the sea at high tide. It is a calm moonlit night. The person addresses someone. While listening to the waves, the person senses a kind of sadness and recalls that Sophocles heard a similar sound and, when he did so, thought of human misery. The person then compares faith to the ebbing and flowing of the tide. The person only hears the ebb now. The person ends by addressing the other person, who is now identified as a lover, and asks that they pledge to be faithful to each other as they acknowledge that the world, though it seems beautiful and new, has no stability. The lightness of the original scene is contrasted with the darkness of the world as a plain "where ignorant armies clash by night."

Scene: The action takes place on the English shore. It is nighttime and the moon lights the water and land. The waves ebb and flow on the shore.

Agent: This is the person who speaks, the narrator, the lyrical self, the person who makes observations about the scene and its meaning for him, the person who addresses his lover. This is the person whose attitude toward the scene seems to change in the poem.

Agency: The poem has four stanzas. The first stanza has 14 lines; the second has 6; the third has 8; the fourth has 9. The poem uses end rhyme but without a discernable conventional pattern. The narrator uses the sea as a central image. He describes the sea in a way that appeals to our eyes and ears. The visual imagery is associated with beauty and brightness until the end of the poem, but the auditory imagery is associated with sadness. The first stanza begins with a scene that is calm, bright, and lovely. After the speaker addresses his companion with the word "Listen," the sounds and the tone gradually seems to become negative. In the second stanza, the central image is dark and disturbed, "the turbid ebb and flow / of human misery." In the third stanza, the narrator compares the ebb and flow of the tide to the "Sea of Faith," and again, sounds dominate, but now are compared melancholy sounds with the earlier brightness. The fourth and final stanza associates brightness with the land of dreams and darkness with the reality of human existence with its confusion, struggle, flight, and conflict.

Purpose: This is difficult to answer. The narrator records his reactions to the scene and uses those reactions to make generalizations about the human misery in the time of Sophocles and about melancholy in his present time. He also seems to want the person he addresses to join him in a pledge of faith, as the only stability in a dark, hostile world without joy, love, light, certitude, peace, or help for pain.

Finding Interpretive Questions

The preceding "Dover Beach" analysis, using Kenneth Burke's five key terms, reveals quite a bit about the poem and may help us identify the questions we want to answer, such as:

What was Arnold's attitude toward faith?

What situation was Arnold reacting to when he wrote the poem?

What kind of conflict is Arnold describing in the last line?

Why does Arnold use end rhyme without a conventional pattern?

In addition to analyzing a work by means of the five key terms, you can extend your analysis by examining the relationships among these terms and come up with a wealth of questions that lead you to understand the subject in new ways or see further complexity in the action of the poem. Consider the following questions that examine some of these relationships:

1. How did the situation in which the act occurred influence the agent's decisions? Were the agent's actions controlled by the situation, allowing the person no options? **The Scene-Agent Relationship**
   In what way does the ebbing and flowing of the tide influence the narrator's shift in attitude from delight in the beauty of the moonlit shoreline to melancholy contemplation of human misery?

2. In what way were conditions changed by a particular action? **Act-Scene Relationship**
   In what ways did the narrator's observations and interpretation of the moonlit shoreline change its image in the minds of the reader?

3. Did the personality of the agent change the scene or the values and attitudes it represented? **Agent-Scene Relationship**
   Was there something about the narrator that made him see the scene shift from one of beauty to one of melancholy and strife?

4. How did the literary devices affect the person who chose or used the method? **Agency-Agent Relationship**
   Did the narrator's observation of the visual and auditory imagery affect his mood in a way that made him shift from delight to melancholy?

5. How did the personality of the person who acted affect his or her choice of imagery or form? **Agent-Agency Relationship**
   Does the poem allow us to generalize about the essential nature of the narrator in such a way that would account for his use of the central image of the sea and the light and dark imagery he uses to describe it?

The questions we identified after looking at the five key terms might lead us to interesting studies of biographies of Matthew Arnold, histories of the Victorian period, and literary studies of Victorian poetry in general and Matthew Arnold's poetry in particular. The questions we identified by examining the relationships between pairs of Burke's key terms have the potential to lead to

APPLICATION

Using Analysis to Find Interpretive Questions

Read the short story by Gwendolyn Brooks, "Home," written in 1953 as a chapter of the short novel *Maud Martha*. Identify the **act, scene, agent, agency**, and **purpose.** Then use the questions listed in the "Finding Interpretive Questions" section to examine the relationships among these terms, and write at least five interpretive questions your analysis generates.

much more complex inquiries about the meaning of the action Arnold asks readers to consider. These questions demand that we consider the motives Arnold embedded in the action of the poem.

GWENDOLYN BROOKS

Home

1   What had been wanted was this always, this always to last—the talking softly on this porch, with the snake plant in the jardiniére in the southwest corner, and the obstinate slip from Aunt Eppie's magnificent Michigan fern at the left side of the friendly door. Mama, Maud Martha, and Helen rocked slowly in their rocking chairs, and looked at the late afternoon light on the lawn, and at the emphatic iron of the fence and the poplar tree. These things might soon be theirs no longer. Those shafts and pools of light, the tree, the graceful iron, might soon be viewed possessively by different eyes.

2   Papa was to have gone that noon, during his lunch hour, to the office of the Home Owners' Loan. If he had not succeeded in getting another extension, they would be leaving this house in which they had lived for more than fourteen years. There was little hope. The Home Owners' Loan was hard. They sat, making their plans.

3   "We'll be moving into a nice flat somewhere," said Mama. "Somewhere on South Park, or Michigan, or in Washington Park Court." Those flats, as the girls and Mama knew well, were burdens on wages twice the size of Papa's. This was not mentioned now.

4   "They're much prettier than this old house," said Helen. "I have friends I'd just as soon not bring here. And I have other friends that wouldn't come down this far for anything unless they were in a taxi."

5   Yesterday Maud Martha would have attacked her. Tomorrow she might. Today she said nothing. She merely gazed at a little hopping robin in the tree, her tree, and tried to keep the fronts of her eyes dry.

6   "Well, I do know," said Mama, turning her hands over and over, "that I've been getting tireder and tireder of doing that firing. From October to April there's firing to be done."

7   "But lately we've been helping, Harry and I," said Maud Martha. "And sometimes in March and April and in October, and even in November, we could build a little fire in the fireplace. Sometimes the weather was just right for that."

8   She knew from the way they looked at her that this had been a mistake. They did not want to cry.

9   But she felt that the little line of white, somewhat ridged with smoked purple, and all that cream-shot saffron, would never drift across any western sky except that in back of this house. The rain would drum with as sweet a dullness nowhere but here. The birds on South Park were mechanical birds, no better than the poor caught canaries in those "rich" women's sun parlors.

10 "It's just going to kill Papa!" burst out Maud Martha. "He loves this house! He *lives* for this house!"

11 "He lives for us," said Helen. "It's us he loves. He wouldn't want the house, except for us."

12 "And he'll have us," added Mama, "where ever."

13 "You know," Helen sighed, "if you want to know the truth, this is a relief. If this hadn't come up, we would have gone on, just dragged on, hanging out here forever."

14 "It might," allowed Mama, "be an act of God. God may just have reached down and picked up the reins."

15 "Yes," Maud Martha cracked in, "that's what you always say—that God knows best."

16 Her mother looked at her quickly, decided the statement was not suspect, looked away.

17 Helen saw Papa coming. "There's Papa," said Helen.

18 They could not tell a thing from the way Papa was walking. It was that same dear little staccato walk, one shoulder down, then the other, then repeat, and repeat. They watched his progress. He passed the Kennedys', he passed the vacant lot, he passed Mrs. Blakemore's. They wanted to hurl themselves over the fence, into the street, and shake the truth out of his collar. He opened his gate—the gate—and still his stride and face told them nothing.

19 "Hello," he said.

20 Mama got up and followed him through the front door. The girls knew better than to go in too.

21 Presently Mama's head emerged. Her eyes were lamps turned on.

22 "It's all right," she exclaimed. "He got it. It's all over. Everything is all right."

23 The door slammed shut. Mama's footsteps hurried away.

24 "I think," said Helen, rocking rapidly, "I think I'll give a party. I haven't given a party since I was eleven. I'd like some of my friends to just casually see that we're homeowners."

Conducting Research

When you write an interpretive essay, you are doing more than simply presenting your opinion about the question you are addressing. Your position should result from an inquiry that will give you the information and background to answer the question in an informed and responsible way. And so, research is just as important in an interpretive essay as in any other academic essay because information about the work's context will allow you to enter the conversation with other knowledgeable interpreters. As with other research situations, you may conduct both primary and secondary research. In Chapter 6, we defined primary research as raw material and secondary research as someone's interpretation of that information. What is the raw material of literary or artistic works? First, it is the actual components of the work itself—the words, literary devices, and structures of a literary work, for example—but documents from the time period also function as primary material. To know more about "Dover Beach," you might look at other writings by Matthew Arnold. You might read his essays or letters that would tell you more about the issues he considered important in his time. To learn more about these issues, you could read Darwin's *The Origin of Species*, sermons given in the period that demonstrate religious leaders' responses to the skepticism of the age, articles in 19th-century newspapers and journals, or speeches given by politicians in the mid-19th century. All of these resources would give you primary information about the period in which Arnold was writing.

Primary research is not the only way to find out more about Arnold and his times. You can also read secondary materials such as books and articles that synthesize materials from the time period. You could also read what others have to say about the work. If you do so, you will notice that similar questions come up over and over again in others' studies of the work. Like you, scholars who write about the work address questions about text features, the author's life, the period and culture out of which the work emerged, and the way the structures of the work represent or fail to represent a significant pattern. Reading the publications of experienced readers can help you become a better interpreter as you:

- Investigate an observation that seems significant but for which you have no explanation.
- Provide a context for an observation that, alone, seems inconsequential.
- Cite an experienced reader to lend support to your interpretive statement.
- Cite an interpretive statement made by another reader in order to distance yourself from it or refute it.

Participating in Shared Inquiry

How do you go about answering the questions you generated after your analysis and research? To address this question, we need to return to our discussion of shared inquiry. Throughout this book we have talked about shared inquiry as the way we explore questions with others who share an interest in the issue or work, and we have talked about the responsibilities of the participants in the shared inquiry process. As you begin discussing questions of interpretation, it may be good to recall those responsibilities, which are:

- To be an informed participant, that is, to have read the material or to have thought carefully about the issues to be discussed.
- To be ready to pose questions about the material.
- To be willing to share your responses to the material and answers to questions you and others pose and to give reasons for your responses.
- To listen carefully and respectfully to others' responses and to engage them in discussion about their positions.
- To consider the reasons and support of the positions of others and to be willing to change your mind.

Would you call the conversation between Graff's OMP and YFP an example of effective shared inquiry? Perhaps we left the faculty lounge too soon, but from what we heard, we would say no. Although the two professors shared an interest in the question of whether students should read "Dover Beach" and in what the poem says about the human condition, neither really made an attempt to find assumptions they shared. Instead, they talked at each other, or even past each other. Neither really made an attempt to offer good reasons for their positions.

As with other arguments, your thesis statement for an interpretive essay is the answer to your question and your reason for thinking that it is the best answer. It is the position that you take as a result of your analysis and research. Like arguments that you write for other academic essays, interpretive essays are addressed to readers who share your question and interest in the work but who may not share your interpretation. This means that you will need to give reasons that your reader will find compelling.

People who disagree need to identify their differences before they can find common ground. The OMP identifies an essential difference between his position and that of the YFP when he says "that YFP seemed to be treating 'Dover Beach' as if it were a piece of political propaganda rather than a work of art." And he disagrees; in fact, he says that "the whole point of poetry" is "to rise above such local and transitory problems" and transform them "into universal structures of language and image." This essential difference might lead us to conclude that the two professors have reached an impasse making further discussion impossible. But having seen their differences, they may be able to find common ground.

They seem to have met some of the responsibilities we listed above as necessary for shared inquiry. They pose questions and share their responses, and they are informed participants. But they need to rethink the questions they have raised in response to each other. Finding what they share and how they differ does not mean that the two should interpret the poem in the same way, but merely that they might be able to find better ways to present their positions to each other. They need to listen carefully and respectfully and consider each other's reasons and support. Most importantly, they need to meet the most difficult responsibility, and that is to be willing to change their minds.

If the OMP and the YFP were to share their interpretations in a thesis statement workshop using the shared inquiry model we have been suggesting, they might find ways to argue more productively, to listen to each other, and by doing so improve their readings of "Dover Beach." As they rethink their questions and positions, the two professors might construct new thesis statements that explain their reasoning in a way that the other might be willing to hear.

SHAPING THE INTERPRETATION

As when you write argument essays, when you structure your interpretive essays, you may use your thesis statement as a kind of plan to follow. Some people find that an effective way to begin is by sketching out their line of reasoning and by thinking of what a reader would need to know to understand each point or what questions a reader might ask. The sequence of reflections we provide below is an example of such planning for a research-supported essay on Theodore Roethke's poem "My Papa's Waltz." The argument is based on an analysis of the rhythm and language of the poem, professional interpretations of the poem, biographies of Roethke, and his own comments on his poetry. We begin with the poem.

THEODORE ROETHKE
My Papa's Waltz

The whiskey on your breath
Could make a small boy dizzy;
But I hung on like death:
Such waltzing was not easy.

We romped until the pans
Slid from the kitchen shelf;
My mother's countenance
Could not unfrown itself.

The hand that held my wrist
Was battered on one knuckle;
At every step you missed
My right ear scraped a buckle.

You beat time on my head
With a palm caked hard by dirt,
Then waltzed me off to bed
Still clinging to your shirt.

Sketching Out a Line of Reasoning

Introduction

What is the narrator's attitude toward his father?

A first reading of the poem suggests this is a fond memory of the narrator's father. Yet much of the language seems to undercut the initial reaction.

Although the poem is about a waltz and thus a balanced and predictable dance, the language is surprising, and thus it may be that the narrator's reaction is more complex than it appears on a first reading.

If we examine the rhythm and diction of the poem, we may see whether the patterns suggest a more complicated response to the narrator's father.

Structure of Argument

The rhythm is regular.

Each line has three stressed beats.

The rhythm is like that in a waltz.

"Waltz" is from the old German word *walzen*, to roll, turn, or to glide.

A waltz is a ballroom dance in 3/4 time with strong accent on the first beat.

Despite the regular rhythm, the language is often threatening and potentially violent.

The whiskey on the father's breath.

The battered wrist.

The buckle that scrapes the child's ear.

Biographical details suggest that the poet felt ambivalence toward his own father.

His father died when he was an adolescent.

Walter Kalaidjian claims Roethke had a "conflicted attitude toward" his father because his father died during the time when he felt adolescent resentment of his father.

Speaking of another Roethke poem, Mark Doty says Roethke uses "dancing as a metaphor for ecstatic being in the world" and in that poem, it is "a dance which alternates between the ecstatic and the desperate."

In another Roethke poem, a father's ghost threatens a lost son.

In "Some Remarks on Rhythm" Roethke said, "We all know that poetry is shot through with appeals to the unconsciousness, to the fears and desires that go far back into our childhood."

The contrast between the regular rhythm and unexpected and threatening language seems in tension or a lack of balance that illustrates the narrator's memory of his father.

Conclusion

Therefore we may conclude that the instability caused by the contrast between the regular dance rhythm and the threatening language expresses an ambivalent response to the childhood encounter.

APPLICATION

Planning an Interpretive Essay

Read Anthony Hecht's poem "The Dover Bitch," his response to Matthew Arnold's "Dover Beach," and take notes on your responses and the literary conventions Hecht uses to elicit those responses. Then sketch out a reflective outline of an interpretive essay that answers the question: Why does Hecht call his response to Arnold's poem "The Dover Bitch: A Criticism of Life"?

ANTHONY HECHT

The Dover Bitch: A Criticism of Life

So there stood Matthew Arnold and this girl
With the cliffs of England crumbling away behind them,
And he said to her, "Try to be true to me,
And I'll do the same for you, for things are bad
All over, etc., etc."
Well now, I know this girl. It's true she had read
Sophocles in a fairly good translation
And caught that bitter allusion to the sea,
But all the time he was talking she had in mind
The notion of what his whiskers would feel like
On the back of her neck. She told me later on
That after a while she got to looking out
At the lights of the channel, and really felt sad,
Thinking of all the wine and enormous beds
And blandishments in French and the perfumes.
And then she got really angry. To have been brought
All the way down from London, and then to be addressed
As sort of a mournful cosmic last resort
Is really tough on a girl, and she was pretty.
Anyway, she watched him pace the room
And finger his watch chain and seem to sweat a bit,
And then she said one or two unprintable things.
But you mustn't judge her by that. What I meant to say is,
She's really all right. I still see her once in a while
And she always treats me right. We have a drink
And I give her a good time, and perhaps it's a year
Before I see her again, but there she is,
Running to fat, but dependable as they come,
And sometimes I bring her a bottle of Nuit d'Amour.

A sample interpretive essay is provided below. It was written by a University of Toronto professor and uses the MLA documentation style.

IAN LANCASHIRE

An Interpretation of "Dover Beach"

1   "Dover Beach," like Keats' "Ode to a Nightingale," contrasts the present and the deep past. For Keats, the nightingale uttered a wordless, melancholic beauty that biblical Ruth also heard. A glimpse of time past proves consoling. When Arnold looks out a window onto Dover beach, he instead hears the "grating roar" caused by the waves of the English Channel as they strike the shoreline at the base of the great chalk cliffs, and he thinks of the "mournful roar" of which Sophocles wrote in *Antigone*. At poem's end, Arnold also remembers the chaotic night-battle at Epipolae when Athenian warriors, unable to see, killed friend and enemy alike. Time past for Arnold forewarns humanity of its sad destiny. Keats escaped the miseries of his present by entering the afterdeath ecstasy of the nightingale's world. Arnold escaped ancient reminders of "human misery," "alarm and flight," by dwelling on present tenderness: a calm sea, sweet night air, and his beloved by his side. Time past, yoked to time present, reveals how fragile is the basis of human happiness. Keats closes his ode, asking if he dreams or wakes. Arnold ends his lyric, leaving no doubt that our "land of dreams" is a sham.

2   Both men say that the imagination acts as the gateway between present and past. At first, the mind fixes on haunting music from nature: the nightingale's song, and the waves' "tremulous cadence slow." Next, the mind finds "in the sound a thought" from past literature. For Arnold, it is a passage in Sophocles; Keats refers only to the "viewless wings" of poetry, but he is soon to think consciously of the Bible, and possibly of Wordsworth's "Solitary Reaper." Lyric poetry, more intensely than prose, fuses present experience and memory of the past and then forges something new from their union. For that reason, such poetry is "occasional": its unique insight rises from an instant of immediate experience and binds that moment permanently to something in long-term memory. "Dover Beach" did not become among the most well-known poems in English by accident. Arnold makes explicit the formula by which everyone finds meaningfulness in an experience. You see a landscape by seashore, moonlight and sunset off the French coast, and then, "Listen! you hear the grating roar." These sights and sounds recall what you knew, say, at school. Here it is something from Sophocles. Then, inexplicably, your experience-memory mixture utters a new thought, that the ebbing tide is to nature what the loss of faith is to humanity, inescapably natural and sad. Thus your revelation, finally, ends in a resolution. The faithful love of friends can replace that between man and God. You say to your partner, "Ah, love, let us to be true / To one another!"

3   Before "Dover Beach," no one had purified this thought and this conviction so effectively. In "In Memoriam," grieving for the loss of his best (male) friend Arthur Hallam, Tennyson came close, but finally he retreated from committing so much to so frail a creature. Arnold, however, was holidaying with his new bride in Dover when he evidently had this experience and this resolution. He kept it secret for fifteen years, only publishing the poem in 1867, by which time Charles Darwin's *Origin of Species* had sheared away the myths of Genesis with scientific dispatch. To say openly, in an age before medicine had the knowledge and the techniques to combat illness, that there was no "help for pain" gave away hope for hope in a bleak world. Of course, Arnold would ably defend the civilizing liberal arts from an enterprising economy energized by the new sciences in his *Culture and Anarchy* (1869). Two years before, in "Dover Beach," Arnold showed why he dared do so. He must have concluded that loving someone truly remained the only alternative to a world that gives us "neither joy, nor love, nor light, / Nor certitude, nor peace, nor help for pain," and that only imagination, working on the likes of Sophocles in long-term memory, could prepare us to love truly.

4   Arnold uses his words carefully. When he says that the world does not give us "love," he means, in part, that the world lacks imagination and so can know very little about time past, which is crystallized in ancient literature like a leaf in amber, knowledge of which is an essential precondition for love. Both the world and the armies that "clash by night" are ignorant. Arnold does not mean that love does not exist, but that it comes only from a partner who, unlike the world, can share the exquisite perception and resolution such as Arnold describes in "Dover Beach." Knowledge, shaped by the well-educated imagination, leads to understanding, understanding to empathy, and empathy to "true love." Note that he says "we / Find also in the sound a thought." Of course, Arnold may also have implied, by true loving, sexual intercourse only between partners, not fornication or adultery. Victorian England engaged in sex far more than the "other Victorians" talked about it; and Matthew and his wife Flu had children.

5   Only analogy and metaphor can translate sounds into thoughts. "Dover Beach" advances by three such extended comparisons. Arnold first associates the "grating roar" that accompanies the waves, retreating and returning, casting pebbles on the beach shingles, with what Sophocles thinks of: "the turbid ebb and flow / Of human misery." If humanity is the sea, the waves collapsing ashore resemble the wretched whose cries "bring / The eternal note of sadness in."

6   Next, Arnold and his companion, the "we" overlooking a "northern sea" far from Sophocles' southern Aegean," devise a different metaphor, one more attune with their lives. If the sea is humanity's religious faith, then the "earth's shore" is the irreligious world, ever expanding as the sea's tide, having turned, retreats. Arnold embeds yet another metaphor within this comparison. The sea resembles the world's bright belt, once in folds (spread out in waves) and furled (that is, coiled up and bound).

7   Last, Arnold manages a deft transition to a quite different analogy. The Sea of Faith, which "Lay" like a belt around the earth's land, becomes "the world which seems / To lie before us like a land of dreams." Religious faith becomes a dream. Arnold brings together the two opposites, sea and land joined at their touching edges, in the phrase "naked shingles of the world." So fused, they become a single "darkling plain." The "roar," which in the first two metaphors stands for the sound of the crashing waves, or of the withdrawing tide, becomes "confused alarms of struggle and flight, / Where ignorant armies clash by night."

8   Arnold's three analogies, step by step, transport his beloved from a window overlooking a calm moonlit sea to a dark, war-torn battlefield, from security to immediate danger of death. The transition takes the friend through an argument like the seduction case of Andrew Marvell's "To His Coy Mistress." "Ah, love, let us be true / To one another!" at first appears positive and affirming. By taking vows of faithfulness, the lovers can to some extent offset the loss of religious faith in the world. However, in the lines that follow, "for the world, which seems…", Arnold uses an argument based on mutual fear. Worse, the allusion to Thucydides allows a reader to infer that the lovers are potentially like warriors on the same side who, because they could not see, have fought against rather than for one another. Having stripped his beloved of the comforts of religious faith, he drops her onto a battlefield of males, warring unintentionally against their own comrades.

9   The poem's speaker need not be its author, just as the circumstances of its composition do not supply its meaning. As honeymoon love-talk, "Dover Beach" leaves much to be desired. It sounds like arguments both for not walking out ("it's cold out there!") and for starting divorce proceedings ("he kills his friends?"). Readers have increasingly, over time, learned—mainly in classrooms—to accept the poem as autobiographical in origin. Arnold said nothing about when or for whom the poem was written at its publication in 1867. Its speaker, the "I" at line 24, could be either male or female. The beloved could be of either sex too. Its content addresses broad religious, social, and political events of its own age as much as personal relationships.

10   Perhaps on the model of Robert Browning's dramatic monologues, "Dover Beach" might express what typical well-educated newlywed couples, the sacrament of marriage still echoing in their memories, might feel in the privacy of their room, far from priests and relatives with unexceptional dogmas. On the other hand, the escalating negativism and subtly veiled threat in the last verse paragraph cannot as easily be explained away as a partly flawed transition resulting from its composition earlier than the first three paragraphs. Either Arnold did not see it—not a good sign—or he meant us to recognize the speaker's nervous drift towards suspecting that best loves might become, accidentally, very bad for one another.

11   "Dover Beach" focuses, not just on a thought detected in a sound, but on a mind, an imagination, at work. This invites an autobiographical approach as well as psychological criticism such as Norman Holland's in *The Dynamics of Literary Response*. He analyzes the typical subconscious drives and the "heavy,

massive set of defences" that the poem elicits in the reader. On the one hand, Holland cites "primitive feelings" like the child's love of a mother in the calm, full, fair, moonlit sea as well as "a well-nigh universal sexual symbolism in this heard-but-not-seen, naked fighting by night" (121). The "darkling plain" suggests a bed, the "struggle" an act of rape by a man, and "flight" a woman's reluctance. He asks what happens in the reader's mind when Arnold shifts from pebbles grating on a beach to armies fighting on a plain. One mind might claim that the poem was patched together from two parts written at different times, but another would ask, why did Arnold choose to patch them together? Why combine Sophocles and Thucydides? Holland suggests that a reader, desiring, in a woman, a mother's "protective love," would fear the closing "primal scene," and would seek for refuge in a love that was a-physical.

12   Put crudely, the fantasy involves a wish to take in from a nurturing "world" (ultimately, the mother). Countering that wish is a sound, associated initially with her withdrawal, then with father, finally with a naked clash by night—a primal scene fantasy. The poem counters the despair involved in these sounds by conjuring up the image of lovers asexual and therefore "true to one another" (127).

13   Because Holland speaks here about a reader's typical response—in the context of psychological theories about how the unconscious mind engineers wish-fulfilment fantasies under many guises, while both dreaming and waking—the only defence his analysis needs is a plausible psychological theory. Insofar as Holland implies that Arnold, as his own first reader, shaped the poem's intellectual content (the loss of religious faith, etc.) by means of a mind of whose workings he could not be fully conscious, however, Holland implies that something historically true can be said about Arnold's mind. Holland might also observe that this poem became successful for a reason. Arguably, it is powered by common fantasies.

14   However, Holland maps imagery against things, persons, and ideas with which it has few literal shared points of comparison. Infants do not drown in mother's (sea) milk or rely on their (Dover cliff) breasts as a defence against enemy invasion. People may think penises are weapons, but swords do not "weep," as Aphra Behn's disappointment did. Any mapping is only as strong as both the theoretical system into which it is embedded, and the immediate plausibility of the comparison. For a metaphor to work, it must be consistent in context.

15   For instance, Timothy D. O'Brien's interpretation of Arnold's "naked shingles" as Herpes zoster, the eruptive disease circling the waist like a belt, makes Arnold's world out, not unreasonably, to be diseased (cf. "human misery"), but then how does one interpret the "long, withdrawing roar" that retreats down these shingles? Is this the patient's moaning out in pain at the progress of the disease, or (as O'Brien implies) is it, quite differently, post-coital depression? It is not easy to maintain both meanings simultaneously. Are we supposed to think of sex between consenting sufferers from shingles? The conscious mind giggles at the mixed metaphors, at the comic inconsistency between them in context.

Bibliography

Allott, Kenneth, Michael Thorpe, and J. C. Maxwell. "The Dating of 'Dover Beach.'" *Notes and Queries* 14 (1967): 374-76.

August, Eugene R. "The Dover Switch: Or, The New Sexism at 'Dover Beach.'" *Victorian Newsletter* 77 (Spring 1990): 35-37.

Bidney, Martin. "Of the Devil's Party: Undetected Words of Milton's Satan in Arnold's 'Dover Beach.'" *Victorian Poetry* 20.1 (Spring 1982): 85-89.

Clark, Clarence C. "A Possible Source of Matthew Arnold's Dover Beach," *MLN* 17 (1902): 484-85.

Holland, Norman N. *The Dynamics of Literary Response*. New York: Oxford University Press, 1968.

Joseph, Gerhard. "The Dover Bitch: Victorian Duck or Modernist Duck/Rabbit?" *Victorian Newsletter* 73 (Spring 1988): 8-10.

Morrison, Theodore, "Dover Beach Revisited: A New Fable for Critics," *Harper's Magazine* 1980 (1940): 235-44.

O'Brien, Timothy D. "Hecht's 'The Dover Bitch.'" *Explicator* 44.2 (Winter 1986): 51-54.

The Poems of Matthew Arnold. Ed. Kenneth Allott, 2nd ed., ed. Miriam Allott. London: Longman, 1979.

Robertson, D. A. "'Dover Beach' and 'Say not the struggle naught availeth,'" *PMLA* 66 (1951): 919-20.

Schneider, Mary W. "The Lucretian Background of 'Dover Beach.'" *Victorian Poetry* 19.2 (Summer 1981): 190-95.

—. "Plutarch's Night-Battle in Arnold, Clough, and Tennyson." *The Arnoldian: A Review of Mid-Victorian Culture* 9.2 (Spring 1982): 32-38.

Super, R. H. "The Dating of 'Dover Beach.'" *Notes and Queries* 14 (1967): 61-62.

Svensson, Lars Hakan. "A Note on 'Dover Beach,' Lines 21-23." *English Language Notes* 25.4 (June 1988): 46-53.

Tinker, C. B., and H. F. Lowry. "Arnold's 'Dover Beach,'" *TLS* (October 10, 1935): 631.

—. *The Poetry of Matthew Arnold: A Commentary*. Oxford University Press, 1940.

Trawick, Buckner B. "The Sea of Faith and the Battle by Night in Dover Beach," *PMLA* 65 (1950): 1282-83.

Turner, P. "Dover Beach and The Bothie of Tober-na-vuolich," *English Studies* 28 (1947): 173-78.

Ullmann, S.O.A. "Dating Through Calligraphy: The Example of 'Dover Beach.'" *Studies in Bibliography* 26 (1973): 19-36.

Weinstock, Donald J. " 'Say not we are on a darkling plain': Clough's Rejoinder to 'Dover Beach.'" *Victorian Poetry* 19.1 (Spring 1981): 73-80.

THE VALUE OF INTERPRETATION

We began this chapter with two quotations about interpretation. Erwin Panofsky tells us that interpretation is a natural act. It is something that we do every day as we make meaning from coded messages. When we interpret these messages, we depend upon our shared knowledge of how the codes work. Although few men take off their hats as a sign of greeting, we would recognize the code from watching old movies and thus would be able to read the action as Panofsky does.

Sharing knowledge of social conventions and patterns allows us to communicate effectively in our society, but refining our interpretive skills helps us decode more complicated puzzles. As Toni Cade Bambara suggests, the works we read challenge us with "evasions, self-deceptions," and "the clutter that blinds." In other words, literature makes us confront the complications of human existence, an existence not always easily read.

Learning to be better interpreters of literature can help us to understand the complicated world we live in, to make meaning of ambiguous events, to make the unfamiliar more understandable. Skills of interpretation help us make sense of our various human problems and find new knowledge that will contribute to our search for answers to such problems.

WRITING INVITATIONS

1. Open the Victorian Web home page at http://65.107.211.206/. Find at least three resources that might help you understand the religious skepticism of the mid-19th century. After reading the entries on the Web page, write a one-page summary in which you briefly explain the historical context for Arnold's view of the "sea of faith" in his era.

2. Find the Modern Language Association electronic bibliography, then do a search for articles written about "Dover Beach" or another work chosen by you or your instructor. Go to your library and find three of those articles that would help you answer your interpretive question. After reading the articles, write a one-page research proposal in which you identify the sources that would best help you answer the interpretive questions you have about the poem. Explain why you think they would help you answer your questions.

3. Write a three to five page interpretive essay of "Dover Beach" or another work chosen by your discussion group or your instructor. After writing a first draft, exchange papers with another person in your discussion group. Read each other's papers and write a one-page response to your classmate's interpretation. After reading the other person's response, write a final, revised copy of your interpretive essay.

DEVELOPING A WRITING PROJECT

Reread the questions you wrote after reading Gwendolyn Brooks's story "Home" (or choose another short story or poem that interests you). Discuss your initial answers to your questions with other members of your reading group, then write a research plan in which you identify the questions you need to answer and the primary and secondary materials you will consult as you search for answers to your questions. After consulting your research materials, meet with your reading group again to share and compare your answers to the questions you have explored. After your group discussion, write an interpretive outline of the paper you will write. Exchange your outlines and write a list of questions for each other to help sharpen the argument of the interpretive essay. Write a five to seven page literary interpretation that presents your answer and gives reasons with evidence for your analysis of the work and your research.

CHAPTER 10

Making Judgments

Do not condemn the judgment of another because it differs
from your own. You may both be wrong.

Dandemis

Never judge a book by its movie.

J. W. Eagan

Nobody outside of a baby carriage or a judge's chamber
believes in an unprejudiced point of view.

Lillian Hellman

EVALUATIONS AS ARGUMENTS

Last night, an announcer on a regional sports network asked us to "Stay tuned"
for the next segment, in which "a panel of celebrity athletes will debate the question, 'Who is the best athlete in history?'" Imagine that conversation taking place.
What do you suppose happened? Each athlete made a case for his choice, and
in the end, they jovially agreed to disagree, pronouncing each other to be in some
way judgmentally impaired. The same thing happens any time people discuss
matters of preference or taste. They don't see their positions as arguments—each
participant is simply expressing and defending a choice; sometimes they are
aware of the criteria underlying their judgment, and sometimes they are not.

In Chapter 8, you learned that all reasons are based on assumptions, and
unless those assumptions are held in common, no agreement will be reached;
no argument will be persuasive. All judgments are based on criteria, whether
we are aware of them or not, and these criteria are the assumptions on which
our judgment is based. When your assumptions differ from those of your audience, you will be unlikely to resolve any differences, because you will just be
asserting your sets of assumptions "against" each other.

That is precisely what the athletes did. Their criteria began to emerge as the conversation progressed, but it became clear that each panel member had a different set. Even when they shared some characteristics that would qualify someone to be judged "the best athlete in history," those characteristics might be differently prioritized, as in "Sure Michael Jordan was a fierce competitor, but there's no way he could match Pele's all-around athleticism, and that's more important."

We often have conversations about issues of taste or preference like the one the panel of athletes engaged in, and they can be fun and entertaining. But if we really engage in dialogue with the purpose of understanding each other, then we have to try to be clear about our criteria, and either make sure they are shared by the other participants, or make a case that our criteria should be applied in the particular situation.

An evaluation argument explores a question at issue—a question that has more than one possible answer. It is one of the most common forms of argument in our culture, and one that is often misused, because the criteria that form the basis of the judgments made are often not stated, and are sometimes even strategically hidden in order to manipulate an audience. Sometimes people who make judgments, whether about small, personal issues, or large, culturally significant ones, aren't even aware of the criteria they are assuming. Occasionally in our classes, when students become aware of what assumptions underlie their judgments, they are surprised and may even change their minds.

In this chapter you will practice the art of informed judgment by reading and writing evaluations, a skill useful in college when you are required to compare and make judgments about the relative value of things, and in everyday life when you wish to make decisions that depend on good judgments of relative value.

The skills you practiced in other chapters of this book will be useful for the reading and writing practices in this chapter. For example, if you write a review of a written text such as a book or an article, you will need to summarize an author's ideas, to analyze the purpose of the writing and the writer's success at achieving that purpose, and to evaluate the validity of the writer's assumptions in relation to alternative perspectives. To evaluate anything, it is necessary to know of or imagine different versions of the same thing, to analyze and com-

 ## KEY CONCEPT

Evaluations Are Arguments Based on Criteria

- Evaluations are arguments about value.
- The underlying assumptions in any evaluative argument are criteria.
- To engage in a genuine dialogue about the value of anything, the participants must agree on specific criteria, or the person making the judgment must make a prior case that his or her criteria are appropriate for the situation.

pare those differences, and to argue for one version over another. These arguments are what we mean by evaluation.

READING EVALUATIONS

Identifying Criteria

In Chapter 5 you were introduced to stasis questions, or types of questions that can help you analyze the purpose of a message. In the context of the stasis question categories, the questions at issue in evaluations are question of value. We read evaluations for the writer's judgment of a product or process. Is it the best of what is available? Is it sufficient, beneficial, necessary, morally justifiable, or appropriate for the occasion? The question will usually be directly raised or implied in an introduction or a title, but the criteria are a different story. In some instances, they are directly stated. In others, they are implied.

It is important to be able to identify implied criteria as underlying assumptions if you are to understand the writer's points enough to know how to agree or disagree with them. The primary strategy for identifying unstated criteria is a bit like what participants do on the television game show *Jeopardy*. They see an answer, and they have to come up with the question that would lead to the answer. Similarly, if you read a statement in a television series review like "Occasional sexual escapades also offend, but the banter is subdued and the scenes haven't been graphic," you can see the criterion "Good television shows avoid graphic, explicit references to sexuality" behind the judgment.

Making judgments in print should involve more than simply expressing the writer's preference or taste. Writing evaluations requires the writer to take responsibility for judgments by making a case for the evaluation that a reader might consider valid.

 STRATEGY

How to Analyze Evaluations

In a well-written evaluation, you will find that the writer:

1. Orients the reader to the context of the evaluation.
2. Describes the product or process being evaluated.
3. States or implies his or her criteria.
4. States his or her own thesis about the value of the product or process.
5. Gives reasons for his or her thesis, including evaluations of credibility or believability.
6. Draws a conclusion about the value of the product or process based on how well it fulfills the criteria.

Reading Media Reviews

The purpose of film, television, video game, or other media reviews is to evaluate a product's success in meeting its entertainment goals. In addition, reviews are often invitations to watch or play, or they may offer cautions to the audience or consumer. They aren't necessarily comprehensive—for example, film reviews don't reveal surprise endings—but they do include generalizations about quality based on criteria and details to substantiate those generalizations. The following two reviews evaluate different award-winning television shows, one a comedy and one a drama. As you read them, think about the criteria on which the writers are basing their judgments.

JOHN G. NETTLES

Watch It or Else

1   No one told you life was gonna be this way…trapped in a room for half an hour every week with six people you wouldn't think twice about excising from your life if given the choice. Unfortunately, it's been made abundantly clear to you that failure to comply will make things decidedly uncomfortable around the office, and you just can't afford that. So you watch their antics, laugh at their little jokes, and furrow your brow at their tribulations as if they're somehow real or interesting, because it's something you've been told that you *must do*.

2   Who knew your very life would depend on a sitcom?

3   *Friends*, a show about six neurotic Manhattanites with fabulous apartments, is the flagship of NBC's "Must-See TV" lineup of "water-cooler" shows, those programs that would strong-arm us into believing that if you don't watch, you'll have no idea what your co-workers are talking about on Friday morning, and so, you'll find yourself ostracized, pilloried perhaps, condemned to sit alone and friendless at your desk, gazing longingly at the hip cognoscenti just a few feet away. This insulting attempt at social extortion alone is reason enough not to watch, but lord, there are so many more.

4   The Friends in question are Rachel (Jennifer Aniston), a spoiled Long Island brat with a track record of hamstringing her friends by elaborate deception in order to get what she wants; Monica (Courteney Cox Arquette), a shrill, anal-retentive control freak; Monica's brother Ross (David Schwimmer), a paleontologist so eager for validation that he repeatedly barrels into disastrous relationships; Chandler (Matthew Perry), an unrelenting jokester with serious masculinity issues that are unlikely to resolve themselves while he's engaged to Monica; Joey (Matt Le Blanc), a loveable out-of-work actor who thinks with his dick; and Phoebe (Lisa Kudrow), a former teenage runaway turned New Age space cadet, who is nonetheless the most *together* person in this crowd. Despite living in Manhattan, the six of them have managed to find unbelievably spacious apartments within sight of each other, and they spend their time hanging out in these or at Rachel's former place of employment, a coffee shop

FIGURE 10.1

THE CAST OF *FRIENDS*

named Central Perk (she works for Ralph Lauren now). The show's hook is that these people are like the cool friends you always wished you had. I *have* friends like these. I avoid them.

5   As sitcoms go, *Friends* is actually above-average, for what that's worth. The lines are fairly clever and the actors deliver them more or less humorously. The first few seasons were directed by James Burrows, an acknowledged master at handling ensemble casts (*Taxi, Cheers*), and under his tutelage this cast developed excellent timing and rapport. The comedic weaknesses of Aniston and Cox Arquette are ably countered by the precision of Perry and Kudrow (a veteran of improv groups). If it's a choice between *Friends* or any of CBS's achingly unfunny shows, line for line this bunch wins.

6   If only NBC were satisfied with funny. *Seinfeld* notwithstanding, the key to "Must-See TV" has never been comedy but continuity—making sure that if the viewer misses even one episode he or she will be thoroughly lost. In order to maintain a berth in the hallowed lineup, an NBC show must provide story arcs, ongoing threads, and "very special" episodes. Niles must crash Daphne's wedding and run away with her on a very special *Frasier*. Susan and Jack must realize their long-denied love on a very special *Suddenly Susan* (shudder). Finch marries the supermodel on a very special *Just Shoot Me* and loses the supermodel on another very special *Just Shoot Me*. On the Peacock network, sitcoms last if they're more "sit" than "com."

7   And no show slings more "sit" than *Friends*. If I'm counting right, the on-again/off-again romance between Ross and Rachel has entered its eighth season where, despite numerous outside relationships inevitably foiled by their raging codependence, the pair continues to wrestle with something the writers insist are "feelings" for each other. Monica and Chandler became engaged last season but only after old flame Tom Selleck was hauled out of secondary-character limbo to provide a gratuitous obstacle. Joey was offered another part on the soap opera that killed off his character years ago, as if the soap opera he's *in* isn't enough. The show is becoming more and more self-referential, cannibalizing ancient plotlines, confident that its viewers who remember history are eager to repeat it.

8   Evidently they're right—you can't argue with *Friends'* rampant success in the ratings—but it's a bit disturbing to think that so many people find nothing whiffy about this group dynamic. All six characters have enjoyed varying degrees of success in their chosen professions despite the fact that, save for Rachel's carrying coffee mugs at Central Perk, none of them ever seems to *work*, yet none of them have been forced to move, except to one or another of the same three apartments. They pair up but the couples never spend time alone. Even when they flat-out despise each other, *they still hang out*. Friends though they may be, these characters appear to be living in a more spacious version of Sartre's *No Exit*, stuck with each other and nowhere else to go. In the end, *Friends* has become the epitome of "Must-See TV"—not because it's in our best interest to watch it, but because without us, these people have no reason to be together. We're the only friends they've got.

STEVEN ISAAC

The West Wing

1   In September of 2000, *The West Wing* won 9 Emmy Awards for everything from Outstanding Drama to Outstanding Cinematography. It deserved every one. Its writing is riveting, the acting superb. Martin Sheen shines as President Bartlet. And his luster is reflected by an all-star ensemble Beltway staff played by Rob Lowe, Richard Schiff, John Spencer, Bradley Whitford and Allison Janney. With that kind of cast, every episode feels like a mini-movie, and *that* has made the series a bona fide hit.

2   Naturally, *The West Wing* is awash in politics. But here, unlike the programming on C-Span, viewers skip past all the dull parts and tap directly into the seamier side of Washington. No dry homilies on the House floor. No grueling analysis of statistics. No gridlock in the Senate. *The West Wing* wrings out the sensational stuff. Like heated arguments in the hallways. Saucy banter between assistants. Scandalous secrets about staffers' sex lives. Back room deals. Oval Office intrigue. Deputy communications director Sam Seaborn (Lowe), who has been secretly seeing a call girl, is a perfect example. His actions not only eerily mirror the profligate history of the actor who plays him, but provide an

FIGURE 10.2

THE CAST OF *THE WEST WING*

endless stream of gossip for the press, entertainment for the aides and headaches for his bosses.

3   Commendable, though, is an emphasis on humanity. It is stressed repeatedly that the decisions made by the White House staff affect *real* people. When a fleet of U.S. warships sails into the path of a hurricane, Bartlet agonizes over the fate of his soldiers. When an FBI negotiator is attacked trying to resolve a hostage situation, the staffer responsible for sending him torments herself over the decision. When a fighter pilot is shot down over Iraq, the president spares nothing to arrange a rescue.

4   Chief of Staff Leo McGarry (Spencer) sets *The West Wing's* tone when he makes an impassioned plea for doing the right thing, even if it costs the administration an election or dampens popular opinion. That's great rhetoric when your decisions are based on truth. His are not always so. The "right thing" to this administration includes maintaining abortion rights and supporting homosexuality.

5   Mild profanity coarsens the dialogue and alcohol gets the better of a few characters. God is both honored and abused. Occasional sexual escapades also offend, but the banter is subdued and the scenes haven't been graphic. As in real-life politics, it is in the arena of moral and social *issues* (homosexuality, abortion, faith) that the series errs most often.

APPLICATION

Analyzing Media Reviews

In groups, discuss the reviews of the television series *Friends* and *The West Wing*, and identify where the writers do the following:

1. Orient the readers to the context of the evaluation.
2. Describe the product or process being evaluated.
3. State or imply their criteria.
4. State or imply their own thesis about the value of the product or process.
5. Give reasons for and evidence supporting the thesis.
6. Draw a conclusion about the overall value of the product or process based on how well it fulfills the criteria.

Then, discuss the quality of the reviews in terms of their strengths and weaknesses. Would you add any criteria to the list of six above when describing what makes a "good" media review?

READING CRITIQUES OF PRINT MATERIAL

Critiques are more formal assessments of value than reviews, and they usually have a more specific audience. Critiques of a written work scrutinize the purposes of the work and evaluate the degree to which the writer achieves those purposes, looking specifically at rhetorical strategies beyond general appeals. When you read a critique of a book, article, or other writing, you need to be aware that the degree to which you find it persuasive will depend on whether you (1) agree with the writer's criteria, stated or not, or (2) come to accept the writer's criteria in the context of reading the critique. It is important to remember that well-written critiques have two purposes: they are intended to review strengths and weaknesses, and at the same time, they are arguments—persuading you to accept the criteria they are applying. Sometimes writers just assume that readers share their criteria, so they don't worry much about justifying them. Other times, when critics assume that their audiences may resist their judgments, they may decide to identify and justify their criteria and to do so explicitly.

Analyzing Evaluations

The following evaluation essay by Richard Bernstein reviews a book by Peter Brimelow on immigration policy. In the right margin, student reading notes indicate where Bernstein orients the reader to the context of the discussion and where his own thesis about the book appears. The notes also indicate where he describes the content of the book and the writing strategies, judges the credibility of the writer, sets his criteria, and forms his judgment. As you read the essay and the student analysis, consider what criteria are being applied. Which criteria, according to Bernstein, does Brimelow's book meet? Which does he not meet?

RICHARD BERNSTEIN

The Immigration Wave: A Plea to Hold It Back

1   Three years ago, Peter Brimelow, a writer for *Forbes* magazine and an immigrant from Britain, Writer's credibility wrote a powerful and elegant article, published in *National Review*, in which he argued that current American immigration policies were leading to disaster. For many conservatives Mr. Brimelow's argument was a kind of heresy, because it contradicted the faith in immigration as an aspect of the free market. Liberals do not generally read *National Review*, Context for the question but many of them have tended to view immigration as an enriching process, certainly a humanitarian requirement.

2   *Alien Nation* is Mr. Brimelow's book-length treatment of this subject. He has included more data Content of the book this time around than he did in his *National Review* article, and yet some of the force of his original position has been strangely lost in the book. This is in part because Mr. Brimelow has opted for a choppy polemical style, with chapters broken up into brief sub-chapters and almost every page in turn festooned with indented, boldfaced or itali- Strategies cized segments in which Mr. Brimelow highlights certain points. Mr. Brimelow's personality also comes through, and it is entirely engaging. But the Credibility essay as a whole reads too much like one of those solicitations you get in the mail urging a contribution to a political cause.

3   Still, Mr. Brimelow has made a highly cogent pre- Strategies sentation of what is going to be the benchmark case against immigration as it is currently taking place. Those who think that the system needs no fixing Bernstein's thesis cannot responsibly hold to that position any longer unless they take Mr. Brimelow's urgent appeal for change into account.

4   His starting point is the Federal legislation in 1965 that, after a pause of nearly half a century, opened up the gates to the country's third great post-independence wave of immigration, one that is far larger in absolute numbers than its predecessors, and one that is conspicuously non-European and nonwhite in nature. Sometime in the middle of the next century, if current trends continue unchanged, whites will no longer be a majority, and blacks will no longer be the largest minority.

Summary of content

5   The strong racial element in current immigration has made it more than ever before a delicate subject. It is to Mr. Brimelow's credit that he attacks it head on, unapologetically. Among his most telling points is that a certain sentimental indulgence toward immigration, combined with the fear that to be opposed to it will be seen as racist, has blinded us to its disastrous consequences. Mr. Brimelow demonstrates what he sees as the looming danger with a concept called "the wedge." By 2050, he argues, the total American population will be nearly 400 million, of whom more than one-third ("a staggering 139 million people") will be post-1970 immigrants and their descendants.

Writer's credibility

Content

6   To those of us who have seen neighborhoods revitalized by recent arrivals, and who have been heartened by the well-publicized success of some groups, especially the Asians, the obvious question is: what is so threatening about this wedge? Mr. Brimelow demonstrates (and he is well furnished with statistics) that by putting the stress on family reunification, rather than job skills, the country has made immigration a kind of civil right for the inhabitants of a small number of third world countries.

Concerns of the reader

Content

7   And, he says, the new immigrants are disproportionately prone to poverty, crime and welfare dependency. In the great immigrant wave of 1890 to 1920, Mr. Brimelow argues, about one-third returned home. Largely because of the welfare system today, he says, that has changed: "The failures are no longer winnowed out. Instead, they are encouraged to stay—at the expense of the American taxpayer."

Concerns of the reader

8   Those most likely to be harmed by the current wave of immigration, moreover, are American-born blacks, Mr. Brimelow says. Citing the economist Simon Kuznets, he argues that a major reason for black progress in this century is that immigration virtually halted between 1920 and 1965. The new wave, it stands to reason, will drive blacks out of jobs. In addition, the emergence of new racial minorities—especially Asian and Hispanic—will fundamentally alter the nature of the American nation-state, which has for most of our history been white, with a strong black minority. What Mr. Brimelow calls "the new American Anti-Idea" will produce "a sort of bureaucratically regulated racial spoils system, rather like Lebanon before its ethnic divisions finally erupted."

Assumption shared by Bernstein and Brimelow

9   Mr. Brimelow does very little on-the-scene reporting, which makes his stress on statistics seem not only abstract but also detached from the concrete human and spiritual reality involved in immigration. He is critical of the press, which, he argues, has given us only the bright side of the picture and left out other matters, like the fact that 25 percent of the prisoners in Federal penitentiaries are immigrants. And yet he himself passes rather too quickly over what the press has perhaps overstressed: the genuinely moving spectacle of millions of people making better lives for themselves in this country than they could in the countries they came from. He may also underestimate the force of assimilation, the eagerness of immigrants to adopt American values as their own.

Strategies

Assumption

10   But Mr. Brimelow also shows that America is not so much a country of immigration as it is one of "intermittent immigration." The periods where there was almost no immigration are more characteristic of our history than the briefer periods when the door was open. The lulls provided time to digest and Americanize the masses of strange and different newcomers. Mr. Brimelow's argument that without a lengthy new lull we will be in trouble is too persuasively made to be ignored.

Conclusion

Restates thesis

WRITING EVALUATIONS

In Chapter 8 we explored ways for you to develop reasoned arguments that take a position on an question at issue, give reasons for that issue, provide evidence that supports your reasons, and draw a conclusion that is supported by your reasoning and evidence. Many of the same critical thinking processes that apply to any other form of academic argument also apply to writing evaluations.

Finding Questions

What are good evaluation questions? There are three criteria. First, good evaluation questions, like all good questions, don't have obvious answers. Second, they pass the "so what" question: why should the answer matter to anyone other than you, and who are those others? Third, good evaluation questions are focused enough that you can answer them with credibility and thoroughness.

Your questions can be about anything requiring a reasoned decision about the value of something. You can judge television shows or books, as the examples in this chapter have done. You can evaluate music, cooking knives, or desktop computers with Pentium 4 processors. You can evaluate restaurant versions of the same dish, or candidates for public office. You can, and do, evaluate college classes. In all cases, though, it is important to consider whether there is a question to be answered or a decision to make, whether the evaluation has implications for sales, purchases, choices, or voting opportunities.

Identifying Criteria

To evaluate anything, you need to be able to describe what a good process, product, concept, or outcome would be like. Your description will constitute your criteria. For example, here is a list of criteria that we believe describes the good student, regardless of area of study:

1. Understands the process of inquiry.
2. Reads responsibly and responsively.
3. Reasons critically.
4. Invents imaginatively.
5. Represents ideas effectively.
6. Plans carefully.
7. Revises thinking and language choices to improve communication.
8. Collaborates well.

Could you write a self-evaluation of your strengths and weaknesses as a student based on these criteria?

To begin thinking about your criteria, state your responses and reactions to your question honestly and clearly. The process you go through may be quite revealing, because we rarely take the time to consider our judgments. Why do

I react the way I do? What makes me feel that way? Beliefs? Values? Would it be the same for others? What are the odds that other people share the beliefs and values that I have?

Then, translate those assumptions into criteria and consider whether your audience shares them. If you have good reason to believe that they are shared, you can simply state them. But if you think they may be at issue for your audience, you may need to begin your evaluation by establishing why your criteria are legitimate. Some evaluators even adopt criteria based on beliefs and values held by their audience in order to prove that something the audience seems to support actually contradicts their beliefs.

To identify criteria that might be used to evaluate something, first consider relevance, which is related to purpose and audience. It wouldn't be fair to evaluate a sitcom negatively for lacking seriousness when the purpose of the sitcom is humor. It might, however, be fair to evaluate a sitcom negatively for turning unexpectedly serious, because that would be a violation of purpose and audience expectation. In addition, make sure the group of things you are comparing something to is as specific as possible. A guitar used to perform a Vivaldi concerto in an acoustically sensitive hall would be valued for the clarity of its tone; the same guitar would not meet the criteria for use by a heavy metal band in an auditorium. The classical guitar shouldn't be compared to the rock guitar; each has standards within its own class. The more specific your knowledge, the more precisely defined the groups and classes become.

Another way to consider relevance is to consider your purposes for judging. First, are the criteria going to tell you what you need to know? Colleges are always discussing what criteria they should use to select new students. Test scores and grade point averages are convenient, but how relevant are they to what the colleges are looking for in a member of that community? Most invite some kind of writing sample, but the criteria for judging that sample are rarely stated, making the process of evaluation seem mysterious.

Second, are your standards appropriate for your purpose? Are you evaluating to determine what example of the thing is *best*, which is the best within a particular range (cost or color, for example), or are you determining whether particular things meet minimum or sufficient standards? Most of you have taken achievement tests. Some measure all students at a particular grade level against all others; others measure particular skills and determine whether each student has met them. This example points out the importance of purposeful standards. On the one hand, the best score is almost impossible to achieve, so evaluating with perfection as the ultimate standard may make it seem impossible to satisfy the evaluator. On the other hand, standards that measure acceptability, or minimums, may cause the lowering of expectations and, as a result, of achievement.

Identifying Your Purpose and Position

The primary purpose for an evaluation is always to persuade someone of the value of something, and your criteria and reasons are your means of doing that. However, you may also have secondary purposes. Evaluations regarding public policy will almost always seek to inform. Evaluations of popular culture will almost always seek to entertain as well as persuade. Evaluations of ideas may seek to challenge, or subvert, the biases of the audience.

Your evaluative argument will be based on a thesis statement like this one:

_____ is a good/best/poor/worst/unjustifiable/reasonable _____, because it has/does not have these features or meets/does not meet these criteria _____.

This thesis statement may appear at the beginning of your critique, or it may appear for the first time in your conclusion, depending on what organizing strategy you choose. However, it will guide your strategy for the whole critique—what to include, what to exclude, in what order, with what kinds of stylistic features.

How you want your audience to respond to your subject will be evident in your position. What you want your audience to do or know or think or feel about your subject may be less obvious, but it is always worth thinking about.

Developing Your Position with Reasons and Evidence

In Chapter 5, you learned to analyze the strategies writers use to persuade readers in terms of three kinds of appeal:

ethos or the ethical appeal: it appeals to readers' value systems.

pathos or the emotional appeal: it appeals to readers' emotions.

logos or the logical appeal: it appeals to readers' reasoning.

Any evaluation can employ reasoning based on any of the appeals. Evaluations about everyday judgments that have as their purpose creative personal exploration may make effective emotional appeals. One of our students once wrote a very entertaining piece titled "Nestle makes the Very Best Chocolate—or Do They?" taking the title from an old advertising slogan. The entire development compared the experience of eating various types of chocolate to other physical experiences using metaphors, similes, and sense imagery. Another wrote about deciding which college to attend, and his answer finally rested on criteria that had more to do with his comfort on the campuses than it did with tuition rates or nationally-recognized program excellence.

Writers of evaluations almost always need to appeal to the readers' value systems because, in order for readers to accept the writer's judgments, they must accept his or her credibility as a judge. We usually find it very difficult to accept the judgments of people we do not respect.

Of course, evaluations are also grounded in observations and evidence. For every criterion, the judgment of whether the thing being evaluated meets it or not will depend on how persuasive are the observations and reasons a writer brings to bear. In a book critique, for example, evaluators observe the rhetorical strategies and determine how they are meant to appeal to the reader. Is the strategy designed to help us identify emotionally with the situation? Is it designed to appeal to our sense of order and logic? Is it meant to create in us a sense of shared values, of community? Chapter 5 demonstrates how the choice of words, the arrangement of sentences, the selection of examples, or the structure or sequence of the ideas may all appeal to us in any of these ways, and often in all of them simultaneously. If the writing is successful, then the combination of the strategies works to create in the reader a sense of purpose and comprehension. If they do not work, then the strategies have failed to bring a particular reader into the rhetorical situation that the writer is attempting to share.

As you develop your reasons and evidence, challenge your knowledge and observations and test your assumptions. Read, talk, listen. Watch for points others make that validate, modify, or contradict your position, and adjust your ideas as your thinking is clarified. Use secondary sources as relevant to help contextualize and substantiate your evaluation.

Drawing Conclusions

The conclusion of an evaluation will summarize the match of criteria to features and characteristics, and generalize about the value of the subject in broader terms. It may include generalizations, as well, about the implications of the evaluation for your understanding of yourself, the larger context of the subject (e.g., the implications of the comparisons of two NBA centers for the future of professional basketball strategy), or in the case of public practice or policy issues, for society or the world.

WRITING BOOK AND ARTICLE CRITIQUES

In a critique that argues the value of a book or other piece of writing, we analyze the assumptions either stated or implied in the writing to see if we agree with them. If we don't agree with them, then the reasons based on the assumptions will also be unacceptable. How do we determine whether the assumptions are valid? As we do when we respond to other kinds of arguments, we may test them against known evidence, against other possible beliefs that seem equally or more likely, and even against our own experience and personal knowledge. But in all cases, when we evaluate the work of others, we must be prepared to submit our own assumptions and our reasons for believing them to the scrutiny of others.

The thesis statement for a book critique will include both your conclusion about the value of the writing and your main reasons for your conclusion. The development of the critique will establish criteria for the book, describe the strategies of the writer, and explain how the strategies do or do not meet the criteria.

As part of the process of judging how well a piece of writing works, you match the elements of the work with its stated purpose. If the purpose is primarily to inform, then the writer of a critique might pay attention to clarity, order, and specificity. If the purpose is primarily persuasive, then the critique must address the quality of the reasoning and the validity of the evidence. If the purpose is primarily to entertain, then the evaluation should ask what effect was intended, what effect was achieved, and to the extent that the intention was or was not realized, why that was the case.

All writers of evaluations have to establish their own credibility, but they also must contend with judging the credibility of the author. Do you believe this writer? Why or why not? In writing critiques, as in courts of justice, we think about the degree to which the writer's knowledge is "firsthand." If it is not, we ask whether he or she is relying on other sources we can count on. We think about whether the writer expresses, directly or indirectly, prejudices that would strongly bias his or her way of looking at the subject. The writer's bias doesn't necessarily render the information useless, but it does mean we, as readers and observers, will be encouraged to seek out other voices on the subject whose perspectives are different. In assessing credibility we think, too, about how knowledgeable the writer is, how much he or she seems to know about the subject, how much research and inquiry and observation were involved in shaping the ideas. These are some criteria for judging the credibility of the writer.

Where it is relevant to the type of book, writers of critiques must also examine the strength of the reasoning. Do you accept the evidence that supports the reasons? Why or why not? Generally, we like evidence that seems to be specific, clear, and precise. We want sufficient evidence, enough to ensure that the picture is as complete as possible. We want evidence that is consistent with other accounts of the same information, or we want an explanation of why the evidence is inconsistent with other accounts. These are some criteria for judging the validity of evidence.

Structure the critique for clarity and readability. If your readers know the work you are critiquing, they still may need to recall the writer's position. If they do not know the work, you may need to give them more information. You need not include a paragraph of summary at the beginning of your critique, although some people do. You may include statements of summary throughout your piece as you address your criteria. The main thing to remember is that the point of your critique is not to rephrase the material you are critiquing, but to share with your reader your informed opinion about the work's value.

Specific details always help readers understand complex ideas. A good way to illustrate a writer's key ideas is by paraphrasing (restating) or citing specific instances of each idea. The specific references to the text are especially necessary when you are disagreeing with a writer's ideas because you will need to persuade your readers that you are reading and reasoning carefully and not overstating or misstating the writer's positions.

As you describe the contents of a book, article, or essay, you must be especially careful to represent the work responsibly and objectively. This is how you establish your own credibility as someone who should be trusted to offer a useful and reliable representation of the work's value.

Certainly, the features of critiques that we have described above will not appear in the order given. There are many ways to organize your information. See the "Writing a Critique" strategy box for a basic structure that can be used as you create your first draft.

STRATEGY

Writing a Critique

There are many ways to organize your information to present the best critique you can. However, you might keep in mind the following basic structure as you draft; then you can add, delete, and reorder as you revise in accordance with your purpose.

1. Introduce the title and the writer of the piece you are going to critique.

2. Note the key question the writer raises and answers in the work.

3. Place the question in a context that helps explain its significance for other readers. You might include information about the writing: does it come from a larger work or a collection? Information about the writer: do the circumstances under which it was written help to explain its purpose and strategies? Information about the subject: is it related to a larger controversy or current issue?

4. State the writer's main answer to his or her question.

5. Summarize the writer's key arguments and assumptions.

6. State your response to the work in a thesis statement, accompanied by the criteria you will use to evaluate the writing. (If you choose, you may summarize the writer's arguments and assumptions one at a time as you evaluate them.)

7. Match each criterion with evidence from the text illustrating how the work does or does not meet the criterion.

8. Draw one or more conclusions about the validity and value of the writing as a whole.

Sample Student Writing: Critique

Before reading this critique, you may want to read Deborah Tannen's "Can't We Talk?" in Casebook 3. It will give you a context for some of the concepts that Takeuchi mentions in her evaluation of Tannen's *You Just Don't Understand*.

Deborah Tannen's *You Just Don't Understand*

Mayo Takeuchi

In her best-selling book *You Just Don't Understand*, Dr. Deborah Tannen makes a number of observations about the problems that men and women encounter when trying to communicate with each other. As a sociolinguist, Tannen attempts to identify and explain the origins of such phenomena as unbalanced talking, metamessages, and inherent value differences and purposes of communication between the sexes. It is my opinion that her book actually undermines her intention to help society because of its very premise: Tannen implies that, because of the problems she has seen, communication between men and women is fundamentally riddled with insurmountable obstacles.

The last paragraph of the book's preface mentions that one of Tannen's students had such difficulty in communicating with her husband that the marriage nearly failed. Tannen quotes the husband as saying "Dr. Tannen had better...write that new book, because this business of men and women talking has got to be the biggest problem around!" Then she dedicates the book to "women and men everywhere who are trying their best to talk to each other."

By implying that the problem of communication between women and men is so prevalent that the most people can do is "try their best," Tannen perpetuates stereotypes that serve to inhibit the behavior and to increase the breadth of misconceptions that would widen the gap between the sexes. Although Tannen's remarks about political and economic inequity and psychological causes of behavioral traits are valid and even useful, her book barely acknowledges the fact that there are plenty of people who do not communicate in a gender-typed manner, and who do not even identify with the societal forces that Tannen describes because of the shifts in cultural views and family structure.

It is unclear how culturally diverse Tannen's students might be, but the couples she refers to appear to be at least in their 30's, and are thoroughly Americanized. The age group of these students means that they were brought up under a different social stigma—specifically, Tannen's theories about male and female conversational role models work for these people because they were more likely to have been exposed to the "appropriate" adult model within a nuclear family. In more recent times there has been a rapid increase in families consisting of single mothers and their children. This would mean that boys are more likely to be brought up with only a strong female conversational model; thus they should develop a more feminine style of communicating. Indeed, of my own experiences with male peers who grew up without a masculine figure, none of them demonstrate the supposedly pervasive traits of male talk (whether it be discomfort in rapport-talk, a tendency to lecture rather than listen, or impolite interrupting) as defined by Tannen.

None of my friends' speaking styles supports Tannen's theories about consistent gender-defined behavior in conversations. Even in situations where a male peer has more information to impart than I or another female acquaintance may have, he tends to hold back or at least allow an egalitarian distribution of floor time. The instances where there is a clear lecturer/listener dichotomy as described by Tannen do not consistently occur in a gender-typed manner within my circle of peers at MIT. Moreover, I have witnessed numerous examples of cooperative overlap and of rapport-talk between male students, as well as partaken in report-talk (or conversations lacking in personal references or emotional content) with female friends.

In the seventh chapter, Tannen discusses various kinds of interrupting, suggesting that men and more aggressively communicating ethnic and religious groups such as New York Jews tend to dominate in both report and rapport talk scenarios. Although she vaguely cautions against generalizations (206 and 207), the vast majority of her examples and statements work toward enforcing cultural stereotypes. Even if her assertions of there being consistently identifiable ethnic differences are accurate, she has not taken into account the factor of Americanization, and how later generations of immigrants from most backgrounds assimilate easily and eagerly into Western modes of communication. Of the classmates I had when I used to attend Japanese language school in Canada, the majority was there because they were forced to go. They stubbornly resisted being viewed or treated as Japanese, and used English first names and interacted in a manner identical to non-Japanese students their age. If they have since grown up to be adults who could be described stereotypically, they would certainly have avoided behavior that would be consistent with the Japanese culture, such as polite or understated approaches they typically take when instigating and participating in conversations.

Given this phenomenon it might also be construed that, given the rebellious tendency of adolescents, one might also expect the trend that Tannen mentions of parental roles being emulated by children to be weaker than assumed, if adolescents realize the limitations of expected gender-specific conversation styles, or simply decide to rebel against this and other concepts that restrict both women and men. Thus the problems that Tannen has identified would naturally decrease as social structures and expectations change.

Another disturbing aspect of Tannen's writing is how she falls into the very traps that she observes and encourages others to avoid. On page 209 she mentions how she would like to avoid negativity in describing behavioral traits (such as that of rude interrupting, which she describes in the same chapter); however, the examples she chooses, such as the interchange between Zoe and Earl, on pages 212 through 214, and the exaggeratedly dysfunctional dialogue from an Ingmar Bergman movie (cited on page 220) evoke skewed views of society today. While claiming to have a feminist perspective, Tannen also implies on page 215 that women might be strong but cannot help but be different from men. The "rules of the game" seem to be fixed in Tannen's opinion; although her defense of what she perceives is the quintessential woman's situation is laudable, she is not acknowledging that it is actually possible to bend or even take away those boundaries that her patients have difficulties in surmounting.

In my personal conversational experiences, I have been constantly reminded of a fundamental concept that Tannen fails to mention in her book. I have observed that people are capable of portraying different characters, or expressing different aspects of their personality and behavior in front of different audiences. Although there are varying degrees of this phenomenon, I and others around me are aware that we will converse in a manner that will elicit not only the desired reactions from whomever we address, but also enable us to communicate the most effectively. While I am capable of expressing sympathy and concern towards someone in distress, and reveal personal details about my own situations that might comfort them, I am also able to exchange facts with someone in a "no-nonsense" manner that Tannen attributes to a masculine frame of mind.

Conversely, I have heard profoundly emotional and private confessions of insecurities and fears from men, just as I have listened to assertive, educational lecture-like monologues from my women acquaintances. Even if one could label these supposedly aberrant examples of conversations as role-reversing behavior, it would still lead to the logical conclusion that, if men and women are capable of conversational styles that do not stereotypically fit them, they should also have the ability to put themselves in the shoes of the opposite sex. This, in turn, must mean that there is much more hope than Tannen has admitted to regarding men and women reconciling their differences, since obstacles of communication and understanding would be half solved if only one side could see the other's perspective.

Near the end of the eighth chapter, which deals with the double standards and linguistic oppression experienced by women, Tannen cites numerous studies (236 and 237) that she believes validate her remark that both girls and women adjust conversationally to male standards and forms of conversing. Again, I have never found this to be consistently true. In my experience everywhere, the dominant personality tended to determine the nature of the discussion or conversation, regardless of the sex of the said personality.

Despite the accessible prose and vivid case studies, Tannen's purpose of providing what one reviewer claimed was a "manageable perspective" on male-female communication problems is sadly unfulfilled. As long as researchers dealing with popular psychology or linguistics such as Tannen continue to confidently assert that there are such aggrandized barriers between men and women, the public will continue to be misled into examining issues of communication from a more hopeless angle. Eventually, one must realize that these problems, while significant, can be dealt with readily if only we stop refusing to see the common aspects of humanity and our individual uniqueness as well as ability to truly understand other people's situations.

APPLICATION

Analyzing a Critique

Read Mayo Takeuchi's review of Deborah Tannen's Book *You Just Don't Understand.* Identify where she orients the reader to the context of the discussion and where her own thesis about the book appears. Then note where she describes the content of the book and the writing strategies, judges the credibility of the writer, sets her criteria and forms her judgment. What criteria are being applied? Which criteria, according to Takeuchi, does Tannen's book meet? Which does she not meet?

 STRATEGY

Writing a Researched Evaluation

To write a credible evaluation, you will need to:

1. Identify your question.
2. Identify your purpose.
3. Orient your reader to the context of the discussion.
4. State your criteria directly or indirectly.
5. Identify as clearly as possible the assumptions that underlie your evaluation.
6. State your thesis about the value of the product or process being evaluated.
7. Write a thesis statement that includes both your conclusion about the value of the subject and your main reasons for your conclusion.
8. Challenge your knowledge and observations and test your assumptions through reading research and listening to the opinions of others. Read, talk, listen. Acknowledge fairly any alternatives to your position, and address those ideas with respect.
9. Develop your ideas by matching each criterion to features of the alternative, and support your points with evidence and reasoning.
10. Conclude your evaluation with generalizations about the value of the alternative and the significance of your position for your audience.

WRITING A RESEARCHED EVALUATION

In college, you may be called on to research, synthesize, and evaluate a number of alternatives and reach a conclusion about the most reasonable or advisable option within a particular set of circumstances. You may also be asked to evaluate a particular alternative and determine whether it fills the requirements, or criteria, for a specific situation or need. A researcher might be asked to use criteria to evaluate several prospective options for the best among alternatives, or she might be asked to evaluate a specific option to determine its degree of acceptability in terms of the criteria. Either way, the critical thinking processes described in this chapter can guide the development of an appropriate response to the situation.

The researched evaluation will rely on print and non-print resources to provide evidence and support for a position. These kinds of evaluations will follow all of the conventions and expectations of any other academic argument, but the structure of the argument will match criteria to features, measuring the value of the alternative or alternatives under consideration.

This kind of writing assignment utilizes the skills of summary, research, synthesis, argument, and interpretation (of data) to draw a conclusion about the value of something.

Sample Student Writing: Researched Evaluation, MLA Documentation Style

Orca Whales: Are They Endangered?

Charlotte Bemis

All their lives, the three men in the tiny boat had been told that orca whales are killers, "wolves of the sea." Yet undeterred, they sat hunched in their small zodiac craft, watching as a pod of orcas circled in a small inlet. They thrust their headphones on and listened for sounds from the underwater microphone, but the normally vocal orcas were silent. Some fishermen had tipped off the three researchers that a pod of whales was exhibiting strange behavior, and when they arrived on the scene the reports were confirmed. Three female whales were lined up side by side in the center of the inlet with the others in a circle around them, as if intently watching or protecting them. As the researchers looked closer, they saw that two of the females in the center appeared to be lowering the third female into the water and then bringing her up to breathe. They sat quietly and unobtrusively pondering the strange, stationary behavior of the normally mobile whales. All of a sudden, their headphones erupted with vibrant vocalizations from the whales. They seemed to be celebrating. As the bemused researchers watched, they suddenly saw a terrifying sight. Sitting only three feet out of the water, they saw the six-foot tall dorsal fins of three gigantic male orcas racing toward them. A lifetime full of fisherman's tales of the brutal "killer whales" raced through their minds as they sat paralyzed and watched their death coming closer. Six feet from the tiny zodiac, the males stopped their headlong rush, and what the researchers saw next nearly stopped their frantically beating hearts. The three males held among them a tiny newborn orca calf. The males had not been attacking the men. Like proud new uncles, they seemed to be showing off the newest member of the pod, and the researchers were touched that they had been made part of the celebration of a new life. Think what you like, but whales watch us, as we watch them.

This story is a favorite of naturalist and wildlife guide Andrew McNeil of the Glacier Spirit, a whale watching boat on which I worked as a crew member this past summer. He loves to tell the story at the end of a long day of whale watching in the San Juan Islands. The best part about the story is that it's true, a fact not doubted in the slightest by any of the listener-passengers who are spending the day observing these magnificent creatures.

In the past twenty years, we have come to know a myriad of impressive and inspiring qualities of the orcas, but recently researchers have made some discoveries that inspire less awe and more concern. The population of the Southern Resident Community of orcas, their range extending from lower Puget Sound through British Columbia, is declining at an alarming rate. Researchers cite several possible causes for this decline, including high levels of toxins in the blood, a decrease in their food source, the stress put on them by private and commercial boats, and a reduced breeding population due to live captures in the 1960s and 1970s (Cahape). It is our responsibility and will be to our benefit and that of the whole ecosystem to remedy the problem of the orca population decline. One proposed way to help the situation is to try to put the orcas of the Southern Resident Community on the Endangered Species List as "threatened." But do they qualify, and would it help to list them?

Because the Southern Resident Community of Orcas fit the criteria for a "threatened" species under the Endangered Species Act of 1973, we must act to correct the decline of the species by protecting them under the provisions of that act. For a species to be considered threatened, it must fit just one of the many criteria listed. The orcas fit two. These are (1) "the present or threatened destruction, modification, or curtailment of its habitat or range," and (2) "other natural or manmade factors affecting its continued existence" (Endangered Species 7).

Certainly research supports the qualification of the Southern Resident Community in terms of the first criterion. Researchers tend to agree that the habitat has suffered great damage in the past few decades. The most serious threat to the orcas seems to be the extremely high levels of toxins in their systems, especially polychlorinated hydrocarbons (PCBs), which affect immune and reproductive systems. Though PCBs were banned in the United States more than twenty years ago, they are still persistent in the environment because they do not break down. In addition, Mexico and much of Asia continue to allow the use of PCBs which can travel widely, both in the oceans and as airborne particles (Cahape). According to Heather Harding, a whale researcher and naturalist aboard the Glacier Spirit, "these toxins accumulate in the systems of whales because [they] have no way of biologically processing them." Whales are mammals like us, so "essentially, while they nurse their young, the first sip of milk has toxins in it" (qtd. in Cahape). Orcas primarily get these toxins by ingesting contaminated fish, which leads to another factor in their decline that qualifies them for Endangered Species protection under the first criterion.

The favorite meal of these orcas is salmon, but as there has been a drastic decline in the salmon population, the orcas are probably eating more rockfish or bottomfish. These species carry even higher levels of

PCBs than do salmon, so the orcas are probably accumulating even higher levels of toxins (Whale Museum, "Pacific"). In addition, orcas are at the top of several food chains and toxic substances accumulate as they move up a food chain. As a result, these top predators of the ocean tend to be more affected by pollutants than are other sea creatures (Whale Museum, "Issues").

The factors discussed so far are evidence both of the destruction of the habitat of the orcas, the first criterion, and evidence of the second. There is other strong evidence that both natural and manmade factors are affecting the continued existence of the Southern Resident Population. Before we can accurately assess whether the Southern Resident Community meets the second criterion, we need to define it as a specific population. The orcas of this community include the members of three pods, or family groups, known as J, K, and L. It is these three pods in particular that researchers are concerned about. According to researchers at the Center for Whale Research on San Juan Island, the population has plummeted from 98 in 1995 to the current count of 83. This year alone, eight orcas died while only three were born (Whale Museum, "Pacific"). This mortality rate is alarming not just because of the whales lost this year, but because of the effect current deaths will have on future populations. Orcas do not take a permanent mate, but breed with many different mates throughout their lifetimes. Because of this "random" breeding, the bloodlines are traced through the mother. Armed with the matrilineal family tree and the record of which whales have died, researchers are able to make population projections. Current predictions assert that of the 15 matrilineal lineages in L pod, half are threatened with extinction, along with two or three lineages in K pod (Whale Museum, "Pacific"). The disappearance of these bloodlines would cause an even more serious population crash from which it would be difficult to recover. Thus this specific population is in dire need of consideration for legal protection through the Endangered Species Act.

One underlying, devastating, manmade factor affecting the orca population is a mistake we made a long time ago. 1967 to 1973 was the "live capture" era during which 48 orcas were captured, or killed in the attempt, from the Southern Resident Community by such companies as Sea World. This is not to put all the blame on Sea World, because back then no one had any idea what an enormous loss the captures would inflict on the orca population. But by the time people realized the damage that was being done and the captures were stopped, much of a generation had been wiped out. It is these missing whales that would now be the breeding stock (Cahape). The orcas still have not recovered their pre-capture era numbers, and their struggle to do so is being further inhibited by the new problems of diminishing salmon and toxic pollution.

Like the canaries that miners took into the mines, the death of the orcas is an indicator that something drastic is wrong with our ecosystem. In light of this message, the complete solution to the problem would necessitate, unfortunately, broad social changes on many fronts. To get to the root of the problem, to, in effect, cure the disease, the large issues of global pollution and habit degradation must be addressed. Though countless attempts to clean up the environment are underway, it is nonetheless our responsibility to take the legal precautions we have available to protect the orcas living now. Until we can find a cure, we must treat the symptoms. Because the orcas fit the criteria of the Endangered Species Act of 1973 for the determination of endangered and threatened species, they should be listed and receive the protection the law allows. In fact, Canada has already listed the Southern Resident Community as threatened in their version of the Endangered Species List, but their listing has no "teeth" (Cahape). In the United States, listing the orcas would mean more stringent protection of the orcas and their habitat. The Endangered Species Act of 1973, like most legal documents, is long and cumbersome. But it holds within it the guidelines for producing "recovery plans" for the protection and survival of threatened species. There are also certain instances where a state can receive federal funding for programs to benefit the threatened or endangered species (Endangered Species).

There are, of course, arguments against listing the orcas. Industries such as logging, commercial fishing, and even whale watching may be threatened by a listing on the Endangered Species List (Cahape). Though their arguments have all been heard before, the industry fears are definitely significant. The key argument will come once again, as with the spotted owl and the salmon, to saving jobs versus saving nature. This is a double-edged sword. No one wants to put people out of work, but there won't be any work for them if the ecosystem starts to shut down. There must be a compromise in which industry and conservation work together, and this is not as impossible as it seems. Most conservationists aren't radical, nor are the loggers and fishermen as backward and self-serving as the media often make them out to be. However, there will be no negotiation unless the listing prods the groups to move beyond the bickering and mudslinging coming from both sides.

Another argument against listing the Southern Resident Community is that there are plenty of orcas throughout the world, so the species as a whole is not really threatened. It is true that there is a large orca population. In fact, the Northern Resident Community of orcas that ranges from midway through British Columbia to Alaska has a healthy population. But just because there are orcas elsewhere doesn't mean that it is acceptable to allow the extinction of the orcas in Puget Sound. The three pods of the Southern Resident Community—J, K, and L—are each a unique family group. Orcas stay with their mothers their entire lives, leaving only to breed with one of the other pods in the community. Because of this, each pod is a closely-knit family that functions as an independent community. In fact, each pod has its own language with which to communicate. When J, K, and L pods get together to breed, they must communicate with a second, more "generic" language because they don't understand other pods' "talk." On the occasions when the resident orcas cross paths with transient orcas from off the coast, they have no communication at all (McNeil). In essence, each community and its constituent pods is a different ethnic group. To destroy one pod would be akin to genocide. If for some this brutal analogy is too idealistic, a more practical, utilitarian answer to the argument can be made. The health of the Southern Resident Community reflects the health of the Puget Sound ecosystem as a whole. To ignore the death of the orcas would be to ignore the larger issue of environmental imbalance. Disturbingly, we really do not know what unforeseen consequences a species missing from the web of nature may have on us.

The ecosystem is a complex web interconnected in more ways than we can imagine. Despite our vast amounts of research, we are only beginning to catch a glimpse of the incredibly intricate workings of nature. Walter Beacham puts it eloquently when he says, "No one knows the value of most species to humans or to lower life forms. From this ignorance should arise the importance of preservation" (1). If the loss of a beautiful species is not reason enough to help protect the orcas, fear for our own precious health should tip the scales in favor of conservation.

In the end, it is the general public that really needs to be convinced to change its ways. If enough people believe in a cause, something usually gets done. This is evidenced by the recent attempts to return Keiko, of the "Free Willy" films, to the wild. Though it is opposed by many, including whale researchers who doubt that he will survive, there is tremendous public support of the "rescue" attempt, and vast amounts of money have been pumped into saving one whale. If such vigorous support was to be directed at the problem of the Southern Resident Community, the results could be phenomenal. But if people are to care, they must see the problem. One way to show people the problem is to attempt to list the Southern Resident Community orcas as threatened on the Endangered Species List. If the listing were approved, the legal benefits would be a good first step in the effort to help the whales. But even if the listing does not go through, the increased public awareness and subsequent support could greatly help the orcas and the environment.

Works Cited

Beacham, Walter, and Loyal H. Mehrhoff, eds. <u>The World Wildlife Fund Guide to Extinct Species of Modern Times</u>. Osprey, FL: Beacham Publications, 1997.

Cahape, Beth. "What's Killing Our Orcas" <u>The Port Townsend Leader</u>, 22 Sept. 1999: B1+.

Endangered Species Act of 1973 (as amended through Dec. 1996). Compiled for the use of Committee on Resources, U.S. House of Representatives, One Hundred Fifth Congress, First session, Committee print 105-C. 29 Nov. 1999. <http://www.house.gov/resources/105cong/reprts>.

McNeil, Andrew. Personal interview. 26 Nov. 1999.

The Whale Museum, San Juan Island. Pacific Northwest Orca Population Declining. 23 Nov. 1999 <http://www.whalemuseum.org/issues.html>.

———. Issues. 23 Nov. 1999 <http://www.whalemuseum.org/issues.html>.

■ APPLICATION

Analyzing a Researched Evaluation

Analyze the components of Charlotte Bemis's essay on orca whales in terms of the strategies in the "Writing a Researched Evaluation" strategy box (page 304). What is her question? What is her purpose? Where does she orient the reader to the context of the discussion? What criteria is she applying? Where does she reveal assumptions and biases? Is there evidence that she has researched and listened to the opinions of others who agree and disagree with her position? Does she address alternate views with respect? Does she match her criteria with reasoning and evidence? Does she conclude her evaluation with generalizations about the significance of her position for her audience?

THE RESPONSIBILITY OF JUDGING

As you observed when reading evaluations, the questions at issue in writing evaluations are questions of value. Sometimes these are everyday issues of personal concern. Which cell phone company is best for me? Which desktop computer meets my needs? Which class would I recommend to others? Sometimes the issues are academic, as in book or article critiques related to your areas of study. Sometimes the issues relate to public policy. As we write this textbook, for example, the United States is in a nationwide dialogue that will, by the time our book reaches a public audience, have been answered in one way or another—whether to engage in military action against the country of Iraq. Nearly every article about this issue includes criteria that would, for each author, constitute sufficient grounds for engaging militarily. The phrase "smoking gun" is used often as a criterion, a metaphor for evidence that would irrefutably prove that Iraq poses an immediate threat to the United States. How this dialogue is to be resolved is unclear as we write, and its resolution may take a form as yet unexpressed in the public forum. But the importance of being able to carefully consider, and repeatedly and conscientiously reconsider, criteria could have no more significant illustration than this kind of public debate.

WRITING INVITATIONS

1. Review a movie, a recording, or a work of art. Begin by examining other items in the same category to develop criteria for judgment. Make your criteria as specific, clear, and precise as possible. Evaluate the subject according to your criteria, and then draw conclusions regarding its relative value. Then write a three to five page review of the work you have evaluated.

2. Locate two articles on the same subject, either in one of the casebooks in this book or in the library. (College instructors and reference librarians can be very helpful in identifying interesting reading material related to particular disciplines.) Write a three to five page essay in which you critique the articles, and then compare them according to criteria that you identify.

DEVELOPING A WRITING PROJECT

1. Having identified and selected several pieces of writing on the same issue for an extended evaluation research project, reflect on what judgments are being made in the pieces of writing and identify the criteria that form the basis of those judgments. Evaluate the relevance and trustworthiness of your source material in terms of the extent to which the writers' criteria are appropriate and acceptable to you and to your purpose. Reflect on and record the results of your

critical reading. How do your observations affect the ways you may or may not use particular sources in your research project?

2. As you plan, identify ways in which the purpose of your writing project involves judgments. What are *your* criteria for judging? Is it likely that your audience will support them? If not, can you support their validity through reasoning and evidence?

3. Write a researched evaluation in which you do the following:

Identify your question.

Identify your purpose.

Orient your reader to the context of the discussion.

State your criteria directly or indirectly.

Identify as clearly as possible the assumptions that underlie your evaluation.

State your thesis about the value of the subject being evaluated.

Write a thesis statement that includes both your conclusion about the value of the subject and your main reasons for your conclusion.

Challenge your knowledge and observations and test your assumptions through reading research and listening to the opinions of others. Read, talk, listen. Acknowledge fairly alternatives to your position on your subject, and address those ideas with respect.

Develop your ideas by matching each criterion to features of the subject, and support your points with evidence and reasoning.

Conclude your evaluation with generalizations about the value of the subject and the significance of your position for your audience.

PART 3

Designing and Refining Your Writing

CHAPTER 11

Visual Rhetoric and Document Design

Everyone designs who devises courses of action aimed at
changing existing situations into preferred ones.

Herbert Simon, *The Science of Design: Creating the Artificial*

VISUAL RHETORIC

Rhetoric, as we defined it in Chapter 1, is the art of testing ideas with people who share our questions. The Greek rhetorician Aristotle defined rhetoric as the art of finding "in any given situation the available means of persuasion." He believed that those who could arouse emotions in listeners and create an image of credibility with them were more likely to move an audience to accept the evidence and reasoning being presented. Certainly in our times, visual media are pervasively available and often very persuasive. Some would say pictures, sounds, and multimedia experiences are more persuasive than print on a page can ever be. It is essential, then, that if we are to be literate, we will understand not just the purposes and rhetorical effects of words, but also the purposes and rhetorical effects of images.

As we explained in Chapter 5, to read and write rhetorically is to be conscious of the effects of the signs and symbols we are using. To the extent that we are conscious of the effects of words when we comprehend them or use them to compose, we are considered verbally literate. To the extent that we are conscious of the effects of images and other non-verbal signs and symbols, we are considered visually literate. This chapter will introduce some ways that we, as readers and writers, can begin to develop our ability to link visual meaning with verbal meaning.

You already "read" visually. Depending on your culture and background, you will be able to cite examples of colors, clothing choices, and hand gestures that have particular meanings. To develop that visual vocabulary, you need to know some of the assumptions that guide the selection and arrangement of visual elements for persuasive purposes. Images may deliver messages, such as when data are presented graphically in a chart or diagram. In that case, the image appeals logically to the reader. Images also create feelings, as in the case of advertisements that associate a product with a beautiful place or with a nurturing family unit. Images can also move people to identify with or believe in a message, as is the case when a photograph accompanying a news story presents visual evidence of a reporter's proximity to the situation and, thus, his credibility. So readers can analyze visual images just as they can verbal messages, by examining purpose, context, appeals, and strategies.

VISUAL LITERACY

Reading Images for Purpose and Context

As is the case with verbal messages, visual images may have complex and multiple purposes. An image may be used to educate, to support, to share values, opinions, or interests; it may be used to move someone to action, or to move someone to fear, tears, laughter, or awe. We appreciate visual images because they help us identify with a moment, and the more remote the moment from our experience, the more helpful it is to have the assistance of visual information. However, we need to be cautious because images are not rhetorically neutral. They are purposeful arrangements of elements designed to have a specific effect on a viewer, which opens them to rhetorical analysis. (See, for example, Figures 11.1 and 11.2.)

FIGURE 11.1   TIMOTHY H. O'SULLIVAN, *INCIDENTS OF THE WAR: A HARVEST OF DEATH, GETTYSBURG, JULY 1863*

FIGURE 11.2   THOMAS HART BENTON, *THE SOWERS* (1941–1945)

There has existed a long-standing belief in the credibility of the photograph as visual evidence of an incident or event. "Seeing is believing," the saying goes. But this belief is beginning to be challenged because of the manipulation that is possible as a result of digital imaging. However, it is not just recent developments that challenge the status of photographs as visual evidence. Photos do not just convey information; the scene they depict is framed and composed to emphasize a particular view of things.

Consider the image in Figure 11.1, a photographer's view of the aftermath of the Battle of Gettysburg in the Civil War. The photographer, Timothy H. O'Sullivan (1840–1882), chronicled the events of his time through the lens of his camera. On the one hand, we use images like this as factual representations of historical events. We can also engage with the pictures personally, identifying with either the photographer or another observer of the casualties. We can look at the photograph as art, considering the framing of the scene, the arrangement of elements, the effects of light. We can also consider the photographer's intentions and perspective. What was he trying to say with his picture? What clues are there to that message? How else might the scene have been recorded, assuming different intentions and a different perspective?

Certainly it is more than an objective perspective. O'Sullivan titled this photograph "Incidents of the war. A harvest of death, Gettysburg, July, 1863." Does the title confirm your sense of the message the picture conveys, or does it interpret the photograph in a way you hadn't considered? In either case, it is clear from

■ APPLICATION

Observing the Rhetorical Appeal of Visual Images

Examine the painting in Figure 11.2, *The Sowers* by Thomas Hart Benton, which depicts his vision of the political situation underlying World War II. The figure at the center is meant to depict a Nazi. Identify the message, the rhetorical appeals that persuade you to accept his message, and the assumptions implied. How does the message about war in Benton's painting differ from that suggested by O'Sullivan's photograph in Figure 11.1?

the title that O'Sullivan's purpose was more than simply to objectively record events. The words "harvest of death" suggest that he might be composing an anti-war message in the midst of the most cataclysmic conflict in American history.

Reading Visual Information as Rhetorical Appeals

If visual images have purposes and contexts, they can also be said to carry persuasive intent. Considering visual information in terms of the classical appeals—logos, ethos, and pathos—can help us read and understand consciously and critically. O'Sullivan's photograph appeals to us as historical fact in that it presents information about the specific conditions of the Battle of Gettysburg. It appeals to us emotionally: the bodies lie strewn and discarded, their physical contact not a relationship but an accident of circumstance, like garbage thrown from a death cart traveling too fast. The light draws the eye back and away, as if lives rising from the dead bodies are moving toward the light. More ominously, the light reveals the barbarous acts of countryman against countryman. The photograph also appeals to our values, our ethics. It asks that we understand one dark truth of war: death.

Advertisers intend to persuade us by appealing to our logic, our emotions, and our values to accept their claims about a particular choice. There's noth-

■ STRATEGY

How to Observe the Rhetorical Appeal of Visual Images

1. What message does the image convey?
2. What assumptions underlie the message?
3. How does the image appeal to our logic, our emotions, and our values?
4. Which appeals seem to have merit, and why?

ing inherently wrong about this practice unless they make false claims, but it is impractical and inadvisable not to be fully aware of the practices they employ to move us to accept their premises. Awareness of the appeal of particular strategies allows us to consider the elements of visual images as rhetorical, in the same way that we can analyze verbal messages rhetorically.

Seeing Images as Strategies

As it is possible to examine any verbal text for the ways in which diction, syntax, examples, structure, and persona affect the message, it is also possible to examine visual images for their rhetorical elements and for their cumulative effect on the viewer. To analyze elements as strategies, we ask "What does each choice have to do with the artist's or designer's purpose?"

Elements of visual images include the sizes, shapes, and arrangement of objects, colors and tones, and the use of space. Just as the relationships among verbal elements in verbal messages shape the reader's experience, so the relationships among visual elements produce certain effects in the observer. Connecting objects through color or space conveys association among the ideas behind the objects. Distance or distinction in space or color may convey tension or conflict. An evident hierarchy of size or arrangement lets the observer know that the message has something to do with relative power. Harmony among elements conveys a sense of calm. In writing, we may use short sentences or long, or we may use active or passive verbs. In the same way, composers of images may try for simplicity or complexity, stability or tension. These kinds of meaningful relationships are expressed differently, but most rely on sets of correspondences.

As elements of written rhetoric can be associated with particular effects on the reader, so the elements of visual images can be consistently associated with effects on the observer. This list will identify only a few of the correspondences between image and effect that have been observed by people who study visual images, but they can be useful in helping us learn to observe images as rhetorical

 ## KEY CONCEPT

Elements of Visual Images

Grammar as a part of language knowledge is a description of the elements we use to compose our messages. If visual images can be said to have a grammar, then those elements would include:

- Shape
- Arrangement
- Space
- Color
- Size

strategies. Because they are always used in combination, and always in a particular context, specific elements may create different effects, so be sure, first, to note what effect the visual has on you, as a responding reader.

Shape

- Horizontal, flat shapes can suggest calm, stability, relaxation.
- Vertical, tall shapes can suggest excitement, strength, energy.
- Diagonal shapes can suggest motion, tension, activity.
- A triangle on a flat surface can suggest stability.
- A triangle set on a diagonal plane can suggest instability, motion.
- Similar shapes can suggest harmony, association.
- Contrasting shapes can suggest tension, dissociation.
- Points and angles can suggest threat, fear, challenge.
- Curves and circles can suggest comfort, security, rest.
- Overlapping shapes can suggest crowding and pressure, or sometimes intimacy.

Arrangement

- Upper portion of the frame can suggest lightness, freedom, even spirituality.
- Bottom portion of the frame can suggest weight and constraint, or stability and solidity.
- Heavy objects suspended at the top of the frame create tension because they defy gravity.
- Objects at the center of the frame can draw attention, attraction, emphasis.
- Objects at the edges of the frame may be seen as marginalized, less important, or cornered, or escaping the frame.
- Objects suspended in the upper part of the frame can suggest vulnerability or tension.
- Repeating elements can suggest order, stability, or sometimes monotony.
- Irregular or random elements can suggest confusion, chaos, or sometimes excitement, change.

Space

- Space around an element can suggest isolation, independence, vulnerability.
- Increasing or decreasing space between elements can suggest depth.
- Wide space between similar elements can suggest tension.

Color

- Light colors can suggest safety, simplicity.
- Dark colors can suggest danger, complexity, mystery.

- Objects of the same color can suggest association, harmony.
- Objects of contrasting color can suggest dissociation, tension, conflict.
- Colors as symbols: e.g., white can suggest purity, light; red can suggest blood, fire, love; green can suggest nature; blue can suggest cool, sea, sky.

Size

- Large objects can suggest stength, importance, superiority.
- Small objects can suggest vulnerability, insignificance, subordinate status.

Shape, arrangement, space, color, and size are not the only elements visual artists use to compose meaningful images, but identifying these alone can help you practice understanding and articulating how images make you feel. The photograph in Figure 11.3, for example, is a simple picture of fishing nets being hauled up. But it conveys much more than factual information. The triangle shapes arranged on the diagonal suggest motion, and the sharp angles suggest effort and challenge. The parts of the boat, just out of the picture, draw the eye up vertically—they actually pull our eyes up and out of the picture, in the same direction the nets are pulling the weight of the fish. That helps us experience the sensation of effort, as if we are assisting the fishermen. We're in the middle

FIGURE 11.3 JACK LEIGH, *NETS AND DOORS* (1986)

of an unresolved, unfinished action, and this creates suspense. The top of the photo, lighter in color, also lifts our eyes up from the darker sea, the line between sea and sky drawing the contrast between the mysterious depths and the simple, clear daylight, where the fish will soon appear. The excitement is enhanced by the hovering of the gulls over the nets, creating tension and anticipation. In the way that they suggest motion opposite to the way the nets are being drawn, they seem to act as elements of the natural world pulling back against the strong pull toward the boat—but they are small, suspended, and subordinate to the strength of the action that is the central focus of the photo. Look how many words it took us just to observe some of the elements of a simple, black and white photo!

STRATEGY

How to Analyze the Effects of Visual Elements

The relationships among visual elements shape the effect of the message by matching the strategies with the purpose. To analyze these elements, we can ask ourselves questions like these:

- Is the visual effect one of sharpness or roundness?
- Is our eye directed vertically or horizontally?
- What is bold or exaggerated; what is subtle or understated?
- Are specific elements close or distant?
- What is in harmony or association; what is in conflict or dissociation?
- Are some elements dominant or subordinate?
- Are elements passive and stable, or is there tension and instability?
- Are there consistent patterns, or a sense of randomness and variation?

APPLICATION

Observing the Effects of Visual Elements

With the strategies for analyzing the elements of visual images in mind, revisit the painting *The Sowers* by Thomas Hart Benton in Figure 11.2. What message does it seem to convey? How does it appeal to the observer? Now examine the visual elements and relationships in the painting. Make a list, independently or with a group, of strategies, and link them to what you saw as the message. How do the strategies reinforce or complicate the message?

DOCUMENT DESIGN

The first section of this chapter examined how visual images can be seen as rhetorical strategies. Visual images are one element of document design, which focuses on how we choose strategies of presentation that complement our purpose. Document design focuses on how graphics, typographical features, and verbal elements are combined. Elements of good document design can function like traffic signals. As the lights and signs point direction, set the pace, and prevent collisions, so a well-designed document helps the reader move easily and comfortably through the intersections of ideas. In addition, a good design differentiates the primary from the secondary, helping us perceive the relationships among sets of ideas. Attention to design also conveys the message that you care about what you are saying. Your readers will assume that a readable design is a sign of clear thinking. All of these functions of design are part of your message to your reader and make your documents more persuasive.

Each situation, each combination of subject and writer and audience and context, requires a different set of choices in order to help people understand each other. As the authors of this book, *our own* rhetorical situation keeps us mindful that most of our readers are college students who need to produce writing for various academic situations, who want clear guidance and direction, and whose time is precious. Therefore, we have worked with editors and experts in book production to integrate techniques and strategies to help you understand and use the information and ideas we are sharing. These document designers helped us use headings, boxes, bullets, graphics, and other features as information organizers.

Document design includes all elements of presentation, such as font type and size, underlining, italics and boldface; page layout, margins, and indentations; numbered and bulleted lists; white space; and graphic illustrations. It also includes the final packaging of a document, including the cover, binding, color, and even the size and quality of paper.

 ## KEY CONCEPT

Document Design

Document design is the practice of combining graphics, typographical features, and verbal elements. Good document design:

- Meets the needs of a specific purpose and audience.
- Enhances the readability and clarity of the message.
- Differentiates primary information from secondary.
- Encourages focus and reflection, through headings and white space.
- Makes information easy to find.

Designing Documents for a Purpose and Audience

We all know that presentation matters. The way we dress may give the impression that we are casual, efficient, playful, rebellious, independent, outgoing, or cooperative. For different situations, we can create images with our clothing that actually help us communicate better with particular audiences. In the same way, we can present written documents that convey similar impressions. Effective document design matches presentation to rhetorical situation. Good presentation cannot make up for a lack of information or reasoning, but it can complement and enhance our purpose.

In addition to the fact that many of you, our readers, are college students, we can also assume three other truths about you. First, like us, most of you will be working at jobs that involve writing and communicating for different audiences. Of course, college English professors write, but we don't just write for academic purposes. In fact, we compose memos, letters, reports, proposals, recommendations, evaluations, and practical arguments much more often than we compose articles, essays, or poems.

Second, most of you will belong to multiple and intersecting communities. Your community memberships may require or inspire you to produce public writing addressed to others like you or to public leaders, designed to influence opinion or policy or decision-making. You might, for example, write your congressperson about backing a particular proposal that will affect your neighborhood. You might, as several writers included in this book have done, write a letter to the editor about an observation or event that prompted you to respond. You might encourage your church to extend its charity to a particular cause, or your local grocery store to permit students to have a fund-raiser in its parking lot, or your local Parent-Teacher Association to fund classes in conflict resolution for teens.

Third, most of you have had *and will increasingly have* writing and reading experiences in "cyberspace," on virtual pages of information or advertising or e-mail or bulletin boards or chat room exchanges. Computers have not reduced the need for effective communication skills. In fact, we are communicating more than ever—opportunities for negotiating meaning with other minds have multiplied in number and type. What challenges do these opportunities present to us as readers and writers? How can we manage rhetoric artfully to make the best use of the opportunities?

The worlds of work, of community, and of cyberspace are rhetorically complex. It helps to know as much as possible about how to analyze and respond to each situation. Thus the skill of analyzing the ongoing and practiced rhetoric of any specific place—real or virtual—is extremely useful in navigating our communications needs effectively.

When considering how to design a document for a particular audience, you begin, as with all writing choices, by identifying your **purpose** and your **audience.**

STRATEGY

Designing Documents for a Purpose and Audience

When designing a document, ask yourself:

1. What needs are you addressing, and whose needs are they?
2. What question are you answering, and who requires the answer?
3. What do your readers already know?
4. What design elements will help them access the information they need?
5. What do you want your reader to do or know or think or feel about your subject, and what design elements will make that happen?

Designing Documents for Readability and Clarity

To design for readability, consider the habits and expectations of your readers. Encourage and reassure them by arranging and selecting elements to set the mood, look, and feel of a document. When we read, our eyes move across the page in a "Z" pattern, so think of the page as a grid, and see if the elements draw the vision back and forth comfortably.

Readers expect and value a sense of unity, and this can be achieved in several ways. When all of the elements are appropriate to the message, the result is thematic unity. When all of the elements have the same "feel," the result is tonal unity. Compare this sense of tone to the unity you try to achieve verbally by using a consistent level of diction. Think about your document on a spectrum between formal and informal, and adjust your design elements to complement each other. Make the structure apparent by "chunking" information and using white space and alignment to relate information. Use headings to invite readers to scan the page for what is relevant to their needs. For emphasis, break established patterns. Achieve visual unity with simplicity and typographic unity by making sure the fonts complement each other.

If conventional forms exist for a specific task, understand that those forms are expected by your audience. To ignore or misuse the conventional forms is to risk alienating your audience. The point of conventional forms in writing is to assist communication; readers and writers begin to understand each other through their shared understanding of the shape writing takes.

White Space

In the simplest sense, white space is about vision. White space allows the eye to rest. It separates what should be distinct; it clarifies relationships by directing the line of sight; it encourages reflection and assimilation of information.

KEY CONCEPT

Elements of Design

- White space
- Graphics (pictures, illustrations, graphs, tables, icons)
- Typography
- Headings
- Boxes and Lines
- Lists: Bullets and Numbering
- Color and Shading
- Conventions of a specific genre or form

Thinking of the page as a grid, align parallel elements for a clean, polished look. To add interest or emphasis, break the grid pattern in a way that parallels a shift in your message.

Academic papers usually call for double-spacing all information, which assumes a concept-heavy purpose requiring close attention and reflection. In other documents, white space adds emphasis by framing or isolating what is significant; it calls attention to relationships if used as a patterned visual cue; it divides key sections; and it directs and rests the eye. Documents that do not use white space effectively—think of Internal Revenue Service documents—are difficult to read and give the impression that the ideas are complicated, even if they are not.

Graphics

The term *graphics* includes all visual material. Pictures, illustrations, graphs, tables, icons, maps, and other graphics present information in forms other than sentences and paragraphs. Graphics should be used purposefully, not decoratively, although they can be arranged to assist with the function of the overall design. They need a context, like quotes do, so introduce them in writing before they appear in the text, making sure the relationship between the graphics and your purpose is evident. They should convey information better than it can be conveyed in prose, and they should be accurate, clear, and worth the attention they draw.

Typography

Typography refers to the way characters, numbers, and symbols look on the page. Although typical word processing software offers us hundreds of font options, for the purposes of writing college papers and workplace documents, only a few are really relevant.

Sanserif Font Examples	Serif Font Examples
Arial	Times New Roman
Helvetica	Garamond
Franklin Gothic Book	Century Schoolbook
Cronos	Courier New

FIGURE 11.4

SANSERIF AND SERIF FONTS

The best way to study the effects on the reader and on readability of various font sizes, shapes, and colors is to surf the Internet. Huge, messy, ungainly headings often appear in rainbow colors, sometimes even flashing. They distract and frustrate as much as small, complicated fonts slow us down and irritate us.

Most typefaces can be divided into two groups: serif, and sanserif (see Figure 11.4). The serif fonts have little bars or "ears" across the top and bottom lines of letters. Sanserif (*sans* means "without") lack these lines. Generally, sanserif fonts are less complicated, so many documents use them. The most readable typefaces are usually considered to be sanserif fonts between 10 and 12 points. It's best to avoid novelty fonts altogether unless your project is unusual and the style would add to the context or purpose of the message.

Fonts carry associations for many people. Serif fonts are often considered "classic," while sanserif fonts are considered "modern." Many people associate feelings with particular fonts. For example, the Bradley Hand is casual and friendly. Examine some of the fonts available to you and imagine a circumstance in which they might be used to enhance a particular purpose.

Other suggestions for font readability include avoiding the overuse of italics and passages in all capital letters; both are difficult to read. In addition, it is better to limit your fonts to two, perhaps one for the body of the document and one for headings. A rule of thumb, though, is to avoid using two fonts in the same family (serif, sanserif) on the same page, because if they are too similar, it looks like a mistake rather than an intentional choice.

Headings

Headings are reader cues. They let the reader know when the focus is shifting. Most importantly, they allow a reader to get an overview of the important topics in a document just by skimming the headings. Generally, the headings represent the same information a reader could glean from having access to your outline. Readers can tell what you will cover, in what order, and how the key sections relate to each other in level of importance.

The most important headings are generally centered. Those of secondary importance are aligned with left margins. Yet another level of division can be signaled with headings indented from the left margin.

Boxes and Lines

Boxes highlight and emphasize key ideas. The key ideas may be included in narrative form within paragraphs, then reformatted in boxes to enhance understanding or to appeal to readers with visual learning styles. They may also be used to summarize key ideas found in a whole document or in document sections, to increase reading speed and focus attention on what is most significant. Lines signal a sharp division in function between one section and another. They do not convey relationship, but instead, a significant separation.

Lists: Bullets and Numbering

It can be challenging to comprehend and retain blocks of information presented in paragraph form. Breaking out sets of ideas into lists is helpful, because our attention and memory are both aided by the change in format and additional white space. When the list includes information of equal importance, separate the items with "bullets": dots, small boxes, checkmarks, or other symbols appropriate to the type of information. When the list includes information in a specific sequence, number or alphabetize the items.

Color and Shading

Now that color printers are inexpensive and widely available, documents are more likely to use color as a reader cue, another way to interpret your material for your reader. It is good to remember that color, like all other elements, should be used purposefully. Color does not necessarily provide added value, because black text on white is actually the most readable format. When documents use too much color, readers can be confused. Where am I supposed to look? How do these sections and ideas relate?

On the other hand, color can attract and engage readers; it can also be helpful as an organizing device and to highlight important information. It is especially helpful for information in graphs or diagrams.

CONVENTIONS OF A GENRE OR FORM

Conventions of a specific genre or form can include any or all of the elements we have previously discussed. Because many work situations involve repeating processes and tasks, conventional forms have been created to make that work efficient and also to make communication clearer. Some people who enjoy the creativity involved in composing resist filling out forms because forms sometimes seem to strip language of meaning rather than enhance it. But forms themselves have meaning. When you look at conventional forms, try to think about what meaning the form itself conveys. What values does the form suggest? What priorities does it set?

One way to analyze formal expectations is to find out what has been done before. Ask supervisors and co-workers for examples of writing with a purpose similar to yours, and think about the effectiveness of the forms for the task. The

STRATEGY

How to Analyze Models of Conventional Forms

1. What ideas are included, and in what order?
2. What shapes the writing? How is it divided into parts? How does it begin? How does it end? How are key ideas integrated with supporting details? Are there additional elements that reveal a standard format?
3. What characterizes the sentences and words? Are certain patterns repeated? Are they formal or informal, complex or simple?
4. How would you imagine the writer? What values and attitudes does the writing convey about the subject? About the reader? About the writer?
5. What conventions are followed?
6. What visual and design elements are included, and what impact do they have on the message?

 APPLICATION

Analyzing a Model of a Conventional Form

In this book, you have learned to observe and analyze many writing purposes and the language choices that match those purposes. Visit a college or university department and ask for samples of the kinds of writing they require. Discover the purposes that inform the writing. Examine the features, and think about why the writer may have made each choice. Write a "style guide" for the document. Describe and illustrate directions for producing an effective document of its type.

library and the Internet are both sources of models for different forms of writing that are used by businesses, organizations, and institutions. Review these models stylistically to help you think about the best ways to address your audiences.

Designing Papers for College

In addition to the summaries, responses, arguments, interpretations, and evaluations that we explore in this text, other forms of writing are used in college classes. These forms, laboratory reports, technical reports, proposals, market studies, and other documents have their own conventional forms. Being familiar with the types of elements listed and discussed in this chapter can help you understand and produce effective writing for many situations. You will generally find that there is a match between the rhetorical conventions expected by any academic area and the kinds of information and data typical of that area.

Your instructors want to understand you, but you need to do what you can to make it easy for them. They need to know you have taken the assignment seriously. They appreciate readability and don't want to be distracted by unnecessary elements, complicated features, or errors.

Before further discussion of specific document design features, we offer this word of caution about final manuscripts: always keep a back-up copy, as well as your drafting and outlining materials. Occasionally, papers get lost either before or after they are evaluated, and you may want to reconstruct a project or develop your ideas further in another context. It also sometimes happens that instructors perceive real effort as possible plagiarism, so documentation of your writing process can help you defend yourself in the case of a misunderstanding.

There are some general document design guidelines, though, for the kinds of college writing assignments we introduce in this book. The key concept box "Design Guidelines for College Essays" lists the basic conventions for college papers.

 # KEY CONCEPT

Design Guidelines for College Essays

If your instructor provides guidelines for submitting your final documents, use them. Otherwise, most instructors appreciate the following:

- Submit papers on 8½ by 11 inch white paper, and type on one side only.
- Use conventional fonts between 10 and 12 points, depending on the font.
- Use one inch margins all around.
- Indent the first line of each paragraph 5 spaces, using the Tab key.
- Align the type at the left margin only.
- Double-space everything, including quotations.
- Use a running "header" to include page numbers and your last name or the name of the paper, placing the information in the upper right corner of each page.
- Place the title of the paper and all identifying information either on a title page or on the first page. If a title page is required, center the title one-third of the way from the top. About 3 inches from the bottom, centered and double-spaced on separate lines, list your name, your instructor's name, the course name and number, and the date. If no title page is required, list and double-space the identifying information at the top left, followed by the title, centered, capitalizing the first and all key words.

Designing a Business Letter: Purpose and Audience Concerns

The business letter conveys efficiency with its letterhead, timeliness by placing the date at the top, and seriousness of purpose with a formal salutation followed by a colon.

Business letters transfer information. They may be used to convey either good news or bad news. They may also be used for public relations purposes, to create acceptance or smooth bad feelings. They may be used to raise questions, negotiate agreements, or clarify meanings. Though the form of the business

 KEY CONCEPT

Rhetoric and Design Guidelines for Business Letters

- Use 8½ by 11 inch paper in white or a light color, nothing that will distract from the information being conveyed.

- If you are writing in your role as a member of a particular business, institution, or organization, use official letterhead. If you are writing on your own behalf, head your letter by including your full name, address, and phone number at the top center of the page. Then, at the left margin, date the letter. These headings acknowledge the way that paper correspondence needs to be managed for reference and retrieval.

- Use a simple font that communicates the attitude you would like your reader to bring to the letter, that is, nothing fancy or reflective of other forms of discourse such as posters, cartoons, or personal letters.

- Use a block style paragraph, with no indentation of the first line. Leave a space between body paragraphs.

- In your greeting, be as specific as possible about the name of the person or at least the category of people you are addressing. Try to avoid "To Whom It May Concern," which may make the real reader feel less responsible for responding and the letter seem as unspecific as the name of the recipient. Unspecific letters often land in trash cans.

- If your information will be welcomed by the recipient, begin with as clear a statement as you can of your purpose. If your information may not be welcomed, provide a context that may soften the reader's attitude toward the message. In any case, say no more than is necessary to make your message complete and clear.

- Unless your entire purpose is to make somebody mad, be reasonable. Accusing or confrontational language will rarely elicit cooperation or respect, because readers rarely respect writers who do not respect them.

- *Proofread very carefully.* Although errors in writing are not measures of intelligence, they do tend to affect readers negatively, if only because they inhibit easy reading and distract the reader from the writer's purpose.

letter is predictable, as seen in the illustration that follows, the rhetoric of the business letter can be complicated. Remember to use your imagination: be the reader of your letter, and consider how you would react if you received it. For the basic conventions, see the key concept box "Rhetoric and Design Guidelines for Business Letters."

Sample Student Writing: Business Letter

206 E. 15th Street #26
Ellensburg, WA 98926
January 22, 2001

Ms. Barbara Fischer, Human Resources Manager
McLane NW Grocery Distribution
Lakewood-Tacoma Industrial Park
Tacoma, WA 98498-0848

Dear Ms. Fischer:

Thank you for your telephone call last week regarding McLane's Management Trainee program targeted to "recruit and select recent college graduates." With the additional information you provided, I have been able to designate three areas of particular interest: distribution, merchandising, and international development. I would greatly appreciate being selected to participate in the program with the goal of developing my career skills in one of these three areas, and I have attached my resumé for your consideration.

My preparation for a management trainee position has included course work in planning and inventory control systems, organizational behavior, international business, and marketing. My core management classes include financial management, human resources operations, and organizational systems.

To anchor my theoretical training with practical experience, I have been involved in a two-year apprenticeship with the Central Washington University Conference Program. With that program, I worked with a team, served customers and facilitated a marketing project. In addition, my involvement with the Human Resource Management Club helped me develop leadership and public speaking skills. Participating as a member of the Ellensburg Beautification Commission, I worked with a diverse group of local officials and community members to craft a long-range plan.

A position at McLane Northwest would offer me exactly the kind of challenge and opportunity that I envision as the next professional step beyond college. I accept your offer to visit your facility and will contact you at the end of March to set up an appointment.

Sincerely,

Melody L. Wollan

APPLICATION

Analyzing a Business Letter

The sample business letter included in this chapter is a letter of application, but the writer's purpose is more complex than simply to add her name to a list of applicants. What does she want her reader to do, know, think, and feel? What choices has she made to address specific aspects of her situation? Are there ways she might have addressed it better? Write Ms. Wollan a letter describing the strengths and weaknesses of her document.

Designing a Resumé: Purpose and Audience Concerns

Many people think a resumé is just a list of your experiences. But a good resumé is strategically crafted to help an employer see you as a person who can do the job; in fact, to the extent that you can, you want to help the employer actually imagine you *doing* the job. Even though resumés look formulaic, yours can say what you want it to say, without your resorting to risky options like floral or perfumed paper, or a picture of you at the top, or a long list of your free-time activities. Your choices should be guided by what the position requires of you, and how your background prepares you for that particular situation.

Before you begin crafting your resumé, do some planning. Take inventory of all of your paid and unpaid experiences that have contributed to the preparation

 KEY CONCEPT

Rhetoric and Design Guidelines for Resumés

- Use 8½ by 11 inch paper of good quality. As for a business letter, choose white or a light color. You may match your resumé shade to an accompanying cover letter.
- Use a professional font, clear and clean.
- There are two types of resumés, the chronological and the functional. The chronological resumé is ordered by date, and ordering your experience from the most to least recent helps you seem current and prepared. The functional resumé organizes experience by skill, and matching the order of the list of skills in the job description will help your reader see you as a match for the job.

continued

- Action verbs and phrases make the applicant seem experienced, active, and involved. Begin descriptions of your experience with verbs or verb forms, where possible.
- Be scrupulously accurate. While you have many opportunities to enhance the presentation of your experience rhetorically, do not try to enhance it substantively. For most entry positions, you should try to fit your resumé onto a single page. However, the more experience you have and the more complex the job, the more difficult the single page limit becomes. Just make sure that if you extend the length, everything you list is essential to your application for the specific position you are applying for. People don't like to hunt for what is relevant.
- The content of a resumé, regardless of which type you choose, will include:

  Your name, address, telephone number, and e-mail address if available at the head of the resumé.

  An objective or goal may be included. If it is, it should be concise and relevant to the position you are applying for.

  Your educational experience. In most cases, and in all cases where a degree is required, education will be placed near or at the top of the page. Include names of colleges, dates attended, degrees, and dates received.

  Your work experience, organized by specific skill or by positions held, most recent first. You can include all relevant experiences, whether paid or unpaid. Also include skills that may be an advantage for the employer, even if they are not specifically listed, such as a second language or computer skills.

  You may include personal interests and activities if they are relevant to the position—for example, if they have given you leadership opportunities or teamwork experience, or if you have earned special recognition. Sometimes people include personal information such as date of birth or marital or parental status, but it is generally irrelevant and often best omitted.

  Include the names of and contact information for two or more references who can verify the information on your resumé, or explain where references can be obtained.

- Proofread scrupulously. You are proving your attentiveness to detail, your seriousness, and your caring attitude toward work and others in your presentation.

you bring to the job. List skills, education, experiences, interests, accomplishments, and goals. Then, select and arrange your lists to best advantage, considering the responsibilities of the job and the impression your credentials will make on your reader.

The conventions that guide the resumé form take into account that the form will be read in comparison to others. This kind of reading requires sim-

plicity and predictability. Full sentences are unnecessary. Information is organized in readily recognizable blocks. The first item on the page is the applicant's name, for emphasis and clarity. You can make use of the rhetoric of
the resumé by using space, headings, and bold or bulleted items to interpret
your experience for your reader. You can also arrange your experience and
qualifications artfully, to best reflect the description of the job expectations
and responsibilities.

Sample Student Writing: Resumé

Melody L. Wollan

206 E. 15th Ave. #26

Ellensburg, WA 98926

(509) 925-4063

wollanm@cwu.edu

Objective A management trainee or management position in an established organization with potential for advancement.

Education <u>B.S. in Business Administration</u>. Organizational Behavior spe-
cialization. Central Washington University, June 2001. GPA
3.417.

Experience <u>Marketing Apprentice</u>: CWU Conference Program, Ellensburg,
WA, 9/99 to the present.
—Prepare pre-conference and post-conference analysis for
marketing.
—Lead internship students in research projects.
—Assist Conference Planner and Conference Services Manager
in administrative duties and scheduling

<u>Registration Assistant</u>: CWU Conference Program, Ellensburg,
WA, 6/99–9/99.
—Trained and supervised seven summer office employees.
—Organized check-in procedures for conferences as well as
apprentice duties.

<u>Registration Apprentice</u>: CWU Conference Program, Ellens-
burg, WA, 2/98–6/99.
—Processed registrations, housed conference groups.
—Prepared daily deposits and trained new employees.

<u>Bookkeeper</u>: 7-Eleven Store, Ellensburg, WA, 11/96–present.
—Prepare shift reconciliation and deposits on weekends.
—Supervise shift employees and problem solve on weekends.

<u>Accounting Assistant</u>: St. Mary's Lodge and Resort, Glacier Park, MT, 6/96–9/96.

—Counted deposits for restaurant, gas station, grocery and gift store, and lodge.

—Recorded intercompany transfers, entered and transmitted bank cards, prepared accounts receivables and payables.

Organizations <u>Beautification Commission Member</u>: City of Ellensburg, WA, 5/96–present.

<u>Public Relations Chairperson, Executive Board Member</u>: Society for Human Resource Management, CWU, 4/96–present.

<u>American Production and Inventory Control Society Member</u>: 1/97–present.

References Available on request from Career Planning and Placement Center, Ellensburg, WA, 98926, (509) 963-1921.

 ## APPLICATION

Analyzing a Resumé

Melody Wollan's resumé accompanied her letter of application. Read the resumé or purpose and audience considerations and design features. What impressions does the resumé convey? Could the resumé be improved?

Designing a Brochure: Purpose and Audience Concerns

A brochure is a pamphlet or booklet that typically introduces services or offers important information for public awareness. Generally brochures have informational, educational, persuasive, and advertising purposes. They nearly always combine verbal and visual elements, as well as columns, boxes, lines, and lists, so that readers will be able to access the essential information quickly and efficiently. The newspaper writer's key questions, "who, what, when, where, how, and why," help define the contents.

Sample Student Brochure

A human community is a group of people who share common ground. Sometimes the ground is simply physical, geographical, as we are members of the towns or cities or regions in which we reside. Most of our community affiliations, though, are based on shared occupations, histories, genetics, values,

KEY CONCEPT

Rhetoric and Design Guidelines for Brochures

- Plan for the brochure by listing all of the information that might be included. Space is at a premium, so you must select the essential information carefully. Remember to consider what you want your reader to do, know, think, or feel in response to the brochure. Consider these factors: What need is being addressed? Why should readers address it? What concerns will the audience have? Make sure you include complete and accurate contact information.

- Plan the layout to attract readers. Include as many graphic elements as is feasible among blocks of text, leaving white space around all components of the brochure.

- Include sentences that are relatively short, though somewhat varied in length and pattern for readability. Use active verbs to help your readers feel involved and participatory.

- Chunk your information. Divide paragraphs with bold or otherwise eye-catching headings. This type of presentation helps readers focus and feel confident that they understand the essential ideas.

- Design principles include harmony, balance, and color. Combine elements that complement each other. Make sure that your text and graphic elements are in balance with each other and evenly distributed throughout the brochure. Whether the color you use is bold or soft, make sure that your text clearly stands out against its background.

- Proofread carefully. Errors not only distract readers but challenge the credibility of the brochure.

beliefs, or needs. As communicators, you can put your writing skills to use to connect members of communities in essential ways—sharing ideas and information, solving problems, and articulating questions and concerns.

Our community roles are essential to our participation in participatory democracy, in religions, as consumers and health advocates, as humans concerned about equity and justice and personal rights, and in public and private education systems. Many colleges and universities have instituted programs to encourage student writers to use their skills to address community needs. These **service learning** programs have not just provided authentic situations in which writers can hone their skills, they have also encouraged an awareness of community service as a component of a balanced, healthy life.

The brochure reproduced in Figure 11.5 was written by a student in a service learning program, and it also advertises Central Washington University's service learning program.

MISSION

Academic Service-Learning enhances student learning by promoting opportunities for faculty and students to connect course content and theoretical knowledge to real life situations with community partners.

Student Reflection:

"The AS-L experience has helped me understand our complex society. It made me think of ways I can assist others to help themselves."
Carlos Sobers - Information Tech. & Admin. Management Major
Allied People Offering Year Round Outreach to Spanish Migrants (APOYO)

Campus/Community Partners

Allied People Offering Yearound Outreach (APOYO)

Central Washington Disability Resources

Chamber of Commerce

Child Protective Services

Citizens Police Academy

Crisis Line: ASPEN and Comprehensive Mental Health

Dispute Resolution Center of Yakima & Kittitas Counties

Ellensburg Pregnancy Care Center

Ellensburg Youth Community Center

Ellensburg Schools

Elmview

High School Equivalency Program

Hospice

Kittitas County Action Council (KCAC)

Kittitas County Head Start / ECEAP

Kittitas County Volunteer Legal Services

Retired & Senior Volunteer Program (RSVP)

Royal Vista Center

United Way of Kittitas County

Youth Services of Kittitas County

(this is not an inclusive list)

External Support for CWU AS-L

- **Funding for Improvement of Post Secondary Education – Faculty Fellow Program** – Supports ten faculty per year, for three years in utilizing AS-L as a teaching pedagogy.

- *Higher Education Board – Work Study Project*- Students are paid and/or receive university credit for helping faculty conduct research and serve communities.

- *Campus Compact* – Faculty Development

  Partners in Service – training programs for faculty, students, and community partners.

  Building Virtual Service Learning Partnerships – supports University consultation with national leaders.

CWU AS-L Priorities

- Develop and implement institutionalization plan.

- Increase faculty use of AS-L teaching pedagogy.

- Increase faculty incentives for using AS-L.

- Increase student participation in AS-L.

- Develop and facilitate community partnerships.

- Increase campus support and visibility.

Academic Service Learning

Definition
Academic Service-Learning is a course-based, credit-bearing educational experience in which students:

(a) participate in an organized service activity that meets identified community needs and

(b) reflect on the service activity in such a way as to gain further understanding of the course content, a broader appreciation of the discipline, and an enhanced sense of civic responsibility. (Bringle & Hatcher, *A Service-Learning Curriculum For Faculty* , 1995)

The Value of the AS-L Pedagogy

- Facilitates effective teaching.
- Enhances student comprehension.
- Motivates students to learn.
- Prepares students for careers.
- Engages students in citizenship.
- Strengthens communities.
- Enhances understanding of issues and subject matter.
- Requires reflective thinking and journal writing.
- Builds community and university relationships.

CWU 2003 Faculty Fellows

Joan Amby	Family & Consumer Sciences
Dorothy Chase	Leisure Services
Irene Cheyne	ITAM
Christina Curran	Teacher Education Programs
Nancy Hultquist	Geography & Land Studies
Fred McDonald	Department of Accounting
Jeff Penick	Psychology
Carrie Rehkopf	Music
Shari Stoddard	Art

CWU 2002 Distinguished Faculty Fellows

Tracy Andrews	Anthropology
Wendy Bohrson	Geology
Gregory Cant	Business Administration
Beatrice Coleman	Communication
Ruth Lapsley	Business Administration
Mufeed Rawashdeh	Department of Accounting

CWU 2001 Distinguished Faculty Fellows

Glen Bach	Art
Lois Breedlove	Communications
Shawn Christiansen	Family & Consumer Sciences
Martha Kurtz	Science Education / Chem.
Barbara Masberg	Leisure Services
Luetta Monson	Curriculum & Supervision
Rex Moody	Business Administration
Bruce Palmquist	Physics / Science Education
Tom Wellock	History

Management Team Members

Jan Bowers	Family & Consumer Sciences
Osman Alawiye	Curriculum & Supervision
Glen Bach	Art
Barbara Masberg	Leisure Services
Beatrice Coleman	Communication

Contact person: James G. Pappas
Director of AS-L
Department of Teacher Education Programs
Email: Pappasj@cwu.edu
Tel: 509-963-3075 FAX: 509-963-1162

Contact Person: Jan Bowers
Project Director of FIFSE Grant
Family & Consumer Sciences Department Chair
Email: bowersj@cwu.edu
Tel: 509-963-2766 FAX: 509-963-2787

Central Washington University
Ellensburg, Washington

Academic Service Learning

www.cwu.edu/~asl

A student reflection statement:

"Before doing an AS-L project, I had no sense of belonging to a community. I was aware of community needs that could be met around me, but never understood how I could use my expertise and energy to become part of the solution. Now I know how to build a community".
Kristy Walker - *Special Education Major*
The EDGE project

FIGURE 11.5 STUDENT-DESIGNED SERVICE LEARNING BROCHURE

APPLICATION

Analyzing a Brochure

Identify the audiences and purposes for the brochure in Figure 11.5. Then list the design features, and evaluate their effectiveness.

RHETORIC, ARGUMENT, AND THE INTERNET

The purpose of our book is to provide guided practice in the ways that readers and writers engage in the exchange of shared ideas for the purposes of testing and clarifying those ideas. Many rhetorical issues arise in the reading and writing arena of cyberspace, but those most relevant to our purposes have to do both with the facility the computer offers readers and writers, and with the change in the shape and sense of argument that hypertext invites. We do not intend to give a thorough overview of Web page design in this section, but only to introduce rhetorical issues raised by hypertext related to the roles of reader, writer, and subject, and to the nature of argument.

It is in this section that the information on visual rhetoric and document design are integrated. All of the concepts and strategies related to visual rhetoric will be relevant to reading and writing on the Internet, where graphics and text are presented side by side as sources of related ideas. All of the strategies and concepts related to document design will provide guidance in comprehending and composing pages of your own. Although we are relying on other resources to help you develop your technical expertise, we consider this section an opportunity for you to bring your critical reading, viewing, and writing awareness to your Internet experiences.

The Changing Roles of Reader, Writer, and Subject

The computer screen as a writing and reading environment certainly provides us with a new component to our rhetorical situation, and its characteristics and effects are still being explored and described. The roles of reader, writer, and subject as we considered them in earlier chapters need to be re-evaluated in light of the way the Internet presents information.

What is the reader's role? Certainly the way we read is changing. Hypertext, or the type of text that allows you to leap from one Internet location to another with a click of the mouse, has made written material seem three rather than two dimensional. The writer establishes an organization for the material, but readers control and change that order in the way that they choose to make use of the hypertext links. Readers are also becoming habitual skimmers and scanners because while our eyes, reading traditional text, are accustomed to moving left to right, back and forth, the tools at the edge of the computer document or World Wide Web page allow us to move vertically, rapidly, searching for what is relevant.

Hypertext is particularly suited for this kind of information management and retrieval. It may be less suited for the kind of reflective, linear argument structures that academic writers often read. Physically, it is less comfortable to read a computer screen than it is a traditional page. You can't arrange and rearrange yourself as you contemplate and reflect on what you are reading. Responding with marginal notes and questions for later use is also complicated. There is, as well, a sense of tentativeness to the cyber-document, at least for those of us who didn't grow up with Internet access, maybe because we don't yet see what method of storage will permit the retrieval of documents which gain significance and value over time. Because of that, words tend to have less a sense of permanence than of transition and transformation.

Access to computers has radically changed the role of the writer, too, and more change is to come. You might be fairly deep into the revision of a piece of writing when a new idea or a better way of expressing your ideas occurs to you. Writing on paper, you might experience some resistance to making use of your new understanding. Do you have the time and energy to change your structure, or change your mind? Because adding, deleting, and modifying writing are all made simpler tasks, composing on a computer may actually allow you to express your thinking and learning more accurately.

Beyond the convenience of word processing capabilities, your computer-generated writing is being influenced and will be influenced by the rhetoric of hypertext. The appearance of highlighted or underlined words and phrases in the context of screen-text is an invitation to digress, to take a detour to investigate related information. In some ways, this non-linear strategy takes readers away from a carefully constructed train of thought, and as composers, you may find that disconcerting. However, integrating hypertext references into your writing may allow you to represent more accurately the actual thinking process that led you to your conclusions. Writers who are frustrated by the linear limits of the outline may find the branching, expansive structures permitted by hypertext exciting and liberating.

The subject or the argument is, with the introduction of hypertext, a co-construction of the reader and writer. Traditionally, an argument is a line of reasoning constructed with a specific purpose by one person for others. The author of an argument creates a persona that is the authority in the work. But in a hypertext environment where readers shift between documents, an argument has multiple authors, multiple voices. The author of a hypertext document is an information-giver who sets up a whole range of possibilities, and every reader will follow a different path through that information.

Of course, writers in print also collect and present information, often from different sources. But in the medium of hypertext, the experience isn't linear, the sequence of information isn't controlled by the writer, and most importantly, the conclusion of the text created by the writer is not necessarily where a reader will finish the experience. Instead of the writer's purpose guiding the reading experience, the reader's needs and interests will clearly guide it. We argued in Chapter 4 that readers' backgrounds, experiences, and ideas influence the way they respond to what they read; in hypertext documents, readers can actually pursue those associations actively while reading.

Designing for the Web: Visual Rhetoric

University departments that have been solely concerned with verbal literacy are becoming more and more concerned with visual literacy. Partly, this is because of the prevalence and availability of film as a medium. More significantly, however, it is because communication expectations go beyond verbal sources to multimedia sources. We are becoming educated in thinking about which medium best communicates which ideas. Teaching, learning, networking, and decision-making are occurring in cyberspace, and it is important to producers and consumers to understand how to enhance and assimilate meaning in this emerging environment.

According to Web page designers, much of what they know about visual literacy applies to page design. Of course, we can select individual visuals to include in our Web pages on the basis of what they communicate rhetorically, but we can also think of the page itself as communicating visually (see Figures 11.6 and 11.7).

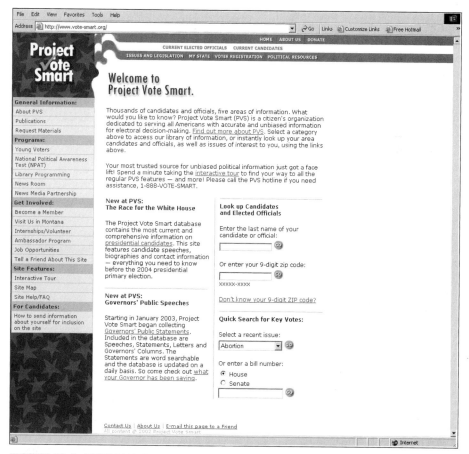

FIGURE 11.6 VOTE SMART HOME PAGE

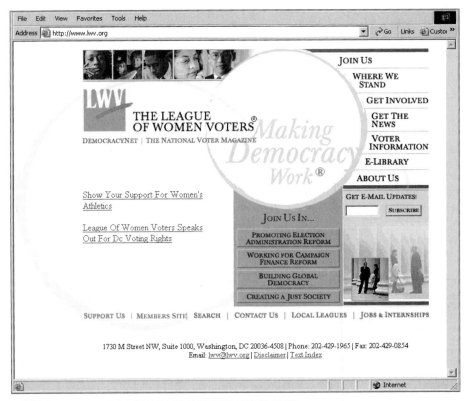

FIGURE 11.7   LEAGUE OF WOMEN VOTERS HOME PAGE

When we introduced visual elements and relationships earlier in this chapter, we referred to them in the context of the "frame" of the visual. If you think of the computer screen as the frame, many of the same elements and relationships can be observed. Some of the elements of a Web page are visual and some are verbal, but if we see them as the objects composing a picture, we can more easily reflect on the way visual rhetoric relates to Web pages.

The visual elements, shape, arrangement, space, color, and size, can be used to create harmony, balance, conflict, or tension. The list in the section of this chapter on "Visual Elements as Strategies" (pages 322–23) is a useful tool for examining the effects Web pages have on you as a reader. It can also help you arrange, revise, and edit Web page elements for best effect.

Seeing the frame visually can also help you guide the reader's eye. When you make the move to the Web page from the paper text, there are a few rhetorical strategies that must be kept in mind. Some of them we already discussed at the beginning of the chapter. Readers are inclined to scan vertically rather than read linearly. They first see pages as shapes and color. Their eyes are first drawn to graphic elements, and then to the verbal information.

APPLICATION

Visual Strategies and Web Pages

Review the list in the section of this chapter on "Visual Elements as Strategies" (pages 322–23). Identify an Internet site that particularly engages or confuses you. Review its elements to see if your response is tied to the effects created by the use of shape, arrangement, space, color, and size. Then see if the elements of the page direct your eye in ways that complicate your reading.

Designing for the Web: Purpose and Audience Concerns

There are many resources—online guides, workshops, and books—to help you learn all of the technical aspects of Web design and publishing. In this book, we intend only to suggest that you be aware of the rhetoric of the Web and of Web resources available to you as readers and writers.

On the WWW, anyone can publish anything, anytime, anyplace. This means, as readers, you must bring all of your critical reading strategies to bear to sort the credible from the incredible. As writers, with some understanding of how to move your words into cyberspace you can be published authors with a ready, wide audience.

We all know there are plenty of ineffective Web pages. One reason for that is a lack of purposeful planning. The best way to plan is precisely the way you plan for any other research project. You identify your question, consider possible answers by listening carefully to others concerned with your question, respond to these other voices respectfully and responsibly, determine your best answer, and craft a document that will take your readers on the exploratory process that you followed. If you translate that process into Web documents, you take into account that your readers need access to as many of your sources as possible, that their process will differ from yours, and that their conclusions, too, may be different. By making your ideas public, you invite the responses of others, as they extend and enrich your inquiry.

Maybe because readers are not fully adapted to the physical process of screen reading, they want concise, efficient prose. A page full of prose unbroken by graphic elements will not engage readers; a page too cluttered with contrasting elements won't permit them to focus. The Internet is changing the way we process information cognitively because its strengths seem to favor efficiency and objectivity and undervalue reflection and higher-level thinking. But information is neutral—what you do with the information depends on your rhetorical purposes and your needs.

KEY CONCEPT

Rhetoric and Design Guidelines for Web Pages

Designing for the Web involves a balance of writer control and reader accessibility and flexibility.

- Be concise. Cut extra words, and use the strategy of hypertext to link to detailed development of ideas that are significant but unnecessary to your key points.
- Use design elements to ensure that the document is easy to visually scan. Typically, Web documents include more of these elements than print text. Use summaries at the top of a long page. Or list in hypertext key ideas at the top of a lengthy document that will help readers quickly link to what they are looking for. Use bulleted and numbered lists and colored text to highlight key words. Add more headings, and shorten paragraphs.
- Chunk text. Divide your information into logical units. Organize them in terms of their sequence and their significance. Leave white space between paragraphs. For visual ease and to limit scrolling, try to limit each block of text to 24 or at most 48 lines.
- Increase the spacing between lines to increase readability and an open, comfortable feel.
- Use left alignment for text blocks. Although some people think justified text, aligned on both left and right, looks neat on a printed page, it doesn't work on a screen because of the low resolution, which can create odd spacing and letter shapes.
- Use frames. Frames are areas of the screen that stay stable while you move through the sections of a document. In the framed area, you can provide links to all of the sections, so that readers can track where they've been and where they're going as they read.
- Use short lines, 10 to 14 words, for readability.
- Typefaces should be screen-friendly (Veranda, New York, and Trebouchet MS are good options). Fancy fonts distract readers and slow reading down.
- Select colors and color schemes carefully and meaningfully. Reds are warm, blues and greens are cool, and pastels create a light and airy feel. Yellows may suggest a warning, browns may suggest earthiness. Limit the number of colors used.
- Use visual elements purposefully and sparingly to enhance meaning and assist readers.
- Give print-accustomed readers help by using some cues that they are familiar with, like left alignment, indenting, and white space.

Though hypertext permits connections beyond the page, the electronic page itself has limits: 24 lines of text, to be specific. The rhetoric of cyberspace almost always values economy and focus. The 24-line screen constitutes a unit of information, verbal and visual, and it should make sense as a unit. Information should be divided into screen-sized portions so that readers can scroll down pages without losing track of the relationship among the parts of the writing.

Where it is possible, include hypertext links to resources available on the Internet. Where that is not possible, link to your bibliography or a note that offers fuller information on the specific subject.

Despite the differences, designing Web pages has much in common with designing printed pages. Your readers need clarity and order, and effective page designs will persuade readers that your site is trustworthy. Of course, good language choices—diction, syntax, structure, and tone—are just as important on the screen as they are on the page.

STRATEGY

Translating Research Projects Into Web Documents

1. Select a writing project you have completed or are in the process of completing.
2. Divide the information into appropriate screen-sized chunks.
3. Revise the prose for maximum concision. Cut all extra words and any repetition.
4. Design the site by sketching the page or series of pages on paper with grid lines. Identify the function of each area in terms of your purpose for the reader.
5. Read your pages visually, identifying where you want your reader's eye to move, and use document design elements to guide the eyes.
6. Identify information that could benefit your reader through hypertext links to your project.
7. Select your design elements, including visual elements (colors, shapes, arrangement, size, and space) and textual elements (typography, headings, boxes and lines, lists with bullets and numbering.)
8. Edit and proofread carefully.
9. Using available authoring software or your HTML knowledge, craft your page. Your instructor or a computer technician can help you launch your page within your college network.

APPLICATION

Evaluating Web Page Design

The screen shots in Figures 11.6 and 11.7 present Web sites for two organizations concerned with young voters. Compare their rhetoric and design, and evaluate their effectiveness.

WRITING INVITATIONS

1. Collect examples of one kind of professional writing from two employers in the same field. Compare the models rhetorically. What is the purpose of each? What language choices reveal that purpose? How are they similar? How are they different? Can the reader identify the professional field from the language? How? Write a rhetorical analysis comparing the features of the samples.

2. If you are currently interested in a particular job, write a resumé and a cover letter for the position. Ask your writing group members to respond to your draft in terms of the rhetorical considerations listed in this chapter. If you are not currently interested in a particular job, find a description for a job you might apply for, and write your resumé and cover letter to address the requirements and expectations of the description.

3. In response to two different job descriptions, write a version of your resumé to address each description, and then write a comparative analysis of the features of each, explaining why you made the choices of rhetorical strategy that you did.

4. List all of the communities you belong to. For each community, write at least one question at issue shared by the group. Select one question and research it in all the ways that make sense to you. Interview people, search documents, discuss the issue with members. Then write a proposal for addressing the question, using the membership as your audience.

5. Research a local organization and create two versions of an informational brochure for public distribution. For the brochure, use the typical format of the tri-folded 8½ by 11 inch paper. Ask classmates, friends, and other community members for responses to the two brochures to discover which sets of elements they prefer and why.

6. Design and produce a brochure as a public service for a local agency or organization. Identify a need and an audience. Plan your brochure by collecting information and graphic elements that might enhance interest and readability. Then construct your brochure to be informative, attractive, and efficient.

7. Pick a subject of interest to you and research it in the library and on the World Wide Web. Focus the topic, and try to identify two published works, one in print and one from the Internet, that answer exactly the same question. Compare the rhetorical strategies of the print document and the Internet site. How do they differ in purpose and presentation? Why do you think that is the case? Which is more effective? On what criteria did you base your judgment?

DEVELOPING A WRITING PROJECT

1. Select a writing project you have completed or are in the process of completing. Translate the project for a Web site.

2. Divide the information into appropriate screen-sized chunks.

3. Revise the prose for maximum concision. Cut all extra words and any repetition.

4. Design the site by sketching the page or series of pages on paper with grid lines. Identify the function of each area in terms of your purpose for the reader.

5. Read your pages visually, identifying where you want your reader's eye to move, and select design elements that will guide the eyes.

6. Identify information that could benefit your reader through hypertext links to your project.

7. Select your design elements, including visual elements (colors, shapes, arrangement, size, and space) and textual elements (typography, headings, boxes and lines, lists with bullets and numbering.)

8. Edit and proofread carefully.

9. Using available authoring software or your HTML knowledge, craft your page. Your instructor or a computer technician can help you launch your page within your college network.

CHAPTER 12

Revising Effectively

Rhetoric, I shall urge, should be a study of misunderstandings—
and their remedies.

I. A. Richards

REVISION IN THE WRITING PROCESS

In Chapter 2, we analyzed writing as a process and identified three categories
of cognitive strategies that go into constructing a piece of writing: *planning,
drafting, and revising.* These categories help us compose consciously and keep
on track as we match our meaning to language strategies that work.

It is possible, though, to think of the whole writing process, from the
moment that you have an idea and an impulse to write about it, as revision. It
helps, as we said in Chapter 2, to do some thinking on paper without committing to a particular shape or sequence of thought. It also helps to set a goal of
producing a complete draft, one that contains all of the ideas you think you
want to include, in order to be able to test your work—by re-reading it yourself, or by sharing it with others. In between and beyond these benchmarks in
composing are revising decisions: cutting, rearranging, adding, experimenting,
clarifying, elaborating, changing your mind, making up your mind, and as the
quotation above suggests, finding remedies for misunderstandings. Revising is
surprising, unpredictable, risky, and often frustrating. It's kind of like trying to
build a plane while you are flying it. Certainly it can be time consuming. But
without careful and thoughtful revision, your writing will not be as good as it
could be.

Revising means *seeing again: re-seeing.* When you revise you are considering and reconsidering your words as you come to understand what you really
want to say. Your most significant growth as a writer and the most significant
improvement of your writing take place as you revise and rewrite with your
purpose and audience in mind.

One goal of revising is to clarify your own understanding. Another goal is to meet your reader's needs. It helps all writers to have in mind a set of expectations for what constitutes "good" writing.

Reader Expectations: Qualities of Good Writing

There are many reasons why something might be misunderstood. If you are a reader, it may be that you are so put off by the writer's tone that you don't *want* to understand him or her. Or it may be that the writer assumes you know things about the subject that you don't know. Most often, writing is hard to understand because a writer has not done a good job of matching writing strategies to the situation. Almost always, messages will be unclear if the writer has not chosen the most effective rhetorical strategies for getting the messages across. Almost always, writing will be sensible and interesting if the rhetorical strategies are carefully chosen.

As a reader, you may have difficulty understanding the reading material because of any of the following characteristics.

Characteristics of Ineffective Writing

- The writer's purpose isn't clear.
- The ideas aren't significant or aren't clearly connected to the purpose.
- The reasoning is flawed or too narrow to accept.
- The development is insufficient—you are left with big questions.
- The form or order of the ideas is unfamiliar or unclear.
- The paragraphs are unfocused—the sentences don't follow logically or the topic of the paragraph shifts.
- The sentences are difficult to read because of errors or confused structures.
- Some words are used imprecisely, are too general, or are too specialized.
- The writing contains frequent errors that distract you from the ideas.
- The writer's tone puts you off.

When your reading makes sense, it may be because the reading material meets the general criteria for good writing listed below.

Criteria for Good Writing

- The purpose of the writer is clear.
- The ideas are significant and are clearly relevant to the purpose.
- The reasoning is persuasive, respectful and inclusive.
- The development is sufficient to meet the needs of readers.
- The sequence of ideas is apparent and provides a sense of unity.

- The paragraphs are focused and coherent.
- The sentences are clear and correct.
- The vocabulary is precise and appropriate.
- The writer consistently uses the conventions of standard academic English.
- The writer's tone is acceptable and engaging.

These are some basic qualities of writing that readers often appreciate. There are others; certainly we also appreciate originality, thoughtfulness, sophistication, thoroughness, specificity, concision, vividness, variety, and precision, all of which can raise the level of effectiveness of a piece of writing. But writing that satisfies the basic qualities will often accomplish its intention.

Evaluating Writing with Criteria

At least three kinds of evaluation can help you meet your responsibilities as a writer. **Self-evaluation** requires you to read with objectivity, honesty, and respect for your audience. Sometimes it is difficult to spot your own mistakes because you already know what you meant to say. We have a few ideas for coping with this problem. First, take a break before you try to evaluate your own work. A full day or two is preferable, but if that's not possible, take a walk or a dinner break, or do some work unrelated to your writing. Second, try reading your writing out loud. Yes, it may get you strange looks if you are working in the library, but reading your work aloud helps you hear where the writing is effective and where it may need revising. Ideas expressed in an unclear way may cause you to hesitate as you read, or even cause you to reread a passage. Third, try reading your work into a tape recorder and then listening to your recording, or using your computer's "speech" to read your words back to you. Students report that this strategy makes it easier for them to be objective and honest about the qualities of the writing. They advise reading a printed copy as you listen to the recording, revising or noting questions on the hard copy in the margins, just as a peer revising partner or an instructor might. A fourth strategy requires a friend—read the work aloud to someone whose intelligence you respect and whose opinion you value, and then talk to that person about it.

Peer evaluation involves working with a partner or a group on revision and editing. Partners or group members exchange their work and discuss strengths and weaknesses. Peer evaluation is not an easy process, but with a focused agenda and a clear task, it can be very valuable. We, too, are often called on to evaluate our colleagues' work, and it is difficult to find a balance between honesty and kindness, but we know that our peers expect help from us, or they would not have bothered to share their work.

Peer evaluation is helpful not just because you may get useful advice from your readers but also because you can learn to read your own work better by reading with others who bring different strengths and concerns to the

FIGURE 12.1

PEER EVALUATION

process. If you have opportunities in a writing class or on your own to share written work with others, remember three things. First, you don't have to name errors; you only need to indicate where you see a problem or have a question. Second, try first to discover the writer's purpose, and if you can't identify it, ask the writer. If you can identify it, read with the writer's purpose in mind—don't feel compelled to tell the reader what you would have said if you had been writing the paper. Third, listen to the writer of the work. What help does he or she need? What questions does he or she have?

Instructor evaluation is offered sometimes when your writing is in process, and other times when it is complete, as a justification of or explanation for a grade. Either way, it is your instructor's job to comment on your writing in a way that will help develop your rhetorical awareness. Instructors are experienced, knowledgeable readers, but because writing is not an exact science, instructors may give you suggestions or make judgments you don't agree with. That can be frustrating, especially when you have put a lot of effort into a writing assignment and know how it has changed and improved since the beginning of its development. However, you should try to regard the instructor's critique of your written work as you would like another writer to regard your critique of their writing. Know that much of the instruction in a writing class can happen in the careful, thoughtful responses that appear in the margins or at the end of your draft or final copy. This advice and guidance is individualized to fit your own writing skills and habits.

The instructor's comments are also an invitation to dialogue. If you have questions about the comments on your writing, it is your right and responsibility to talk to the instructor about what was meant, or what you should do to solve a problem. It is not, however, always useful to seek out a teacher to argue about a grade. Grades have a different purpose from evaluative comments. In his or her comments, an instructor is offering advice and guidance to help you become a better writer. When assigning a grade, an instructor is judging how a particular piece of writing compares to a set of expectations. A grade does not indicate your capabilities as a writer, but only the extent to which one writing attempt met the assignment's description and the evaluative criteria. So if you talk to your instructor about a grade, be prepared to discuss the writing not in terms of how hard you worked or how crazy your schedule was or how you have done on past writing assignments, but only in terms of how it met the assignment's specifications and the instructor's expectations.

If you are allowed to revise a paper that the instructor has already evaluated, be sure to read the comments as indications of places where your meaning or structures need adjustment, not necessarily as a set of instructions. As readers, instructors can't know what meaning you intended, only where your meaning wasn't completely clear or clearly expressed. It's important to revise *strategically*, making changes that clarify and support your purpose.

In a composition class, you have the assistance of other readers, including the instructor, as you revise. However, the goal of all class-based conversations about your writing is to help you internalize other voices so that you can be a thoughtful, objective, and independent reviser of your own work.

Revising Attitudes

We have noticed that some students think revising is the same as editing. But when you revise, you are changing more than grammar, spelling, and mechanics. Those things are crucial for a reader's understanding and are the focus of Chapter 13: Editing Effectively. When you revise, you must be willing to look at what you've said as if you were someone else trying to understand your thoughts. You must be willing to clarify not just how you have expressed yourself but also what you have said. It's a tricky business. We have some suggestions for how to make it work.

- **Plan to revise.** Manage your writing schedule to make sure you have time left for revision. When an instructor (or an employer) gives you an assignment, begin writing. Get words onto paper—words you can change or develop later.

- **Be objective.** We find that it is very difficult to revise what we have just written. A few days, or a day, or a few hours, or at least time for a meal or a walk will make objective reflection and revision easier. But you can't do it if you don't have time!

- **Read as a friend.** Read your work with an attitude of acceptance and see what your writing invites you to do or think or feel or believe. See if there are places where your willingness to accept the ideas is tested.

FIGURE 12.2

SEEK OUT RESPONSE

- **Read as a critic.** Read your work with an attitude of doubt. See what arguments occur to you that challenge your ideas or your presentation of them.

- **Seek out response.** Many writers dread getting responses from others because readers will raise questions that will require them to make changes. Get over it! This whole writing effort doesn't matter much if you don't care whether your readers understand you. It's better to have those questions raised so that you have an opportunity to address them.

- **See it all over again.** When you revise, remember that as you write, you make up your mind. We mean you *make up what's in your mind,* creating and re-creating the ideas. Through writing, but especially through revising, you see yourself and your subject in new ways, ways you can share with other minds that are also in the process of being *made up.*

REVISING FOR COMPELLING IDEAS

One of the most important reasons to revise is to make sure that your ideas are clear, supported, and compelling—that is, they are worth the time it took to write them down. Sometimes your first draft may include statements that are obvious or unnecessary, though you need to have them in front of you as you complicate your thinking. Sometimes a first draft includes distractions—interesting, but not directly related to your purpose—that need to be cut so they don't confuse the reader. Sometimes you will discover in reading your draft that some of your most important ideas are ones you take for granted as true because you have been persuaded of them yourself, but all statements about issues require substantiation and support. Sometimes you state all of your major arguments but neglect to imagine a reader who may not already agree with you; in that case, you will need to make sure to consider other points of view than your own, both for the sake of your own credibility and to increase the likelihood that readers will hear what you have to say.

It is important that you try to revise your ideas first, and probably separately from revising for organization or style. Why? Because why should you go to the trouble of carefully crafting sentences in a paragraph that will be cut? While you can't, of course, separate your ideas from the structures that give them their shape, you can keep from doing unnecessary work by first deciding what ideas need to be included in the first place.

All basic revision of content includes the following tasks:

- Ensure that your purpose is clear.
- Cut unnecessary material.
- Add supporting material where necessary.
- Consider other points of view when they are relevant.

"What I Really Mean Is…"

One important goal of revising for compelling ideas is to keep on track, to stay focused. It's easy to include material that interests us which is only marginally related to our purpose. Peter Elbow, a professor of rhetoric, has suggested that writers simply begin to write whatever comes into their minds in response to an impulse to write; he also suggests that every ten minutes or so, writers pause to clarify their thinking by saying to themselves, "What I really mean is…" and finishing the sentence, taking stock of the progression of their thinking. The strategy can work as you draft. Keep pulling yourself back to your purpose, and in the process, your purpose, too, will become clearer.

Speak It/Tape It

Several of our students have found it especially helpful to rely on their ears as well as their eyes when they are revising. Sometimes, confused sentence structures draw your attention away from the ideas you are trying to revise. (Remember: your readers will experience this same kind of distraction when they read your work if you have not edited thoroughly.) One strategy for hearing what you are thinking is to summarize out loud your ideas for a friend, one whose intelligence you respect and one who cares enough about you to want to understand what you have to say. If you struggle with the oral summary, note that significant connections may be missing or unclear. If, in summarizing, you are tempted to ignore significant parts of your paper, note that they may not be relevant to your purpose. Where your listener questions your thinking, be aware that you will need an especially effective transition.

Another strategy for hearing what you are thinking involves reading your paper into a tape recorder and listening as you play it back. Several of our students over the years have found this method very revealing—lapses in logic or absences of support that may be difficult to notice on the page sometimes become apparent when you play the role of listener.

The Descriptive Outline

Rhetoric professor Kenneth Bruffee describes the strategy of using a descriptive outline for guiding the selection and sequencing of key ideas. Many instructors call this the "says/does" outline because Bruffee suggests that the writer identify the content and function of each paragraph. This strategy, like those above, helps you be more objective about what you have or have not included in your draft and how the sequence of ideas flows.

The following draft of an essay on gender communication was written by a student in a composition class to share with a peer review group. Her readers thought that her draft lacked focus and that some of her ideas weren't very interesting. These comments can be devastating to a writer unless he or she has a strategy for testing the validity of the comments objectively. Following the draft of the paper is the writer's descriptive outline, which helped her see for herself not just what her readers had noted but also how she might go about fixing the problems.

Sample Student Writing: Draft of an Argument Essay

The draft essay below is followed by the student's descriptive outline. But before you review the outline, play the role of a peer reviewer. Read each paragraph of the essay for what it says and what it does, and think about what might help the writer revise the draft.

Communication Barriers

Katie Dickison

The problems facing couples today seem to be based on the lack of communication between the man and the woman. It is an ongoing problem that people seem to have a hard time solving. Whether the couple is married or not, communication is a big part of a relationship and must be dealt with. One of the main reasons people find it hard to talk to people of the opposite sex is just that, they are the opposite. Men and women have been having conflicts for years and not understanding why. The issues of sex, money, and power in the home and in the workplace are the main conflicts that our society faces every day. Another reason conflicts arise are because of a difference in values and moral beliefs. Values that people possess are very important to them, and if the person they are sharing their lives with does not share the same belief system, then the chances of the relationship working out is slim. If people can learn to deal with their differences, then communication can be established and the gap between men and women will lessen.

Early arising conflicts, like the fear of intimacy and the "ultimate trap" (Brown 72) of getting married, were the start of the downfall in male and female relationships. The fear of getting involved in a relationship has grown over the past twenty years. In the early 1970's, relationships were strong and the need for marriage seemed unnecessary. The marriage contract seemed to have lost "its binding character" (Brown 72). Sexual relations were something more solid than legal papers. This strong, intimate bond in relationships was followed by a decrease in the number of children. This made the connection between men and women improve because it increased the time spent together meeting each other's emotional needs. As time passed and men's and women's needs changed, it was harder to please one's partner. In women's lives the ideas of feminism and sisterhood were introduced. Those ideas made it harder for men and women to communicate with each other. Soon "male and female relationships became increasingly risky" (Brown 73). Both men and women sought escape from emotions and there was little for couples to relate to in each other's lives. Men found it difficult to express their emotions. People of both genders increased their expectations of each other. In recent decades, though, expectations, emotional issues, and values in marriage have changed drastically. "Today people see marriage as being held together by the strength and significance of the couple's interpersonal relationship" (Brown 35). This relationship is dependent on love, respect, friendship and communication. After a couple has achieved these things in a relationship, most strive for "happy couple" status (Brown 134). Those who can achieve this level in a relationship seem to lead healthier lives with each other.

Another problem facing couples, which is widening the communication gap, is the amount of stress put on sex, power, and money. The combination of those three stressors can make for an unhappy home life, which can ultimately lead to bigger problems. The overpowering issue of sex, and using it as a means to get what you want, is a huge thing in our society. People use sex and sex appeal to achieve a higher status in the work place, as well as in home life. The use of sex in a relationship is one way of communicating with, but also controlling, your partner. If one partner in the relationship has significantly more power and control, it can lead to power struggles and loss of communication. The topic of making money, who does it, and who keeps control of it is also a largely recognized problem. In most societies, the women handle the majority of the money while the male counterparts go out and make it. If the couple is not communicating about how the money is spent and exactly what it is going towards, that is when the major problems arise. A struggle to be the one in charge and holding the power begins and communication is cut off. If the issue of power can be split evenly between the partners, enough so that one is not consistently dominant over the other, it will make for a healthy relationship.

One of the most important things in a relationship is to have good communication, and another way of making sure that is established is to have common values and beliefs. Before starting a rapport with someone, we normally look for those underlying values that connect us to each other. "The assumption here is that individuals in choosing someone to marry make use of their personal values, and by doing so they tend to select people who have values similar to their own" (Whyte 118). Personal values are what sets everyone apart from everyone else, and in most cases what keep people together. Your own values come from numerous different places, but the majority of them seem to come from how you were raised as a child. Early in life we are taught that talking things out is a good way to fix a problem. As we get older, though, the lessons learned as children seem to fade away and we are left, in a way, speechless. The values taught to us, which seemed so important, are forgotten. The art of communication is as well. Communication is one value that everyone should be able to maintain. The ability to communicate well with others is an important value that can make a relationship reliable and lasting.

Through discovering how men and women differ emotionally and how they handle stress, power, and personal beliefs, we can determine how to handle ourselves in a relationship. Using communication to discuss these things can greatly enhance our chances at a healthy and meaningful relationship. Despite the many differences men and women have, one thing that can be agreed on is that it is hard to communicate with the opposite sex. Through listening, observing, and knowing your role in the relationship, anyone can communicate what he or she is feeling and let the other person know what exactly is going on. Overall, communication is the key to a happy and healthy relationship.

Works Cited

Brown, Phillip M. *The Death of Intimacy: Barriers to Meaningful Interpersonal Relationships*. New York: Haworth, 1995.

Whyte, Martin. *Dating, Mating and Marriage*. New York: De Gruyter, 1990.

Example Descriptive Outline

This descriptive outline of "Communication Barriers" by Katie Dickison both indicates what the writer intended, and also what she planned to do based on her observations and the peer critique offered by her classmates. As you read it, compare her reading of the essay to yours. Did you notice the same problems? Different problems? Did you suggest the same solutions? Different solutions?

Paragraph 1

What it says: This paragraph says that communication is a problem for couples because they are opposites; because of sex, money, and power in the home; and because of different value systems.

What it does: Introduces the problem.

Writer's comments: It introduces the problem in several different ways. No wonder my readers didn't know what I was going to say. Some of the things I bring up in this paragraph I don't really deal with, like communication problems are caused by differences in men and women. I need to decide what my real question is and stick to it.

Paragraph 2

What it says: This paragraph says that communication problems got worse over the last two decades. Although initially a decline in marriages led to stronger interpersonal relationships, change in both partners and the growth in feminism caused conflicts. But there is hope, because a new understanding of marriage is emerging which is based on equality.

What it does: Provides context for the issue and supports the importance of communication to a good relationship.

Writer's comments: I have to confess I was very confused as to what my own points were in this paragraph until I sorted it out here. Most of this paragraph paraphrases Brown's interpretation of the history of the issue. I need to rewrite it to clarify the sequence in Brown's thinking and make sure that readers know where it came from and why it's important to my purpose—right now the paragraph doesn't do that.

Paragraph 3

What it says: This paragraph says that issues of control over sex, power, and money create problems in relationships.

What it does: Complicates the issue, showing how many factors are working against the goal of healthy and open communication.

Writer's comments: This paragraph doesn't work at all. I have to unpack it. First of all, it deals with three topics instead of one, though they all have to do with control and power. Second, only one sentence focuses on power, which may be the real topic of the paragraph. I could either split the paragraph into two, and go back to my research to find support for my statements, or I could rewrite the paragraph with power as the topic and use sex and money as two instances where power gets in the way of communication.

Paragraph 4

What it says: It says that common beliefs and values help communication, and then it says that we tend to lose the value of communication as we get older.

What it does: It's supposed to show how values and beliefs complicate or help communication.

Writer's comments: There's no support of this point. Not only that, but it contradicts itself. I'm embarrassed by this one—it sounds like I was just trying to fill space. Even though this is an idea I believe very strongly and wanted to include, I didn't back it up through reasoning or evidence or even illustrations. I just restated it.

Paragraph 5

What it says: It says that we can communicate better if we understand how the factors of emotional difference, stress, power, and personal beliefs affect our relationships.

What it does: It's supposed to unify the paper by referring to the key ideas that came up in my paper.

Writer's comments: This paragraph doesn't unify my paper, and now it's very clear why my readers got lost. I don't deal with the ideas I've promised to deal with. I don't show how men and women differ emotionally or handle stress. I don't show how hard it is to communicate with the opposite sex. I don't describe how we can improve communication; I just say we can. And I don't support the concluding statement that communication is the key to a happy and healthy relationship, although I believe that. When I started, I wanted to answer the question "Is communication the key to a healthy relationship?" but what I did was answer the question "What can get in the way of healthy communication in relationships?" I should revise with that question in mind, and develop the points that I had no support for.

As this example shows, the Descriptive Outline is a very effective way to distance yourself from your writing in order to test what it is accomplishing. This writer had worked hard on her ideas and if she had not been able to review her work with this strategy, she might have felt helpless in the face of the peer critique. The critique, rightly, evaluated her paper with higher-order criteria— does the essay do what it set out to do? If they hadn't done that, they might have directed the writer to fix grammar problems in sentences that should be cut, or to write better transitions between ideas that may not live through the revision process. So, when you revise, do so first for your ideas, to make sure that your purpose is clear, your ideas are relevant and related to your purpose, and your key points are supported. Then make a plan for revising that will guide you through the process and keep you focused on revisions that are strategic.

Example Revision Plan

After reading her group's critique and writing her descriptive outline, Katie devised a plan for the ways she might rethink and improve her essay.

1. I will clarify my question. What I'm now most interested in exploring is what factors work against healthy communication in relationships?

2. I will need to revise my introduction for clarity and cohesion, cutting out the repetition and finding a more personal or engaging way to introduce the problem.

3. I will rewrite the history of the issue as a paraphrase of Brown's ideas, but my topic in this paragraph should be that changing social and cultural expectations have influenced communication.

4. I will rewrite the third paragraph to focus on power issues, using money and sex as examples but building in better, more persuasive support.

5. Paragraph 5 also needs specific support, and when I do additional research, I will decide whether this point is the best one for the final paragraph of development. My strongest point should go here.

6. One of my readers suggested I have a paragraph supporting alternative views, but my thesis is that healthy communication in relationships is difficult because of cultural issues, power issues, and differences in values and

beliefs. What I need, instead, is some recognition at the end that healthy communication is possible, with some ideas for what will encourage it. This should be a part of the conclusion.

REVISING FOR UNITY AND FORM

When you draft, you often make connections mentally that propel your writing forward. But these connections don't always get written down. One frequent problem in unfinished writing is that it contains many interesting ideas but the connections between and among them aren't clear. The connections may be clear to the writer, but they aren't clear to the reader. Rhetoric professor Linda Flower calls a draft that is clear to a writer "writer-based prose," and a revised draft that anticipates a reader's needs "reader-based prose." She explains that writers need to make a shift from one to the other, sometimes repeatedly, in the process of composing in order to discover their own meaning and design their writing for readability.

Some English classes have taught writers particular forms and models for their writing, but unfortunately these models don't always easily contain the ideas you might want to express. For example, you may be familiar with the tradition of composing the "Five Paragraph Essay" with one paragraph each for an introduction and conclusion, and three paragraphs of development. Instructors sometimes rely on these predictable forms to help beginning writers understand the importance of unity and shape in writing. However, the more mature our thinking becomes, the less useful such forms are to our writing needs. Ben Shahn, an artist, wrote a book about painting called *The Shape of Content*, in which he explains that form, in art, is the shape our particular and unique content must take. So as your ideas develop and become more complex, you will need a flexible and strategic understanding of form to accommodate the richness of your thinking.

You can witness the limits of predictable forms in the sample student essay above. The writer forced three possible topics—the effects on communication in relationships of sexual politics, finance, and power—into a single paragraph, and our guess is that she did it to retain the form of the "Five Paragraph Essay," which she may have learned in another class. This prevented her from developing three very provocative ideas that could have been the most compelling in her essay.

When you consider unity and form, think about:

- What to include,
- In what order,
- With what interconnections,
- In what proportion,
- For your particular audience and situation.

Selecting and sequencing ideas, marking clearly the connections among them, and paying an appropriately balanced amount of attention to each—these are your goals in revising for shape and unity. Writing works well when the parts fit with each other. Often instructors make an analogy between revising for shape and doing a jigsaw puzzle, because in both cases you are looking for fit and seeking to reveal the whole picture. It would be great, in our opinion, if we knew, as writers, that the jigsaw puzzle of our ideas included all the necessary pieces and no extras. Our job is a little more complicated, but we have better tools and greater rewards—we can cut and paste, we can use putty and sandpaper, and we can create a picture unlike the one on the box, one that no one else has created before.

Strategies for Selecting and Arranging Ideas

When you allow yourself to complicate ideas and issues, it may feel as if you are creating chaos, because you are challenging your preconceived ideas. But chaos is essential. One of the most complicated tasks of writing is to find order in that chaos. Some people are born to outline and have no trouble with this task. Others are less linear and more spatial; their ideas don't come to them in order but in fits and jerks, in pieces and parts. Here are a couple of strategies for finding the shape of your content.

The "Rainbow Notepad"

Some students have been freed from the limits of the page and some of the writing time involved in multiple drafts through the "rainbow notepad" strategy, named for the cheap pads of multicolored paper first used for this activity. Once you have collected all of the ideas you believe are relevant to your writing situation, sit in a soft chair in a comfortable room and write each (a phrase is enough) on a separate slip of notepaper. Throw the notes onto the floor. When you have exhausted your supply of ideas, get down on the floor. Pick up the slips one at a time and arrange them in piles that seem to go together. If a slip doesn't fit into any pile, throw it away. Look at each pile and identify what ties the ideas together. Write out the connection and put that statement on the top of the pile. Then arrange the piles in an order that seems to make sense. If a pile doesn't fit in the sequence of other groups of ideas, throw the pile away. Write statements that link each pile to the one that came before, and the one that comes after, and add these notes to the piles. Pick up the piles in order, and write your way through the stack. Sound crazy? At least you save yourself the struggle of thinking, after each sentence, "Now what will I say next?" It sounds like an additional activity in your writing process, but it usually saves time that might have been spent deleting, adding, and ordering ideas.

Colors and Numbers

To take advantage of color and number organizers, make sure you draft or list on only one side of your paper. To select and sequence your ideas, you can color code chunks of thought that seem to go together, or you can add numbers to your points. Some people number their key ideas and color code their support for each idea. This strategy is especially helpful when you do research. Often another writer's sequence of ideas will take over your thinking and impose itself on your own purpose. Establishing your own order on the material before you draft ensures that the source material will be used to support your purpose.

Strategies for Creating Coherence

Although the "Five Paragraph Essay" is too constraining for most writing situations, it is true that most readers of prose about issues and ideas expect strategic beginnings, middles, and ends. The introduction sets up the writer's commitment to the reader; in the introduction, the wandering mind of the writer chooses a specific path for the reader to follow. In the middle, the ideas should follow each other without distraction or confusion; the writer takes the reader's arm, using structures that will support the reader's confidence and understanding. The conclusion provides a sense of arrival, of the appropriateness and necessity of all that came before.

The expectation of beginnings, middles, and ends is a specific cultural form, certainly. Non-Western cultures have other expectations for entering and concluding an inquiry that are as compelling as our classical expectation of unity. It is helpful, though, for writers to have strategies that will help them address these audience expectations when the situation calls for them, as they do in most college and professional writing.

Beginnings

Introductions are difficult because they need to accomplish several things at once. They introduce the subject, they usually introduce the writer's purpose and perspective on the subject, they need to invite the reader into the subject and motivate further reading, and they need to make the reading seem achievable and worth the time and effort. Some people write their introductions last, so that they can ensure the introduction really reflects the writing that is to follow. Some people write a tentative introduction, and return to it at the end to make sure that they have met the commitment to the reader that they made in the beginning.

Rhetorical strategies for introductions include these:

- Set up a conflict by presenting a view to refute or by presenting alternate perspectives on an issue that will engage the reader intellectually ("Although this may seem to be the case, I assert that…")

- Begin with a personal story about what led you to this particular inquiry that will engage the reader imaginatively in your situation.

- Begin with an anecdote or a particular instance, real or even hypothetical, that will allow the reader to see the significance or relevance of the subject.

- Begin with the question at issue, a strategy we have advocated repeatedly throughout the book, to engage readers' curiosity and challenge them to participate in seeking an answer.

- Begin with a compelling image, metaphor, or quotation that interests the reader for its own sake, in order to build on the idea from your own perspective.

Middles

If you find that your ideas link neatly one to the next in a sequence that is logical and compelling, you don't need specific design strategies to help you arrange your development. Composing doesn't always work that way, though, especially in writing that relies on research. Many chapters of this book present purposes for writing that compel you to use evidence, explanation, description, narration, statistics, examples, analogies, reasons, and rhetorical appeals in developing your points, and the sheer volume of the material can overwhelm the most experienced writers. Often, writers rely on familiar, tried-and-true methods of development like those in the following list. Others use these methods as ways of thinking about their content as they work to discover their own best design, one which may combine strategies or which may be guided by an entirely different principle. The tried-and-true designs, then, are not rules to follow but tools to use as you find a shape that suits your content.

Familiar designs for development include:

- Chronological order: This design arranges the ideas according to their appearance or occurrence over a specific period of time. This is useful when you are writing about personal experiences and events, but it is also important when you are tracing the evolution of an idea or linking causes to effects.

- Deductive order: In this pattern, you make a general statement and support it with specifics, in each paragraph, and across the essay as a whole. This is useful when you can begin a presentation with generalizations or assumptions that your reader also accepts. This pattern suggests an authoritative attitude on the part of the writer: "I am right in what I am saying, and let me tell you why."

- Inductive order: The reverse of deductive order, in this case you offer particular examples that lead to a general statement. This is useful when your readers may not agree with your position, because you can guide them through specific instances to see the validity of your general ideas.

- Causal order: This pattern of development moves either from known consequences to probable causes, or from known causes to predicted consequences. Sometimes this pattern blends well with chronology, because causes and effects happen across time; sometimes it blends well with inductive order, because it can be rhetorically effective to describe consequences and then establish why they occurred, or might occur.

- Rank order, or order of hierarchy: This pattern relies on a writer being able to establish either an order of importance or of dramatic effect. You might progress, for example, from the argument that is least acceptable to the one that is most acceptable, or from the smallest consequence to the largest, or from the most predictable outcome to the most surprising. Rank order is very important in situations that require reasoning and the presentation of evidence. Anyone who has heard a real or dramatized closing argument in a court of law has witnessed a hierarchical presentation. The most damning evidence, or the evidence casting the most doubt on the guilt of the accused, will be presented last.

As we have said before, the writing process is not so predictable that we can identify a point in the composing process where choosing a design will be necessary. Some writers like to commit to a particular structure early. Some rearrange the order of information right up to the last minute. Either way, the design should be perceptible to your reader and supportive of your purpose.

Endings

The purpose of the conclusion is for the reader to find satisfaction and closure. As you draw your ideas to a close, ask yourself, "So what?" Just as you would ask that question when you read someone else's work, ask it of yourself. Take responsibility for your reader's need to understand clearly both the content and the significance of your writing. A "therefore" statement followed by a summary of the paper often seems like a formulaic conclusion, and effective conclusions go beyond this form. You can imagine the conclusion of a piece of writing as the summit of a mountain peak. You have guided your reader to the top, and now you share the view of the whole landscape. Interpret that landscape for your fellow traveler. What do you point out? What generalizations might you share about the vista? The goal of the conclusion is to help your reader see your subject the way you do.

To discover what essential ideas you will need in your conclusion, get a friend to ask you what you wrote about. It's a simple but effective way to focus your thoughts. If you stumble or repeat yourself, keep talking, and keep answering questions your friend asks, until the clear and essential information reveals itself—you'll know you have succeeded when your friend says, "Oh, now I get it!"

Rhetorical strategies for conclusions include these:

- Restate the purpose: Identify your controlling idea, but now state it in terms of the key ideas that you used to develop it.

- Use a frame: If you used a story or an image to introduce your writing, come back to it in your conclusion. If you began with a quotation or a metaphor, refer to it again.

- Repeat key words: Remind readers of what has come before by using important or striking words and phrases in your conclusion.

- Use structures for emphasis and emotional charge: Parallel structures (repeated phrase or clause or sentence structures) make key points sound authoritative. Using repetition and rhythm for emphasis can work, as can syntactic contrast—long sentences followed by a very short statement of a crucial point.

- Develop a situation or image included in the paper to add emotional charge to the conclusion.

REVISING FOR VOICE AND TONE:
PERSONA AND ATTITUDE

Every piece of writing conveys a particular voice and tone. Voice, in writing, means the person, or persona, that is evident behind the words. (*Persona* is a word used to indicate a voice evident in the language of writing without suggesting that the voice is the writer's own or only one.) The voice of a piece of writing includes its tone, or the attitude of the writing toward the subject and audience. Writing can sound friendly, condescending, gossipy, thoughtful, energetic, calm, suspicious, warm, cold—use any adjective for describing a personality, and it can be used to describe the way writing sounds to a reader. Voice is conveyed by style, or the language choices you use to express yourself. Finally, voice includes authority, or the ways you establish your control and self-confidence, whether through your knowledge or your honesty or your powers of observation.

It is important to understand how to modulate your voice to support your purpose. You can't completely control how a reader will hear you, but to the extent that you can, you will want to know how to do it. In writing this book, we had to determine what persona to convey through the voice of the language we chose, and we had to reflect on what attitude we wanted to take toward our subject. We are teachers; you are students. But we are all readers and writers. Sometimes in the book we needed to be experts, sharing information that may be useful to you. Sometimes, too, we needed to be frustrated, struggling writers, sharing honestly our learning experiences and mistakes. In all, we have tried not to be too professorial, which might persuade you that this reading and writing business is a matter for professionals only; and we have tried not to be too casual, which might suggest that we take reading and writing as skills and subjects of study less seriously than we do.

As readers, you are aware of many different voices in writing, including the familiar and comfortable, the poetic and reflective, the scientific and technical, and the academic and authoritative. As writers, you have certainly expressed a range of voices in your writing, possibly including the private voice of journals, the personal voice of letters, the informative voice of reports or research papers, and the public, persuasive voice of a letter to the editor. You don't have just one style. Each set of language elements you choose becomes the style you adopt to convey a particular persona and attitude. Use them to help you achieve your writing purpose.

Here are some tips for modulating your voice and tone effectively:

- No one will care about your subject unless you do. Be confident, but not arrogant, and invite your reader to share your interest.

- Unless your subject is *you*, try to focus on your subject and your audience more than on yourself.

- No one will respect what you say unless you respect your listeners. You don't have to restrict yourself to pleasantries, of course, and certainly do not say things just to flatter your audience. Just accept that you will do better to imagine an audience who would *like* to understand your point of view; then you will be more likely to take alternate perspectives into account as you develop the reasons for seeing things your way.

- Don't say things just for effect. It's dishonest, and it rarely creates anything but confusion or aggravation.
- Write clearly, and as simply as the complexity of your ideas will allow. Sounding smart is not the same thing as sounding stuffy. In writing, unlike in speaking, you have the opportunity to revise and clarify. When people have to sift through your words for your meaning, they may mistrust you.

REVISING PARAGRAPHS, SENTENCES, AND WORDS

Strategies for Creating Cohesion

It isn't enough to have good ideas. Readers' attention will fade if you can't keep them connected to what you are saying. In conversation, we may often use connecting phrases like "Do you follow me?" and "Does that make sense?" as well as hand gestures, eye contact, and other body language to move the conversation forward and keep our listeners engaged. In writing, we lack all such physical communication, and yet the need for cohesion, for linking ideas together, is very real.

It isn't even enough to have good ideas and a good design. A good design provides coherence, but readers may still not follow your ideas unless you give them help in figuring out the design. That help is provided by cohesion. It is created by signals that indicate to readers exactly where they have been and where they are going.

As readers and writers, you are already familiar with many of the cohesive devices that are often used. Many are obvious, like beginning sentences with "First," "Second," and Third," to introduce a series of points. Others are less evident but even more important to a reader's comprehension. But all good writing makes use of strategies that create cohesion.

To create cohesion within paragraphs and sentences, try the following strategies.

Tie old ideas to new ideas, linking what came before to what follows.
Example:

> It isn't even enough to have good ideas and *a good design*. *A good design* provides coherence, but readers may still not follow your ideas unless you give them *help* in figuring out the design. That *help* is provided by cohesion.

Repeat key words and synonyms of key words.
Example:

> Every piece of writing conveys a particular *voice*. *Voice*, in writing, means the person, or *persona*, that is evident behind the words. (*Persona* is a word used to indicate a *voice* evident in the language of writing without

suggesting that the *voice* is the writer's own and only one.) The *voice* of a piece of writing includes its *tone*, or the attitude of the writing toward the subject and audience. Writing can *sound* friendly, condescending, gossipy, thoughtful, energetic, calm, suspicious, warm, cold—use any adjective for describing a personality, and it can be used to describe the way writing *sounds* to a reader. *Voice* is conveyed by style, or the language choices you use to express yourself, as well as authority, or the ways you establish your control and self-confidence, whether through your knowledge or your honesty or your powers of observation.

Use referring words, especially pronouns and demonstrative adjectives (that *story,* those *reasons*).

Pronouns can help by referring back to something that came before. But be careful that the pronouns refer clearly to something specific. The first set of sentences that follows lacks cohesion because it isn't clear what both "this" and "it" refer to. The second sentence makes use of pronouns as cohesive devices.

> *Ineffective Pronoun Use*: A good design provides coherence, but readers may need help in following your ideas. *That* is provided by the cohesion in your writing. *It* is created by signals that indicate to readers exactly where they have been and where they are going.
>
> *Effective Pronoun Use*: A good design provides coherence, but readers may still not follow your ideas unless you give them *help* in figuring out the design. *That help* is provided by cohesion. *It* is created by signals that indicate to readers exactly where they have been and where they are going.

Use transition words and phrases to indicate relationships.

Transition words and phrases link sentences, parts of sentences, and paragraphs, wherever a particular turn in thought needs to be marked. Transition words and phrases are not just glue used to hold ideas together. When you are writing to learn, you are responding to ideas that already exist, but the connections you make between and among those ideas represent your original intellectual effort. Transition words and phrases indicate specific relationships. They are your tools for acting on and creating something unique out of the intellectual materials you are confronting.

Be aware, though, that transition words cannot create cohesion in a piece of writing that lacks a good design. If you find yourself struggling to find an appropriate transition, or if you notice that you are using transitions frequently, check to see if your ideas are ordered in the most effective way. Effectively organized writing requires only infrequent use of transition words.

Transition words and phrases can relate one idea to the next by:

Adding: *and, in addition, also, furthermore*

Comparing: *similarly, likewise, in the same way*

Contrasting: *although, but, while, yet, whereas, instead, on the other hand*

Emphasizing: *clearly, obviously, certainly, indeed, in fact*

Exemplifying: *for example, for instance, namely, specifically*

Showing cause or effect: *accordingly, as a result, so, therefore, thus*

Showing order: *next, finally, first/second/third*

Summarizing: *finally, in conclusion*

Using Paragraphs and Sentences as Rhetorical Strategies

Paragraphs

You all know what paragraphs look like, but not everyone knows that they are rhetorical strategies just like any other strategy. Writers have used paragraphs since the time of the ancient Greeks, although they didn't use indentation to indicate a shift. They used an asterisk (*) in the margins of the writing to say to the reader "Pay attention here—this is important." In the same way, paragraphs are now used to divide sections of writing to emphasize what is important and to help readers understand how to tell the general statements from the specific support.

Have you ever tried to read a long block of prose without paragraph divisions? Your mind, if it works like ours, quickly fatigues, because it is difficult to sustain the same level of intensity and focus. Paragraphs allow our brains to establish a predictable rhythm in our thinking and understanding. One function of paragraphs is to mark the beginnings and ends of discussions of particular topics. However, if the topic is large, paragraphs are also used to mark shifts within the topic just so the reader can break the ideas into smaller chunks for easier comprehension. You have probably noticed this kind of paragraph style in journalism and magazine writing, in which paragraphs are relatively short; on the other hand, in fiction writing, where the writer desires a sustained intensity of attention from the reader, paragraphs can extend for several pages.

Paragraphs can function rhetorically to create unity and focus.

Unity: Each paragraph should have a single, clear purpose. The sequence of sentences should be clearly related, without unproductive repetition or irrelevant ideas. Through her "Descriptive Outline," the student writer of the argument essay "Communication Barriers" discovers the problems with her own paragraphing scheme, and her plan for revision notes the problems. Although there is no fixed length for a paragraph, length provided an important clue. In the original double-spaced copy, one paragraph was longer than a page and contained three ideas that might have been developed separately. However, when she tried developing the ideas separately, she was left with one paragraph consisting of a single sentence. For the revision to be effective, that sentence would require support.

Focus: Each paragraph needs a generalization that explains the paragraph's significance to the essay. Even if a subsequent paragraph continues to explore the same topic, it will often require a generalization to indicate its relationship to what came before. Sometimes topic sentences come at the end of a paragraph, especially in introductions. Most of the time, though, they appear at the beginning, often functioning as transition sentences.

Sentences

Sentences, too, are rhetorical strategies. A change in the order of sentences within a paragraph can radically affect its readability and meaning. In the same way, a change in the order of the parts of a sentence can radically affect its emphasis and tone. So often, we have seen frustrated writers trying to work out awkwardly worded sentences by substituting words but not changing the order of the parts. Remember: the parts of sentences are *movable*. Moving parts around can help you create effective sentences by revealing the order that will move the reader forward toward the important information, eliminating extra words (especially transition words), and increasing vividness and grace.

You may not be aware of all the (frequently subconscious) decisions you make when you construct or revise a sentence. As we explained earlier, when you repeat key words, use familiar information to introduce new information, and use pronouns and demonstrative adjectives, you promote readability by creating cohesion. You also choose the arrangement of parts—words, phrases, clauses—for emphasis and clarity. You may indicate structurally what is more and less important, using coordination and subordination. You may choose the sentence types and lengths, remembering that sentence variety is one of the consistent qualities of good writing.

The following examples from Katie's essay demonstrate such strategies.

Order the parts for emphasis and clarity.

> *Original*: She and my father would argue about any small issue for hours on end.
> *Revised*: She and my father would argue for hours on end about any small issue.

Grammatically speaking, the phrases that end the sentence could go in either order. But in the revision, the last words, "small issue," point the way for the paragraph to exemplify the small issues that would result in arguments.

Use coordination and subordination to clarify relationships and indicate emphasis.

> *Original*: We know now that they were working on solving their problems. That wasn't clear at the time to us though.
> *Revision 1* (Coordination): We know now that they were working on solving their problems, but at the time, that wasn't clear to us.

This revision coordinates equal but contrasting independent clauses and thus clarifies the relationship between the statements. Ending on "us" is also more emphatic and suggests that the people in the sentence will be the subject of the sentence that follows.

> *Revision 2* (Subordination): Though it wasn't clear to us at the time, we know now that they were working on solving their problems.

Putting the second clause first and making it dependent clarifies the relationship between the statements, and it also suggests that the topic of the following sentence will be the parents' problems.

Vary your sentence types and lengths to keep your readers interested and your writing rhythmic and graceful.

> *Original*: The problems facing couples today seem to be based on a lack of communication between the partners. It is an ongoing problem that people seem to have a hard time solving. Communication is a big part of any relationship and it must be dealt with. Men and women have been having communication conflicts for years and not understanding why. People may find it hard to talk to a partner of the opposite sex.
>
> *Revision*: Today, couples face many problems, some of which seem to be based on a lack of communication between the partners. Communication is crucial to a healthy relationship, and communication problems can be difficult to solve. There are many causes of communication problems. One of the causes for communication difficulties between the opposite sexes is just that—they are opposites.

The range in length in the original is 14–17 words per sentence; two sentence patterns are represented. In the revision, the range in length is 7–20 words per sentence; three sentence patterns are included. Revising for sentence variety also suggested to the writer shifts in words and phrases that clarified meaning as well.

Sample Student Writing: Revised Argument Essay, MLA Documentaion Style

The following revision of "Communication Barriers" follows the plan Katie established but incorporates many additional changes as well.

Communication Barriers

Katie Dickison

When I was fourteen, my parents got a divorce. My mother tried to help us deal with our confusion, but we wouldn't let her because we saw her as part of the problem. My two sisters and I knew, of course, that there was a problem. She and my father started to argue for hours on end about any small issue. The car had a scratch on the fender. They both had a commitment on the afternoon that I had a doctor appointment. The garage needed paint, but the living room also needed new carpet. In retrospect, these things seem so unimportant. We wondered then, as we have wondered often since then, why they couldn't communicate. What makes it so difficult for partners in marriage to talk to each other? Though it wasn't clear to us at the time, we know now that our parents were working on solving their communication problems. But even with professional help, healthy communication in a marriage is not easy to achieve; changing expectations, issues related to power, and differences in beliefs and values can all get in the way of good communication.

In his book <u>The Death of Intimacy: Barriers to Meaningful Interpersonal Relationships</u>, Philip M. Brown outlines the social and cultural changes that have complicated healthy communication between men and women in relationships. In the early 1970s, the idea that marriage was necessary to a strong relationship started to be questioned. The marriage contract seemed to have lost "its binding character" (72). Sexual relations, rather than legal papers, formed the basis of ongoing relationships. The good thing about this challenge to the idea of marriage was that it encouraged personal connections between men and women, because as marriages declined, so did the number of children. Couples had more time alone with each other for intimacy and for addressing each other's emotional needs. The bad thing about this challenge was that as men and women grew and changed as individuals, there was less reason to stay together. Both men and women sought escape from emotional traps. "Male and female relationships became increasingly risky" (73) as feminism challenged traditional roles for women and men began to see marriage as "the ultimate trap" (72). Both men and women brought expectations to their relationships, and in the middle of the social transformation intensified by feminism, those expectations changed. The idea that relationships end, marriage or no marriage, became more accepted.

However, as Brown sees it, this period of change has been good for relationships overall. Now men and women generally see marriage not in terms of traditional roles but as an equal partnership in which roles need to be negotiated. "Today people see marriage as being held together by the strength and significance of the couple's interpersonal relationship" built on love, respect, friendship and communication (35).

Those who can achieve this kind of relationship seem to sustain healthy relationships. Unfortunately, my parents were caught in the middle of these changes in cultural expectations.

One set of changing expectations that complicates communication has to do with power. Many communication problems arise not just because of differences of opinion but because of power struggles: not which answer is the best, but who has the right to decide. Some power struggles are financial. For example, when it is time to pay bills or make financial decisions, disagreements about options may be replaced by a discussion of who makes more. In our culture, making more money is one of the ways we measure success and importance. In relationships where men make more money, women can feel that they have no say in financial matters. They may overcompensate by insisting on their position in a disagreement, just to make sure that they are not being ignored. In relationships where women make more money, men may feel that their importance in the relationship is threatened and may overcompensate by insisting on their positions. Either way, who has the power can become a barrier to communicating about whatever financial decision is being made.

Another set of expectations which can interfere with healthy communication relates to values. People don't set out to marry somebody different from themselves. As Martin Whyte says, "individuals...tend to select people who have values similar to their own" (118). But our values aren't always evident until they are revealed in the middle of some decision-making situation. In the stress of the situation, marriage partners may be arguing about unstated values instead of what they think they are arguing about. For example, an issue could come up over how bills are paid. That seems like something people could agree on. However, what if one partner insists that bills be paid as soon as they are received, and the other wants to hold onto the bills and pay them as late as possible? One or the other will be stressed about this disagreement potentially for weeks, every month. Even if they decide that one of them will do the job, there is still an underlying conflict that goes unresolved. One partner values promptness and feels uncomfortable owing people. The other values money and wants to hold onto it as long as possible. This difference in values may interfere with communication over and over again.

An article from <u>Women Today</u>, an online magazine, states that "Traditionally, when couples fight, have misunderstandings, discover a lack of things in common, or confront the challenge of incompatibility, their first instinct is to flee while rationalizing to themselves 'this will never work, we're just too different.'" My parents tried to get help for their communication problems, but in the end, they bought into the idea that their problems weren't solvable. However, even now, they can't remember any significant differences, but only that the small disagreements made life too unpleasant for both of them. It's possible that if they had understood better the reasons why communication can be so difficult, they might have developed strategies for understanding each other, too.

Works Cited

Brown, Phillip M. <u>The Death of Intimacy: Barriers to Meaningful Interpersonal Relationships</u>. New York: Haworth, 1995.

Shervan, Judith, and James Sniechowski. "There is Hope for Your Marriage: Using the Differences as Opportunities to Grow." <http://www.womentodaymagazine.com/relationships/ savemarriage.html>.

Whyte, Martin. <u>Dating, Mating and Marriage</u>. New York: De Gruyter, 1990.

WRITING INVITATIONS

1. Analyze the revised argument essay "Communication Barriers" by comparing it to the earlier draft and answering the following questions about the changes the writer has made:

   - Which ideas are more compelling, and why?
   - How has the shape changed? Is the essay more unified? Why?
   - How have the voice and tone changed?

   The paragraphs and sentences barely resemble those in the original. Why do you think that happened? Are there paragraphs or sentences you see as especially effective?

Evaluate the revision in terms of the "Criteria for Good Writing" list at the beginning of this chapter. What are the essay's strengths and weaknesses? What further suggestions for revision would you offer the writer?

2. Find and bring to class examples of effective and ineffective writing. Discuss the samples with others. Are there characteristics of ineffective writing that you would like to add to the list of "Characteristics of Ineffective Writing" at the beginning of this chapter? Are there qualities of good writing that you would like to add to the "Criteria for Good Writing" list?

DEVELOPING A WRITING PROJECT

1. Review a draft of any writing project you are currently working on. Reread the section of this chapter on "Revising Attitudes." Establish your purpose for reading, and review your writing with your purpose in mind.

2. Complete a Descriptive Outline, and make a Revising Plan. Share your work with other readers.

3. With their guidance and suggestions in mind, use the revision strategies most relevant to the paper's strengths and weaknesses. Consider unity and form; voice and tone; and sentences, paragraphs, and words.

4. Prepare a finished draft, and compare it with your earlier writing.

CHAPTER 13

Editing Effectively

The problem—and the challenge—of English prose is that, with every sentence we write, we have to strike the best compromise between the principles of local clarity and directness...and the principles of cohesion that fuse separate sentences into a whole discourse.

Joe Williams

WHAT IS EDITING?

Editing is what we do when we have completed all other revisions. It is what professional writers do when they prepare their final copy for publication. They proofread, check the clarity and correctness of each sentence, and correct for grammar, punctuation, and sense.

Most people correct their papers after they have completed the kind of rethinking that is necessary for revising. Although some people correct their work as they write, most find that doing so pulls them out of the flow of getting ideas down on paper and, as a result, creates stilted or awkward writing. If you know that you can always edit, you may feel more freedom to simply get your ideas down on paper. In addition, many people have found that focusing on grammar, diction, and punctuation before revision may make you fail to notice larger problems with the development of the ideas of your writing. Besides, if you edit before revising the entire essay, you may spend a great deal of time rewriting sentences that you then cut. Instead, we suggest that you first revise for purpose, development, and organization of ideas, and then read for clarity and correctness.

In this chapter, we will look at ways to address the most typical problems with sentences as well as provide a list of common proofreading and editing marks to use as you edit. First, we want to talk a bit about sentences.

SENTENCE SENSE

Sentences are ideas that need to make sense to the reader. When you construct sentences, you find key words to act as subjects (what you are talking about) and predicates (what you are saying about the subject). Look at the following simple sentence:

Jane walked.

Jane is the subject you are talking about and walk is what you are telling us about the subject—she did something and that something was **walked**.

To these central elements, you may add words and groups of words that describe or define the subject or the predicate, resulting in an endless variety of sentence shapes. Notice the various ways you could rewrite the simple sentence about Jane by adding different words and groups of words:

Jane walked quickly.

Jane walked quickly to the store.

On Monday Jane walked quickly to the store.

On Monday Jane and her friend walked quickly to the store.

On Monday, when the electricity was off, Jane and her friend walked quickly to the store.

The more you know about the parts of a sentence, shapes, and types, the more likely it is that you will find a sentence shape that fits your unique message. To make sense of these unique messages for others, you need to use language conventions that meet community expectations so that you show respect for your audience and your subject. Remember, you've been using varied, meaningful sentences since you were two years old, perfecting your ability to match language choices to situation and purpose. But you may not have had many opportunities to think carefully about how sentences function, how they work, and what powers they give you. Looking carefully at how sentences work will allow you to play with familiar structures as you consider how "sense" is shaped rhetorically.

Imagine the internal connections of sentences as the internal workings of cars. A car can have all the necessary parts but still not run. Or it may run, but one problem in the engine will keep it from running well. It is frustrating to drive a car like that, just as it is frustrating to read a sentence that isn't working well. You may have been taught grammar as a set of rules, but really, grammar is the knowledge of how the parts work best together. If a sentence doesn't move well or sound good, a part needs adjusting.

Using Your Sentence Sense to Read for Correctness

Often writers who feel unsure about their understanding of grammar will write what we might call "safe sentences" such as the simple sentence "Jane walked."

They may do so because they are reluctant to use any complex structures that might be incorrect. We hope that the following discussion of the most common errors found in student papers will help you become more secure in your sentence sense.

This fear of error is neither unique nor new. English is a confusing language. Commas and apostrophes, for instance, have confused students of the language throughout its history because English is a language that has undergone more changes than almost any other modern language. This makes its history fascinating but at the same time makes its conventions somewhat confusing. However, despite its confusions, there are ways to understand contemporary conventions. We hope the following explanations added to your understanding of how sentences work and help you in learning how to identify English language conventions and correct common errors.

Parts of a Sentence

In the examples about Jane, we show ways to expand the most simple sentence by adding words and groups of words, and we talked about how the parts of a sentence work together by comparing the sentence to the engine of a car. Let's return to that metaphor for a moment. If you were a mechanic working on a car, you would need to recognize all the parts of the engine before you decided what part needed adjusting. Likewise, when you are editing your sentences, you will need to recognize the parts of a sentence to understand how to make the sentences work. So, before looking at common problems and how to fix them, let's review the names for the parts of a sentence. The basic structure of a simple sentence, as we explained before, is the subject and the predicate.

> *Subject*: The subject of a sentence is its central focus. It will be either a noun or a pronoun.
>
> *Predicate*: The predicate is the part of the sentence that expresses what is being said about the subject. It tells us how the subject acts or what it is, and its central word is a verb.

The predicate may also include a complement, a direct object, and sometimes an indirect object. A *complement* is either a noun or a modifier that can replace the subject. A *direct object* is a noun or pronoun in the predicate the verb acts upon. An *indirect object* is a second object that receives the direct object.

Look, for example, at the following simple sentences.

1. A basketball bounces.
   This sentence expresses a simple action. The subject (*A basketball*) acts in a particular way (*bounces*). *Basketball* is a noun. *Bounces* is a verb.

2. The class is Biology.
   This sentence tells us what the subject (*The class*) is (*is Biology*). *Class* is a noun. *Is* is a verb. *Biology* is a complement.

3. The ball hit the floor.

   This sentence also expresses an action. It differs from the first two sentences because it has a verb (*hit*) that acts upon something else (*the floor*). The subject is *ball*. The verb is *hit*. The direct object is *floor*.

4. The boy gave the girl a book.

   This sentence also expresses an action and has a direct object. The boy gave something, a book. Because *book* is the word the verb acts upon, it is the direct object. The girl receives the book and therefore *the girl* is the indirect object.

We can expand these sentences with words that modify, define, or qualify either the subject or the predicate. We do so with words, phrases, and clauses. The difference between a phrase and a clause is that a phrase is a group of words that will function together in the sentence and a clause has a subject and a predicate.

Phrases:	*Clauses:*
in the house	because I came late
by the door	when the team won the tournament
to look down	although I wanted to go
after school	after Joan saw the film
full of water	who was an old man

So we might take our simple sentences and add words to modify or define the subject:

1. A new basketball bounces.
2. The first class is Biology.
3. The red ball hit the floor.
4. The young boy gave the girl a book.

Or we might add phrases to modify the subject:

1. A basketball full of air bounces.
2. The class down the hall is Biology.
3. The ball in his hand hit the floor.
4. The boy with the red hair gave the girl a book

Or we might add clauses to modify the subject.

1. A basketball that is full of air bounces.
2. The class that I enjoy the most is Biology.
3. The ball that I gave my sister hit the floor.
4. The boy who lives next door gave the girl a book.

We can also expand a sentence by adding words, phrases, and clauses to modify the predicate. We can modify the verb, complement, or either object.

1. A basketball bounces well.
   A basketball bounces on the floor.
   A basketball bounces when you drop it.

2. The class is always Biology.
   The class is the Biology of Humans.
   The class is Biology, which is my favorite subject.

3. The ball hit the waxed floor.
   The ball hit the floor hard.
   The ball hit the floor with great force.
   The ball hit the floor when I threw it.

4. The boy shyly gave the girl a book.
   The boy gave the young girl a book.
   The boy gave the girl a new book.
   The boy gave the girl a book on Monday.
   The boy gave the girl a book that he had enjoyed.

These basics will help you understand how sentences work and how you might fix them when they are not working, but we will need to add to these basics by discussing grammar, syntax, punctuation, and diction.

GRAMMAR

Grammar is the term we use to identify the classes of words such as nouns, pronouns, and verbs that make up the parts of a sentence. It is also the term we use to explain how those words work together to make sense to a reader. Our language has conventions that speakers and readers share. These conventions are what help us make sense when we communicate.

Modifiers

When you modify words, you need to let the reader know what word you are modifying. Not doing so leads to humor at best, confusion at worst. Look, for example, at the following sentences:

1. Having discovered the right answers, the test seemed easy.
2. Lying in a dusty corner of the library, the student found a valuable 17th-century book.

Do these sentences make sense? You may be able to determine what the writer really meant, but the lack of precision makes a reader work to find that sense. The first sentence tells us that the test discovered the answers. This is probably not what the writer intended. To make the sentence clearer, the writer could say, "Having discovered the right answers, the student found the test easy." The second sentence tells us that the student was lying in the corner. To make the sentence clearer, the writer could say, "Lying in a dusty corner of the library, a 17th-century book fell into the hands of a student."

Using modifying phrases to introduce a sentence can add variety to your writing, but you should remember that readers expect the phrase in this position to modify the subject of the sentence. As you read the following examples and their corrections, notice how much easier it is to read the corrected sentence. Some examples may be easier to read than others, but all suffer from a lack of precision.

1. Noticing the ice on the road too late, the car slid into the snow bank.
   Corrected: Noticing the ice on the road too late, the driver slid the car into the snow bank.

2. By revising carefully, my paper grades have improved this term.
   Corrected: By revising carefully, I have improved my paper grades this term.

3. To find the best price for airline tickets, a travel Web page is helpful.
   Corrected: To find the best price for airline tickets, most people find a travel Web page helpful.

4. Circling the city, the sights were breathtaking.
   Corrected: Circling the city, we found the sights breathtaking.

5. Seen from the air, a person might think the cars were toys.
   Corrected: Seen from the air, the cars looked like toys.

We call this error a dangling or misplaced modifier. While most of these errors are found with modifying phrases used to introduce sentences, they may also occur in other positions, as in the sentence, "The time seemed endless waiting for the bus." The sentence is confusing because the phrase "waiting for the bus" is not modifying any noun or pronoun. The writer could say, "Waiting for the bus, I found the time endless." As you proofread your papers, check to see that all modifying phrases have nouns or pronouns that they modify and, if so, are adjacent to the nouns or pronouns they modify.

Prepositions

Prepositions are the most common words in our language, but they are also the ones you notice the least because they are never found without a noun or pronoun. Common prepositions include:

above	around	at
before	behind	below
in	of	on
to	upon	

As you read the list, you may have thought "above what?" or "around what?" As your response indicates, prepositions introduce a noun or pronoun and form a phrase that modifies another word in the sentence. You would use the phrase "above the door" only if you wished to describe something in that location. Despite the fact that we rarely think about prepositions, they play an important function in sentences because they allow us to express the relationship between two elements in the sentence. In the sentence "The keys are on the shelf" *on* indicates the relationship between keys and shelf.

Prepositions cause problems for non-native speakers because the relationship the preposition expresses is not obvious. Why, for example, do people in the West say "I stood in line" and people in the Northeast say "I stood on line"? Another interesting dialect characteristic associated with the preposition is the omitted preposition as in "I plan to work home" in place of "I plan to work at home."

In addition to exhibiting a few different dialect conventions in pronoun usage, some writers may hesitate to use prepositional phrases because they have heard that they should never end a sentence with a preposition. They avoid the prepositional phrase rather than write "Which of the books did you find the quotation in?" The informal usage is called the "the postponed preposition." This usage occurs often when the element the preposition introduces takes the first position in the sentence and the preposition is in the final position. In formal writing, we would say, "In which of the books did you find the quotation?" Grammarians disagree about the usage. A good rule of thumb is to read the sentence aloud and let your ear help you make the decision.

Pronouns

Pronouns are used in the place of nouns. Like nouns, they may be subjects, objects, and complements, as the following sentences show:

She is my friend.	*She* is the subject.
Brian saw *her*.	*Her* is the direct object.
I gave *her* the book.	*I* is the subject. *Her* is the indirect object.
It came from *me*.	*It* is the subject. *Me* is the object of the preposition *from*.

Pronoun Reference

We use pronouns because we assume our readers know what nouns the pronouns replace, or refer to. Sometimes, however, what seems clear to us when we are writing may be confusing to readers. In the following sentence, for example, the reader might have difficulty understanding whether the *its* refers to the window or the landscape.

While the woman looked at the landscape outside the window, her host pointed out its beauty.

In such sentences, the writer might consider repeating the noun rather than use a pronoun. The following sentences demonstrate the confusion that results from vague pronoun reference.

1. On the first day of class a fire alarm sent all the students into the courtyard where they waited 30 minutes until it stopped.
    Less confusing: On the first day of class a fire alarm sent all the students into the courtyard where they waited 30 minutes until the alarm stopped.

2. It was not until I saw that the assignment required us to conduct a survey that I realized it was going to be difficult.
    Less confusing: It was not until I saw that the assignment required us to conduct a survey that I realized such an assignment could be difficult.

Agreement

A pronoun needs to be the same number as the noun or pronoun to which it refers. If we are writing about a student, for example, the pronoun we use to refer to that student needs to be singular, as in: "The student brought his book" or "The student brought her book." The following examples represent common agreement errors.

1. Everyone brought their books.
    Corrected: Everyone brought his or her books. (*Everyone* is singular, but *their* is plural, and the two must agree.)

2. Nobody thought their papers were due.
    Corrected: Nobody thought his or her paper was due. (*Nobody* is singular, but *their* is plural.)

3. Somebody believed they could skip the class.
    Corrected: Somebody believed he (or she) could skip the class. (*Somebody* is singular, but *they* is plural.)

4. Anybody who wants to join the group should sign their name on the roster.
    Corrected: Anybody who wants to join the group should sign his or her name on the roster. (*Anybody* is singular, but *their* is plural.)

Pronouns in Compound Constructions

Many writers have difficulty distinguishing the appropriate convention when using pronouns in compound constructions like "my friend and I." They often write "She gave it to my friend and I" instead of the correct form, "She gave it to my friend and me." Or they may write "Just between you and I" instead of the correct "Just between you and me." Because we hear this usage so often, we need to read carefully to identify the appropriate use. The easiest way to catch the error is to cover the first part of the construction with your hand and read the sentence aloud. The pronoun should sound correct when it stands alone.

1. Me and my friend went to the ballgame.
   Without the first half of the compound construction: Me went to the ballgame.
   Corrected: I and my friend went to the ballgame. (Or: My friend and I went to the ballgame.)

2. The professor gave the assignment to John and I.
   Without the first half of the construction: He gave the assignment to I.
   Corrected: The professor gave the assignment to John and me.

"Self" Pronouns

"Self" pronouns are ones such as myself, himself, herself. They are used tradition-ally when writers wish to be emphatic, as in the sentence "I did it myself." The self pronoun is also appropriate when the pronoun is a second reference to the same person, as in the sentence "I hurt myself" or "She reminded herself." Some writers use the self pronoun inappropriately because they think it sounds more elegant.

1. He wants to see you and myself.
   Corrected: He wants to see you and me.

2. The professor spoke to my roommate and myself.
   Corrected: The professor spoke to my roommate and me.

3. Myself and my friend went to the concert.
   Corrected: I and my friend (or my friend and I) went to the concert.

Verbs

Subject-Verb Agreement

Most people have little difficulty making their subjects and verbs match in number. It seems a simple notion that if the subject is singular, the verb is also. Few of us would write "I were there," or "She go to the store." Some people may write awkward sentences when it is difficult to identify the subject of the verb. One such instance occurs when the writer adds plural modifiers after a singu-lar subject. Sometimes doing so leads the writer to make the verb agree with the noun in the phrase.

1. The pile of leaves are very large.
   The subject of the sentence is *pile*.
   Corrected: The pile of leaves is very large.

2. A group of many kinds of people were gathered.
   The subject of the sentence is *group*.
   Corrected: A group of many kinds of people was gathered.

3. The directions in my grandmother's recipe for pecan pie was confusing.
   The subject of the sentence is *directions*.
   Corrected: The directions in my grandmother's recipe were confusing.

A second instance where we may have difficulty making subjects and verbs agree is when the subject is compound but joined by *or, either-or,* or *neither-nor,* and one element is plural and the other singular, as in "Neither the girl nor the men." When this is the case, the convention is to make the verb agree with the closer element, so we would say "Neither the girl nor the men were listening."

Verb Tense

English has a fairly simple verb tense system, but there are a few constructions that cause writers some difficulty. Most writers have little difficulty with the simple present, past, and future forms, but some writers find tenses that include auxiliary verbs such as *be* and *have* confusing. Look at the following forms and the explanations to help you decide which will be the most appropriate choice.

Verb Form	*When to Use It*
I write	if you are doing so now
I am writing	if you wish to note that the writing is an ongoing process
I wrote	if you did so in the past
I was writing	if you wish to note that the writing was an ongoing process
I have written	if you wish to note that you did so in the past and continued to do so until the present
I had written	if you wish to note that you did so in the past but do not now
I have been writing	if you wish to note that you did so in the past and continue in the present as an ongoing process
I had been writing	if you wish to note that you did so in the past as an ongoing process but do so no longer

Some verbs that change form in their past tense cause confusion for writers. We call such verbs irregular verbs. Until you learn them well enough, you may wish to keep a list of ones that are particularly confusing. Here are some that many students have difficulty remembering:

Present	*Simple past*	*Past with have (or had)*
I cut myself today	I cut myself yesterday	I have cut myself often.
She bends the rules.	She bent the rules then.	She has bent the rules often.
He comes to class.	He came to class then.	He has come to class all term.

I drink the soda now.	I drank the soda then.	I have drunk soda often.
I meet you today	I met you yesterday.	I have met you often.
I swim daily.	I swam yesterday.	I have often swum there.
I lie in the sun now.	I lay in the sun yesterday.	I have lain in the sun.
I lay the book down.	I laid the book down then.	I have laid the book down.

Tense Agreement

Shifting from past to present for no obvious reason confuses readers. We often find ourselves shifting verb tense when we are writing about something that happened in the past but we are using what we might call a timeless present. For example, if we are writing about choices an author made in writing a novel, it is conventional to do so in the present. We say, "Virginia Woolf writes that every writer needs a room of her own." If we suddenly shift to the past tense and say, "She believed that writing required a private space," we have shifted from the eternal present to the past and doing so may puzzle the reader.

Infinitives

The infinitive form of the verb, *to be* for example, is sometimes called the base form. Some grammarians believe that writers should never insert any words between the two elements of the infinitive—resulting in a "split infinitive." Others think that avoiding split infinitives may result in stuffy and awkward language. There are no absolute rules, but a good rule of thumb is to avoid inserting more than one word because doing so may confuse the reader.

1. "I will run if the party sees fit to so honor me." (Adlai Stevenson)
   Without the split infinitive: I will run if the party sees fit so to honor me.
2. The room seems large enough to fully hold all the cast members.
   Without the split infinitive: The room seems large enough to hold fully all the cast members.
3. "To boldly go where no man has gone before." (*Star Trek*)
   Without the split infinitive: To go boldly where no man has gone before.
4. The drama club wanted to in a completely new way renovate the old theater.
   Without the split infinitive: The drama club wanted to renovate the old theater in a completely new way.

Syntax

Syntax is what we call sentence structure. It is the way writers put words together to form or shape the idea. The English sentence is very flexible and thus gives writers many opportunities to shape its elements for variety and emphasis. Before looking at some of the opportunities and problems associated with them, we need to identify the basic types of sentences writers may use: simple, compound, complex, and compound-complex. Each sentence is made up of one or more clauses.

A clause is a group of words with a subject and a predicate. There are two kinds of clauses: independent and dependent. An independent clause is the main clause of a sentence and could function alone as a separate sentence. When a sentence has two or more independent clauses, they may be joined by coordinating words. These coordinating words join equal structures in a sentence and are called coordinating conjunctions: *and, but, or, nor, for,* and *yet.*

A dependent clause could not stand alone as a separate idea. Dependent clauses begin with words that link them to the main clause. These words may be either subordinators or relative pronouns:

Subordinators	*Relative Pronouns*
after	who
because	whose
before	whom
how	which
since	that
until	
when	
why	
while	

Simple Sentence

A simple sentence has one main clause. The form may include a single unmodified subject and verb, or it may include a compound subject and a series of verbs, or it may include many modifying words and phrases, as the following examples demonstrate.

1. Jane walked.
2. Jane, Fred, and I walked in the warm sun all afternoon.
3. The frightened old woman and her dog cowered in the bushes, peered around the tree, and watched the hunters at the edge of the clearing.

Compound Sentence

A compound sentence has two or more independent clauses. Clauses are called independent when they could function as simple sentences without the connecting term, as in the following examples.

1. Jane walked, and Fred followed.
   Each clause has a subject and a verb, and each could function alone: Jane walked. Fred followed.
2. Fred, Jane, and I played basketball in the sun all afternoon, and we decided to play together again the next day and bring water with us.
   Each clause has a subject. The first is compound; the second is simple. Each clause has a verb—the first a single verb, the second a compound.

Complex Sentence

A complex sentence has one independent clause and one or more dependent clauses. Clauses are called dependent when they are introduced by words that would not allow them to function alone.

1. When the child found his toy, he was overjoyed.

    The first clause has a subject and a verb but because it is introduced by the word *when*, it could not function alone. "When the child found his toy" does not express a complete idea. This makes it a dependent clause. The second clause has a subject and verb and expresses a complete idea.

2. After I learned about the benefits of joining a health club and realized how out of shape I had become in the first few weeks of school, I decided to join and to ask a friend to exercise with me.

    The first clause is dependent because beginning with the word *after* means that it could not function as complete idea. The second clause expresses a complete idea.

Compound-Complex Sentence

A compound-complex sentence has at least two independent clauses and one dependent clause.

1. After Sarah's family decided to visit Williamsburg, Sarah logged on to a Web site to find a hotel, and her brother searched for area parks.

    The first clause is dependent because it begins with *After*. The second and third clauses are both independent.

2. When Jim realized that he would have to write a paper about the potential changes in environmental law, he decided that he was most concerned with laws concerning air quality, and he began his research by interviewing his environmental studies professor about how the current statutes regulate pollution.

    This sentence begins with a dependent clause introduced by the word *when*. It also includes two independent clauses: the clause that begins "he decided" and the clause that begins "and he began." What makes this sentence more complicated is that each of the independent clauses includes a dependent clause: "that he was concerned with laws concerning air quality" and "how the current statutes regulate pollution."

Problems with Syntax

Knowing about syntax can help you vary your sentences for style and focus. It can also help you recognize problems you may be having with the clarity of the sentences you write. In the following sections we discuss some of the common syntactic problems.

Fused Sentences

A fused sentence (also called a run-on sentence) results from joining two clauses without coordinators or appropriate punctuation. Sometimes writers fuse sentences because they are writing so quickly that they omit the punctuation, as in "The goal of such a study is to find answers to questions scientists have always had about cell growth appropriate arenas for the study include the NIH and CDC." Other times, writers may simply write quickly or combine sentences from an early draft. When they do so, they often forget to add the necessary punctuation.

1. My brother will receive his Ph.D. next June if he is able to complete his dissertation it is a study of the contributing factors to elementary children's literacy.

   Correction: My brother will receive his Ph.D. next June if he is able to complete his dissertation. It is a study of the contributing factors to elementary children's literacy.

2. Visitors to the University of Oregon's campus always want to see the fraternity house that was the site of the film *Animal House* they never recognize.

   Correction: Visitors to the University of Oregon's campus always want to see the fraternity house that was the site of the film *Animal House*, but they never recognize it.

Faulty Parallelism

Often we wish readers to see several elements as a series because they contrast or relate to each other. When we wish to do so, we place them in parallel structures. A simple example is parallel verbs, all governed by the same subject, as in "Jack cleaned, stuffed, and baked the Thanksgiving turkey." Faulty parallels occur when the items do not have the same grammatical structure, as in the following sentences.

1. The professor is giving the exam on Friday and grade over the weekend.

   The verbs *giving* and *grade* need to be parallel. Both should be in the same form.

   Corrected: The professor is giving the exam on Friday and grading it over the weekend.

2. The writer began her revising by rereading all that she had written and noted all the errors.

   Both *rereading* and *noted* should be objects of the preposition *by*— *rereading* and *noting*.

   Corrected: The writer began her revising by rereading all that she had written and noting all the errors.

3. I hope that either I will find the errors or have a good editor.

   Putting *either* before *I* contrasts *I* and *have*, instead of the verbs. The writer needs to place *either* before the first of the two contrasted verbs, *find*.

   Corrected: I hope that I will either find the errors or have a good editor.

4. The cook not only has all the best kitchen equipment but also the exper-
    tise to use it.

    As in the preceding sentence, the words that establish the contrast, *not
    only* and *but also*, need to signal the contrasted elements—*the best kitchen
    equipment* and *the expertise*.

    Corrected: The cook has not only all the best kitchen equipment but
    also the expertise to use it.

Sentence Fragment

A sentence fragment is any group of words punctuated as if it were a sentence but
without expressing a complete idea, either because it does not have both a subject and a predicate or because it is a dependent clause. Sometimes a long phrase
may seem to be a complete idea, but if you read it carefully to find its subject and
predicate, you will see that it is incomplete, as in "Living by the shore with many
other peace activists who travel to Georgia every November." The reader will need
to know who was living by the shore with the other peace activists.

When we are writing very complicated ideas, we often begin a sentence
with a long dependent clause then forget that we have begun it with a subor-
dinating word, as in "When we are deeply into the idea of our argument and
considering all the possible ramifications and potential outcomes of such a
complex proposition." Because this dependent clause is so long and complex,
we might not notice that we have not completed the idea by saying what happens in such a case.

Occasionally, you might choose to use a sentence fragment to draw special
attention to a point. Doing so can be very effective but only if the meaning is
clear and the reader can see that you have done so intentionally. Notice the way
the following example highlights and makes emphatic the fragmentary element:
"You might think that you can never use a sentence fragment. Wrong!"

1. Until the weather clears up and the sidewalks dry.

    Corrected: I will wear my boots until the weather clears up and the side-
    walks dry.

2. Although you have taken all the classes necessary to complete your major
    and have fulfilled all the university's core requirements.

    Corrected: Although you have taken all the classes necessary to com-
    plete your major and have fulfilled all the university's core requirements,
    you will not be able to graduate until you have taken the required hours.

3. When the time has come to apply for graduation and you discover that you
    need to meet with your advisor one last time so that you are certain that
    you will have no problems.

    Corrected: When the time has come to apply for graduation and you
    discover that you need to meet with your advisor one last time so that you
    are certain that you will have no problems, you will need to make an
    appointment.

PUNCTUATION

Punctuation is simply the marks writers use to help readers make sense of the written work. The English language uses apostrophes, colons, commas, dashes, exclamation points, parentheses, periods, question marks, and semicolons. The following discussion looks at punctuation marks that might give you problems.

Apostrophes

The apostrophe is the punctuation symbol we use to indicate that we have omitted a letter or letters in a word or phrase, as in the contraction *don't* for *do not*. We also use apostrophes to indicate the possessive form of nouns, as in the phrase *Brian's book*—the book belonging to Brian. However, we do not use the apostrophe for possessive pronouns like *hers, ours, theirs,* or *its.*

Writers have three main problems with the apostrophe. Some people omit the apostrophe and write *Brians book* instead of *Brian's book*. Some people add apostrophes when they use plural forms of nouns and write, "The boy's went to town" in place of "The boys went to town." Others use the apostrophe for possessive pronouns and write *her's* instead of *her*, or *it's* for *its*, as in the following sentences.

1. The book was her's.
    Corrected: The book was hers.
2. The building showed it's age.
    Corrected: The building showed its age.

Remembering that we do not use apostrophes with possessive pronouns may help you remember not to use *it's* when you mean "belonging to it." *It's* is the contraction of *it is*, as in "It's a beautiful morning."

Colons

Colons are marks we use to introduce a quotation, a series, or an explanation, as in the following circumstances.

- To indicate that the next words are quoted, as in "The fragrance in the room reminder her of Shakespeare's famous line: 'A rose by any other name would smell as sweet.'"
- At the end of an independent clause to indicate that we will be listing words or phrases that illustrate the central meaning of the main idea, as in the following: "A successful racquetball player requires three things: a racquet, balls, and lots of energy."
- To join two independent clauses if the second clause is an illustration of the central meaning of the first: "Credit card solicitors called us almost daily with new offers: they were a persistent group."

In addition, colons are used in numbers between the hour and minute, as in 3:30 a.m., between a chapter number and verse or line number, as in John 4:15, between the title of a work and its subtitle, as in *The Company We Keep: An Ethics of Fiction*, and after a salutation in a formal letter, as in "Dear Professor Martin:"

When used in a sentence to introduce a quotation, a series, or an explanation, the colon should be used only when the independent clause is complete. It should never separate a verb from a direct object or a preposition from its object.

1. A successful racquetball player requires: a racquet, balls, and lots of energy.
   The colon separates the verb from its direct objects.
   Corrected: A successful racquetball player requires three things: a racquet, balls, and lots of energy.

2. The mayor showed his understanding of: the fears of the citizens, their strength, and their sense of community.
   The colon separates the preposition from its objects.
   Corrected: The mayor showed his understanding of three things: the fears of the citizens, their strength, and their sense of community

Commas

Commas are punctuation marks we use to separate ideas or elements in a sentence. We use them in the following circumstances.

- To join independent clauses in compound sentences when we also link them with a coordinating word: "Jim crashed his truck, and he scraped his arm in the wreck." "Jim crashed his truck, but he was unhurt."

- To separate a dependent clause from an independent clause that follows it: "When Jim crashed his truck, he scraped his arm in the wreck."

- To enclose words, phrases, or clauses when we add parenthetical information: "Jim, an excellent driver, had a strange accident yesterday." "Jim, who is an excellent driver, had a strange accident yesterday."

- To separate words or phrases in a series: "His favorite colors were blue, green, and gold." "She hit the ball from the baseline, ran to the net, and slammed the return."

- To separate longer introductory phrases from the subject of the sentence: "Before the beginning of the basketball game, the coach called her players into a huddle."

Problems with Commas

Comma Splice

When you join two independent clauses with a coordinating word, you need to place a comma at the end of the first clause before the coordinating conjunction. When you join the two without a coordinating conjunction, you need to use a semicolon. For example, "Jane brought the turkey; Jack brought the pie." Using just the comma where you need the semicolon is called a comma splice. It creates problems for readers because they expect a different kind of relationship—that the clauses will be part of a series of clauses, for example.

1. The construction on the highway caused gridlock for days, further construction will require better planning by the highway commission.

    Corrected: The construction on the highway caused gridlock for days; further construction will require better planning by the highway commission.

2. The storm knocked out power to three neighborhoods in the city, the college campus, and government buildings, it shut down much of the city for the afternoon.

    Corrected: The storm knocked out power to three neighborhoods in the city, the college campus, and government buildings; it shut down much of the city for the afternoon.

Lack of a Comma in a Series

Many sentences include a series of elements. These elements may be simple nouns, pronouns, adjectives, verbs, and occasionally adverbs or clauses or phrases. When you include such a series of three or more, you need to separate them with commas, as in the following sentences.

Mary bought oranges, apples, cherries, and bananas.

The puppy jumped, yapped, and ran madly around the room.

The old blanket was dusty, black and white, and full of moth holes.

Last summer my little brother fell in the lake, in a creek, and off the roof.

The only time you will not use the comma is when two elements are to be seen in a unit—as in the third sentence where "black and white" is a unit referring to color.

1. We spent the time in our writing group rereading the drafts of our papers, looking for problems with grammar and suggesting ways to improve the final paper.

    Corrected: We spent the time in our writing group rereading the drafts of our papers, looking for problems with grammar, and suggesting ways to improve the final paper.

2. We drove up the Maine coast, stopped for a lobster dinner and ended up making it to our Bed and Breakfast by midnight.

    Corrected: We drove up the Maine coast, stopped for a lobster dinner, and ended up making it to our Bed and Breakfast by midnight.

Missing Comma After an Introductory Element

One way to expand and develop the idea represented in a sentence is by adding modifing words, phrases, and clauses. When we begin sentences with modifying phrases and clauses that are more than a few words in length, we need to separate them from the subject so that readers do not have difficulty seeing where the phrase ends.

1. With very little difficulty the instructor found the error.
   Corrected: With very little difficulty, the instructor found the error

2. Because he knows grammar well the instructor found the error.
   Corrected: Because he knows grammar well, the instructor found the error.

3. In the final moments of the game the third baseman hit a homerun.
   Corrected: In the final moments of the game, the third baseman hit a homerun.

4. Beside the river on a rock the child found the skeleton of a small mammal.
   Corrected: Beside the river on a rock, the child found the skeleton of a small mammal.

5. To find the best doctor you should ask friends for advice.
   Corrected: To find the best doctor, you should ask friends for advice.

Unnecessary Comma with Restrictive Phrase or Clause

Often we modify or clarify a noun or pronoun by adding a phrase or clause after the noun. We modify *man* by saying "the man with the red hat" or *child* by adding "the child who was late this morning." Sometimes we set the phrase or clause off with a comma, but other times we do not. The guideline to remember is that if the phrase or clause is necessary for the reader to understand the noun—in other words, if it restricts the meaning—we do not use a comma. If the phrase or clause is parenthetical, or adds additional information, we call it nonrestrictive and set it off with commas. Look at the following examples that illustrate the difference between restrictive and nonrestrictive modifiers.

1. The president who was elected in 1960 was the first Roman Catholic president.
   John F. Kennedy, who was elected in 1960, was the first Roman Catholic president.

2. The town where my father was born had only two restaurants.
   Stigler, where my father was born, had only two restaurants.

3. The city that I remember was on the northern coast of Georgia.
   Savannah, which is on the northern coast of Georgia, is a charming Southern city.

The following sentences show the confusion created when the writer does not use commas that tell the reader whether the modifying word, phrase, or clause is essential to the meaning of the word it modifies or parenthetical.

1. The tallest structure in Washington, D.C. the Washington Monument is my favorite place to take tourists.
   Corrected: The tallest structure in Washington, D.C., the Washington Monument, is my favorite place to take tourists.

2. The old stone church which is where my mother was married burned to the ground last year.
   Corrected: The old stone church, which is where my mother was married, burned to the ground last year.

3. The best class, that I took last term, was History of the Civil War.
   Corrected: The best class that I took last term was History of the Civil War.

As the second and third examples demonstrate, when the modifying clause is necessary to the meaning of the word it modifies, we begin the clause with *that*; when it is parenthetical, we begin the clause with *which*.

Dashes

Dashes are punctuation marks that often replace commas or colons. Writers choose to use dashes when they wish to draw the reader's attention to an element in the sentence. Dashes may be effective punctuation in the following circumstances.

1. In place of a colon to draw attention to the second clause of a compound sentence: "Credit card solicitors called us almost daily with new offers—they were a persistent group."

2. In place of commas around parenthetical words, phrases, or clauses: "My morning class—which was at 7:30 a.m.—was the most difficult course I have taken this year."

3. To highlight a phrase in a sentence: "She was overjoyed to find such amazing shoes—until she received the bill."

Semicolons

Semicolons are used to connect two independent clauses with no conjunction, as in "Susan brought the poster board and markers; I designed the posters." The semicolon is also used in a series of clauses or phrases that include commas within one or more of the clauses or phrases: "I decided to volunteer in the following agencies: the food bank, a collection agency near my apartment; the soup kitchen, which is on the campus; and a shelter for abused women."

DICTION

Diction is simply word choice. When you proofread, you need to consider whether your reader will understand what your language means. Using the wrong word misleads the readers. Spelling errors may cause some of this confusion, but some may result from the writer's lack of understanding the word he or she has chosen.

Spelling Errors

Spelling is not a problem of grammar, but it is an ongoing problem for writers of all levels of education. Spelling errors often result in humorous sentences, as in the unfortunate error found in a church bulletin: "This evening at 7 P.M. there will be a hymn sing in the park across from the Church. Bring a blanket and come prepared to sin." Such spelling errors are usually merely "typos," but others may be habits or lack of familiarity with a word. Your computer has a "spell check" operation that will help you find some misspellings, but it will not find errors in usage such as substituting *to* when you mean *too* or *its* when you mean *it's*. To identify and correct such errors, you need to be aware of your own bad habits. You can improve your spelling by keeping a log of words that you frequently misspell. Doing so will help you change your spelling habits. You also might edit with a dictionary at your elbow so that you can check the spelling of any words you are unsure of. Some people check spelling as they write drafts but we have found that too often this makes the writer self-conscious and thus unable to write a first draft as an exploration of an idea.

Wrong Word

Using the wrong word is not a grammar error but rather a problem of diction, or word choice. Usually, we use the wrong word when we have heard or read it but not understood the meaning. Then we may use it inappropriately. Sometimes we have heard a word or phrase used but have never seen it written and don't really know the meaning, as in the following: "It's a doggy-dog world" (for "a dog-eat-dog world") or "for all intensive purposes" (for "for all intents and purposes").

One distinction many people have difficulty remembering is the distinction between *affect* and *effect*. When we wish to use the verb meaning to influence, we use *affect*, as in the sentence: "Having you take the class affected what books I would teach." When we are referring to a change, the noun form is *effect*, as in "Your choice had an effect on my planning." If we need a verb that means to bring about or to bring into existence, we may use *effect*, as in the sentence: "The economic slump effected a change in policy."

The following is a list of commonly confused pairs of words.

To adapt: to adjust or make suitable to a specific use
To adopt: to choose
She adapted her actions to fit with those around her, but she did not adopt their ideas.

To allude: to make indirect reference to
To elude: To avoid something
The instructor's comments on her paper alluded to the difficulties she was having with diction. The student realized that the meaning of several words eluded her.

Among: in the middle of, in a group of more than two
Between: in the position joining two elements
I sat among the other fans at the concert and between an elderly man and a two-year-old child.

Bad: an adjective meaning unfavorable
Badly: an adverb meaning in a bad way
I felt bad when I played the game so badly.

Can: physically able
May: given permission
May I drive you to class if my car can start?

Continual: happening frequently, repeated at intervals
Continuous: happening without interruption
The children's continuous chatter during class occurred continually all year.

To impact: to pack firmly together or strike with force
To affect: to influence or have an effect upon
The falling crane impacted the earth, and as a result, the accident affected the public's attitude concerning the road construction.

Capital: the place where the government is located
Capitol: the building housing the government
Washington, D.C., is our nation's capital, where you might visit the Capitol.

Complement: to complete
Compliment: to praise
I complimented her on how well her shoes complemented her outfit.

To evoke: to call to mind
To invoke: to appeal to or call on or put into use
The report of the bombing evoked memories of past conflicts and so the leaders of both countries invoked the understanding of all parties involved in the dispute.

Farther: a greater physical distance
Further: to a greater degree, time, or space
He walked farther than he had ever, and he realized that he would need further repairs to his hiking boots.

Gourmet: a person who is an expert about fine food
Gourmand: a lover of good food, often meaning someone who eats to excess
The owner of the restaurant hoped that the food critic was a gourmet not a gourmand.

To immigrate: to come into a new country to live
To emigrate: to leave one country to live in another
She emigrated from the United States to live in Canada, and when she did so, immigrated into Canada.

Imminent: about to happen
Eminent: outstanding
The ceremony in which the eminent scientist is to be honored is imminent.

To imply: to suggest
To infer: to draw a conclusion
The professor implied that she might give a quiz and the students inferred from her actions that she probably would.

To insure: to guarantee against financial loss
To ensure: to make sure or certain
Mrs. Smith insured her home to ensure that its contents would be replaced in case of a fire.

Less: not as great an amount of (used with mass terms)
Fewer: not as great a number of (used with countable items)
We have less homework and fewer papers.

Mantel: the facing around a fireplace
Mantle: a cloak
She wore a mantle as she stood next to the fireplace's mantel.

Memento: a souvenir or keepsake
Momentum: force in motion
The crater fell with great momentum and crushed the car in which she had left a cameo, a memento given to her by her grandmother.

Unnecessary Words

Extra or extraneous words detract from the clarity of a piece of writing. Often, we think that the more words we use, the more sophisticated our writing sounds. Wrong! Extraneous words make us sound less in control of our writing, and cutting excess is one of the most important tasks of revising.

Some words are empty; they provide no necessary information. The following list gives several common examples and an appropriate revision:

Empty Words	*Revision*
At this point in time	now
Due to the fact that	because
Each and every	each
In view of the fact that	because

Some phrases are worth omitting altogether, such as the following.

now at the present time

for all intents and purposes

the function of

needless to say

EDITING

Editing Sentences for Clarity of Meaning

Editing our drafts for clarity requires us to hear our prose. We suggest that you read your papers aloud and ask yourself whether you have any questions after hearing each sentence. The following sentence illustrates how a lack of clarity raises questions for readers.

> If the embryo is a possibility that some people believe should be given the same rights as you and I needs to sit and think a bit.

This comes from a student paper on abortion rights, and the writer has taken on the complex question of whose rights are paramount in pregnancy. In the process of adjusting the ideas to fit better, something got lost. Who needs to sit and think a bit? After reading the sentence aloud, the writer revised it to say

> Anyone who believes that an embryo should be given the same rights as you and I needs to sit and think a bit.

What needs adjusting in the following sentence, which comes from a very well-researched paper on the question of how incidents of rape can be reduced?

> Among criminologists and sociologists who study rape, there are four types: displaced aggression or anger, compensatory or sexual fantasies, sexual aggression, and explorative or impulsive acts.

We're sure the writer didn't intend to suggest that criminologists and sociologists were rapists. When she rewrote, she clarified the list:

> Criminologists and sociologists who study rape have identified four types of motives for rape incidents: displaced aggression or anger, compensatory or sexual fantasies, sexual aggression, and explorative or impulsive acts.

Editing Sentences for Readability

Sometimes there is no confusion in the content of a sentence, but the language needs adjusting for the sentence to run smoothly. In the following sentence, the list of projections mixes phrases and clauses, making the sentence difficult to read.

> The Washington State Research Council also projects losses to freight mobility programs, state supported Amtrak service between Portland and Vancouver, B.C. would be reduced, ferry service cut backs, and delays in road maintenance.

The writer revised the sentences so that the phrases were all of the same type, creating parallel structures and making the sentence much easier to read:

> The Washington State Research Council also projects losses to freight mobility programs, reductions in Amtrak service between Portland and Vancouver, B.C., cutbacks in ferry service, and delays in road maintenance.

Editing Sentences for Conciseness

Being concise means saying what you need to say with the fewest, best-chosen words. The two sentences below come from the first draft of a paper on the question of whether school uniforms should be required in high schools.

> Everyone in my high school wore the latest trends in clothes and usually never wore the same outfit twice and you were considered uncool if you wore something that was out of style or old or worn out. By wearing uniforms it takes the attention off popularity and materialistic materials and puts the attention back on academics and studies.

After meeting with a peer-editing group, the writer incorporated the suggestions of her readers into a final draft:

> Everyone in my high school wore the latest trends in clothes, and tried never to be seen in the same outfit twice or in something old. Wearing uniforms helps students focus less on popularity and values and more on academics.

Down from 59 words to 43, the revised sentences are clearer and easier to read because of the conciseness; but we think the revision also makes the writer more believable because her thoughts are more carefully constructed. Editing, then, is not just correcting. It is also an essential part of helping your audience care about what you are saying.

Common Editing Symbols

Many writers use a form of shorthand when they edit their drafts. Figure 13.1 shows the most common symbols that writers and editors use. English professors often use the abbreviations shown in Figure 13.2 when commenting on students' papers.

To improve your proofreading skills, you might try the following.

- Print a "hard copy" of your paper.
- Read slowly with a pencil in hand, marking all places you think might be errors.

COMMON EDITING SYMBOLS

Symbol	Meaning	Example
⌄	insert a comma	The mayor's brother, I tell you, is a crook.
⌄	apostrophe or single quotation mark	I wouldn't know where to put this vase.
∧	insert something	I know it, in fact, everyone knows it. ;
⌄ ⌄	use double quotation marks	My favorite poem is Design.
⊙	use a period here	This is a declarative sentence.
ℓ	delete	The elephant's trunk is is really its nose.
∿	transpose elements	He only picked the one he likes.
◡	close up this space	Jordan lost his favorite basket ball.
#	a space needed here	I have only three friends: Ted, Raoul, and Alice.
¶	begin new paragraph	"I know it," I said. "I thought so," she replied.
No ¶	no paragraph	"I knew it," she said. No ¶ "He's no good."

FIGURE 13.1 COMMON EDITING SYMBOLS

- Reread sections of this chapter that give explanations of usage.
- Identify common errors your instructor has marked on your papers in the past and check for those as you read.
- Read your paper sentence by sentence from the end of the paper back to the beginning.
- Exchange papers with a peer editor.

Proofreading and editing your writing are not easy but are necessary and important activities. All writers, even professionals, commit grammatical errors, misspell some words, or type incorrectly. Consequently, all writers must proofread. Professional writers know that they must have error-free copy if they wish to have readers take them seriously. Good student writers know this as well; they know that errors distract readers from the message they wish to communicate, either because errors confuse the reader or suggest that the writer does not care enough to take the time to produce a clean copy.

COMMON EDITING ABBREVIATIONS

Abbreviation	Meaning	Example
Ab	a faulty abbreviation	She had earned a **PHd** along with her M.D.
Agr *See also P/A* *and S/V*	agreement problem: subject/verb *or* pronoun/antecedent	The piano as well as the guitar **need** tuning. The student lost **their bo**ok.
Awk	awkward expression or construction	The storm **had the effect of causing** millions of dollars in damage.
Cap	faulty capitalization	We spent the **Fall** in Southern **spain.**
CS	comma splice	Raoul tried his best, this time that wasn't good enough.
DICT	faulty diction	Due to the fact that we were wondering **as to** **whether it would rain**, we stayed home.
Dgl	dangling construction	**Working harder than ever,** this job proved to be too much for him to handle.
-ed	problem with final *-ed*	Last summer he **walk** all the way to Birmingham.
Frag	fragment	Depending on the amount of snow we get this winter and whether the towns buy new trucks.
||	problem in parallel form	My income is bigger than my **wife.**
P/A	pronoun/antecedent agreement	A student in accounting would be wise to see **their** advisor this month.
Pron	problem with pronoun	My aunt and my mother have wrecked **her** car. The committee has lost **their** chance to change things. You'll have to do this on **one's** own time.
Rep	unnecessary repetition	The car was blue **in color**.
R-O	run-on sentence	Raoul tried his best this time that wasn't good enough.
Sp	spelling error	This sentence is **flaude** with two **mispellings**.
-s	problem with final *-s*	He **wonder** what these teacher think of him.
STET	Let it stand	The proofreader uses this Latin term to indicate that proofreading marks calling for a change should be ignored and the text as originally written should be "let stand."
S/V	subject/verb agreement	The problem with these cities **are** leadership.
T	verb tense problem	He **comes** into the room, and he **pulled** his gun.
Wdy	wordy	Seldom have we perused a document so verbose, so ostentatious in phrasing, so burdened with too many words.
WW	wrong word	What **affect** did the movie have on Sheila? She tried to hard to **analyze** its conclusion.

FIGURE 13.2 COMMON EDITING ABBREVIATIONS

WRITING INVITATIONS

1. Revise the following paragraph for clarity, readability, and conciseness.

> My proposal as a partial solution to the problem of binge drinking is to lower the drinking age from 21 to 19. This would probably not erase totally the very questionable problem of binge drinking, but I think it would curb much of the binge drinking that goes on in colleges today. By lowering the drinking age from 19 instead of 21 the thrill or novelty of doing something wrong or something that one is not supposed to do is gone, this makes it so most high school students are till not allowed to drink by law. The solution would probably not have an instant impact, but I believe that a couple of years or so after it is implemented there will be a very large and sudden decrease in the amount of binge drinking that goes on in colleges all around the U.S. I am sure that right after this law would go into effect that there would be a short increase in binge drinking. Due to the fact that those people who are 19 and 20 will buy alcohol and they might go a little crazy at first.

2. Connect the following groups of clauses into clearer, more readable sentences. Compare your new version with the original. Which version is shortest? Which version is best? Are they different? Why?

> Divorce is common in society.
> People fail to notice its effects on adolescents.
> People generally think about its effects on adults.
> Over 1 million children experience parental divorce each year.

> Courts have recognized that some divorcing couples need counseling.
> Few places implement this kind of counseling.
> Some focus on the needs of the children as well as the adults.

> Mediation is used in 29 states.
> Mediation was started in 1980.
> Mediation involves using a third party to help parents resolve disputes.
> The disputes regard custody and family issues.

DEVELOPING A WRITING PROJECT

1. Proofread a draft of any writing project you are currently working on. Using the "Common Editing Symbols" found in Figure 13.1 and the "Common Editing Abbreviations" found in Figure 13.2, mark all spelling, grammatical, and syntactic errors. You may wish to exchange papers with someone in your writing group and proofread each other's papers.

2. Reread sections in this chapter that discuss the errors you (or your peer editor) mark. After reading the section, correct the errors, then complete a final error-free draft of your paper.

PART 4

A Meeting of Minds: Dialogues on Issues

The Vote

The readings in this casebook span two and a half centuries, from the beginnings of American Democracy to the 2000 Presidential Election. Each reading asks and answers different questions about the nature of voting rights and responsibilities. The right to vote, to participate in one's own governance, is the focus of one of the most significant discussions in contemporary world politics. This right is recognized by the United Nations as fundamental for all people everywhere. Yet in countries where voting is not mandatory, participation levels vary and are often surprisingly low. This casebook examines the phenomenon of the vote from different perspectives, in different forms and genres, for various audiences.

The Declaration of Independence
IN CONGRESS, July 4, 1776

The unanimous Declaration of the thirteen united States of America

1   When in the Course of human events, it becomes necessary for one people to dissolve the political bands which have connected them with another, and to assume among the powers of the earth, the separate and equal station to which the Laws of Nature and of Nature's God entitle them, a decent respect to the opinions of mankind requires that they should declare the causes which impel them to the separation.

2   We hold these truths to be self-evident, that all men are created equal, that they are endowed by their Creator with certain unalienable Rights, that among these are Life, Liberty and the pursuit of Happiness.—That to secure these rights, Governments are instituted among Men, deriving their just powers from the consent of the governed,—That whenever any Form of Government becomes destructive of these ends, it is the Right of the People to alter or to abolish it, and to institute new Government, laying its foundation on such principles and organizing its powers in such form, as to them shall seem most likely to effect their Safety and Happiness. Prudence, indeed, will dictate that Governments long established should not be changed for light and transient causes; and accordingly all experience hath shewn, that mankind are more disposed to

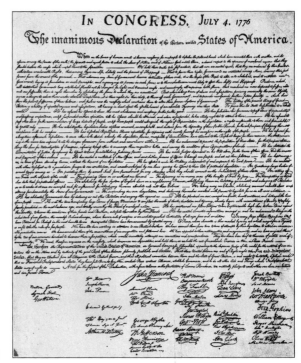

FIGURE C1.1

THE DECLARATION
OF INDEPENDENCE

suffer, while evils are sufferable, than to right themselves by abolishing the forms to which they are accustomed. But when a long train of abuses and usurpations, pursuing invariably the same Object evinces a design to reduce them under absolute Despotism, it is their right, it is their duty, to throw off such Government, and to provide new Guards for their future security.—Such has been the patient sufferance of these Colonies; and such is now the necessity which constrains them to alter their former Systems of Government. The history of the present King of Great Britain is a history of repeated injuries and usurpations, all having in direct object the establishment of an absolute Tyranny over these States. To prove this, let Facts be submitted to a candid world.

3   He has refused his Assent to Laws, the most wholesome and necessary for the public good.

4   He has forbidden his Governors to pass Laws of immediate and pressing importance, unless suspended in their operation till his Assent should be obtained; and when so suspended, he has utterly neglected to attend to them.

5   He has refused to pass other Laws for the accommodation of large districts of people, unless those people would relinquish the right of Representation in the Legislature, a right inestimable to them and formidable to tyrants only.

6   He has called together legislative bodies at places unusual, uncomfortable, and distant from the depository of their public Records, for the sole purpose of fatiguing them into compliance with his measures.

7   He has dissolved Representative Houses repeatedly, for opposing with manly firmness his invasions on the rights of the people.

8   He has refused for a long time, after such dissolutions, to cause others to be elected; whereby the Legislative powers, incapable of Annihilation, have returned to the People at large for their exercise; the State remaining in the mean time exposed to all the dangers of invasion from without, and convulsions within.

9   He has endeavoured to prevent the population of these States; for that purpose obstructing the Laws for Naturalization of Foreigners; refusing to pass others to encourage their migrations hither, and raising the conditions of new Appropriations of Lands.

10   He has obstructed the Administration of Justice, by refusing his Assent to Laws for establishing Judiciary powers.

11   He has made Judges dependent on his Will alone, for the tenure of their offices, and the amount and payment of their salaries.

12   He has erected a multitude of New Offices, and sent hither swarms of Officers to harass our people, and eat out their substance.

13   He has kept among us, in times of peace, Standing Armies without the Consent of our legislatures.

14   He has affected to render the Military independent of and superior to the Civil power.

15   He has combined with others to subject us to a jurisdiction foreign to our constitution, and unacknowledged by our laws; giving his Assent to their Acts of pretended Legislation:

16   For Quartering large bodies of armed troops among us:

17   For protecting them, by a mock Trial, from punishment for any Murders which they should commit on the Inhabitants of these States:

18   For cutting off our Trade with all parts of the world:

19   For imposing Taxes on us without our Consent:

20   For depriving us in many cases, of the benefits of Trial by Jury:

21   For transporting us beyond Seas to be tried for pretended offences:

22   For abolishing the free System of English Laws in a neighbouring Province, establishing therein an Arbitrary government, and enlarging its Boundaries so as to render it at once an example and fit instrument for introducing the same absolute rule into these Colonies:

23   For taking away our Charters, abolishing our most valuable Laws, and altering fundamentally the Forms of our Governments:

24   For suspending our own Legislatures, and declaring themselves invested with power to legislate for us in all cases whatsoever.

25   He has abdicated Government here, by declaring us out of his Protection and waging War against us.

26   He has plundered our seas, ravaged our Coasts, burnt our towns, and destroyed the lives of our people.

27   He is at this time transporting large Armies of foreign Mercenaries to compleat the works of death, desolation and tyranny, already begun with circumstances

of Cruelty & perfidy scarcely paralleled in the most barbarous ages, and totally unworthy the Head of a civilized nation.

28   He has constrained our fellow Citizens taken Captive on the high Seas to bear Arms against their Country, to become the executioners of their friends and Brethren, or to fall themselves by their Hands.

29   He has excited domestic insurrections amongst us, and has endeavoured to bring on the inhabitants of our frontiers, the merciless Indian Savages, whose known rule of warfare, is an undistinguished destruction of all ages, sexes and conditions.

30   In every stage of these Oppressions We have Petitioned for Redress in the most humble terms: Our repeated Petitions have been answered only by repeated injury. A Prince whose character is thus marked by every act which may define a Tyrant, is unfit to be the ruler of a free people.

31   Nor have We been wanting in attentions to our Brittish brethren. We have warned them from time to time of attempts by their legislature to extend an unwarrantable jurisdiction over us. We have reminded them of the circumstances of our emigration and settlement here. We have appealed to their native justice and magnanimity, and we have conjured them by the ties of our common kindred to disavow these usurpations, which would inevitably interrupt our connections and correspondence. They too have been deaf to the voice of justice and of consanguinity. We must, therefore, acquiesce in the necessity, which denounces our Separation, and hold them, as we hold the rest of mankind, Enemies in War, in Peace Friends.

32   We, therefore, the Representatives of the united States of America, in General Congress, Assembled, appealing to the Supreme Judge of the world for the rectitude of our intentions, do, in the Name, and by Authority of the good People of these Colonies, solemnly publish and declare, That these United Colonies are, and of Right ought to be Free and Independent States; that they are Absolved from all Allegiance to the British Crown, and that all political connection between them and the State of Great Britain, is and ought to be totally dissolved; and that as Free and Independent States, they have full Power to levy War, conclude Peace, contract Alliances, establish Commerce, and to do all other Acts and Things which Independent States may of right do. And for the support of this Declaration, with a firm reliance on the protection of divine Providence, we mutually pledge to each other our Lives, our Fortunes and our sacred Honor.

MARTIN LUTHER KING, JR.

I Have a Dream

Delivered on the steps at the Lincoln Memorial in Washington, D.C., on August 28, 1963.

1   Five score years ago, a great American, in whose symbolic shadow we stand, signed the Emancipation Proclamation. This momentous decree came as a great beacon light of hope to millions of Negro slaves who had been seared in the

flames of withering injustice. It came as a joyous daybreak to end the long night of captivity. But one hundred years later, we must face the tragic fact that the Negro is still not free.

2   One hundred years later, the life of the Negro is still sadly crippled by the manacles of segregation and the chains of discrimination. One hundred years later, the Negro lives on a lonely island of poverty in the midst of a vast ocean of material prosperity. One hundred years later, the Negro is still languishing in the corners of American society and finds himself an exile in his own land.

3   So we have come here today to dramatize an appalling condition. In a sense we have come to our nation's capital to cash a check. When the architects of our republic wrote the magnificent words of the Constitution and the Declaration of Independence, they were signing a promissory note to which every American was to fall heir.

4   This note was a promise that all men would be guaranteed the inalienable rights of life, liberty, and the pursuit of happiness. It is obvious today that America has defaulted on this promissory note insofar as her citizens of color are concerned. Instead of honoring this sacred obligation, America has given the Negro people a bad check which has come back marked "insufficient funds." But we refuse to believe that the bank of justice is bankrupt. We refuse to believe that there are insufficient funds in the great vaults of opportunity of this nation.

5   So we have come to cash this check—a check that will give us upon demand the riches of freedom and the security of justice. We have also come to this hallowed spot to remind America of the fierce urgency of now. This is no time to engage in the luxury of cooling off or to take the tranquilizing drug of gradualism. Now is the time to rise from the dark and desolate valley of segregation to the sunlit path of racial justice. Now is the time to open the doors of opportunity to all of God's children. Now is the time to lift our nation from the quicksands of racial injustice to the solid rock of brotherhood.

6   It would be fatal for the nation to overlook the urgency of the moment and to underestimate the determination of the Negro. This sweltering summer of the Negro's legitimate discontent will not pass until there is an invigorating autumn of freedom and equality. Nineteen sixty-three is not an end, but a beginning. Those who hope that the Negro needed to blow off steam and will now be content will have a rude awakening if the nation returns to business as usual. There will be neither rest nor tranquility in America until the Negro is granted his citizenship rights.

7   The whirlwinds of revolt will continue to shake the foundations of our nation until the bright day of justice emerges. But there is something that I must say to my people who stand on the warm threshold which leads into the palace of justice. In the process of gaining our rightful place we must not be guilty of wrongful deeds. Let us not seek to satisfy our thirst for freedom by drinking from the cup of bitterness and hatred.

8   We must forever conduct our struggle on the high plane of dignity and discipline. We must not allow our creative protest to degenerate into physical violence. Again and again we must rise to the majestic heights of meeting physical force with soul force.

9   The marvelous new militancy which has engulfed the Negro community must not lead us to distrust of all white people, for many of our white brothers, as evidenced by their presence here today, have come to realize that their destiny is tied up with our destiny and their freedom is inextricably bound to our freedom.

10   We cannot walk alone. And as we walk, we must make the pledge that we shall march ahead. We cannot turn back. There are those who are asking the devotees of civil rights, "When will you be satisfied?" We can never be satisfied as long as our bodies, heavy with the fatigue of travel, cannot gain lodging in the motels of the highways and the hotels of the cities. We cannot be satisfied as long as the Negro's basic mobility is from a smaller ghetto to a larger one. We can never be satisfied as long as a Negro in Mississippi cannot vote and a Negro in New York believes he has nothing for which to vote. No, no, we are not satisfied, and we will not be satisfied until justice rolls down like waters and righteousness like a mighty stream.

11   I am not unmindful that some of you have come here out of great trials and tribulations. Some of you have come fresh from narrow cells. Some of you have come from areas where your quest for freedom left you battered by the storms of persecution and staggered by the winds of police brutality. You have been the veterans of creative suffering. Continue to work with the faith that unearned suffering is redemptive.

12   Go back to Mississippi, go back to Alabama, go back to Georgia, go back to Louisiana, go back to the slums and ghettos of our northern cities, knowing that somehow this situation can and will be changed. Let us not wallow in the valley of despair. I say to you today, my friends, that in spite of the difficulties and frustrations of the moment, I still have a dream. It is a dream deeply rooted in the American dream.

13   I have a dream that one day this nation will rise up and live out the true meaning of its creed: "We hold these truths to be self-evident: that all men are created equal." I have a dream that one day on the red hills of Georgia the sons of former slaves and the sons of former slaveowners will be able to sit down together at a table of brotherhood. I have a dream that one day even the state of Mississippi, a desert state, sweltering with the heat of injustice and oppression, will be transformed into an oasis of freedom and justice. I have a dream that my four children will one day live in a nation where they will not be judged by the color of their skin but by the content of their character. I have a dream today.

14   I have a dream that one day the state of Alabama, whose governor's lips are presently dripping with the words of interposition and nullification, will be transformed into a situation where little black boys and black girls will be able to join hands with little white boys and white girls and walk together as sisters and brothers. I have a dream today. I have a dream that one day every valley shall be exalted, every hill and mountain shall be made low, the rough places will be made plain, and the crooked places will be made straight, and the glory of the Lord shall be revealed, and all flesh shall see it together. This is our hope. This is the faith with which I return to the South. With this faith we will be able to

hew out of the mountain of despair a stone of hope. With this faith we will be able to transform the jangling discords of our nation into a beautiful symphony of brotherhood. With this faith we will be able to work together, to pray together, to struggle together, to go to jail together, to stand up for freedom together, knowing that we will be free one day.

15   This will be the day when all of God's children will be able to sing with a new meaning, "My country, 'tis of thee, sweet land of liberty, of thee I sing. Land where my fathers died, land of the pilgrim's pride, from every mountainside, let freedom ring." And if America is to be a great nation, this must become true. So let freedom ring from the prodigious hilltops of New Hampshire. Let freedom ring from the mighty mountains of New York. Let freedom ring from the heightening Alleghenies of Pennsylvania! Let freedom ring from the snowcapped Rockies of Colorado! Let freedom ring from the curvaceous peaks of California! But not only that; let freedom ring from Stone Mountain of Georgia! Let freedom ring from Lookout Mountain of Tennessee! Let freedom ring from every hill and every molehill of Mississippi. From every mountainside, let freedom ring.

16   When we let freedom ring, when we let it ring from every village and every hamlet, from every state and every city, we will be able to speed up that day when all of God's children, black men and white men, Jews and Gentiles, Protestants and Catholics, will be able to join hands and sing in the words of the old Negro spiritual, "Free at last! free at last! thank God Almighty, we are free at last!"

SUSAN B. ANTHONY

Women's Right to Vote

Susan B. Anthony delivered this address after she was arrested for voting illegally in the presidential election of 1872. Not until August 1920, fourteen years after Anthony died, was the 19th Amendment to the U.S. Constitution ratified, securing voting rights for women.

1   Friends and fellow citizens: I stand before you tonight under indictment for the alleged crime of having voted at the last presidential election, without having a lawful right to vote. It shall be my work this evening to prove to you that in thus voting, I not only committed no crime, but, instead, simply exercised my citizen's rights, guaranteed to me and all United States citizens by the National Constitution, beyond the power of any state to deny.

2   The preamble of the Federal Constitution says:

> "We, the people of the United States, in order to form a more perfect union, establish justice, insure domestic tranquility, provide for the common defense, promote the general welfare, and secure the blessings of liberty to ourselves and our posterity, do ordain and establish this Constitution for the United States of America."

FIGURE C1.2

SUSAN B. ANTHONY

3   It was we, the people; not we, the white male citizens; nor yet we, the male citizens; but we, the whole people, who formed the Union. And we formed it, not to give the blessings of liberty, but to secure them; not to the half of ourselves and the half of our posterity, but to the whole people—women as well as men. And it is a downright mockery to talk to women of their enjoyment of the blessings of liberty while they are denied the use of the only means of securing them provided by this democratic-republican government—the ballot.

4   For any state to make sex a qualification that must ever result in the disfranchisement of one entire half of the people, is to pass a bill of attainder, or, an ex post facto law, and is therefore a violation of the supreme law of the land. By it the blessings of liberty are forever withheld from women and their female posterity.

5   To them this government has no just powers derived from the consent of the governed. To them this government is not a democracy. It is not a republic. It is an odious aristocracy; a hateful oligarchy of sex; the most hateful aristocracy ever established on the face of the globe; an oligarchy of wealth, where the rich govern the poor. An oligarchy of learning, where the educated govern the ignorant, or even an oligarchy of race, where the Saxon rules the African, might be endured; but this oligarchy of sex, which makes father, brothers, husband, sons, the oligarchs over the mother and sisters, the wife and daughters, of every household—which ordains all men sovereigns, all women subjects, carries dissension, discord, and rebellion into every home of the nation.

6   Webster, Worcester, and Bouvier all define a citizen to be a person in the United States, entitled to vote and hold office.

7   The only question left to be settled now is: Are women persons? And I hardly believe any of our opponents will have the hardihood to say they are not. Being persons, then, women are citizens; and no state has a right to make any law, or to enforce any old law, that shall abridge their privileges or immunities. Hence, every discrimination against women in the constitutions and laws of the several states is today null and void, precisely as is every one against Negroes.

LINDA FELDMANN

Why the Poll Booths of America Are Empty

This commentary appeared in The Christian Science Monitor *on October 3, 2000, a month before the presidential election of 2000 between Vice President Al Gore and Texas Governor George W. Bush.*

1   Mark Mills cares passionately about community issues. He calls local officials and writes letters to the editor about everything from school spending to local tax rates. Yet he rarely votes. Currently, he's not even registered.

2   "To me, politicians have become so removed from the real world," says the middle-aged Mr. Mills, a computer technician with a PhD who lives in Denver. "Politics is just so political."

3   As the nation's politicians, parties, and press gear up for the first elections of the millennium, more and more Americans are dropping out of the conventional political process—even civic-minded people like Mills.

4   Indeed, while the United States often holds itself up as a model of democracy, it has chronically produced one of the lowest voter participation rates in the Western world since World War II. It hardly seems what the Founding Fathers had in mind 224 years ago when they set forth a blueprint for a new kind of representative government, one deriving "just powers from the consent of the governed."

5   Since 1960, when modern-day U.S. presidential voting peaked at 63 percent, turnout has declined by 14 percent, to less than half the voting-age population. This November, it could drop even further. Experts have been grappling with the downward drift for years, but never more than now. Dozens of groups, from Harvard University to the World Wrestling Federation, are devoting resources to understanding and, they hope, reversing the decline in voting.

6   "We have a crisis of the erosion of democracy at the grass roots," says Curtis Gans, director of the Committee for the Study of the American Electorate. Walter Dean Burnham, another expert on voting, says the attitudes associated with low participation—the apathy, the anger, the negative views of government—may be even more dangerous than low turnout itself. In fact, he notes, studies show that people who do vote are just as cynical about politics as people who don't.

7   "You've got all this surging just below the surface, even at a time when the context—peace and prosperity—is so favorable," says Mr. Burnham, a professor at the University of Texas at Austin. Still, many people, like Mills, are finding new ways to participate in politics—just not at the ballot box. So, at the start of a new century, the question looms: Is American democracy broken, or just being transformed?

"Doers" Who Don't

8   Karl Stoecker of Miami, a lanky, blond magazine photographer in his late 50s, has one foot inside the mainstream and one foot outside. Every morning, he likes to go to the ocean to chat with the young surfer/philosopher crowd. He also has two daughters in public school—and says he's fine with paying taxes to support their education.

9   "But I won't help [politicians] push their system by voting," says Mr. Stoecker. They "cater to business interests, not to the public's."

10   Jill Davidson, a 30-something massage therapist and restaurant hostess in Miami, laughs when asked if she votes. "I don't know where to go register," she says, flush from a workout at the gym. "And reason No. 2, I'm just lazy."

11   Consciously or not, these two people represent a significant element in the American psyche: the notion that the right not to vote is as valid as the right to vote.

12   If they were from Australia or Belgium, where voting is mandatory, they would face a fine on the order of a parking ticket for a "no-show" on election day. In Australia's two most recent elections, turnout there broke 80 percent.

13   Stoecker and Ms. Davidson represent another important observation about nonvoters in America: Those over age 45 tend to be more angry and alienated, while those below 45 tend toward indifference.

14   It may be, observers say, that older nonvoters grew up with higher expectations of what government can accomplish, while the younger generation came of age when disillusionment with government was already in place. Since the 1960s, a steady stream of events—the Vietnam War, Watergate, Iran-Contra, the Lewinsky matter—has reinforced cynicism about Washington.

15   Still, attitudes and behaviors of nonvoters vary widely: Some appear so intimidated by the complexity of the issues involved that they don't vote, almost out of respect for democracy. Others are absorbed by concerns at home and work, and don't see the need to become civically engaged.

16   And then there are those like Mills, the activist in Colorado, who feels he can have a greater impact through direct, local action, rather than handing his mandate for action to someone else by voting.

17   In a 1996 poll of 1,001 likely nonvoters, the Medill Journalism School at Northwestern University in Evanston, Ill., found that nearly one-third of nonvoters are so-called "doers" like Mills: They are active in their communities, pay attention to the news, and tend to be educated.

18   Still, they often don't vote because they "don't have time" or because "politicians spend too much time on petty things."

19   If such social connectedness and community involvement were rising over-all, then the decline in voting might not be as troublesome to observers. But, in fact, the nation's "social capital"—involvement in community networks—has steadily eroded for the past two generations, according to Robert Putnam, author of *Bowling Alone*.

20   Once-robust civic organizations, like the League of Women Voters, are strug-gling to remain active in some communities. Weekly church attendance—which correlates strongly with voting—is down. Newspaper reading and TV-news viewing, which also tie closely to voting, are declining significantly as each gen-eration gives way to the next.

21   "Generational replacement," in fact, is the single biggest factor in the decline in turnout, says Mr. Putnam, a professor at Harvard University in Cambridge, Mass. As the World War II generation—known for high civic involvement—dies off and is replaced by their grandchildren, voting levels are going to con-tinue to decline.

22   Young adults typically vote at lower levels than older, more settled adults. But fewer and fewer young people are converting into voters as they grow older.

23   Putnam himself places the largest share of blame on television: Since 1984, household viewing has averaged more than seven hours a day. "It's really quite lethal to civic engagement," he says. "And I'm not talking about watching *The NewsHour*."

Dinner-Table Index

24   Dan Bryan, a judge from Auburn, Neb., stands at the foot of the Jefferson Memorial in Washington and quietly reads the inscriptions on the wall.

25   "I always vote," says Judge Bryan. "Voting is a way of memorializing them," he adds, gesturing toward the statue of the author of the Declaration of Inde-pendence and the third president.

26   He lobbies his three children to vote, too, even though they exhibit the usual characteristics that weigh against voting among young adults—such as being away at school or simply on the move.

27   Daughter Colleen, an undergrad at Loyola University in Chicago, confirms that she does indeed vote. Usually. She missed the Nebraska primary, even though dad had sent her an absentee ballot. "I didn't know any of the issues," she admits.

28   Behaviors learned from our first teachers—parents—are perhaps the most deeply instilled. But as families get busier and spend less leisure time together, including at dinner, that becomes less true. In some families, dedication to vot-ing may be a casualty.

29   Another factor, alluded to by Ms. Bryan, is the amount of work it takes to cast an informed vote. As initiatives and referenda proliferate, voters joke that they need to enroll in graduate school to understand all the issues. In Cali-fornia, for example, this year's voters' guide explaining ballot measures is a Michener-esque 74 pages long.

30   Beyond the explosion in initiatives—some of which involve hot topics and actually drive up turnout—Americans are asked to vote far too often, analysts

say. Between primary and general elections, from president down to dogcatcher, voters can end up going to the polls four times a year.

31   "We have this system that's gotten more and more complicated and is asking more and more of citizens," says Martin Wattenberg, a political scientist at the University of California at Irvine. "Basically, people don't want to have this much control."

32   Even many Americans who try to vote regularly say the political system isn't working. "I think the system's sick," says Ken Kozol, an electrical engineer from Long Grove, Iowa, who nevertheless votes "as much as I can."

33   Mr. Kozol blames the dual party system, for one thing, saying he'd "sure like more diversity" among candidates. His wife, Sandy, who home-schools daughters Amy and Lara, adds, "You pick the top two candidates, and that's all you hear about, and then you're sick of hearing about them."

34   But for those Americans who vote less often than the Kozols, overexposure of the major-party candidates isn't the problem. It may be too little exposure. In recent years, the parties have used increasingly sophisticated technology to pinpoint where "their" voters are, and target them, to the exclusion of non- or sometime-voters, who don't get the phone calls, e-mails, and regular mail that drive up turnout.

35   In other words, parties and candidates are not in the business of producing large turnouts. The key, for them, is to get more votes than the other guy, not to promote the lofty goal of greater democratic involvement.

36   Many nonvoters also point to the explosion of money in politics as a reason for staying away. Rick Romero, a construction worker and father of three from Denver, says he feels his vote doesn't count: Those who get into office are simply the ones with the biggest "war chests."

37   Likewise, poll after poll shows that the public intensely dislikes negative campaigning. Yet negative races often attract big turnouts—usually because they're closely contested. And in races where the most money is spent, turnout is highest, because they also tend to be the tightest battles.

38   Another player that takes some blame for declining turnout is the media, which tend to focus on campaign tactics and brawls rather than issues. The "civic journalism" movement, an effort to report news in a way that is more responsive to a community's needs, was launched in the early 1990s, but with mixed results.

39   Ultimately, though, it may be candidates themselves who can spur greater interest in voting. When John McCain, the Republican senator from Arizona, captivated the nation with his drive for the GOP presidential nomination, it was his air of straight-shooting "authenticity" that brought some nonvoters into the "small d" democratic fold.

40   What Mr. McCain's candidacy showed is that, when people feel inspired, they will turn out. In this year's New Hampshire primary, which featured hot races in both major parties, voter turnout topped 80 percent.

It's Not All Bad

41   Declining turnout has become the poster child for the view that the American political system is in distress—or, at least, has lost the faith of the people.

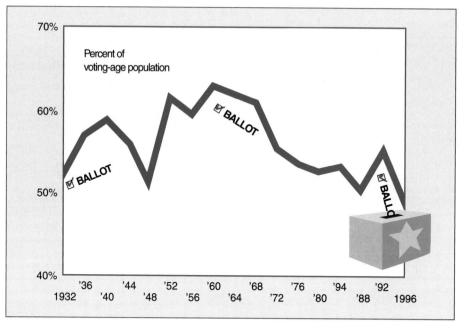

FIGURE C1.3 VOTER TURNOUT IN U.S. PRESIDENTIAL ELECTIONS, 1932–1996

Source: U.S. Bureau of the Census, and Curtis Gans, Committee for the Study of the American Electorate, Peter King—Staff.

42   But, in fact, the two phenomena may be unrelated, says Ruy Teixeira, author of two books on voter turnout. Turnout now is not catastrophically lower than it was in 1960—63 percent—when government was viewed as more responsive, he says.

43   He also notes that turnout in most other major democracies has been dropping as well. Switzerland, the only country in the Organization for Economic Cooperation and Development with lower turnout than the U.S., has declined by 39 percentage points since the 1950s. Only two countries have seen an increase: Denmark and Sweden.

44   To some, low turnout is a sign of satisfaction with government. Indeed, turnout in the U.S. spiked up to 55 percent in 1992, when voters were unhappy with the state of the economy. But the low-turnout-equals-satisfaction argument fails to acknowledge the overwhelming survey evidence of public cynicism and unhappiness with government. In fact, it is older Americans—those with the highest turnout—who are most satisfied with government.

45   Still, many experts predict turnout this fall could be slightly higher than it was in 1996, when the nation approved of President Clinton's job performance and Republican nominee Bob Dole looked weak. This time around, the race is expected to be one of the closest in the post-WWII era, which could add to turnout.

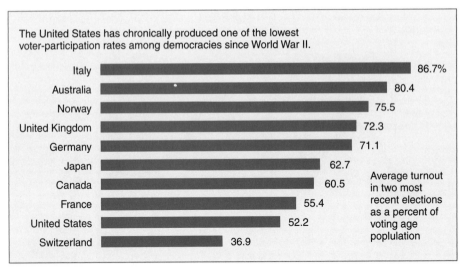

FIGURE C1.4 VOTER TURNOUT IN TEN DEMOCRACIES

Source: Martin Wattenberg, University of California at Irvine, Peter King—Staff

46   Weighing against that is growing public sentiment that Washington just isn't as important as it used to be. Betsy Siegel, a wardrobe stylist for TV commercials in Miami, never voted in a presidential election until recently. Yet her real interest remains local issues—the neighborhood park, Christmas lunches for needy children.

47   "I don't know enough about Congress," she says. "I don't know how much they really do. And I think the president is more or less a symbol."

TAIPANONLINE

Why People Don't Vote

This commentary appeared on the Taipanonline Web site shortly after the 1996 presidential election, which resulted in Bill Clinton being elected to a second term.

1   The 1996 election will be remembered for three important statistics: 1) a Democrat won a second term for the presidency (first time since FDR); 2) for the first time in the 20th Century, Republicans maintained control of the House and Senate for two consecutive terms; and 3) it was the lowest voter turnout in American history—approximately 49 percent. For the first two, I would agree they are important events. But for the 49 percent voter turnout, I say: Big deal! Let me elaborate.

2   This year an important book accomplished a rather unusual achievement. Anthony Downs's *An Economic Theory of Democracy*—published in 1957—

became the most cited book in the discipline of political science. Think about this now: In the span of 40 years, a book written by an economist (Downs is an economist) is cited more often than any other "political" book (or article for that matter) written by a political scientist. More than de Tocqueville's *Democracy in America*...more than Woodrow Wilson's *Congressional Government*...more than Charles Beard's *An Economic Interpretation of the Constitution*...heck, even more than *The Federalist Papers*.

3   Why would an economist's dissertation be so widely cited and read? Simple. *An Economic Theory of Democracy* explains—in accurate, economic terms—what hundreds of political philosophers could not: why people vote...or don't vote in a democracy. But it is more than just an academic treatise on democracy. What Downs explains goes against everything you've ever heard from liberal elites, media pontificators, and even your favorite school teacher. And what you've been hearing (more like brainwashed) is: YOU MUST VOTE!

4   You hear it a million times come election season: "If you don't vote, you're un-American...you don't deserve to complain about government...our forefathers died for the right to vote..." The morons who exclaim such nonsense need to get a few things straight. For starters, many people who don't vote are actually exercising a democratic principle known in intelligent circles as "the freedom of speech." People who don't vote sometimes will tell you that their abstinence from the voting booths is a form of protest. Besides, voting isn't the only element of a democracy. There are other things people do (other than voting) that allow them to participate in a democracy—like abiding by democratically enacted laws.

5   I hate to draw this out, but concerning our forefathers and their fight for a right to vote, well, it is not exactly accurate history. The main reason the American colonies rebelled against England was due to King George's usurpation of legislative powers—a violation of the separation of powers doctrine. If you don't believe that, read the Declaration of Independence. Jefferson gives a long litany of grievances against King George...not Parliament. And even when the colonies won independence, the newly formed nation prohibited 2/3 of the populace from voting. Women, blacks, and non-propertied (poor) white males were disenfranchised. So why do so many of the self-righteous cite "the forefathers" when voting began as a right for uppity white males? (If these people, who are complaining about low voter turnout, would simply cite the civil rights movement...and the deaths that occurred in that period—instead of the forefathers—they might have a more persuasive case.)

6   One woman—on election night—even told me that America should have a law forcing people to vote! What a frightening proposition. I'm reminded of Rousseau's *Social Contract*. In his argument about the "General Will," Rousseau claims that every "rational" person would want to be a part of his community—exercising pure democracy and being truly free. A critic of the *Social Contract* challenged Rousseau with this: What if a person doesn't want to be a part of your social contract? To which Rousseau replied: "We will have to force him to be free!"

Hollywood Herrings

2   You see, people like Barbara Streisand and Madonna think that people who don't vote are somehow apathetic buffoons. But that's not the case…and Downs proves as much. According to Downs, people who do not vote, don't vote on the basis of a rational, economic decision. The pin that holds Downs's theory together is the economic phenomena known as the "free rider." In a free rider, a person receives a benefit without absorbing the cost of receiving the benefit. For example, let's say my neighborhood is collecting funds for a parade. My neighborhood is fairly large, so I know they'll get enough (without my money) to pay for the parade. Why would I contribute money (a cost) to enjoy a parade (a benefit) that I can watch regardless if I pay or don't pay? Strictly speaking, a person acting rationally wants to maximize benefits at a minimal cost…at no cost if possible.

8   Well, as Downs argues, the same logic applies to voting. A person who wants to make a "rational decision" in a vote would absorb substantial costs. Namely, reading "everything" about the issues and candidates…attending debates, etc. After reading everything, a fully informed person could then vote rationally. But why do that? Especially when polls tell you who will most likely win. For instance, in October, Clinton held a strong 15-point lead. So why would a Clinton supporter—acting rationally—go to the polls knowing his vote really wouldn't make a difference? He'll receive the benefit without absorbing the cost of voting. Well, the answer is: Some people have different values when it comes to democracy. They view voting as their civic duty…regardless of the outcome. That's perfectly valid. But so is the view of the person who doesn't vote.

9   How does Downs's theory explain the 1996 presidential election? Easily. Polls had a major effect on voting turnout. For 6 months, every major poll had Clinton leading Dole anywhere from 12 to 20 points. This influenced people coming to the voting booth…namely, it influenced them to stay home. Clinton supporters knew Clinton would win…so why vote? Dole supporters knew Dole would lose…so why waste the time? Besides, even if 100 percent of the voting population voted, I guarantee the results would reflect exactly the same returns reflected in the 49 percent turnout.

10   My recommendations for people like Babs, Madonna, Ted Danson, Alec Baldwin et al.: Stick to what you do best, entertainment. After all, this isn't amateur night at the debate club.

RICHARD ROSE

Evaluating Election Turnout

This essay was written by the Director of the Centre for Public Policy, University of Strathclyde, Glasgow, Scotland. It was published online in 2000 by the Center for Voting and Democracy and then reprinted by the International Institute for Democracy and Electoral Assistance.

1   In the contemporary world, virtually every country holds elections of one kind or another. The right of citizens to vote is now a defining attribute of democracy, and the franchise is a right of every adult citizen and no longer a privilege restricted to a narrowly defined group. Yet the fact that everyone has a right to vote is not sufficient to make a country democratic.

2   Global surveys invariably conclude that the majority of regimes in the world today are not democratic; the median regime has been aptly described as "partly free" (Freedom House, 1996). In countries of this nature, the failure to achieve democracy is not the result of denying most citizens the right to vote. It stems from the fact that such elections as are held are not freely competitive, and that regimes do not fully respect the rule of law, which includes the need to limit their own coercion. As long as it has the power to control competition and the counting of votes, a regime has nothing to fear from holding elections which are unfree and unfair.

3   Democrats are not the only rulers to promote a high voter turnout; a distinguishing feature of modern totalitarian regimes is the compulsory mobilization of subjects to show public commitment to them. Totalitarian rulers share the goal of 100 percent turnout, even when this is combined with no choice at all of parties or candidates. Thus, when it comes to electoral participation, it is certainly possible to have too much of a good thing. Virtual unanimity in turnout and in voting for a single party produces an election result too good to be true. This essay discusses firstly what constitutes "free and fair" elections and the inter-relationship of turnout and choice in both democratic and totalitarian countries. Secondly, it shows that, although a comparative perspective does make it possible to evaluate turnout as higher or lower by comparison with other countries or a nation's past record, there is no consensus on evaluation, on what a "good" turnout actually is; rational choice theorists can argue that "whatever is, is right," while at the other extreme democratic idealists can argue that anything below 100 percent turnout is not good enough. And thirdly, this essay concludes by showing what a government can do to make a good turnout better. It examines the question of compulsion to vote, whether it is a worthwhile option, and why a government can never produce "perfect" turnout and still hold an election that is fair and free.

Freedom of Choice

4   Two conditions must be met before citizens are free to choose their governors. The right to vote is a necessary but not a sufficient condition; in addition, elections themselves must be both free and fair. An election is free if a multiplicity of parties are able to compete for votes; without this, the only choice open to an elector is whether to turn out or, if compelled to, whether to vote for the sole party, publicly abstain, or spoil the ballot paper. An election is fair if officials administer the law in ways that protect the rights of each elector and of competing parties, and if the counting of the votes is accurate. As Mackenzie (1958: Part Four) shows in his classic discussion of "electoral morality and its enforcement," the pathology of elections takes many different forms: an unfair election can be corrupt, muddled, stolen or manufactured.

5   The evaluation, as opposed to the counting, of turnout must not only take into account who can vote but also the radically different significance of voting in unfair and unfree as against free and fair elections….The democratic ideal is an election in which all adults have the right to vote, many parties compete and the election is administered fairly. If the franchise is granted to relatively few adults, but there is free and fair competition for the support of those who can vote, the political system is an oligarchy, and meets at least one condition for democracy; this arrangement may be described as proto-democratic, since the expansion of the franchise will make it democratic.

6   At the other extreme, if competition is very limited and very few adults are allowed to vote, an election is repressive. Under these conditions, restrictions are imposed not only on citizens but also on politicians, since those who oppose the ruling powers are unable to voice their opposition effectively. This type of election can be found in poor countries with low literacy rates, when governments decide to go through the formalities of an election without wishing to stir up either their opponents or their subjects. In contrast, a totalitarian regime wants everyone to vote, but it does not want the result to be decided by the free and fair choice of its citizenry; it therefore eliminates competition, and the ruling party campaigns aggressively to make everyone turn out to vote for it.

Interview with David Pryor
One Expert's Opinion on Election 2000

This interview with former Arkansas Senator David Pryor was published by the Kennedy School of Government at Harvard University reflecting on youth voter participation.

1   October 18, 2000—Many analysts suggest that this generation of young people is more disengaged from politics than previous ones. In the 1996 presidential election, about one-third of 18- to 24-year-olds voted compared to an overall turnout of 49 percent. With the election just weeks away, efforts nationwide to register younger votes and to encourage them to go to the polls have heightened. Former Arkansas Senator David Pryor is the Director of the Institute of Politics, which has been conducting a Harvard-wide effort to achieve 100 percent registration among undergraduates. He says young people think there are better ways than politics to effect change.

2   Q: Are there specific reasons why young people have turned away from voting?

3   Pryor: Surveys indicate that young people do not feel that government and politicians are the best way of implementing change. Students are very active about volunteering and giving back to their community and country. They feel that becoming involved in politics is not the best method for change.

4   Q: Are candidates sufficiently focused on issues that younger voters care about?

5   Pryor: No! And it's simple. Candidates focus on the issues that affect voters and if young people don't vote, politicians will pay very little attention. Politicians go where the voters are and right now voters are not represented by the younger generation.

6   Q: What do you say to those who argue that younger generations don't vote because of apathy?

7   Pryor: The younger generation is not apathetic. This generation is temporarily tuned out. Politicians don't speak to their interests. Younger voters feel they want to make a difference and they can be effective in other ways. In a national survey of college undergraduates conducted by the Institute of Politics, 85 percent of college students prefer community volunteerism to political involvement to solve issues in their community and 60 percent prefer it to solve important issues facing the country.

8   Q: How can the political process be better at courting the youth vote?

9   Pryor: It is important for us not only to talk about how to get involved but why you should be. For example, Senator John McCain turned on younger voters by talking about campaign finance reform. Ralph Nader reached out by talking about student loans. Both of these politicians spoke clearly to the "why" of getting involved.

GEORGE WILL

The Framers' Electoral Wisdom

George Will's columns are syndicated nationally. This one appeared in the Sacramento Bee *on Nov. 2, 2000, just before the presidential election took place.*

1   Political hypochondriacs again are urging Americans to fear and be offended by the system of choosing presidents by electoral votes. Criticism of this system recurs whenever a close contest poses the possibility that a candidate might win an electoral vote victory while receiving fewer popular votes than his opponent. It is said, with more passion than precision, that this happened three times— 1824, 1876, 1888.

2   Even if that is true, it means that in 50 of 53 elections since 1789—in 94 percent of elections, and in 27 consecutive elections—the system has not produced the outcome that troubles the sleep of its critics. Besides, the assertions about those elections can be true without being pertinent.

3   In 1824, before the emergence of the two-party system, all four candidates appeared on the ballots in only six of the 24 states. Six states, including New York, had no elections: their state legislatures picked the electors. Nationally, only about 350,000 of the 4 million eligible white males voted. Andrew Jackson received 38,149 more votes than John Quincy Adams, but neither received a majority of electoral votes. So the House of Representatives decided, picking Adams. In 1888 fraud on both sides may have involved more votes than the victory margin (90,596).

4   There never has been an Electoral College victory by a candidate who lost the popular vote by a substantial margin. And only simple-minded majoritarianism holds that "the nation's will" would be "frustrated" and democracy "subverted" (this is the language of Electoral College abolitionists) were an electoral vote majority to go to a candidate who comes in a close second in the popular vote count. In such a case, the framers' objective—a president chosen through state-by-state decisions—would be achieved.

5   The Electoral College has evolved, shaping and being shaped by the two-party system, which probably would not survive abandonment of winner-take-all allocation of electoral votes. Direct popular election of presidents, or proportional allocation of states' electoral votes, would incite minor parties to fractionate the electorate. This might necessitate runoff elections to guarantee that the eventual president got at least 40 percent of the vote—and runoffs might become auctions in which minor parties sold their support.

6   The electoral vote system shapes the character of winning majorities. By avoiding proportional allocation of electoral votes, America's system—under which Ross Perot in 1992 got 19 percent of the popular votes and zero electoral votes—buttresses the dominance of two parties, and pulls them to the center, producing a temperate politics of coalitions rather than a proliferation of ideological factions with charismatic leaders.

7   Furthermore, choosing presidents by electoral votes is an incentive for candidates to wage truly national campaigns, building majorities that are geographically as well as ideologically broad. Consider: Were it not for electoral votes allocated winner-take-all, would candidates campaign in, say, West Virginia? In 1996 Bill Clinton decisively defeated Bob Dole there 52 percent to 37 percent. But that involved a margin of just 93,866 votes (327,812 to 233,946), a trivial amount compared to what can be harvested in large cities. However, for a 5–0 electoral vote sweep, West Virginia is worth a trip or two.

8   Some Electoral College abolitionists argue that a candidate could get elected with just 27 percent of the popular vote—by winning the 11 largest states by just one vote in each, and not getting a single popular vote anywhere else. But it is equally pointless to worry that a candidate could carry Wyoming 220,000 to 0, could lose the other 49 states and the District of Columbia by an average of 4,400 votes, and be the popular vote winner while losing the electoral vote 535 to 3. Serious people take seriously probabilities, not mere possibilities. And abolitionists are not apt to produce what Madison was too sober to attempt, a system under which no unwanted outcome is even theoretically possible.

9   Critics of the Electoral College say it makes some people's votes more powerful than others'. This is true. In 1996, 211,571 Wyoming voters cast presidential ballots, awarding three electoral votes, one for every 70,523 voters, whereas 10,019,484 California voters awarded 54 electoral votes, one for every 185,546 voters.

10   So what? Do critics want to abolish the Senate as well? Delaware, the least populous state in 1789, understandably was the first to ratify the Constitution with its equal representation of states in the Senate: Virginia, the most popu-

lous, had 11 times more voters. Today Wyoming's senators' votes can cancel those of California's senators, who represent 69 times more people. If that offends you, so does America's constitutional federalism.

11   The electoral vote system, like the Constitution it serves, was not devised by, and should not be revised by, simple-minded majoritarians.

BOB WING

The Structure of White Power and the Color of Election 2000

Bob Wing is the executive editor of ColorLines *magazine and www.colorlines.com. In this article he explores the racial implications of the Electoral College system and the 2000 presidential election.*

1   What if there was an election, and nobody won?

2   Thank you, Florida, for exposing as fraud the much-vaunted sanctity of the vote in this country and placing electoral reform back on the country's agenda. Reports indicate that black and Haitian voters were harassed by police, their names removed from the rolls, and their ballots left uncounted by outdated machines. Thirty-five years after passage of the Voting Rights Act, racist

FIGURE C1.5

A BLACK VOTER PROTESTS THE 2000 FLORIDA PRESIDENTIAL ELECTION.

violations of election law are rampant and should be pursued to justice in Florida and elsewhere.

3   But beyond these immediate issues, this election reveals again just how central race is to U.S. politics and how racism is institutionally structured into the electoral system. The election reaffirms that people of color are the most consistent liberal/progressive voters in the country and that their clout is increasing—but that electoral racism effectively nullifies almost half of their votes. The Civil Rights movement destroyed the monopoly over power by whites, but the tyranny of the white majority is still institutionalized in the winner-take-all, two-party, Electoral College system.

4   Unless we place fighting electoral racism at the top of the racial justice agenda, we cannot challenge the political stranglehold of conservative white voters or maximize the growing power of people of color.

By the Numbers

5   The idea that race and racism are central to American politics is not just a theory that harkens back to the days of slavery. It's a current-day lived reality that is particularly evident in this country's biggest and most sacred political event: the presidential pageant.

6   According to the Voter News Service exit polls for Election 2000, 90 percent of African Americans voted for Gore, as did 63 percent of Latinos, and 55 percent of Asians. (No exit poll data on the Native American vote is available, but most have historically voted Democratic.) Combined, people of color accounted for almost 30 percent of Gore's total vote, although they were only 19 percent of voters.

7   Latinos, the country's fastest growing voters, went heavily Democratic—even in Texas—despite extensive efforts by the Republicans to sway them. Most Asians followed suit. People of color are becoming a larger portion both of the U.S. population and of the electorate, and voting largely in concert with each other in presidential elections.

8   On the other hand, whites constituted almost 95 percent of Bush's total vote. Conventional electoral wisdom discounts race as a political factor, focusing instead on class, the gender gap, union membership, etc. But, the only demographic groups that had a fairly unified vote—defined as 60 percent or more for one of the candidates—were: blacks, Latinos, Jews (81 percent for Gore), union members (62 percent for Gore), residents of large cities (71 percent for Gore), and white males (60 percent for Bush). All but union members and big-city residents are racial or ethnic groups.

9   And, the large numbers of people of color in unions (about 25 percent) and big cities largely account for the heavy Democratic vote of those demographic groups. White union members and city dwellers vote to the left of whites who live more racially isolated lives, but they barely tilt Democratic. Similarly, women voted 54–43 for Gore, but white women actually favored Bush by one point. Women of color create the gender gap.

10   The same can be said of the poor: although 57 percent of voters with incomes under $15,000 voted for Gore, poor whites—who make up just under half of eligible voters in this category—broke slightly for Bush. The income gap in presidential politics is thoroughly racialized. As the sociologist William Form pointed out long ago, if only a bare majority of white working-class people voted consistently Democratic, we could have some kind of social democracy that would provide much more social justice than the conservative regimes we are used to.

11   Despite the pronounced color of politics, Ralph Nader (and his multi-hued progressive pundits) blithely dismiss the fact that he received only one percent of the votes of people of color and that the demographics of his supporters mirrored those of the Republicans (except younger).

Electoral College: Pillar of Racism

12   The good news is that the influence of liberal and progressive voters of color is increasingly being felt in certain states. They have become decisive in the most populous states, all of which went to Gore except Ohio, Texas, and (maybe?) Florida. In California an optimist might even envision a rebirth of Democratic liberalism a couple of elections down the road, based largely on votes of people of color.

13   The bad news is that the two-party, winner-take-all, Electoral College system of this country ensures, even requires, that voters of color be marginalized or totally ignored.

14   The Electoral College negates the votes of almost half of all people of color. For example, 53 percent of all blacks live in the Southern states, where this year, as usual, they voted over 90 percent Democratic. However, white Republicans out-voted them in every Southern state (and every border state except Maryland). As a result, every single Southern Electoral College vote was awarded to Bush. While nationally, whites voted 54–42 for Bush, Southern whites, as usual, gave over 70 percent of their votes to him. They thus completely erased the massive Southern black (and Latino and Native American) vote for Gore in that region.

15   Since Electoral College votes go entirely to whichever candidate wins the plurality in each state, whether that plurality be by one vote or one million votes, the result was the same as if blacks and other people of color in the South had not voted at all. Similarly negated were the votes of the millions of Native Americans and Latino voters who live in overwhelmingly white Republican states like Arizona, Nevada, Oklahoma, Utah, the Dakotas, Montana—and Texas. The tyranny of the white majority prevails.

16   Further, the impact of the mostly black voters of Washington, D.C., unfairly denied statehood, is undermined by its arbitrary allocation of only three electoral votes. And the peoples of Puerto Rico, the U.S. Virgin Islands, American Samoa, and Guam—which are colonies ruled by the U.S. and have greater populations than more than a quarter of the U.S. states—get no Electoral College votes at all.

Slave Power

17   In his *New York Times* op-ed, Yale law professor Akhil Amar reveals that the hitherto obscure Electoral College system was consciously set up by the Founding Fathers to be the mechanism by which slaveholders would dominate American politics.

18   The Constitution provided that slaves be counted as three-fifths of a person (but given no citizenship rights) for purposes of determining how many members each state would be granted in the House of Representatives. This provision vastly increased the representation of the slave states in Congress.

19   At the demand of James Madison and other Virginia slaveholders, this proslavery allocation of Congresspersons also became the basis for allocation of votes in the Electoral College. It is a dirty little secret that the Electoral College was rigged up for the express purpose of translating the disproportionate Congressional power of the slaveholders into undue influence over the election of the presidency. Virginia slaveholders proceeded to hold the presidency for 32 of the Constitution's first 36 years.

20   Since slavery was abolished, the new justification for the Electoral College is that it allows smaller states to retain some impact on elections. And so it does—to the benefit of conservative white Republican states. As Harvard law professor Lani Guinier reports, in Wyoming, one Electoral College vote corresponds to 71,000 voters, while in large-population states (where the votes of people of color are more numerous) the ratio is one electoral vote to over 200,000 voters. So much for one person, one vote.

21   This year the Electoral College will apparently enable the winner of the conservative white states to prevail over the winner of the national popular vote—a tyranny of the minority.

Two-Party Racism

22   The two-party system also structurally marginalizes voters of color.

23   First of all, to win, both parties must take their most loyal voters for granted and focus their message and money to win over the so-called undecided voters who will actually decide which party wins each election. The most loyal Democrats are strong liberals and progressives, the largest bloc of whom are people of color. The most loyal Republicans are conservative whites, especially those in rural areas and small towns. The undecideds are mostly white, affluent suburbanites; and both parties try to position their politics, rhetoric, and policies to woo them. The interests of people of color are ignored or even attacked by both parties as they pander to the "center."

24   Another consequence is that a disproportionate number of people of color see no reason to vote at all. The U.S. has by far the lowest voter participation rate of any democracy in the world. The two-party system so demobilizes voters that only about 65 percent of the eligible electorate is registered, and only 49 to 50 percent usually vote (far less in non-presidential elections).

25   Not surprisingly, the color and income of those who actually vote is skewed to higher income, older, and more conservative white people. In the 1996 presiden-

tial election, 57 percent of eligible whites voted compared to 50 percent of blacks and 44 percent of Latinos. Seventy-three percent of people with family incomes over $75,000 voted compared to 36 percent of those with incomes below $15,000.

26   In addition, current electoral law disenfranchises millions of mainly Latino and Asian immigrants because they are not citizens. And, according to Reuters, some 4.2 million Americans, including 1.8 million black men (13 percent of all black men in America), are denied the right to vote because of incarceration or past felony convictions.

Proportional Representation

27   To remedy these racist, undemocratic electoral structures, Lani Guinier and many others propose an electoral system based on proportional representation. New Zealand, Australia, all of the European countries except Great Britain, and many Third World countries have proportional electoral systems. In such systems, all parties that win a certain minimum of the popular vote (usually five percent) win representation in the Congress (or Parliament) equal to their vote. To win the presidency, a party must either win an outright majority or form a governing coalition with other parties.

28   Thus, for example, the German Green Party, which gets about seven percent of the vote, is part of the ruling coalition in that country. If we had such a system, a racial and economic justice party could be quite powerful. Instead, in our current system, voting for a third-party candidate like Nader takes votes from Gore and helps Bush. And someone like Jesse Jackson, who won 30 percent of the Democratic popular vote in 1988, is not a viable candidate, and his supporters have little clout in national politics.

29   If we fail to place fighting electoral racism at the very top of a racial justice agenda, we will continue to be effectively disenfranchised, and white people, especially conservative white Republicans, will enjoy electoral privileges that enable them to shape the policies and institutions of this country at our expense. We must eliminate the role of big money in elections and make voting readily accessible to poor folk.

30   Until we win a proportional system—or unless there is some other major political shake-up—the vast majority of people of color will continue to participate in the Democratic Party. Therefore we must resist the racist, pro-corporate right wing of the Democratic Party, led by people like Al Gore, and demand that the Democrats more strongly represent the interests of people of color. However, our ability to do this—or to build anti-racist third parties that include our peoples—depends upon our ability to form mass, independent racial justice organizations and to build alliances with other progressive forces both inside and outside the electoral realm.

31   Building electoral alliances—around issues, referenda, and candidates, both inside and outside the Democratic Party—is key to the maturation of a racial justice movement that functions on the scale necessary to impact national politics, social policy, or ideological struggle in this country.

ROB RICHIE AND STEVEN HILL

The Dinosaur in the Living Room

Richie and Hill's essay was published in 1997 by the Center for Voting and Democracy.

1   Pardon me, but do you see the dinosaur in the living room? It's standing there in the middle of the carpet, and nobody wants to talk about it. We all just tiptoe around it, year after year, pretending it's not there and hoping it will go away.

2   In spinning the recent elections for partisan implications, commentators generally ignored the glaring fact that, once again, fewer and fewer of us participate. It is typical for any election from overseas to report voter turnout on a near-equal basis with election results, but you had to work mighty hard to find references to turnout in the latest round of voting—or rather, non-voting.

3   Let's take Virginia. Turnout in the 1997 governor's race among registered voters was 48 percent—as opposed to 67 percent and 61 percent in the state's last two gubernatorial elections. And that doesn't even count eligible voters who never registered. Turnout among all eligible adult Virginians was an abysmal 34 percent.

4   But Virginians can take heart. Their turnout was better than Broward County, Florida, where a mere 7 percent of registered voters made their way to the polls. Such shockingly low numbers were found in numerous localities.

5   Detroit's mayoral primary turnout was 17 percent of registered voters; in Charlotte's primary, it was 6 percent. General election turnout was under 40 percent of registered voters in Miami and New York City and under 30 percent in Boston and San Francisco. And of course 25 percent of eligible voters typically remain unregistered.

6   The United States now has on average the lowest voter turnout in the world among mature democracies. The long-term implications of our plunging voter turnout surely are as serious as fluctuations in the stock market. But because it is creeping up slowly, like a crippling disease, the crisis of our "political depression" generally goes unrecognized.

7   At what point does a democracy cease to be democratically governed? Bill Clinton was re-elected with the support of fewer than one in four eligible voters. Republicans won control of the House of Representatives with even fewer votes. We maintain the corner posts of representative democracy, but with the active consent of less than half our citizens.

8   It is time for prominent national and state discussions about this political depression. Thomas Jefferson wrote in his twilight years that "Laws and institutions must go hand in hand with the progress of the human mind. As that becomes more developed, more enlightened, as new discoveries are made, new truths disclosed, institutions must advance also, and keep pace with the times."

9   Our political leaders and concerned citizens must be as bold as Jefferson and his contemporaries, and consider changes that will allow voters to see a real connection between their votes and policy. Here are some proposals to consider:

10   •Non-partisan redistricting: One-seat legislative districts give incumbents the opportunity to gerrymander district lines using sophisticated computers and census data. They quite literally choose their constituents before their constituents choose them. This consigns most Americans to "no-choice" legislative races.

11   •Election holidays, weekend voting and mail-in-balloting: Making the practice of voting more convenient will have a beneficial effect on voter turnout.

12   •Unicameral state legislatures: Two houses in a state legislature undercut accountability and increase costs; bicameralism is simply redundant in state government, since both houses represent overlapping geographic areas.

13   •Increased size of legislatures: The U.S. House has remained at 435 representatives since 1910, despite our population nearly tripling. Many state legislatures also are small; California's state senate districts are larger than its congressional districts. Big districts make elections costly and keep representatives distant from constituents.

14   •Instant runoff voting: As more important races are won by a simple plurality—like the Clinton presidency, or the recent New Jersey governor's race—it becomes more important to use this Australian system that insures a majority winner in a single round of voting. It also should replace current two-round runoffs or primaries, thereby maximizing turnout and saving candidates and taxpayers the cost of the second election.

15   •Proportional representation voting systems: Used in nearly all mature democracies, proportional systems mirror a free market economy; voters have the multiplicity of choices they treasure so highly as consumers. A political force winning 51 percent of votes earns a majority, but not all; winning 10 percent wins 10 percent of representation, not nothing. Proportional systems increase voter turnout substantially because voters have more choices and a greater chance to elect their favorite candidates.

16   Debating such rule changes is only the beginning. Pulling us out of our political depression will not be easy, but we must not wait. If President Clinton seeks a place in history, calling for a national campaign to address our political depression would be a lasting legacy.

17   Call it a new deal for democracy. It's time to talk in earnest about that dinosaur standing in the middle of the living room.

EMILY B. COMPTON, STUDENT

Why You Should Vote

1   Look, guys, here's how it works: whenever we don't vote, we are allowing them to take whatever they want from us.

2   I am so sick of hearing twenty-somethings blah-blah-blahing, as if they are political sophisticates, "One vote doesn't matter. The system is corrupt anyway. I'm expressing my disgust by not voting." Gen-Xers perceive that it's all about polling and demographics anyway, and not about doing what is right or best for

the country. Unfortunately, many think that silence is as good as speaking out, for making a statement.

3   The history of our electoral process is one of continual expansion of voting rights, from white landholders to African-Americans to women, thus to all citizens of our country. And, truly, it is daunting to consider oneself only one of 50,000,000 voices. I understand that. It's nothing like raising your hand in class and being heard by twenty of your closest friends.

4   Meanwhile, the vote is a right, subject to no conditions on property ownership or personal morality. The only legal way to restrict voting rights is to convict a citizen of a felony. The illegal ways to restrict voting rights are numerous, however: voting procedures can be made so inconvenient or complicated that only voters of the preferred demographics are able to cast legal ballots.

5   But the youth of America were not disenfranchised in 2000 the way African-Americans and Jewish senior citizens were in Florida. We didn't even show up. We completely failed to say anything at all.

6   It's hard for an entire generation to agree, for sure. I think a lot more of us support environmentalism and gay rights than our parents do. I think we are the only ones with the technical knowledge to protect the Internet from breaking down into the personal fiefdoms of Bill Gates and Jack Warner. I even think it's possible that our generation holds the fate of organized religion in our disenchanted hands.

7   But here's a fact: right now Gen-Xers and Gen-Yers, many of us with outrageous debts and beautiful children and leftover step-parents and pit-hole apartments of our own, are being taxed at 5 percent to pay out Social Security benefits to retirees playing golf in Florida. We know it too, and we are aware that, with our Boomer parents and step-parents retiring, we will, in the near future, be taxed at 10 percent, then 15 percent, in addition to federal income tax, before the Social Security system goes bankrupt.

8   A 1994 poll found 28 percent of Gen-Xers believed they would ever receive Social Security. 46 percent believed UFOs exist.

9   And yes, many retirees worked very hard all their lives and are receiving what they were promised. Moreover, it seems awfully cold-hearted to turn our backs on the Christmas laps and cookie-bakers we remember from when we were this big. But the system cannot last forever. It can't. Even President Bush's whacko scheme of individualized retirement accounts cannot create a social safety net for all of us.

10   Unfortunately for us young'uns, senior citizens vote, and their vote is essential to any party that would like to win an election. So no politician with any sense at all is going to fight the fight to reduce Social Security benefits or raise the retirement age.

11   Not one politician is going to take up our interests until we young people start showing up on Election Day and telling Grandma and a few million of her closest friends that robbing us of our economic futures is not how America will treat her young people.

12   Social Security is just one example of how voters whose demographic are not adequately represented at the polls will LOSE, and will LOSE BIG, until they start showing up. Have you noticed how media accounts of the Social Security budget crisis never point out that today's twenty-somethings are the ones who will be hungry and medication-less when we are sixty-five? Guys, it's because we don't vote!

13   One vote doesn't matter at all. And I've only got one vote, and it's worth just as much as yours, except in certain senatorial races. But your vote and my vote together exactly equal two votes cast by a couple of our respected elders with way more money, influence, and respect than you and I might think we'll ever see. And if you and I and a few million of our closest friends would just show up, then the parties would be able to take on Great-Uncle Mooch, and maybe, in their spare time, even clean up some of the industrial filth that is poisoning our world.

14   If I can talk anyone down from the "I'm too self-aware to vote" pedestal today, perhaps if I can talk you down, then I think that you and I together can change the world. Please vote in 2002.

English Only

Should English be the only official language of the United States of America? These readings examine arguments and implications that constitute the many sides of the issue.

RICHARD RODRIGUEZ

Public and Private Language

This reading is from Rodriguez's book Hunger of Memory. *He has written two other books,* Brown: The Last Discovery of America, *and* Days of Obligation: An Argument with my Mexican Father, *as well as many articles in* Harper's Magazine, U.S. News & World Report, *and the Sunday "Opinion" section of the* Los Angeles Times.

1   I remember to start with that day in Sacramento—a California now nearly thirty years past—when I first entered a classroom, able to understand some fifty stray English words.

2   The third of four children, I had been preceded to a neighborhood Roman Catholic school by an older brother and sister. But neither of them had revealed very much about their classroom experiences. Each afternoon they returned, as they left in the morning, always together, speaking in Spanish as they climbed the five steps of the porch. And their mysterious books, wrapped in shopping-bag paper, remained on the table next to the door, closed firmly behind them.

3   An accident of geography sent me to a school where all my classmates were white, many the children of doctors and lawyers and business executives. All my classmates certainly must have been uneasy on that first day of school—as most children are uneasy—to find themselves apart from their families in the first institution of their lives. But I was astonished.

4   The nun said, in a friendly but oddly impersonal voice, "Boys and girls, this is Richard Rodriguez." (I heard her sound out: *Rich-heard Road-ree-guess.*) It was the first time I had heard anyone name me in English. "Richard," the nun repeated more slowly, writing my name down in her black leather book. Quickly I turned to see my mother's face dissolve in a watery blur behind the pebbled glass door.

FIGURE C2.1

RICHARD RODRIGUEZ

5   Many years later there is something called bilingual education—a scheme proposed in the late 1960s by Hispanic-American social activists, later endorsed by a congressional vote. It is a program that seeks to permit non-English-speaking children, many from lower-class homes, to use their family language as the language of school. (Such is the goal its supporters announce.) I heard them and am forced to say no: It is not possible for a child—any child—ever to use his family's language in school. Not to understand this is to misunderstand the public uses of schooling and to trivialize the nature of intimate life—a family's 'language.'

6   Memory teaches me what I know of these matters; the boy reminds the adult. I was a bilingual child, a certain kind—socially disadvantaged—the son of working-class parents, both Mexican immigrants.

7   In the early years of my boyhood, my parents coped very well in America. My father had steady work. My mother managed at home. They were nobody's victims. Optimism and ambition led them to a house (our home) many blocks from the Mexican south side of town. We lived among *gringos* and only a block from the biggest, whitest houses. It never occurred to my parents that they couldn't live wherever they chose. Nor was the Sacramento of the fifties bent on teaching them a contrary lesson. My mother and father were more annoyed than intimidated by those two or three neighbors who tried initially to make us unwelcome. ("Keep your brats away from my sidewalk!") But despite all they achieved, perhaps because they had so much to achieve, any deep feeling of ease, the confidence of "belonging" in public was withheld from them both. They regarded the people at work, the faces in crowds, as very distant from us. They

were the others, *los gringos*. That term was interchangeable in their speech with another, even more telling, *los americanos*.

8   I grew up in a house where the only regular guests were my relations. For one day, enormous families of relatives would visit and there would be so many people that the noise and the bodies would spill out to the backyard and front porch. Then, for weeks, no one came by. (It was usually a salesman who rang the doorbell.) Our house stood apart. A gaudy yellow in a row of white bungalows. We were the people with the noisy dog. The people who raised pigeons and chickens. We were the foreigners on the block. A few neighbors smiled and waved. We waved back. But no one in the family knew the names of the old couple who lived next door; until I was seven years old, I did not know the names of the kids who lived across the street.

9   In public, my father and mother spoke a hesitant, accented, not always grammatical English. And they would have to strain—their bodies tense—to catch the sense of what was rapidly said by *los gringos*. At home they spoke Spanish. The language of their Mexican past sounded in counterpoint to the English of public society. The words would come quickly, with ease. Conveyed through those sounds was the pleasing, soothing, consoling reminder of being at home.

10   During those years when I was first conscious of hearing, my mother and father addressed me only in Spanish; in Spanish I learned to reply. By contrast, English (*ingles*), rarely heard in the house, was the language I came to associate with *gringos*. I learned my first words of English overhearing my parents speak to strangers. At five years of age, I knew just enough English for my mother to trust me on errands to stores one block away. No more.

11   I was a listening child, careful to hear the very different sounds of Spanish and English. Wide-eyed with hearing, I'd listen to sounds more than words. First, there were English (*gringo*) sounds. So many words were still unknown that when the butcher or the lady at the drugstore said something to me, exotic polysyllabic sounds would bloom in the midst of their sentences. Often, the speech of people in public seemed to me very loud, booming with confidence. The man behind the counter would literally ask, "What can I do for you?" But by being so firm and so clear, the sound of his voice said that he was a *gringo*; he belonged in public society.

12   I would also hear then the high nasal notes of middle-class American speech. The air stirred with sound. Sometimes, even now, when I have been traveling abroad for several weeks, I will hear what I heard as a boy. In hotel lobbies or airports, in Turkey or Brazil, some Americans will pass, and suddenly I will hear it again—the high sound of American voices. For a few seconds I will hear it with pleasure, for it is now the sound of *my* society—a reminder of home. But inevitably—already on the flight headed for home—the sound fades with repetition. I will be unable to hear it anymore.

13   When I was a boy, things were different. The accent of *los gringos* was never pleasing nor was it hard to hear. Crowds at Safeway or at bus stops would be noisy with sound. And I would be forced to edge away from the chirping chatter above me.

14   I was unable to hear my own sounds, but I knew very well that I spoke English poorly. My words could not stretch far enough to form complete thoughts. And the words I did speak I didn't know well enough to make into distinct sounds. (Listeners would usually lower their heads, better to hear what I was trying to say.) But it was one thing for *me* to speak English with difficulty. It was more troubling for me to hear my parents speak in public: their high-whining vowels and guttural consonants; their sentences that got stuck with "ch" and "ah" sounds; the confused syntax; the hesitant rhythm of sounds so different from the way *gringos* spoke. I'd notice, moreover, that my parents' voices were softer than those of *gringos* we'd meet.

15   I am tempted now to say that none of this mattered. In adulthood I am embarrassed by childhood fears. And, in a way, it didn't matter very much that my parents could not speak English with ease. Their linguistic difficulties had no serious consequences. My mother and father made themselves understood at the county hospital clinic and at government offices. And yet, in another way, it mattered very much—it was unsettling to hear my parents struggle with English. Hearing them, I'd grow nervous, my clutching trust in their protection and power weakened.

16   There were many times like the night at a brightly lit gasoline station (a blaring white memory) when I stood uneasily, hearing my father. He was talking to a teenaged attendant. I do not recall what they were saying, but I cannot forget the sounds my father made as he spoke. At one point his words slid together to form one word—sounds as confused as the threads of blue and green oil in the puddle next to my shoes. His voice rushed through what he had left to say. And, toward the end, reached falsetto notes, appealing to his listener's understanding. I looked away to the lights of passing automobiles. I tried not to hear anymore. But I heard only too well the calm, easy tones in the attendant's reply. Shortly afterward, walking toward home with my father, I shivered when he put his hand on my shoulder. The very first chance that I got, I evaded his grasp and ran on ahead into the dark, skipping with feigned boyish exuberance.

17   But then there was Spanish. *Español:* my family's language. *Español:* the language that seemed to me a private language. I'd hear strangers on the radio and in the Mexican Catholic church across town speaking in Spanish, but I couldn't really believe that Spanish was a public language, like English. Spanish speakers, rather, seemed related to me, for I sensed that we shared—through our language—the experience of feeling apart from *los gringos*. It was thus a ghetto Spanish that I heard and I spoke. Like those whose lives are bound by a barrio, I was reminded by Spanish of my separateness from *los otros, los gringos* in power. But more intensely than for most barrio children—because I did not live in a barrio—Spanish seemed to me the language of home. (Most days it was only at home that I'd hear it.) It became the language of joyful return.

18   A family member would say something to me and I would feel myself specially recognized. My parents would say something to me and I would feel embraced by the sounds of their words. Those sounds said: *I am speaking with ease in Spanish. I am addressing you in words I never use with los gringos. I recognize you as someone special, close, like no one outside. You belong with us. In the family.*

19   *(Ricardo.)*

20   At the age of five, six, well past the time when most other children no longer easily notice the difference between sounds uttered at home and words spoken in public, I had a different experience. I lived in a world magically compounded of sounds. I remained a child longer than most; I lingered too long, poised at the edge of language—often frightened by the sounds of *los gringos*, delighted by the sounds of Spanish at home. I shared with my family a language that was startlingly different from that used in the great city around us.

21   For me there were none of the gradations between public and private society so normal to a maturing child. Outside the house was public society; inside the house was private. Just opening or closing the screen door behind me was an important experience. I'd rarely leave home all alone or without reluctance. Walking down the sidewalk, under the canopy of tall trees, I'd warily notice the—suddenly silent—neighborhood kids who stood warily watching me. Nervously, I'd arrive at the grocery store to hear there the sounds of the *gringo*—foreign to me—reminding me that in this world so big, I was a foreigner. But then I'd return. Walking back toward our house, climbing the steps from the sidewalk, when the front door was open in summer, I'd hear voices beyond the screen door talking in Spanish. For a second or two, I'd stay, linger there, listening. Smiling, I'd hear my mother call out, saying in Spanish (words): "Is that you, Richard?" All the while her sounds would assure me*: You are home now; come closer; inside. With us.*

22   "*Sí,*" I'd reply.

23   Once more inside the house I would resume (assume) my place in the family. The sounds would dim, grow harder to hear. Once more at home, I would grow less aware of that fact. It required, however, no more than the blurt of the doorbell to alert me to listen to sounds all over again. The house would turn instantly still while my mother went to the door. I'd hear her hard English sounds. I'd wait to hear her voice return to soft-sounding Spanish, which assured me, as surely as did the clicking tongue of the lock on the door, that the stranger was gone.

24   Plainly, it is not healthy to hear such sounds so often. It is not healthy to distinguish public words from private sounds so easily. I remained cloistered by sounds, timid and shy in public, too dependent on voices at home. And yet it needs to be emphasized: I was an extremely happy child at home. I remember many nights when my father would come back from work, and I'd hear him call out to my mother in Spanish, sounding relieved. In Spanish, he'd sound light and free notes he never could manage in English. Some nights I'd jump up just at hearing his voice. With *mis hermanos* I would come running into the room where he was with my mother. Our laughing (so deep was the pleasure!) became screaming. Like others who know the pain of public alienation, we transformed the knowledge of our public separateness and made it consoling—the reminder of intimacy. *We are speaking now the way we never speak out in public. We are alone—together,* voices sounded, surrounded to tell me. Some nights, no one seemed willing to loosen the hold sounds had on us. At dinner, we invented new words. (Ours sounded Spanish, but made sense only to us.) We pieced together new words by taking, say, an English verb and giving it Spanish endings. My mother's instructions at bedtime would be lacquered with mock-urgent tones. Or a word

like *si* would become, in several notes, able to convey added measures of feeling. Tongues explored the edges of words, especially the fat vowels. And we happily sounded that military drum roll, the twirling roar of the Spanish *r*. Family language: my family's sounds. The voices of my parents and sisters and brother. Their voices insisting: *You belong here. We are family members. Related. Special to one another. Listen!* Voices singing and sighing, rising, straining, then surging, teeming with pleasure that burst syllables into fragments of laughter. At times it seemed there was steady quiet only when, from another room, the rustling whispers of my parents faded and I moved closer to sleep.

25   Supporters of bilingual education today imply that students like me miss a great deal by not being taught in their family's language. What they seem not to recognize is that, as a socially disadvantaged child, I considered Spanish to be a private language. What I needed to learn in school was that I had the right— and the obligation—to speak the public language of *los gringos*. The odd truth is that my first-grade classmates could have become bilingual, in the conventional sense of that word, more easily than I. Had they been taught (as upper-middle-class children are often taught early) a second language like Spanish or French, they could have regarded it simply as that: another public language. In my case such bilingualism could not have been so quickly achieved. What I did not believe was that I could speak a single public language.

26   Without question, it would have pleased me to hear my teachers address me in Spanish when I entered the classroom. I would have felt much less afraid. I would have trusted them and responded with ease. But I would have delayed— for how long postponed?—having to learn the language of public society. I would have evaded—and how long could I have afforded to delay?—learning the great lesson of school, that I had a public identity.

27   Fortunately my teachers were unsentimental about their responsibility. What they understood was that I needed to speak a public language. So their voices would search me out, asking me questions. Each time I'd hear them, I'd look up in surprise to see a nun's face frowning at me. I'd mumble, not really meaning to answer. The nun would persist, "Richard, stand up. Don't look at the floor. Speak up. Speak to the entire class, not just to me!" But I couldn't believe that the English language was mine to use. (In part, I did not want to believe it.) I continued to mumble. I resisted the teacher's demands. (Did I somehow suspect that once I learned the public language my pleasing family life would be changed?) Silent, waiting for the bell to sound, I remained dazed, diffident, afraid.

28   Because I wrongly imagined that English was intrinsically a public language and Spanish an intrinsically private one, I easily noted the difference between classroom language and the language of home. At school, words were directed to a general audience of listeners. ("Boys and girls.") Words were meaningfully ordered. And the point was not self-expression alone but to make oneself understood by many others. The teacher quizzed: "Boys and girls, why do we use that word in this sentence? Could we think of a better word to use there? Would the sentence change its meaning if the words were differently arranged? And wasn't there a better way of saying much the same thing?" (I couldn't say. I wouldn't try to say.)

29   Three months. Five. Half a year passed. Unsmiling, ever watchful, my teachers noted my silence. They began to connect my behavior with the difficult progress my older sister and brother were making. Until one Saturday morning three nuns arrived at the house to talk to our parents. Stiffly, they sat on the blue living room sofa. From the doorway of another room, spying the visitors, I noted the incongruity—the clash of two worlds, the faces and the voices of school intruding upon the familiar setting of home. I overheard one voice gently wondering, "Do your children speak only Spanish at home, Mrs. Rodriguez?" While another voice added, "That Richard especially seems so timid and shy."

30   *That Rich-heard!*

31   With great tact the visitors continued, "Is it possible for you and your husband to encourage your children to practice their English when they are home?" Of course, my parents complied. What would they not do for their children's well-being? And how could they have questioned the Church's authority which those women represented? In an instant, they agreed to give up the language (the sounds) that had revealed and accentuated our family's closeness. The moment after the visitors left, the change was observed, "*Ahora*, speak to *us en inglés*," my father and mother united to tell us.

32   At first, it seemed a kind of game. After dinner each night, the family gathered to practice "our" English. (It was still then *inglés*, a language foreign to us, so we felt drawn as strangers to it.) Laughing, we would try to define words we could not pronounce. We played with strange English sounds, often overanglicizing our pronunciations. And we filled the smiling gaps of our sentences with familiar Spanish sounds. But that was cheating, somebody shouted. Everyone laughed. In school, meanwhile, like my brother and sister, I was required to attend a daily tutoring session. I needed a full year of special attention. I also needed my teachers to keep my attention from straying in class by calling out, *Rich-heard*—their English voices slowly prying loose my ties to my other name, its three notes, *Ri-car-do*. Most of all I needed to hear my mother and father speak to me in a moment of seriousness in broken—suddenly heartbreaking—English. The scene was inevitable: One Saturday morning I entered the kitchen where my parents were talking in Spanish. I did not realize that they were talking in Spanish however until, at the moment they saw me, I heard their voices change to speak English. Those *gringo* sounds they uttered startled me. Pushed me away. In that moment of trivial misunderstanding and profound insight, I felt my throat twisted by unsounded grief. I turned quickly and left the room. But I had no place to escape to with Spanish. (The spell was broken.) My brother and sisters were speaking English in another part of the house.

33   Again and again in the days following, increasingly angry, I was obliged to hear my mother and father: "Speak to us *en inglés*." (*Speak.*) Only then did I determine to learn classroom English. Weeks after, it happened: One day in school I raised my hand to volunteer an answer. I spoke out in a loud voice. And I did not think it remarkable when the entire class understood. That day, I moved very far from the disadvantaged child I had been only days earlier. The belief, the calming assurance that I belonged in public, had at last taken hold.

34   Shortly after, I stopped hearing the high and low sounds of *los gringos*. A more and more confident speaker of English, I didn't trouble to listen to *how* strangers sounded, speaking to me. And there simply were too many English-speaking people in my day for me to hear American accents anymore. Conversations quickened. Listening to persons who sounded eccentrically pitched voices, I usually noted their sounds for an initial few seconds before I concentrated on *what* they were saying. Conversations became content-full. Transparent. Hearing someone's *tone* of voice—angry or questioning or sarcastic or happy or sad—I didn't distinguish it from the words it expressed. Sound and word were thus tightly wedded. At the end of a day, I was often bemused, always relieved to realize how "silent," though crowded with words, my day in public had been. (This public silence measured and quickened the change in my life.)

35   At last, seven years old, I came to believe what had been technically true since my birth: I was an American citizen.

36   But the special feeling of closeness at home was diminished by then. Gone was the desperate, urgent, intense feeling of being at home; rare was the experience of feeling myself individualized by family intimates. We remained a loving family, but one greatly changed. No longer so close; no longer bound tight by the pleasing and troubling knowledge of our public separateness. Neither my older brother nor sister rushed home after school anymore. Nor did I. When I arrived home there would often be neighborhood kids in the house. Or the house would be empty of sounds.

37   The silence at home, however, was finally more than a literal silence. Fewer words passed between parent and child, but more profound was the silence that resulted from my inattention to sounds. At about the time I no longer bothered to listen with care to the sounds of English in public, I grew careless about listening to the sounds family members made when they spoke. Most of the time I heard someone speaking at home and didn't distinguish his sounds from the words people uttered in public. I didn't even pay much attention to my parents' accented and ungrammatical speech. At least not at home. Only when I was with them in public would I grow alert to their accents. Though, even then, their sounds caused me less and less concern. For I was increasingly confident of my own public identity.

38   I would have been happier about my public success had I not sometimes recalled what it had been like earlier, when my family had conveyed its intimacy through a set of conveniently private sounds. Sometimes in public, hearing a stranger, I'd hark back to my past. A Mexican farmworker approached me downtown to ask directions to somewhere. "¿*Hijito*...?" he said. And his voice summoned deep longing. Another time, standing beside my mother in the visiting room of a Carmelite convent, before the dense screen which rendered the nuns shadowy figures, I heard several Spanish-speaking nuns—their busy, singsong overlapping voices—assure us that yes, yes, we were remembered, all our family was remembered in their prayers. (Their voices echoed faraway family sounds.) Another day, a dark-faced old woman—her hand light on my shoulder—steadied herself against me as she boarded a bus. She murmured something I couldn't quite comprehend. Her Spanish voice came near, like the face of a

never-before-seen relative in the instant before I was kissed. Her voice, like so many of the Spanish voices I'd heard in public, recalled the golden age of my youth. Hearing Spanish then, I continued to be a careful, if sad, listener to sounds. Hearing a Spanish-speaking family walking behind me, I turned to look. I smiled for an instant, before my glance found the Hispanic-looking faces of strangers in the crowd going by.

39   Today I hear bilingual educators say that children lose a degree of "individuality" by becoming assimilated into public society. (Bilingual schooling was popularized in the seventies, that decade when middle-class ethnics began to resist the process of assimilation—the American melting pot.) But the bilingualists simplistically scorn the value and necessity of assimilation. They do not seem to realize that there are two ways a person is individualized. So they do not realize that while one suffers a diminished sense of *private* individuality by becoming assimilated into public society, such assimilation makes possible the achievement of *public* individuality.

40   The bilingualists insist that a student should be reminded of his difference from others in mass society, his heritage. But they equate mere separateness with individuality. The fact is that only in private—with intimates—is separateness from the crowd a prerequisite for individuality. (An intimate draws me apart, tells me that I am unique, unlike all others.) In public, by contrast, full individuality is achieved, paradoxically, by those who are able to consider themselves members of the crowd. Thus it happened for me: Only when I was able to think of myself as an American, no longer an alien in *gringo* society, could I seek the rights and opportunities necessary for full public individuality. The social and political advantages I enjoy as a man result from the day that I came to believe that my name, indeed, is *Rich-heard Road-ree-guess*. It is true that my public society today is often impersonal. (My public society is usually mass society.) Yet despite the anonymity of the crowd and despite the fact that the individuality I achieve in public is often tenuous—because it depends on my being one in a crowd—I celebrate the day I acquired my new name. Those middle-class ethnics who scorn assimilation seem to me filled with decadent self-pity, obsessed by the burden of public life. Dangerously, they romanticize public separateness and they trivialize the dilemma of the socially disadvantaged.

SENATOR S. I. HAYAKAWA

The Case for Official English

S. I. Hayakawa was a U.S. senator from 1977 to 1983, following a distinguished career as a professor of semantics. He is the author of the widely used textbook Language in Thought and Action. *Hayakawa sponsored the original English Language Amendment in 1981 and then founded the organization U.S. English to promote it.*

1   What is it that has made a society out of the hodgepodge of nationalities, races, and colors represented in the immigrant hordes that people our nation? It is language, of course, that has made communication among all these elements possible. It is with a common language that we have dissolved distrust and fear. It is with language that we have drawn up the understandings and agreements and social contracts that make a society possible.

2   But while language is a necessary cause of our oneness as a society, it is not a sufficient cause. A foreigner cannot, by speaking faultless English, become an Englishman. Paul Theroux, a contemporary novelist and travel writer, has commented on this fact: "Foreigners are always aliens in England. No one becomes English. It's a very tribal society....No one becomes Japanese....No one becomes Nigerian. But Nigerians, Japanese, and English become Americans."[1]

3   One need not speak faultless American English to become an American. Indeed, one may continue to speak English with an appalling foreign accent. This is true of some of my friends, but they are seen as fully American because of the warmth and enthusiasm with which they enter into the life of the communities in which they live.

4   Even as the American nation was coming into being, it had become obvious that the American experience was creating a new kind of human being. Among the first to comment on this fact was Thomas Paine, who wrote:

> If there is a country in the world where concord, according to common calculation, would be least expected, it is America. Made up, as it is, of people from different nations...speaking different languages, and more different in their modes of worship, it would appear that the union of such a people was impracticable. But by the simple operation of constructing government on the principles of society and the rights of man, every difficulty retires, and the parts are brought into cordial unison.[2]

5   Hector St. John de Crevecoeur, in *Letters from an American Farmer*, wrote in 1782:

> What then is the American, this new man?...I would point out to you a family whose grandfather was an Englishman, whose wife was Dutch, whose son married a French woman, and whose present four sons have four wives of different nations. He is an American who, leaving behind him all his ancient prejudices and manners, receives new ones from the new mode of life he has embraced....The Americans were once scattered all over Europe. Here they are incorporated into one of the finest systems of population which has ever appeared....The American ought therefore to love his country much better than that wherein he or his forebears were born. Here the rewards of his industry follow with equal steps in the progress of his labor.[3]

6   Herman Melville, in *Redburn*, published in 1849, wrote: "You cannot spill a drop of American blood without spilling the blood of the whole world....We are not a narrow tribe of men. No: our blood is the flood of the Amazon, made

up of a thousand noble currents all pouring into one. We are not a nation, so much as a world."[4]

7   Despite the exclusion of the Chinese after 1882, the idea of immigration as "a thousand noble currents all pouring into one" continued to haunt the American imagination: Israel Zangwill's play *The Melting Pot* opened in New York in 1908 to enthusiastic popular acclaim, and its title, as Nathan Glazer and Daniel P. Moynihan remark, "was seized upon as a concise evocation of a profoundly significant American fact." In the play David Quixano, the Russian Jewish immigrant—"a pogrom orphan"—has escaped to New York, and he exclaims:

> Here you stand, good folk, think I, when I see them at Ellis Island...in your fifty groups with your fifty languages and histories, and your fifty blood hatreds and rivalries, but you won't be long like that, brothers, for these are the fires of God you've come to....A fig for your feuds and vendettas! German and Frenchman, Irishman and Englishman, Jews and Russians—into the Crucible with you all! God is making the American.[5]

8   In the past several years, strong resistance to the "melting pot" idea has arisen, especially for those who claim to speak for the Hispanic peoples. Instead of a melting pot, they say, the national ideal should be a "salad bowl," in which different elements are thrown together but not "melted," so that the original ingredients retain their distinctive character. In addition to the increasing size of the Spanish speaking population in our nation, two legislative actions have released this outburst of effort on behalf of the Spanish language and Hispanic culture.

9   First, there was the so-called "bilingual ballot" mandated in 1975 in an amendment to the Voting Rights Act, which required foreign language ballots when voters of selected language groups reached 5 percent or more in any voting district. The groups chosen to be so favored were Asian-Americans (Chinese, Filipino, Japanese, Korean), American Indians, Alaskan Natives, and "peoples of Spanish heritage," that is, Puerto Ricans, Cubans, and Mexican Americans.

10   Sensitive as Americans have been to racism, especially since the days of the civil rights movement, no one seems to have noticed the profound racism expressed in the amendment that created the bilingual ballot. Brown people, like Mexicans and Puerto Ricans, red people, like American Indians, and yellow people, like the Japanese and Chinese, are assumed not to be smart enough to learn English. No provision is made, however, for non-English-speaking French-Canadians in Maine or Vermont, or for the Hebrew-speaking Hasidic Jews in Brooklyn, who are white and are presumed to be able to learn English without difficulty. Voters in San Francisco encountered ballots in Spanish and Chinese for the first time in the elections of 1980, much to their surprise, since authorizing legislation had been passed by Congress with almost no debate, no roll-call vote, and no public discussion. Naturalized Americans, who had taken the trouble to learn English to become citizens, were especially angry and remain so.

11   Furthermore, there was the *Lau* decision of the U.S. Supreme Court, in response to a suit brought by a Chinese of San Francisco who complained that

his children were not being taught English adequately in the public schools they were attending. Justice William O. Douglas, delivering the opinion of the court, wrote: "No specific remedy is urged upon us. Teaching English to the students of Chinese ancestry who do not speak the language is one choice. Giving instructions to this group in Chinese is another. There may be others. Petitioner asks only that the Board of Education be directed to apply its expertise to the problem and rectify the situation." Justice Douglas's decision, concurred in by the entire court, granted the *Lau* petition. Because the *Lau* decision did not specify the method by which English was to be taught, it turned out to be a go-ahead for amazing educational developments, not so much for the Chinese as for Hispanics, who appropriated the decision and took it to apply especially to themselves.

12 The new U.S. Department of Education, established during the Carter administration, was eager to make its presence known by expanding its bureaucracy and its influence. The department quickly announced a vast program with federal funding for bilingual education, which led to the hiring of Spanish-speaking teachers by the thousands. The department furthermore issued what were known as the Lau Regulations, which required under the threat of withdrawal of federal funds that (1) non-English-speaking pupils be taught English, and that (2) academic subjects be taught in the pupils' own language. The contradiction between these two regulations seems not to have occurred to the educational theorists in the Department of Education. Nor does it seem to trouble, to this day, the huge membership of the National Association for Bilingual Education.

13 Bilingual education rapidly became a growth industry, requiring more and more teachers. Complaints began to arise from citizens that "bilingual education" was not bilingual at all, since many Spanish-speaking teachers hired for the program were found not to be able to speak English. Despite the ministrations of the Department of Education, or perhaps because of them, Hispanic students to a shocking degree drop out of school, educated neither in Hispanic nor in American language and culture. "Hispanics are the least educated minority in America, according to a report by the American Council on Education," writes Earl Byrd. "The report says 50 percent of all Hispanic youths in America drop out of high school, and only 7 percent finish college. Twelve percent of black youths and 23 percent of whites finish college. Eighteen percent of all Hispanics in America who are 25 or older are classified as functional illiterates, compared to 10 percent for blacks and 3 percent for whites."[6]

14 I welcome the Hispanic—and as a Californian, I welcome especially the Mexican—influence on our culture. My wife was wise enough to insist that both our son and daughter learn Spanish as children and to keep reading Spanish as they were growing up. Consequently, my son, a newspaperman, was able to work for six months as an exchange writer for a newspaper in Costa Rica, while a Costa Rican reporter took my son's place in Oregon. My daughter, a graduate of the University of California at Santa Cruz, speaks Spanish, French, and after a year in Monterey Language School, Japanese.

15 The ethnic chauvinism of the present Hispanic leadership is an unhealthy trend in present-day America. It threatens a division perhaps more ominous in the long run than the division between blacks and whites. Blacks and whites

have problems enough with each other, to be sure, but they quarrel with each other in one language. Even Malcolm X, in his fiery denunciations of the racial situation in America, wrote excellent and eloquent English. But the present politically ambitious "Hispanic Caucus" looks forward to a destiny for Spanish-speaking Americans separate from that of Anglo-, Italian-, Polish-, Greek-, Lebanese-, Chinese-, and Afro-Americans, and all the rest of us who rejoice in our ethnic diversity, which gives us our richness as a culture, and the English language, which keeps us in communication with each other to create a unique and vibrant culture.

16   The advocates of Spanish language and Hispanic culture are not at all unhappy about the fact that "bilingual education," originally instituted as the best way to teach English, often results in no English being taught at all. Nor does Hispanic leadership seem to be alarmed that large populations of Mexican Americans, Cubans, and Puerto Ricans do not speak English and have no intention of learning. Hispanic spokesmen rejoice when still another concession is made to the Spanish-speaking public, such as the Spanish-language Yellow Pages telephone directory now available in Los Angeles.

17   "Let's face it. We're not going to be a totally English-speaking country any more," says Aurora Helton of the governor of Oklahoma's Hispanic Advisory Committee. "Spanish should be included in commercials shown throughout America. Every American child ought to be taught both English and Spanish," says Mario Obledo, president of the League of United Latin American Citizens, which was founded more than a half-century ago to help Hispanics learn English and enter the American mainstream. "Citizenship is what makes us all American. Nowhere does the Constitution say that English is our language," says Maurice Ferre, mayor of Miami, Florida.

18   "Nowhere does the Constitution say that English is our language." It was to correct this omission that I introduced in April 1981 a constitutional amendment which read as follows: "The English language shall be the official language of the United States." Although there were ten co-sponsors to this resolution, and some speeches were given on the Senate floor, it died without being acted upon in the 97th Congress.

19   But the movement to make English the official language of the nation is clearly gaining momentum. It is likely to suffer an occasional setback in state legislatures because of the doctrinaire liberals' assumption that every demand made by an ethnic minority must be yielded to. But whenever the question of English as the official language has been submitted to a popular referendum or ballot initiative, it has won by a majority of 70 percent or better.

20   It is not without significance that pressure against English language legislation does not come from any immigrant group other than the Hispanic: not from the Chinese or Koreans or Filipinos or Vietnamese; nor from immigrant Iranians, Turks, Greeks, East Indians, Ghanaians, Ethiopians, Italians, or Swedes. The only people who have any quarrel with the English language are the Hispanics—at least the Hispanic politicians and "bilingual" teachers and lobbying organizations. One wonders about the Hispanic rank and file. Are they all in

agreement with their leadership? And what does it profit the Hispanic leadership if it gains power and fame, while 50 percent of the boys and girls of their communities, speaking little or no English, cannot make it through high school?

21   For the first time in our history, our nation is faced with the possibility of the kind of linguistic division that has torn apart Canada in recent years; that has been a major feature of the unhappy history of Belgium, split into speakers of French and Flemish; that is at this very moment a bloody division between the Sinhalese and Tamil populations of Sri Lanka. None of these divisions is simply a quarrel about language. But in each case political differences become hardened and made immeasurably more difficult to resolve when they are accompanied by differences of language—and therefore conflicts of ethnic pride.

22   The aggressive movement on the part of Hispanics to reject assimilation and to seek to maintain—and give official status to—a foreign language within our borders is an unhealthy development. This foreign language and culture are to be maintained not through private endeavors such as those of the Alliance Française, which tries to preserve French language and culture, but by federal and state legislation and funding. The energetic lobbying of the National Association for Bilingual Education and the Congressional Hispanic Caucus has led to sizable allocations for bilingual education in the Department of Education: $142 million in fiscal 1985, of which the lion's share goes to Hispanic programs. The purpose of this allocation at the federal level is to prepare administrators and teachers for bilingual education at the state level—which means additional large sums of money allocated for this purpose by state governments. In brief, the basic directive of the *Lau* decision has been, for all intents and purposes, diverted from its original purpose of teaching English.

23   One official language and one only, so that we can unite as a nation. This is what President Theodore Roosevelt also perceived when he said: "We have room for but one language here, and that is the English language, for we intend to see that the crucible turns our people out as Americans, of American nationality, and not as dwellers in a polyglot boarding house." Let me quote in conclusion a remark from the distinguished American novelist, Saul Bellow, when he agreed to serve on the advisory board of our national organization, U.S. English: "Melting pot, yes. Tower of Babel, no!"[7]

Notes

1. Interviewed by James T. Yenchel, *Washington Times*, Dec. 30, 1984.
2. Quoted in J. A. Parker and Allan C. Brownfield, "The Jackson Campaign and the Myth of a Black-Jewish Split," *Lincoln Review* (Summer 1984): 21–22.
3. Ibid.
4. Ibid.
5. Quoted in Nathan Glazer and Daniel P. Moynihan, *Beyond the Melting Pot* (Cambridge, Mass.: M.I.T. Press, 1963), p. 289.
6. *Washington Times*, July 3, 1984.

7. [This essay appeared in an edited collection called *Legislating Language* by James Crawford. Crawford added the following note for historical context and clarification.] Crawford's note: Through his literary agent, Saul Bellow has denied any involvement with U.S. English. But the organization, claiming to "have a letter on file" from the author, has continued to use his name in its fundraising; William Trombley, "Norman Cousins Drops His Support of Prop. 63," *Los Angeles Times*, Oct. 16, 1986, Pt. 1, p. 3.

SUSAN HEADDEN, LINDA RODRIGUEZ BERNFIELD, SALLY DENEEN, MISSY DANIEL, MONIKA GUTTMAN, BARBARA BURGOWER HORDERN, SCOTT MINERBROOK, DEBRA A. SCHWARTZ, AND JILL JORDAN SIEDER

One Nation, One Language? Only English Spoken Here

Would making English the nation's official language unite the country or divide it?

1   For a Sherman Oaks, Calif., election worker, the last straw was hanging campaign posters in six languages and six alphabets. For a taxpayer in University Park, Texas, it was a requirement that all employees of the local public utility speak Spanish. For a retired schoolteacher from Mount Morris, N.Y., it was taking her elderly and anxious mother to a Pakistani doctor and understanding only a fraction of what he said.

2   As immigration, both legal and illegal, brings a new flood of foreign speech into the United States, a campaign to make English the nation's official language is gathering strength. According to a new *U.S. News* poll, 73 percent of Amer-

FIGURE C2.2

Silent Language of the Soul/El Lenguaje Mudo del Alma, © 1990 Susan Kelk Cervantes and Juana Alicia. On Cesar Chavez Elementary School, at Shotwell between 22nd and 23rd Streets.

icans think English should be the official language of government. House Speaker Newt Gingrich, Senate Majority Leader Bob Dole and more than a third of the members of Congress support proposed federal legislation that would make English America's official tongue; twenty-two states and a number of municipalities already have English-only laws on the books.

3   Like flag burning and the Pledge of Allegiance, the issue is largely symbolic. Without ever being declared official, American English has survived—and enriched itself from—four centuries of immigration. It is not much easier for today's Guatemalan immigrant to get a good education and a good job without learning English than it was for his Italian, Polish or Chinese predecessors. And at best, eliminating bilingual education might save about a dollar per student per day. But many Americans are feeling threatened by a triple whammy of growing economic uncertainty, some of it caused by foreign competition; rising immigration, much of it illegal; and political pressure to cater to the needs of immigrants rather than letting them sink or swim. "Elevating English as an icon," says author and bilingual expert James Crawford, "has appeal for the insecure and the resentful. It provides a clear answer to the question: Who belongs?"

Nation of Strangers

4   There is no question that America is undergoing another of its periodic diversity booms. According to the Census Bureau, in 1994 8.7 percent of Americans were born in other countries, the highest percentage since before World War II. More tellingly, at least 31.8 million people in the United States speak a language other than English at home. Of the children returning to urban public schools this fall, a whopping one third speak a foreign language first. "It blows your mind," says Dade County, Fla., administrator Mercedes Toural, who counts 5,190 new students speaking no fewer than 56 different tongues.

5   English-only advocates, whose ranks include recent immigrants and social liberals, believe that accommodating the more than 300 languages spoken in the United States undercuts incentives to learning English and, by association, to becoming an American. Massachusetts offers driver's tests in 24 foreign languages, including Albanian, Finnish, Farsi, Turkish and Czech. Federal voting rights laws provide for ballots in multiple translations. Internal Revenue Service forms are printed in Spanish. And in Westminster, Calif., members of Troop 2194 of the Boy Scouts of America can earn their merit badges in Vietnamese. "It's completely insane," says Mauro Mujica, the chairman of the lobbying group U.S. English and himself an immigrant from Chile. "We are not doing anybody any favors."

Pulling the Plug

6   The proposed official-English laws range from the barely noticeable to the almost xenophobic. A bill introduced by Missouri Republican Rep. Bill Emerson would mandate English for government use but provide exceptions for

health, safety and civil and criminal justice. Although it is the most viable of the bunch, it would change the status quo so little that it begs the question of why it is needed at all. The most extreme official-English measures would pull the plug on what their sponsors consider linguistic welfare, ending bilingual education and bilingual ballots.

7   Advocates of official-English proposals deny that their measures are draconian. Says U.S. English's Mujica: "We are simply saying that official documents should be in English and money saved on translations could go to help the people learn English. We're saying you could still take a driver's test in another language, but we suggest it be temporary till you learn English."

8   U.S. English, which reports 600,000 contributors, was founded by the late U.S. Sen. S. I. Hayakawa, a Japanese-American linguistics professor, and boasts advisory board members such as Saul Bellow and Alistair Cooke. The group was tarred eight years ago when its founder, John Tanton, wrote a memo suggesting that Hispanics have "greater reproductive powers" than Anglos; two directors quit, Tanton was forced out and the group has been rebuilding its reputation ever since. Its competitor, English First, whose founder, Larry Pratt, also started Gun Owners of America, is more hard-line.

9   Defenders of bilingual education, multilingual ballots and other government services ask whether legal immigrants will vote if there are no bilingual ballots. If foreign speakers can't read the street signs, will they be allowed to drive? Such thoughts bring Juanita Morales, a Houston college student, to tears. "This just sets up another barrier for people," she says. "My parents don't know English, and I can hardly speak Spanish anymore and that's painful to me."

10   Go it alone, the hard-liners reply, the way our grandfathers did. But these advocates don't mention that there is little, if any, evidence that earlier German or Italian immigrants mastered English any faster than the current crop of Asians, Russians and Central Americans. And it's hard to argue that today's newcomers aren't trying. San Francisco City College teaches English to 20,000 adults every semester, and the waiting list is huge. In De Kalb County, Ga., 7,000 adults are studying English; in Brighton Beach, N.Y., 2,000 wait for a chance to learn it.

11   The economic incentives for learning English seem as clear as ever. Yes, you can earn a good living in an ethnic enclave of Chicago speaking nothing but Polish. But you won't go far. "Mandating English," says Ron Pearlman of Chicago, "is like mandating that the sun is going to come up every day. It just seems to me that it's going to happen."

12   What worries many Americans are efforts to put other languages on a par with English, which often come across as assaults on American or Western culture. Americans may relish an evening at a Thai restaurant or an afternoon at a Greek festival, but many are less comfortable when their children are celebrating Cinco de Mayo, Kwanzaa and Chinese New Year along with Christmas in the public schools. In Arlington, Va., a classically trained orchestra teacher quit the public school system rather than cave in to demands to teach salsa music.

13   But diversity carries the day. The U.S. Department of Education policy is not simply to promote learning of English but also to maintain immigrants' native tongues. And supporters of that policy make a good case for it. "People

ask me if I'm embarrassed I speak Spanish," says Martha Quintanilla Hollowell, a Dallas County, Texas, district attorney. "I tell them I'd be more embarrassed if I spoke only one language."

Language Skills

14   That may be what's most disturbing about the English-only sentiment: In a global economy, it's the monolingual English speakers who are falling behind. Along with computer skills, a neat appearance and a work ethic, Americans more and more are finding that a second language is useful in getting a good job. African-Americans in Dade County, now more than half Hispanic, routinely lose tourism positions to bilingual Cubans. Schoolteachers cry foul because bilingual teachers earn more money while monolingual teachers are laid off. "There is no way I could get a job in the Los Angeles public schools today," says Lucy Fortney, an elementary school teacher for 30 years.

15   The proliferation of state and local English-only laws has led to a flurry of language-discrimination lawsuits and a record number of complaints with the U.S. Equal Employment Opportunity Commission. Ed Chen, a lawyer with the San Francisco office of the American Civil Liberties Union, says clients have been denied credit and insurance because they don't speak English. But courts increasingly have endorsed laws that call for exclusive use of English on the job. Officials at New York's Bellevue Hospital, where the vast majority of nurses are Filipino, say an English-only law was necessary because nurses spoke Tagalog among themselves.

16   Other employers have wielded English-only laws as a license to discriminate, giving rise to fears that a national law would encourage more of the same. A judge in Amarillo, Texas, claimed a mother in a custody case was committing "child abuse" by speaking Spanish to her child at home. Another Texas judge denied probation to a drunk driver because he couldn't benefit from the all-English Alcoholics Anonymous program. In Monterey Park, Calif., a citizens' group tried to ban Chinese signs on businesses that served an almost all-Asian clientele. In Dade County, a since-repealed English-only law was so strict that it forbade using public funds to pay for court translations and bilingual signs to warn metrorail riders against electrocution.

17   Though it is not intended as such, the English-first movement is a reminder of a history of prejudice toward speakers of foreign tongues. Many American Indians were prohibited from speaking their own languages. The Louisiana Legislature banned the use of Cajun French in public schools in 1912, but instead of abandoning their culture, many Cajuns dropped out of school and never learned English. French was finally allowed back in the schools in the 1960s. As recently as 1971, it was illegal to speak Spanish in a public school building in Texas, and until 1923 it was against the law to teach foreign languages to elementary school pupils in Nebraska. At Ellis Island, psychologists tested thousands of non-English-speaking immigrants exclusively in English and pronounced them retarded.

18   Champions of diversity say it's high time Americans faced the demographic facts. In Miami, with leading trade partners Colombia and Venezuela, businesses

would be foolish to restrict themselves to English. If emergency services suffer because of a shortage of foreign-speaking 911 operators, it is downright dangerous not to hire more. As for embattled teachers, Rick Lopez of the National Association of Bilingual Education says: "Why should we expect students to learn a new language if teachers can't do the same? We have to change the product to fit the market. The market wants a Toyota and we're still building Edsels."

19   Many Americans still value the melting pot: General Mills's new Betty Crocker is a digitized, multiethnic composite. But Skokie, Ill., educator Charlene Cobb, for one, prefers a colorful mosaic. "You don't have to change yourself," she says, "to make a whole thing that's very beautiful." The question is whether the diverse parts of America still make up a whole.

ROBERT D. KING

Should English Be the Law?

Language is tearing apart countries around the world, and the proponents of "Official English" may be ready to add America to the list.

1   We have known race riots, draft riots, labor violence, secession, anti-war protests, and a whiskey rebellion, but one kind of trouble we've never had: a language riot. Language riot? It sounds like a joke. The very idea of language as a political force—as something that might threaten to split a country wide apart—is alien to our way of thinking and to our cultural traditions.

2   This may be changing. On August 1 of last year the U.S. House of Representatives approved a bill that would make English the official language of the United States. The vote was 259 to 169, with 223 Republicans and thirty-six Democrats voting in favor and eight Republicans, 160 Democrats, and one independent voting against. The debate was intense, acrid, and partisan. On March 25 of last year the Supreme Court agreed to review a case involving an Arizona law that would require public employees to conduct government business only in English. Arizona is one of several states that have passed "Official English" or "English Only" laws. The appeal to the Supreme Court followed a 6-to-5 ruling, in October of 1995, by a federal appeals court striking down the Arizona law. These events suggest how divisive a public issue language could become in America—even if it has until now scarcely been taken seriously.

3   Traditionally, the American way has been to make English the national language—but to do so quietly, locally, without fuss. The Constitution is silent on language: the Founding Fathers had no need to legislate that English be the official language of the country. It has always been taken for granted that English is the national language, and that one must learn English in order to make it in America.

4   To say that language has never been a major force in American history or politics, however, is not to say that politicians have always resisted linguistic jin-

goism. In 1753 Benjamin Franklin voiced his concern that German immigrants were not learning English: "Those [Germans] who come hither are generally the most ignorant Stupid Sort of their own Nation....they will soon so out number us, that all the advantages we have will not, in My Opinion, be able to preserve our language, and even our government will become precarious." Theodore Roosevelt articulated the unspoken American linguistic-melting-pot theory when he boomed, "We have room for but one language here, and that is the English language, for we intend to see that the crucible turns our people out as Americans, of American nationality, and not as dwellers in a polyglot boarding house." And: "We must have but one flag. We must also have but one language. That must be the language of the Declaration of Independence, of Washington's Farewell address, of Lincoln's Gettysburg speech and second inaugural."

Official English

5   Roosevelt's linguistic tub-thumping long typified the tradition of American politics. That tradition began to change in the wake of the anything-goes attitudes and the celebration of cultural differences arising in the 1960s. A 1975 amendment to the Voting Rights Act of 1965 mandated the "bilingual ballot" under certain circumstances, notably when the voters of selected language groups reached five percent or more in a voting district. Bilingual education became a byword of educational thinking during the 1960s. By the 1970s linguists had demonstrated convincingly—at least to other academics—that black English (today called African-American vernacular English or Ebonics) was not "bad" English but a different kind of authentic English with its own rules. Predictably, there have been scattered demands that black English be included in bilingual-education programs.

6   It was against this background that the movement to make English the official language of the country arose. In 1981 Senator S.I. Hayakawa, long a leading critic of bilingual education and bilingual ballots, introduced in the U.S. Senate a constitutional amendment that not only would have made English the official language but would have prohibited federal and state laws and regulations requiring the use of other languages. His English Language Amendment died in the Ninety-seventh Congress.

7   In 1983 the organization called U.S. English was founded by Hayakawa and John Tanton, a Michigan ophthalmologist. The primary purpose of the organization was to promote English as the official language of the United States. (The best background readings on America's "neolinguisticism" are the books *Hold Your Tongue*, by James Crawford, and *Language Loyalties*, edited by Crawford, both published in 1992.) Official English initiatives were passed by California in 1986, by Arkansas, Mississippi, North Carolina, North Dakota, and South Carolina in 1987, by Colorado, Florida, and Arizona in 1988, and by Alabama in 1990. The majorities voting for these initiatives were generally not insubstantial: California's, for example, passed by 73 percent.

8   It was probably inevitable that the Official English (or English Only—the two names are used almost interchangeably) movement would acquire a conservative,

almost reactionary undertone in the 1990s. Official English is politically very incorrect. But its cofounder John Tanton brought with him strong liberal credentials. He had been active in the Sierra Club and Planned Parenthood, and in the 1970s served as the national president of Zero Population Growth. Early advisers of U.S. English resist ideological pigeonholing: they included Walter Annenberg, Jacques Barzun, Bruno Bettelheim, Alistair Cooke, Denton Cooley, Walter Cronkite, Angier Biddle Duke, George Gilder, Sidney Hook, Norman Podhoretz, Arnold Schwarzenegger, and Karl Shapiro. In 1987 U.S. English installed as its president Linda Chávez, a Hispanic who had been prominent in the Reagan Administration. A year later she resigned her position, citing "repugnant" and "anti-Hispanic" overtones in an internal memorandum written by Tanton. Tanton, too, resigned, and Walter Cronkite, describing the affair as "embarrassing," left the advisory board. One board member, Norman Cousins, defected in 1986, alluding to the "negative symbolic significance" of California's Official English initiative, Proposition 63. The current chairman of the board and CEO of U.S. English is Mauro E. Mujica, who claims that the organization has 650,000 members.

9   The popular wisdom is that conservatives are pro and liberals con. True, conservatives such as George Will and William F. Buckley Jr. have written columns supporting Official English. But would anyone characterize as conservatives the present and past U.S. English board members Alistair Cooke, Walter Cronkite, and Norman Cousins? One of the strongest opponents of bilingual education is the Mexican-American writer Richard Rodriguez, best known for his eloquent autobiography, *Hunger of Memory* (1982). There is a strain of American liberalism that defines itself in nostalgic devotion to the melting pot.

10   For several years relevant bills awaited consideration in the U.S. House of Representatives. The Emereson Bill (H.R. 123), passed by the House last August, specifies English as the official language of government, and requires that the government "preserve and enhance" the official status of English. Exceptions are made for the teaching of foreign languages; for actions necessary for public health, international relations, foreign trade, and the protection of the rights of criminal defendants; and for the use of "terms of art" from languages other than English. It would, for example, stop the Internal Revenue Service from sending out income-tax forms and instructions in languages other than English, but it would not ban the use of foreign languages in census materials or documents dealing with national security. "*E Pluribus Unum*" can still appear on American money. U.S. English supports the bill.

11   What are the chances that some version of Official English will become federal law? Any language bill will face tough odds in the Senate, because some western senators have opposed English Only measures in the past for various reasons, among them a desire by Republicans not to alienate the growing number of Hispanic Republicans, most of whom are uncomfortable with mandated monolingualism. Texas Governor George W. Bush, too, has forthrightly said that he would oppose any English Only proposals in his state. Several of the Republican candidates for President in 1996 (an interesting exception is Phil Gramm) endorsed versions of Official English, as has Newt Gingrich. While

FIGURE C2.3

BILINGUAL EDUCATION:
DOES IT WORK?

governor of Arkansas, Bill Clinton signed into law an English Only bill. As President, he has described his earlier action as a mistake.

12   Many issues intersect in the controversy over Official English: immigration (above all), the rights of minorities (Spanish-speaking minorities in particular), the pros and cons of bilingual education, tolerance, how best to educate the children of immigrants, and the place of cultural diversity in school curricula and in American society in general. The question that lies at the root of most of the uneasiness is this: Is America threatened by the preservation of languages other than English? Will America, if it continues on its traditional path of benign linguistic neglect, go the way of Belgium, Canada, and Sri Lanka—three countries among many whose unity is gravely imperiled by language and ethnic conflicts?

Language and Nationality

13   Language and nationalism were not always so intimately intertwined. Never in the heyday of rule by sovereign was it a condition of employment that the King be able to speak the language of his subjects. George I spoke no English and spent much of his time away from England, attempting to use the power of his kingship to shore up his German possessions. In the Middle Ages nationalism was not even part of the picture: one owed loyalty to a lord, a prince, a ruler, a family, a tribe, a church, a piece of land, but not to a nation and least of all to a nation as a language unit. The capital city of the Austrian Hapsburg empire

was Vienna, its ruler a monarch with effective control of peoples of the most varied and incompatible ethnicities, and languages, throughout Central and Eastern Europe. The official language, and the lingua franca as well, was German. While it stood—and it stood for hundreds of years—the empire was an anachronistic relic of what for most of human history had been the normal relationship between country and language: none.

14 The marriage of language and nationalism goes back at least to Romanticism and specifically to Rousseau, who argued in his *Essay on the Origin of Languages* that language must develop before politics is possible and that language originally distinguished nations from one another. A little-remembered aim of the French Revolution—itself the legacy of Rousseau—was to impose a national language on France, where regional languages such as Provençal, Breton, and Basque were still strong competitors against standard French, the French of the Ile de France. As late as 1789, when the Revolution began, half the population of the south of France, which spoke Provençal, did not understand French. A century earlier the playwright Racine said that he had had to resort to Spanish and Italian to make himself understood in the southern French town of Uzès. After the Revolution nationhood itself became aligned with language.

15 In 1846 Jacob Grimm, one of the Brothers Grimm of fairy-tale fame but better known in the linguistic establishment as a forerunner of modern comparative and historical linguists, said that "a nation is the totality of people who speak the same language." After midcentury, language was invoked more than any other single criterion to define nationality. Language as a political force helped to bring about the unification of Italy and of Germany and the secession of Norway from its union with Sweden in 1905. Arnold Toynbee observed—unhappily—soon after the First World War that "the growing consciousness of Nationality had attached itself neither to traditional frontiers nor to new geographical associations but almost exclusively to mother tongues."

16 The crowning triumph of the new desideratum was the Treaty of Versailles, in 1919, when the allied victors of the First World War began redrawing the map of Central and Eastern Europe according to nationality as best they could. The magic word was "self-determination," and none of Woodrow Wilson's Fourteen Points mentioned the word "language" at all. Self-determination was thought of as being related to "nationality," which today we would be more likely to call "ethnicity"; but language was simpler to identify than nationality or ethnicity. When it came to drawing the boundary lines of various countries— Czechoslovakia, Yugoslavia, Romania, Hungary, Albania, Bulgaria, Poland—it was principally language that guided the draftsman's hand. (The main exceptions were Alsace-Lorraine, South Tyrol, and the German-speaking parts of Bohemia and Moravia.) Almost by default language became the defining characteristic of nationality.

17 And so it remains today. In much of the world, ethnic unity and cultural identification are routinely defined by language. To be Arab is to speak Arabic. Bengali identity is based on language in spite of the division of Bengali-speakers between Hindu India and Muslim Bangladesh. When eastern Pakistan seceded from greater Pakistan in 1971, it named itself Bangladesh: *desa* means "country";

bangla means not the Bengali people or the Bengali territory but the Bengali language.

18   Scratch most nationalist movements and you find a linguistic grievance. The demands for independence of the Baltic states (Latvia, Lithuania, and Estonia) were intimately bound up with fears for the loss of their respective languages and cultures in a sea of Russianness. In Belgium the war between French and Flemish threatens an already weakly fused country. The present atmosphere of Belgium is dark and anxious, costive; the metaphor of divorce is a staple of private and public discourse. The lines of terrorism in Sri Lanka are drawn between Tamil Hindus and Sinhalese Buddhists—and also between the Tamil and Sinhalese languages. Worship of the French language fortifies the movement for an independent Quebec. Whether a united Canada will survive into the twenty-first century is a question too close to call. Much of the anxiety about language in the United States is probably fueled by the "Quebec problem": unlike Belgium, which is a small European country, or Sri Lanka, which is halfway around the world, Canada is our close neighbor.

19   Language is a convenient surrogate for nonlinguistic claims that are often awkward to articulate, for they amount to a demand for more political and economic power. Militant Sikhs in India call for a state of their own: Khalistan ("Land of the Pure" in Punjabi). They frequently couch this as a demand for a linguistic state, which has a certain simplicity about it, a clarity of motive—justice, even, because states in India are normally linguistic states. But the Sikh demands blend religion, economics, language, and retribution for sins both punished and unpunished in a country where old sins cast long shadows.

20   Language is an explosive issue in the countries of the former Soviet Union. The language conflict in Estonia has been especially bitter. Ethnic Russians make up almost a third of Estonia's population, and most of them do not speak or read Estonian, although Russians have lived in Estonia for more than a generation. Estonia has passed legislation requiring knowledge of the Estonian language as a condition of citizenship. Nationalist groups in independent Lithuania sought restrictions on the use of Polish—again, old sins, long shadows.

21   In 1995 protests erupted in Moldova, formerly the Moldavian Soviet Socialist Republic, over language and the teaching of Moldovan history. Was Moldovan history a part of Romanian history or of Soviet history? Was Moldova's language Romanian? Moldovan—earlier called Moldavian—is Romanian, just as American English and British English are both English. But in the days of the Moldavian SSR, Moscow insisted that the two languages were different, and in a piece of linguistic nonsense required Moldavian to be written in the Cyrillic alphabet to strengthen the case that it was not Romanian.

22   The official language of Yugoslavia was Serbo-Croatian, which was never so much a language as a political accommodation. The Serbian and Croatian languages are mutually intelligible. Serbian is written in the Cyrillic alphabet, is identified with the Eastern Orthodox branch of the Catholic Church, and borrows its high-culture words from the east—from Russian and Old Church Slavic. Croatian is written in the Roman alphabet, is identified with Roman Catholicism, and borrows its high-culture words from the west—from German,

for example, and Latin. One of the first things the newly autonomous Republic of Serbia did, in 1991, was to pass a law decreeing Serbian in the Cyrillic alphabet the official language of the country. With Croatia divorced from Serbia, the Croatian and Serbian languages are diverging more and more. Serbo-Croatian has now passed into history, a language-museum relic from the brief period when Serbs and Croats called themselves Yugoslavs and pretended to like each other.

23   Slovakia, relieved now of the need to accommodate to Czech cosmopolitan sensibilities, has passed a law making Slovak its official language. (Czech is to Slovak pretty much as Croatian is to Serbian.) Doctors in state hospitals must speak to patients in Slovak, even if another language would aid diagnosis and treatment. Some 600,000 Slovaks—more than 10 percent of the population— are ethnically Hungarian. Even staff meetings in Hungarian-language schools must be in Slovak. (The government dropped a stipulation that church weddings be conducted in Slovak after heavy opposition from the Roman Catholic Church.) Language inspectors are told to weed out "all sins perpetrated on the regular Slovak language." Tensions between Slovaks and Hungarians, who had been getting along, have begun to arise.

24   The twentieth century is ending as it began—with trouble in the Balkans and with nationalist tensions flaring up in other parts of the globe. (Toward the end of his life Bismarck predicted that "some damn fool thing in the Balkans" would ignite the next war.) Language isn't always part of the problem. But it usually is.

Unique Otherness

25   Is there no hope for language tolerance? Some countries manage to maintain their unity in the face of multilingualism. Examples are Finland, with a Swedish minority, and a number of African and Southeast Asian countries. Two others could not be more unlike as countries go: Switzerland and India.

26   German, French, Italian, and Romansh are the languages of Switzerland. The first three can be and are used for official purposes; all four are designated "national" languages. Switzerland is politically almost hyperstable. It has language problems (Romansh is losing ground), but they are not major, and they are never allowed to threaten national unity.

27   Contrary to public perception, India gets along pretty well with a host of different languages. The Indian constitution officially recognizes nineteen languages, English among them. Hindi is specified in the constitution as the national language of India, but that is a pious postcolonial fiction: outside the Hindi-speaking northern heartland of India, people don't want to learn it. English functions more nearly than Hindi as India's lingua franca.

28   From 1947, when India obtained its independence from the British, until the 1960s blood ran in the streets and people died because of language. Hindi absolutists wanted to force Hindi on the entire country, which would have split India between north and south and opened up other fracture lines as well. For as long as possible Jawaharlal Nehru, independent India's first Prime Minister, resisted nationalist demands to redraw the capricious state boundaries of British

India according to language. By the time he capitulated, the country had gained a precious decade to prove its viability as a union.

29   Why is it that India preserves its unity with not just two languages to contend with, as Belgium, Canada, and Sri Lanka have, but nineteen? The answer is that India, like Switzerland, has a strong national identity. The two countries share something big and almost mystical that holds each together in a union transcending language. That something I call "unique otherness."

30   The Swiss have what the political scientist Karl Deutsch called "learned habits, preferences, symbols, memories, and patterns of landholding": customs, cultural traditions, and political institutions that bind them closer to one another than to people of France, Germany, or Italy living just across the border and speaking the same language. There is Switzerland's traditional neutrality, its system of universal military training (the "citizen army"), its consensual allegiance to a strong Swiss franc—and fondue, yodeling, skiing, and mountains. Set against all this, the fact that Switzerland has four languages doesn't even approach the threshold of becoming a threat.

31   As for India, what Vincent Smith, in the *Oxford History of India*, calls its "deep underlying fundamental unity" resides in institutions and beliefs such as caste, cow worship, sacred places, and much more. Consider *dharma*, *karma*, and *maya*, the three root convictions of Hinduism; India's historical epics; Gandhi; *ahimsa* (nonviolence); vegetarianism; a distinctive cuisine and way of eating; marriage customs; a shared past; and what the Indologist Ainslie Embree calls "Brahmanical ideology." In other words, "We are Indian; we are different."

32   Belgium and Canada have never managed to forge a stable national identity; Czechoslovakia and Yugoslavia never did either. Unique otherness immunizes countries against linguistic destabilization. Even Switzerland and especially India have problems; in any country with as many different languages as India has, language will never not be a problem. However, it is one thing to have a major illness with a bleak prognosis; it is another to have a condition that is irritating and occasionally painful but not life-threatening.

33   History teaches a plain lesson about language and governments: there is almost nothing the government of a free country can do to change language usage and practice significantly, to force its citizens to use certain languages in preference to others, and to discourage people from speaking a language they wish to continue to speak. (The rebirth of Hebrew in Palestine and Israel's successful mandate that Hebrew be spoken and written by Israelis is a unique event in the annals of language history.) Quebec has since the 1970s passed an array of laws giving French a virtual monopoly in the province. One consequence—unintended, one wishes to believe—of these laws is that last year kosher products imported for Passover were kept off the shelves, because the packages were not labeled in French. Wise governments keep their hands off language to the extent that it is politically possible to do so.

34   We like to believe that to pass a law is to change behavior; but passing laws about language, in a free society, almost never changes attitudes or behavior. Gaelic (Irish) is living out a slow, inexorable decline in Ireland despite enormous government support of every possible kind since Ireland gained its

independence from Britain. The Welsh language, in contrast, is alive today in Wales in spite of heavy discrimination during its history. Three out of four people in the northern and western counties of Gwynedd and Dyfed speak Welsh.

35   I said earlier that language is a convenient surrogate for other national problems. Official English obviously has a lot to do with concern about immigration, perhaps especially Hispanic immigration. America may be threatened by immigration; I don't know. But America is not threatened by language.

36   The usual arguments made by academics against Official English are commonsensical. Who needs a law when, according to the 1990 census, 94 percent of American residents speak English anyway? (Mauro E. Mujica, the chairman of U.S. English, cites a higher figure: 97 percent.) Not many of today's immigrants will see their first language survive into the second generation. This is in fact the common lament of first-generation immigrants: their children are not learning their language and are losing the culture of their parents. Spanish is hardly a threat to English, in spite of isolated (and easily visible) cases such as Miami, New York City, and pockets of the Southwest and southern California. The everyday language of south Texas is Spanish, and yet south Texas is not about to secede from America.

37   But empirical, calm arguments don't engage the real issue: language is a symbol, an icon. Nobody who favors a constitutional ban against flag burning will ever be persuaded by the argument that the flag is, after all, just a "piece of cloth." A draft card in the 1960s was never merely a piece of paper. Neither is a marriage license.

38   Language, as one linguist has said, is "not primarily a means of communication but a means of communion." Romanticism exalted language, made it mystical, sublime—a bond of national identity. At the same time, Romanticism created a monster: it made of language a means for destroying a country.

39   America has that unique otherness of which I spoke. In spite of all our racial divisions and economic unfairness, we have the frontier tradition, respect for the individual, and opportunity; we have our love affair with the automobile; we have in our history a civil war that freed the slaves and was fought with valor; and we have sports, hot dogs, hamburgers, and milk shakes—things big and small, noble and petty, important and trifling. "We are Americans; we are different."

40   If I'm wrong, then the great American experiment will fail—not because of language but because it no longer means anything to be an American; because we have forfeited that "willingness of the heart" that F. Scott Fitzgerald wrote was America; because we are no longer joined by Lincoln's "mystic chords of memory."

41   We are not even close to the danger point. I suggest that we relax and luxuriate in our linguistic richness and our traditional tolerance of language differences. Language does not threaten American unity. Benign neglect is a good policy for any country when it comes to language, and it's a good policy for America.

U.S. ENGLISH, INC.

Advertisement

"Immigrants Want And Need To Learn English. It's Time Politicians Got The Message."

Mauro E. Mujica, Architect
Chairman/CEO, U.S.English
Immigrant

"Multilingual ballots. U.S. citizenship ceremonies in foreign languages. Drivers' license tests in dozens of different languages. Bilingual education programs that fail to teach children English language proficiency.

"Programs invented by politicians and implemented by bureaucrats, all designed to help immigrants assimilate into American culture. In reality, they do just the opposite. They keep immigrants linguistically isolated. And they seriously limit an individual's earning potential.

"My native language is Spanish, yet I know the value of learning the language of this country. I am Chairman of U.S.ENGLISH. With over 600,000 members nationwide — we are the largest, non-partisan, non-profit organization committed to making sure government — at all levels — not waste money and energy providing services in foreign languages when money could be better spent simply teaching new immigrants English.

"We're supporting a bill in Congress which would make English the official language of government. Of course, common sense applications such as emergency services and foreign language teaching would be exempted. This bill would in no way restrict an individual's use of any language.

"Around the nation we're at the forefront of legislation on a state by state level. To date, 19 states have passed official language bills. We have a lot of work ahead of us and we can't do it without your help. It's time for you to speak up in a language politicians and bureaucrats can't ignore."

To join our grassroots movement, or to find out more, call 1-800 U S E N G L I S H (1 800-873-6454). Or write: Dept T10, 818 Connecticut Avenue, NW. Suite 200, Washington, DC 20006

THE LANGUAGE OF EQUAL OPPORTUNITY™

FIGURE C2.4 ADVERTISEMENT FOR U.S. ENGLISH, INC.

CASEBOOK 3

He Said, She Said

Many writers have explored the question of how men and women seem to think, act, and communicate in different, gender-influenced ways. Does our gender condition our behavior, or does society shape the way we perceive behavior as gendered? The articles in this section focus on how we see and define gender and how gender may relate to language.

DEBORAH TANNEN

Can't We Talk?

Deborah Tannen is a professor of linguistics at Georgetown University and the author of several books on gender relationships including You Just Don't Understand: Women and Men in Conversation, *from which this article is condensed.*

1   A married couple was in a car when the wife turned to her husband and asked, "Would you like to stop for a coffee?"

2   "No, thanks," he answered truthfully. So they didn't stop.

3   The result? The wife, who had indeed wanted to stop, became annoyed because she felt her preference had not been considered. The husband, seeing his wife was angry, became frustrated. Why didn't she just say what she wanted?

4   Unfortunately, he failed to see that his wife was asking the question not to get an instant decision, but to begin a negotiation. And the woman didn't realize that when her husband said no, he was just expressing his preference, not making a ruling. When a man and woman interpret the same interchange in such conflicting ways, it's no wonder they can find themselves leveling angry charges of selfishness and obstinacy at each other.

5   As a specialist in linguistics, I have studied how the conversational styles of men and women differ. We cannot lump all men or all women into fixed categories. But the seemingly senseless misunderstandings that haunt our relationships can in part be explained by the different conversational rules by which men and women play.

6   Whenever I write or speak about this subject, people tell me they are relieved to learn that what has caused them trouble—and what they had previously ascribed to personal failings—is, in fact, very common.

7   Learning about the different though equally valid conversational frequencies men and women are tuned to can help banish the blame and help us truly talk to one another. Here are some of the most common areas of conflict:

Status vs. Support

8   Men grow up in a world in which a conversation is often a contest, either to achieve the upper hand or to prevent other people from pushing them around. For women, however, talking is often a way to exchange confirmation and support.

9   I saw this when my husband and I had jobs in different cities. People frequently made comments like, "That must be rough," and "How do you stand it?" I accepted their sympathy and sometimes even reinforced it, saying, "The worst part is having to pack and unpack all the time."

10   But my husband often reacted with irritation. Our situation had advantages, he would explain. As academics, we had four-day weekends together, as well as long vacations throughout the year and four months in the summer.

11   Everything he said was true, but I didn't understand why he chose to say it. He told me that some of the comments implied: "Yours is not a real marriage. I am superior to you because my wife and I have avoided your misfortune." Until then it had not occurred to me there might be an element of one-upmanship.

12   I now see that my husband was simply approaching the world as many men do: as a place where people try to achieve and maintain status. I, on the other hand, was approaching the world as many women do: as a network of connections seeking support and consensus.

Independence vs. Intimacy

13   Since women often think in terms of closeness and support, they struggle to preserve intimacy. Men, concerned with status, tend to focus more on independence. These traits can lead women and men to starkly different views of the same situation.

14   When Josh's old high-school friend called him at work to say he'd be in town, Josh invited him to stay for the weekend. That evening he told Linda they were having a house guest.

15   Linda was upset. How could Josh make these plans without discussing them with her beforehand? She would never do that to him. "Why don't you tell your friend you have to check with your wife?" she asked.

16   Josh replied, "I can't tell my friend, 'I have to ask my wife for permission'!"

17   To Josh, checking with his wife would mean he was not free to act on his own. It would make him feel like a child or an underling. But Linda actually enjoys telling someone, "I have to check with Josh." It makes her feel good to show that her life is intertwined with her husband's.

Advice vs. Understanding

18   Eve had a benign lump removed from her breast. When she confided to her husband, Mark, that she was distressed because the stitches changed the contour of her breast, he answered, "You can always have plastic surgery."

19   This comment bothered her. "I'm sorry you don't like the way it looks," she protested. "But I'm not having any more surgery!"

20   Mark was hurt and puzzled. "I don't care about a scar," he replied. "It doesn't bother me at all."

21   "Then why are you telling me to have plastic surgery?" she asked.

22   "Because you were upset about the way it looks."

23   Eve felt like a heel. Mark had been wonderfully supportive throughout her surgery. How could she snap at him now?

24   The problem stemmed from a difference in approach. To many men a complaint is a challenge to come up with a solution. Mark thought he was reassuring Eve by telling her there was something she could do about her scar. But often women are looking for emotional support, not solutions.

25   When my mother tells my father she doesn't feel well, he invariably offers to take her to the doctor. Invariably, she is disappointed with his reaction. Like many men, he is focused on what he can do, whereas she wants sympathy.

Information vs. Feelings

26   A cartoon shows a husband opening a newspaper and asking his wife, "Is there anything you'd like to say to me before I start reading the paper?" We know there isn't—but that as soon as the man begins reading, his wife will think of something.

27   The cartoon is funny because people recognize their own experience in it. What's not funny is that many women are hurt when men don't talk to them at home, and many men are frustrated when they disappoint their partners without knowing why.

28   Rebecca, who is happily married, told me this is a source of dissatisfaction with her husband, Stuart. When she tells him what she is thinking, he listens silently. When she asks him what is on his mind, he says, "Nothing."

29   All Rebecca's life she has had practice in verbalizing her feelings with friends and relatives. But Stuart has had practice in keeping his innermost thoughts to himself. To him, like most men, talk is information. He doesn't feel that talk is required at home.

30   Yet many such men hold center stage in a social setting, telling jokes and stories. They use conversation to claim attention and to entertain. Women can wind up hurt that their husbands tell relative strangers things they have not told them.

31   To avoid this kind of misunderstanding, both men and women can make adjustments. A woman may observe a man's desire to read the paper without seeing it as a rejection. And a man can understand a woman's desire to talk without feeling it is a manipulative intrusion.

Orders vs. Proposals

32   Diana often begins statements with "Let's." She might say "Let's park over there" or "Let's clean up now, before lunch."

33   This makes Nathan angry. He has deciphered Diana's "Let's" as a command. Like most men, he resists being told what to do. But to Diana, she is making

suggestions, not demands. Like most women, she formulates her requests as proposals rather than orders. Her style of talking is a way of getting others to do what she wants—but by winning agreement first.

34   With certain men, like Nathan, this tactic backfires. If they perceive someone is trying to get them to do something indirectly, they feel manipulated and respond more resentfully than they would to a straightforward request.

Conflict vs. Compromise

35   In trying to prevent fights, some women refuse to oppose the will of others openly. But sometimes it's far more effective for a woman to assert herself, even at the risk of conflict.

36   Dora was frustrated by a series of used cars she drove. It was she who commuted to work, but her husband, Hank, who chose the cars. Hank always went for cars that were "interesting" but in continual need of repair.

37   After Dora was nearly killed when her brakes failed, they were in the market for yet another used car. Dora wanted to buy a late-model sedan from a friend. Hank fixed his sights on a 15-year-old sports car. She tried to persuade Hank that it made more sense to buy the boring but dependable car, but he would not be swayed.

38   Previously she would have acceded to his wishes. This time Dora bought the boring but dependable car and steeled herself for Hank's anger. To her amazement, he spoke not a word of remonstrance. When she later told him what she had expected, he scoffed at her fears and said she should have done what she wanted from the start if she felt that strongly about it.

39   As Dora discovered, a little conflict won't kill you. At the same time, men who habitually oppose others can adjust their style to opt for less confrontation.

40   When we don't see style differences for what they are, we sometimes draw unfair conclusions: "You're illogical," "You're self-centered," "You don't care about me." But once we grasp the two characteristic approaches, we stand a better chance of preventing disagreements from spiraling out of control.

41   Learning the other's ways of talking is a leap across the communication gap between men and women, and a giant step towards genuine understanding.

ROBIN TURNER

"Male Logic" and "Women's Intuition"

Robin Turner is a graduate of Surrey University's English Language Institute and teaches at Bilkent University in Turkey.

1   The split in our thinking between "masculine" and "feminine" is probably as old as language itself. Human beings seem to have a natural tendency to divide things into pairs: good/bad, light/dark, subject/object and so on. It is not surprising, then, that the male/female or masculine/feminine dichotomy is used to

classify things other than men and women. Many languages actually classify all nouns as "masculine" or "feminine" (although not very consistently: for example, the Spanish masculine noun *pollo* means "hen," while the feminine *polla* is slang for "penis"). This is perfectly natural; it is part of the way categorization works in language. This does not, however, mean that it is right. It is probably unimportant whether a table or a chair is thought of as masculine or feminine. It may not even be very important these days whether we think of the sun as male and the moon as female (like the ancient Greeks) or vice versa (like most of the German tribes). However, when we start associating abstract concepts like Reason or Nature with men and women, we run into serious difficulties.

2   The association of Reason with men and Nature with women is well-known, and has been widely criticized. Aristotle defined Man as a "rational animal," and by that he really meant men, not human beings. Unlike Plato, he saw women as less able to reason, hence less "human" and more "animal." In Europe, well into the twentieth century, women were generally seen as somehow intellectually deficient. An English woman recently became Oxford's oldest graduate because although she had completed her degree course in the 1920's, at that time the university did not award degrees to female students. Presumably it would have decreased the status of the university to award degrees to an intellectually inferior sex!

3   Nearly all societies, from hunting and gathering tribes to post-industrial nations, offer some kind of compensation to those who lose out in the status game. For example, among the practically matriarchal Zuni Indians of New Mexico, the economically powerless men were credited with the ability to make rain. Black slaves in the American South were thought to be naturally stronger (which they generally were), better at music and dancing (which they may have been) and more cheerful (highly unlikely for slaves, but a good justification for treating them badly). In the same way, women are compensated for their supposed inability to think rationally by a mysterious "women's intuition." Attempts were made to justify this in biological terms; women were seen as naturally more emotional and/or in touch with Nature because of their strange biology (menstruation, hormones, "vapours" or whatever). This was about as scientific as the Zuni Indians' theory that men could make rain.

4   Men and women are, of course, biologically different. There are even significant differences in male and female brains; women, for example, have a thicker corpus callosum (the thing that connects the two halves of the brain). However, it is a giant leap from observing that there are neurological differences between the sexes to assuming that these differences correspond to the classic Reason/Nature or logic/emotion dichotomies. In fact, some of these differences may even indicate the opposite. The left hemisphere of the brain generally deals with linear processing, as found in language and some types of mathematics, and this hemisphere develops faster in girls than in boys. The old "11 plus" test of verbal reasoning used in British schools was actually adjusted to bring boys' scores up to the level of girls! Whatever the case, it is a mistake to look at people's brains and then decide that they must think in a certain way;

it would be far better to try and find out how people actually think, and then to see if this corresponds to brain structure.

5   When we talk about the way men and women think, we are actually dealing with not one, but at least three separate things: how men and women usually think, how men and women can think, and how we think men and women think. Usually when we think we are looking at the first or second subjects, we are actually only describing the third. Since our main guide to how people think is their language, the fact that in most cultures men and women talk in different ways, and about different things, may lead us to false conclusions about the way they think in general. Women's conversation tends to emphasize feelings more, which may also mean that they think about feelings more. It does not, however, mean that women are more emotional. It is perfectly possible that men are just as emotional, but for social reasons they talk (and think) about their feelings less. Similarly, the fact that in most cultures men argue more about abstract things does not mean that men are naturally more logical, it just means that the things men prefer to talk about require logical argument more than they require expression of feelings. Obviously the more you argue, the better you get at it, hence the prejudice that men are somehow biologically more logical. This would be like assuming that I am biologically better at speaking English (my first language) than Turkish (my second).

6   Problems also arise with the actual words we use: logic, reason, intuition and emotion. Logic is simply a set of principles for getting from something we already knew, to something we didn't. If we know that all cows eat grass, and we know that Daisy is a cow, we can use very simple logic to say that Daisy eats grass, even if we have never seen her eat anything. The more complex logic that we use in constructing philosophical arguments or designing computers is really only doing the same kind of thing. The word "rational" is a little more problematic, since it involves an assessment of aims and actions. If our aims are consistent with each other and our actions achieve our aims, then we can fairly say that we are behaving rationally. If we act in a way that prevents us from realizing our aims, then we are behaving irrationally, or in other words, stupidly. For example, if I know that I will have a better relationship with my wife if I don't shout at her, but I still shout at her because I am in a bad mood, my problem is not that I am being emotional, it is that I am being stupid.

7   The opposite of "rational" is not, then, "emotional" but "irrational." If we set up a pair of opposites, rational/emotional, we are likely to make the assumption that women are more emotional and therefore irrational, which is a polite way of saying that women are stupid. While having strong emotions can sometimes interfere with your thought processes, this is not automatically the case. For example, I often get quite excited when I am working on a new theory or project, but this usually makes my thinking better, not worse. Strong "negative" emotions such as rage, jealousy or depression are usually the result of irrational thinking as much as a cause of it, and men are just as vulnerable to this type of stupidity as women.

8   "Intuition" is an even trickier concept. We usually say that we arrive at an idea or solution to a problem "intuitively" when we know something without

knowing how we came to know it. A scientist may arrive at a new theory because the idea just "pops into" his or her head, or even turns up in a dream. You may get an "intuitive" feeling that a person is dishonest without actually having heard them say something you know to be untrue. In both these cases, what seems to be happening is that the mind stores and sorts information unconsciously, providing us only with the end result of this process. There is no guarantee, of course, that this conclusion will be true; a scientist would still have to perform experiments to prove their intuitive theory, and you would probably want some hard evidence to prove that the person you feel is dishonest really does tell lies.

9   There is therefore nothing particularly strange or mystical about intuition; it is something we do all the time. Why, then, do we talk about "women's intuition" as though men never arrive at a conclusion without consciously following all the stages that were necessary to reach it? Again, the answer is probably linguistic. As we have seen, traditionally women's conversation is less formal, less argumentative, and more concerned with feelings than men's conversation. Intuitive conclusions are therefore more acceptable in an all-female group. Men, on the other hand, are expected to argue more, and to argue more logically, presenting evidence in a systematic way to back up their conclusions. It is less socially acceptable in an all-male conversation (or a conversation where the men are doing most of the talking) to say "Well guys, I don't know why, but I just get this kind of *feeling* that e = mc^2."

10   We can see, then, that these artificial pairs of opposites, logic/intuition and rational/emotional, are not only false, but also damaging, particularly to women. It is therefore surprising that some feminists actually support a version of this patriarchal nonsense. Particularly at the more "spiritual" end of the Radical Feminist community, there is a tendency to glorify women's "intuition" and "closeness to Nature," and to avoid "logic" as somehow "male," as though it were a psychological problem resulting from too much testosterone. The fact that men often use logic, or at least logical-sounding arguments, to "put women in their place" is not a fault of logic, it is the fault of those men's sexism and lack of social skills. More innocently, men are often accused of being too "cold" and "logical," not because there is anything wrong with their ideas, but because they do not understand the unspoken rules of female conversation, in the same way that women are often accused of being "illogical" or "emotional" because they do not argue using the same language as men.

11   If women reject logic and rely solely on feelings, they are left in the weak position of having to argue with feelings. Feeling that something is true does not make it true, and it will not convince anyone else that it is true either. You can say, "I feel X," but the person you are arguing with can just as well reply, "Well I don't." The result is that the argument usually goes nowhere. This is particularly damaging in arguments between men and women, since both sides are likely to go away with their prejudices strengthened; the men think women are subjective, emotional and illogical, and the women think men are impersonal, cold and over-intellectual.

12   To justify their feelings of hurt at being "beaten" in an argument, the women concerned may go further and dismiss the whole thing as "male logic," as though there were two types of logic, one for men and another for women. This then

places the men in an impossible position, since if they attempt to be reasonable, they are accused again of using "male logic," in the same way that if a woman gets upset in an argument, it is taken as proof that she is overly emotional, and hence irrational. This does not only lead to a lack of communication between the sexes, it leads to a lack of communication in which women come off worse, since policy is generally made as the result of argument, not sharing feelings.

13   A further criticism of "male logic" extends the argument to take in the whole of science and technology, which are seen as "aggressive," "phallic" and "toys for the boys." While it is true that science and technology were at least initially male inventions (largely because at that time only men had the time and resources to do this), and while it is also true that a lot of early scientific thinking used sexist and even violent terminology (e.g. Bacon's "putting Nature to the rack," where the physical world is seen as a woman who must be tortured to give up her secrets), this does not mean that there is anything inherently masculine about a chemistry experiment or a digital watch. Again, if women leave science and technology to the men, they will be left in a world which is understood and shaped by men. By all means criticize the sexist and unscientific metaphors that scientists and technologists use, but (to use a more feminine metaphor) let's not throw the baby out with the bathwater. By all means think of the Earth as a Mother Goddess if you like that metaphor, but remember that it is only a metaphor; the Earth is a planet, not a woman.

14   As I said initially, language categorizes. If it didn't, it wouldn't work, as you would have to have a separate word for everything in the world. Categorization works largely through prototypes, stereotypes and maybe even archetypes, and these types frequently use metaphorical and symbolic imagery borrowed from other categories. Nature tends to be seen, metaphorically, as a woman, but that doesn't make her (or rather it) a woman. The modern personification of logic is *Star Trek*'s Mr. Spock, pointy-eared, unemotional, and of course male. This does not mean, however, that to be logical you need to be unemotional or masculine, any more than it means that you have to have pointy ears. After all, in much European literature and painting (especially during the Enlightenment) both Reason and Nature were personified as women. They are, after all, not opposites; Stoic philosophers such as Epictetus frequently used the words "nature" and "reason" to talk about the same thing. What feminists, like any intelligent people, need to do is analyze and criticize the false polarization and dubious metaphors that distort our thinking, not repeat them in a different form.

SONDRA THIEDERMAN

He Said, She Said: Differences to Be Admired

Dr. Sondra Thiederman is one of the nation's leading experts on workplace diversity and cross-cultural business. She contributed this piece to Monster.com's continuing discussions of workplace communication issues.

1   Let's face it: As aggravating and frustrating as they can be, gender differences are also great fun. No, I don't mean that way. I mean that gender differences strike our funny bone. I suppose it has something to do with our past experiences and the vulnerability many of us feel in our personal relationships with the opposite sex. And we are even more vulnerable when it comes to male-female relationships in the workplace.

2   While it's always risky to generalize about gender differences, it's possible to make certain flexible generalities that can be valuable when communicating across the gender line.

Giving Orders

3   Men and women often differ in the way they manage people and give orders. Several well-respected studies have shown women tend to soften their demands and statements, whereas men tend to be more direct. Women, for example, use tag lines, phrases like, "don't you think" following the presentation of an idea, "if you don't mind" following a demand or "this may be a crazy idea, but" preceding a suggestion.

4   Many women are conditioned by culture to maintain harmony in relationships. That conditioning is manifested in softened demands, hedged statements and a generally more tentative communication style. The important thing to remember is that tentative communication does not mean the speaker actually feels tentative or is lacking in confidence. Similarly, more direct communication—as seen with some men and, because we can't generalize, some women too—does not mean the person is arrogant, bossy or feels superior. These are nothing more than learned ways of communicating.

Asking Questions

5   Another difference often seen between men and women is women generally ask more questions than men. We have all heard or experienced the anecdote about the man who refuses to stop to ask directions when lost. We get a good chuckle out of this story, but differences in how and when questions are asked can create real confusion in the workplace.

6   Asking questions means different things to men and women. Men ask questions for one purpose only: To gather information. For women, asking questions serves two purposes: One is to gather information but, as you've probably noticed, women will also ask questions when they already know the answers. Why? They want to show interest in what the other person has said to cultivate the relationship.

Overcoming Misunderstandings and Misinterpretations

7   Both management style and asking questions raise fundamental issues about the role of women in the workplace. There is nothing intrinsically wrong with different communication styles. Men are perfectly right to be more direct and ask fewer questions, while women and some men are simply more comfortable

with a softer style of communicating. The problem arises when these differences lead to misunderstandings and misinterpretations, which can ultimately disrupt teamwork and even derail someone's chances for upward mobility.

8   We need to look past our assumptions about the meaning of a particular manner of speaking to build better gender-mixed teams. Just because one person may be more abrupt does not mean he or she is cold, uncaring or uninvolved. On the other hand, a more tentative approach is not necessarily a sign of weakness, fear or lack of confidence. We communicate the way we do, because it is what we are taught. What matters is that we give each other a chance, that we get to know what lies behind the communication style and, most important, that we resist the urge to jump to premature conclusions about the meaning of a particular style.

EUGENE R. AUGUST

Real Men Don't: Anti-Male Bias in English

Eugene R. August is the author of The New Men's Studies: A Selected and Annotated Interdisciplinary Bibliography0. *In this article, he calls attention to the ways in which language can express an anti-male bias that should no more be tolerated than is language bias against women.*

1   Despite numerous studies of sex bias in language in the past fifteen years, only rarely has anti-male bias been examined. In part, this neglect occurs because many of these studies have been based upon assumptions which are questionable at best and which at worst exhibit their own form of sex bias. Whether explicitly or implicitly, many of these studies reduce human history to a tale of male oppressors and female victims or rebels. In this view of things, all societies become *patriarchal societies*, a familiar term used to suggest that for centuries males have conspired to exploit and demean females. Accordingly, it is alleged in many of these studies that men control language and that they use it to define women and women's roles as inferior.

2   Despite the popularity of such a view, it has received scant support from leading social scientists, including one of the giants of modern anthropology, Margaret Mead. Anticipating current ideology, Mead in *Male and Female* firmly rejected the notion of a "male conspiracy to keep women in their place," arguing instead that

> the historical trend that listed women among the abused minorities…lingers on to obscure the issue and gives apparent point to the contention that this is a man-made world in which women have always been abused and must always fight for their rights.
>
> It takes considerable effort on the part of both men and women to reorient ourselves to thinking—when we think basically—that this is

a world not made by men alone, in which women are unwilling and helpless dupes and foils or else powerful schemers hiding their power under their ruffled petticoats, but a world made of mankind for human beings of both sexes. (298, 299–300)

The model described by Mead and other social scientists shows a world in which women and men have lived together throughout history in a symbiotic relationship, often mutually agreeing upon the definition of gender roles and the distribution of various powers and duties.

3   More importantly for the subject of bias in speech and writing, women—as well as men—have shaped language. As Walter J. Ong reminds us,

> Women talk and think as much as men do, and with few exceptions we all...learn to talk and think in the first instance largely from women, usually and predominantly our mothers. Our first tongue is called our "mother tongue" in English and in many other languages....There are no father tongues....(34)

4   Feminists like Dorothy Dinnerstein agree: "There seems no reason to doubt that the baby-tending sex contributed at least equally with the history-making one to the most fundamental of all human inventions—language" (22). Because gender roles and language are shaped by society in general—that is, by both men and women—anti-male bias in language is as possible as anti-female bias.

5   To say this, however, is emphatically not to blame women alone, or even primarily, for anti-male usage. If guilt must be assigned, it would have to be placed upon sexist people, both male and female, who use language to manipulate gender role behavior and to create negative social attitudes towards males. But often it is difficult to point a finger of blame: except where prejudiced gender stereotypes are deliberately fostered, most people evidently use sex-biased terminology without clearly understanding its import. In the long run, it is wiser to concentrate not on fixing blame, but on heightening public awareness of anti-male language and on discouraging its use. In particular, teachers and writers need to become aware of and to question language which denigrates or stereotypes males.

6   In modern English, three kinds of anti-male usage are evident: first, gender-exclusive language which omits males from certain kinds of consideration; second, gender-restrictive language which attempts to restrict males to an accepted gender role, some aspects of which may be outmoded, burdensome, or destructive; and third, negative stereotypes of males which are insulting, dehumanizing, and potentially dangerous.

7   Although gender-exclusive language which excludes females has often been studied, few students of language have noted usage which excludes males. Those academics, for example, who have protested *alumnus* and *alumni* as gender-exclusive terms to describe a university's male and female graduates have failed to notice that, by the same logic, *alma mater* (nourishing mother) is an equally

gender-exclusive term to describe the university itself. Those who have protested *man* and *mankind* as generic terms have not begun to question *mammal* as a term of biological classification, but by categorizing animals according to the female's ability to suckle the young through her mammary glands, *mammal* clearly omits the male of the species. Consequently, it is as suspect as generic *man*.

8   In general, gender-exclusive usage in English excludes males as parents and as victims. Until recently, the equating of *mother* with *parent* in the social sciences was notorious: a major sociological study published in 1958 with the title *The Changing American Parent* was based upon interviews with 582 mothers and no fathers (Roman and Haddad 87). Although no longer prevalent in the social sciences, the interchangeability of mother and parent is still common, except for noncustodial parent which is almost always a synonym for father. A recent ad for *Parents* magazine begins: "To be the best mother you can be, you want practical, reliable answers to the questions a mother must face." Despite the large number of men now seen pushing shopping carts, advertisers still insist that "Choosy mothers choose Jif" and "My Mom's a Butternut Mom." Frequently, children are regarded as belonging solely to the mother, as in phrases like *women and their children*. The idea of the mother as primary parent can be glimpsed in such expressions as *mother tongue, mother wit, mother lode, mother of invention*, and *mothering* as a synonym for parenting.

9   The male as victim is ignored in such familiar expressions as *innocent women and children*. In June 1985, when President Regan rejected a bombing strike to counter terrorist activities, newspapers reported that the decision had been made to prevent "the deaths of many innocent women and children in strife-torn Lebanon" (Glass). Presumably strife-torn Lebanon contained no innocent men. Likewise, *rape victim* means females only, an assumption made explicit in the opening sentences of this newspaper article on rape: "Crime knows no gender. Yet, there is one offense that only women are prey to: rape" (Mougey). The thousands of males raped annually, in addition to the sexual assaults regularly inflicted upon males in prison, are here entirely overlooked. (That these males have been victimized mostly by other males does not disqualify them as victims of sexual violence, as some people assume.) Similarly, the term *wife and child abuse* conceals the existence of an estimated 282,000 husbands who are battered annually (O'Reilly et al. 23). According to many expressions in English, males are not parents and they are never victimized.

10   Unlike gender-exclusive language, gender-restrictive language is usually applied to males only, often to keep them within the confines of a socially prescribed gender role. When considering gender-restrictive language, one must keep in mind that—as Ruth E. Hartley has pointed out—the masculine gender role is enforced earlier and more harshly than the feminine role is (235). In addition, because the boy is often raised primarily by females in the virtual absence of close adult males, his grasp of what is required of him to *be a man* is often unsure. Likewise, prescriptions for male behavior are usually given in the negative, leading to the "Real Men Don't" syndrome, a process which further

confuses the boy. Such circumstances leave many males extremely vulnerable to language which questions their sense of masculinity.

11   Furthermore, during the past twenty years an increasing number of men and women have been arguing that aspects of our society's masculine gender role are emotionally constrictive, unnecessarily stressful, and potentially lethal. Rejecting "the myth of masculine privilege," psychologist Herb Goldberg reports in *The Hazards of Being Male* that "every critical statistic in the area of [early death], disease, suicide, crime, accidents, childhood emotional disorders, alcoholism, and drug addiction shows a disproportionately higher male rate" (5). But changes in the masculine role are so disturbing to so many people that the male who attempts to break out of familiar gender patterns often finds himself facing hostile opposition which can be readily and powerfully expressed in a formidable array of sex-biased terms.

12   To see how the process works, let us begin early in the male life cycle. A boy quickly learns that, while it is usually acceptable for girls to be *tomboys*, God forbid that he should be a *sissy*. In *Sexual Signatures: On Being a Man or a Woman*, John Money and Patricia Tucker note:

> The current feminine stereotype in our culture is flexible enough to let a girl behave "boyishly" if she wants to without bringing her femininity into question, but any boy who exhibits "girlish" behavior is promptly suspected of being queer. There isn't even a word corresponding to "tomboy" to describe such a boy. "Sissy" perhaps comes closest, or "artistic" and "sensitive," but unlike "tomboy," such terms are burdened with unfavorable connotations. (72)

13   Lacking a favorable or even neutral term to describe the boy who is quiet, gentle, and emotional, the English language has long had a rich vocabulary to insult and ridicule such boys—*mama's boy, mollycoddle, milksop, muff, twit, softy, creampuff, pantywaist, weenie, Miss Nancy*, and so on. Although sometimes used playfully, the current popular *wimp* can be used to insult males from childhood right into adulthood.

14   Discussion of words like *sissy* as insults has been often one-sided: most commentators are content to argue that the female, not the male, is being insulted by such usage. "The implicit sexism" in such terms, writes one commentator, "disparages the woman, not the man" (Sorrells 87). Although the female is being slurred indirectly by these terms, a moment's reflection will show that the primary force of the insult is being directed against the male, specifically the male who cannot differentiate himself from the feminine. Ong argues in *Fighting for Life* that most societies place heavy pressure on males to differentiate themselves from females because the prevailing environment of human society is feminine (70–71). In English-speaking societies, terms like *sissy* and *weak sister*, which have been used by both females and males, are usually perceived not as insults to females but as ridicule of males who have allegedly failed to differentiate themselves from the feminine.

15   Being *all boy* carries penalties, however; for one thing, it means being less lovable. As the nursery rhyme tells children, little girls are made of "sugar and

spice and all that's nice," while little boys are made of "frogs and snails and puppy-dogs' tails." Or, as an American version of the rhyme puts it:

> Girls are dandy,
> Made of candy—
> That's what little girls are made of.
> Boys are rotten,
> Made of cotton—
> That's what little boys are made of.
> (Baring-Gould 176n116)

16   When not enjoined to *be all boy*, our young lad will be urged to *be a big boy*, *be a brave soldier*, and (the ultimate appeal) *be a man*. These expressions almost invariably mean that the boy is about to suffer something painful or humiliating. The variant—*take it like a man*—provides the clue. As Paul Theroux defines it, be a man means: "Be stupid, be unfeeling, obedient and soldierly, and stop thinking."

17   Following one boy further into the life cycle, we discover that in school he will find himself in a cruel bind: girls his age will be biologically and socially more mature than he is, at least until around age eighteen. Until then, any ineptness in his social role will be castigated by a host of terms which are reserved almost entirely for males. "For all practical purposes," John Gordon remarks, "the word 'turkey' (or whatever the equivalent is now) can be translated as 'a boy spurned by influential girls'" (141). The equivalents of turkey are many: *jerk, nerd, clod, klutz, schmuck, dummy, goon, dork, square, dweeb, jackass, meathead, geek, zero, reject, goofball, drip*, and numerous others, including many obscene terms. Recently, a Michigan high school decided to do away with a scheduled "Nerd Day" after a fourteen-year-old male student, who apparently had been so harassed as a nerd by other students, committed suicide ("'Nerd' day"). In this case, the ability of language to devastate the emotionally vulnerable young male is powerfully and pathetically dramatized.

18   As our boy grows, he faces threats and taunts if he does not take risks or endure pain to prove his manhood. Coward, for example, is a word applied almost exclusively to males in our society, as are its numerous variants—*chicken, chickenshit, yellow, yellow-bellied, lily-livered, weak-kneed, spineless, squirrelly, fraidy cat, gutless wonder, weakling, butterfly, jellyfish*, and so on. If our young man walks away from a stupid quarrel or prefers to settle differences more rationally than with a swift jab to the jaw, the English language is richly supplied with these and other expressions to call his masculinity into question.

19   Chief among the other expressions that question masculinity is a lengthy list of homophobic terms such as *queer, pansy, fag, faggot, queen, queeny, pervert, bugger, deviant, fairy, tinkerbell, puss, priss, flamer, feller, sweet, precious, fruit, sodomite*, and numerous others, many obscene. For many people, gay is an all-purpose word of ridicule and condemnation. Once again, although homosexuals are being insulted by these terms, the primary target is more often the heterosexual male who fails or refuses to live up to someone else's idea of masculinity. In "Homophobia Among Men," Gregory Lehne explains, "Homophobia is used as a technique of social control…to enforce the norms of male sex-role behavior.…[H]omosexuality is not the real threat, the real threat is change in the male sex-role" (77).

20   Nowhere is this threat more apparent than in challenges to our society's male-only military obligation. When a young man and a young woman reach the age of eighteen, both may register to vote; only the young man is required by law to register for military service. For the next decade at least, he must stand ready to be called into military service and even into combat duty in wars, "police actions," "peace-keeping missions," and "rescue missions," often initiated by legally dubious means. Should he resist this obligation, he may be called a *draft dodger, deserter, peacenik, traitor, shirker, slacker, malingerer,* and similar terms. Should he declare himself a conscientious objector, he may be labeled a *conchy* or any of the variants of coward.

21   In his relationships with women, he will find that the age of equality has not yet arrived. Usually, he will be expected to take the initiative, do the driving, pick up the tab, and in general show a deferential respect for women that is a left-over from the chivalric code. Should he behave in an *ungentlemanly* fashion, a host of words—which are applied almost always to males alone—can be used to tell him so: *louse, rat, creep, sleaze, scum, stain, worm, fink, heel, stinker, animal, savage, bounder, cad, wolf, gigolo, womanizer, Don Juan, pig, rotter, boor,* and so on.

22   In sexual matters he will usually be expected to take the initiative and to perform. If he does not, he will be labeled *impotent.* This word, writes Goldberg, "is clearly sexist because it implies a standard of acceptable masculine sexual performance that makes a man abnormal if he can't live up to it" (*New Male* 248). Metaphorically, *impotent* can be used to demean any male whose efforts in any area are deemed unacceptable. Even if our young man succeeds at his sexual performance, the sex manuals are ready to warn him that if he reaches orgasm before a specified time he is guilty of *premature ejaculation.*

23   When our young man marries, he will be required by law and social custom to support his wife and children. Should he not succeed as breadwinner or should he relax in his efforts, the language offers numerous terms to revile him: *loser, deadbeat, bum, freeloader, leech, parasite, goldbrick, sponge, mooch, ne'er-do-well, good for nothing,* and so on. If women in our society have been regarded as sex objects, men have been regarded as success objects, that is, judged by their ability to provide a standard of living. The title of a recent book—*How to Marry a Winner*—reveals immediately that the intended audience is female (Collier).

24   When he becomes a father, our young man will discover that he is a second-class parent, as the traditional interchangeability of mother and parent indicates. The law has been particularly obtuse in recognizing fathers as parents, as evidenced by the awarding of child custody to mothers in ninety percent of divorce cases. In 1975 a father's petition for custody of his four-year-old son was denied because, as the family court judge said, "Fathers don't make good mothers" (qtd. in Levine 21). The judge apparently never considered whether *fathers* make good *parents.*

25   And so it goes throughout our young man's life: if he deviates from society's gender role norm, he will be penalized and he will hear about it.

26   The final form of anti-male bias to be considered here is negative stereotyping. Sometimes this stereotyping is indirectly embedded in the language, sometimes it resides in people's assumptions about males and shapes their response to seemingly neutral words, and sometimes it is overtly created for political rea-

sons. It is one thing to say that some aspects of the traditional masculine gender role is limiting and hurtful; it is quite another to gratuitously suspect males in general of being criminal and evil or to denounce them in wholesale fashion as oppressors, exploiters, and rapists. In *The New Male* Goldberg writes, "Men may very well be the last remaining subgroup in our society that can be blatantly, negatively and vilely stereotyped with little objection or resistance" (103). As our language demonstrates, such sexist stereotyping, whether unintentional or deliberate, is not only familiar but fashionable.

27   In English, crime and evil are usually attributed to the male. As an experiment I have compiled lists of nouns which I read to my composition students, asking them to check whether the words suggest "primarily females," "primarily males," or "could be either." Nearly all the words for lawbreakers suggest males rather than females to most students. These words include *murderer, swindler, crook, criminal, burglar, thief, gangster, mobster, hood, hitman, killer, pickpocket, mugger,* and *terrorist.* Accounting for this phenomenon is not always easy. *Hitman* may obviously suggest "primarily males," and the –er in *murderer* may do the same, especially if it reminds students of the word's feminine form, *murderess.* Likewise, students may be aware that most murders are committed by males. Other words—like *criminal* and *thief*—are more clearly gender neutral in form, and it is less clear why they should be so closely linked with "primarily males." Although the dynamics of the association may be unclear, English usage somehow conveys a subtle suggestion that males are to be regarded as guilty in matters of lawbreaking.

28   This hint of male guilt extends to a term like suspect. When the person's gender is unknown, the suspect is usually presumed to be a male. For example, even before a definite suspect had been identified, the perpetrator of the 1980–81 Atlanta child murders was popularly known as *The Man.* When a male and female are suspected of a crime, the male is usually presumed the guilty party. In a recent murder case, when two suspects—Debra Brown and Alton Coleman—were apprehended, police discovered *Brown's* fingerprint in a victim's car and interpreted this as evidence of *Coleman's* guilt. As the Associated Press reported:

> Authorities say for the first time they have evidence linking Alton Coleman with the death of an Indianapolis man.
> A fingerprint found in the car of Eugene Scott has been identified as that of Debra Brown, Coleman's traveling companion…" ("Police")

29   Nowhere does the article suggest that Brown's fingerprint found in the victim's car linked Brown with the death: the male suspect was presumed the guilty party, while the female was only a "traveling companion." Even after Brown had been convicted of two murders, the Associated Press was still describing her as "the accused accomplice of convicted killer Alton Coleman" ("Indiana").

30   In some cases, this presumption of male guilt extends to crimes in which males are not the principal offenders. As noted earlier, a term like *wife and child abuse* ignores battered husbands, but it does more: it suggests that males alone abuse children. In reality most child abuse is committed by mothers (Strauss,

Gelles, Steinmetz 71). Despite this fact, a 1978 study of child abuse bears the title *Sins of the Fathers* (Inglis).

31   The term *rape* creates special problems. While the majority of rapes are committed by males and the number of female rape victims outdistances the number of male rape victims, it is widely assumed—as evidenced by the newspaper article cited above—that rape is a crime committed only by males in which females are victims. Consequently, the word *rape* is often used as a brush to tar all males. In *Against Our Will* Susan Brownmiller writes: "From prehistoric times to the present, I believe, rape…is nothing more or less than a conscious process of intimidation by which *all men* keep *all women* in a state of fear" (15; italics in original). Making the point explicitly, Marilyn French states, "All men are rapists and that's all they are" (qtd. in Jennes 33). Given this kind of smear tactic, rape can be used metaphorically to indict males alone and to exonerate females, as in this sentence: "The rape of nature—and the ecological disaster it presages—is part and parcel of a dominating masculinity gone out of control" (Hoch 137). The statement neatly blames males alone even when the damage to the environment has been caused in part by females like Anne Gorsuch Burford and Rita Lavelle.

32   Not only crimes but vices of all sorts have been typically attributed to males. As Muriel R. Schulz points out, "The synonyms for *inebriate*…seem to be coded primarily 'male': for example, *boozer, drunkard, tippler, toper, swiller, tosspot, guzzler, barfly, drunk, lush, boozehound, souse, tank, stew, rummy,* and *bum*" (126). Likewise, someone may be *drunk as a lord* but never *drunk as a lady*.

33   Sex bias or sexism itself is widely held to be a male-only fault. When *sexism* is defined as "contempt for women,"—as if there were no such thing as contempt for men—the definition of sexism is itself sexist (Bardwick 34).

34   Part of the reason for this masculinization of evil may be that in the Western world the source of evil has long been depicted in male terms. In the Bible the Evil One is consistently referred to as *he*, whether the reference is to the serpent in the Garden of Eden, Satan as Adversary in Job, Lucifer and Beelzebub in the gospels, Jesus' tempter in the desert, or the dragon in Revelations. *Beelzebub*, incidentally, is often translated as *lord of the flies*, a term designating the demon as masculine. So masculine is the word *devil* that the female prefix is needed, as in *she-devil*, to make a feminine noun of it. The masculinization of evil is so unconsciously accepted that writers often attest to it even while attempting to deny it, as in this passage:

> From the very beginning, the Judeo-Christian tradition has linked women and evil. When second-century theologians struggled to explain the Devil's origins, they surmised that Satan and his various devils had once been angels. (Gerzon 224)

35   If the Judeo-Christian tradition has linked women with evil so closely, why is the writer using the masculine pronoun *his* to refer to Satan, the source of evil according to that tradition? Critics of sex-bias in religious language seldom notice or mention its masculinization of evil: of those objecting to *God the Father* as sexist, no one—to my knowledge—has suggested that designating Satan as the *Father of Lies* is equally sexist. Few theologians talk about Satan and her legions.

36   The tendency to blame nearly everything on men has climaxed in recent times with the popularity of such terms as *patriarchy*, *patriarchal society*, and *male-dominated society*. More political than descriptive, these terms are rapidly becoming meaningless, used as all-purpose smear words to conjure up images of male oppressors and female victims. They are a linguistic sleight of hand which obscures the point that, as Mead has observed (299–300), societies are largely created by both sexes for both sexes. By using a swift reference to *patriarchal structures* or *patriarchal attitudes*, a writer can absolve females of all blame for society's flaws while fixing the onus solely on males. The give-away of this ploy can be detected when patriarchy and its related terms are never used in a positive or neutral context, but are always used to assign blame to males alone.

37   Wholesale denunciations of males as oppressors, exploiters, rapists, Nazis, and slave-drivers have become all too familiar during the past fifteen years. Too often the academic community, rather than opposing this sexism, has been encouraging it. All too many scholars and teachers have hopped the male-bashing bandwagon to disseminate what John Gordon calls "the myth of the monstrous male." With increasing frequency, this academically fashionable sexism can also be heard echoing from our students. "A white upper-middle-class straight male should seriously consider another college," declares a midwestern college student in *The New York Times Selective Guide to Colleges*. "You [the white male] are the bane of the world....Ten generations of social ills can and will be strapped upon your shoulders" (qtd. in Fiske 12). It would be comforting to dismiss this student's compound of misinformation, sexism, racism, and self-righteousness as an extreme example, but similar yahooisms go unchallenged almost everywhere in modern academia.

38   Surely it is time for men and women of good will to reject and protest such bigotry. For teachers and writers, the first task is to recognize and condemn forms of anti-male bias in language, whether they are used to exclude males from equal consideration with females, to reinforce restrictive aspects of the masculine gender role, or to stereotype males callously. For whether males are told that *fathers don't make good mothers*, that *real men don't cry*, or that *all men are rapists*, the results are potentially dangerous: like any other group, males can be subtly shaped into what society keeps telling them they are. In *Why Men Are the Way They Are* Warren Farrell puts the matter succinctly: "The more we make men the enemy, the more they will have to behave like the enemy" (357).

Works Cited

Baring-Gould, William S., and Ceil Baring-Gould. *The Annotated Mother Goose Nursery Rhymes Old and New, Arranged and Explained*. New York: Clarkson N. Potter, 1962.

Brownmiller, Susan. *Against Our Will: Men, Women and Rape*. New York: Simon, 1975.

Burdwick, Judith. *In Transition: How Feminism, Sexual Liberation, and the Search for Self-Fulfilment Has Altered Our Lives*. New York: Holt, 1979.

Collier, Phyllis K. *How to Marry a Winner*. Englewood Cliffs, NJ: Prentice, 1982.

Dinnerstein, Dorothy. *The Mermaid and the Minotaur: Sexual Arrangements and Human Malaise*. New York: Harper, 1976.

Farrell, Warren. *Why Men Are the Way They Are: The Male-Female Dynamic*. New York: McGraw-Hill, 1986.

Fiske, Edward B. *The New York Times Selective Guide to Colleges*. New York: Times Books, 1982.

Gerzon, Mark. *A Choice of Heroes: The Changing Faces of American Manhood*. Boston: Houghton, 1982.

Glass, Andrew J. "President wants to unleash military power, but cannot." *Dayton Daily News* 18 June 1985: 1.

Goldberg, Herb. *The Hazards of Being Male: Surviving the Myth of Masculine Privilege*. 1976. New York: NAL, 1977.

———. *The New Male: From Self-Destruction to Self-Care*. 1979. New York: NAL, 1977.

Gordon, John. *The Myth of the Monstrous Male, and Other Feminist Fables*. New York: Playboy P, 1982.

Hartley, Ruth E. "Sex-Role Pressures and the Socialization of the Male Child." *The Forty-Nine Percent Majority: The Male Sex Role*. Ed. Deborah S. David and Robert Brannon. Reading, MA: Addison-Wesley, 1976, 235–44.

Hoch, Paul. *White Hero, Black Beast: Racism, Sexism, and the Mask of Masculinity*. London: Pluto P, 1979.

"Indiana jury finds Brown guilty of murder, molesting." *Dayton Daily News* 18 May 1986: 7A.

Inglis, Ruth. *Sins of the Fathers: A Study of the Physical and Emotional Abuse of Children*. New York: St. Martin's, 1978.

Jennes, Gail. "All Men Are Rapists." *People* 20 Feb. 1978: 33–34.

Lehne, Gregory. "Homophobia Among Men." *The Forty-Nine Percent Majority: The Male Sex Role*. Ed. Deborah S. David and Robert Brannon. Reading, MA: Addison-Wesley, 1976, 66–88.

Levine, James A. *Who Will Raise the Children? New Options for Fathers (and Mothers)*. Philadelphia: Lippincott, 1976.

Mead, Margaret. *Male and Female: A Study of the Sexes in a Changing World*. New York: Morrow, 1949.

Money, John, and Patricia Tucker. *Sexual Signatures: On Being a Man or a Woman*. Boston: Little, 1975.

Mougey, Kate. "An act of confiscation: Rape." *Kettering-Oakwood [OH] Times* 4 Feb. 1981: 1b.

"'Nerd' day gets a boot after suicide." *Dayton Daily News* 31 Aug. 1984: 26.

Ong, Walter J. *Fighting for Life: Contest, Sexuality, and Consciousness*. Ithaca, New York: Cornell UP, 1981.

O'Reilly, Jane, et al. "Wife-Beating: The Silent Crime." *Time* 5 Sept. 1983: 23–4, 26.

"Police Print links Coleman, death." *Dayton Daily News* 31 Aug. 1984: 26.

Roman, Mel, and William Haddad. *The Disposable Parent: The Case for Joint Custody*. 1978. New York: Penguin, 1979.

Schulz, Muriel R. "Is the English Language Anybody's Enemy?" *Speaking of Words: A Language Reader.* Ed. James MacKillop and Donna Woolfolk Cross. 3rd ed. New York: Holt, 1986, 125–27.

Sorrels, Bobbye D. *The Nonsexist Communicator: Solving the Problems of Gender and Awkwardness in Modern English.* Englewood Cliffs, NJ: Prentice, 1983.

Straus, Murray A., Richard J. Gelles, and Suzanne K. Steinmetz. *Behind Closed Doors: Violence in the American Family.* 1980. Garden City, NY: Doubleday, 1981.

Theroux, Paul. "The Male Myth." *New York Times Magazine* 27 Nov. 1983: 116.

LISA J. KING

Gender Issues in Online Communities

1   The Internet is imagined as an all-inclusive technology that will allow everyone, regardless of social status, gender, or ability, to communicate equally. The full title of a recent book is *The Control Revolution: How the Internet Is Putting Individuals in Charge and Changing the World We Know.* But has the offline world really changed? Or is what is happening online merely a reflection of real-world power structures and communications?

2   One possible answer is: the world has changed because online communities allow geographically diverse people to form relationships, whereas previously the mere accident of living in the same town or some other artificially constructed border conferred a sense of belonging.

3   Another possible answer is that nothing has changed. The same people who hold power in the real world do so online as well. They are the same people who created and control the technologies that make up the Internet. Only when other groups have a say in how and which new technologies are implemented will the world begin to change.

4   A combination of these two answers leads to this examination of gender issues in online communities. The physical isolation from peers felt by many women leads them to explore new technologies as a way of reaching others. The environment they discover in the traditional Internet forums is, in many ways, hostile to their interests and discussions.

5   Should women learn to adapt to the prevailing style of discourse online? Alternatively, should they instead strive to create their own spaces, whether specifically women-friendly or women-only? Are online communities of any sort better than traditional, public areas for gender-equitable discussions?

6   I will discuss theories of online communications as they relate to community and gender, what makes an online community different from other areas on the Internet, my own experiences in various online communities, both women-only and mixed-gender, and will examine my experiences in relation to the theories, and attempt to draw some larger lessons.

7   There is extensive literature on gender issues in online or computer-mediated communications (CMC). In addition, much has been written about online communities. While there is some common ground, there is not much recent literature concerning gender issues in online communities.

8   The information available on gender issues in online communications can be divided into two major theories. The first theory maintains that online communication is more equal, that women (and possibly other marginalized groups) are able to participate and complete thoughts, in effect "softening social barriers" (Shapiro 1999). One man, responding to a survey on gender issues, wrote, "Women get heard more because they can finish a thought without being interrupted. In addition, men tend to deal with the content of what women say rather than dismissing it because it comes from a woman....I see women taken more seriously than I think they would be if the communication were face to face" (We 1993).

9   The second theory is that online interaction is merely a reflection of real world conversation where men dominate. Men introduce more new topics, ignore topics introduced by women, and provide most of the traffic in a mixed-gender environment (Herring 1993 and Herring 1994). Herring cites research that "men (and to a lesser degree, women) perceive women as talking more than men at a time when women actually talk only 30% of the time" (Herring 1993).

10   Herring summarizes gender characteristics in online interactions with a comparison between the language used by women and men:

Women's Language	Men's Language
Attenuated assertions	Strong assertions
Apologies	Self-promotion
Explicit justifications	Presuppositions
Questions	Rhetorical questions
Personal orientation	Authoritative orientation
Supports others	Challenges others
	Humor/sarcasm

11   Finally, Herring concludes than there is no possibility of gender-neutral communication, since gender-cues are scattered through online communications. Therefore, the ideal of free and equal participation is impossible (Herring 1993).

12   However, all of this research was done regarding public spaces on the Internet: Usenet newsgroups, open electronic mailing lists, and Internet Relay Chat (IRC) channels. No one has addressed issues specific to online communities.

What's An Online Community?

13   The following appeared as a job advertisement on the DC Web Women electronic mailing list in May 1999:

> womenCONNECT.com seeks Community Builder—helping to manage bulletin board and chat discussions, scheduling chat guests, writing opportunities with opportunities to grow as a writer.

14   The Netpreneur Ad/Marketing list frequently has discussions on community building and increasing traffic to web sites. The perception is that a feeling of

community will bring repeat traffic to the web site and result in additional revenue. Toward that end, many commercial sites such as e-bay now provide newsletters and chat opportunities. WomenConnect is a content-driven site, depending on advertising for revenue. Demographic information captured during the course of community participation is useful in attracting new advertisers. However, community building is proving to be an elusive goal for many sites.

What differentiates a community from any other space on the Internet?

15   To be a community, rather than merely a group of people, there must be a way of excluding others and a feeling of belonging (Watson 1997). Alternately, "to be an 'Us' there must be a 'Them'" (Horn 1998). In addition, there must be rules of accepted behavior, preferably "home-grown" or self-imposed (Watson 1997). In many cases, a community is solidified by a threat, whether internal, such as the Rape in Cyberspace (Stefik, 1997), or external. Ideally, members act for the good of the community and come to identify with the community goals (Thomsen et al. 1998 and Dyson 1998).

16   A feeling of community is also enhanced by private spaces and a lack of anonymity (Horn 1998 and Dyson 1998). A feeling of security—a "safe place" to express ideas—is also vital (Borg 1996). Finally, some real world or face to face interaction often solidifies virtual communities (Anderson 1996).

17   Building online communities is difficult, because leaving does not entail moving to another physical location, but merely surfing the Internet to find another group. The main challenge facing communities is that if members do not like the rules, they can easily leave. In a community, traditionally, the ultimate punishment is banishment. Members of the community must fear ostracism; such fear is difficult to evoke when leaving is so easy (Dyson 1998).

How do real online communities compare to the theories?

18   From my own experience, community comes from a combination of private space and lack of anonymity. On Echo and the Well (two of the best known Internet communities), a basic credo is "you own your words." Real names of all users are easily obtained while on the systems. This limits the number of pure flames, while increasing vigorous discussion in an open atmosphere. In addition, both the Well and Echo are open only to subscribing members. In effect, one must "move" into the community in order to take part. This solidifies feelings of community. Since there are few transients, everyone present has a stake in making the community pleasant and livable.

19   In addition, a user is not considered a true "Echoid" (member of Echo) until she has attended a face to face gathering. Echo provides numerous possibilities for this including meetings at their offices, museum discussions, happy hours, open mike nights, bands, and a softball team (Horn 1998 and Echo discussions).

20   DC Web Women provides private spaces for members as well. Posting to the electronic discussion list is possible only for members. Special Interest Groups, with topics ranging from Cold Fusion programming to organizing play groups

for single mothers, are also closed to the public. Face to face monthly meetings, workshops, networking and purely social events provide a "real world" completion to the community. Another perceived community-building feature, off-topic posts, are used to advertise concert tickets, apartments needed or for rent, recommendations for hairdressers, car repair shops, and doctors, as well as other daily life conversation. The group's membership chair recently found her new job, new apartment and furniture from such posts to the list. However, at over 2000 members, the community is beginning to show the strain. A recent, heated discussion over off-topics posts has resulted in the creation of a social list solely for off-topic postings. It remains to be seen how this will affect feelings of community.

21   Tae-Bo is a commercial site that has given rise to an online community. Again, there is no anonymity in posting. While aliases are allowed in the threaded discussions, registration is required to participate. The feeling of identity comes from enthusiasm for the Tae-Bo videotapes. Many participants are also dealing with health and weight issues that provide a common ground for their discussions. While there are currently no face-to-face events planned, members share the daily event of working out with their tapes and use this as a bonding experience, similar to that gained from real world group interaction.

22   MenWeb provides a forum for men's issues with articles, interviews and resources. There is apparently a related discussion area that I was not able to access. There are face-to-face events that help reinforce the feeling of community the web site attempts to build. However, the lack of private space makes it questionable how much community actually exists.

How does gender figure in such communities?

23   While Echo is closed to "outsiders" or non-members, there are additional private spaces available within its boundaries. There are separate discussion areas for different age groups as well as for men and women. Such a structure allows a further retreat and a provision of safe space to vent, ask for advice, or test out new ideas. I am not privy to the discussions in the men-only area of Echo, and so cannot comment. However, the mixed-gender discussion areas of Echo are not dominated by men. Anyone can start and pursue a discussion—indeed many discussions have been continuing for years. Echo, however, may be a unique case since it was founded by a woman, Stacy Horn. Horn has strived through the years to maintain a near equal balance of men and women. In addition, she provides training and mentoring to women who wish to participate (Shade 1993 and Echo discussions). Therefore, Echo has gained a reputation as a women-friendly space while not resorting to women-only membership.

24   DC Web Women is a women-only forum. As a result, Herring's gender cues discussed earlier are particularly obvious in those discussions (Herring 1993). Even though they are not attempting to placate flaming men, women use the communication styles of attenuated assertions, support and questions. Many posts to the electronic discussion list contain such phrases as "I'm sorry if this has been asked before;" "I had the same problem and here is how I fixed it;" and "This worked for me, but I'd be interested to hear what others think." In addition, questions are often accompanied by detailed explanations of why the

information is required. Indeed, a man lurking on the list was unmasked by his strong assertions and rhetorical questions. This supports Herring's claim that gender-neutral communication is impossible. There are discussions about allowing men to participate in the electronic mailing list. If it comes to pass, it will bear watching to see if men adjust their communication style to the accepted norms of the list or if they follow traditional gender-cued styles.

25   The Tae-Bo site, the most public of the examples, is also geared toward weight and fitness issues, traditional female concerns. As a result, most threads are started by women. In addition, due to its focus this community may be atypical. It is offered as a support system for Tae-Bo users. Therefore, the main thrust of discussion is supportive and encouraging. Achievements such as moving from the basic to the advanced tape are celebrated by all participants. In such an environment there is little room for the challenging and self-promotion Herring finds in men's online communications. It is likely that people with such a style would not bother to participate in this discussion.

26   MenWeb provides articles and interviews by and about community members and activities. Most articles are written in line with Herring's gender-cued communication. The prevalent style is making strong assertions and presuppositions from an extremely authoritative orientation. There is little room to question the content or conclusions. However, without accessible chat or threaded discussion areas, it is difficult to judge the interaction between members.

Are women-only communities the only way to give women a voice?

27   From the literature and the real world experience, the answer is a qualified no. However, there is a difference between women-only and women-friendly spaces. Where there are no women-friendly spaces, women-only forums may be the best alternative.

28   Women-friendly spaces consist of an equitable mix of genders and actual participation in the discussion commensurate with their numbers. At Echo, half the members are women; in addition, half of the discussion moderators are also women—the common model is for each discussion area to have a male and female moderator. This helps ensure equitable participation and even-handed enforcement of the rules (Horn 1999).

29   In the context of technology-based groups, there is substantial evidence that women-only groups are beneficial to the participants. Truong writes that for members of Berkeley Mac Women, "the all-women format has proven to be a more comfortable environment for women computer users to ask questions" (Truong 1993). In her justification of women-only groups, "Why Systers?" Borg points to the working world isolation many female computer scientists feel—they are often the only women in their workgroup and have no professional social contacts with other women. Therefore, Systers provides what is otherwise missing from their professional lives (Borg 1996).

30   DC Web Women was founded for similar reasons. Three women who were working in Internet development were the only women in their respective offices. By reaching out for support, they began the DC chapter of Webgrrls,

which has now grown into DC Web Women. It is precisely the nurturing environment not provided by "mixed gender" groups (which in technology groups are de facto men-majority if not men-only) that led to the explosive growth of Webgrrls International, Systers, Spiderwoman, San Francisco Women on the Web and DC Web Women. It is ironic that once these groups become successful and are perceived to be providing valuable resources they are forced to defend their women-only status.

So, what about gender issues in online communities?

31   The majority of issues in existing research regarding equitable gender communication online concern Usenet newsgroups and other public discussion areas. This is largely a result of the public nature of the discussions and the feelings of anonymity. It is easy to flame someone you do not know and will never know or see in person. In addition, IRC suffers from its impermanence. Something said on IRC is gone with a scrolling of the screen. This leads to a tendency to say things that would not be said if a record of the interaction were being kept, such as on a threaded discussion board. A true community, with its common goals, private spaces and revealed users, does not suffer from the same gender-based difficulties that hinder other forms of computer mediated communications.

32   Commercial sites face more difficulty in building community, because by their nature they are public spaces. However, by providing private discussion areas (not merely chat) some feelings of community can begin to form. Care must be taken that communication is not dominated by men, thereby silencing female members. In addition, moderators or other authority figures must be sensitive to gender communication issues. This can be done as simply as encouraging discussion on topics introduced by women.

33   However, groups that have a non-commercial purpose or activity in common must be careful not to compromise what gives the community its identity. If a women-only community is thriving because of its gender-based membership, it is extremely difficult to surrender the "us" and "them" aspects and have the community survive.

34   Recently the necessity and desirability of women-only groups has been questioned, even within my own group, DC Web Women. However, there are ample mixed gender groups available in all fields, so the existence of a few women-only groups does not threaten or truly exclude anyone. As Borg succinctly stated, "I have not addressed whether a forum such as Systers would be necessary in an ideal and egalitarian world or even in a world similar to our own but with many more women in computing. When we get there, we can make that decision" (Borg 1996).

Conclusion

35   I believe that allowing women to find their own voices in a women-friendly and/or women-only environment will leave them better equipped to face mixed-gender online communications, whether in other communities or in the

more public areas of the Internet. By gaining confidence and experience in a safe environment, women will later be able to hold their own when faced with flaming and challenging men. In addition, by learning to see other women as experts in the closed communities, women will value their input more in mixed-gender discussions.

Resources

Ad/Marketing Electronic Discussion List administered by the Netpreneur Program. <http://www.netpreneur.org>

Anderson, Judy. (1996). "Not for the Faint of Heart: Contemplations on Usenet." In Lynn Cherny and Elizabeth Weise, eds., *wired_women, Gender and New Realities in Cyberspace*. Seattle, WA: Seal Press.

Borg, Anita. (1996). "Why Systers?" In Lynn Cherny and Elizabeth Weise, eds., *wired_women, Gender and New Realities in Cyberspace*. Seattle, WA: Seal Press.

DC Web Women electronic mailing list. <http://www.dcwebwomen.org/resources/archives/>

DC Web Women special interest groups (SIGs). <http://www.dcwebwomen.org/cgi-bin/ubb/sig/Ultimate.cgi?action=intro>

DC Web Women web site. <http://www.dcwebwomen.org>

Dyson, Esther. (1998). *Release 2.1*. New York: Broadway Books.

Echo web site and BBS community. <http://www.echonyc.com>

Herring, Susan. (1995). "Politeness in Computer Culture: Why Women Thank and Men Flame."

Herring, Susan. (1993). "Gender and Democracy in Computer-Mediated Communication." <http://www.cios.org/getfile/HERRING_V3N293>

Herring, Susan. (1994). "Gender Differences in Computer-Mediated Communication: Bringing Familiar Baggage to the New Frontier." <ftp://cpsr.org/cpsr/gender/herring.txt>

Horn, Stacy. (1998). *Cyberville*. New York: Warner Books.

MenWeb web site. <http://www.vix.com/menmag>

Regan Shade, Leslie. (1993). "Gender Issues in Computer Networking." <http://eng.hss.cmu.edu/cyber/gendernet.txt>

Shapiro, Andrew. L. (1997). *The Control Revolution*. New York: Century Foundation.

Stefik, Mark. (1997). *Internet Dreams*. Cambridge, MA: MIT Press.

Tae-Bo web site. <http://www.taebo.com/home.html>

Thomsen, Steven, Joseph Straubhaar, and Drew Bolyard. (1998). "Ethnomethodology and the Study on Online Communities: Exploring the Cyber Streets" <http://sosig.esrc.bris.ac.uk/iriss/papers/paper32.htm>

Truong, Hoai-An. (1993). "Gender Issues in Online Communications." <http://students.cec.wustl.edu/~cs142/articles/GENDER_ISSUES/ gender_issues_in_online_communications—bawit>

Vaugh Trias, Jennifer. (1999). "Democracy or Difference? Gender Differences in the Amount of Discourse on an Internet Relay Chat Channel." <http://nimbus.temple.edu/~jvaughn/summary.html>

Watson, Nessim. (1997). "Why We Argue About Virtual Community: A Case Study of the Phish.Net Fan Community." In Steven Jones, ed., *Virtual Culture: Identity and Communication in Cybersociety.* London: Sage.

We, Gladys. (1993). "Cross-Gender Communication in Cyberspace." Unpublished graduate research paper for Simon Fraser University available from author. <email we@sfu.ca>

WomenConnect web site. <http://www.womenconnect.com>

NATASHA JOSEFOWITZ

He vs. She

This set of comparisons between men and women in the workplace is variously attributed when it appears in several different iterations on the Internet. These parallel statements reflect well-recognized but still evident attitudes, and the pattern of the writing has inspired others to extend the list with their own observations and experiences.

The family picture is on HIS desk: Ah, solid, responsible family man
The family picture is on HER desk: Her family will come before her career.

HIS desk is cluttered: He's obviously a hard worker and busy man.
HER desk is cluttered: She's obviously a disorganised scatterbrain.

HE is talking with his co-workers: He must be discussing the latest deal.
SHE is talking with her co-workers: She must be gossiping.

HE's not at his desk: HE must be in the meeting.
SHE's not at her desk: She must be in the ladies' room.

HE's not in the office: He's meeting customers.
SHE's not in the office: She must be out shopping.

HE's having lunch with the boss: He's on the way up.
SHE's having lunch with the boss: They must be having an affair.

The boss criticised HIM: He'll improve his performance.
The boss criticised HER: She'll be very upset.

HE got an unfair deal: Did he get worried?
SHE got an unfair deal: Did she cry?

HE's getting married: He'll get more settled.
SHE's getting married: She'll get pregnant and leave.

HE's having a baby: He'll need a raise.
SHE's having a baby: She'll cost the company money in maternity benefits.

HE's going on a business trip: It's good for his career.
SHE's going on a business trip: What will her husband say?

HE's looking for a better job: He knows how to recognize a good opportunity.
SHE's leaving for a better job: Women are not dependable.

APPENDIX:
A GUIDE TO DOCUMENTATION

INTRODUCTION

As we explained in Chapters 6 and 7, academic writing will always include research. Participating in academic discussions means finding out what others have said or discovered about the question you are exploring. When you use ideas and information that you have found through your research, you need to acknowledge what you have borrowed and the author, title of the author's work, and place of publication.

Documenting your research allows your reader to find your sources, but more importantly, documentation is a part of your own ethical appeal in your work. When you acknowledge the sources you have used, you are giving credit to each person whose work you have used. If you do not do so, you are asking your reader to consider the work your original ideas. This is called plagiarism, which is a kind of cheating or fraud and is a serious offense. On most college campuses, plagiarism is grounds for receiving a failing grade on the assignment or the class. Or it may be grounds for dismissal from the college. If you publish plagiarized work, you may be subject to legal action.

The two major forms of documentation used in most college classes are Modern Language Association (MLA) style and American Psychological Association (APA) style. Classes in English, languages, philosophy, and most of the humanities will require you to use MLA style. Social science classes will generally require APA style. The following descriptions are based on the *MLA Handbook*, Sixth Edition, and the *Publication Manual of the American Psychological Association*, Fifth Edition.

MLA DOCUMENTATION

The MLA style of acknowledging sources is to include very short citations in the text itself. After using a quotation, paraphrase, or information from a source, you will include a brief reference to that source in parentheses. This reference gives your reader just enough information to find the more detailed entry in the Works Cited section of your paper, which lists all the sources you have used in your work. Your list of references is a resource for your reader to learn more about the issue you address in your paper.

Citing Sources in Your Text

MLA documentation style requires that you acknowledge your sources within the text of your paper. This way of telling your reader where you found your information resembles the way you would acknowledge your use of someone else's information in everyday conversation. For example, you might say, "A head-on crash on I-25 closed the northbound lanes this afternoon, according to Channel 7 news reports."

Because parenthetical citations interrupt the flow of your writing, you should keep them as short as possible. Your Works Cited section provides the complete information about the reference. To acknowledge your source, you use a parenthetical citation that includes the author's name, if you have not included it in the text itself, and the page number. If you have more than one entry for the author you are citing, you add a short version of the title of the work after the author's name.

Citing Books and Articles

The following examples—some hypothetical, some real, some taken from "Real Men Don't: Anti-Male Bias in English" by Eugene R. August, reprinted in Casebook 3—show the MLA in-text citation style used with printed books and articles:

Author named in the text
Because you include the author's name in the sentence, you need only a page reference in the parentheses.

> When considering gender-restrictive language, one must keep in
>
> mind that—as Ruth E. Hartley has pointed out—the masculine gender
>
> role is enforced earlier and more harshly than the feminine role is (235).

Author not named in the text
If the author's name is not included in your text in a signal phrase, then you need to include the author's last name and a page number in parentheses.

> "The implicit sexism" in such terms, writes one commentator,
>
> "disparages the woman, not the man" (Sorrells 87).

Two or more books or articles by the same author
If you have used more than one book or article by the same author, you need to let the reader know which source you are citing. You do so by including a short version of the title.

> This word, writes Goldberg, "is clearly sexist because it implies a
>
> standard of acceptable masculine sexual performance that makes a
>
> man abnormal if he can't live up to it" (New Male 248).

A book or article by two or more authors
If two or three authors wrote the work you are citing, include the last name of each author in the parenthetical citation, using the order you find on the title

page of the book. For more than three authors, either use the last name of the first author followed by "et al." (which means "and others"), or use all of the names, whichever style is used in the Works Cited listing.

Until recently, the equating of <u>mother</u> with <u>parent</u> in the social

sciences was notorious: a major sociological study published in 1958

with the title <u>The Changing American Parent</u> was based upon

interviews with 582 mothers and no fathers (Roman and Haddad 87).

In reality most child abuse is committed by mothers (Strauss,

Gelles, and Steinmetz 71).

Similarly, the term <u>wife and child abuse</u> conceals the existence of

an estimated 282,000 husbands who are battered annually (O'Reilly et

al. 23).

A work with no author

If the source you are using does not list an author, use a short version of the title in your parenthetical citation.

A fingerprint found in the car of Eugene Scott has been identified

as that of Debra Brown, Coleman's traveling companion ("Police").

An indirect source

If you quote words that are in a quotation in your source, use "qtd. in" before the reference to the source you consulted, and include the page number of that text.

In 1975 a father's petition for custody of his four-year-old son was

denied because, as the family court judge said, "Fathers don't make

good mothers" (qtd. in Levine 21).

An idea developed in an entire work

When you make reference to an entire work, use the author's name or, if the work is anonymous, the title of the work in your text rather than in a parenthetical citation.

All too many scholars have maligned the male, as John

Gordon pointed out in his book, *The Myth of the Monstrous Male,*

and Other Feminist Fables.

One volume in a multivolume work with the author's name and title in the text

When you refer to a particular quotation or paraphrase from one volume of a multivolume work, you may include the author's name or the title in the text itself. If you do so, you include both the volume number and page in parentheses, separated by a colon and space. Do not include the words "volume" and "page" in the parenthetical reference.

> In his <u>Topics</u>, Aristotle suggests that enthymemes depend upon
>
> contingencies (1: 1).

If your Works Cited list includes more than one work by an author and you do not mention the title in your text, cite it parenthetically with the volume number and page number.

> Aristotle suggests that enthymemes depend upon contingencies
>
> (<u>Topics</u> 1: 1).

An idea developed in an entire volume of a multivolume text

If you wish to make reference to an idea that the author develops throughout the entire volume, cite either the author's name or the title parenthetically followed by a comma and "vol." and the volume number.

> Aristotle makes the point that enthymemes depend upon
>
> contingencies (<u>Topics</u>, vol. 1).

A biblical passage

When you cite a passage from the Bible, include the version of the Bible, the abbreviated title of the book, the chapter number, a period, and the verse number.

> "And I saw in the right hand of him that sat on the throne a book
>
> written within and on the backside, sealed with seven seals" (<u>King</u>
>
> <u>James Bible</u>, Rev. 5.1).

A literary work

When quoting a play, include the act, scene, and line numbers in parenthesis. When referring to a poem, include line numbers.

For example, if you are quoting Richard Brinsley Sheridan's play *The School for Scandal,* include act number, scene number, and lines quoted:

> "Walk in gentlemen, pray walk in?—here they are, the family of
>
> Surfaces, up to the Conquest" (IV, 1.1-3).

If you are quoting Robert Frost's "Stopping by Woods on a Snowy Evening":

> But I have promises to keep,
>
> And miles to go before I sleep,
>
> And miles to go before I sleep. (14-16)

Citing Electronic Sources

The following examples are based on the research from the student essay "An Answer to Gridlock" and illustrate ways to cite electronic sources. Electronic sources have no pages as such, so you will simply list the author or short version of the title in the parenthetical citation.

An electronic source by a corporate author

When referring to a corporate author in a parenthetical citation, use recognizable abbreviations, as in the following reference to the Regional Transportation District Home Page.

> In 1994, Denver built its first light rail line, called the Central
>
> Corridor Light Rail System (Regional Trans.).

Two or more electronic sources by the same author

If you use more than one electronic source by the same author, add a short title reference.

> This would mean a tax of 4 cents on each $10 purchase, making
>
> the transportation tax 1 percent, "a penny on every dollar's purchase"
>
> (Leib "RTD").

An indirect source

As you would when quoting a quotation from a printed source, include "qtd. in" to indicate that your source quoted the material.

> "The Regional Transportation District is considering a delay for a
>
> FasTracks vote because a private poll shows the ballot measure might
>
> have trouble passing as one of the few items on the November 2003
>
> ballot" (qtd. in Leib "Public").

A numbered section or paragraph

If the electronic source has sections or paragraphs, include the name or number of the relevant section in your parenthetical reference.

> "In October 1970, RTD participated in a comprehensive
>
> transportation study for the Boulder Valley area" (Regional Trans.,
>
> Transit Planning History, par. 1).

PREPARING THE WORKS CITED LIST IN MLA STYLE

When you write papers that include research, you are entering into dialogue with researchers who have published their ideas and information they have gathered about the issue, and with readers who wish to know more about that conversation. It is therefore important that you be very precise in telling readers where to find the information and ideas you include in your paper.

You may have learned to call the list of works you have consulted your "bibliography." In MLA style, the list of all your sources is called the "Works Cited" list. As the name indicates, the items you list in this section of your paper include only those you have made explicit reference to in your text. Include any book, article, electronic source, film or other non-print sources, and alphabetize the entries by the author's last name or, if there is no author, the title of the work. If your sources include two or more authors with the same last name, alphabetize those entries by the first letter of the first name.

Double space the Works Cited section. Indent subsequent lines of each entry one-half inch from the left margin. The following examples demonstrate the format you will follow when using MLA style.

Books

A book by a single author is the format you will use most often and is the basic form of the entry. This entry includes the author's name, title of the book (underlined), and the publication information: city of publication, publisher, and date of publication.

A book by a single author

Booth, Wayne C. <u>The Company We Keep: An Ethics of Fiction</u>.

Berkeley: U of California P, 1988.

Notice that the author's name is given last name first, followed by a comma and then the first name and, if listed on the title page of the book, the middle name or initial. After the author's name, put a period.

The title will be the full title as given on the title page of the book. If there is a subtitle, it will follow a colon and space. After the title, put a period. (Underline the title of the work but not the period.)

The publication information includes the city of publication and sometimes the state. You will find this information on the copyright page, which is the other side of the title page. If more than one city is listed for the place of publication, use the first listed. After the place of publication, put a colon and a space, then the publisher's name followed by a comma, and the date of publication, followed by a period.

If the title includes the title of another book within it, do not underline the contained title.

Crane, Susan. <u>Gender and Romance in Chaucer's</u> Canterbury Tales.

Princeton: Princeton UP, 1994.

A book with two or three authors

Roman, Mel, and William Haddad. <u>The Disposable Parent: The Case for</u>

<u>Joint Custody</u>. 1978. New York: Penguin, 1979.

Notice that the second author's name is listed first name first.

A book with more than three authors

Either include all of the authors names, or use just the name of the first author followed by "et al." (meaning "and others").

> Edens, Walter, et al., eds. <u>Teaching Shakespeare</u>. Princeton: Princeton
>
> UP, 1977.

Two or more books by the same author

> Frye, Northrup. <u>Anatomy of Criticism: Four Essays</u>. Princeton:
>
> Princeton UP, 1957.
>
> ---, ed. <u>Sound and Poetry</u>. New York: Columbia UP, 1957.

Notice that the author's name is listed only with the first entry. For all subsequent entries, type three hyphens then a period. If the subsequent book is one edited or translated by the author, you will also add that abbreviation after a comma following the hyphens.

An anthology or edited book

If the book has an editor instead of an author, place a comma after the editor's name, then add "ed."

> Hunt, Douglas, ed. <u>The Riverside Anthology of Literature</u>. 2nd ed.
>
> Boston: Houghton Mifflin, 1991.

A book by a corporate author

> Modern Association Group on Children's Literature. <u>Children's</u>
>
> <u>Literature</u>. Ed. F. Butler. New Haven: Yale UP, 1993.

An anonymous book

> <u>Beowulf</u>. New York: Heritage Club, 1939.

An essay in an anthology or collection of essays

> Faulkner, William. "Barn Burning." <u>The Compact Bedford:</u>
>
> <u>Introduction to Literature</u>. Ed. Michael Meyer. 5th ed. Boston:
>
> Bedford/St. Martin's, 2000. 397-409.
>
> Wormald, Patrick. "Anglo-Saxon Society and Its Literature." <u>The</u>
>
> <u>Cambridge Companion to Old English Literature</u>. Ed. Malcolm
>
> Godden and Michael Lapidge. Cambridge: Cambridge UP, 1991. 1-22.

A translation

Begin with the author, then give the translator's name after the title, preceded by "Trans."

Gide, André. <u>The Immoralist</u>. Trans. Richard Howard. New York:

Knopf, 1970.

If the work is anonymous, begin with the title, then give the translator's name after the title, preceded by "Trans."

<u>Beowulf</u>. Trans. E. Talbot Donaldson. Ed. Nicholas Howe. New York:

Norton, 2001.

A work edited by someone other than the author

If the book has an editor, add the editor's name after the title, preceded by "Ed."

O'Connor, Flannery. <u>Mystery and Manners</u>. Ed. Sally Fitzgerald and

Robert Fitzgerald. New York: Farrar, Straus & Giroux, 1983.

A book published in a second or subsequent edition

Booth, Wayne C. <u>The Rhetoric of Fiction</u>. 2nd ed. Chicago: U of Chicago

P, 1983.

A multivolume work

When using two or more volumes of a multivolume work, include the number of volumes in the work followed by "vols." If the work is an ongoing project and is continuing in the present, add "to date" after "vols." and then leave a space after the hyphen that indicates that the project is ongoing.

Bales, Mitzi. <u>The Supernatural</u>. 11 vols. London: Danbury Press, 1975-6.

If you are using only one volume of the work, list the volume number after "Vol."

<u>The Works of Sir Thomas Malory</u>. 2nd ed. Ed. Eugène Vinaver. Vol. 1.

London: Oxford UP, 1967.

A book in a series

Owens, Louis. <u>Bone Game: A Novel</u>. American Indian Literature and

Critical Studies Series 10. Norman: U of Oklahoma P, 1994.

A republished book

If you use a paperback version of a book originally published in a clothbound version, you will need to provide the dates of both publications. The date of the original publication follows the name of the book, and the date of the book you are citing follows the publisher.

Wheatley, Phyllis. <u>The Poems of Phyllis Wheatley</u>. 1966. Chapel Hill: U

of North Carolina P, 1989.

A book with multiple publishers

Include all publishers, separated by semicolons, in the order given in the book.

> Milovoyevitch, M. The Marvels of Coffee. 1990. Louisville: Gulp;
>
> Johannesburg: Roberts, 1991.

A pamphlet

Treat a pamphlet as you would a book.

> Kaladi Brothers' Coffee Is for the Birds! Denver: Kaladi Brothers
>
> Coffee, 2000.

A government publication

If no author is listed, use the name of the government, then the agency. You may use abbreviations if your readers will understand them.

> United States. Department of Labor. Bureau of Statistics. Salary
>
> Listings of the Service Industries. Washington: GPO, 1999.

Published proceedings of a conference

The published proceedings of a conference follow the format of a book reference except that you will need to add information about the conference if it is not a part of the title of the work.

> Szarmach, Paul E., and Bernard S. Levy, eds. The Fourteenth Century.
>
> Proc. of the Fourth Annual Acta Conf., March 1977. Binghamton:
>
> Center for Medieval and Early Renaissance Studies, 1978.

An unpublished dissertation

> Kastely, Jay. "An Ethical Poetics: The Art of Critically Reconstituting
>
> and Evaluating Fictional Experience." Diss. U of Chicago, 1980.

Journals, Periodicals, and other Print Sources

An article in a scholarly journal

Enclose the title of the article in quotation marks. Underline the title of the journal, then list the volume number with the year of publication in parentheses, followed by a colon and then the page numbers of the article.

> Mailloux, Steven. "Evaluation and Reader Response Criticism: Values
>
> Implicit in Affective Stylistics." Style 10 (1976): 329-43.

If the journal numbers its pages by separate issues, you will need to include the issue number as well as the volume number. Place a period after the volume number, then add the issue number.

Ross, Matthew J. "Literary Alliances Make Strange Bedfellows:

Feminism and Racism in Cooper's <u>Last of the Mohicans</u>."

<u>Nineteenth Century American Literature</u> 29.3 (1958): 125-39.

An article in a magazine

If the magazine is published weekly, or twice monthly, include the entire date (with month abbreviated) followed by a colon and the page number or inclusive page numbers of the article.

Martin, David. "The Whiny Generation." <u>Newsweek</u> 1 Nov. 1993: 10.

If the article is not written on consecutive pages in the magazine but rather continues later in the volume, include only the first page and a plus sign:

Zinn, Laura. "Move Over, Boomers: The Busters are Here—and They're

Angry." <u>Business Week</u> 14 Dec. 1992: 74+.

An article in a newspaper

Give the name of the newspaper as it appears on the top of the front page, but omit any article such as *a, an,* or *the.* Underline the title. If the city is not part of the name and the paper is not well known, include that in brackets following the name, but without underline. Then give the complete date of publication, with the month abbreviated. If the edition is named, such as late edition, add it after the date and a comma. Then after a colon, add the page number or numbers.

Hanford, George H. "We Should Speak the 'Awful Truth' about College

Sports." <u>Chronicle of Higher Education</u> 30 May 2003: B10-12.

Jones, Mary. "Hoping for Change." <u>Joneston Herald</u> 15 Feb. 2000, late

ed.: B12.

An anonymous article

If the source does not identify an author, begin your citation with the title.

"Times Gone By." <u>The News</u> 15 Jan. 1998: 60-62.

An editorial

If the editorial is signed, include the author's name, followed by the title, then add "Editorial."

Greene, David. "A Time to Question." Editorial. <u>News of Today</u> 1 Feb.

2000: 7.

A letter to the editor

If the letter is to the editor of a newspaper or journal, add "Letter" after the author's name.

Jones, Frederick S. Letter. <u>News of Today</u> 3 Nov. 1991, late ed.: 15.

If the letter is a response to another letter, add "Reply to letter of…"

> Haverford, Gilbert. Reply to letter of James Walton. <u>Victorian Tensions</u>
>
>   28 (1985): 53.

A review

When you cite a review, include "Rev. of" and the title of the work reviewed, and "by" followed by the name of the author.

> Ward, Judith R. "Harry's Magic." Rev. of <u>Harry Potter and the Order of</u>
>
>   <u>the Phoenix</u>, by J. K. Rowling. <u>Joneston Herald</u> 30 June 2003: 18.
>
> Erard, Michael. Rev. of <u>Spoken and Written Discourse: A Multi-</u>
>
>   <u>disciplinary Perspective</u>, by Khosrow Jahandarie. <u>Rhetoric Society</u>
>
>   <u>Quarterly</u> 33 (2003): 139-42.

Miscellaneous Print and Nonprint Sources

A television or radio program

Include the title of the episode or show in quotation marks, the title of the program underlined, the title of the series, the name of the network, the call letters of the station and the city if it is a local station, and the broadcast date. You will also need to include the author's name if you know it, the narrator, the director, or whatever information is significant.

> "Well Schooled in Murder." By Elizabeth George. Dir. Robert Young.
>
>   <u>Mystery</u>. The Inspector Lynley Mysteries, Series 2. PBS. KMRA,
>
>   Denver. 31 Oct. 2003.

Sound recording

Include either the conductor, composer, or performer first in the entry. Which you choose will depend upon the way you have used the information in your paper. After the title of the recording, underlined, list the manufacturer and the year of issue. If you are citing anything other than a compact disc, indicate the medium.

> Berlioz, Hector. <u>Symphonie Fantastique</u>, op. 14. Philadelphia
>
>   Orchestra. Cond. Riccardo Muti. EMI Seraphim, 1999.

A film or video recording

Include the title underlined, the director, distributor, and year of release. If it seems significant, include the name of the writer, performers, and producer after the title.

> "Jane Austen's <u>Emma</u>." Dir. Diarmuid Lawrence. New Video Group, 1996.
>
> "Jane Austen's <u>Emma</u>." Dir. Diarmuid Lawrence. Perf. Bernard Hepton,
>
>   Prunella Scales, Kate Beckinsale, Mark Strong, Raymond

Coulthard, Dominic Rowan, Lucy Robinson, Samantha Bond,

James Hazeldine, Olivia Williams, Samantha Morton. New Video

Group, 1996.

A performance

Include the title of the performance underlined, author, director, performers, the site of the performance, and the date.

Coriolanus. By William Shakespeare. Dir. David Farr. Perf. Greg Hicks.

The Old Vic Theatre, London. 6 June 2003.

A musical composition

Include the composer's name, the title underlined, and any additional information that identifies the work. For a published score, treat it as you would a book.

Mozart, Wolfgang Amadeus. Complete String Quartets. New York:

Dover, 1970.

A painting, sculpture, or photograph

Begin with the artist's name, then the title underlined, followed by the museum, gallery, or place where the work is housed, and the city. If you are citing a published source in which the artwork appears, include the title of the publication, the author, and publisher information.

Rexlie, Jean. Peacocks in the Garden. London Transport Museum,

London.

Rexlie, Jean. Peacocks in the Garden. London Transport Museum,

London. British Travel Painting to 2000. By Eleanor Rinkle.

London: Ronahue, 2002. Slide 192.

If you wish to include the date the work was painted, include it immediately after the title.

Rexlie, Jean. Peacocks in the Garden. 1991. London Transport

Museum, London. British Travel Painting to 2000. By Eleanor

Rinkle. London: Ronahue, 2002. Slide 192.

An interview

List the name of the person interviewed, the title in quotation marks or just Interview if there is no title, the interviewer's name if significant, and significant publishing information.

Henley, Patricia. "Taking the Soulful Journey: An Interview with

Patricia Henley." Writer's Chronicle 35.6 (2003): 4-8.

Levertov, Denise. "A Poet's Valediction." <u>At the Field's End: Interviews</u>

<u>with 22 Pacific Northwest Writers.</u> Ed. Nicholas O'Connell.

Seattle: U of Washington P, 1998. 28-34.

If you have conducted an interview, list the name of the person interviewed, the kind of interview (e.g., personal, telephone, e-mail), and the date.

Brown, John. Personal interview. 15 May 2001.

Brown, John. Telephone interview. 3 Mar. 1999.

Brown, John. E-mail interview. 24 Dec. 1999.

An advertisement

List the name of the product, the word Advertisement, and the publishing information.

Budweiser Beer. Advertisement. NBC. 21 June 2001.

A letter or memo

For a published letter, cite as you would a work in a collection but add the date of the letter and number, if given.

Silko, Leslie Marmon. "To James Wright." 29 May 1976. Letter 16 of

<u>The Delicacy and Strength of Lace: Letters between Leslie Marmon</u>

<u>Silko and James Wright</u>. Ed. Anne Wright. St. Paul: Greywolf,

1986. 39-40.

Electronic Publications

Whenever you cite an electronic source that includes a Web address, enclose the URL in angle brackets.

A document from an Internet site

List the author's name, the title of the document in quotation marks, information about the print publication if pertinent, information about the electronic publication, and access information, the date of access, and the URL.

Rondolini, Marcus. "The Joys of Organic Coffee." 12 May 2002. <u>Oxford</u>

<u>Dictionary of Food</u>. Ed. Ronald Carlyle. Institute of Culinary

Innovation. 16 June 2003 <http://www.ICI/organ.coffee.html>.

An Internet site

Include the title of the site, underlined, the name of the editor of the site if given, the electronic publication information, the date of access, and the URL.

<u>Smithsonian</u>. 2003. Smithsonian Institute. 16 June 2003 <http://si.edu>.

A home page for a course

Include the name of the instructor, the title of the course, a description of the page, the dates of the course, the names of the department and institution, date of access, and the URL.

> Kuhn, Cynthia. Introduction to Children's Literature. Course home
>
> page. Summer 2003. Dept. of English, Metro. State U. 4 June 2003
>
> <http://clem.mscd.edu/~kuhnc/childrenslitsum03.html>.

A home page for an academic department

List the department name, description of the page, the name of the institution, date of access, and the URL.

> Department of English. Home Page. U of Denver. 5 June 2003 <http://
>
> www.du.edu/english/>.

An online book

Cite as you would a published book but add electronic information—the title of the Internet site, the editor of the site, version number, date of electronic publication, and the name of any sponsoring organization.

> Du Bois, W.E.B. The Souls of Black Folk. Chicago, 1903. Project Bartleby.
>
> Ed. Steven van Leeuwen. Dec. 1995. Columbia U. 2 Dec. 1997
>
> <http://www.bartleby.com/114/>.

If you are citing only part of an online book, add the title or name of the part you are citing between the author's name and the title of the book. If the part is a poem or essay, place it within quotation marks.

> Hawthorne, Nathaniel. "The Custom House." The Scarlet Letter. The
>
> Harvard Classics. New York, 1907-1917. Bartleby.com. 18 July 2003
>
> <http://www.bartleby.com/310/1/>.

An online posting

List the author's name, the title of the document in quotation marks, the description, the date when the material was posted, the name of the forum, the date of access, and the online address of the list's Internet site.

> Peri, Doreen. "See?" Online Posting. 22 June 2003. Utterances.
>
> 25 June 2003 <http://www.litkicks.com.Beatpages/
>
> profile.jsp?who+doreen=peri>.

An online government publication

Include the information usually given for a governmental publication: author, if known, the name of the government, then the agency as the author. Add the electronic information.

United States. Dept. of Human Services. <u>Aging Better</u>. By Susan E.

Tyler. Dec. 2001. 18 June 2002 <http://www.dhs.org./sua/

aging-better.html>.

An article in an online periodical

Include the author's name, title in quotation marks, name of the periodical underlined, volume and issue number, date of publication, total number of pages, paragraphs, or sections, date of access, and URL.

Digliano, Roberto. "Hysteria and the End-Times." <u>Millennium</u> 2.6

(1999) 43 pars. 23 June 2003 <http://www.ReligionDept.uccd.edu/

millenium/digliano.html>.

An article in an online newspaper

Sarche, Jon. "AFA to Ease Training for New Cadets." <u>Denver Post</u> 24

June 2003. 24 June 2003 <http://www.denverpost.com/stories

/0,1413,36~1474798.00.html>.

An online review

Vidimos, Robin. "'Phoenix' Rises Even Higher than Harry Hype." Rev.

of <u>Harry Potter and the Order of the Phoenix</u>. <u>Denver Post</u>.

24 June 2003. 25 June 2003 <http://www.denverpost.com/stories/

0,1413,36~78~1472792,00.html>.

A publication on CD-ROM, diskette, or magnetic tape

In addition to information on publishing, add the publication medium.

<u>The Oxford English Dictionary</u>. 2nd ed. CD-ROM. Oxford: Oxford UP,

1992.

"Jape." <u>The Oxford English Dictionary</u>. 2nd ed. CD-ROM. Oxford:

Oxford UP, 1992.

SAMPLE STUDENT WRITING: MLA PAPER

Author's name

Instructor's name

Course number

Date

Megan Keating

Ms Kuhn

ENGG 1122

March 10, 2002

Author's name and page number

Title centered

An Argument Worth Howling Over:

The Reintroduction of Wolves

Paragraph's first line indented one tab

Paper double spaced throughout

He will huff and puff and blow your house down! He will devour your dear old granny and then pretend to be her, so he can gulp you down as well. He is the bloodthirsty creature in the shadows waiting for you when there is a full moon. These are the legends of the big bad wolf, the tales that have been handed down from one generation to the next, creating a false perception of wolves.

The reality of the matter is that there are very few cases of a wolf ever attacking a human. The few incidences that have occurred have been under unusual circumstances. This misconception of wolves, along with man's need for land, and his love of the warmth of the wolf's fur coat, has led to the destruction of wolves over the last two hundred years. The attempt to reintroduce wolves to their natural surroundings has begun. However, not everyone is pleased with this idea. The reintroduction of wolves into Yellowstone National Park in 1996 has created a very strong debate between environmentalists, ranchers, and hunters. Wolves inhabited almost all of the United States sixty years ago, but today they are extinct in most of the connecting forty-eight states. Ranchers are against the reintroduction of wolves because of fear that the wolves will eat their livestock. Hunters are opposed to wolves because of the possible decrease in the number of animals they hunt. However, the reintroduction of

1"

Keating 2

the wolf is important for ecological, emotional, and economical reasons. Wolves balance ecosystems because they are predators. Wolves are beautiful, wild creatures and attract many visitors to Yellowstone National Park, which increases revenue at the park. For these reasons, laws should be passed that allow wolves to be reintroduced into all of the areas they once inhabited.

Before the settlement of Europeans in North America, wolves freely roamed the North American continent. Native Americans considered them mankind's brothers. However, in the 1800s when more Europeans came to North America, forests were cut down to provide land for farming and housing. Unfortunately, the loss of forest also meant the loss of habitat for the wolves. Their food supply also became less plentiful as settlers increased their hunting of deer and elk, prey for the wolves (Noecker par. 2). As settlers began to raise cattle, they feared that the wolves would prey on their herds, so they poisoned, trapped, and shot the wolves. Even though the number of wolves had already been greatly decreased, "In 1914, Congress authorized funding for the removal of all large predators, including the wolves, from federal lands " (Noecker par. 2). The howl of the wolf that was once heard all across North America was by the 1940s silenced by this systematic extermination of wolvas (Noecker par. 2).

Not until over half a century later did the debate of wolf reintroduction begin. Douglas Pimlott, a columnist for *Defenders* magazine and a Canadian wolf expert, proposed the idea of wolf reintroduction into Yellowstone National Park in his column in 1968 (Ridgley 9). Pimlott thought that Yellowstone was the perfect habitat to begin restoring wolves, not only because it is protected, but also because of the vast amount of wildlife it contains. Yellowstone National Park is located in the northern part of Wyoming and was declared a national park by Congress

Parenthetical citation: author's last name plus paragraph number in electronic source

Parenthetical citation: author's name plus paragraph number in source

Keating 3

Parenthetical
citation with
no author:
short title
plus paragraph
number in elec-
tronic source

in 1872 because of its unique ecosystem and its natural wonders ("Yellowstone" par. 1). However, the Endangered Species Act, which gives authorization to the reintroduction of endangered animals, was not passed until 1973. So it was not until 1974 that the wolf recovery team formed ("Yellowstone" par. 9). In 1987, the Fish and Wildlife Services approved the reintroduction of grey wolves into Yellowstone ("Restoring" par. 3). Ridgley describes how the supporters of wildlife organized themselves: Defenders, the supporters of the wildlife magazine, then battled on the wolf's behalf, conducting public education campaigns, promising to compensate ranchers for verified livestock losses to wolves, suing FWS [Fish and Wildlife Service] to force reintroduction, fighting for federal funding, garnering public support and rewarding ranchers that allowed wolves to breed on their property (10).

The hard work of Defenders was not a waste. In 1995 14 wolves were reintroduced into Yellowstone (Ridgley 10). Over the years, more wolves were released into Yellowstone, and the wolves formed packs, which are an average often wolves that live together like a family, and produced offspring (Julivert 10). More packs have since been created and there are about one hundred wolves now living within the Yellowstone area.

The reintroduction of wolves back into areas that they once roamed is important for ecological reasons. Ecosystems are the environment and species working together as one unit (Enger 91). Ecosystem that have been disrupted do not function as well as those that are unaltered. When humans began to interfere with the location and existence of the wolves, it affected the ecosystems in which they lived. The number of deer and elk significantly increased because there were few predators to keep their numbers at a reasonable level. The overpopulation of animals is the reason why hunting is allowed; however, hunting

Keating 4

is not allowed in the national parks, so there is no way to control the number of animals living there. An example of this is the ecosystem of Yellowstone prior to the reintroduction of wolves. There were enormous herds of elk, deer, and buffalo, all of which feed on vegetation, and in the harsh winter of 1988 there were not enough plants to feed all the grazing animals ("Wolves Promote" par. 2). Had there been more predators—animals that feed on live prey like wolves—there would have been more vegetation because fewer animals would have been eating it (Clark 19). The wolves also help strengthen the herds of their prey by weeding out the weaker animals such as the old and sick. By eating the more vulnerable members of the herd, the group benefits because they are now quicker as a whole, and there is more food for the stronger animals so they can maintain strength for survival ("Wolves Promote" par. 4).

The reintroduction of the wolf is also important for emotional reasons. The emotional experience that comes from seeing an animal in the wild is like no other experience. Sure many of us have seen wolves at the zoo, but how many of us have seen them in their natural surroundings? How many of us have come across them while hiking? The majority of us have most likely never encountered a wolf in the wild, even though wolves used to live in many of the North American biomes, areas with different climates that have certain types of plants and animals living in them because they are best suited for the conditions (Enger 91). The possibility of seeing a wolf in the wild is very unlikely. I had to travel to Alaska to encounter my first wild wolf, but the trip was well worth it because I saw the mystical creature, full of beauty, pace its way through the thick green forest.

The reintroduction of wolves is also important for economical purposes. Wolves, for many people, are a sign of the wild, and

Keating 5

their mysterious eyes and shy nature make them fascinating creatures; there are few places left in the world where people can observe the wolf's beauty. Therefore, people are willing to travel great distances to see them, as I did. As a result, people come from all over the world to visit Yellowstone National Park because of its beauty and wildlife and the possibility of seeing a wolf. In 1999 it was estimated that 30,000 Yellowstone visitors saw wolves in the park (Ridgley 10). Since 1995, when wolves were reintroduced into Yellowstone, there has been a $10 million increase in revenue, and it is believed that the wolves will eventually bring in $23 million a year ("Restoring Wolves" par. 8). The popularity of the wolf has created marketing opportunities. The sales of t-shirts, stuffed animals, posters and other wolf memorabilia items, along with wolf tours, have also contributed to revenues ("Restoring Wolves" par. 9). Not only have the wolves generated a great deal of funds for Yellowstone, but they have also increased revenue in cities neighboring Yellowstone because people pass through these towns on their way to Yellowstone. Cooke City in Montana had over a 22 percent increase in their tourism in 1996 because of the wolves ("Restoring Wolves" par. 10). The wolves in Yellowstone bring people to Wyoming and Montana and thus generate needed funds for the states as well as the park.

Wolves are very beneficial to the environment because they provide a balance in wildlife, and they are beneficial to humans because they enrich the beauty in our lives and provide revenue. Despite this, ranchers and hunters are still opposed to the wolves being returned to the areas where they once roamed free. Ranchers are against the reintroduction of wolves because of the fear that the wolves will kill their livestock. Many ranches have been owned by the same family for generations, and they require money and hard work to be successful. The loss of a cow or sheep

Keating 6

results in the rancher losing the profit they would have made from selling the animal. Sharon Beck is the owner of a ranch that has been in her family for four generations, and she is against the reintroduction of wolves because she fears that they will kill her cattle and cause her to lose money: "Environmentalists say 'What's a calf or two? You can spare that!' We're not raising beef for wolves. We're raising them for profit" (qtd. in "Wolves Add Fuel" par. 5). Although some ranchers have lost livestock because of wolves, only 42 sheep and 52 cattle were killed in the Montana area in 11 years by wolves; of all the possible ways for livestock to die, wolves are the reason behind less than .0004 percent of their deaths ("Wolves and Livestock" par. 3). Furthermore, all the verified losses of livestock due to wolves are reimbursed by the Wolf Compensation Trust. The Wolf Compensation Trust is a $100,000 fund that is used specifically to pay ranchers the market value price for any animals they lose due to wolves. The fund was set up in 1987 by Defenders of Wildlife (Noecker par. 15). A rancher from Missoula, Montana, named Tom Ruffatto, realizes that the wolves are going to eat some of his cattle, but he does not believe other ranchers should be getting worked up about it: "Some cattle are going to die. That's just how life is....Of all the problems I have to deal with, wolves are not that big of a problem" (qtd. in Long 16). Ranchers are worried about losing money because of wolves eating their livestock, but there are very few livestock killed by the wolves, and the ones that are lost are paid for by the Wolf Compensation Fund. So the possibility of a wolf killing livestock is not reason enough to stop wolf reintroduction programs.

Hunters are opposed to wolves because of the balance a wolf provides for an ecosystem. Without wolves, there is not a steady balance of predators and prey, and the prey population increases to

(margin note) Quotation from an indirect source

(margin note) Omitted material indicated by an ellipsis, three spaced periods

Keating 7

the point where there is not enough food to support all of the prey; many die because of starvation. The lack of predators is the reason why hunting is allowed—to help balance the population of prey. Since the wolves will provide a balance, the hunters see the wolves as competitors. Hunters fear that the reintroduction of wolves will drop the population of game such as deer and elk, which in turn will lower the number of hunting licenses that are allowed each season; therefore, fewer people will be able to hunt. For many, hunting is a serious hobby. Groups of people plan trips and vacations for the sole purpose of hunting. However, most hunters will not be affected by the reintroduction of wolves because they are being reintroduced into national parks and forests where hunting is not allowed in the first place. A few wolves will probably venture out of the national parks and feed on the game that is outside of the park; however, if wolves help to decrease the number of deer and elk, the animals that are left will be healthier animals. This results in bigger and stronger animals left to be hunted.

The loss that ranchers and hunters believe they will experience because of the reintroduction of wolves is not as significant as they think. Very few livestock are actually killed by wolves, and the ranchers that do experience losses are reimbursed for the animal. The hunters are not greatly affected by the wolves either, because reintroduction is occurring in national parks, and a decrease in population benefits the deer or elk. Although, there are some sacrifices to be made, the benefits of the reintroduction of wolves outweigh the costs.

The struggle to reintroduce wolves to their natural habitats has been long and hard, and there is still a lot more work to do. Having seen a wolf in the wild has only fed my desire to see more wolves in the wild. I visit Yellowstone National Park every summer with my family in the hope of seeing a wolf. Just

Keating 8

imagine the crisp, pine-scented air lingering in the night, the silver light of the moon filling the valley as you see the proud wolf standing among the timber. His green eyes jump out from his black face. He raises his head towards the stars and lets out a ghostly howl that creeps through the valley and up your spine. You are captured by his beauty and freedom. Though I have not yet seen a wolf in Yellowstone, thanks to the reintroduction of wolves into Yellowstone, there is a greater possibility that I, along with many others, will have the pleasure of seeing wolves in the wild. There are many places where the wolf still needs to be returned, such as Rocky Mountain National Park in Colorado. The Yellowstone experience shows that wolf recovery programs can be successful. Although most ranchers and hunters still disagree with the reintroduction of wolves, the majority of humans have seen the recklessness of their ancestors' actions and has begun to try to correct them. Thanks to them, wolf howls are being heard in the Northwest again, and they are benefiting animals and humans alike. But the question still remains: Will there be a happy ending to the tale of the wolf?

Works Cited
new page
Double spaced
throughout

Keating 9

Works Cited   *Title centered*

*Article in a
magazine*

Clark, Tim, and A. Peyton Curlee. "Nature's Movers and Shakers."

Defenders Spring 1995: 18–25.

Book

Enger, Eldan, and Bradley F. Smith. Environmental Science: A

Study of Interrelationships. New York: McGraw, 2002.

*Second and
subsequent
lines of each
entry indented
one tab*

Julivert, Maria Angels. The Fascinating World of ... Wolves. New

York: Barron's Educational Series, 1996.

Long, Ben. "Reversal of Fortune." Defenders Spring 2000: 14–19.

*Congressional
Report found
on CSR web-
page, para-
graphs of
reference*

Noecker, Robert J. "Reintroduction of Wolves." CRS Report for

Congress 1 August 1997: pars. 1–15 <http://cnie.org/NLE/

CRSreportsBiodiversity/biodv-13.cfm>.

"Restoring Wolves to Yellowstone National Park." Defenders.

Accessed 27 January 2002: pars. 1–12

<http://www.defenders.org/wildlife/wolf/ynpfact.html>.

*Electronic
journal,
paragraphs
of reference*

Ridgley, Heidi, et al. "Opening the Door to Wolf Recovery."

Defenders Fall 1999: 7–15.

*Newspaper
article*

"Wolves Add Fuel to Grazing Battle." Gazette Telegraph

3 Feb 2002: A11.

"Wolves and Livestock: Living Together." National Wildlife

Federation. 28 January 2002. 15 December 2001

<http://www.nwf.org/wolves/predcont.html>.

"Wolves Promote Healthy Ecosystems." National Wildlife

Federation. 28 January 2002. 15 December 2002

<http://www.nwf.org/wolves/ecosystem_health.html>.

"A Yellowstone Chronology." Defenders. 27 January 2002. 24

October 2002 <http://www.defenders.org/wildlife/wolf/

ynpchro.html>.

APA DOCUMENTATION

APA documentation style requires that the in-text citation of a source include the date of publication as well as the author, or title if no author is identified in the work. Because the timeliness of the information is significant for research in the social sciences, APA citations include the date.

Citing Sources in Your Text

Like MLA style, APA style requires that you provide parenthetical citations to your sources in the text of your paper. As you would with MLA style, you need to integrate your research into the flow of your writing. Again, you should keep parenthetical interruptions as short as possible. To acknowledge your source, you will use a parenthetical citation that includes the author's name, if you have not included it in the text itself, and the date of publication. APA guidelines suggest that you try to integrate the author's name into the text of your paper.

The following citations are either hypothetical or from the essay "Real Men Don't: Anti-Male Bias in English" by Eugene R. August, reprinted in Casebook 3, modified to show the APA in-text citation style used with printed books and articles.

Author named in the text

Place only the publication date within parentheses immediately following the author's name. If using a direct quotation or paraphrase, indicate the page number after the quotation or paraphrase.

> When considering gender-restrictive language, one must keep in mind that—as Ruth E. Hartley (1976) has pointed out—the masculine gender role is enforced earlier and more harshly than the feminine role is (p. 235).

> Ruth E. Hartley (1976) suggests that males have more difficulty with socialization than females.

Author not named in the text

Place the author's last name and the date of publication (and if necessary a page number for a quotation or paraphrase) within parentheses at an appropriate reference point within or at the end of the sentence.

> "The implicit sexism" in such terms, writes one commentator, "disparages the woman, not the man" (Sorrells, 1983, p. 87).

Two or more books published in the same year by the same author

> Mann (2000a, 2000b) has argued that we ought to look closely at the results of the 2000 election.

A book by two authors

For two authors, either use their last names in the text and the date of publication in parentheses, or place their names within parentheses along with the date. If the names are within the parentheses, join the names with an ampersand (&).

> Until recently, the equating of <u>mother</u> with <u>parent</u> in the social sciences was notorious: a major sociological study published in 1958 with the title <u>The Changing American Parent</u> was based upon interviews with 582 mothers and no fathers (Roman & Haddad, 1979, p. 87).

A book by three to five authors

For the first textual reference to a work by three to five authors, use all of the last names. In subsequent references, use the first author's last name and "et al." (meaning "and others").

> The study demonstrated the need for close monitoring of election results (James, Frederick, & Johnson, 2003).

Next citation:

> (James et al., 2003).

A book by six or more authors

Use only the first author's last name and "et al." for all references.

> One study examined a group of 80 children who had lived in foster families for five to seven years (Trapp et al., 2002).

A work with no author or an anonymous work

If a work has no author, use the first two or three words of the title, and capitalize each major word of your shortened version. Italicize your shortened title if the source is a book. However, if "Anonymous" appears as the author on the title page, then use Anonymous as the author.

> A major study found that the new drug was effective in nine out of 10 cases of early stage melanoma (*New Hope*, 1998, p. 352).

An indirect source

If you quote words that are in a quotation in your source, include "as cited in" before the reference to the source you consulted, and include the page number of that text.

> In 1975 a father's petition for custody of his four-year-old son was
>
> denied because, as the family court judge said, "Fathers don't make
>
> good mothers" (as cited in Levine, 1976, p. 21).

An entire work

When you make reference to an entire work, use the author's name or, if no author is indicated, the title of the work in your text rather than in a parenthetical citation.

> All too many scholars and teachers have hopped the male-bashing
>
> bandwagon to disseminate what John Gordon (1982) calls "the myth of
>
> the monstrous male."

A reference cited in another work

If you mention a work that is cited in your source but that you did not consult directly, use "as cited in" before your source information.

> Brown's earlier study had found that the skin cancer may be
>
> stopped if caught in the early stages (as cited in Abrams, 2001).

Multiple references

Alphabetize multiple references within parentheses and separate author groups with a semicolon.

> Several studies found the new medicine to be a promising
>
> treatment (Partesel, 1990; Tundell, 1992; Black, 1994).

A work by a corporate author

If a corporation is the author of a work, use the name of the corporation in your reference. If a corporation is recognizable by its initials, use the full name in the first citation with the initials in brackets, and thereafter use the initials.

> The study showed great promise according to one report (National
>
> Institutes of Health [NIH], 2001).

> The new drug was tested on a control group of 500 people (NIH,
>
> 2001).

A personal communication

For personal communications such as letters, e-mail, telephone conversations, and interviews that you conduct, use the name of the source, the phrase "personal communication," and the date of the communication. Do not include the reference in the References list.

The students explained that they had not realized that their

actions were illegal (Susan Hawthorne, personal communication,

September 15, 1989).

An electronic source with paragraph or section numbers

If the electronic source has paragraph or section numbers, include the number in the citation.

Busing had been in place for 15 years in the district (Hopewell,

2001, para. 15).

PREPARING THE REFERENCES LIST IN APA STYLE

In APA style, the list of your sources is called References. Include all sources you have cited in your paper, alphabetized by authors' last names or, if there is no author, the title of the work. If two or more authors have the same last name, alphabetize those entries by the first letter of first name.

Double space the References section. Indent subsequent lines of each entry one-half inch from the left margin. Italicize the titles of books and journals, but do not enclose article titles within quotation marks. Capitalize only the first word of a book or article title and subtitle, and any proper nouns. The following examples demonstrate other details of APA style.

A book by a single author

Begin with the author's last name followed by the initial of the first name, and second initial if it is given on the title page. Then comes the date of publication in parentheses followed by a period. The title should be italicized, but only the first word of the title and subtitle are capitalized, as well as any proper noun. Finally, provide the city of publication and, if not recognizable alone, the state abbreviation, then a colon followed by the publisher.

Booth, W. C. (1988). *The company we keep: An ethics of fiction*.

Berkeley: University of California Press.

Omit superfluous terms such as "Publishers," "Co.," and "Inc." but retain "Press."

A book by two to five authors

When a work has two, three, four, or five authors, include the names of all authors.

Eemeren, F. H., Van Grootendorst, R., & Kruiger, T. (1987).

A handbook of argumentation theory. Dordrecht: Foris.

A book by six or more authors

Use the name of the first author followed by "et al."

> Recquerst, A. A., et al. (1993). *The history of women in higher education from 1900 to 1965*. Chicago: Green Brothers.

Two or more books by the same author

Repeat the author's name and list the entries chronologically from the oldest to the newest. If two entries have the same date, list those works alphabetically by title, and distinguish between them by adding lowercase letters (a, b, etc.) after the date.

> Booth, W. C. (1990a). *The company we keep: An ethics of fiction*.
> Berkeley: University of California Press.
> Booth, W. C. (1990b). *Modern dogma and the rhetoric of assent* (Vol. 5).
> Chicago: University of Chicago Press.
> Booth, W. C. (1999). *For the love of it: Amateuring and its rivals*.
> Chicago: University of Chicago Press.

An anthology or edited book

If the book has an editor instead of an author, provide the editor's name in place of an author's name, then add "Ed." in parentheses, followed by a period.

> Hunt, D. (Ed.). (1991). *The Riverside anthology of literature* (2nd ed.)
> Boston: Houghton Mifflin, 1991.

A book by a corporate author

> Modern Language Association Group on Children's Literature. (1993).
> *Children's literature*. Ed. F. Butler. New Haven: Yale University
> Press.

An essay in an anthology or collection of essays

> Wormald, P. (1991). Anglo-Saxon society and its literature. In M. Godden
> and M. Lapidge (Eds.), *The Cambridge companion to Old English
> literature* (pp. 1-22). Cambridge: Cambridge University Press.

A translation

Begin with the author, date, and title, then in parentheses give the translator's name followed by a comma and "Trans."

> Gide, A. (1970). *The immoralist* (R. Howard, Trans.). New York: Alfred
> A. Knopf.

A book with no author

Beowulf. (1939). New York: Heritage Club.

A work edited by someone other than the author

O'Connor, F. (1983). Mystery and manners. (S. Fitzgerald & R.
Fitzgerald, Eds.). New York: Farrar, Straus & Giroux.

A second or subsequent edition

After the book's title, include the number of the edition in parentheses.

Booth, W. C. (1983). The rhetoric of fiction (2nd ed.). Chicago:
University of Chicago Press.

One volume of a multivolume work

Kingston, J. (1976). The supernatural: Witches and witchcraft (Vol. 7).
London: Danbury Press.

A republished book

Wheatley, P. (1989). The Poems of Phyllis Wheatley (Rev. ed). Chapel
Hill: University of North Carolina Press. (Original work published
1966)

A government publication

Department of Labor. (1999). Salary listings for the service industry.
Washington, DC: U.S. Government Printing Office.

An article in a scholarly journal

Do not use quotation marks with the title of the article. Italicize the title of the
journal and volume number, and after a comma list the page numbers of the
article. Capitalize major words in the title of the journal.

Mailloux, S. (1976). Evaluation and reader response criticism: Values
implicit in affective stylistics. Style, 10, 329-343.

If the journal numbers its pages by separate issues, you will need to include the
issue number in parentheses after the volume number.

Ross, M. J. Literary alliances make strange bedfellows: Feminism and
racism in Cooper's Last of the Mohicans. Nineteenth Century
American Literature, 29(3), 125-139.

An article in a magazine

After the year of the publication in parentheses, add a comma and the month of publication. Do not abbreviate months. Include a day date if the magazine is published weekly.

> Branaird, S. (1998, October). On ways to change your looks. *Women's*
>
> *world of living*, 30.

An article with no author

> With best wishes. (1995, September). *Creative living at the end of the*
>
> *century*, 15.

An editorial

> Greene, D. (2000, February 1). A time to question [Editorial]. *The News*
>
> *of Today*, p. 7.

A review

> Ward, J.R. (2003, June 30). Harry's magic [Review of the book
>
> *Harry Potter and the order of the phoenix*]. The Joneston Herald,
>
> p. 18.

Letter to the editor

> Goldblatt, C. (1993, October 31). Looking for an idea [Letter to the
>
> editor]. *The News of Today*, p. 24.

A document from an Internet site

List the author's name, Internet publication date in parentheses, the title of the document with no quotation marks, information about the print publication if pertinent, information about the electronic publication, the date of access, retrieval information, and the URL.

> Rondolini, M. (2002, May 12). The joys of organic coffee. In Ronald
>
> Carlyle (Ed.), *Oxford dictionary of food* [Online]. Institute of
>
> Culinary Innovation. Retrieved June 16, 2003, from
>
> http://www.ICI/organ.coffee.html

Article in an online journal also available in print

> Mann, R. (1999). The silenced Miami: Archeological and
>
> ethnohistorical evidence for Miami-British relations, 1795-1812

[Electronic version]. *Ethnohistory, 46*(3), 399-427. Retrieved June 24, 2003, from http://links.jstor.org/sici?sici=0014.html

Article in an online journal not available in print

Digliano, R. (1999). Hysteria and the end-times. *Millennium*. Retrieved June 23, 2003, from http://www.ReligionDept.uccd.edu/ Millenium/digliano.html

A document from a university program or department Web site.

Barker, J. C. (2003). Evaluating web pages: Techniques to apply and questions to ask. Retrieved June 23, 2003, from University of California at Berkeley, Library Web site: http:// www.lib.berkeley.edu/TeachingLib/Guides/Internet/Evaluate.html

SAMPLE STUDENT WRITING: APA PAPER

Unlike the sample MLA style paper, this paper in APA style requires a title page and a separate abstract page. The abstract should be no more than 120 words.

Educational Vouchers 1

Running head is short version of the title, in all upper case letters, below the manuscript page header

The manuscript page header consists of the running head plus page number. Title page is page number one

Running Head: EDUCATIONAL VOUCHERS

Title centered, double spaced, in upper and lower case letters

Educational Vouchers: The Solution to the Problems in Public Education?

Title begins in upper half of the page

Author's name   Peter Briggs

School affiliation   Central Washington University

Educational Vouchers 2

Abstract

One proposed solution to the problems plaguing public education is implementing a tax-funded educational voucher system. Freedom of choice might motivate improvement in all schools, but would significantly harm public schools and not achieve the desired outcome of overall educational improvement. It would not, for example, prepare public schools to compete adequately in a free market system, with very different educational goals and without the burden of meeting the needs of students of all ability levels. In addition vouchers would privilege higher income families at the expense of the economically disadvantaged who rely on the public schools. It is possible to improve the present system by focusing resources on specific problem areas in alignment with recent research on effective schools.

Label typed in upper and lower case, centered, at top of page

Abstract typed as a single paragraph in block format, not to exceed 120 words

Page header plus page number

Title centered and double-spaced

Educational Vouchers:

The Solution to the Problems in Public Education?

First line of paragraph indented one tab

By all accounts, our public education system is in trouble, and of the many proposed solutions, educational vouchers have recently gained popularity as a way to address the problems seen within our current system. Vouchers were originally proposed as

Double space throughout

a way to create a free market system, breaking the stranglehold of government on the educational world. However, the implementation of a tax-funded voucher system would significantly harm the public schools and would not achieve the desired outcome of overall educational improvement.

The concept of giving a voucher to students that could then be used to pay for any school of their choosing is not a recent idea. "The proposal, though not the name, is literally older than the United States, first appearing in Adam Smith's *Wealth of Nations*

Parenthetical citation: book author's name plus date of publication and reference page

in 1776, and even more specifically in Tom Paine's *The Rights of Man* in 1792" (Kirkpatrick, 1990, p. 1). While many of those who propose ideal societies have toyed with the voucher idea, its primary appeal seems to be as a way to create a free-market system of education. Tannenbaum holds that "The original supporters of the idea focused on the concept of competition, which would supposedly improve educational offerings, and the mechanisms of the free market, which would destroy the government monopoly on schools" (1995, p. 7).

Book with author's name given in sentence, date and page reference in parentheses

More recently, vouchers have captured the public interest in Washington State as a way to solve some of the problems with the current system of education, problems acknowledged by many but which also have complex causes. "Education experts claim

Educational Vouchers 4

that the deterioration in educational quality is caused by several factors including the subpar performance of schools, urban blight, drugs, the prevalence of television, the abject failure of national leadership, and the erosion of the family" (Hakim,

Book with three authors   Seidenstat, & Bowman, 1994, p. 3). What is more, our country now seems to expect the public schools to address these social and cultural issues in the classroom. In essence, "the schools are expected to babysit children of working parents, to eliminate the roots of racism, to prevent drug use, to teach children to become responsible parents, and to perform a dozen other tasks that were earlier considered the responsibility of the family and church"

Book with two authors   (Hanus & Cookson, 1996, p. 5). And yet, disregarding how complex the task has become, many charge the public schools with failure. Kirkpatrick sees the interest in a voucher system not as a desire for a solution but as an emotional response to this sense of dissatisfaction with the current system: "Many supporters of vouchers seem not so much to be really committed to educational choice and/or student welfare as they seem to be motivated by anti-teacher and anti-public school feelings or by an interest to get money for their own projects" (1990, p. 165). The public dissatisfaction can be noted when one considers the recent increases in the number of students being home-schooled. In addition, many school districts across Washington State are having difficulty finding public support to pass the local property tax levies that substantially support their needs.

Stemming from the recent dissatisfaction in the educational system, the public support for a voucher program in Washington and across the nation has grown, as evidenced by an increase in voucher-focused legislative proposals and court cases that seek

Educational Vouchers 5

voucher-type options. There is danger, however, in too quickly
accepting a particular path to school improvement without
carefully considering whether the proposal would achieve the
desired outcome of general educational improvement.

One assumption underlying the voucher movement is that a
truly competitive free-market environment improves quality in
all cases. Would this assumption hold if a voucher system
encouraged competition with the public schools? In an editorial
in the *Bremerton Sun*, Maggie Gallagher claims that forcibly
breaking up monopolies creates competition, which leads to
better products and/or innovation at less cost. She makes a
comparison of the governmental involvement in the Microsoft
anti-trust case to the public school's monopolization of tax dollars
and students (1999, p. c3). Ideally, allowing students to choose
schools would motivate continuous improvement, causing all
schools to produce quality results in order to keep enrollments
viable. However, the voucher system does not prepare public
schools to compete adequately with private and parochial schools;
furthermore, the competing schools could potentially promote
widely varying educational goals, and the choices would
therefore be based primarily on the type of school rather than on
the quality of the learning.

One of the most significant deterrents of a supposed free-
market educational system is a result of how the funding would
be redistributed. "We have a real fight on our hands. These
vouchers are literally taking dollars away from our public
schools," says Karen Gutloff, a National Education Association
member and activist against legislation which gives public tax
dollars to private schools (1999, p. 8). According to Gutloff, the

Educational Vouchers 6

voucher program in Milwaukee is shifting a total of $25 million a year away from public schools (p. 9). Instead of leveling the playing field to yield a truly free market economy, these cuts in tax funding damage the public schools to the point that they are unable to compete with privately funded schools which gain supplemental funding from voucher/tax money.

Funding is not the only area where the voucher program hinders the public schools while aiding the private. Because the private schools are able to choose their students, there is a good chance that they will accept the excellent students, thereby "skimming the cream" from the public schools, further complicating the public school efforts to demonstrate improvement. "Private schools have the right to reject or accept any student, regardless of whether the student holds a voucher. Private school officials often choose the so-called 'desirable' students and leave those they would find more difficult to educate for the public schools" (Gutloff, 1999, p. 9). Supporters of the vouchers claim that equal opportunity for all social classes is a better ideal to strive for than equality through integration. Further, they point out that the current area-division, or "neighborhood" organization of schools creates just as much socioeconomic division as the voucher system would. However, it seems as though the public system is and should be able to serve all, gifted and challenged, from upper and lower economic classes. Diana Herrera, a teacher and NEA member in Texas, believes that "As public school educators, we need to meet the needs of all students, from those with low abilities to the gifted. If a child is in special education, private schools won't meet the child's needs" (as cited in Gutloff, 1999, p. 8). What is more, if the

Educational Vouchers 7

voucher system is adjusted to include a truly equal opportunity for all, many private schools would balk at the idea. According to a U.S. Department of Education report published in 1998, "46 percent of private schools would not accept the vouchers if they had to accept students randomly. Even more, 68 percent, would not accept vouchers if they had to accept special-needs students" (as cited in Gutloff, 1999, p. 9).

Even if the best students remained in the public education system, voucher systems would still negatively impact students from lower-income families. The NEA claims that "some low-income families may benefit from vouchers, but the vast majority of poor people depend on public schools. These schools have fewer resources if taxpayer dollars are sidetracked into private tuition," (as cited in Gutloff, 1999, p. 9). Though some claim that an educational voucher system would make it possible for those who can't pay tuition to attend a private school, opponents of the vouchers are afraid that those most negatively affected by the voucher system would be the members of racial and social class groups already suffering from prejudice and inequity (Tannenbaum, 1995, p. 8).

These complications of implementing a voucher system are not just speculation, because we can see what is happening in areas currently under a voucher program. Findings from voucher programs in California and Milwaukee are showing that the quality of learning is not necessarily improving. "Voucher students' test scores in reading and math have stayed on a par with those of students in Milwaukee public schools....As a result the Center [for Advancement of Public Education] continues to argue that vouchers are the wrong answer" (DiLorenzo, 1997, p. 38). Furthermore, according to the NEA, official studies

Educational Vouchers 8

of the voucher plans in Cleveland and Milwaukee conclude that
vouchers don't improve overall student achievement (Gutloff, 1999,
p. 9).

If it is true that the voucher system does not improve the
overall education of the students and has such negative effects on
public schools, students from low income families, and students
with special needs, what alternatives might better address the
existing problems? Rather than undermine the existing system,
it seems more rational to attempt to improve and enhance what
we have, focusing repairs specifically on problem areas, and it
appears that there is support for such an effort. National Public
Radio pollsters randomly phoned 1442 people nationwide and
found that "75 percent of Americans would be willing to pay an
additional $200 in taxes to improve their public schools, while 55
percent would be willing to pay an additional $500" (as cited in
Gutloff, 1999, p. 9). While these figures may seem difficult to
reconcile with the recent decline in levy support, they do suggest
that there is still enough support for public education to attempt
to find ways to improve the existing system.

Much educational research has focused on possibilities for
focused improvement. For example, "The recent research of
Chubb and Moe has emphasized the importance of the
organizational features of schools for explaining academic
performance....They found that the characteristics of an effective
school include strong leadership by the principal, clear goals,
strong academic programs, teacher professionalism, shared
influence, and staff harmony" (Hanus & Cookson, 1996, p. 72).

Research is also examining how education is impeded by
governmental bureaucracy. Because school boards must adhere to

Educational Vouchers 9

multiple levels of regulations and policies, the process of

educational decision-making can be slow.

Block quotation, indented one tab

One of the most serious obstacles to the development of

policies that would bring about [beneficial] characteristics is

excessive bureaucracy, a danger to which all institutions are

prey but which seems to be particularly endemic to

governmental organizations. [Chubb and Moe's]

recommended cures for this ill are to increase the autonomy

of the individual school, reduce the size of schools, and

reduce or abolish the close supervision by school boards.

(Gutloff, 1999, p. 73)

Not only would smaller schools be academically efficient, but

they would also be financially efficient. The NEA states that "for

the same money that Milwaukee spends on vouchers for 6500

students, the district could put 13,000 students in smaller

classes—with better academic results" (Gutloff, 1999, p. 9).

Though the current organization of community members on

a school board may need adjusting, it is essential for the public to

remain involved in the public school system. Eliminating the

presence of community members who participate in directing the

public schools would most likely cause the general public to be less

supportive of the system. When the communities have a sense of

ownership in the schools, they are more likely to work toward

improving the quality of education.

Therefore it is important to find solutions that reduce the

bureaucracy and increase school autonomy while increasing

public participation and ownership. Some schools have already

attempted such changes. The Selah, Washington School District

has been on the cutting edge of educational problem solving.

Educational Vouchers 9

They have worked to create a smaller, more intimate school atmosphere while maintaining the high standards required by the state. To do so they have restructured the large elementary and intermediate schools in to a "benchmark band" system. This would place student in kindergarten through the fourth grade in one benchmark, students in fifth through seventh in the second, and those in eighth through twelfth in the third. Within these benchmarks, students join smaller learning communities. Students remain with the same group for the entire time they remain in the benchmark. To implement the structure, the school district has assigned teachers to faculty teams of 12 to 15 teachers who share the groups, approximately 350 to 450 students, and reconfigured school buildings so that instead of housing 900 students, each building has 300 (Pohlig, 1999, p. 7A).

The results of the changes in Selah are still new, but the outlook is good. Test scores have consistently improved. The "schools within a school" structure has reduced the teacher/administrator ratio. The largest hurdle they face now is not the changes themselves but the pace of change. While many strongly support the rapid advances and efforts of the school district, others feel that there have been too many changes made too quickly. Kathy Lambert, a Selah kindergarten teacher, feels that the rapid changes are putting pressure on students, parents, and teachers. What is more, she feels that parents should have been more involved in the reform process to increase the sense of community ownership (Pohlig, 1999, p. 7A).

Though the educational voucher system has emerged as a potential solution to a shared sense of the problems faced by

Educational Vouchers 10

public education, its implementation could cripple the public

system and compromise the goal of overall educational

improvement. Whatever solution does evolve in response to

educational needs, it should capitalize on the research already

conducted and the progress already made. Rather than discard

public education as we know it, we should attempt to improve it,

care for it, recognize its responsibilities and limits. Whether we

choose reforms like those of the Selah School District or attempt

to find other locally appropriate solutions, it is important to

involve the public and educators in reform decision-making. Such

solutions would ideally bind parents, teachers, and students in a

unified quest to better our educational system for all.

Educational Vouchers 11

References

Gallagher, M. (1999, November 26). Go after a real monopoly [Editorial]. *The Bremerton Sun*, p. C3.

Gutloff, K. (1999, November). Talking turkey. *NEA Today*, 8-9.

Hakim, S., Seidenstat, P., & Bowman, G. W. (Eds). (1994). *Privatizing education and educational choice: Concepts, plans, and experiences*. Westport, CT: Praeger.

Hanus, J. J., & Cookson P. W., Jr. (1996). *Choosing schools: Vouchers and American education*. Washington, D.C.: American University Press.

Kirkpatrick, D. W. (1990). *Choice in schooling: A case for tuition vouchers*. Chicago: Loyola University Press.

McGroarty, D. (1996). *Break these chains: The battle for school choice*. Rocklin, CA: Prima Publishing.

Pohlig, C. (1999, November 22). Too much too fast? *Yakima Herald-Republic*, pp. A1, A7.

Tannenbaum, M. D. (1995). *Concepts and issues in school choice*. Lewiston, NY: Edwin Mellen Press.

References on a new page, double spaced throughout

Title centered

Editorial in a newspaper

Article in a journal

Book with three editors

Book by two authors

Article in newspaper

CREDITS

Text Credits

"'Male Logic' and 'Women's Intuition'" by Robin Turner. Published online in August 5, 2002 on http://neptune.spaceports.com. Reprinted by permission of Robin Turner.

Student essay "The Problem of Textbook Prices" by Lisa Dell Vandever is included by permission of Lisa Dell Vandever.

WebLab.org discussion on Health Care System is reprinted by permission of Web Lab/Digital Innovations Group, Inc.

"The Framers' Electoral Wisdom" by George Will, *Sacramento Bee* (November 2, 2000). Copyright © 2000, The Washington Post Writers Group. Reprinted with permission.

"The Structure of White Power and the Color of Election 2000" by Bob Wing, *ColorLines Magazine.* Reprinted with permission from ColorLines Magazine (www.colorlines.com).

"Sample Student Business Letter" and "Sample Student Resume" by Melody L. Wollan are included by permission of Melody L. Wollan.

"U.S. English" by Guy Wright, *The San Francisco Examiner* (March 28, 1983). Reprinted by permission.

The examples in Figure 13.1, "Common Editing Symbols," and Figure 13.2, "Common Editing Abbreviations," are taken from The Guide to Grammar and Writing, an online resource of Capital Community College, Hartford, CT, http://www.ccc.commnet.edu/writing/symbols.htm, Charles Darling, editor. Used by permission of Charles Darling.

Photo Credits

Page 9: *The Conversation*, pastel by Lois Bajor. Courtesy of the artist; **18:** Photo courtesy of the *Yakima Herald-Republic*, Washington; **29:** Photofest; **55:** © Charles Ommanney/Contact Press Images; **61:** *Blackfoot River #1,* Mark Alan Wilson/<picturetomorrow.org>; **63 (bottom):** © David Allocca/Time Life Pictures/Getty Images; **63 (top):** AP/Wide World Photos; **93:** Courtesy of Rock the Vote; **100:** Hulton Archive/Getty Images; **116:** Courtesy of the California Department of Health Services; **130:** AP/Wide World Photos; **188:** © AFP/CORBIS; **195:** AP/Wide World Photos; **259:** © Kevin Schafer/CORBIS; **287:** NBC/Everett Collection; **289:** NBC/Everett Collection; **318:** Library of Congress. Timothy H. O'Sullivan, *Incidents of the War: A Harvest of Death, Gettysburg, July, 1863;* **319:** National Archives. Thomas Hart Benton, *The Sowers,* 1941–1945; **323:** *Nets and Doors,* 1986. © Jack Leigh; **353:** Courtesy of the author; **355:** Courtesy of the author; **410:** Hulton Archive/Getty Images; **416:** © Bettmann/CORBIS; **429:** ©Reuters/NewMedia Inc./CORBIS; **439:** © Roger Ressmeyer/CORBIS; **452:** *Silent Language of the Soul/El Lenguaje Mudo del Alma,* On Cesar Chavez Elementary School, at Shotwell between 22nd & 23rd Streets. © 1990 Susan Kelk Cervantes and Juana Alicia/<www.precitaeyes.org>; **465:** U.S.ENGLISH, Inc. is the nation's oldest and largest citizens' action group dedicated to preserving the unifying role of the English language in the United States (website: <www.us-english.org>).

INDEX

DOCUMENTATION CHECKLIST